Microsoft

Project 2013
IN DEPTH

Scott Daley

800 East 96th Street
Indianapolis, Indiana 46240

PROJECT 2013 IN DEPTH

ISBN-13: 978-0-7897-5095-2

ISBN-10: 0-7897-5095-3

Library of Congress Cataloging-in-Publication Data:

Printed in the United States of America

First Printing: July 2013

Trademarks

All terms mentioned in this book that are known to be trademarks or service marks have been appropriately capitalized. Que Publishing cannot attest to the accuracy of this information. Use of a term in this book should not be regarded as affecting the validity of any trademark or service mark.

Warning and Disclaimer

Every effort has been made to make this book as complete and as accurate as possible, but no warranty or fitness is implied. The information provided is on an "as is" basis. The authors and the publisher shall have neither liability nor responsibility to any person or entity with respect to any loss or damages aris-ing from the information contained in this book.

Bulk Sales

Que Publishing offers excellent discounts on this book when ordered in quantity for bulk purchases or special sales. For more information, please contact

U.S. Corporate and Government Sales

1-800-382-3419

corpsales@pearsontechgroup.com

For sales outside of the U.S., please contact

International Sales

international@pearsoned.com

Associate Publisher
Greg Wiegand

Executive Editor
Loretta Yates

Development Editor
Sondra Scott

Managing Editor
Sandra Schroeder

Project Editor
Seth Kerney

Copy Editor
Geneil Breeze

Indexer
Erika Millen

Proofreader
Sarah Kearns

Technical Editor
Alan Wright

Publishing Coordinator
Cindy Teeters

Designer
Anne Jones

Compositor
Jake McFarland

30021006195093

CONTENTS AT A GLANCE

CONTENTS

3 Microsoft Project and the Project Management Domain   57

II Organizing for Success—Project Initiation and Planning

4 Getting Started After the Business Initiative Is Approved   71

5 Setting Up Project for Your Use   89

6 Creating Your Project Schedule   131

7 Defining Task Logic   183

III Project Execution Through Completion

13 Tracking Your Project Progress   431

14 Analyzing Performance   459

ABOUT THE AUTHOR

Scott Daley has been updating *Project In Depth* since the Project 2010 edition. He has been working with Project and Project Server for over a decade as a consultant, a Microsoft employee, and an independent consultant. Scott believes that project management done well is a highly underrated discipline.

This book was written with the intent to explain more than just what Project does or why it does it, and to go beyond the standard narratives surrounding Project. Scott has seen Project put to use managing many different kinds of projects, and hopes that this book will clarify some of the reasons why these efforts can succeed or fail.

ABOUT THE TECHNICAL EDITOR

Alan Wright has worked professionally in and around IT for nearly 10 years. He has provided enterprise-level support in the Detroit, Michigan, area and continues to provide software and hardware support for small business and residential users. He holds several certifications from CompTIA and Microsoft and enjoys working with technology and teaching others how they can make technology work for them.

DEDICATION

This book is dedicated to all the deliberate and accidental project managers who, in the end, just want to deliver.

ACKNOWLEDGMENTS

Scott would like to thank QuantumPM for the contribution they made to this edition of *Project In Depth* by writing the 2007 edition.

Scott would also like to acknowledge the hard-working staff at Que Publishing who have helped make this book what it is today. He would especially like to thank Executive Editor Loretta Yates. It has been his pleasure working with her over the years.

WE WANT TO HEAR FROM YOU!

As the reader of this book, *you* are our most important critic and commentator. We value your opinion and want to know what we're doing right, what we could do better, what areas you'd like to see us publish in, and any other words of wisdom you're willing to pass our way.

We welcome your comments. You can email or write to let us know what you did or didn't like about this book—as well as what we can do to make our books better.

Please note that we cannot help you with technical problems related to the topic of this book.

When you write, please be sure to include this book's title and author as well as your name, email address, and phone number. We will carefully review your comments and share them with the author and editors who worked on the book.

Email: feedback@quepublishing.com

Mail: Que Publishing
              ATTN: Reader Feedback
              800 East 96th Street
              Indianapolis, IN 46240 USA

READER SERVICES

Visit our website and register this book at www.quepublishing.com/register for convenient access to any updates, downloads, or errata that might be available for this book.

POWER OF MICROSOFT PROJECT 2013

Unsurprisingly, if you are familiar with the other Microsoft Office products, you'll find Microsoft Project both instantly familiar and instantly different. Project is a mature, feature-packed application designed to help you manage your project more effectively. Consequently, while Project shares many features in common with other Office products, if you are a first-time user, expect to be surprised by just how deep and unique the Project feature set is.

> **note**
>
> Microsoft has released several tools for project and portfolio management that are designed to work together. However, only the desktop tools are addressed in this book.

This chapter provides an overview of new 2013 features and how you should use Project to improve your role of project manager. Subsequent chapters explain individual areas in greater depth.

 *For more of a quick-start guide to using Project 2013, which includes a walkthrough overview of how to use the tool, **see** Chapter 2, "Microsoft Project Quick Start," **p. 15**.*

Essentials of Project Management

Before getting started using the tool itself, it is important that you take the time to understand the essentials of project management so that the tool can be used in its proper context. Project is one of several tools that should be used to help project managers bring in their projects on time, on budget, and with the expected quality and functions. Project is a scheduling engine first and foremost. It does an excellent job of helping you keep track of what work needs to be done and the status of that work. Use the information provided throughout Part I, "Getting Started with Microsoft Project 2013," of this book to help you set up the project properly.

The remainder of the book explores specific features and functions that will be much more useful if your project schedule is organized correctly.

Managing a project is different from the operational management of a business or a department. By definition, successful projects result in *change*; they usually have one primary goal and a definite start and finish. Operational management is primarily concerned with a continuously repeated set of processes: many small tasks that start and complete. Because projects are designed to change the ways things are and they have a conclusive finish, the approach to project management is different from the approach to operational management.

Project management includes creating an overall plan (including a project schedule), leading a team to execute the plan, monitoring and adapting the schedule to changes, communicating progress to the project stakeholders, keeping the team focused on the project scope (the work that needs to be done to reach the objective), managing risks, and much, much more.

The upcoming sections discuss the concept of managing a project, as well as provide a basic understanding of Project. The chapters throughout this book describe implementing successful project management ideas using Project.

 caution
Project has certain limitations. For example, it cannot control the scope of your project, and it cannot be used as a substitute for effective communication. So before you begin to enter tasks into the tool, take the time to organize your project for success.

 note
Project helps you organize your project data, creates your project schedule, and manages your project overall. However, just as Microsoft Word will not make you a better writer, Project will not automatically make you a better project manager. Your ability in this field improves as you increase your knowledge and experience, and Project contributes to that growth.

 note
There is a difference between a project plan and a project schedule. A project *schedule* is the course of actions you intend to follow over time to reach the endpoint of your project. A project *plan* includes the project schedule but is much larger overall. A project plan also involves defining the objective of the project, the team that will work to reach the objective, the budget, and so on. Project is *primarily* a scheduling engine; it creates a project schedule based on the information you enter into the project file. It also aids in tracking the progress on your project and organizing all your project data.

➡ *For more information on project management, **see** Chapter 3, "Microsoft Project and the Project Management Domain," **p. 57**.*

Projects Are Temporary

As stated previously, projects have a definite start and finish. A project is a temporary endeavor that is finished when the project objective is reached. Each project is unique and should have a clear goal. Projects can be similar, but no project is ever duplicated exactly. Even if the plan and objective are the same on two separate projects, the project team and time period will be different. Thus, each project is unique.

Temporary is a relative term when applied to projects. Some projects can take one week, whereas others can last for decades. A project is temporary in that its life span is less than that of the organization working on the project. It is temporary because it ends, and the end is intentional.

> **note**
>
> Of course Project can and should be used for operational endeavors with a significant scheduling requirement. Project's scheduling engine is effectively a device for predicting the future, so it's incredibly useful for managers who need to predict whether a complex process or interconnected set of tasks will finish on time.

Project Objectives Are Specific and Measurable

For a project to be successful, the project objective(s) must be specific and measurable—that is, a project must have a specific goal that clearly can be labeled "complete" when reached. Vague generalizations do not provide a focus for the project to be successful. Projects like this result in a lot of work completed and resources expended but an endpoint that's never reached. For example, perhaps your organization takes on a project to design a new kind of car. You cannot simply say that the objective is to design a new car. You must develop a specific, measurable set of criteria as the goal, so you have an idea of exactly what to work for. Maybe the car must be a certain size, fall under a specific price range for the consumer, be a certain percentage more efficient than previous models, and so on. These are the kinds of things to identify before a project begins.

As a project manager, it is your responsibility to reach a clear goal with your stakeholders and then focus on executing the details of task management to reach the goal. Without defining this focus up front, it is easy to lose direction of the individual task work that must be done to reach the end.

➡ *For more information about the scope statement of a project,* **see** *Chapter 4, "Getting Started After the Business Initiative Is Approved,"* **p. 71**.

Projects Are Constrained by Time, Cost, Scope, and Quality

Besides being temporary, with defined, unique sets of measurable objectives (scope and quality), projects are bound by time and cost. In other words, all projects have limitations on the amount of time that can be allotted to work on them, the amount of money that can be spent, and the satisfactory quality level of the objective delivered at the end of the project.

Well-designed and managed projects balance three things: delivery of the desired *result* in as little *time* and for as little *cost* as possible. However, a tradeoff always needs to be made to determine which of the three is the most important. Individual task activities of the project also might be subject to constraints. Discussion of the tradeoffs with the stakeholders helps you prioritize so you can develop your plan and schedule.

Consider the following scenarios:

- The deliverable is required to be high quality, which likely will increase the cost or time spent working on the project. Projects in biotechnology or aerospace tend to fit in this scenario because the product produced by the project must protect human life.

- The project might be required to finish quickly, which might cost more to have additional people working to finish on time or lower the quality to finish in time. Competitive situations such as a desire to be the "first to market" prioritize time ahead of budget and quality.

- The cost is reduced, which might in turn reduce the quality of the deliverable or increase the time spent working, as less-expensive resources might require more time to finish their work. "Do-it-yourself" projects tend to fit in this category.

As you can see, the project constraints are all related to each other. They form a type of push-pull relationship within the project; when one constraint is put into effect, the others are affected as well. This relationship is often illustrated by the triple constraint diagram, or the constraint triangle, as shown in Figure 1.1.

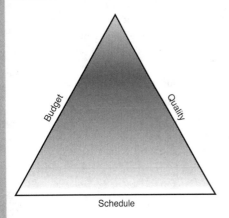

Figure 1.1
As a project manager, you must operate within the constraints of time (schedule), cost (budget), and scope or quality.

➡ *For more information about the domain of project management as it relates to Microsoft Project,* **see** *Chapter 3, "Microsoft Project and the Project Management Domain," **p. 57**.*

What Project Can Do for You

Project is extremely helpful for organizing, scheduling, recording, calculating, tracking, reporting, and analyzing schedule data for any project. The tool will help you achieve your project goals on time and within budget. However, using Project does not guarantee you successful project execution. Project can help you in a number of ways, including:

- **Project helps you create a better project plan and schedule**—Project forces you to think carefully about the details of your project because you must accurately enter all tasks necessary for successfully completing the project as defined in the scope statement. Thus, you create a better schedule and overall project plan because you can easily monitor activity and communicate information.

- **Project helps you organize your project**—Dozens of screen views, tables, and reports that organize your project data in various ways are contained within Project. This makes it easy for you to visualize, organize, and adjust the project plan and schedule as work progresses. All of these screens are customizable, and you have the ability to create your own if none of the existing ones fully meets your requirements.

  ➡ *For more information about the screens in Project, **see** Chapter 11, "Using Standard Views, Tables, Filters, and Groups to Review Your Schedule," **p. 357**.*

  ➡ *For more information about creating and customizing views and tables, **see** Chapter 22, "Customization Almost Beyond Reason: Views, Tables, Filters, Groups, Fields Toolbars, Menus, and Forms," **p. 699**.*

  ➡ *For more information about creating and customizing reports, **see** Chapter 20, "Reports Part I: 2013 Reports," **p. 625**, and Chapter 21, "Reports Part II: Visual Reports," **p. 653**.*

- **Project accurately and automatically performs calculations**—Project calculates a precise schedule based on the data you enter that illustrates when each task should begin and end. Additionally, if you enter cost data, Project makes budget calculations and provides schedule data for a variety of reporting needs.

- **Project makes it easier to search for the best possible project schedule and plan**—You can experiment with different scenarios by creating mock schedules for all possible circumstantial data for your project, and choose to work with whatever scenario produces the most desirable outcome.

- **Project helps detect problems or inconsistencies in the schedule**—Project identifies when resources are overallocated (assigned more work than their schedule allows). Resources include the people, equipment, and facilities used to work on the project. Project also detects when deadlines are impossible to meet according to any constraints you have included in the schedule. The tool helps you resolve resource overallocation and deadline issues.

➡ *For more information about resolving resource overallocation, **see** Chapter 24, "Resolving Resource Allocation Problems," **p. 801**.*

➡ *For more information about working with constraints and resolving deadline issues caused by constraints, **see** the "Defining Constraints" section on **p. 211** in Chapter 7.*

- **Project helps communicate project data and the schedule to stakeholders and team members**—Poor communication is one of the primary causes for project failure. Use Project to help you communicate better. You can produce textual and visual reports with ease to illustrate any aspect of your project to clients, stakeholders, partners, team members, or anyone else who might be interested in project information of any kind. This makes it easier for you to obtain approval from supervisors and keep clients satisfied and informed with accurate, professional reporting data.

  ➡ *For more information about working with reports, **see** Chapter 15, "Using Reports for Tracking and Control," **p. 497**.*

- **Project helps you track progress and detect deviations from your plan**—After the schedule is created and approved and work begins on a project, you should enter actual data into the project file based on the progress. Project compares this data to what was planned and calculates any difference, or variance. You can then adjust accordingly to compensate for any deviation from the plan. Project also reschedules any remaining tasks and revises the finish date for the project based on the actual data.

  ➡ *For more information about tracking progress on your project, **see** Chapter 13, "Tracking Your Project Progress," **p. 431**.*

- **Project helps adjust the schedule when the situation changes**—A project is never executed exactly as it is planned. Situations will arise when you need to adjust what was planned, sometimes quickly, and adapt to the new circumstances. Team members might leave the organization, work takes longer than expected, the scope of work changes, costs increase, and so on. Project helps to adjust and adapt to the changes.

  ➡ *For more information about adjusting and adapting to changes, **see** Chapter 16, "Revising the Schedule," **p. 527**.*

The preceding list is just an overview of some of the things Project can do for you. As you examine this book further, apply its concepts, and become more familiar with using Project, you will find it to be a helpful tool for project management. Of course, keep in mind that Project only multiplies the effort you put into it. Plan on taking the necessary time to accurately and carefully enter all project data into the project file and establish a regular update cycle to keep it accurate.

Enterprise Versus Standard Thinking

Project scheduling is an important function on its own, but many organizations also need enterprise project management capabilities. They need to monitor an entire portfolio of projects, share resources across the organization, store project artifacts, and collaborate more effectively. Microsoft Project Server was designed to perform these functions and also integrate with the desktop scheduling engine. The combination of tools provides a powerful software system that supports the needs of many users, including leadership, the Portfolio/Project/Program Management Offices, project managers, resource/staff managers, and project team members.

A few additional features in Project Professional enable it to work with Project Server. Project Server features are discussed only briefly in this book.

Desktop Tools: Project Standard and Project Professional

As mentioned earlier in this chapter, Project Standard and Project Professional are desktop scheduling tools. With the exception of collaboration and a few items discussed later in this chapter, the features in both tools support the functions of creating and executing a schedule.

Project scheduling, as described in this book, focuses on managing one project at a time. With few exceptions, the features of the desktop tools are designed to affect only one project schedule at a time.

There are really three key differences between Project Standard and Project Professional:

- The Team Planner is a Project Professional only feature that is frequently referenced in this book.

- The ability to make tasks "Inactive" is useful for schedule modeling but isn't critical and is explained where appropriate.

- Synchronizing with SharePoint and publishing to Project Server are of course useful but are only mentioned in passing. Both are outside the scope of this book, as making good use of each requires an in-depth understanding of either/both SharePoint and/or Project Server.

 tip

If you are not connecting to an instance of Project Server, Team Planner is by far the most significant difference between Project Professional and Standard.

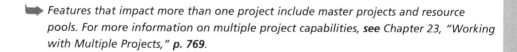 *Features that impact more than one project include master projects and resource pools. For more information on multiple project capabilities,* **see** *Chapter 23, "Working with Multiple Projects,"* **p. 769**.

What's New in Project 2013

Although Project 2013 works in largely the same way as past versions, the user experience has been significantly updated in keeping with Microsoft's Windows 8 style guidelines.

Reports

By far the most significant new feature in Project 2013 is called simply Reports. These reports are not the Visual Reports that debuted in Project 2007; these Reports finally replace the ancient reporting feature set that had not changed significantly since the mid-1990s (see Figure 1.2).

➡ *For more information about Project's new reports,* **see** *Chapter 20, "Reports Part I: 2013 Reports," **p. 625**.*

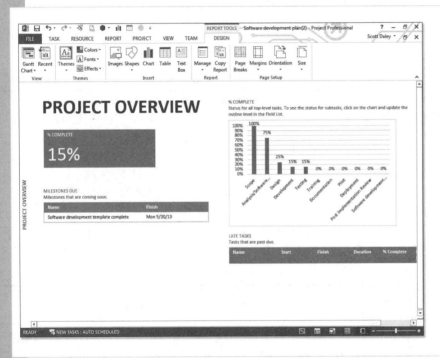

Figure 1.2
At last! Project Reports enter the twenty-first century.

The flexibility of Project 2013's new reports really cannot be overstated, especially relative to Project's old reports. Report design tools are now part of the Ribbon, and they are significantly more flexible and feature complete (see Figure 1.3).

Project 2013 enables you to add charts to reports, and to control the appearance of those charts in great detail (see Figure 1.4).

Figure 1.3
Report design can
be controlled in
great detail.

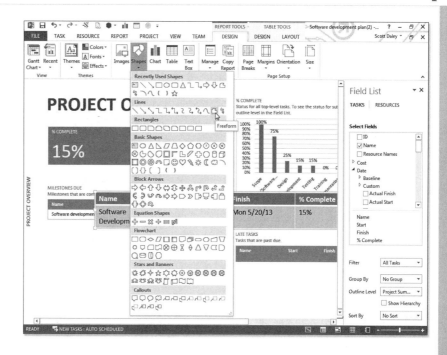

Figure 1.4
Adding charts to
a report in Project
2013 is easy and
flexible.

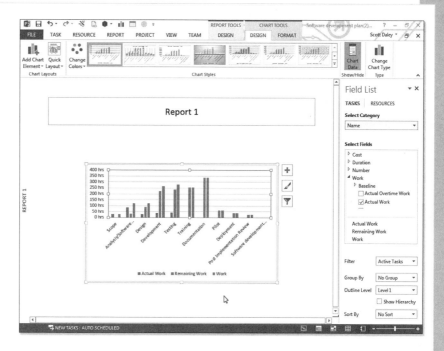

Tables are also easy to add to reports, and they can of course be combined with charts. Once they are, the same powerful, flexible formatting tools available for charts are available for tables (see Figure 1.5).

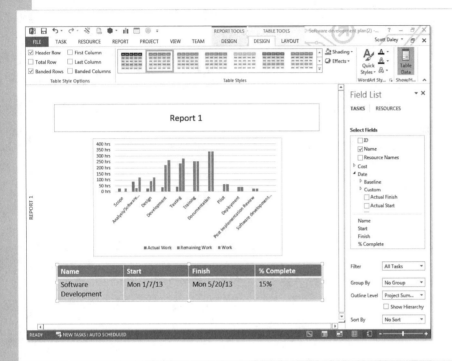

Figure 1.5
Tables can look any way you want them to.

Finally, Project 2013 ships with a set of reports that are immediately familiar and immediately usable for any project manager (see Figure 1.6). The good news is they can be modified to suit your situation precisely.

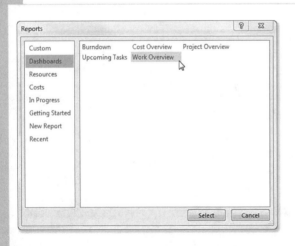

Figure 1.6
Project still includes a standard report set.

Consultants' Tips

Project 2013 is an excellent tool that can help a project manager be successful. There is much more to success than scheduling, however, so it is important that you understand what the tool can and cannot do. The following set of recommendations is intended to help you put Project in context as a tool that can support you but cannot be used as a substitute for leadership. Project is a key component of project success, but it does not stand alone.

Go Ahead and Ignore Project Management If It Suits Your Role

Many people who find themselves with a Project license really need to manage a team of resources working on many projects, not a single project. The Team Planner—especially when it is coupled with user-controlled scheduling—is a powerful, versatile, but, most importantly, *simple* tool for planning and managing your team's work. It does not require a complex task network or an identifiable critical path to provide exactly what you need: a simple way to plan work and resolve allocation issues in real time.

For skilled project managers, user-controlled scheduling and the Team Planner are a boon during the early stages of project planning, but also for managing and resolving near-term resource allocation issues during project execution.

Alternately, many people find themselves managing highly repeatable yet complex processes that require proactive correction if finish dates are at risk. This type of "project" typifies many operational environments. There's no need for a project charter or other kinds of typical project artifacts, but the Project scheduling engine, if used well, can make the entire difference between being blindsided by a slipped date and being a hero who just always seems to get it done.

Communicate

People skills and the ability to communicate in a healthy, understandable way are perhaps the most important parts of project management. You can have the greatest ideas in the world, but if you cannot communicate those ideas to your team members, you are on your own. Use the data in Project to help you, but do not depend on it to be your only communication tool.

Define Project Roles

Obtain clarity regarding the roles of everyone on your project team. Do not assume that your role as the project manager is clear just because you put a schedule together. Many things can complicate project roles. For example, in matrix-managed organizations, the team members might be assigned tasks by many other project managers on many other projects, so you need to make sure they are as engaged in and committed to your project as you are.

Define Project Deliverables Prior to Building the Schedule

Involve your team in the planning stage of the project. Build the schedule interactively by first defining what deliverables need to be created and only then determine how the work will be done and who will do it. You will have a more complete schedule and a team that understands what they need to do.

> ➡️ *For more information about defining a project's scope deliverables, and creating a Work Breakdown Structure (WBS), **see** Chapter 4, "Getting Started After the Business Initiative Is Approved," **p. 71**.*

Define the Project Goal

State the goal of the project as concisely and as clearly as possible. Everyone associated with the project should be able to understand the project goal, including your supervisors who approve the project, other project managers involved with the project, and team members who perform the work on the project. Document the project goal in a summary statement, with language that is easy to understand. The goal should be realistic and measurable. You can only measure your success if you can measure your goal. "Design a new car" is not an acceptable goal, but "Design a new car that is 20% more efficient than last year's model" gives you a specific direction.

> ➡️ *For more information about measuring goals, **see** Chapter 4, "Getting Started After the Business Initiative Is Approved," **p. 71**.*

Create the Work Breakdown Structure

Avoid the tendency to create a schedule with chronological phases and tasks when you first open Project. Instead, first complete a Work Breakdown Structure (WBS) to define the deliverables at the level of work packages. This is probably the most important thing you can do to fully define and manage the scope of your project successfully.

> ➡️ *For more information about defining and managing the scope of your project, **see** Chapter 4, "Getting Started After the Business Initiative Is Approved," **p. 71**.*

Communicate the Schedule to Your Project Team

Document and distribute the planned project schedule to all people who are supervising or working on the tasks. Be sure you answer any questions they have, and ensure that they fully understand and agree with their roles in the schedule. Address their disagreements and revise the schedule as necessary based on their comments, and redistribute the revised schedule, complete with charts and tables that clearly identify the work flow and scope of the project. Be sure that everyone understands their responsibilities for successfully completing the project.

Acquire Commitment from the Project Team

Secure a firm commitment from all project team members and outside resources (such as subcontractors and so on) to do the work assigned to them as outlined in the project plan, with no deviation unless otherwise approved by you.

Track Your Project Performance During Execution

When work on the project begins, carefully monitor the progress by tracking actual performance, and enter that data into the project file regularly. When variances arise, adjust the plan accordingly.

Tracking accurate performance information also helps document the history of the project, which will be useful for future similar projects. This is especially useful if unforeseen problem areas arise and will be valuable in explaining why project goals were not met. Also, if problems arise that are significant enough to delay the project's completion, you can give ample warning to stakeholders who are expecting the project to finish on time, so they can prepare for the adjustments on their end.

Close Your Project and Retain History

When work on a project is finished, document the entire process. This serves not only as a summary and closure to the project, but also as a history of what lessons were learned to improve performance on the next project.

MICROSOFT PROJECT QUICK START

Okay, so you have acquired Microsoft Office Project Standard or Professional, you have installed it on your computer, and you are ready to go. Now, only one small obstacle stands in the way of your rise to Supreme Project Manager: How does this thing work?

This chapter provides an overview that helps you to get started immediately without having to read nearly a thousand pages first. Think back to when you were younger: Did you ever receive a present you just wanted to dive into and figure out its intricacies later? That is what this chapter is for—to help you dive into using Microsoft Project without going into too much detail.

Maybe Project is the present you have been asking for all year, or maybe it is something that was simply installed by your company for you to use (perhaps even against your will). Whatever the case may be, this chapter aids you tremendously in getting started with the tool and introduces you to many of the concepts discussed in greater detail throughout this book.

 note

This chapter is a "quick start," and it mostly assumes you are managing a project. You might in fact be managing a team of resources engaged on multiple projects—in this case, you will want to reference the Team Planner section.

Five Process Groups for Projects

There are five main functions that are referred to as *process groups* for any project:

- Initiating

- Planning

- Executing

- Monitoring and controlling

- Closing

 For more information about the five process groups, **see** *the "Project Management Body of Knowledge (PMBOK)" section on* **p. 58** *in* **Chapter 3**.

The process groups have a logical, iterative flow (you begin with Initiating, cycle through Planning, Executing, and Monitoring and Control, and then end with Closing), with a recommended set of components to consider in each group. Project methodologies vary, and complex projects or programs might be in several of these stages at once, but all projects share these same basic processes. They should be used to help you account for all the components that might be required during your project's life.

Initiating Process Group

During Initiation, the purpose and goals of the project are clarified with the stakeholders. It is here that a project manager should be assigned to the project, and the first scope statement is created. The *scope* includes the agreed-upon objective and set of project deliverables that must be completed to reach the end goal. The upcoming section, "Define Project Scope," discusses this concept further.

The scope is decomposed into a set of deliverables (*what* the project will deliver) and then further decomposed into activities and assignments (*how* work will be done). In Project, you break up work into *tasks* as defined by the scope's deliverables. The work on these tasks is performed by different types of *resources*, which can be anything from people and machinery to ink and camera film. A resource is anything you might use to complete a task. Therefore, resources you define within the project are assigned to different tasks throughout the project during the Planning process group. This quick start focuses on how you assign resources that are people.

> **note**
>
> In contrast with Microsoft Project *Server*, Project will probably not be that significant during the Initiating phase. Its use typically begins during Planning and continues through Execution and Monitoring. Like Initiation, Closing is also better handled with Project Server.

In Project, there are two possible *task modes*. The default mode is Manually Scheduled. This means that tasks stay wherever you first put them, with whatever attributes you apply, such as duration or cost. The second mode is Auto Scheduled. This task mode enables Project to calculate task attributes for you. You can switch the task mode at any time. For the sake of simplicity, this section assumes that tasks are in Auto Scheduled mode. These modes are discussed throughout the book.

> ### note
>
> Manually Scheduled mode might be the preferred way to plan, depending on the constraints your project has to fit within. In essence, Project is a predictive tool that uses what you tell it to predict the future. In the real world, stakeholders and bosses have often already predicted a different future in terms of deadlines and budgets. In these situations, having a realistic picture of the future is significantly less important than simply knowing what's going on today and tomorrow. Manually Scheduled mode will make that much easier.

When tasks are in Auto Scheduled mode, Project calculates the start and finish dates for each task (and thus the entire project) based on the amount of work hours or duration you estimate for the task and its relationship to other tasks in the project. The upcoming section, "Create a Project Schedule Using Microsoft Project," provides more information.

Planning Process Group

People sometimes use Project in the planning process to create a schedule for the project, but do not maintain it for execution of the project. This happens because the schedule has become too difficult to maintain. If it was not organized in a logical decomposition from scope to deliverables to tasks, the schedule can become a disjointed set of activities that might or might not be focused on completion of deliverables. Using the Manually Scheduled task mode often hides this lack of focus.

Executing Process Group

If the project is organized correctly, you should have a detailed understanding of what needs to happen, and when, to successfully execute the work on your project. Auto Scheduled mode enables Project to act as a check on your assumptions and organization.

There has never been a project that was executed exactly as it was planned, and there likely never will be. Situations arise where resources cannot work on a task at the time they are scheduled to, additional work needs to be added as tasks in the schedule, one task is delayed, which in turn delays additional tasks that are dependent on its completion, and so on. You need to continuously review the schedule to see if it is executing according to plan.

Monitoring and Controlling Process Group

The fourth process group, Monitoring and Controlling, occurs in conjunction with the Executing process group. Although most of the execution activities are performed by your resources and project team, as a project manager, you are essentially responsible for tracking the progress as compared to the plan. Project provides many helpful features that enable you to accurately track your progress, compare it to your original plan, and calculate the variance between what is actually happening and what was supposed to happen. Then, with that information, you can adjust your plan of action and the schedule itself to make sure you can accomplish the project goals. The upcoming section, "Track Your Project," discusses in greater detail how Project can aid in executing, monitoring, and controlling your project.

note

The Planning, Executing, and Monitoring and Controlling process groups are cyclical. Changes occur as work is performed in the Executing process group based on tracking data you analyze in the Monitoring and Controlling process group, and you might have to go back and adjust the plan. Expect to repeat this cycle throughout your project. It is normal to revert to Planning as you track your project because you need to add a new task or reduce the scope of an activity. In fact, it would be considered bad practice if you did not readjust the plan based on the actual progress of the project.

Closing Process Group

Finally, when all work on a project is complete and all deliverables are accounted for, it is time to close the project, which is discussed near the end of this chapter in the section, "Close Your Project."

This chapter demonstrates the use of the process groups using a real-life example to give you a feel for how to manage a successful project using Project. A kitchen remodeling project is used to illustrate.

Navigating Project

Before you start to create your project schedule using Project, it is important that you understand the functionality of the tool itself. Users of Microsoft Office tools might be familiar with many standard navigating aspects, but some features are unique to Project.

Figure 2.1 illustrates the appearance of your screen when you first open Project based on the default settings. Notice the following features of the interface:

- Microsoft Fluent Interface (also known as the Ribbon)
- The Quick Access toolbar
- The timeline
- The task entry grid
- The time-phased Gantt Chart
- The status bar

It is fairly easy to customize this interface, so your first use of Project might not look exactly the same as the example shown in Figure 2.1. Moreover, your screen resolution is probably significantly higher than shown in the figure; like all Microsoft Office products, the Project interface expands to make the most of available space.

Figure 2.1
When you first open Project, your screen looks similar to this illustration.

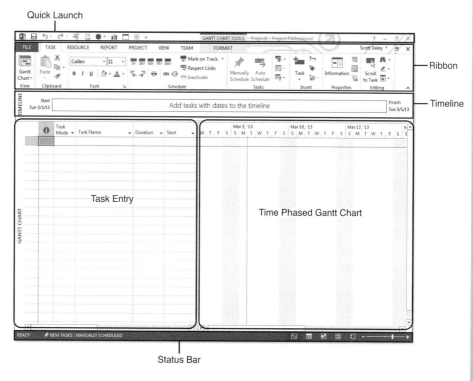

The following list briefly describes the six areas called out in Figure 2.1:

- **The Ribbon**—The Project Ribbon is organized roughly according to what you might want to do: Plan and manage tasks, resources, or the project itself. The View tab centralizes organization (grouping, sorting, and so on) that might be applied to all views. The Format tab is context dependent: It presents options that only apply to the active view type. Finally, the File tab is similar to the File tab in other Office products, with some unique options for Project.

  ➡ *For more information about Project-specific features of the File tab, **see** Chapter 5, "Setting Up Project for Your Use."*

- **The Quick Access Toolbar**—The Quick Access toolbar should be familiar to most users of other Office products or Internet Explorer. It can appear above or below the Ribbon, and you can customize it with oft-used controls. By default, it shows the Save, Undo, and Redo controls.

- **The Timeline**—The timeline provides a graphical view of your project along a single left-right axis. It can be copied to a presentation or emailed. You can select tasks and milestones for display on the timeline, and you can manually add annotations (if the timeline isn't visible, select the View tab and check the Timeline box).

- **Task Entry Table**—The task entry table on the left is one half of the Gantt Chart view (next section), which is the default view (you can change the default view by selecting the File tab, Options, General, Default view). It displays task information. Type a name directly into the Task Name column to create a new task and define its information using this or other tables you can display.

➡️ *For more information and helpful tricks for creating and manipulating the task list, **see** the "Manipulating the Task List" section on **p. 148** in **Chapter 6**.*

- **Gantt Chart**—The right half of the Gantt Chart view is the time-phased display of the tasks. This area displays task bars that correspond to the tasks listed to the left in the task entry table. You can move the separator bar between the timescale and the task entry table to the left or right to display more of either area, or you can use the scrollbars as with other Microsoft tools. The next section discusses in greater detail the Gantt Chart view.

- **The Status Bar**—By default, the status bar includes a Task Mode for New Tasks control, quick links to the Gantt Chart, Task Usage, Team Planner, and Resource Sheet views, and Zoom control. Right-clicking on the status bar shows several other options, all of which are discussed in detail later.

➡️ *For more information on the status bar, **see** the "Customizing the Quick Access Toolbar" section on **p. 762** in **Chapter 22**.*

Like other Microsoft tools, you navigate and control Project through the Ribbon and other toolbars. Select the File tab on the Ribbon to open, save, or print new or existing project files. The easiest way to change the view is through the status bar in the bottom-right corner, although the Ribbon offers many more options for changing and manipulating views.

More navigating options are discussed throughout this chapter and throughout this book in general. The following sections describe the minimum specific navigation options you should familiarize yourself with before creating your project schedule.

 tip

If you are unsure of the function of a particular button on any of the toolbars, hover your mouse pointer over the button, and a ScreenTip appears. To display or hide any of the toolbars, right-click in the toolbar area and select the toolbar from the resulting list.

 tip

As in previous versions of Project, you can also opt to enter information by selecting the cell and typing into the Edit field above the table *if* you have selected the check box next to File tab, Options, Display, Entry Bar. This area functions similarly to what you might have seen in Excel.

 tip

The right-click function can also be a helpful navigating shortcut. You can right-click almost anywhere on your screen to display various options for formatting, viewing, editing, and so on.

Introducing the Gantt Chart View

As previously mentioned, the Gantt Chart view is the default view when you open Project. It has two main areas: the task table and the timescale. The task table lists the tasks and their accompanying information in a text or entry table, whereas the timescale is the visual aspect of the schedule showing task bars for each task listed in the table. The task bars show the duration of each task, from their planned start date to their planned finish date, over time.

Figure 2.2 shows a simple example of a Gantt Chart view. Notice that the task bars on the timescale side are displayed on the same row as the tasks they represent.

 note

The Gantt Chart is a popular graphic representation of a project. It provides an effective way of visually examining the overall timeline of a project, task by task, and is therefore the default view in Project.

Figure 2.2
In the Gantt Chart view, tasks are listed on the table and visually represented on the timescale.

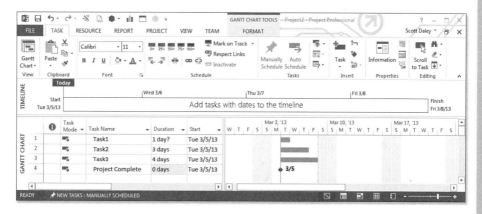

The timescale side of the Gantt Chart view displays time-phased information. You can choose to zoom in or out to show more or less of the task bars over time. For longer projects, it might be advantageous to zoom out on the timescale, allowing you to see more of your projects' task bars. Or, you can zoom in to specific time periods across your project. There are several ways to zoom in and out; for now, use the zoom control in the lower-right corner on the status bar.

As an alternative, you can also right-click on the timescale headings and select Zoom. This opens the Zoom dialog box, as shown in Figure 2.3.

Choose from the list of zoom options in the Zoom dialog box. You can also choose to display the entire project or customize the zoom value. The smaller the time unit you select, the less will be displayed on your screen. In other words, zooming into one week shows less information than one month, but also enables you to see more time-phased detail on the task bars. When you make your selection, click OK.

Figure 2.3
Zoom in or out of the timescale using the Zoom dialog box.

You can move the vertical divider bar between the timescale side and the task table on the Gantt Chart to the left or right to show more of either side. To do so, follow these steps:

1. Hover your mouse pointer over the divider bar. The mouse pointer becomes a double-sided arrow pointing left and right.

2. Press and hold the mouse button, and drag the bar either left or right.

3. When you have reached the desired location, let go of the mouse button.

You can display many "tables" in the task grid. In Project, "views" display tables of project information. By default, the task entry table is displayed in the Gantt Chart view, which displays the task ID field, Indicator, Task Name, Duration, Start date, Finish date, Predecessors, and Resource Names. To display another table, follow these steps:

1. Select the View tab, Tables. A list of the more popular tables appears, as well as an option for more tables.

2. Choose from any of the tables in the list, or choose More Tables to open the More Tables dialog box. The More Tables dialog box contains additional tables to choose from.

> *For more information about using tables in Project,* **see** *the "Understanding Standard Tables" section on* **p. 389** *in* **Chapter 11**.

You can display many different tables on the left-hand side; however, the timescale side of the Gantt Chart view will still be displayed. Each table is still the same task list, but different information about those tasks is shown depending on which table you choose to display.

You can also opt to insert other data columns into any table. Perhaps you do not want to display a different table entirely, but just want to add a few additional columns. For example, the Work field is not displayed in the task entry table on the default Gantt Chart view. It might be useful to see the Work field, especially if your estimates for tasks are provided via hours of work rather than duration.

To add another column into a table, follow these steps:

1. Select the place you want to insert the new column by clicking the header of the column that is currently there. When you insert the new column, the selected column, and all columns to the right of it, shift to the right to make room for the newly inserted column.

2. Right-click the column header and choose Insert Column. This opens a drop-down list of all the fields available for a task table.

3. Select a field. You can give it a different name right-clicking the column (or any column) and opening the Field Settings dialog. Type a new title into the Title field. The title will be the field name if you don't enter anything into the Title field. If you do rename the column, you can hover your mouse over the column title, and you see Project's original name of the column.

4. Also in the Field Settings dialog, you can define the alignment of the column heading and the data it holds. You can also define the width of the column. Both of these items are optional; if you do not define the alignment and width specifically, Project formats the column automatically.

5. Click OK when you are finished. You have to perform the same operation for each column you want to insert; you cannot insert multiple columns at the same time.

*For detailed information on customizing views, **see** Chapter 22, " Customizing Views, Tables, Filters, Groups, Fields, Toolbars, Menus, and Forms," **p. 699**.*

Scrolling, Selecting, and Entering Data Fields

Most of the views you can display in Project are interactive, enabling you to use your mouse and keyboard to navigate and modify the data. As with other Microsoft Office products, Project contains scrollbars when information is available beyond the current screen size. You can use the arrows to scroll vertically or horizontally, or you can drag the mouse through the scrollbar to your desired destination. If your mouse has a scrolling wheel, you can scroll up or down using that wheel.

To select or work with data in any field in a task table, click the mouse in the field. You can also use the arrow keys on your keyboard to navigate through the fields. If you double-click on any field in a task table, the Task Information dialog box appears. It provides more details about the selected task and can be used to update information.

*For more information about using the Task Information dialog box, **see** the "Editing Tasks Using the Task Information Dialog Box" section on **p. 146** in **Chapter 6**.*

When entering data in a table, you can either type directly into the cell, or select the cell and type into the Edit field located above the table *if* the Entry Bar is visible (File tab, Options, Display, Entry Bar), as in Excel. Sometimes, a cell will be grayed out, meaning that data cannot be entered into the cell. In general, that means that particular data is calculated automatically using other project or task information.

Exploring the Look and Feel of Project

Project contains dozens of views to display and enter data in your project, and perhaps dozens of ways to select them. On the Task, Resource, and View tabs, the far-left control should be the View control. Click and select More Views. Selecting More Views opens the More Views dialog box, which contains all the standard views available in Project. Each view has its advantages; some views show task information, some show resource information, some show tracking information, and so on.

➡️ *For more information about using the standard views for specific situations, **see** Chapter 11, "Using Standard Views, Tables, Filters, and Groups to Review Your Schedule," **p. 357**.*

Three views worth noting are the Team Planner, the Resource Sheet view, and the Resource Usage view. These views are helpful when you are entering and assigning your resources to tasks or reviewing existing assignments. They are discussed in the upcoming section "Create Your Team and Assign Resources." To display either of these, select the Resource Tab.

Although each view displays different kinds of project information, they all function similarly and can be navigated by using the methods described thus far in this chapter.

It is also worth noting that each view is customizable to varying degrees, and you have the ability to create a new view from scratch if none of the standard views meets your needs.

➡️ *For more information about creating and customizing views, **see** the "Creating and Customizing Views" section on **p. 708** in **Chapter 22**.*

Exploring the Project Window

This chapter has already discussed the Ribbon and various toolbars, as well as the task table and timescale sides of the Gantt Chart view. You can also split each view to display a second view on the bottom half of the screen. Whereas the Gantt Chart view contains two parts divided by a vertical bar, a split view is divided horizontally.

To split the window in any view, select the View tab, Details. Unlike a lot of other Microsoft applications that provide a duplicate display of the content in the new window, the split window in Project provides a totally different display of the content to help you analyze or review your data. To remove the split and return to the original view (the one displayed in the top pane of a split window), uncheck the Details box, or, alternately, right-click almost anywhere in the lower half and uncheck Show Split.

Figure 2.4 displays the Gantt Chart view after checking the Details box on in the Split View group on the View tab.

By default, the Task Form view is displayed on the bottom half of the screen when you split the window in a task view (such as the Gantt Chart view). The Resource Form view is displayed when you split the window in a resource view (such as the Resource Sheet view). You can display any view you want by selecting the View tab and using the drop-down control next to the Details check box.

The Task Form view (or Resource Form view) shows specific information in the bottom pane for the task (or resource) that is selected in the top pane. In Figure 2.4, the task "Task3" is selected in the top pane, and the Task Form in the bottom pane shows its detailed information. If the task had any resources assigned to it, they would appear in the left column under the Resource Name heading. Similarly, if the task had any predecessor task relationships, they would appear in the right column under the Predecessor Name heading. Task dependency relationships are discussed in the upcoming section "Create Task Dependency Relationships."

Figure 2.4
Splitting the window in any view displays a second view in the bottom pane, which shows more detailed information.

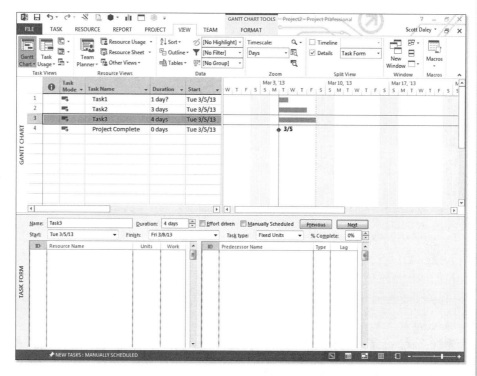

Splitting the window is advantageous for viewing more detailed information for the items in the top pane, or to display two different views at once to compare the information contained in both views simultaneously.

Project's Help Feature

The Help feature in Project is also handy when you are stuck in a situation you are unsure how to resolve. Many dialog boxes in Project have a Help button that opens the Help feature to information regarding that specific area or dialog box you are working in. Additionally, the Tab bar has a Help option, denoted with a question mark to the right. Choose from the categories listed in the window, or type in the area you want to find help for in the Search box at the top of the Project Help box. For example, you could type in a question, or the key words of your question, and Project searches helpful information related to your entry. Figure 2.5 shows the context-sensitive help available within Project. Finally, many settings and fields have a small circle with an "i" (for Information) in the center next to them. Hovering over the Information icon displays a tooltip.

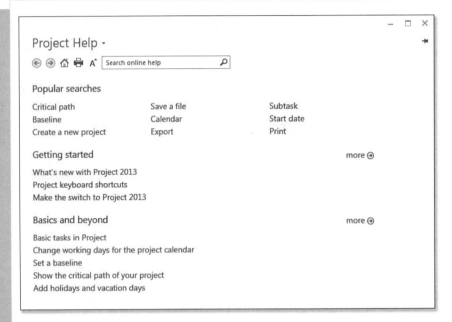

Figure 2.5
Choose Help, Project Help to open the Project Help box. Type in the keywords to search for, or select from the categories listed in the box.

Using Team Planner to Start Managing Resources Quickly

The Team Planner (see Figure 2.6) enables a radically different approach to managing effort. With the addition of Team Planner and Manually Scheduled task mode, resource managers can use Project in a resource-centric fashion. This includes people who do not want or need to concern themselves with approved project management techniques, such as Work Breakdown Structures (WBS), critical paths, or task Network Logic.

The Team Planner (Resource tab, View, Team Planner) consists of four key areas: Resource names, Unassigned tasks, Unscheduled tasks, and Gantt Charts for tasks that are scheduled and both assigned (top) and unassigned (bottom).

Using the Team Planner depends first on creating tasks and then creating resources to perform those tasks. By default, Project creates tasks in Manually Scheduled mode. This means that task start and end dates will not be recalculated without explicitly converting them to Auto Scheduled mode. Use the Gantt Chart to simply enter tasks you need your team to perform. This is the default view, but if you change to a different view and then need to return to the Gantt Chart, it is on the Task tab, View, Gantt Chart.

Next, you need to create resources. Select the Resource tab, View, Resource Sheet from the drop-down under the Team Planner control. Enter resource names and whatever other information you see fit.

Figure 2.6
The Team
Planner is
separated
into four
areas, each
with a dis-
tinct pur-
pose.

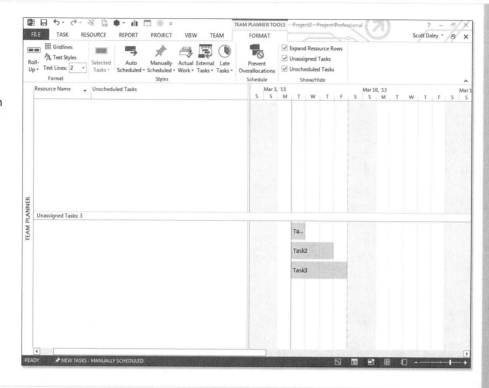

When used with Manually Scheduled tasks, the Team Planner is a drag-and-drop interface, without the usual restrictions associated with using Project. You can drag unassigned tasks to resource names or to the dates you'd like to schedule their start. Overallocated resources are highlighted in red; simply drag tasks to resolve overallocations.

In some ways, using Team Planner and Manually Scheduled task mode resembles using the world's most common project management tool, Excel. But Team Planner makes the process of scheduling resources easy, straightforward, and drag-and drop. Moreover, it opens up the possibility of using Project's more goal-oriented features, discussed in this chapter and throughout this book.

Define Project Scope

Before you begin to create the schedule for your project, you must first define and document the project's scope.

The stakeholder and fulfiller build a joint vision of the end result of the project. This joint vision sets the framework for the *scope* of the project. Therefore, to create your project's scope, you must identify exactly what the goals and limitations of the project are, define how you will measure the project's success, and what specific deliverables will be required to declare that the project is complete. In other words, defining a project's scope is defining exactly what you are trying to achieve, how you will achieve it, and how you will know you have achieved it.

Determining and documenting your project's objectives is an important part of your scope statement. Discuss with all project stakeholders exactly what the objectives of the project are, what is expected to be delivered at the end of the project, and what limitations will be enforced when working on the project's tasks.

As mentioned previously, every project has to have a defined end goal. This is generally broken down into two parts: the Measure of Success (MOS) and the final deliverables. The MOS is the framework for what is and is not included in the project. The MOS focuses on the desired result, and not the process of reaching it.

 tip

It is important to work through the scope and deliverables before you create a schedule. This seems like common sense, but that concept can be easy to forget when you factor in all other elements of beginning a project.

The final deliverables are a measurable set of components that must be met for the project to be considered successful and complete. Unless the criteria is specifically defined and documented up front, it is difficult to decide when a project is "good enough," because the stakeholders have different expectations.

For example, the reason for remodeling the kitchen could be to increase its efficiency, make it wheelchair friendly, or simply modernize an outdated look. Whatever the case might be, the MOS and final deliverables have to be measurable. In this example, there are hundreds of possible interpretations of what is meant by "efficient" or "modern." Until the reasons and measurements for the remodel are clear and the deliverables are defined, you cannot create a schedule that the stakeholders will agree meets their expectations.

The MOS sets the direction for the remodel and should drive all decisions behind what is included in the scope and what is out. After that is clear, the final deliverables can be determined. There can be a difference in defining *a* remodeled kitchen and *this* remodeled kitchen. The more clarity you can achieve here, the easier it will be to measure success.

➡ *For more information about defining a project's scope,* **see** *Chapter 4, "Getting Started After the Business Initiative Is Approved,"* **p. 71**.

Build and Decompose the WBS

Building your WBS, as part of defining your project's scope, is an important step between defining your scope statement and creating your schedule. It is imperative to build and decompose your WBS to give you an idea of the breakdown of work. With a WBS, it will be easier to construct your project schedule by breaking the work into logical deliverable components that further break down into tasks.

Think of your WBS as an outline of the work, designed in a tree diagram. The lowest level of the WBS contains the work packages—that is, the tasks and actions to complete the work. You can create this diagram using Microsoft Office Word, Visio, and a variety of other tools, or you can draw it on a whiteboard. No matter how you choose to build it, creating a WBS is a project management best practice and an opportunity to brainstorm and organize before creating the actual schedule.

➡ *For more information about building a WBS,* **see** *the "Work Breakdown Structure" section on* **p. 76** *in* **Chapter 4**.

Generally, your WBS will have at least three levels. The first level is the project itself. From this top level, you *decompose* the work on your project. The next level lists all the major products, services, or common components in the project, and the third level and below decomposes the components from the second level. Decomposition below the third level varies with the complexity of the project and the specific deliverable.

As you are drilling into each level, you are decomposing your work. Avoid the initial tendency to break the work into process groups because this tends to limit your thinking and you might miss some pieces of the scope. Use nouns when building the WBS, as opposed to an action verb-noun combination.

In the example of the Kitchen Remodel project, the first level of the WBS is Kitchen Remodel. The next level is organized by major deliverable categories and includes Management, Preparation, Vendors, Surfaces, Storage, and Appliances. The third level, partially decomposed in Figure 2.7, lists further decomposition of each item in the second level.

 note

Building a WBS is a step that often gets overlooked. However, it is an important step because it enables you to lay out all the work elements in front of you, and gives you a foundation for creating your task list. Similar to constructing an outline before writing a research paper or drawing up blueprints for a new house, building a WBS organizes the work on your project.

When it is time to create your project schedule, you can build a task list by using the organization through the lowest level in your WBS (the work package level). This process is discussed in the upcoming section "Build Your Project Schedule Using the WBS."

Figure 2.7 shows an example of a WBS, created using Microsoft Office Visio. Notice the three levels and the tree diagram format. This is a basic example; not all items of the Kitchen Remodel project have been listed, but this example gives you an idea of the look and feel of the WBS and its content.

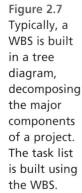

Figure 2.7
Typically, a WBS is built in a tree diagram, decomposing the major components of a project. The task list is built using the WBS.

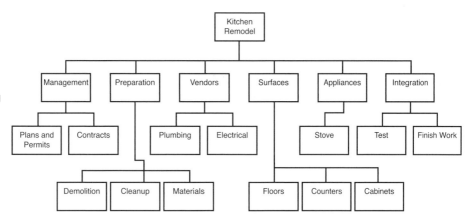

Create a Project Schedule Using Microsoft Project

After you have created your scope statement, have documented and distributed it to all project stakeholders, and have the approval to move forward, it is time to create your project schedule.

As mentioned previously, Project is a scheduling tool. You use Project to create a project schedule based on task information you define. Using Auto Scheduled mode, it is best to avoid entering start or finish dates for any tasks when you begin. Entering start or finish dates for tasks creates date constraints for those tasks. Instead, enter educated estimates of the tasks' durations or work hours, and be sure to accurately define all task dependency links, and Project will schedule them to start and finish accordingly. Upcoming sections discuss entering task information and dependency links more thoroughly.

Table 2.1 is a quick checklist of how you would create a project schedule. It might be helpful for you to use this checklist as a quick reference when you create a schedule for your project. The items in the left column (the "Step" column) are discussed in the upcoming sections. The kitchen remodel example is used to maintain consistency in illustrating the steps involved with properly creating a project schedule in Project.

Table 2.1 Checklist for Creating Your Project Schedule

Step	Complete? (Y/N)
Use project schedule templates or create a new project.	
Set project attributes.	
Set the project start date.	
Select a project calendar.	
Set the project summary task.	
Build your project schedule using the WBS:	Enter or adjust summary tasks and subtasks.
	Create milestones.
	Set deadlines.
Create task dependency relationships.	
Create your team and assign resources in Project.	
Enter estimates in Project.	

Step	Complete? (Y/N)
Adjust schedule based on estimates and resources.	
Baseline your schedule.	
Track your project:	Obtain project status.
	Enter your tracking data.
	Analyze your status.
	Adjust the schedule based on status.
Close your project.	

Use Project Schedule Templates or Create a New Project

There are two primary ways to begin to create your project schedule: Use one of the templates or create a new project from scratch. To view the project templates that come with Project, follow these steps: Open Project and select the File tab, New. A New Project pane appears to the right.

There are many options for starting templates beyond those that you might create and save (see Figure 2.8). They include Excel workbooks, SharePoint tasks lists (if you are using a version of Project Professional that is not associated with a Project Server), and Office.com templates, if you have an Internet connection.

➡ *For more information about creating a project template in Project,* ***see*** *Chapter 18, "Managing Project Files Locally and in the Cloud," **p. 549**.*

You or your organization might have your own templates for similar projects that you can also use. Although using a template can be advantageous, creating a new project from scratch might be more beneficial for you in terms of familiarizing yourself with the overall functionality of Project.

To create a new project, select the File tab, New and then select Blank Project. For the example of a kitchen remodel, a blank project will be used.

If you choose to create your project schedule from an existing template, you have to modify the data stored in the template to tailor it to your specific project. To do so, use the same methods described in the upcoming sections.

Figure 2.8
Select a template to use for your new project from the new Project section of the File tab.

Set Project Attributes

The first step in creating your project schedule is to set your overall project attributes. To do so, open the Project Information dialog box by selecting the Project tab, Project Information. The Project Information dialog box appears, as shown in Figure 2.9.

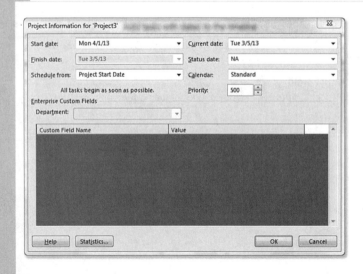

Figure 2.9
Define your general project attributes in the Project Information dialog box.

Set the Project Start Date

In the Start Date field of the Project Information dialog box, choose the date you want to begin the actual work on your project. When you begin entering tasks, Project automatically plans to have the first task start on this date, and continue scheduling forward from there. The first task will be assigned to begin at the time your working day starts on the date you enter in the Start Date field. The working time is discussed in the upcoming section "Select a Project Calendar."

When you have entered the start date for your project, you cannot enter a finish date. Project automatically defines the project's finish date based on the task information. In other words, if you enter a start date of January 7, 2013, Project schedules the first task to begin on January 7, 2013. Project then schedules the rest of the tasks based on the durations and dependency links you define, and the finish date will be automatically defined as the day the last task is scheduled to finish. If you are entering dates other than the project start date or if you are using Manually Scheduled as the task mode, you are not utilizing Project as a scheduling engine.

 tip

Be sure that the Current Date field in the Project Information dialog box is accurate. The Status Date field is used for tracking, controlling, and reporting on your project; leave it "NA" for now.

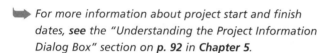 *For more information about project start and finish dates, **see** the "Understanding the Project Information Dialog Box" section on **p. 92** in **Chapter 5**.*

Select a Project Calendar

The project calendar is selected in the Calendar field in the Project Information dialog box and is important to the schedule of your project. The project calendar defines the working time for your project: which days are working days, which hours are considered working time in a typical workday, and which days are nonworking time (such as holidays and so on). For the Kitchen Remodel project, the Standard calendar is used.

Three default project calendars already exist for you to select in the Calendar field drop-down list, as follows:

- **24 Hour**—Continuous time from midnight to midnight, 24 hours a day.

- **Night Shift**—Used for overnight work that begins at the end of one night and finishes the following morning.

- **Standard**—The standard work week in the United States: 40 hours, 5 days (M–F), 8:00 a.m. to 5:00 p.m., with an hour lunch break from 12:00 p.m. to 1:00 p.m.

If none of these three calendars match your typical working time, you need to create a new project calendar and assign the newly created calendar in the Project Information dialog box.

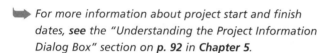 *For more information about creating a new project calendar, **see** the "Defining Calendars" section on **p. 101** in **Chapter 5**.*

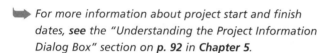 *The preceding explanation on project calendars is more of an overview to help get you started. To learn more about calendars **see** the "Defining Calendars" section on **p. 101** in **Chapter 5**.*

tip

You can define working time exceptions, such as holidays, vacation, and so on, in the Exceptions tab of the Change Working Time dialog box. This process is discussed in detail in the "Defining Calendars" section of Chapter 5, "Setting Up Project for Your Use."

Figure 2.10 provides an illustration of the Change Working Time dialog box. Notice the Exceptions tab. Select Tools, Change Working Time to open this dialog box.

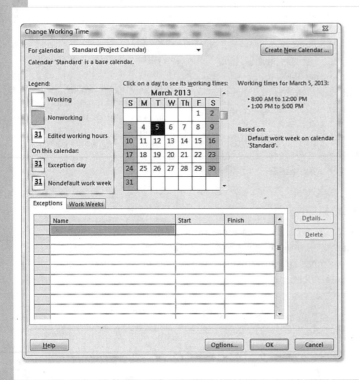

Figure 2.10
Create new project calendars in the Change Working Time dialog box.

caution

If you do not specify a project calendar, Project uses the default (Standard) calendar. This is acceptable if you are working on the remodel during normal U.S. business hours. However, if you plan on working on the remodel during different hours, such as evenings and weekends, you need to create and define those working hours on a new calendar and apply it to your project as described in this section. If not, Project schedules your tasks based on incorrect working time, and your project will likely get off track quickly in terms of schedule.

Set the Project Summary Task

Set up the project summary task (task ID number "0") on your project so you can see rolled-up information that summarizes your entire project at a glance. Also, the name of your project shows as the task name in the project summary task. To display the project summary task, select the Format tab and check the Project Summary Task box.

*For more information about the project summary task, **see** the "Selecting the Display Options for Outlining" section on **p. 158** in **Chapter 6**.*

Build Your Project Schedule Using the WBS

When you have defined your project calendar, it is time to start building your task list in the project schedule. As mentioned previously, work on a project is broken down into tasks. Whereas the WBS lists your work breakdown, the task list is the breakdown of the WBS into actions. The WBS is discussed in the previous section "Build and Decompose the WBS."

To enter a task into the project, simply type the task name into the Task Name field on the Task Entry table (the task grid) in the Gantt Chart view. Be sure to use an action verb and a noun, and be as specific as possible. A person should be able to read your task name knowing nothing about your project, and know exactly what the task is trying to accomplish.

After you type the task name into the Task Name field, you can press Enter or use your arrow keys to move out of the cell. The task will be entered into the list. Because we are assuming Auto Scheduled mode (task mode can be changed for all new tasks by selecting the New Task mode control in the status bar at the bottom of the screen, and for existing tasks by selecting the Task tab, Tasks, Auto Schedule) some of the other fields will be filled in automatically (such as Duration, Start, and Finish). Do not worry for now about entering any other data into these fields; they are discussed throughout this chapter. For now, enter the task names only.

Use your WBS to enter each major component, followed by each task within that component. List the major components ahead of the corresponding tasks. It is not required to list the tasks in chronological order, but it is recommended. You can always go back and move tasks, or insert new ones you might have forgotten.

For example, the WBS for the kitchen remodel project has Surfaces listed, with items such as Cabinets and Floors listed underneath it. You would likely create one or more tasks below Floors, such as Install Flooring, based on the items in the WBS. Underneath that task, you would enter more detailed tasks, such as Install Underlayment and Install Tile, to provide more specific activities. The task names contain a comprehensive, descriptive action verb-noun format, and are organized as specific activities within a project process group.

Therefore, to build your project schedule using your WBS, do the following:

1. Enter a task by typing it directly into the Task Name field, and press Enter. Use the WBS to guide you in your task entries, and name your tasks using an action verb-noun format.

 tip

If you use the convention recommended for the WBS, it is easy to see the difference between the WBS components and the tasks. WBS components are expressed as nouns (for example, Cabinets), and tasks are expressed as actions with a verb and a noun (Install Lower Cabinets).

2. Determine whether the task is at the lowest level of detail needed for the work to be assigned to one or more resources. If it is not, enter more detailed tasks related to the original task directly underneath it. Later, you will indent these specific tasks, making the original task a summary task in the project (more about that later).

3. Double-check that all items from your WBS have been entered as tasks and that all work is accounted for.

To insert a new task in between two existing tasks, right-click on the row ID number where you want to insert the new task and choose New Task. A blank task row is inserted above the row you selected, and you can enter its task name as described previously. To delete a task from the list, right-click in its row ID number and choose Delete Task. The row ID number is located on the left side of the task entry table; clicking in it highlights the entire task row.

> 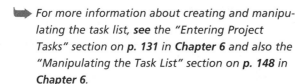 *For more information about creating and manipulating the task list,* **see** *the "Entering Project Tasks" section on **p. 131** in **Chapter 6** and also the "Manipulating the Task List" section on **p. 148** in **Chapter 6**.*

 note

It is unlikely that you will get your entire task list right the first time; you might have to enter new tasks, remove tasks, or move tasks around as you continue to build your project schedule. Do not get discouraged if you find yourself constantly adjusting your task list; this should be expected as you learn more details about your project.

Enter or Adjust Summary Tasks and Subtasks

The next step in creating your project schedule is to adjust your task list. Be sure that the Gantt Chart view is displayed. If it is not, select the Gantt Chart from your status bar at the bottom of the screen.

There are two types of tasks: summary tasks and subtasks. Summary tasks are larger, more general tasks, whereas subtasks are more detailed tasks that specify the actual work. Summary tasks are composed of subtasks; you do not actually work on a summary task. A summary task is complete when all of its subtasks are complete. Therefore, a summary task's duration is the total sum of all of its subtasks' durations. A summary task is scheduled to begin when its first subtask begins, and end when its last subtask ends. If you make changes at the summary task level, the summary task is automatically put into Manually Scheduled mode. For this reason, you should not enter duration or start and finish date data for a summary task unless you are sure you understand that you are "breaking" the scheduling functionality.

Summary tasks and subtasks are organized in an outline format, divided into task levels. For example, if a summary task is at outline level 1, its subtasks are at outline level 2. Those subtasks can then have subtasks of their own, displayed at level 3. Therefore, a task can function both as a summary task and a subtask simultaneously. Figure 2.11 shows a quick illustration of task levels.

Figure 2.11
This illustration demonstrates how the task at outline level 2 functions as both a summary task for outline level 3 tasks as well as a subtask for outline level 1.

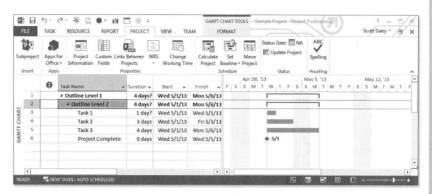

To adjust the outline levels of your tasks, select the task(s) to adjust and then use the Indent and Outdent buttons located on the Task tab (refer to Figure 2.14). The right arrow is the Indent button, and the left arrow is the Outdent button. Outdenting a task moves it to a higher outline level (a lower number), whereas indenting a task moves it to a lower outline level (a higher number). Therefore, to make a task or group of tasks subtasks, select them and click the Indent button. They become subtasks of the tasks directly above them.

 note
Hold down the Ctrl button and click on multiple tasks to select them simultaneously and indent or outdent them. They must be directly located underneath their prospective summary task.

You can choose to display or hide a summary task's subtasks. Sometimes it might be beneficial to hide the subtasks to save screen space, especially when all the subtasks for a particular summary task are complete. Next to each summary task is an expand/collapse control to hide or display subtasks in the shape of a triangle (refer to Figure 2.11). You can also use the Show Subtasks or Hide Subtasks buttons, located on the View tab under the Outline control.

➡ *For more information about manipulating and adjusting the task list, including more information about summary and subtasks,* ***see*** *the "Manipulating the Task List" section on* ***p. 148*** *in* ***Chapter 6.***

Create Milestones

A *milestone* is a significant turning point, landmark, or decision in your project. You should create a milestone attached to the last task in each section in your project, at the end of the project itself, and anywhere else you feel is a place of significance in your project.

Milestones are created as tasks with zero duration. Therefore, to create a milestone, enter it as a task, with a specific name (such as "Phase 1 Complete"), and enter zero (0) in the duration field. Project automatically creates the task as a milestone.

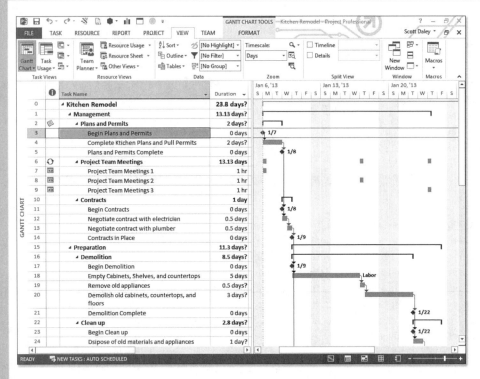

Figure 2.12
Task numbers 3, 5, 11, 14, 17, and 21 are milestones. Notice the diamond shape that appears in the timescale side as opposed to a task bar.

Figure 2.12 shows the task list for the Kitchen Remodel project. Notice the milestones at the end of each process group. Also, notice the components from the WBS in (refer back to Figure 2.7) are now decomposed into tasks.

In Figure 2.12, the milestones are linked to the last task in each process group. The upcoming section "Create Task Dependency Relationships" discusses the concept of linking tasks in greater detail.

 *For more information about using and creating milestones, **see** the "Defining Milestones" section on **p. 160** in **Chapter 6**.*

> **tip**
>
> Always place a milestone at the end of your project, attached to the last task. Call it "Project Complete" or something to that effect. This adds a final, official close to your project and avoids the all-too-often scenario of a project dragging on after legitimate work is complete.

Set Deadlines

Sometimes, you might need to clearly identify a task that must finish by a certain date. The recommended practice is to use the task deadline feature. For example, perhaps you are remodeling your kitchen around the busy season for the distributor, and you must order the materials by a certain date to receive them in time. Rather than assign a finish date, which would put a constraint on that task, you could set a deadline.

To set a task deadline, do the following:

1. Double-click on the task to open its Task Information dialog box.

2. On the Advanced tab of the Task Information dialog box, select the deadline date in the Deadline field (see Figure 2.13).

3. Click OK to close the Task Information dialog box, applying the deadline.

Figure 2.13
Set a deadline date for a task on the Advanced tab of the Task Information dialog box.

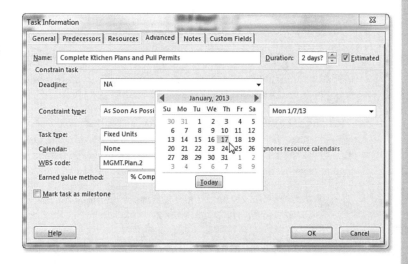

If the project schedule changes in any way that would push the completion of the task past its deadline, the task will be highlighted to alert you of the potential missed deadline, and you can make the appropriate adjustments.

> *For more information about using the Task Information dialog box, **see** the "Editing Tasks Using the Task Information Dialog Box" section on **p. 146** in **Chapter 6**.*

Create Task Dependency Relationships

Often in your project, you will find that certain tasks rely on the start or completion of other tasks for their own start or finish dates. For example, in the Demolition phase, you cannot remove the old appliances without first emptying the kitchen compartments. The start of the task Remove Old Appliances depends on the finish of the task Empty Cabinets, Shelves, and Countertops. Project enables you to link these tasks so it can schedule the start date of the Remove Old Appliances task to coincide with the finish date of the Empty Cabinets, Shelves, and Countertops task.

Linking tasks is key to enabling Project to predict the future. In Auto Scheduled mode, you have created your task list, but the planned start and finished dates for tasks are determined by two primary items: the dependency relationships and the planned duration for each task. Entering task duration is discussed in the upcoming section "Enter Estimates."

This type of relationship between tasks is called a *task dependency relationship*. There are two types of tasks in dependency relationships: the predecessor and the successor. Successor tasks are dependent on predecessor tasks. In this case, Remove Old Appliances is the successor and Empty Cabinets, Shelves, and Countertops is the predecessor, because the removal of the old appliances is dependent on the emptying of kitchen compartments. This is called a Finish-to-Start relationship, because the finish of the predecessor determines the start of the successor. This is the most common type of dependency relationship. The four types of dependency links are as follows:

- **Finish-to-Start (FS)**—Predecessor's finish determines successor's start.

- **Start-to-Start (SS)**—Predecessor's start determines successor's start.

- **Finish-to-Finish (FF)**—Predecessor's finish determines successor's finish.

- **Start-to-Finish (SF)**—Predecessor's start determines successor's finish. This is a rarely used task dependency relationship.

There are many ways to link tasks. For now, select the two tasks by holding down Ctrl and clicking on them; then click the Link Tasks button on the Task tab. The task you select first is the predecessor, and the task you select second is the successor. By default, Project places a Finish-to-Start dependency link on the two tasks (see Figure 2.14).

➡ *To learn more about these alternate methods for linking tasks,* **see** *the "Linking Tasks" section on* **p. 186** *in* **Chapter 7.**

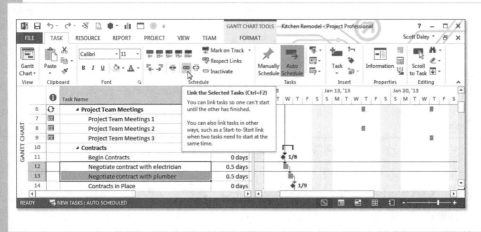

Figure 2.14
Link predecessor and successor tasks using the Link Tasks button on the Standard toolbar.

When tasks are linked, an arrow is drawn on the timescale side of the Gantt Chart from the predecessor to the successor.

To remove a task dependency link, select the two tasks and click the Unlink Tasks button, located next to the Link Tasks button on the Standard toolbar.

You can change the dependency link type in the Task Information dialog box. Double-click on the successor task to open its Task Information dialog box. On the Predecessors tab, you see the predecessor task(s) listed. Choose from the four task dependency relationship types in the drop-down list in the Type column and then click OK. The relationship type will be changed accordingly.

note

Tasks do not have to be adjacent to each other to be linked. You can link a task on row 2 with a task on row 13.

You will notice on the Predecessors tab of the Task Information dialog box that there is a Lag field for the dependency relationship. This is used in situations where the tasks have a dependency relationship, but need to allow for some time in between the predecessor and successor start or finish dates. For example, if the tasks can follow each other without delay, Project would schedule the Remove Old Appliances task to start immediately after the Empty Cabinets, Shelves, and Countertops task finishes. However, for other tasks, you might need to wait some time before the next task can begin. For example, Install Grout cannot begin until the task Install Tile has been completed for at least a day so that the tile adhesive has time to cure. In that case, you would enter a one-day (or more) lag (type **1d**) in the Lag field, and Project would link the two tasks and schedule the grout installation to begin one day after the tile is installed.

Some tasks have a dependency relationship but can overlap a bit; that is, the successor task can start before the predecessor task is completely finished. An example of this in the Kitchen Remodel project would be during the preparation stage. Cleanup of one area of the kitchen can begin before demolition of the entire kitchen is complete. In this case, you can enter a lead time, which starts the successor task early. There is no Lead field; leads are entered in the Lag field using negative numbers. Therefore, to enter a lead of one day for Cleanup Kitchen, you would enter **-1d** in the Lag field, and Project would schedule the Cleanup Kitchen task to begin one day before the Demolish Cabinets task was scheduled to finish.

> *For more information about task dependency relationships and linking tasks,* ***see*** *the "Linking Tasks" section on* ***p. 186*** *in* ***Chapter 7****.*

As you are creating dependency links, you are also beginning to create what is called the *critical path*. The critical path is composed of those tasks whose finish dates affect the finish date of the overall project. In other words, if a critical task finishes late, the project will likely finish late also, unless you are able to adjust to the delay and make up time elsewhere. Some tasks can finish late and the project's finish date will be unaffected, but those tasks that will push the finish date are a part of the critical path.

> *For more information about the critical path,* ***see*** *the "Reviewing the Big Picture: Critical Path Analysis" section on* ***p. 417*** *in* ***Chapter 12****.*

Create Your Team and Assign Resources

When you have defined your dependency links, the next logical step in creating your project schedule is to enter your planned estimates for each task (such as duration, cost, and so on). However, before you do that, it is wise to create your project team and assign resources to work on the tasks. That way, you can gather input from your team to better assist in entering more accurate estimates.

A plumber might be able to give you a better idea of how long it takes to install a new sink; therefore, it is important to build your team first before entering estimates so the team members can contribute to the process.

As you are creating your resource team, bear in mind that the members have crucial roles in the successful completion of your project. You are the project manager, but your team performs most of the actual work on the tasks. Just like a quarterback in football depends on his teammates, you rely on the individual success of your project team members for the overall success of your project.

To enter your resource information in Project, display the Resource Sheet view by selecting the View tab, Resource Sheet. Enter all resources you will use: people, facilities, equipment, and so on. Note that there are three types of resources in the Type field: work, material, and cost. Work resources are resources that work on tasks, such as people. Material resources are resources that are consumed while working on tasks, such as camera film, ink, or in the case of the Kitchen Remodel project, wood stain. A cost resource identifies specific project costs, such as travel expenses or delivery charges for appliances.

A fourth type of resource exists—the budget resource. A budget resource enables you to allocate the budget for the entire project. However, this is not an option in the Type field of the Resource Sheet view because a budget resource is assigned at the top (project summary) level, and not at the individual task level.

> ➡️ *For more information about the four resource types,* **see** *the "Defining Resources and Resource Information" section on* ***p. 237*** *in* ***Chapter 8.***

This quick start focuses on entering people resources for building your schedule. After you enter the resource name, you define its type in the Type field. Work is the default resource type (people are work resources).

The following list describes the remaining major fields you might need to complete on the Resource Sheet to set resource attributes:

- **Max. Units (Maximum Units)**—The maximum amount of units the work resource is available to work on the project. If a resource works 8 hours a day, and can only devote 4 hours a day to your project, that resource's Max. Units is 50%.

- **Std. Rate (Standard Rate)**—The amount of money the resource costs, such as $20/hour or $32,000/year. Project calculates the total cost of a task by multiplying the rate by the work on the task for the resource.

- **Cost/Use**—For work resources, the amount of money the resource costs per use. You can use this instead of the standard rate when you want to indicate a one-time use cost for a resource.

- **Base Calendar**—Which calendar the resource follows for workdays. By default, the project calendar is used (defined in the Project Information dialog box).

Figure 2.15 shows what a Resource Sheet view might look like for the Kitchen Remodel project.

> ➡️ *For more information about entering resource information,* **see** *the "Using the Resource Fields to Define Resource Details" section on* ***p. 242*** *in* ***Chapter 8.***

Figure 2.15
Enter all your resources and resource information on the Resource Sheet view. Due to screen space, not all fields are shown in this example.

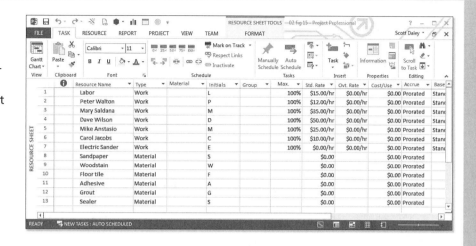

When you have created your resource list using the Resource Sheet, it is time to assign resources to tasks. To do so, follow these steps:

1. Return to the Gantt Chart view (select the View tab, Gantt Chart).

2. Double-click on a task to open the Task Information dialog box.

3. On the Resources tab in the Task Information dialog box, assign resources to the task by choosing the resource from the drop-down list in the Resource Name field. The drop-down list contains all the resources you have listed on the Resource Sheet view. You can also enter different values for Units and Cost if those values are different from what is defined on the Resource Sheet view (see Figure 2.16).

4. Click OK to close the Task Information dialog box, assigning the resources as you defined.

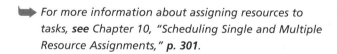 *For more information about assigning resources to tasks, **see** Chapter 10, "Scheduling Single and Multiple Resource Assignments," **p. 301**.*

 note

Sometimes you do not know the specific resources that will be available to work on your project. If this is the case, use the Resource Sheet view to create generic resources, and go back later to replace the generic resources with actual resources. That way, you have an idea of what kind of resources you will need and can assign generic resources to tasks to give you an idea.

 note

You can assign multiple resources to one task.

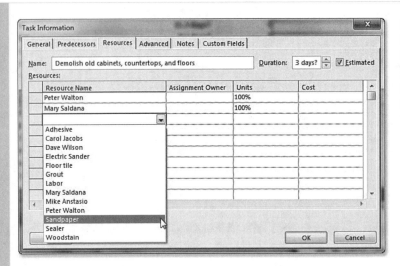

Figure 2.16
On the Resources tab of the Task Information dialog box, you can assign resources to work on the task.

How Duration, Work, and Resource Units Affect Your Project Schedule

Before discussing estimates, it's important to take a moment to discuss the work formula. For auto-scheduled tasks, Project uses a work formula to calculate either Work, Duration, or Resource Units. The work formula is as follows:

Work = Duration * Units

Therefore, you can only enter two of these three fields (usually Units and Duration or Units and Work); Project calculates the third.

These three data fields are important to your project schedule. They affect the amount of time scheduled to work on each task. For example, if you receive an estimate of 10 days (Duration) and the resource can work at 100% of an 8-hour work day (Resource Units), the assignment will be completed in 80 hours (Work). In other words, 10 days * (100% of 8 hrs/day) = 80 hours of effort, or work. However, if you obtain a work estimate of 20 hours, and your resource can only work at 50% of capacity because of other projects, the Duration will be calculated as 5 days (20 hours / 4 hours per day = 5 days). It is wise to remember that resources are rarely able to work at 100% efficiency, so it's important to be realistic regarding resource units so that either the work or duration is calculated by Project.

▶ *For more information about using Project's work formula,* **see** *Chapter 9, "Understanding Work Formula Basics," p. 269.*

Enter Estimates

Together with task dependency links, planned estimates help Project shape your schedule. Enter your estimates—with the help and guidance of your project team—directly into the entry fields in the Gantt Chart view. Obtain from them how much they can work (units) and either the duration or work estimate for the task.

The five fields that exist to the right of the task names on the default Gantt Chart view are Duration, Start, Finish, Predecessors, and Resource Names. It is often most accurate to get your estimates for tasks in hours, so you need to insert the Work field into this table and enter the hours in that field. The table, called the task entry table, is the default table displayed with a timescale in the Gantt Chart view.

You should only concern yourself with entering the durations of tasks in the Duration field or the work effort for the tasks in the Work field. When the task mode is Auto Scheduled, the Start and Finish fields will be calculated automatically based on the Project start (or finish) date, which you defined in the Project Information dialog box, as well as the task dependency links and duration or work estimates. The predecessors have already been determined when you created your task links, and the resources have already been assigned.

Duration is the amount of time scheduled to work on a task, usually shown in days. By default, when you create a new task, the duration of "1d?" is entered in its Duration field, meaning it is scheduled for one day, and the question mark indicates that this is a tentative estimate. You can specify a more solid estimate by entering a specific number and time unit in the Duration field. Or, you can enter a work estimate (usually hours for the task to be completed) in the Work field and let the Duration be calculated by the work formula. It is best to first consult your team members who have expertise in particular areas of your project, and make duration or work estimate entries in all of your subtasks.

Some organizations consider work hours the best way to obtain estimates. For instance, it will take 10 hours to complete the task. Other organizations consider duration the best way to provide estimates, such as two days. Generally, work hours are more accurate, but many organizations are successful at creating schedules using duration. In this example, duration has been used.

Figure 2.17 shows a portion of the kitchen remodel project with all task links defined and all durations entered. Notice now how the task bars on the timescale side create a chronological timeline for the project. Also, the assigned resources appear next to the task bars.

 note

You can enter other time units in the Duration field, such as hours. However, "days" is the default time unit. Similarly, you can enter alternate time units in the Work field, but "hours" is the default time unit.

 tip

Make your estimates as accurate as possible. Do not overcompensate to buy yourself more time, and do not underestimate to give the impression that you will get the project done sooner than expected. Enter realistic estimates, and try to ensure that the project stays consistent with those estimates, and things will run much more smoothly.

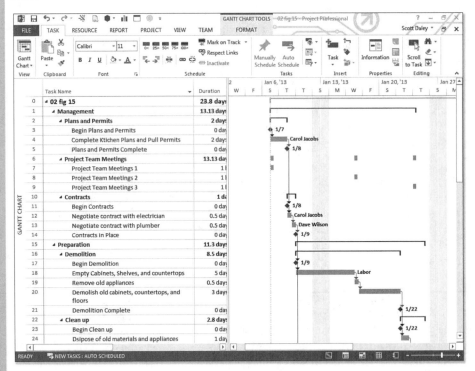

Review the Schedule for Overallocation or Other Potential Issues

At this point, you have created your initial project schedule, using Project as a scheduling engine. However, there are two more things you need to do before moving to the next process group of your project. The first is to double-check everything to make sure it looks correct, and the second is to fix any issues or complications.

There are many ways to check for resource overallocation. For now, display the Resource Usage view (using Team Planner for this same purpose is described in detail elsewhere). Resource overallocation is when a resource is assigned to more work than can be completed in the default 8-hour day (or whatever capacity has been set to work in a day).

Figure 2.18 shows the Resource Usage view for the kitchen remodel project. You can see that Peter Walton and Mary Saldana are both overallocated; their names appear in red, and there is an Overallocation indicator next to each name.

If you have any resources that are overallocated, you might want to go back and reassign other resources to take some of the work from the overallocated resources, or rearrange the schedule to spread the overallocated resources' workload out across time. In this case, Peter and Mary are the owners of the kitchen and will be doing most of the work themselves. They can hire other workers to take some of the workload, but that would cost more money. So in this case, they will remain overallocated to save money.

Figure 2.18
The Resource Usage view shows whether any resources are overallocated.

	①	Resource Name	Work	Add New Column	Details	S	Jan 27, '13 S	M	T	W	T	F	S
1		Labor	0 hrs		Work								
2	◇	◢ Peter Walton	59 hrs		Work			1.6h	8h	6.4h		1.6h	
		Begin Plans and	0 hrs		Work								
		Complete Ktche	16 hrs		Work								
		Plans and Permi	0 hrs		Work								
		Project Team M	1 hr		Work								
		Project Team M	1 hr		Work								
		Project Team M	1 hr		Work								
		Begin Counters	0 hrs		Work			0h					
		Install Counterto	8 hrs		Work			1.6h	6.4h				
		Install Sink and F	8 hrs		Work				1.6h	6.4h			
		Counters Compl	0 hrs		Work					0h			
		Begin Appliance	0 hrs		Work							0h	
		Install Appliance	8 hrs		Work							1.6h	
		Appliance Install	0 hrs		Work								
		Begin Test	0 hrs		Work								
		Test wiring and (	8 hrs		Work								
		Test plumbing fc	8 hrs		Work								
		Test Complete	0 hrs		Work								
3	◇	◢ Mary Saldana	177.4 hrs		Work		8h	8h	8h	8h	6.4h		
		Project Team M	1 hr		Work								
		Project Team M	1 hr		Work								
		Project Team M	1 hr		Work								
		Begin Contracts	0 hrs		Work								
		Negotiate contr	4 hrs		Work								
		Negotiate contr	4 hrs		Work								

 For more information about resolving resource overallocation, **see** Chapter 24, "Resolving Resource Allocations Problems," **p. 801**.

Besides checking for resource overallocation, review the timeline of your schedule to make sure no work is scheduled during any nonworking time you might have forgotten to define. Also check for any missing tasks or tasks without resource assignments, and make sure your dependency links are correct.

In short, double-check everything, because the next step is the last step in creating your project schedule!

 For more information about reviewing your schedule for other potential issues, **see** Chapter 12, "Performing a Schedule Reality Check," **p. 411**.

Inactivating Tasks

Sometimes you'll want to tell Project to ignore a task. There are a variety of reasons for it; maybe you want to remember that a particular task might be important, but it isn't yet. Or maybe you are working from a project template, and you want to retain all possibly useful tasks, without actually having them impact your project schedule in anyway.

If you have Project Professional, any task can be made inactive by selecting the task on any view, clicking on the task tab, and then clicking Inactivate in Schedule group. The task will no longer affect resource availability or any other tasks in the schedule. Tasks that are inactive appear with a line through the center and are grayed out.

> 🔍 **note**
>
> The control in the Ribbon is called Inactivate, but the task field is called Active. So, if you need to filter out, highlight, or sort by Inactive tasks, use the Active field.

Baseline Your Schedule

When you have verified that everything is in order, it is time to baseline your schedule. A baseline is essentially a snapshot of your project at a given time. Therefore, when you baseline your project after you have created the schedule, it is a snapshot of the planned schedule, with no actual work tracked or recorded yet.

This baseline will be important later in the project as you compare actual data with planned data; the baseline enables you to compare what is happening with what was planned to happen according to the schedule you have just created. This is important because the Work and Duration fields are actually planned fields that start to change as actual work is entered. Your original estimates that you entered into those fields will perhaps be changed if you do not capture the baseline.

To baseline your project schedule, select the Project tab, Set Baseline. The Set Baseline dialog box appears. Be sure Set Baseline is selected, as well as Entire Project, as illustrated in Figure 2.19. Then, click OK to set your baseline.

Figure 2.19
In the Set Baseline dialog box, set the baseline for your project schedule, which will be useful for future tracking and reporting processes.

➡ *For more information about capturing the baseline, **see** the "Working with Project Baselines" section on **p. 432** in **Chapter 13**.*

Track Your Project

When you have created your schedule and set your baseline, you are ready to begin the Executing and the Monitoring and Controlling process groups of your project. As mentioned previously, these two process groups overlap and recur cyclically during the project life cycle. Work on a project begins (Execution), and you must track and analyze the actual work as compared to the baseline and make adjustments based on actual data (Monitoring and Controlling).

To accurately analyze your project's progress, two things must happen. First, you must set your baseline when your schedule is complete before any work begins, as discussed in the previous section. Then, you must accurately track the actual progress on your project.

Communication with your team is important for gathering tracking information, so after you find what works best, stick with it consistently.

After you enter actual progress data into your project file, it is necessary to review the schedule to see the effect of the actual data. It might be necessary to modify the schedule to account for the changes and reset the baseline. Use the Tracking Gantt Chart view to help you review the changes caused by entering the actual data. Select View, Tracking Gantt to display the Tracking Gantt Chart view.

The following sections discuss tracking and controlling your project data.

 tip

It is important to be consistent in your tracking habits. Develop a routine that works best for you, and stick with it. For example, you can hold a meeting every few days or every week with your project team members to get their latest progress updates and then enter that data into your project.

Obtain Project Status

Regular meetings with your project team are essential for collecting actual data for the tasks they are working on. Keep the lines of communication open. Discuss any problems your team members are experiencing, and whether any solutions are available to resolve these issues. Team meetings are also a great place to discuss future tasks and prepare the team members for the work that lies ahead.

Get actual work or duration based on the kind of estimate you used. For instance, if you entered duration estimates, ask for how much the resource has completed in duration. If you had work estimates, ask how much work has been completed. You can also ask for %Complete to enter progress. However, no matter which way you get the progress status, you need to ask one more question: How much duration or work is left to complete the task? A common tendency is for team members to report that a task is 85% or 90% complete because they believe that most of their work is done, but in reality, they have quite a bit more work to finish. If you talk with them about how many more hours remain or what date they believe they will finish, you can get a better idea of the actual work that remains.

As you get progress information from your team, you need to enter that data into Project, which is discussed in the next section.

note

Project has fields for both remaining work and remaining duration, and it is important to track these fields as well as the actual data. A task might have 16 hours of planned work, and a resource might have worked 5 hours on it, so Project would assume there are 11 hours left. However, the actual remaining work might be only 3 hours, because the work estimate was too much. That is why it is important to gather not only actual work but remaining work as well.

Enter Your Tracking Data

When you have obtained project data from your team, you must enter it into Project. There are many ways to do this as well. A good way to display and enter tracking data is by using a split view. In the top pane, use the Tracking Gantt view with the Tracking table displayed. Select the View tab, and select the Tracking Gantt; then display the Tracking table by clicking Tables and selecting Tracking. The Tracking table has entry fields for actual data, percentage complete, and Remaining Duration.

You can also see the Baseline Work and Remaining Work for each resource on the task. To do so, follow these steps:

1. On the Tracking Gantt view with the Tracking table displayed, split the window (check the Details box in the Split View group on the View tab).

2. In the bottom pane, right-click in the gray area and select Work. The bottom pane now displays Baseline, Actual, and Remaining Work for each resource assigned to the task selected in the top pane.

Splitting the window also makes it easier for you to enter Remaining Work for each resource. This split window is displayed in Figure 2.20.

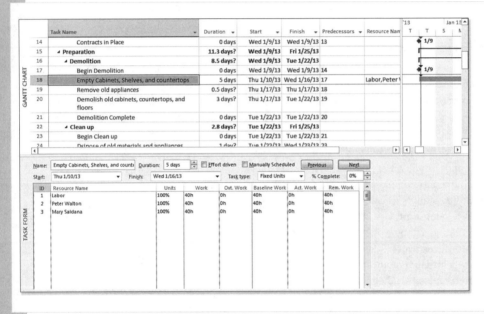

Figure 2.20 Split the window to view each resource's Baseline, Actual, and Remaining Work for the task selected in the top pane, and for easy entry for Remaining Work.

Before you enter any tracking data, it is important to set the Status Date field to the date through which you have collected data. For example, you might have a team meeting on a Tuesday, where you gather actual progress data from your team through the previous Friday. You would need to set the Status Date field to the previous Friday, because the data you enter is current only through that

Friday. Because an entire week has passed since the data was collected by the team and obtained by you, Project should use the status date instead of the current date for updating the project schedule. To set the status date, select the Project tab and set the status date in the Status Date field (refer back to Figure 2.9).

Enter data into the Actual Work and Actual Cost fields directly from the information you gather from your project team. You can enter Actual Work as hours they spent working on their tasks, or you can enter %Complete for how far they are percentage-wise to completing their tasks. If a task has an estimated duration of one day, and the resource has worked four hours as of the status date on the task, you could enter **4 hours** in the Actual Work field, and the %Complete field automatically displays 50%. Or, you could enter **50%** in the %Complete field, and the Actual Work field would display four hours automatically (you can also use the 0%, 25%, 50%, 75%, and 100% controls on the Task tab).

However, if the task has been worked on for four hours but is not yet 50% complete, you would enter the remaining duration in the Remaining Duration or Remaining Work field. Therefore, you could enter **4 hours** in the Actual Work field to show that four hours have been worked on the task, and then enter **6 hours** in the Remaining Work or Remaining Duration field to show that six hours of work remain to be done to finish the task. The %Complete field would show 40% instead of 50% to account for the remaining time, as well as the actual time spent working on the task.

Figure 2.21 shows the Tracking Gantt view with the Tracking table displayed. Notice how the task bars on the timescale side display the percentage complete on the right, and for those tasks that have started but have not completed, the task bars display progress in a darker shade.

Figure 2.21 When you enter tracking data into your project, the task bars on the Tracking Gantt Chart display percentage complete.

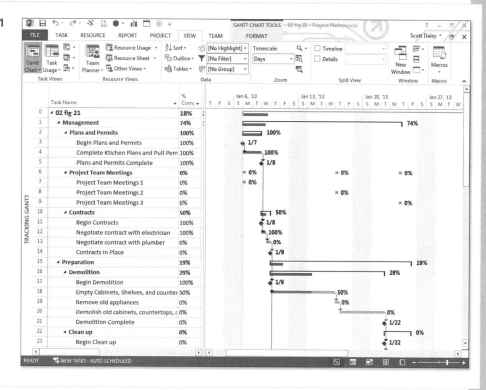

note

When tasks are entirely complete, it is important that you zero out Remaining Work or Duration rather than just entering **100%** in the %Complete field. This practice enables you to capture data on the current project to use as the basis for future project estimates. If you enter **100%** in the %Complete field, Project always assumes that the Remaining Work should be added to what is in the Actual Work or Actual Duration field. If the Remaining Work was not accurate, your historical record will also be inaccurate. Entering the actual work or duration and then zeroing out the Remaining Work or Duration field makes the task 100% complete. If you are not trying to capture estimates for historical reasons, entering 100% in the %Complete field is fine.

It is especially important to enter **100%** in the %Complete field for milestones. The check marks next to tasks visually indicate that all tasks are closed, and you can have a clean project finish.

After each time you enter project data, you should update the changes to your project. To do so, follow these steps:

1. Select the Project tab, Update Project.

2. In the Update Project dialog box, select Reschedule Uncompleted Work to Start After and then enter the status date used for the most recent tracking update.

3. Click OK to update the project and close the dialog box. Any uncompleted work is scheduled to begin after the status date.

After your project is updated, review the schedule impacts caused by the tracking updates on the Tracking Gantt view. If the actual values are less than your estimates (through the status date), your schedule dates might move out and show a later finish date than what was originally planned, because the project is taking longer than expected. If more work was accomplished than planned, the finish date might be scheduled sooner than originally planned, because you have completed more work through the status date than you estimated.

You might need to make adjustments to help get the schedule back on track if your project update is undesirable, such as reducing the scope or adding resources to help finish tasks faster. Keep in mind that this might increase your budget.

➡ *For more information about tracking your project,* **see** *Chapter 13, "Tracking Your Project Progress," **p. 431**.*

Analyze Your Status

Reports are an excellent method of analyzing your progress as compared to your baseline plan. Project offers two kinds of reports, confusingly called *reports* and *visual reports*. Think of reports as your primary reporting tool and visual reports as your primary export tool for further analysis or presentation using Visio or Excel. These reports are all customizable. In addition, you can create your own reports from scratch to display exactly the data fields you want included in the report.

To access Project's existing reports, select the Report tab and choose either Reports or Visual Reports. You see that Project comes with a default set of reports, as well as the ability to create reports from scratch.

If you select Visual Reports from the Report tab, the Visual Reports – Create Report dialog box appears. You can choose from six categories, displayed on the tabs in the dialog box: Task Usage, Resource Usage, Assignment Usage, Task Status, Resource Status, and Assignment Status. The All tab contains all the reports found on these six tabs.

Visual reports are created using either Microsoft Office Excel or Microsoft Office Visio. Each report contains different dimensions of data and is accompanied by a visual representation of that data.

> ➡ *For more information about using reports and visual reports in Project,* ***see*** *Chapter 15, "Using Reports for Tracking and Control,"* ***p. 497***.

> ➡ *For more information about creating and customizing reports,* ***see*** *Chapter 20, "Reports Part I: 2013 Reports,"* ***p. 625***.

> ➡ *For more information about creating and customizing the visual reports,* ***see*** *Chapter 21, "Reports Part II: Visual Reports,"* ***p. 653***.

Because it is impossible to plan the perfect project, project analysis is important while you're working on a project. Unforeseeable issues will arise that delay certain tasks, and possibly delay the project in general. In short, life happens. All you can do is prepare as best as possible, stay patient and calm when things do not go as planned, and communicate issues to the proper members of your organization so they are not surprised by the changes and have the opportunity to help the project get back on track. Track and analyze your progress, make adjustments, and use Project to help you communicate the alternatives for project adjustments when the issues arise.

> ➡ *For more information about analyzing your project's progress,* ***see*** *Chapter 14, "Analyzing Performance,"* ***p. 459***.

Close Your Project

When you are at the end of the work on your project, you are not quite finished. All too often, work on a project finishes, and the project just kind of fizzles out with no official ending. Do not let this happen to you. Take the time to properly close your project, and you will benefit greatly.

Before you officially close the project, examine your task list to be sure all tasks are completed and their %Complete field is 100% (including milestones). If for some reason a task is not complete, be sure to specifically document the reason by attaching a note to the task (double-click on the task, and in the Task Information dialog box, select the Notes tab). Also, be sure all project deliverables are delivered as agreed upon in the scope statement.

After all tasks are completed and accounted for, it is time to close the project. Save the project file in the appropriate location on your computer or network for future reference.

One of the most important steps in closing a project is conducting a Lessons Learned session. This is a chance to sit down with your team and other project stakeholders and discuss what worked well and why, as well as what did not work well and why. No matter what the outcome of the project was, you have learned something. It is important to focus on the positive and not the negative, and close the project on a good note, no matter how successful or unsuccessful it was.

Even if you installed your cabinets upside-down in the kitchen remodel project, you are still better at remodeling a kitchen than you were before the project began. Document all the lessons learned, and give all persons involved with the project a chance to voice their opinions about how everything went. It will enable them to leave their opinions with the project, and move on without feeling like they had more to say.

After you have closed the project and conducted a Lessons Learned session, celebrate the completion and hard work by having a party with your team and stakeholders. Projects are hard work, and the people involved deserve to celebrate their efforts.

And, at the end of a kitchen remodel project, what better place to host the party than the new kitchen itself—the project deliverable!

> 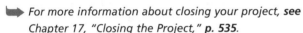 *For more information about closing your project,* **see** *Chapter 17, "Closing the Project,"* **p. 535**.

 note

When conducting a Lessons Learned session, it is important to stay positive and light-hearted. Even if there was tension during the project, your team members will feel better about their performance if you leave things on a good note.

 tip

Document the lessons learned. If they involve specific tasks or phases of the project, attach them as notes to the task or phase for future reference. Above all else, projects are learning experiences, and it is important to welcome the lessons learned. You will only improve your ability as a project manager for the next project you work on.

Consultants' Tips

The intent of this chapter was to give you a quick overview of the power of Project so that you can begin to benefit immediately. Hundreds of great features are available in the tool that were not even mentioned in this chapter, so keep reading and discover many capabilities that help you become a better project manager.

Formulas That Affect Your Schedule

The primary complaint that people have about using a scheduling tool such as Project is that the tool "changed my data." Introduced in Project 2010, Manually Scheduled task mode has changed that. It is now possible to use Project's scheduling capability selectively, on some tasks, no tasks, or all tasks, depending on how you need to use it.

The key to using Project well—to use Project to make your life easier—is that you must learn how Project uses formulas to help you predict the future of your project. When things do not go according to plan, the scheduling engine helps you figure out what the ripple effect will be. Learn these formulas and rules so that it is not a surprise to you. Manually Scheduled task mode defeats the predictive mechanisms of Project.

Duration = Actual Duration + Remaining Duration

The total duration of a task includes all that has happened before today and all that is scheduled to happen in the future. You cannot reduce duration without considering both the past and the future.

Work = Actual Work + Remaining Work

The same rule applies to work. It is made up of whatever work has happened before (Actual Work) and all work yet to be completed (Remaining Work).

Work Formula (Work = Duration × Units)

This is the basic formula that drives most of the behavior of the scheduling engine. You can only change two of the three items; the remaining item will be calculated by the software. Memorize this formula and practice changing two of the three items until you become comfortable with its properties.

Create a WBS

The vast majority of projects that fail do so because the scope and requirements were not clear. The use of the WBS is the single most important thing you can do to ensure that a project comes in on time, within budget, and with the quality and functions expected. Do not skip this step.

80/20 Rule

When you start a project, there are always some things that are unknown. Focus on the big picture (the 80%) and make progress on what you do know. Clearly identify the things that are not yet resolved (the 20%), but do not let them keep you from making progress.

Project Is a Tracking Tool

Project is a scheduling and tracking tool. Use it to help you keep your project on target. If you only use it to create the initial schedule, you have left most of its value unused.

Always Baseline!

A baseline is like a map. If you don't know where you planned to go or how long it would take you to get there, it is difficult to know when you have arrived. You cannot learn from your mistakes or celebrate your accuracy if you don't keep track of your original plan. It is an excellent tool for helping you keep your project's scope on target.

Split Window and Views

Get comfortable with the use of the split window and with these four important views: Gantt Chart, Tracking Gantt, Resource Sheet, and Resource Usage. Between them, they display most of the data that tells you what is happening in your project. If you get comfortable with them, you can quickly make Project the most powerful tool on your desktop.

MICROSOFT PROJECT AND THE PROJECT MANAGEMENT DOMAIN

This chapter is about using Microsoft Project within the domain of project management. It identifies accepted standards and methodologies that are in use within the field and provides some examples of how they are used with Project.

History of Project Management

When Patrick Henry said, "I know of no way of judging the future but by the past," he could have been talking about project management. When faced with projects that have never been done before, all project managers can do is look at what has come before them.

Although project management has been practiced for thousands of years, evidenced by the Egyptian and Roman dynasties, modern project management can be traced back to the late nineteenth century and the rise in large-scale government projects and growing technological advancements. Fredrick Taylor, the Father of Scientific Management, applied scientific reasoning to analyzing and improving labor, and Henry Gantt studied management of Navy ship construction during World War I. Gantt's use of charts, task bars, and milestone markers is still practiced today, and they bear his name. One of the major projects that brought detailed project planning, controlling, and coordination to the forefront was the Hoover Dam project, which involved $175 million dollars, six different companies, a major worksite with no existing infrastructure, and approximately 5,200 workers. The project was brought in under budget and ahead of schedule.

After developments in project management during two World Wars and the growing Cold War, major changes to project management were brought about with the launch of Sputnik. Fearful that the United States was falling behind in the race to space, the United States introduced several major programs to focus on science and exploration. Several agencies, including the Advanced Research Project Agency, a high-level research and development program that later became DARPA, and NASA were founded. These agencies led the way in the development of project management.

Two other major developments for project management to grow out of this period were the Critical Path Method (CPM) and the Program Evaluation and Review Technique (PERT). CPM was devised by Du Pont and Remington Rand for use with the UNIVAC-1 computer mainframe. PERT was invented by the Program Evaluation Branch of the Special Projects office of the U.S. Navy, for use with the POLARIS missile program, and was also used on the Apollo program for NASA. CPM/PERT gave managers more control over extremely large and complex projects, but could only be calculated within large mainframe computer systems and were used mainly for government sector projects.

With the computer revolution of the 1980s and the move from mainframe computers to personal computers with the ability to multitask, project management software became more accessible to other companies. The Internet and networked systems only made project managers more efficient at controlling and managing the different aspects of their projects. More information on previously completed projects is available today than ever before, making the project manager's job of estimating the future by looking at the past easier than ever.

Exploring Project Management Industry Standards

Almost anyone can create a schedule with Project. Organizing that schedule into a logical flow of work, however, requires a solid understanding of how projects should be managed and decomposed into logical units. To understand project management, you must understand the standards and methodology behind it. Although Gantt Charts and other similar resources are used in almost all project management schedules, there are several different ways of using those resources.

This chapter discusses prominent industry standards often used to set a framework for building schedules. A variety of methodologies, team styles, and life cycles also are explored. The approach and techniques vary, but the software can still be used to support virtually any approach to scheduling that an individual or organization chooses to use.

Project Management Body of Knowledge (PMBOK)

The Project Management Institute, or PMI, is an internationally recognized organization that has developed standards for the domain of project management including standards for portfolio management, program management, project management, and Work Breakdown Structures. PMI has several hundred thousand members in more than 65 countries. It is widely recognized for its certification programs and continues to grow through a combination of volunteer efforts, certification programs, local chapter events, international seminars, and special interest groups.

The standards created by PMI are authored by a vast network of project management professionals who volunteer their time to create and update these standards on a regular basis. The standards groups are from many different countries across the globe; they research topics and collaborate to bring together the latest thinking and techniques from their collective experience.

The PMI standard that is of primary importance for this chapter of the book is in its fifth edition and is known as "A Guide to the Project Management Body of Knowledge," also known as the PMBOK Guide. It is discussed in some detail in this chapter to help in understanding all the components that should be considered when creating a schedule.

Because PMI is a standards and certification organization, it does not prescribe methodologies or "how to" approaches; rather, it defines specific standards and offers certifications in the field of project management. The PMBOK provides a context for a way to do things, rather than the process that should be followed.

Inexperienced project managers often try to make their schedules follow PMBOK as if it were a recipe for success. This can lead them into traps and complexity that is not useful in completion of their projects. Instead, they should look to the PMBOK for support of the methodology and life cycle that they choose to follow.

The PMBOK Guide has established five process groups to define the project management process. These processes are as follows:

- **Initiating Process Group**—Defines and authorizes the project or a project phase

- **Planning Process Group**—Defines and refines objectives, and plans the course of action required to attain the objectives and scope that the project is to address

- **Executing Process Group**—Integrates people and other resources to carry out the project management plan

- **Monitoring and Controlling Process Group**—Regularly measures and monitors progress to identify variances from the project management plan so that corrective action can be taken when necessary to meet project objectives

- **Closing Process Group**—Formalizes acceptance of the product, service, or result and brings the project or a project phase to an orderly end

 tip

PMI makes a clear distinction between a *project plan* and a *project schedule*. The *plan* is a formal document that includes narrative on communication approaches, assumptions, deliverables, and execution of the project. The *schedule* is one component of the plan that focuses on the timeline for the activities to be performed. As scheduling tools become more sophisticated, they are gradually including more elements that used to reside only in the plan. Project Desktop still focuses on scheduling functions, but the server components have added capabilities to support more of the plan functions.

Projects are created and implemented in environments that are larger in scope than the projects themselves. All projects must have a beginning and an end, as shown by the Initiating and Closing process groups. In between, a project will be engaged continually with the other three process groups, as shown in Figure 3.1.

The PMBOK identifies nine knowledge areas that a project manager should consider throughout the entire life cycle of a project. Knowledge areas focus on a specific aspect of the overall domain and identify the elements that need to be considered to properly manage a project:

- **Project Integration Management**—This knowledge area looks at the processes and activities needed to identify, define, combine, unify, and coordinate the different actions within a project management process group.

- **Project Scope Management**—This knowledge area handles scope planning, scope definition, creating a WBS (decomposition of the scope into smaller components), scope verification, and scope control.

- **Project Time Management**—This knowledge area concerns five different steps: activity definition, activity sequencing, activity resource estimating, activity duration estimating, and schedule development.

- **Project Cost Management**—This knowledge area involves planning, estimating, budgeting, and controlling costs so a project can be finished within budget.

- **Project Quality Management**—This knowledge area determines policies, objectives, and responsibilities to meet a project's quality standards.

- **Project Human Resource Management**—This knowledge area helps organize and manage a project's team, the people necessary for the completion of the project.

- **Project Communications Management**—This knowledge area involves the processes that ensure timely generation, collection, distribution, storage, retrieval, and disposition of information.

- **Project Risk Management**—This knowledge area envelopes risk management planning, identification, analysis, responses, monitoring, and controlling of a project.

- **Project Procurement Management**—This knowledge area involves the processes necessary to purchase products, services, or results from outside the project team.

- **Project Stakeholder Management**—This knowledge area involves the processes necessary to manage the expectations of and results for the many people and things that can have a stake in the execution and outcome of your project.

The ten knowledge areas are specifically designed to work with the five process groups to identify possible areas for management within the scope of the project. When the two components are combined, they provide guidance for what elements should be considered at what time in a project.

In the context of the Project desktop, the key knowledge areas are scope, time, and cost. These components help you build the initial project schedule framework.

The emphasis for each knowledge area varies by phase of project; some are more important in one phase than another, but all of the nine are used throughout the project.

 note

Do not confuse the PMBOK process groups with life cycle phases of projects. This is a common tendency when a project manager tries to decompose a project into logical components. Process groups pertain to all projects; life cycles vary by the type of project, the domain of the work, the complexity and timeframe, and many other factors. Details about phases are covered later in this chapter.

Figure 3.1
The relationship among the PMBOK process groups (taken from Figure 3.3, *PMBOK Guide, Fifth Edition*).

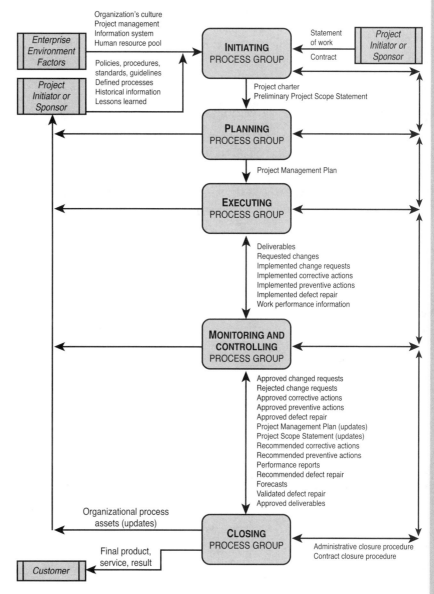

PRINCE2

PRINCE2, which stands for *Projects in Controlled Environments*, is a project management methodology developed by the United Kingdom government. It is in its second release and was originally known as the PRINCE technique. The first release was established in 1989 by the Central Computer and Telecommunications Agency (CCTA) as a standard for information technology project management. Because of its success in IT, the methodology was republished about seven years later in a version that could be applied across many other disciplines. PRINCE2 was again updated in 2005 by the Office of Government Commerce (OGC), has become the standard for project management in the United Kingdom, and is now used in 50 other countries. You can become certified in the use of PRINCE2 at either one of two levels: Foundation and Practitioner.

PRINCE2 uses a simple four-step process to explain what each project needs, as shown in Figure 3.2. This process is explained in more detail using the following eight different processes, sometimes known as the Validation, Quality, Verification, and Approval steps:

- **Start-up**—This is when a project manager is chosen. The need for the project is defined and outlined as to how it will be executed.

- **Direction**—The project manager, who reports to the Project Board, is responsible for managing the details. The Project Board is responsible for the overall success of the current project and defines the direction in which the project will be heading.

- **Initiation**—The Project Initiation Document is prepared and submitted to the Project Board for approval and possible revision.

- **Stage Control**—During this stage, the project is broken down into several different manageable stages. The number of stages depends on the size and risk level of the project, and each stage must also plan for the succeeding stage. Before any new stage can begin, the current stage must be fully finished.

- **Stage Boundary Management**—At this stage, the Project Board must review the current stage and then develop the process for the next stage. It is only after the approval for the execution of the current stage and the planning of the next stage that the project can continue.

- **Planning**—This stage is used for deciding what products will be produced and what is required for their production. Then, estimates are made for cost, time, and any other resources, plus any risk analysis, activity scheduling, and process streamlining that is necessary for the project.

- **Product Delivery Management**—This is the production stage, where the project manager confirms that the right goods are being produced correctly and on schedule.

- **Closing**—After everything is finished, the project manager must perform a post-project review, which evaluates the outcome of the project. When this review is approved by the Project Board, the project is complete.

In addition to consideration of these standards and methods, project managers need to understand the environment in which they will be working before they create a schedule. They need to be aware of the various methodologies and approaches that can be used to help them (or confuse them, if they do not understand how and when the methodologies and approaches should be applied). The following section provides an introduction to this information.

 note

There is no conflict between PMBOK and PRINCE2. They can be used together if a project manager chooses to use both. PRINCE2 is a methodology and focuses more on deliverables, whereas PMBOK is a standard and focuses on the process and knowledge areas. PRINCE2 establishes a Validation of Process (through a specific focus on deliverables and the activities around them), whereas PMBOK focuses on the processes used to manage the deliverables.

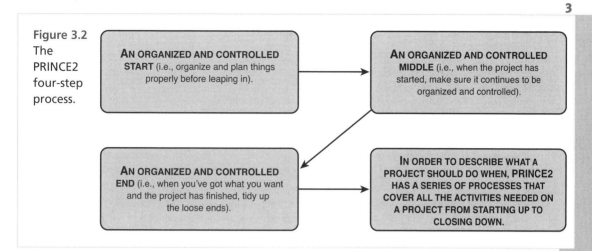

Figure 3.2
The
PRINCE2
four-step
process.

WBS, Phases and Control Points, Methodologies, and Life Cycles

 note

Many of the preceding terms are used by project managers to describe the approach that is used to define and execute a project. Each of these has been explained in many other texts and references. Because the focus of this book is using Project, the topics are brought up here to provide context only; there is no attempt to provide the definitive use of any of the terms. Rather, the hope is that the reader can apply the concepts and techniques as appropriate when building a schedule. The work that needs to happen during a project's life does not automatically conform to a particular methodology.

Before building any schedule, the project manager must consider two key components: work decomposition (what work needs to be done, the Work Breakdown Structure or WBS) and managerial control (stages, phases, and life cycle requirements). The discipline used for either depends on the environment in which the project is executed, so the formality will vary, but both components must be considered. The tasks or activities and milestones (how the work will be accomplished) should not be defined in a project schedule until the WBS and control framework are determined. WBS helps the project manager set parameters around the scope of work to be done; the life cycle sets the controls in place for decisions during project execution. If these two components are kept in control, the project will have a much higher opportunity for success.

Work Breakdown Structure (WBS)

Step one in building a schedule is to begin with a Work Breakdown Structure (WBS) that allows decomposition of the scope of the project from major components to the smallest set of deliverables, called *work packages*. As a best practice, this process is completed before a true schedule is built. It can be done using Project as long as ongoing "use" rules are defined and followed to keep the WBS components intact after the project is approved and baselined.

As mentioned earlier in this chapter, PMI has developed a standard for the WBS. It is a primary component of good project management practices because it forces the discipline of scope definition and control.

➡ *For detailed information of how to build a WBS,* **see** *Chapter 4, "Getting Started After the Business Initiative Is Approved,"* **p. 71**.

If the scope of your project is managed through a WBS, all the tasks and milestones will be created in support of specific work packages and can be rolled up through the structure for tracking progress using Earned Value Management techniques. This practice eliminates some of the common failure points in project management, such as scope creep and fuzzy requirements. All work is clearly linked to the production of a deliverable, and progress against that deliverable can be monitored.

Managerial Control

So many terms are used in the context of managerial control that a few definitions are in order. Hundreds of resources are available to provide detailed explanations; the purpose here is context only. The hope is that these simple descriptions will help the user's understanding when building a project schedule, as discussed in the following sections.

Phases and Gates

Many organizations have established processes for deciding what projects will be approved and for overseeing the projects after they have been launched. In some organizations, the processes are rigorous and robust; in others, the processes might be simple guidelines that have been put in place to help project managers. In either case, a defined set of standard phases and control points (often called *gates*) simplify the decisions that need to be made when running a project. In most cases, templates can be created that standardize the phases and the required control points for different types of projects.

Phases and gates can allow more management control of the project, as they break down the project into smaller components. This helps to keep executive and team focus aligned on the same set of activities. A change between phases is usually defined by some kind of transfer. In many cases, the transfer requires a formal review before the project is allowed to move into the next phase. It is not unusual, however, for phases to begin before the completion of the previous phase, especially when the risks are judged as acceptable. Each organization will make its own determination of the level of control required.

Building the phases and control points into templates is an excellent way to minimize the amount of work that needs to be done when building a new schedule. Many examples are already available in Project, and the organization can build additional ones as needed.

➡ *For additional information on building and using templates,* **see** *Chapter 18, "Managing Project Files Locally and in the Cloud," on* **p. 549**.

Methodologies

As organizations mature in the project management discipline, they often adopt more formal management control systems. These systems are typically described as methodologies that include processes, rules, standards, and methods for how work will be done. In this section, we identify a few of the ones used in specific industry segments. Each industry has its own set of methodologies, and this chapter does not attempt to identify all of them. The purpose here is to show how managing projects using Project can be included in the methodology to assist in the enforcement and usability of the tools.

Life Cycles

Like methodologies, project life cycles are unique to the industries and disciplines in which they are used. Although all projects have a beginning and an end, they vary greatly in how the work is accomplished. It is nearly impossible to define an ideal life cycle. Some companies and organizations use a single, standardized life cycle for every project, whereas others permit the project manager to choose the best life cycle for the project. In others, a variety of life cycles exists to accommodate different levels of complexity and different styles or types of work.

Regardless of the organization's choices regarding methodologies and life cycles, all organizations can use a scheduling tool to help with project execution. The key to success in every case is that the schedule must be focused on the deliverables to be produced rather than the process. The process must be set up to assist with producing deliverables.

The next section of this chapter provides several examples of methodologies and life cycles in the field of software development to illustrate how Project can be used to enable management of a wide variety of projects.

Using Microsoft Project with Methodologies and Life Cycles

Almost all organizations have at least a small number of technology projects underway, so software development is an excellent example of the wide variety of project-scheduling approaches available to organizations. The types of projects range from simple to complex, short to multiyear, and goal-oriented to open-ended research.

The following examples discuss the associated software development life cycle (SDLC) and how Project can be set up to support the life cycle. As you review the examples, you should also keep in mind that these projects should be planned and executed using the principles described in the previous sections on project standards (the PMBOK Guide and PRINCE2).

Although strict adherence to the standards is not required or necessary on every project, it is useful to remember that there are five major process groups to be managed on each project and that there are nine knowledge areas that should be considered throughout the project's life cycle.

Waterfall Development Process

Traditional software development is often described as a waterfall model because it is sequential in nature. The assumption with this model is that phases can be completed in order with little or no need to repeat the previous activities. Development is described as a waterfall, steadily falling down through traditional phases such as definition, preliminary design, detailed design, coding, testing, implementation, and transition to operations.

This method of development is used in many organizations today, especially those involved in multiyear programs. The phases can be lengthy and the work can be exacting. Although the name suggests that all work from one phase is completed before moving into the next phase, these types of projects are often set up with overlapping phases so that design can begin on certain deliverables as soon as the definition of the work for those deliverables is completed. In addition, there is typically some level of iterative development involved in almost all projects, but the term "waterfall" is still in common use today.

In this type of project, the tendency is to set up the project schedule in the same order as the major phase names. Instead, the project can be set up so that it is broken into logical work packages that can be monitored and measured separately.

Iterative Development

Iterative development provides a strong framework for planning purposes and also flexibility for successive iterations of software development. The Rational Unified Process (RUP) and the Dynamic Systems Development Methods are two frameworks for this type of project life cycle. RUP is not only a methodology for software engineering project management; it also has a set of software tools for using the specific methodology that is the Rational Unified Process. Figure 3.3 depicts the RUP workflow.

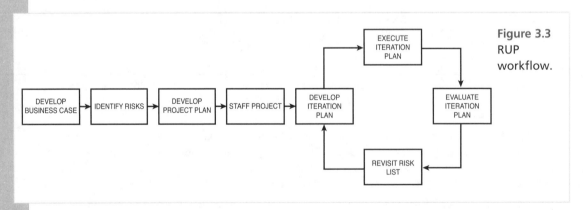

Figure 3.3
RUP
workflow.

The goal for this type of software development life cycle (SDLC) is to allow the developers to learn through incremental development and the use of prototypes instead of trying to complete detailed requirements before the development work begins. Agile and XP can also be considered to be iterative methods.

Agile Development Process

Agile is a philosophy of project management that moves away from the classic project management methods and focuses less on planning and more on execution. In Agile, crucial decisions are made during the project execution phase, instead of the planning phase. As business and project environments become more fluid and dynamic, the amount of time for effective planning becomes less and less. This does not mean that planning is ignored; rather, the focus shifts to supporting decisions during project execution instead of finalizing all decisions during the planning stage.

Agile is not an all-or-nothing methodology either; it is possible to combine Agile with more classic project management ideas. Whereas classic project management is comprehensive and works in diverse situations, Agile can add various ideas for facing new and unique situations that can be found in creative, knowledge-based industries.

Here are some of the attributes of an Agile SDLC:

- Short development cycles are used to produce working software in weeks rather than months.

- Communication between the business users and the developers occurs daily.

- Documentation of working functionality is captured after the software is completed; there is limited documentation of the requirements or design.

- Timeboxing is used to force tough decisions early in the project.

- Changes to requirements are expected; they are a result of early working prototypes and are a goal of the process.

- The project manager for an Agile team is focused on ensuring excellent communication as the primary mechanism to maintain progress.

Agile development can be difficult for large organizations to embrace because it does not require a focus on formal planning of an entire project.

The major difference is that the primary measurement of progress is frequent delivery of small amounts of working software. With a focus on feature delivery, it can sometimes be difficult to understand the overall picture, so strong project management must provide this clarity.

In this type of environment, a project team can still use Project to support its goals. In an Agile environment, the tool is not used to develop a robust schedule with a beginning-to-end flow of tasks and resources. Its use in this case supports communication to management and ensures that changes are captured and the backlog of work is moved through each successive iteration of the project schedule.

 caution

The use of Agile should not be used as an excuse to avoid planning or managing a budget. The approach is meant to provide a lighter and faster method to reach a goal, but the goal is still required.

In the following example, the project manager has established a budget summary task to provide rollup of budget for management purposes. Successive sets of work are defined in small iterations, while the overall timeframe and budget are obvious for all (see Figure 3.4). This approach enables the team to perform iterative planning while still meeting the business requirements of not exceeding a specific timeframe and budget.

By establishing a project schedule with an overall goal, the needs of the team and their management can be met. Refer to Figure 3.4 for an example of a short project that is expected to complete within a target effort of 340 hours. The work is not fully defined at the beginning so that the team has the flexibility to decide what work will happen in what order. Management is still able to see overall metrics of planned work, actual work, and the current estimate of work remaining.

Figure 3.4
An Agile project showing overall budget, work, and timeframe with iterative development.

Agile is an extremely successful method of software development that is well suited to an environment with self-motivated teams, open communications, and leadership that is comfortable with a prototyping approach to work. It does not fit all projects, but when it works, it works well.

The schedule created in Project for this type of approach becomes a tool for communication, overall budget and time goals, and historical tracking purposes.

Extreme Programming

Extreme Programming, or XP, is another method within the Agile family that has become a simple and flexible way for developing software through the writing of tests. It is designed to be used by a group of two to ten programmers who are able to execute tests in a fraction of a day. It uses short cycles of phases, with early

 note

For organizations that use the Project Server, this method enables them to use an Agile approach and yet have oversight of the entire project portfolio. Agile projects coexist with standard iterative projects in their Project Server environment; the projects have planned timeframes, resources, and budgets but are not required to have all the work scoped out at the beginning of the project.

and continuing feedback during each cycle. This flexibility enables it to respond to changing business demands through the implementation of functionality.

XP's use of automated tests, written by the programmers to scrutinize development, helps in early detection of defects and also enables the cycle of phases to evolve as the project continues. These automated tests depend both on the short-term instincts of programmers and also on the long-term interests of the project. XP also relies heavily on a system of oral communication, tests, and source code to help communicate the system structure and intent.

These processes allow for the day-to-day programming of a feature, and then moving on to testing, implementation, design, and integration, all packed into each cycle. The scheduling methods used in the preceding Agile example can again be adapted for XP.

Spiral Development Project

Spiral development was defined by Barry Boehm in 1985 and is often used in fairly large projects that take months to two years or more to complete. The initial focus might be on core functionality, and then the "bells and whistles" such as graphical user interfaces and reporting are added at a later time. This is sometimes considered to be another form of iterative development, but the structure of the plans and schedule focus on a robust core design in the early stages.

Research Project

A research project might be the most difficult type of project to tackle when it comes to constructing a project schedule. Often there is no clear goal in mind, and there might not even be an expectation of a specific end date or budget. On the other side, however, even research projects must be funded by someone, and they must have a working staff, so there is typically some expectation of a result. In most cases, there is also an expectation that the funding is used responsibly, so there must be a process in place to track how the money has been spent.

Project can once again be used to support this type of project as a tracking mechanism and a place to bring together the set of work that will be performed. The schedule will not require all the advanced features of critical path analysis, resource leveling, and predecessor/successor relationships, but it can be used as an easy method of historical support and a loose prediction of the work that is to be accomplished.

Accommodating Teaming Styles

High-performance teams, self-managed teams, and other nontraditional structures began to emerge more than 50 years ago in Great Britain and gained acceptance across the globe as several large corporations began to adopt the concepts. The general idea behind these teaming styles was to loosen managerial constraints in an effort to increase worker performance and make quantum leaps in accomplishment of organizational goals.

When framed correctly, the teams need little direction and excel in accomplishing the goals of their projects. If the dynamics are not understood, however, little is accomplished. From a project management perspective, Agile or XP projects can be a bit intimidating because the team dynamics can overwhelm the designated leader. In reality, successful self-managed teams are not leaderless. They have simply figured out a mechanism to allow many people within the team to play a leadership role.

Even in a team where a project management role has not been defined, someone must take on the job of setting a direction to accomplish a goal. The goal might only be one week in the future, but the team must coalesce around that goal, and the person who makes that happen is a leader. If the project manager understands the dynamics of the team, he or she can use these dynamics to improve the team's focus and increase its performance. The PM must be comfortable with sharing decision making and needs to focus heavily on communication of information within the team and with the stakeholders of the project. Things change quickly in this environment, so communication of status becomes a driving force for the project.

Project is an excellent tool to aid the PM in communication. Two components need to be established to make this successful. The overall goal of the project needs to be clear to the team, and the boundaries of the project (overall timeframe, scope, resources, and budget) must be understood. If these components are established within the tool as a baseline, the remainder of the schedule can be flexible or rigid, as dictated by the project structure and the teaming style.

Consultants' Tips

Determine the Approach to Use in Managing Your Project

Project has a rich set of features that enable the project manager and team to track projects at a detailed level. It also has enough flexibility to allow high-level tracking without a demand for the detail. It can be and has been used to support all industries and all domains within those industries.

Because the software has so many capabilities, it must be well understood to be used correctly. The scheduling engine anticipates your needs and moves the dates or adjusts the amount of work that is to be accomplished based on the parameters that you set. Because it does this, project managers must have a clear understanding of the approach that they want to use on their projects before they begin entering tasks.

Use WBS as a First Step in Project Definition

Always start with a WBS to help you be clear on the goals of the project. Wait to add the task-level details until you are sure that you have decomposed the WBS to the work package level that is right for the type of project you are leading. Do not confuse the listing of activities with the completion of deliverables.

Use the 5×9 Checklist for Planning

Remember the 5×9 checklist and consider it when planning and executing each project. As you move through the phases of your project's life cycle, spend a moment to consider which of the five process groups is most dominant at the moment and which of the nine knowledge areas plays the most important part in the project's evolution.

GETTING STARTED AFTER THE BUSINESS INITIATIVE IS APPROVED

The purpose of this chapter is to position your project for success from the start. Planning a successful project requires leadership and management skills and includes the following tasks:

- **Setting the direction**—Establish a goal that your stakeholders and team members can understand and work to achieve.

- **Sharing the vision**—Provide a framework and sufficient detail so that each member of the team knows what to do and when to do it.

- **Establishing the rules**—Establish methods for work to be accomplished, communication to occur, and methods to track status and manage the changes that will inevitably come your way.

After you set the stage for success, you can use Microsoft Project to do what it does best: help you organize and track the work of your team. If you start with these basics, you can optimize all the features that are available to assist you.

Organizing Projects for Success

A project has been approved and you have been assigned as the project manager. Now what? Before you reach for the keyboard to open Project, you need to set up your project for success.

You can draw upon many resources to help you with this process. Several are used in this chapter as the foundation for the author's approach to running successful projects. Dr. William Casey, principal in the Executive

Leadership Group, has provided the foundation for the work on Measure of Success in the next section. The information regarding Work Breakdown Structures is based on two primary sources: *Practice Standard for Work Breakdown Structures, Second Edition* (PMI, 2006) and *Effective Work Breakdown Structures* (Haugen, 2002).

Much of your work will ultimately be reflected in a Microsoft Project schedule, but if you start that process before you are ready, you can end up with a project that is out of control. This is because Project was designed to help you manage the *details* of your project schedule—the activities, calendars, resources, and many other details that can be captured and managed. Before you dive into the details, however, you need to frame the big picture with the following:

- Where you are going (your goal and objectives)

- What you must provide as results of your project (end products or outcomes, deliverables)

- What boundaries and constraints you must work within (regulatory requirements, budgets, timeframes, quality levels, and more)

- How you will manage change when it happens (and it will happen)

The details that will reside within your Project schedule will become important, but it is equally important to start with a well-designed approach that is easy to explain to your team and to your stakeholders. After that is in place, working out the details and controlling the scope of the project will be much more manageable.

Define Measure of Success

Projects are most successful when they focus on the achievement of *one* clear goal. The goal should be measurable and achievable. Project goals can range from lofty (putting a man on the moon) to simple (reduce errors in a report). If the team can rally behind the goal and understand the purpose, your chances of success are much improved.

After documenting the goal, review all lower-level objectives against this goal to determine whether they should be included in the scope or should be defined as out of scope. The illustration in Figure 4.1 explains the point. Jigsaw puzzles come in all sizes and shapes, but the point of each is to complete a puzzle. You cannot complete the goal of finishing the puzzle if you start with pieces from different puzzles, or without all the necessary pieces. All of the puzzle pieces (objectives) must compose the same picture and none of them should be missing.

A project with multiple goals can result in a lot of churn when things do not go according to plan, because the team cannot easily make a decision on which components are the most critical for project success. Rather than try to accommodate divergent needs, the project must have one driver. All additional objectives should support that goal in some way or they are "out of scope."

 note

Typical projects have multiple legitimate sub-objectives. However, these sub-objectives can also become a diversion. It is extremely important to that all the project team members and stakeholders be clear on the primary objective of the project.

 caution

It is important that a project have one—and only one—driving goal. When stakeholders do not agree on the purpose of the project or have competing needs and objectives, problems occur.

Figure 4.1
If the parts of the puzzle (or deliverables you define for the project) are mixed with another puzzle, are in the wrong place, or are completely left out, the outcome will not be as you expected.

In addition, you must define clear boundaries and rules of fair play to ensure that reaching the goal does not have a negative impact. The next section develops this idea further.

Clarify Constraints and Boundaries

This section addresses two topics essential to building a good project schedule. It will help the team understand what is in scope and what is out of scope. It will also help you and your team define the work that must be accomplished and the manner in which it will be done.

Define Boundaries—Rules of Fair Play

Projects exist in an overall mission context that they must support and not negatively impact. A set of rules helps define and guard project boundaries while building a proper framework that enables flexibility within the project. Rules also protect the overall corporate mission context.

For example, a company that produces playground equipment for schools may need to reduce the costs of its manufacturing process. If the company launches a project to reduce costs of the manufacturing process, there aroe hundreds of ways to accomplish this. Some of the methods could cause consumer safety issues. To prevent this, the project team could set a boundary that states that the injury statistics for the equipment must not increase. The framework will affect both the project planning method and the way the project is measured.

Similarly, putting a man on the moon without getting him back to Earth safely would not be a successful project outcome. Not all projects have boundaries this critical or visible, but it is easy to see how they affect the project's budget, schedule, and quality planning.

The same is true for even the simplest of projects; the team must determine the rules within which the project will operate. Those decisions will help you decide what is truly in scope, what is out of scope, as well as how and when the project will be completed.

Identify Time, Budget, and Quality Constraints

Clarification of the goal and the scope is critical to obtaining some flexibility in time and budget. In many cases, only one of the factors (time, budget, or quality) is extremely important, and it may become a part of the driving goal. For example, it may be important to be the "first to market" with a particular product concept. In this case, being first is more critical than being the best, so the project manager must focus on timely delivery and limit the number of features or the quality of the product.

Projects usually labor under preset expectations of outcome, delivery date, and cost. If this is the case, the project manager's job has little to do with managing a project and much more to do with managing expectations. Often, when one of the factors changes, it directly affects the other two. Similarly, if you were to lengthen or shorten one side of the triangle, one of the other two sides, or both, have to adjust to maintain the shape, as shown in Figure 4.2.

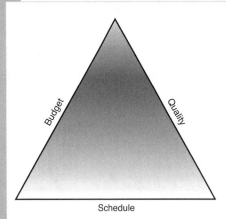

Figure 4.2
Time, budget, and quality are the key variables in a project. Generally, you must pick one as the most important, and vary the other two to accommodate it.

Regardless of the situation, the project team should still work with the stakeholders to clarify the goals and the boundaries before creating a schedule. Even though the tendency is to get resources engaged in activities as soon as you can, it is more critical to have all resources working on meeting one clear goal.

Define the Final Deliverables

If you have ever worked on a project that seemed to never end, it was probably because there was no clear definition of project completion. The project goal must be measurable, and final deliverables must constitute closure.

For a home construction project, the deliverables would include a completed house, landscaping, and a certificate of occupancy (CO). Each deliverable must also include a measurable quality component. Due to the large amount of detail, homebuilders typically list "deliverables" in a walkthrough document for the buyer's approval. The CO may take some time to achieve, but the result is clear and measurable.

For a software project, some of the final deliverables include:

- Software, documentation

- Operational processes

- Training

The quality measures can include things such as response times, number/severity of errors in the system test, user acceptance surveys, or other similar measures. The deliverables and the measures should all relate to the driving goal of the project or at least support one of the subordinate goals or objectives.

The project team may not even have identified some of the work that the stakeholders are expecting or the quality expectations may not be achievable within the time and cost constraints of the project. It is much better to clarify these points during the planning cycle than to reach the end of the project's budget and time and not be able to deliver undefined work.

 note

Without clear, measurable deliverables, there is no way to be sure that all of the stakeholders are in agreement regarding the project's goals.

The process of defining end deliverables will likely require you to go back and reexamine both the goal and the constraints and boundaries of the project. This is an iterative process, and it is time well spent. Without this process working through to completion, you will be creating a list of tasks that may or may not be useful in reaching your goal. The project will certainly expend a large amount of effort but may not earn any true value for the stakeholders.

Establish Change Control Process

The final component of organizing for success is planning for change. Change is inevitable, no matter how perfectly you plan. The only thing that you can do is prepare and have a process ready so that when it happens, your team knows how to respond.

Change control provides the discipline to identify and communicate the impact of scope changes, quality demands, risks, issues, and the day-to-day complexities of resource management. Project will help you identify, manage, and report on project changes, so determining the features that you will use during the planning cycle is a good idea. For example, establish an expectation for when you baseline your project, how often you capture a snapshot of the current schedule, and what criteria you use to determine whether you need to reset the baseline because of scope changes. You should also set up guidelines for how you will track progress and status and what features you will use for reporting.

➥ *For more information about capturing the baseline and tracking your progress,* **see** *Chapter 13, "Tracking Your Project Progress,"* **p. 435**.

Work Breakdown Structure

After you have clarity on the goal, boundaries, and constraints for your project, it is time to begin the process of identifying all of the work by decomposing the goal into manageable pieces. Of all the projects that fail, most are due to a failure to identify all of the changes to scope or to manage these changes.

The *PMBOK Guide* recommends the use of the Work Breakdown Structure (WBS) as the best practice for identifying and managing packages of work in a project schedule. The identification and management of these packages of work are critical to understanding and maintaining project scope.

This section covers key principles of building and using a WBS with a focus on creation of the WBS for accurate and effective management of Project schedules. It is important that your schedule be an accurate reflection of the work required to reach a successful conclusion of your project. Using a WBS helps you reach that goal by ensuring you cover 100% of the scope of your project without adding unrelated activities.

This book does not attempt to cover all of the details; much more thorough reference materials are available for that, as identified at the beginning of this chapter.

Work Breakdown Structure Concepts

You can create a Work Breakdown Structure (WBS) using Project, but it is often more useful to create the first iteration on a whiteboard because it will change multiple times before you are ready to finalize it. The iterative process typically begins with a top-down decomposition of deliverables through successive levels of detail until you reach a level where you can plan and control the work. This level is a *work package*. All levels of decomposition from Level 1 (the project) through the lowest level (work package) are noun-based and focus on the deliverable, not achieving the deliverable.

Many levels may be required, depending on the complexity of the project, and not all branches of the WBS require the same number of sublevels of breakdown. The lowest-level WBS element (the work package) will eventually contain the set of activities or tasks that needed to accomplish the achievement identified by the work package. A work package should be assignable to one work group or an individual for performance. If that is not possible, it should probably be broken down further.

The example in Figure 4.3 shows the levels of decomposition in a WBS to break a project into the appropriate work packages.

Of course, Project supports decomposition, work packages, and their activities. The lowest level of the WBS—the work package—will be represented by a summary task.

Figure 4.4 shows an example of a task activity list in Project that is derived from the WBS example in Figure 4.3.

 tip

You should keep together all activities within the WBS work package and link them with a starting and an ending milestone.

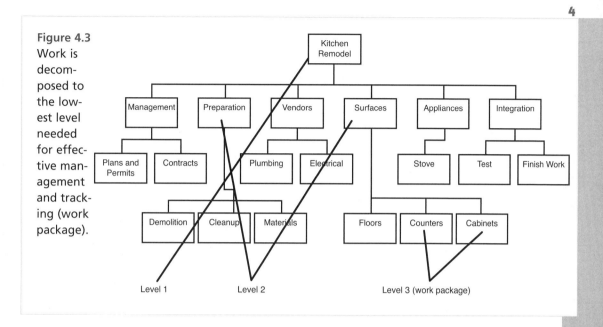

Figure 4.3
Work is decomposed to the lowest level needed for effective management and tracking (work package).

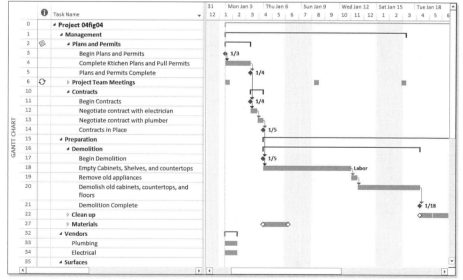

Figure 4.4
Work packages within Project should have a starting and an ending milestone.

Rules for Building WBS

There are a few rules regarding building a WBS that you should keep in mind when developing a schedule in Project:

- **Number of levels**—The number of levels in a WBS will vary with the complexity of the project. Some elements may have more levels of detail than others. Describe elements with nouns and adjectives.

- **Level 2 elements**—This level includes project management and at least one other element, depending on the type of deliverables to be produced by the project: product, service, or result. There may also be additional elements at Level 2 and below that support neighboring elements (cross-cutting elements) or represent the next step in a process. See Figure 4.5 for an example.

- **Level 3 and below (work package elements)**—Decomposition continues as needed until the work package, the lowest element of a WBS, is reached. It must be at a level of decomposition controllable and performed by one individual or one organizational entity. A verb describes the activities and tasks of a work package (see Figure 4.5).

- **WBS dictionary**—Each element of a WBS may be described in more detail in a WBS dictionary. Additional information about the element, including budget, cost, and earned value data may also be included there.

- **100% rule**—Each lower level of decomposition must represent all of the work of the higher-level element; conversely, all higher-level scope must be reflected in one of the lower-level elements. This is the 100% rule, which ensures the capture of all the scope and only the scope, free of extraneous commitments.

As you can see from these examples, you can use Project or a whiteboard to create the WBS. The *Practice Standard for Work Breakdown Structures, Second Edition* (PMI, 2006) recommends that the team be involved in the creation of the WBS. The focus for this process should be on the outputs to be produced so that the team uses nouns to describe what will be produced and can identify all of the cross-cutting elements that are required.

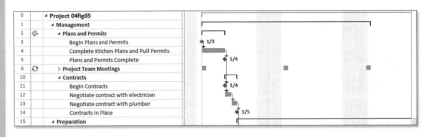

Figure 4.5
Level 2 elements include Management and at least one other element based on the type of deliverables that the project will produce.

WBS and Scheduling

Regardless of the methods used to create the schedule, the process will be iterative. Some groups will choose to begin the process using top-down decomposition. Others may choose to identify all of the work they can using brain-storming techniques and then organize the work into logical packages. Either method is effective as a starting point. The team will perform multiple iterations of each method to identify all the required work.

The iterative nature of building a WBS, and subsequently a schedule, requires a great deal of realignment and reordering of elements. When developing and maintaining the WBS structure, it is important that you remember the 100% rule mentioned previously. You should maintain work packages as units and move them as units within the schedule rather than moving individual tasks below the work package.

After you have identified the work packages, you can rearrange them, but you should have the same set of lowest-level work packages regardless of the realignment. Use the 100% rule to validate the process and always focus on the outputs of the packages rather than the resources required to do the work.

Figures 4.6 and 4.7 show examples of how work packages can exist in different locations in the project schedule. In this case, the work package called Cabinets exists under the Level 2 task Surfaces in Figure 4.6, and under the Level 2 task Storage in Figure 4.7. Remember, a work package is defined as the lowest level of the WBS; the tasks (activities to be performed) are broken out below the work package level.

 note

It is important to remember that only the bottom-up persepctive reveals certain types of work, such as integration of elements. Examples of this include assembly of components in a manufacturing project or quality testing in a software project.

 tip

Remember that the work package is the lowest component of a WBS; after you are sure that you have captured all of them, organize them in a way that is meaningful to the team. Tasks are the level below the work package.

Figure 4.6 Work packages can be aligned in different ways; use the 100% rule to verify the scope.

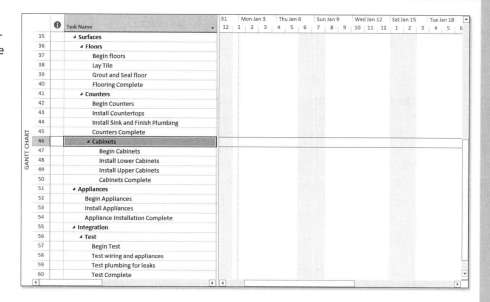

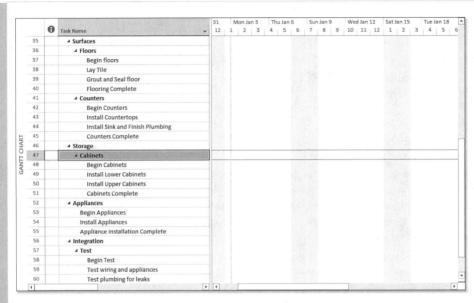

Figure 4.7
The Cabinets work package has been moved. If Storage existed as a Level 2 component in your WBS, this may be a more appropriate place for the Cabinets work package.

After the team is satisfied that all work has been captured and decomposed to the appropriate level, the WBS work packages are set to be the basis for adding precedence and resources and creating a schedule. The work packages should have starting and ending milestones to aid with work flow and to ensure that the focus remains on the production of deliverables. Refer to Figure 4.4 for examples of these milestones.

Use of Templates

Most organizations repeatedly deliver similar projects. Templates can be extremely useful for capturing the best practices developed into repeatable standards and reporting, giving new projects a jumpstart to success. Project-oriented organizations often use the top two levels of the WBS consistently.

 caution
Avoid the tendency to define the work according to the groups that may be performing the work during initial decomposition because this will limit your thinking and make it easier to violate the 100% rule. Instead, focus on the deliverable work and then assign it to a group as appropriate.

The project management elements can be standardized, as can many other cross-cutting elements. Standard templates minimize the amount of startup work required to determine process use for each project and also improve the organization's ability to control scope on the elements consistent across projects.

WBS Numbering

Project has a customizable field called WBS made to support an organization's WBS numbering schema. The default WBS code is identical to the outline numbers that Project generates and stores

Figure 4.8
The Outline Number field and the default WBS code are identical.

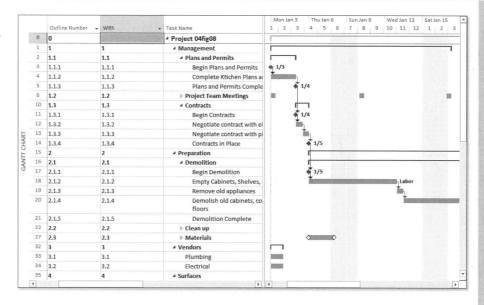

in the Outline Number field. You can display both of these fields in a table by inserting the columns, as shown in Figure 4.8.

To insert these fields onto your screen, follow these steps:

1. Right-click on the column header where you want to insert the column (field), and choose Insert Column. This opens the Column Definition dialog box. All columns to the right, including the column in which you right-clicked, shift to the right to make room for the new column insertion.

2. In the Column Definition dialog box, choose either Outline Number or WBS from the drop-down list in the Field Name field.

3. Click OK to close the Column Definition dialog box and insert the column.

Repeat these steps to insert the other column (the one you did not just insert), either Outline Number or WBS.

If your team chooses to use these fields, you must be aware that the Outline Number field and WBS field are identical in Project's default mode, and the number associated with a work package will change if the package is moved within the project schedule. If the WBS numbering schema must remain the same throughout the life of the project, use a custom field that you must then maintain instead of the automatic WBS field provided by Project.

 note

By default, the value in the Project WBS field automatically changes if you move a work package from one location to another within the schedule.

Creating Custom WBS Codes

To customize the WBS code format in the Project WBS field, you can generate custom codes using a *WBS code mask*. The mask contains numbers or characters for each outline level, with separators between the levels. There is a total limit of 255 characters, which is sufficient to handle even the most complex WBS structure. For projects that are part of a larger program, you can also include a project-level code that will be a prefix for all tasks within the project, or you can leave it blank.

To create a custom WBS code, follow these steps:

1. Choose the Project tab, WBS, Define Code to display the WBS Code Definition dialog box, as shown in Figure 4.9.

2. Enter a code prefix for the project, if needed, in the Project Code Prefix box. Identify a separator, such as a colon or period, to make it easier for the reader to identify the levels.

3. Click the first blank row under the Sequence column in the Code Mask table and select the option from the drop-down menu for numbers or letters, as appropriate for your organization. You can display your options with the pull-down arrow, which are as follows:

   - **Numbers (ordered)**—Project will insert sequential numbers for this part of the code. You can edit these numbers later.

   - **Uppercase Letters (ordered)**—Project will insert sequential uppercase letters.

   - **Lowercase Letters (ordered)**—Project will insert sequential lowercase letters.

   - **Characters (unordered)**—Project will insert an asterisk (*). You can go back and change it to any character later.

4. Specify the length of the field or choose Any to allow flexibility in the number of characters. Use the pull-down arrow in the Length column to show the options for the number of characters you can use for this part of the formatting:

   - Select Any when you want to later edit this part of the code, using a variety of number of characters.

   - Select 1 through 10 when you want to set a fixed number of characters for this section of formatting.

5. Identify a separator from the choices in the drop-down menu or type another symbol directly on the keyboard.

6. Repeat steps 3, 4, and 5 for each additional level of the WBS. The Code Preview field at the top of the dialog box shows you what the custom WBS code looks like as you are creating the mask.

7. If you want Project's automatically generated WBS codes, select the box Generate WBS Code for New Task. If this box is cleared, you will need to enter the codes manually but will be required to follow the format defined in this process.

8. If you want Project to check for duplicate codes, select the box Verify Uniqueness of New WBS Codes. The check only occurs when you edit the codes, and you need to modify the codes

manually to make them unique. It is generally a good idea to have this box selected to avoid confusion with the WBS codes.

9. Click OK to save the mask. Project automatically replaces the default WBS code with the new codes you have designed.

10. Select the column header and double-click the right-hand column border.

 tip

If your project is complex and has many levels, you may need to widen the column to see the entire WBS code.

Figure 4.9
Project creates custom WBS codes through your formatted mask.

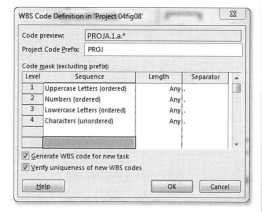

See the "Editing Custom WBS Codes" section later in this chapter to further customize your WBS.

See the "Renumbering the Custom WBS Codes" section later in this chapter for more information on this topic.

If you use the check box to verify the uniqueness for new codes, Project only checks the code when it is created or edited. If your project file has custom WBS codes that were set up when this feature was disabled, and you then decide to enable unique codes, Project will not check the existing codes for uniqueness. If necessary, you can force Project to renumber all of the codes, which is to say generate new codes for the task, to correct your nonunique ones. This also causes you to lose any codes you have entered manually.

If you want to reduce the number of defined levels in the mask, you can delete only the bottom-most level of the Sequence table. Start with the bottom-most level and use the Delete key to clear your mask; then work your way up the list, deleting from the bottom up.

note

If you have not defined enough levels in the mask for all of your WBS, Project will use the default numbering system for the lower levels.

You can force Project to renumber all of the codes in your WBS, but you will lose any special coding that you have done manually.

tip

If necessary, you can edit every task's code, forcing Project to check each task's uniqueness. You can do this quickly and easily by choosing the WBS column, selecting all of the cells, and pressing F2 to edit the first cell. Then press Enter to force Project to make a uniqueness check. If your code is unique, Project moves on to the next cell in the selection. Press F2 and Enter again to process the next cell. It is easy to move down the column this way quickly, provided the codes are unique. If not, you have to stop and change the code before you finish.

Inserting, Deleting, and Moving Tasks with Custom WBS Codes

You should stabilize your WBS and your schedule before adding the custom WBS codes so that you do not have to spend too much time making changes to them. On occasion, however, you will find that you need to add or delete tasks and perhaps move entire work packages to different areas of your WBS. Project makes some automatic numbering changes, and you need to be aware of how these changes work if you use custom WBS codes.

When you insert a new task into a work package (summary task group), Project automatically gives it the next highest codes for the level. If you delete a task, Project renumbers the tasks that follow. If you want a specific code assignment, you need to manage the addition and deletion carefully.

If you move a task to another row within a work package, it keeps its original code even though it is no longer in sequence. Although not a recommended practice, if you move a task from one work package to another, it acquires the correct prefix code for the new work package. The final part of the code may change if it would be a duplicate of an existing task within the package.

Editing Custom WBS Codes

Editing custom codes after creating a code mask is straightforward. Select a summary task by double-clicking any field in the row except the row number. The Summary Task Information window appears, as shown in Figure 4.10. Because you have created a WBS code mask, under the Custom Fields tab, a custom field called WBS should be visible. Select the value field for WBS. Make your change in the entry bar immediately above the Custom Field Name list box.

You will be editing only the last segment of any of the custom codes; all the higher-level segments derive from the higher levels (summary task levels). You can change the segment codes at the summary task level if the assignment made by Project does not fit with what your organization would like to see.

For instance, in Figure 4.11, the major phases have been edited as abbreviations or acronyms for the name of the phase. AA was the default WBS code for the Planning the Move phase, but it has been changed to PLAN. It makes it easier to realize a task's place within the WBS code.

If you want to show the tasks in their WBS code order, select the View tab, Sort, Sort By and then select the WBS field in the Sort By box.

Figure 4.10
You can use the Custom Fields tab of the Summary Task Information dialog box to edit the WBS code.

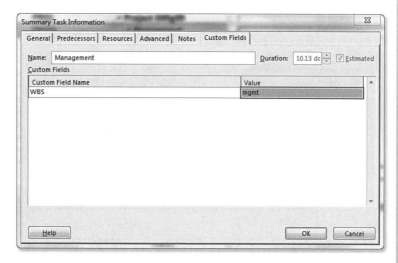

Figure 4.11
Editing the default letters assigned by Project in the custom WBS codes lets you describe how a task fits into the task list.

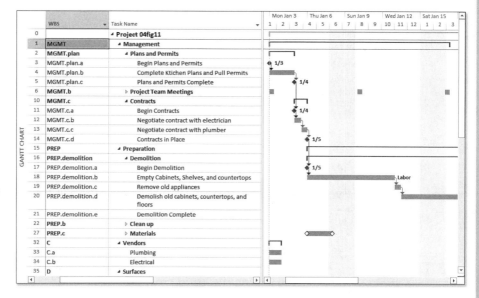

You lose your edited codes if you edit custom codes for summary tasks and then tell Project to renumber the tasks. Use the following steps to prevent that from happening:

1. Using the Gantt view, select the Format tab.

2. Clear the Show Summary Tasks check box. Only the normal and milestone tasks should be displayed.

3. Choose one of the column headings to select all displayed tasks.

4. Select the Project tab, WBS, Renumber to bring up the WBS Renumbering dialog box.

5. Click the Selected Tasks button instead of the Entire Project button.

6. Click OK to begin renumbering.

7. You can then restore the display of summary tasks by selecting the Format tab, Show Summary check box. Click any cell to unselect all tasks.

note

If Renumber is grayed out in Step 4, a custom WBS code mask has not been created. Refer to the earlier section "Creating Custom WBS Codes" in this chapter to rectify this.

Project will display your entire task list again. Your summary tasks have not lost their edited codes, but Project will renumber all of your other tasks using the current order of the outline.

Renumbering the Custom WBS Codes

As you are planning your project, you are likely to revise the task list somewhere along the line. If you have already defined the custom WBS codes by this time, they might not be in sequence after the editing. Project recalculates the WBS codes for the whole project, putting them into sequence for you. Follow these steps to renumber the WBS codes:

1. If you are only renumbering a small, selected set of tasks, choose those tasks first (they must be adjacent to one other). Project will not renumber the first selected task, but it will be the starting point for renumbering the rest of the selection.

2. Go to the Project tab, WBS, Renumber to pull up the WBS Renumber dialog box, shown in Figure 4.12.

3. Pick either Selected Tasks or Entire Project.

4. Click OK to begin renumbering.

5. If you decide to renumber the whole task list, Project asks you to confirm your decision. Click Yes or No as necessary.

Figure 4.12
You can renumber the entire project, or just a small select set of tasks, using the WBS Renumber dialog box.

If, even with a warning to confirm your decision, you still end up realizing that you did not want to renumber, you can go back and use the Undo feature to restore your original codes.

Scope Control and Change Control

If you use the WBS approach to building your schedule, it is much easier to control the scope of the project. The 100% rule defeats the "as long as you are there" phenomenon: the tendency to add features that are not within scope because they would be nice to have.

Using the 100% rule allows you to perform top-down planning and budgeting and enables tracking and reporting at the work package level. This is essential if you will be using any type of the earned value reporting in your project. You will be able to baseline the project and keep track of history at a work package level rather than trying to manage at the individual activity level.

Change control should be implemented at the work package level. Budget and schedule impacts are easier to control in logical units, and it is much easier to see the ripple effect of a requested change at the work package level.

Consultants' Tips

Understanding a Work Breakdown Structure

Project uses the term *Work Breakdown Structure (WBS)* to mean a hierarchical list of working activities. The tasks you create in a Project schedule are really an *Activity Breakdown Structure (ABS)* showing the relationship of tasks throughout the schedule.

The term WBS has a formal definition and United States government MIL-HDBK-881A standard. That standard describes using a WBS to define the cost and management control structures that define the official scope of your project. Even though this is a government military standard, project management discipline has adopted this standard as the basis for defining a Work Breakdown Structure. Reviewing this standard will help you better understand the distinction between Activity Breakdown Structure and Work Breakdown Structure.

You should also consider reviewing ANSI/EIA Standard 748 that defines Earned Value Management (EVM) and specifically refers to the formal WBS definitions. EVM is a well-defined method for measuring project performance against a defined Work Breakdown Structure.

Use your favorite Internet search engine to learn more about WBS and Earned Value Management.

Define the Full Scope of Your Project

When building a schedule, it is always easier to add more detail later than to take it out. If you keep your schedule focused on deliverables, it will be much easier to identify missing deliverables. This allows much greater flexibility in setting the scope for a project. (This is accomplished naturally if you follow the best practice of creating a WBS prior to creating a schedule! It is extremely difficult to keep WBS principles in mind when you jump to creation of a schedule without having gone through prior creation of a WBS.)

Build WBS First

Many project managers skip the process of building a WBS before they build a schedule because project sponsors tend to push for early resource and date commitments. Project is an excellent scheduling tool, and it can be an excellent tool for controlling scope if the project manager takes a disciplined approach to developing a WBS from the beginning.

Avoid the tendency to structure your schedule according to workgroup during initial decomposition because it will limit your thinking and make it much easier to violate the 100% rule. Focus on the deliverable work, describe it completely in a WBS and WBS dictionary, and then assign the logical flow of precedence and the resources. Use other fields to structure your schedule according to workgroups, GL codes, and so on, after the WBS is complete.

Define Project Work Packages

Understand the work package level of your project as the most important component for providing scope management and control. This will keep you "out of the weeds," and you can make decisions based on the impact to the work package rather than trying to deal with many activities. You can rearrange work packages in a variety of ways without altering the scope of the project. There is no single correct structure for WBS; you can legitimately arrange work packages in a variety of ways.

Make sure that all of the work packages within your project support the defined measures of success and that you have an objective method to measure both progress and accomplishment of the project goal. Most project failures are due to not understanding or managing scope; project success requires a clear goal and a scope of work that supports the goal.

SETTING UP PROJECT FOR YOUR USE

One of the many ways Microsoft Project differs from other Office applications such as Excel and Word is how important high-level configuration settings are. This chapter describes how to use these settings to help manage your project.

Setting the Task Mode

The task mode in Microsoft Project was an important new feature in 2010. For the first time, project or resource managers could employ the Project scheduling engine selectively. Manually scheduled tasks do not cause a cascade of response across other tasks. Conversely, auto-scheduled tasks employ the Project scheduling algorithms experienced Project users are familiar with.

Setting the Task Mode

By default, the bottom-left corner of the project window should display a control for a new task's task mode. It should say New Tasks: Manually Scheduled (see Figure 5.1). This means start dates, end dates, work, and so on, all need to be entered and maintained manually by the user. If this control is not visible, right-click the status bar at the bottom of the screen. The Customize Status Bar window should appear. Check the New Tasks control to make it visible.

Selecting the New Tasks control opens the new task window (see Figure 5.2). From here, you can select either Auto Scheduled or Manually Scheduled. Changes made with this control impact only new tasks.

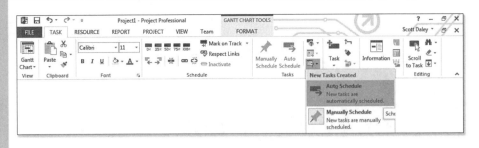

Figure 5.1
Selecting the Task tab and clicking the Mode control also changes the task mode for new tasks.

Figure 5.2
The task mode can be changed for existing tasks using the Task Mode column.

You can change the task mode for existing tasks using one of two ways:

- Right-click any column header and select Insert Column. Select Task Mode. You can use the Task Mode column to change a single or many tasks' task mode.

- Double-click on the task row header. The Task Information window will appear. You can set Schedule Mode to either Manually Scheduled or Auto Scheduled.

Understanding the Task Mode

The addition of Manually Scheduled task mode makes it easier to record estimated task start and end dates, as well as durations, because Project no longer automatically calculates them. Experienced Project users will find this to be disconcerting at first. The fundamental Project equation of Duration × Units = Work no longer applies. Project records tasks dependencies but does not honor them.

Manually Scheduled mode is intended for use during project planning. Auto Scheduled mode is intended for use during execution. In practical terms, users might find that they want a mix of manually scheduled and auto-scheduled tasks at any one time.

For instance, when faced with a series of tasks that must happen in sequence, managers will find auto-scheduling very useful. If Task A is not completed this week, Task B simply must be rescheduled, and why bother doing it by hand if Project will do it for you?

 caution

It is possible, however, that within the same project, some tasks represent likely resource usage. These are tasks (sometimes called *Level of Effort* or *LOE* tasks) that represent the time a resource will spend on the project without any predefined output. These kinds of task should probably remain in Manually Scheduled mode throughout the project.

Defining Project Information

When you sit down to plan the scope of a new project, it is important to ask yourself exactly what your objectives are. Take your time and be thorough. Planning a project can be daunting, especially to the novice planner, but taking the time to plan and organize your project at its beginning provides for much smoother and more efficient execution during later project stages.

There is no such thing as perfect project planning. It is inevitable that you will need to modify your plan as your project progresses. The best defense is a comprehensive, realistic project schedule that anticipates setbacks and provides the foundation for your success as a project manager.

Microsoft Project configuration settings can vary from project to project, and you should make them work for your benefit. You can change many of these settings after you have entered tasks and resources into the project, but by addressing these issues up front, you can make Project work for you, and avoid working against Project.

Microsoft Project is an excellent tool to help you manage the three main areas of information of any project schedule (scope, schedule, and cost), but before you enter any tasks, you should ask yourself the following questions:

 tip

Enter all known information about the project at the beginning. The more information you capture about the project, the more consistent and organized your project will be.

- What makes up my entire project? What is in scope and what is out of scope?

- What expectations have already been set for start and completion dates? Do I have any set constraints on the schedule of this project?

- How much is the project going to cost? Do I have any set constraints on the budget of this project?

Your Project schedule is a model balancing scope, schedule, and cost. Answers to these questions will help you create a useful, realistic schedule.

Understanding the Project Information Dialog Box

You can define, view, and edit some key information about your project using the Project Information dialog box. To view the Project Information dialog box, click the Project tab, Project Information. The Project Information dialog box appears (see Figure 5.3).

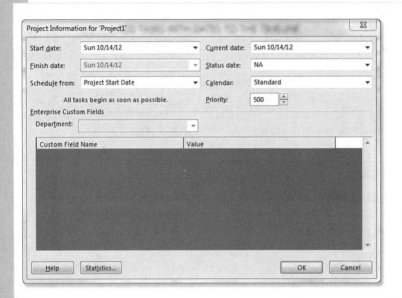

Figure 5.3
The Project Information dialog box enables you to set high-level properties for your schedule dates and scheduling approach, make calendar choices, and enter custom field data if you have created them.

The Project Information dialog box is used for entering basic information about a project. It includes project start and finish dates, as well as the base calendar to use for scheduling. The following sections describe the settings in the Project Information dialog box in detail.

You can also view Summary Project Information by selecting the File tab, Info. The right-hand pane summarizes project information.

Start Date, Finish Date, and Schedule From

One of the key decisions to make in the Project Information dialog box is whether you are going to schedule auto-scheduled tasks in your project from the start date or from the finish date. By default,

 note
The Project Information dialog box in Project Professional also includes additional enterprise fields that are not part of the Project Standard. These fields include Priority and any project-level enterprise custom fields. Note that the Priority field also exists in Project Standard, but the only place where you can specify it is if you display the zero-level project summary task in the Gantt Chart view.

Project uses the start date. This is the preferred method of scheduling because it provides the most flexibility in determining when work must begin. Tasks within the schedule are set to begin as soon as possible so there are no artificial delays in the plan. The finish date will also be as soon as possible, based on the relationships established between tasks. Most project managers use this default option if they can because it is intuitive and the logic is easy to follow.

However, project managers are often given a target end date, making the Schedule From Project Finish Date option attractive. If task mode is set to Auto Scheduled, and (as always) there is too much work and too little time, Project will schedule the project to start in the past. Adjusting the schedule so that the current date is the start date is much more difficult using Schedule From because all tasks are starting as late as possible. Be aware of the consequences if you choose to use it.

In Figure 5.3, the project is scheduled to begin on Sunday, October 14, 2012. You can change the start date by typing the date in the Start Date field, or by clicking the drop-down arrow and choosing the date from the calendar. When you enter a start date, Project schedules the first auto-scheduled task to begin on that date and calculates the project's schedule based on that date and the sequence of auto-scheduled tasks that follow.

Click the drop-down arrow in the Schedule From field and choose Project Finish Date to schedule your project from the finish date. You can enter the date in the Finish Date field by typing it in or choosing from the calendar with the drop-down arrow. Project schedules the final task to finish on the finish date, and schedules the task before it to finish in time for the final task to start, and so on, until the first task is scheduled and the project now has a defined start date.

 note

You cannot choose both a start date and a finish date for your project. If you schedule from the start date, Project automatically calculates the finish date based on the duration of the project's auto-scheduled tasks. If you schedule from a finish date, Project schedules the project's final task to finish on that date, and its start date is determined by the duration of the tasks.

If you choose Project Start Date in the Schedule From field, Project allows you to enter only the start date. If you choose Project Finish Date, you can enter only the finish date. You can change this setting as often as you like, but be aware that the logic at the task level does not automatically change, so the logic for the task constraint type will remain as it was.

 For additional information on constraints and logic applied when scheduling tasks, see Chapter 7, "Defining Task Logic," p. 183.

tip

Although Project provides the ability to schedule the project from a finish date, you should avoid it. Scheduling from a start date is easier to manage. It is more natural for most people to schedule forward instead of backward. If the schedule slips, it is more natural to make adjustments that bring it back to the planned finish. If you do decide to schedule the project from the finish date and the project slips, Project will push the start date further into the past. Unless you are experienced with Project and project management concepts, it will be difficult to manage the situation and figure out the appropriate actions to repair the schedule.

Current Date and Status

Project uses the Current Date and Status Date fields to perform several date-related calculations. Your computer's internal clock supplies the Current Date. When viewing the Gantt Chart, the dashed date line represents the current date defined by this field. You should generally avoid changing the current date unless your computer's internal clock is incorrect. If you leave the Status Date box as NA, Project uses the Current Date as the Status Date.

You can use the Current Date as a point of reference when tracking progress. However, if you want to track progress using a date other than the Current Date, enter that date in the Status Date field. The status date is what Project uses for calculating Earned Value and other tracking purposes.

For example, it is typical that project managers will track a week's progress after the end of that week. If on Monday a project manager wanted to track the progress from the previous week, then he or she would enter the previous Friday's date (or whatever date the workweek ended on) in the Status Date box. Project uses the status date to adjust the project schedule, reflecting the latest information.

➡️ *For more information about tracking progress, see Chapter 13, "Tracking Your Project Progress," p. 431.*

To change the Current Date field or enter a Status Date setting, select the box and either type in the date or choose it from the calendar via the drop-down arrow.

Calendar

Project uses base calendars to define the default working and nonworking days for scheduling both manual and auto-scheduled tasks. In the Project Information dialog box, click the Calendar drop-down field to view all available base calendars, including the ones you have defined yourself. Out-of-the-box Project contains three base calendars:

- **24 Hour**—Continuous time from midnight to midnight, 24 hours a day

- **Night Shift**—Used for overnight work that begins at the start of one night and finishes the following morning

- **Standard**—The standard workweek in the United States: 40 hours, 5 days, 8:00 a.m. to 5:00 p.m., with an hour lunch break

The default base calendar is the Standard calendar. This calendar assumes five days of work each week (Monday through Friday), from 8:00 a.m. to 12:00 p.m., an hour for lunch, and then 1:00 p.m. to 5:00 p.m. This Standard calendar does not designate set holidays; you have to do that yourself. To define the base calendar best suited for your project, you can edit the Standard calendar, use one of the other built-in base calendars, or create your own base calendar.

➡️ *For detailed information on task durations and creating subtasks, see Chapter 6, "Creating Your Project Schedule," p. 131.*

Statistics

Next to the Help button is the Statistics button. Click this button to view the Project Statistics dialog box. This box contains brief summary information about the project. You can also view it by clicking File tab, Info, Project Information, Project Statistics. Figure 5.4 shows the Project Statistics dialog box.

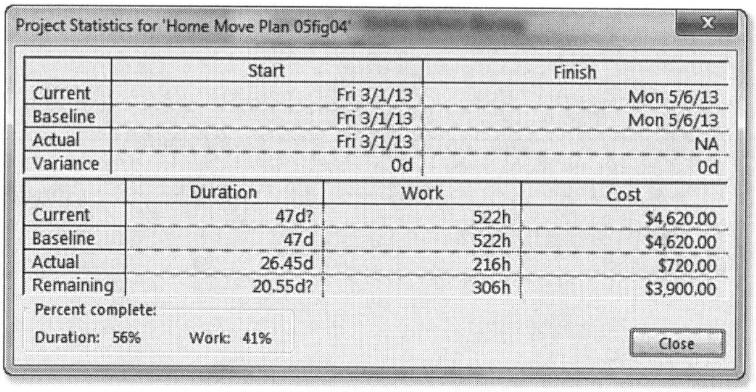

Figure 5.4
The Project Statistics dialog box provides a quick summary of a project's status.

Project Statistics for 'Home Move Plan 05fig04'				☒
	Start		Finish	
Current		Fri 3/1/13		Mon 5/6/13
Baseline		Fri 3/1/13		Mon 5/6/13
Actual		Fri 3/1/13		NA
Variance		0d		0d

	Duration	Work	Cost
Current	47d?	522h	$4,620.00
Baseline	47d	522h	$4,620.00
Actual	26.45d	216h	$720.00
Remaining	20.55d?	306h	$3,900.00

Percent complete:
Duration: 56%   Work: 41%

Close

Data in the Project Statistics dialog box cannot be modified. It is simply a quick reference to view or print.

The top pane shows project Start and Finish dates in relation to current projections, the baselined planning assumptions, actual progress recorded, and the variance between the baseline and the current projections.

The bottom pane shows project Duration, Work, and Cost in relation to current projections, baselined planning assumptions, actual progress recorded, and remaining amounts. Project calculates remainders by comparing the actual progress to current projections.

Finally, in the bottom-left corner, Project Statistics displays the entire project duration and project work in terms of percent complete.

The Project Statistics dialog box in Figure 5.4 displays statistics midway through the project's duration; out of the scheduled 47 days, 26 days have been completed, or 56% overall. The Project Statistics box also includes Start and Finish variance values that enable you to see how many days the Start or the Finish dates vary from those that you planned.

 note
Project Managers rarely use the Project Statistics feature in practice, especially in light of new reporting features in Project 2013.

 tip
You can identify the baseline used for this comparison by selecting the File tab, Options, Advanced, Baseline for Earned Value Calculation.

Priority

The Priority field allows you to set the priority of the project. Although it is visible in the Project Information dialog box only if you are using Project Professional, you can still set it using Project Standard.

The Priority field is helpful when you are sharing a group of resources with other projects. When you use the leveling feature in Microsoft Project, if a resource is assigned to work on tasks from different projects at the same time, the project with the higher priority level is what the resource will be leveled to work on first.

> *For more information about Project's leveling feature, see Chapter 24, "Resolving Resource Allocation Problems," p. 801.*

All projects have the same priority level until you change it. The priority starts at a midpoint, 500. 1000 is the highest priority, and zero is the lowest. See Figure 5.5 for an illustration of the Project Information dialog box in Project Professional, which contains the Priority field.

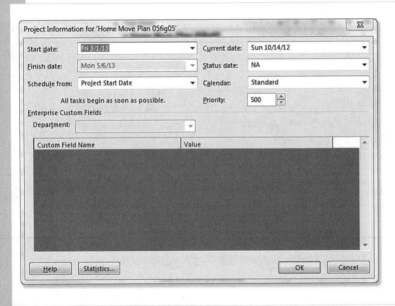

Figure 5.5
The Project Information dialog box in Project Professional has two additional fields: Priority and the Custom Fields.

Unsurprisingly, there are at least three ways to set the project priority:

1. From the Project Information dialog box, which you can reach through either the File tab or the Project tab.

2. By exposing the project summary task (File tab, Options, Advanced, Show Project Summary Task), selecting the task row, selecting the Task tab, and clicking the Information control.

3. By exposing the project summary task, adding the Priority column by right-clicking on one of the columns in the view, selecting Insert Column, and then selecting Priority from the drop-down list.

➡ *For more information about creating master projects and combining projects into a single Project window, see Chapter 23, "Working with Multiple Projects," p. 769.*

 tip

The Priority field can be useful when you want to review project priorities within a program. One way to compare the project priorities is to create a master project. Another is to combine projects into one Project view using the Window command.

Custom Fields

In Project Professional, the Custom Fields Table appears in the Project Information dialog box. The custom fields shown in the Project Information dialog box are Enterprise Custom Fields set within the server environment and do not exist in Project Standard.

➡ *For more information about local custom fields, see the "Defining Custom Fields" section, p. 112, in this chapter.*

Defining Project Properties

The other area to find and define information about your project is the Properties dialog box. Here, you can view and edit a number of options that describe the project. To open the Properties dialog box, select the File tab, Info, Project Information, Advanced Properties.

Figure 5.6 shows the Properties dialog box opened to the Summary tab. You can see five tabs: General, Summary (the default selected tab), Statistics, Contents, and Custom. The following sections discuss the options available within these tabs.

Figure 5.6
The Properties dialog box provides another area to define and edit aspects of your project.

Summary Tab

The Summary tab is the default selected tab when you open the Properties dialog box (refer to Figure 5.6). The first five fields (Title, Subject, Author, Manager, and Company) are general information about the project and who is associated with it.

The remaining fields—Category, Keywords, and Comments—are useful when you search for the project on your computer. If you have several projects in various stages, it might be difficult to keep track of all of them.

- You can keep notes on the project in the Comments field, which, for example, might help you remember where you left off when last working on the project.

- The Properties box is a great way to document metadata (information about data) for your project.

- If in the future you have trouble locating project files, you can search for words entered in the Summary tab in the Open dialog box.

 note

Pressing Enter selects the OK button except when the Comments field is selected. Pressing Enter in the Comments box moves you to the next line of text, like in a Word document.

The Hyperlink Base field is where you would enter the main addresses to the hyperlinks associated with the project, whether they be links to a file on your computer, your server, or a web address.

By default, the Save Preview Picture check box is not selected. To select it, click inside the box. By selecting it, you are telling Project to save a thumbnail sketch of the current view when you save the file. You can browse these pictures when you search for files using the File, Open command.

To enter information in any of the fields in the Properties dialog box, simply select the field and type in the information. Pressing Tab on your keyboard selects the next field below. When you are finished entering the information you want, click OK or press Enter. Click Cancel to exit the box without making any changes. Clicking OK and Cancel have the same function for all five tabs in the Properties dialog box.

 tip

It is good practice to complete the Summary tab at least. Without complete project information, a person viewing the project will need to deduce what the project is and who is managing it by sifting through the project itself. Additionally, many file storage systems use metadata in their searches. Complete project information increases the chances of your document being returned in search results.

General Tab

The General tab provides information about the project file: the filename, type, location where it is saved, and size. It also displays the dates when the file was created, last modified, and last opened. This tab is blank until the project file is saved for the first time.

The Attributes section of the tab displays the current file permission setting. You set the file permissions using the File Properties dialog box, opened by right-clicking the project file using Windows Explorer. By default, the Archive setting is checked when the file is saved, but the file owner can set access settings.

Statistics Tab

The Statistics tab provides helpful information about the work on the file. Included are dates when the file was created, last modified, last accessed, and last printed. The other section of the Statistics tab shows who last saved the file, how many revisions have been made, and how much total time has been spent editing the file. The information in the Statistics tab is especially useful if multiple people are accessing, editing, and saving the project. It helps you to keep track of who did what to the file.

Contents Tab

The Contents tab displays the most commonly reviewed information about the project schedule. Included are the project start and finish dates, the scheduled duration, work and cost amounts, and the percentage complete for both duration and work. This is a handy reference point for a quick project schedule review.

Custom Tab

The concept of custom properties is to give project managers the ability to add project attributes to a project file. In the Custom tab, you can add more properties to a file (or delete them). You can then search for files by the values of these properties. This can bring more meaning to your project file. The properties are listed in the Properties list in the bottom of the Custom tab. Figure 5.7 shows the Custom tab in the Properties dialog box.

Figure 5.7
The Custom tab enables you to customize the fields in the Properties dialog box.

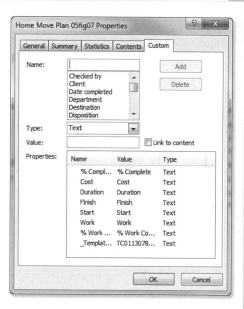

To create a custom property for a project, follow these steps:

1. Open the Properties dialog box (File tab, Info, Project Information, Advanced Properties) and choose the Custom tab.

2. Type a property name in the Name box, or choose from the list. The list includes commonly used properties.

3. In the Type box, use the drop-down list to define the type of data to place in the field. You should use this option only when you type the value of the property instead of linking it to a field in the project file. When you link the property value to a field, the Type drop-down list is unavailable. The allowable data types are Text, Date, Number, and Yes or No.

4. If you chose Text, Date, or Number in the Text box (step 3), type a value in the Value text box. If you chose the Yes or No option in the Type box, you see Yes and No buttons in the Value box. Select either Yes or No.

5. Click the Add button to add the property to the list in the Properties dialog box. The newly created property appears in the Properties list box at the bottom.

If you want to link a property value to a project field, follow these steps:

1. Open the Properties dialog box (File tab, Info, Project Information, Advanced Properties) and select the Custom tab (see Figure 5.8).

2. Type a property name in the Name box.

3. Select the Link to Content check box. The Type box is grayed out, and the Value text box becomes a drop-down list. The name of the Value box changes to Source.

4. In the Source drop-down list box, choose the field that has the value you want the property to reflect.

5. Click the Add button to add the property to the list in the Properties dialog box.

If you want to modify the value for a property, follow these steps:

1. Select the property name in the Properties list. This places the current name and value in the text boxes at the top of the dialog box.

2. Change the Type or Value field as needed, and the Add button automatically changes to Modify.

3. If you change the Name field, you have to use the Add button to include it as a new property.

4. You can then use the Delete button to remove the original, leaving the newly named version.

5. Click Modify to complete the change.

To delete a custom property, select it in the Properties list and click Delete.

When you are finished with the custom properties list, click OK, or select another tab to work in. When you are finished with all the tabs, click OK.

Figure 5.8
Property values can be linked to Project fields using the Custom tab of the Properties dialog box.

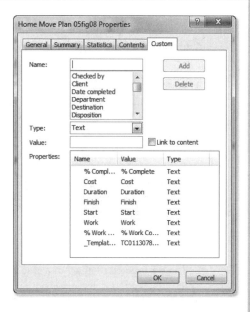

Defining Calendars

One of the first major assumptions you have to make in any schedule is how much time is available to complete tasks. You need to account for all holidays, vacation time, and all other foreseeable non-working time to build a schedule with any degree of accuracy.

As previously mentioned, by default Project applies a Standard calendar of 40 hours a week, Monday through Friday, 8:00 a.m. to 5:00 p.m., with an hour off for lunch. You can modify this Standard calendar, and you can create additional project calendars as well.

 tip

It is important to keep your organization's working environment in mind when constructing base calendars for projects. Choose a calendar so that you can plan for success. If you simply accept the Standard base calendar, you quickly run into an issue: Your people cannot typically spend eight hours a day working only on your project. Your project schedule ought to reflect reality.

A resource might typically spend six out of the eight hours in a day working on your project, and the other two hours on administrative tasks or miscellaneous activity. You could change your base calendar to reflect six hours of working time in a day.

For most organizations, it is recommended that you keep your eight–hour-a-day calendar or another calendar that reflects the general start and finish working times of an average day/week, and instead adjust the percentage of time that resources have available each day. This is accomplished by adjusting the resource Max Units, which is explained in more detail in Chapter 8, "Defining Project Resources." For example, you can use 75% for the Max Units if your resources spend on average two hours a day for every day of the week for miscellaneous activities and only six hours per day for work on your project.

Calendar Hierarchy

Project makes it possible to assign calendars at the Project, Resource, and Task level. Tasks using Auto Schedule mode will honor working and nonworking time according to the following hierarchy of calendars:

1. **The Task Calendar**—If a task has a specific calendar, Project honors the Task Calendar unless a resource assigned to the task also has a specific Calendar; in this case, Project attempts to honor *both* calendars. If the task does not have a specific calendar....

---

 tip

It is also possible to check the Scheduling Ignores Resource Calendars box in the Task Information window, Advanced tab. In the event of a conflict, Project will display an error message, telling you that it will default to this setting to resolve the conflict.

---

2. **The Resource Calendar**—If a resource is assigned to a task and the resource has a specific calendar assigned to it, Project honors that calendar. If the resource does not have a calendar (which is common) and the Task does not have a calendar....

3. **The Project Calendar**—All tasks without specific calendars, lacking resources with specific calendars, will honor the Project Calendar.

This hierarchy is a powerful scheduling feature. Unfortunately, in past versions of Project, it often led to confusion; Project Managers and schedulers found it difficult to understand exactly why some tasks were scheduled to occur when they were. Starting in 2010, the information column clearly identifies the driving calendar unless it is the Project Calendar.

➡️ *For additional information on Max Units and their use, see Chapter 8, "Defining Project Resources," p. 235.*

Modifying and Defining Base Calendars

Many of your calendar modifications will occur on the Change Working Time dialog box. To access it, click the Project tab, Change Working Time. Figure 5.9 shows the Change Working Time dialog box. The Change Working Time dialog box contains a For Calendar field to define which calendar you are viewing, a legend, a calendar, and two tab options (Exceptions and Work Weeks) to modify the calendar. When you open the Change Working Time dialog box, the current date is highlighted in bold on the calendar.

Figure 5.9
The Change Working Time dialog box is used to modify and create base calendars.

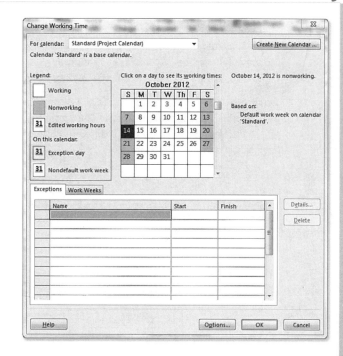

Defining Exceptions

You can define exceptions individually, or you can define a recurrence exception along with its recurrence pattern, so each exception only has to be defined once.

For example, if Labor Day is always a nonworking day at your company, you can tell Project to define every Labor Day as an exception. To do this, follow these steps:

1. Open the Change Working Time dialog box (Project tab, Change Working Time).

2. Scroll to the month of September using the arrows on the right side of the calendar.

3. Click on Labor Day, the first Monday of every September. In 2013, Labor Day is September 2nd.

4. Under the Exceptions tab, type **Labor Day** in the Name column, and click Enter, or press the directional arrow to the right. The Start and Finish columns display the date of the highlighted day in the calendar (in this case, 9-2-13).

5. Select the cell in the Start column next to the exception name (in this case, select the 9-2-13 cell in the Start column next to Labor Day) and click the Details button.

6. The Details dialog box appears, as shown in Figure 5.10. If Labor Day is a nonworking holiday, leave the Nonworking option selected. If you want to define working hours (such as a half day), select Working Times and enter the hours of working times for Labor Day.

7. Under Recurrence Pattern, select Yearly, because Labor Day happens once a year. Figure 5.10 shows this selection.

8. Because the date for Labor Day changes annually, select the The... option, and then the First Monday of September is filled in automatically. Because this is the appropriate description for Labor Day, you do not have to change anything else.

9. The Range of Recurrence automatically fills the selected date from the calendar in the Start field. Because this is the first Labor Day in your project, you do not have to change this field. If you wanted the exception to start on a different date, you can type in the date or use the drop-down list to choose from a calendar.

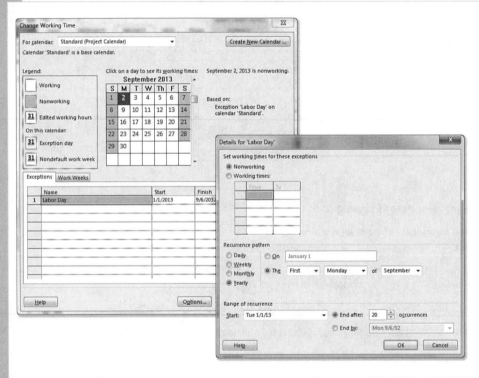

Figure 5.10
The Details dialog box enables you to define the details of your exception, including its recurrence pattern and range.

 tip

The Recurrence Pattern options are Daily, Weekly, Monthly, and Yearly. Click each option to familiarize yourself with defining in detail the recurrence pattern information for all four options. Information appears at the right of the options and varies depending on which one you choose.

10. The final step is defining the end of the range of the exception. You can select End By and fill in a date (type it in or use the drop-down), or you could select End After and fill in the number of occurrences you want the exception to end after. Project supports information up until 12-31-2049, so the maximum number of occurrences you could enter is 39, because there are 39 Labor Days between 9-5-2011 and 12-31-2049.

 note

If you were defining a non-working day that occurs each year on the same date, such as Christmas Eve, you would select the On option and type in the date.

11. Click OK. The date is now highlighted as an Exception Day (as defined in the legend), and if you scroll through every month of September, you will notice the same for every first Monday. Click OK again to close the Change Working Time dialog box, or continue modifying your calendar.

Similarly, if you have a long meeting every Friday, you can simply click on the Friday of the first meeting and repeat the process. Define working hours around the meeting, select a Weekly recurrence pattern on Friday, and define the end of the exception.

Defining Longer Exceptions

You can also define longer exceptions, such as office closures for an extended period. For example, if your company shuts down starting on Christmas until the end of the year, you can define that entire time period as nonworking time. To set this up so that it occurs each year, the changes must be made one day at a time:

1. Open the Change Working Time dialog box by selecting Project Tab, Change Working Time.

2. Scroll to the month of December using the arrows on the right side of the calendar.

3. Click on December 26th.

4. Under the Exceptions tab, type **Holiday** in the Name column, and click Enter, or press the directional arrow to the right. The Start and Finish columns display the date range of the highlighted period in the calendar.

5. To set up the recurrence pattern for this date, click the Details button. Under Recurrence Pattern, select Yearly, and the On (December 26, in this case) option is automatically selected.

6. Under Range of Recurrence, you can either specify the number of years by selecting the End After option and then entering the number (of years, in this case) that this exception will apply to. Or you can also select the End By option and select the specific date (in this case, 12/26/2013) until which the exceptions will apply. The date you provide here is inclusive, so in this example, the last year the exception will be applied is 2013. Click OK.

Repeat this process for each day in the closure period, even if it falls on a weekend in the first year. This enables you to make sure that all days between 12/26 and 12/31 are nonworking days, regardless of where they fall in the week.

Creating New Base Calendars

It is helpful to make exceptions to your base calendar to account for small changes in working time. However, sometimes it is more efficient to create a new base calendar completely and apply that to your project. For example, assume that your resources work 40 hours a week, but only four days a week. Rather than going through and changing every Monday through Thursday to 10 hour days and making Friday a nonworking day, it is easier to just create a new base calendar that more accurately depicts your standard working time.

To do this, follow these steps:

1. Open the Change Working Time dialog box by selecting the Project tab, Change Working Time.

 tip

You can verify that the change is correct by reviewing the number of occurrences shown in the dialog box in Figure 5.11. In this example, the number is "5" because the recurrence time period was established as 5 years. If you have successfully made an exception, the numbers on the dates of the exception appear as defined in the legend.

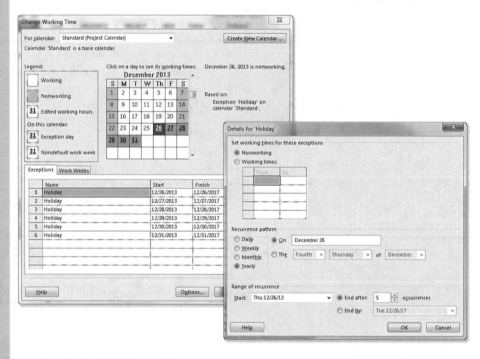

Figure 5.11
The Details dialog box allows you to define the details of your exception period and set up the exact period as well as the recurrence pattern in which it occurs.

2. Click the Create New Calendar button at the top, which opens the Create New Base Calendar box.

3. Type in a distinctive name in the Name field.

4. Select the Create New Base Calendar option if you want to start from scratch on the standard 40-hour workweek, or select the Make a Copy Of option if you want to use an existing base calendar as your template. Click OK.

Notice that the For Calendar field at the top of the Change Working Time dialog box has defined the new base calendar with the name you gave it. Also, when you are finished creating the calendar, if you open your Project Information dialog box (Project, Project Information), you see the new base calendar listed as an option for the project base calendar in the Calendar drop-down list.

5. After you have defined your new base calendar, it is time to define your workweek. Click the Work Weeks tab, and click the Details button or double-click Default in the Name column. The Details dialog box appears, in which you define your workweek (see Figure 5.12).

6. To define a 40-hour, four-day workweek (Monday–Thursday, 10 hours a day), go through each day in the Details dialog box. Sunday is selected first. Because this is a nonworking day, you can select either Set Days to Nonworking Time or Use Project Default Times for These Days.

 note

Selecting Make a Copy Of changes your calendar name from what you named it to Copy of [*name of calendar you are making a copy of*]. If you still want to call it your original name, change it back.

7. Next, highlight Monday. Select Set Day(s) to These Specific Working Times. In the From and To columns, set the appropriate working hours. Be sure to press Enter after each cell entry to save the information. For example, you could type **8:00 a.m.** in the From column, press Enter, and type **12:00 p.m.** in the To column and press Enter. Then for afternoon hours, type **1:00 p.m.** in the From column, press Enter, and type **7:00 p.m.** in the To column and press Enter. This gives you a 10-hour day with an hour off for lunch. If you are satisfied with this schedule, repeat the process for Tuesday, Wednesday, and Thursday.

8. Finally, highlight Friday and select Set Days to Nonworking Times. Do the same for Saturday, and click OK.

 tip

To enter time for multiple days simultaneously, hold down Shift and drag your mouse over the multiple days you want to change. Alternatively, hold down Ctrl and click each day individually.

Notice how the new calendar is created, with all Fridays set as nonworking days, and the working times for Monday through Thursday reflect what you defined.

When you have finished, click OK to close the Change Working Time dialog box, or click Cancel to exit without saving.

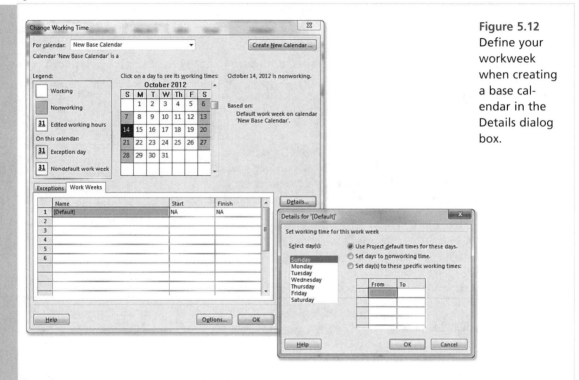

Figure 5.12
Define your
workweek
when creating
a base cal-
endar in the
Details dialog
box.

note

You can enter time in 12-hour clock format or 24-hour clock format (military time). If you're using the 12-hour format, noon is 12:00 p.m. and midnight is 12:00 a.m. If the time is on the hour, you only have to enter the single number (5 p.m. for 5:00 p.m.). Be sure to define a.m. and p.m. Otherwise, Project may misinterpret your times.

Generally, only the first four working hours boxes are defined: the top two for morning hours and the bottom two for afternoon hours. Sometimes you will use the remaining boxes to account for multiple breaks or meals, or for other unusual work schedules. You must define the To and From fields as pairs, and the From field must come later than the To field.

Setting Project and Resources Calendar

Start dates for tasks are generally determined by resource calendars, unless you create a task calendar, in which case the resource will operate based on the task calendar. Resource and task calendars begin as the base calendar for the project. You can modify the resource and task calendars without changing the base calendar. The previous sections talked about the base calendar; the next few sections discuss resource and task calendars.

Resource Calendars

Resources are the people and materials that work on tasks within the projects. This section focuses specifically on resource calendars.

 For information about resources, see Chapter 8, "Defining Project Resources," p. 235.

By default, when you create a resource, the resource calendar is the same as the project calendar. You can modify the resource calendar specifically for the resource without changing the base calendar to the project. To modify the working time of a resource, follow these steps:

> **tip**
>
> Work resources are the only ones that include resource calendars. The other three resource types— material, budget, and cost— do not have calendars associ- ated with them as they are assumed to always be available.

1. Open the Resource Sheet view by selecting the Resource tab, View, Resource Sheet (this can be also done from the Task tab).

2. There are at least two ways to change the resource calendar, as follows:

   a. Double-click the resource row of the resource that needs a resource calendar.

   b. Select the resource row of the target resource and Click Information under the Resource Tab.

   Either of these methods opens the Resource Information dialog box (see Figure 5.13).

3. In the Resource Information dialog box, under the General tab, click the Change Working Time button.

4. The Change Working Time dialog box appears. To change the resource's base calendar, choose from the Base Calendar drop-down list at the top.

5. To make additional modifications, use the same methodology discussed in the section "Defining Exceptions," earlier in this chapter.

6. When you are finished modifying the resource calendar, click OK to save the changes or Cancel to exit without making any changes.

The resource now operates based on the base calendar plus the exceptions defined in his or her resource calendar. Referring back to the example of a four-day workweek, if a resource normally works those hours, but had a three-day vacation coming up, you could define that vacation and Project would schedule work for that resource around the vacation dates. Similarly, if a resource had a standing obligation every week outside of your project, you could define that exception and the appropriate recurrence range, and Project would not assign task work to the resource during that time.

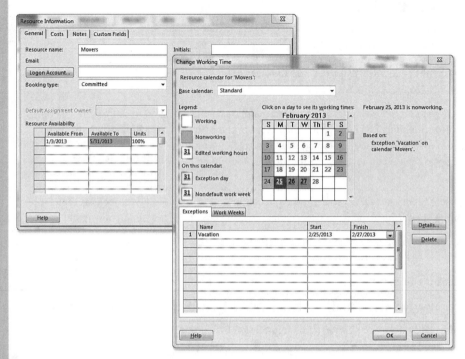

Figure 5.13
Click the Change Working Time button under the General tab of the Resource Information dialog box to make changes to a resource's schedule. In this case, the resource has a three-day-long vacation scheduled for the fourth week of February.

Task Calendars

As mentioned previously, if you assign a resource to a task, the work on the task will follow the resource calendar. If the resource has no specific resource calendar, or if there are no resources assigned to the task, the task will follow the project (base) calendar.

However, you can create a calendar specifically for a task. To do this, create a base calendar specifically for the task by following the process described in the earlier section "Creating New Base Calendars."

After you create the base calendar, assign it to the task by following these steps:

1. In any view where you can see your tasks, such as the Gantt Chart view, select the task to which you want to assign the newly created base calendar.

2. With the task (or tasks) selected, select the Task tab, Information to open the Task Information dialog box. Alternatively, right-click on the task and select Task Information to open the Task Information dialog box.

3. Under the Advanced tab is a Calendar field (see Figure 5.14). Click the arrow to open the drop-down menu with the base calendars listed. If you successfully created a new base calendar, it will be on this list. Select it.

Figure 5.14
Assign calendars to tasks under the Advanced tab of the Task Information dialog box. In this case, the New Base Calendar is being assigned the "Drive to new residence" task.

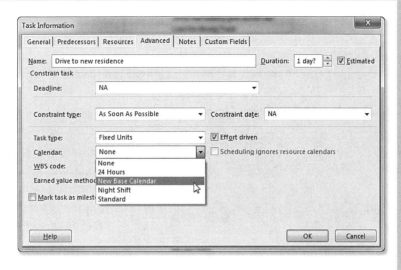

4. Next to the Calendar field is a check box labeled Scheduling Ignores Resource Calendars. If you want your task calendar to override the resource calendar for the resource assigned to the task, select this box. If you want Project to schedule based on the resource calendar *and* the task calendar, leave it blank.

5. Click OK to close the Task Information dialog box with the changes made, or click Cancel to close it without making any changes.

Task Calendars

As the project manager, you must decide whether assigning task calendars makes more sense for your project than using resource calendars.

For example, if you run a newspaper printing facility, you will have tasks that do the actual printing. Often this happens overnight, so the task may cover multiple shifts. In addition to your human resources, you would include the machines used to print the newspaper as resources. Because these machines and people all operate under different schedules, it would be more effective to schedule the task based on its own calendar, instead of the project's base calendar or the resource calendar. Likely you would use a version of the 24 Hour calendar, because the task is constantly being worked on by various resources at all hours of the day.

Compiling the entire newspaper may use a standard base calendar, which does not work for the "printing" task because there would be too many exceptions to enter. It is easier to simply customize a calendar for this specific task and schedule from that.

Defining Custom Fields

Every project is unique. Accordingly, Project enables the use of custom fields in addition to its extensive selection of default fields.

The following sections discuss the tactics and logic behind customizing fields.

Custom Fields Concept

Project has dedicated predefined fields for the user to customize in a variety of ways. All the fields are accessible on the Project tab, Custom Fields. This command opens the Custom Fields dialog box shown in Figure 5.15.

Figure 5.15
Define custom fields in the Custom Fields dialog box.

There are two categories of customizable fields: task fields and resource fields.

 note

Both Project Professional and Project Standard contain custom fields that each project manager can customize within his project. When connected to Project Server, Project Professional also includes enterprise-level task and resource custom fields (as well as a third class of project-level custom fields) that allow an organization to standardize the fields they capture for all projects.

In each of these categories, you can do the following:

- Rename the custom fields permanently so that the new name appears wherever the field name appears.

- Add a value list to a custom field.

- Add a formula to a custom field.

- Designate graphic indicators to appear in a custom field in place of the data.

There are nine types of custom fields, as shown in the Type drop-down list: Cost, Date, Duration, Finish, Flag, Number, Start, Text, and Outline Code. Within these types, there are designated numbers of fields. These are detailed in Table 5.1.

 note

Custom field names appear in any drop-down list in which the predefined fields are accessible. For instance, if you are inserting a new column on a table, the field choices for the column include all the custom field names you define, even if they have not yet been used for data storage.

Table 5.1 The Custom Fields Types (Excludes Enterprise Fields Associated with Project Server)

Type	Number of Available Fields	Description
Cost	10	Can contain currency data you want to enter in your project
Date	10	Can contain dates you want to enter in your project
Duration	10	Can contain duration or work values you want to enter in your project
Finish	10	Can contain finish dates you want to enter in your project
Flag	20	Can contain yes/no flags you want to enter in your project
Number	20	Can contain numeric (positive or negative) values you want to enter in your project
Start	10	Can contain start dates you want to enter in your project
Text	30	Can contain textual information you want to enter in your project alphanumerically, up to 255 characters
Outline Code	10	Create an alternate structure for your project that you can use to sort, filter, or group tasks or resources (in other words, alphanumeric outline structures)

Custom fields can be used in many ways. Perhaps you need to identify the status of a task as something other than percentage complete, such as approved/not approved. Perhaps you want to create a stop-light style status field to show whether the project is on schedule and on budget. The following section explains how to define custom fields for your project.

Defining Custom Fields

All changes to a custom field are done in the Custom Fields dialog box (Project tab, Custom Fields). To work with a particular field, select the general type (Task or Resource) first. Then select a particular category of custom field (such as Cost or Duration) from the Type drop-down list. The list of available fields for that particular category appears in the box; click on the one you want to customize.

Renaming, Deleting, and Importing Custom Fields

To avoid having to change the name label every time you open a new table or display a custom field, you can give the generic name provided in Project an alias that is a more accurate description for your purpose. After you have selected your general type and custom field category, highlight the custom field you want to rename. If you have not renamed any of them yet, their names all appear as the category type and a number after (such as Duration1).

When you have the custom field highlighted, click the Rename button, which opens the Rename Field dialog box. Type in the name you want, and click OK. Notice that the new name appears in the box with the old name in parentheses. The new name will now appear anywhere the custom field appears instead of the generic custom field name.

If you want to delete a custom field alias, click the Rename button, highlight the alias, and click the Delete button.

You can also import a custom field from your project, another project, or from a template. The imported custom field includes all the attributes associated with it, such as formulas or indicators.

Click the Import Custom Field button to open the Import Custom Field dialog box. From there you can import the custom field using the drop-down list in the Project field as your source, selecting the field type and the field. All open projects appear in the Project field drop-down list. The Field drop-down list displays all available custom fields from the source you selected. Click OK to import the custom field, or click Cancel to cancel.

 note

The information relating to custom fields in this chapter is an overview. You can find more detailed information, as well as advanced actions when working with custom fields, later in this book.

For more advanced actions and information about custom fields, see Chapter 22, "Customization Almost Beyond Reason: Views, Tables, Filters, Groups, Fields Toolbars, Menus, and Forms," p. 699.

Defining Environment Options

The Options dialog box in Project 2013 is the same as 2010, which was a complete redesign. It enables you to view, modify, and define assumptions about your project. There are two types of options: global (which affect all your projects) and file-specific (which affect only the specific project file you are working with when you open the Options dialog box). To display the Options dialog box, select the File tab, Options (see Figure 5.16).

In the Options dialog box, you use 11 categories divided into groups to define the environment options of your project. Most of the settings are global options, affecting all of your projects, including previously created projects. If you change these settings, they stay that way until you change them again. However, on the scheduling tab you can choose which projects you want to change, as shown in Figure 5.17.

Figure 5.16
The Options dialog box contains 11 groupings to define elements of your project.

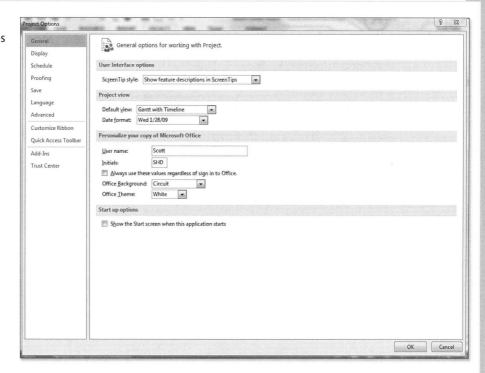

There are also option settings that affect only the project you are currently working on (have the project files open). These settings have a header that is suffixed with "...options for this project" and are next to a drop-down that enables you to specify a particular project or All New Projects.

Project 2013 automatically updates the Global Template when All New Projects is selected. There is no Set as Default button.

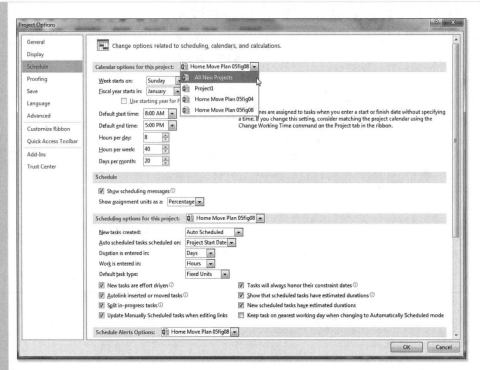

Figure 5.17
Some settings affect all projects, and some affect only the project you select. This is true throughout all tabs in the Options dialog box.

Defining Project Standards

As previously mentioned, there are 11 tabs in the Options dialog box. Option settings are global unless they are grouped under a header suffixed with "...options for this project." The following sections discuss the 11 tabs of the Options dialog box.

General Tab

As the name suggests, the General tab deals with general information (refer to Figure 5.16).

The User Interface options enable you to change the Screentip style. The Project View options enable you to select the view you always see by default, and to specify the date format. Note that the options in the date format are determined by the Calendar type selected in the Display tab. Personalizing your copy of Microsoft Office amounts to specifying your name and your initials, but in Project 2013, you now have the option to set this for all Office applications. Project uses this user name for the Author and Last Saved By properties. You can also choose the Office background. Finally, you have the choice between seeing the Office startup screen every time you open Project, or going straight to a new, blank project.

 tip

Each tab contains a Help button. Use this feature as an alternate resource for any questions or confusion you have relating to the particular tab you have open.

Display Tab

The Calendar type enables you to select which basic international calendar underpins all other calendars. Changes in this option impact views throughout Project. This should be used in places where the default Gregorian calendar is nonstandard (for example, the Hijri Calendar, the Thai Buddhist calendar, and so on; see Figure 5.18).

Currency options can be project specific, or set for all new projects.

The Show Indicators and Options Buttons For group refers to indicators that show in the Indicator column in various views.

Finally, the Entry bar check box in the Show These Elements section displays or hides the text-entry toolbar just below the Ribbon. This was a default feature of Project for many years that is now optional.

Figure 5.18
The Display tab changes how some Project content is displayed.

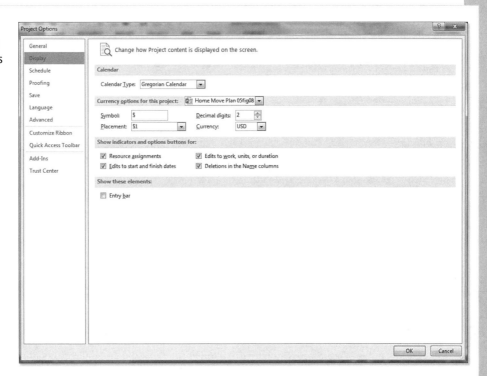

Schedule Tab

The Schedule tab has a significant impact on how Project schedules your tasks.

Calendar Options

The Calendar Options section is one of the more critical sections in the Options dialog box (see Figure 5.19). All fields in the Calendar Options section are file-specific; select the All New Projects item if you want to use the information on all future projects as well as the one you are working on.

The Hours Per Day, Hours Per Week, and Days Per Month fields are crucial to the interpretation and display of your estimates of task duration. Days, weeks, and months are the basic task duration units. However, minutes are the fundamental time unit in Project. Thus, all durations are converted into minutes, and the conversion is based on the information you enter on the Calendar tab. If this information is inaccurate, your schedule will be inaccurate. For example, if you define a day as 8 hours, Project calculates that there are 480 minutes of working time in a day. If you define a day as 10 hours, Project calculates that there are 600 minutes of working time in a day. Even though they are both one day, there is a big difference in the amount of working time in that day.

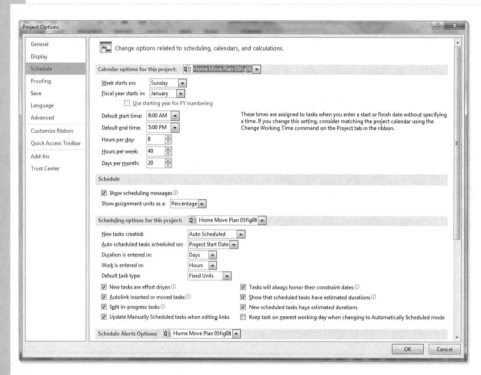

Figure 5.19
Use the Calendar section of the Schedule tab to set Project's calendar options, which include the default calendar used for all of your projects.

You can use the Week Starts On field at the top of the Calendar Options for this project section to change the way that a week is displayed in timescales and dialogs. It does not change any calculations for the project. Similarly, the Fiscal Year Starts In field affects reports and displays that show annual and quarterly information. The default setting is the same as a calendar year, so this field should be changed if your fiscal year does not begin in January.

The Default Start Time and Default End Time fields define the start and end times of the normal working days. Again, it is very important that these times match the times defined in your base calendar, discussed earlier in this chapter.

 tip

To avoid confusion, make your estimates of the amount of work in hours rather than in days and then validate that the duration of the work matches what you expected it to be.

Although you may assign tasks to begin on a certain day, Project does not actually schedule the task until the start time of that day. So, if your workday starts at 6:00 a.m., but you have not changed the Default Start Time from 8:00 a.m., Project will schedule that task to start two hours late. This also affects how you track a task. If a task took a full eight-hour day from 6:00 a.m. to 3:00 p.m. (accounting for an hour lunch break), and you mark the task as 100% complete but still have 8:00 a.m. in the Default Start Time field, Project shows the task as finishing later than it actually did.

If the information you defined in the Calendar options section is the standard calendar information for your organization, select the All New Projects item from the Calendar options for this project drop-down.

In short, be sure to define your calendar options accurately and realistically, and be sure that the Calendar tab on the Options dialog box matches the information defined in the base calendar you use for your project, created in the Change Working Time dialog box.

Schedule

Show Scheduling Messages causes Project to display messages about scheduling inconsistencies, such as successor tasks starting before the finish of predecessor tasks.

The Schedule section enables you to turn scheduling messages on and off, and to show the assignment units as either a percentage or a decimal (see Figure 5.20). This is a matter of personal preference.

Figure 5.20 Use the Calculation section of the Schedule tab on the Options window to set Project's calculation settings, such as whether Project should use automatic calculation or allow you to do it manually.

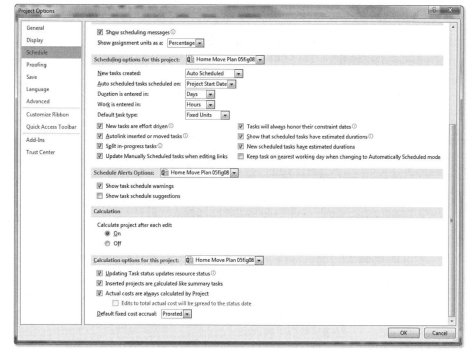

Scheduling Options

The Scheduling Options section pertains primarily to tasks that are auto-scheduled. However, there are two exceptions:

- The option Without Dates for New Tasks Created pertains only to Manually Scheduled tasks.

- Update Manually Scheduled tasks when editing links is self-explanatory.

For New Tasks Created, choose whether you want new tasks to begin on the project start date or on the current date, or as mentioned, without dates in the case of manually scheduled tasks.

The next two fields enable you to enter the unit of duration and work: minutes, hours, days, weeks, or months. Again, this is a personal preference, depending on what is best for you and your project. Be sure your working time and Calendar section entries coincide; if you enter duration in days, be sure you have defined the correct number of hours in a day, and so on. Also, these fields will determine the default units when entering tasks. For example, if you have Days entered in the Duration Is Entered In field, you could simply type **2** in the Duration field for 2 days. However, if you wanted to assign a different time unit, you would have to enter the unit, such as **2 w** for 2 weeks.

Choose the task type: Fixed Duration, Fixed Units, or Fixed Work. The task type defines how Project calculates the schedule, work, and units (this will be described in greater detail later).

The remaining options include the following:

- New tasks are effort driven means that adding resources to a task won't alter how much work actually needs to be done.

- Auto-linking inserted or moved tasks enables Project to create finish to start dependencies automatically.

> ## 📡 caution
> It is unwise to use months as a duration unit because of the inconsistency of the length of months throughout the year. Use hours, days, or weeks as the duration unit.

- Split In-Progress Tasks enables project to discontinuously reschedule unfinished portions of a task when you use Project to automatically reschedule uncompleted work.

- Update Manually Scheduled tasks when editing links means that Project WILL move your manually scheduled tasks if you have linked them to another tasks.

- Tasks Will Always Honor Their Constraint Dates is less significant than it was before Manual Task mode was introduced. Tasks that do not honor their constraint dates will be rescheduled to eliminate negative slack.

- Show that Scheduled Tasks Have Estimated Durations merely toggles off the indicator in the duration field. The Estimated column serves the same purpose.

- New Scheduled Tasks Have Estimated Durations applies only to auto-scheduled tasks.

- Finally, Keep Task on Nearest Working Day When Changing to Automatically Scheduled Mode is self-explanatory. Turning off this option when using Auto Scheduled mode is rarely a good idea because it will result in scheduling that ignores calendars.

Schedule Alerts Options

The Schedule Alerts options (refer to Figure 5.20) enable you to turn task schedule warnings and task schedule suggestions on and off. More experienced users of Project often find these alerts obvious and distracting.

Calculation

The Calculation section enables you to select whether Project recalculates after every change you make, or only when you specify—typically, to turn on Calculate Project After Each Edit, which is the default.

However, if you choose to manually recalculate your project after each edit, you can click the Calculate Project button on the Project tab. This applies not only to the scheduling of your project, but also to the status as compared to the planned estimates (such as how much you are behind or ahead of schedule).

The Manual option can be useful on large projects when you are making updates to the status and want to prevent calculations from occurring until you have entered all the data. This speeds up your entry process and prevents pop-up warnings from showing until you are ready to review the changes.

In addition, the Manual option is effective when you are working on multiple projects that have links established between them, and you are making a lot of changes in one of them. It will speed up your editing process, but keep in mind that links will not be updated between the projects until you manually calculate.

Calculation Options

The calculation options for this project section provide a few more options. Selecting the Updating Task Status Updates Resource Status check box automatically updates the task and resource status together when either is updated. For example, if you update a task's percent complete to 50%, the % Work Complete field is automatically calculated to reflect that task's percent effort complete (50%). The same methodology applies if you update the resource status; Project automatically updates the task status.

The Inserted projects Are Calculated Like Summary Tasks option pertains to whether data is rolled up to a single task in your receiving project schedule. The concepts and usage of multiple project schedules are covered in more detail later.

Using the Actual Costs Are Always Calculated by Project option can be a difficult decision to make. When Project calculates actual costs, you cannot enter a cost that differs from the costs specified in the resource rates. You could, however, use a custom field for those occasions. If you choose to enter actual costs manually, you can then choose to allow Project to spread those costs up to the status date. This is more appealing if a task has not been updated for months. However, if the actual cost incurred represents an invoice, for example, it might not make any sense to spread the costs.

Finally, the Default Fixed-Cost Accrual can be set to Start, Finish, or Prorated.

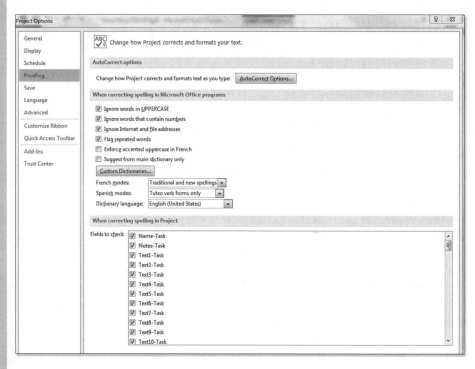

Proofing Tab

Under the Proofing tab, you designate which fields you want Project to spell-check automatically (see Figure 5.21). By default, everything is selected to spell-check. Exceptions are defined with the check boxes on the right.

Save Tab

The Save As tab is where you define what kind of file you want your project to save as and where you want to save it (see Figure 5.22). You can also turn on the Auto Save feature to automatically save your project as you are working.

New in Project 2013, you can also choose to show the Office Backstage when opening or saving files. If you choose not to show the Office Backstage, you will open the standard Windows file browser.

The Cache section refers to an instance of Project Professional that is linked to Project Server. The Cache stores a local copy of project files, allowing Project Server to download only the differences between the published file and the copy in the local Cache. The default of 50MB is plenty, unless you are opening a lot of large project files. Increase the size limit as your available hard drive space allows.

 tip

You can also choose to show Sign In to SkyDrive during save if you intend to use SkyDrive to save your Project files.

Figure 5.22
The Office
Backstage.

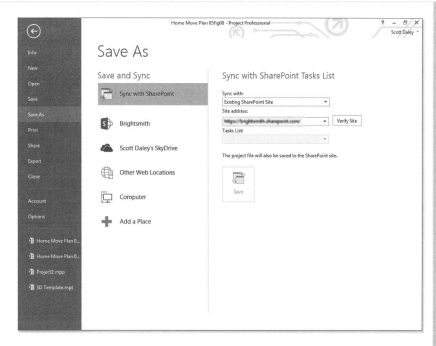

Figure 5.23
Use the Save
tab of the
Options win-
dow to define
the default file
type and loca-
tion for saving
your Project
files.

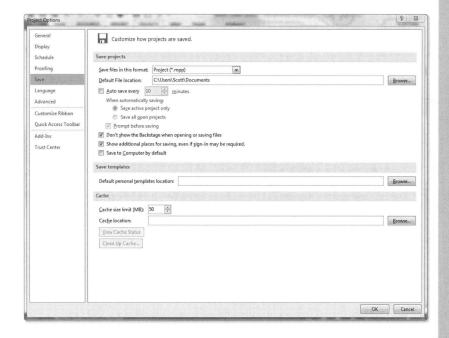

➡ *For additional information on manipulating Project Files Locally and in the Cloud, see Chapter 18, "Managing Project Files Locally and in the Cloud," p. 549.*

Language Tab

As the window describes itself, the Language tab (see Figure 5.24) enables you to add additional languages to edit your documents. In cases where you are working in a language that is different from your local installation of windows (for example, if you've brought your own laptop to a client site, and the client's primary language is different from yours), you can set a different language priority order for Project.

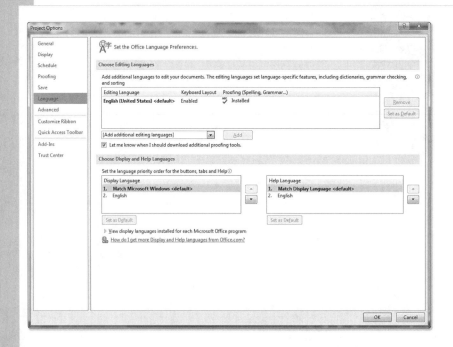

Figure 5.24
The Language tab of the Options screen.

Advanced Tab

The Advanced tab (see Figure 5.25) is a grab-bag of remaining option sets that are used by a minority of managers. However, it's likely that you will at some point need to make a change on this tab.

The options in the General section are as follows:

- **Set AutoFilter on for New Projects**—This refers to a small arrow that appears next to columns in views when this option is selected. Clicking this arrow brings up a sorting and grouping control.

- **Prompt for Project Info New Projects**—This applies only to projects that are associated with a project server instance. When a new project is created, this opens a window allowing the user to enter data in project-level fields (managers can enter this data at any time, regardless).

- **Show add-in user interface errors**—If you've purchased or written an add-in for Project and it attempts and fails to change the UI, checking this box will show the error.

- **Open Last File on Startup**—If you are working with a single project file every day, this saves you the hassle of opening first Project and then the file.

- **Undo Levels**—Although Undo is technically unlimited, it is practically limited by the amount of RAM your computer has. Managers that perform heavy future modeling ("what if-ing") might want to increase this number.

The Project Web App section also only applies to projects that are associated with an instance of Project Server.

The Planning Wizard section should be self-explanatory. Note, however, that there is some overlap with the Scheduling section on the Schedule tab in the Project Options screen.

The General Options for This Project section enables you to set standard rates, but, more interestingly, it enables you to toggle Automatically Add New Resources and Tasks on and off. This feature is useful insofar as it prevents you from creating the same resource repeatedly with slight variations in name.

The Edit section should be self-explanatory, with the exception of the Ask to Update Automatic Links option. Project will ask before updating automatic links (if there are any) when a project is first opened. Automatic links can be made to Excel documents, and so on, just like any other Office application.

The options in the Display section are as follows:

- Show This Number of Recent Projects controls how many recent documents are tracked in the Open File dialog.

- Quickly Access This Number of Recent Projects controls how many projects you see when you hover over Project 2013 in the Start Menu.

- Show Status Bar refers to the bar running along the bottom of your Project window, where things such as the New Task Mode control and the Zoom control are displayed.

- Show Windows in Taskbar refers to your Windows taskbar and controls whether the taskbar will display multiple windows for Project if you have multiple Project files open.

- Use Internal IDs enables Project to ignore local names in favor of internal machine names. This is better left checked in most circumstances, but there might be an instance where you need to control how Project matches things such as Views that you move with the Organizer, particularly if you don't want to have items with duplicate names but different specifications.

- Automatically Add New Views is very much a matter of preference. If you manage your projects in a consistent manner, it makes sense to turn this on. If each project you manage is totally unique, turn it off.

- Show Scroll Bars is self-explanatory.

- Show OLE Links Indicators is self-explanatory. OLE links are links from tasks to other Office applications.

- Disable Hardware Graphics Acceleration is an esoteric that might make sense if your computer lacks hardware acceleration.

The options in the Display options for this project section are mostly self-explanatory with the exception of the Show Project Summary task option. The Project Summary task is a zero-level task with the same name as the project file. It displays summary data for the entire project. Although this is off by default, most experienced Project users prefer to have it on.

The options in the Cross Project Linking Options for This Project section are covered in greater depth in Chapter 23, "Working with Multiple Projects."

The Earned Value Options for This Project Section options are as follows:

- **Default Task Earned Value Method**—There are more than two Earned value methods specified in the ANSI Standard. % Complete—the default—isn't one of them. Physical % complete is specified, however.

- **Baseline for Earned Value Calculation**—This option enables you to use any of the baselines for calculating EV. This can be useful in a variety of scenarios, including situations where the project manager wants to control what appears on his s-curves.

The Calculation Options for This Project section options are as follows:

- **Move End of Completed Parts**—This option causes Project to automatically "fix" completion dates that are in the future.

- **Move Start of Remaining Parts**—This option reschedules unstarted tasks with a start date in the past forward to the status date.

- **Edits to Total Task % Complete**—By default, Project will spread actuals across the entire planned duration of a task. This results in actuals being recorded for future dates. Check this option to prevent creation of future-date actuals.

- **Calculate Multiple Critical Paths**—This will not identify secondary and tertiary critical paths, which beg definition regardless. This will calculate the critical paths for disconnected networks running through the same file.

- **Tasks Are Critical**—Use this option to provide a little leeway in critical path calculation. On a longer project with larger duration tasks, the default of 0 days might not make sense.

Figure 5.25
The Advanced tab of the Options screen.

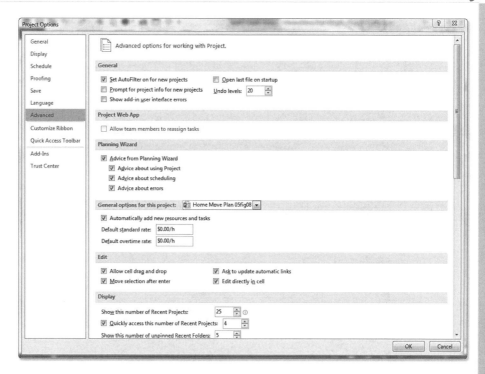

Customize Ribbon Tab

The Customize Ribbon tab is used to add or subtract controls from the Ribbon (see Figure 5.26). Options available in the left pane are filtered by the Choose Commands From drop-down above the left pane. The right pane enables you to specify the location of added controls.

➡️ *For additional information on the Customize Ribbon tab, see Chapter 22, "Customization Almost Beyond Reason: Views, Tables, Filters, Groups, Fields Toolbars, Menus, and Forms," p. 699.*

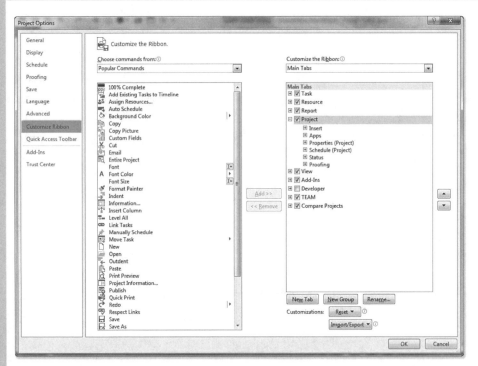

Figure 5.26
The Customize Ribbon tab can be used to change the default layout and controls of the Ribbon.

Quick Access Toolbar Tab

To show the Quick Access Toolbar, right-click on the Ribbon, Show Quick Access Toolbar. By default, the Quick Access Toolbar displays the Save, Undo, and Redo buttons (see Figure 5.27).

Options available in the left pane are filtered by the Choose Commands From drop-down above the left pane. The drop-down above the right pane enables you to customize the Quick Access toolbar for the open project only or all projects. Add controls to the Quick Access Toolbar by clicking Add.

The Reset button at the bottom of the right pane enables you to reset only the Quick Access Toolbar or all customizations made to the Ribbon.

Trust Center Tab

This Trust Center includes several hyperlinks, including the Show the Microsoft Project Privacy Statement, Office.com Privacy Statement, Customer Experience Improvement Program, the Send a Smile Privacy Statement, and the Microsoft Trustworthy Computing links. These are informative only (see Figure 5.28).

Figure 5.27
The Quick Access Toolbar customization screen

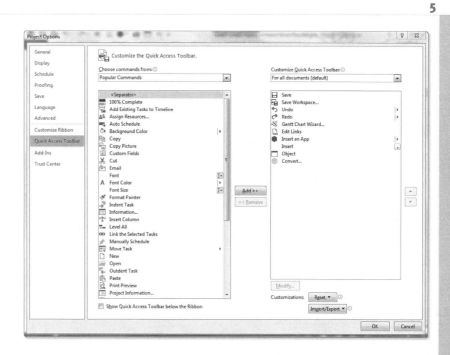

Figure 5.28
The Trust Center tab is mostly informative, except for the Trust Center Settings button.

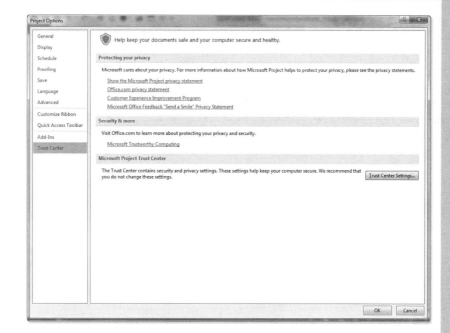

The Trust Center Settings button opens the Trust Center. Third-party software often requires changes in the Trust Center, particularly to Macro Settings (see Figure 5.29).

You can use the Legacy Formats tab to prevent opening non-default or older Project file formats.

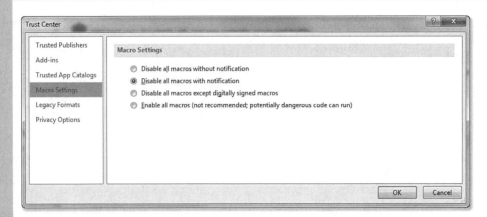

Figure 5.29
The Macro Settings often need to be changed if third-party software is deployed.

Consultants' Tips

It is always a best practice to include as much information about the project with the schedule. Take advantage of Project's capabilities to store project information with the new project when you create it. The project properties, Project Information dialog box, and the custom fields give project managers the ability to include project, task, and resource information within the project schedule. This allows the project manager to use this "metadata" for reporting, filtering, and organizing schedule information for the various audiences that will need it. Project properties settings are very useful when searching project archives for specific types of information.

Custom fields are especially helpful in extending basic schedule information to include your organization's unique information. All companies categorize task, resource, and project information with unique labels that they will use for reporting.

Project-level calendars (as opposed to resource or task calendars) are an effective way to define the basic expectations you have for planning project work. They allow you to model actual, productive time so you can plan project tasks in a realistic manner instead of assuming that 100% of resource time can be devoted to project tasks.

At the same time, developing a good schedule can be difficult, so do not make it any more complicated than it needs to be. Establish a calendar for your project that works for the majority of the requirements you have and then handle exceptions on a case-by-case basis. Do not attempt to account for all possible conditions. Getting in the weeds to account for resource efficiency is not justified in most cases.

6

CREATING YOUR PROJECT SCHEDULE

Creating the project schedule is simultaneously the easiest and most difficult part of managing a project. It is straightforward because there are very few restrictions—it can be created exactly as you'd like it. It is difficult because your schedule affects every other aspect of your project. Keep in mind that the schedule is always a work in progress; it will be out of date almost the minute it is finished.

Entering Project Tasks

After you have created your new project (defined its properties, calendars, and so on, as discussed in Chapter 5, "Setting Up Project for Your Use"), it is time to create the project's schedule. This chapter focuses on doing just that.

As you know, work on a project is broken up into tasks. These tasks are the building blocks of a project's schedule, so it is important that you take the time to enter all the tasks within your project and provide realistic estimates of each task's duration. Often, tasks are dependent on each other; their start or finish dates might rely on the start or finish of another task. Also, a task might be part of a larger task. Thus, organizing your tasks properly is a vital element in successfully creating your schedule and managing your project. This chapter shows you how to properly organize your tasks into a task list.

➡ *For additional information on task dependency relationships, **see** the "Linking Tasks" section, **p. 186**, in Chapter 7, "Defining Task Logic."*

Entering Tasks Using the Gantt Chart View

When you are ready to create the schedule for your new project, the default view you begin in is the Gantt Chart view. The Gantt Chart view is a great example of combining table (linear) and graphical (time-phased) information on one screen.

The Task table has several columns that relate to each task. Figure 6.1 shows the standard Gantt Chart view: the Task Entry table on the left and the Gantt Chart timescale on the right. In addition to the displayed columns, you can insert new ones by right-clicking on any column and selecting Insert Column. You can then select a field name from the drop-down list, and the column will be inserted before the column you clicked on. Typing the first few letters of the column name auto-filters the list for column names beginning with those letters. You can also scroll through the list.

You can take two approaches to creating a task list. The most common approach is to start by listing the major phases of the project and then listing the detailed tasks under each major phase. This approach is called the *top-down* approach.

The other approach is the *bottom-up* approach. In this approach, you list all the detail tasks first. When using this approach, it might be helpful to list these tasks in chronological order. After they are all listed, you can come up with the major phases of the project. This approach might be more useful for smaller projects, but for complex projects that have hundreds of detailed tasks, this approach is not ideal because you will likely forget to list some of the tasks. In the bottom-up approach, you list the entire scope of tasks for the project, whereas in the top-down approach, you concentrate on each phase, one at a time, thus allowing less room for error.

The top-down approach also supports the concept of *scope breakdown*, where you start with the project scope statement and decompose it into smaller and smaller parts. The top-down approach is also often associated with the *Work Breakdown Structure* (WBS) concept. Using WBS, the work and scope of that work are broken down layer by layer, starting at the top project scope statement.

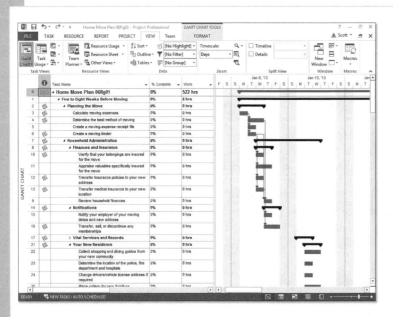

Figure 6.1

The Gantt Chart view displays the Task Entry table on the left and the timescale on the right, separated by the vertical divider bar.

New Home Project Example

This chapter uses moving into a new home as a project example. The top-down approach is used to determine the major phases of a home move, such as Planning the Move and Move Preparation. There are more major phases to a move than this, but they should suffice for illustrating the creation of a task list.

Under the Planning the Move task, you would create separate tasks for events such as Calculate Moving Expenses, Determine the Best Method of Moving, and Schedule the Moving Dates. The Move Preparation task can have detailed tasks, such as Notify Your Employer of Your Moving Dates, Obtain Estimates from Several Moving Services, Prepare Packing Materials, and so on (refer to Figure 6.1).

You can see how each major task breaks down into detailed tasks, sometimes on several levels, but they all relate to the original major phase. The major phases are called *summary* tasks, and the detailed tasks are called *subtasks*. Subtasks are displayed as indented under the summary tasks. Summary tasks and subtasks are discussed in greater detail later in this chapter.

As described in Chapter 4, "Getting Started After the Business Initiative Is Approved," you should consider building the WBS first, and then build your task list from it. It will help you organize your thoughts and understand the scope of the work of the project, prior to entering tasks into Microsoft Project.

> *For more information on the project summary task, see the "Selecting the Display Options for Outlining" section later in this chapter.*

Creating a task begins when you enter the task's name into the project. The most common way of doing this is by typing the name of the task directly into the Task Name field in the Task Entry table. After you have typed in the name, press Enter or use the arrow keys to exit the cell. If you are using the Auto Scheduled task mode, Project will automatically supply values in the ID, Duration, Start, and Finish fields if new tasks are auto-scheduled. The following sections describe the default Gantt Chart view entry fields.

> 🌐 **tip**
>
> Microsoft Project automatically creates the project-level summary task, but it is not displayed by default. To display it, select the Format tab. It should be identified as Gantt Chart Tools because the Format tab is context-sensitive. Check the box next to Project Summary Task. The project summary task is shown in Figure 6.1 at the top of the task list.

Task Modes

The task mode is mentioned throughout this book. As detailed in Chapter 4, by default, the task mode for new tasks is set to Manually Scheduled. In Manually Scheduled mode, Project does very little work for you. You can't set a task finish date before a start date—Project sets the Task start date to equal the finish date. But dates in the Start, Finish, Duration, and Work fields will no longer match their "Scheduled" counterparts.

Because working in Manually Scheduled mode is similar to working in a spreadsheet, for the most part, this book assumes you are working in Auto Scheduled mode. Where relevant, differences caused by the two modes are highlighted.

ID Field

The ID field is the column all the way on the left. Although you cannot see the label on the field, if you were to insert a column, you would see the column identified as ID at the top. This field is defined automatically when you type in a task and cannot be manually edited. The ID numbers refer to a task's position in the Task table, beginning with 1 and continuing in ascending numeric order (1, 2, 3, and so on). The ID field is also used to reference a task in the task outline. These numbers are not permanently associated with the task; if you move a task from row 5 to row 2, for example, the task's ID field changes according to the move (from 5 to 2 in this case).

 note

Although the ID number is not permanent, Project does create some permanent numbers it associates with each task. Unique ID associates the original ID number permanently with the task for review within the project itself and the GUID (generated unique identifier) creates a 32-character number that might be used for integrating custom programs or programming macros.

Indicators Field

The Indicators field is the column to the right of the ID field. At the top of the column is an icon with a small *i* in white surrounded by a blue circle. If a task has additional information that is not revealed in the other columns, an indicator icon often appears in this field next to the task. Hover your mouse pointer over the indicator to view a tip about what the icon indicates. For example, a check mark appears in this field when the task is complete. Not all tasks have an indicator.

Table 6.1 shows all the Project indicators and their meaning.

Table 6.1 Indicator Icons and Their Descriptions

Indicator Icon	Description
Note Attached	Indicates that a note is attached.
HyperLink	Indicates that a hyperlink is attached.
Overallocated Resource	Indicates that the resource needs leveling.
Deadline	Indicates that the task will finish later than its Deadline date.
Inflexible Constraint	Indicates that the task has an inflexible constraint; the task is tied to a specific date (such as Must Finish On, Must Start On, and so on).
Moderately Flexible Constraint	Indicates that the task has a moderately flexible constraint; the task is constrained but not to a specific date (such as As Soon As Possible, As Late As Possible, and so on).
Missed Constraint	Indicates that the task has missed its constraint deadline; it has not been scheduled or completed within the constraint's timeframe.

Indicator Icon	Description
Recurring	Indicates that the task is recurring.
Complete	Indicates that the task is complete.
Inserted Project	Indicates that the task is a subproject, or inserted project (a project file consolidated as a summary task in another project).
Inserted Project Read Only	Indicates that the task is a read-only inserted project.
Task with Calendar	Indicates that the task has a calendar related to it (a task calendar).
Task with Conflicting Calendars	Indicates that the task calendar and a resource calendar conflict for accomplishing the work on the task.
Backloaded	A contour indicator that means scheduled work is back-loaded (the work assigned is heaviest toward the end of the task).
Bell	A bell contour indicator that means assigned work is heaviest in the middle and lighter at the beginning and end of the task.
Double-Peak	A double-peak contour indicator that means scheduled work is distributed over time in peaks and valleys.
Early Peak	An early-peak contour indicator that means scheduled work peaks shortly after it starts and becomes increasingly lighter.
Edited	An edited contour indicator that means scheduled work has been manually entered.
Front Loaded	A front-loaded contour indicator that means scheduled work is heaviest at the beginning of the task and decreases over time.
Late Peak	A late-peak contour indicator that means scheduled work starts light, increases over time, and peaks near the end of the assignment, but not the very end.
Turtle	A turtle contour indicator that means scheduled work starts and ends the same but becomes heaviest in the middle.

Task Name Field

The Task Name field contains the text you defined as the name of the task. Task names should not be vague; they should make sense out of context.

See the "Creating Task Names" section later in this chapter, for more information about task names.

Duration Field

The Duration field is extremely important for scheduling tasks. If you are using Auto Scheduled mode, the new task duration will also be one day with a question mark next to it. If you are using Manually Scheduled mode, the task duration will not be calculated. The question mark signifies that the duration in this field is tentative, and you should enter the actual estimated duration for the task later as you confirm and enter more confident estimates. For more information about the Duration field, see the section, "Entering Task Durations," later in this chapter.

Start and Finish Date Fields

In Auto Scheduled mode, the Start field displays the date the task is scheduled to begin, and the Finish field shows the date it is scheduled to finish (based on the duration).

Manually Scheduled mode disables the predictive capabilities of Project. That does not mean you should never use it. On the contrary, a sophisticated Project user will probably have schedules with a mix of task modes. However, it is best used in early planning stages of a task or a project, or for tasks or projects where anticipating the future is less important than understanding the present.

Helpfully, Project still actively calculates what your schedule would look like if your tasks were auto-scheduled. These values are in the Scheduled Start, Scheduled Finish, and Scheduled Duration columns.

Although you can enter dates in the Start and Finish fields while using Auto Scheduled mode, it is best to let Project calculate these dates based on the durations you enter. If you enter the dates on your own, Project places a date constraint on the task. You should enter only Start and Finish dates for tasks if in fact they must start or finish on a certain date and time. For example, you might not be able to get into your new house until a certain date, so you would have to schedule your tasks that involve moving in to start no earlier than that specific date.

 note

As you build your task list and the Gantt Chart expands based on the start and end dates of your tasks, you might have problems finding the task's Gantt bar on the Gantt Chart. You can select the task and then use the Scroll to Task button on the Standard toolbar. This shows you the beginning of the selected task's Gantt bar.

tip

To take full advantage of Auto Scheduled mode, you should not enter start or finish dates when you are initially building your schedule. Microsoft Project builds a schedule based on estimated durations, logical dependencies, resource assignments, and calendars. If you find yourself consistently entering specific start and finish times for tasks, you are not utilizing the full benefits and potential of Project. After you have built your schedule using Microsoft Project's scheduling engine, you might then want to consider entering constraints for those tasks that are date-constrained, like your set move-in date, or a specific date and time your new refrigerator is being delivered.

Default Start and Finish Dates

When you set up your project, you need to decide if you want to set a fixed start date (a *forward-scheduled project*) or, less commonly, set a finish date (*backward-scheduled project*). Projects that need to be scheduled backward from a finish date might benefit from using Manually Scheduled mode. This is usually a sign that the finish date has been imposed from by a project sponsor, without much concern how much time the project will actually take. Projects that use tasks in Auto Scheduled mode insist on showing "the truth" as far as Microsoft Project can interpret it. Manually Scheduled mode makes it easier to paint the right picture, even if in fact it is not possible.

 caution

You should be aware that scheduling from the project's finish date in Auto Scheduled mode can complicate building the schedule. You might find that as you build your backward-scheduled project, your schedule shows you should have started the project two months prior to the current date.

If you have scheduled your project from a fixed start date, Microsoft Project automatically enters the project's start date as the task's start date. Similarly, if you scheduled your project from a fixed finish date, Project sets the tasks to finish on the project's finish date and calculates the start date by subtracting the duration from the finish date. Project automatically recalculates and changes this date as you link and assign dependency relationships to tasks and make other modifications.

You can tell Project to schedule tasks from the current date (if it is different from the project's start date) or with no dates. This is especially helpful when scheduling tasks after the project has already begun, because the project start date has already occurred.

To do this, perform the following steps:

1. Select the File tab, Options, Schedule.

2. On the Schedule tab, select Auto Scheduled or Manually Scheduled from the drop-down list in the New Tasks created field. However, if you are planning for a future project, it is best to leave the default as the project start date, and let Project recalculate the start date for the task for you. The project start and finish dates and the current date are defined in the Project Information dialog box (select the Project tab, Project Information).

You can also move the entire project, which is particularly useful when you are starting from a Project template. To do this, perform the following steps:

1. Select the Project tab, Move Project.

2. In the Move Project dialog box, select the new start date for the project, and optionally move all the deadlines as well by the same difference in time.

The Default Time of Day Project automatically includes both the time of day and the date in the date field, even if it has not been formatted to show the time. If you do not enter a time of day when you enter a task with a start date, Project uses the default start time, usually 8:00 a.m. The same is true when you enter a finish date for a task with no time of day; Project sets it at 5:00 p.m. You can, however, change the default start and end times in the Options dialog box (see Figure 6.2).

You can also enter the time of day manually, even if the date field does not show it. For instance, if you wanted a task to start at noon on October 13, you would enter **10/13/ 12:00 PM**.

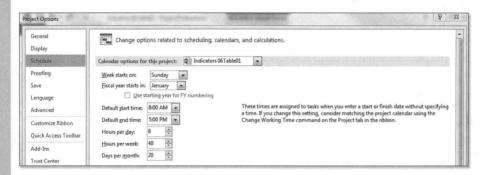

Figure 6.2
You can change the start and end times for a work-day using the Options dialog box.

You can also enter time in the 24-hour clock format (14:00), but Project displays it as 2:00 p.m. To display time in the 24-hour format, you must change the format outside Project in the Windows Control Panel. In Windows 7, Project honors changes made by the computer's administrator in the Adjust Date/Time dialog boxes.

Perform these steps to set the default time of day:

1. Select the File tab, Options, Schedule.

2. Enter the time you want Project to use if you do not include the time of date with a start date, using the Default Start Time field.

3. Enter the time you want Project to use if you do not include the time of day with a finish date, using the Default End Time field.

4. You can set your changes as the default for any open project or all new projects using the Calendar Options for This Project drop-down list.

Displaying the Time of Day with Dates You can turn on the time display in the Start and Finish fields by selecting the File tab, Options, General, Date Format drop-down. From the drop-down list of different date formats, you can choose the one that works best for you. The first one on the list has both the time and the date; however, others in the list have both the time and date, simply in different formats.

tip

Use capital letters to define morning or afternoon. For example, to schedule a task to start at 2:00 p.m., enter **2:00 PM** next to the date in the Start field. However, enter time sparingly in your project schedules, unless you truly need to control a project task so discretely.

tip

It is best to make sure that these default start and finish times match up to the calendar start and finish times. It is not required, but if they do not match, it can create some confusion.

 note

You might have trouble with the Start and Finish fields when you add time to the date format. If you see a column displaying pound signs, it is an indicator that the column is not wide enough to display the new format. You can double-click the column header and then select the Best Fit button to expand it.

Predecessors Field

The Predecessors field displays the ID numbers for any tasks linked to the selected task. As previously mentioned, tasks often are dependently linked to each other, so one task often cannot start or finish until another task has started or finished. For example, you cannot install new carpeting until you have measured the square footage of each room for which you're getting new carpet. Therefore, the task ID number for Measure Room Square Footage for New Carpeting would be in the Predecessors field for the Install New Carpeting task. As a note, each task should have a task, called a successor task, that starts after the previous task. The Install New Carpeting task is a successor task for Measure Room Square Footage for New Carpeting. The Successor field does not show by default.

 For details about task predecessor/successor relationships, **see** *the "Linking Tasks" section,* **p. 186**, *in Chapter 7, "Defining Task Logic."*

Resource Names Field

The Resource Names field displays the names of any resources assigned to work on the task. When multiple resources are assigned to the task, their names are separated using a comma. If a resource is assigned at less or more than 100% units, you see the number of units assigned in brackets next to each resource name.

 For additional information about assigning resources to tasks, **see** *the "Assigning a Resource to a Task" section,* **p. 274**, *in Chapter 9.*

Creating Task Names

As previously mentioned, when you enter a name into the Task Name field, you create a task. You must include several critical pieces of information when you create a task, all of which are discussed in this chapter, but the first step is choosing the name itself.

Task names can contain any combination of characters and spaces, up to 255 characters long. Most project managers advocate using a verb-noun format when creating task names, such as Assemble Boxes or Load Truck. This is because action verbs provide more information to you and your resources on what action is supposed to be performed and remove any possible confusion.

As another example, if you have a task named System Test Plan, it can be confusing as to what needs to be done—whether the system test plan is being created, reviewed, approved, and so on. However, if you specify Create System Test Plan as the task name, there is no question about what exactly the task entails.

> ## ⚡ caution
>
> A task is created when you make an entry in any of the Task Entry table fields, not just the Task Name field. If you create a task by accident and want to remove it, simply click the ID number for the accidentally created task and press the Delete key on your keyboard. You can also select any field in the task row, press the Delete key, and then select Delete the Entire Task from the smart tag that appears.

Nevertheless, it is important that you take the time to ensure the task name is clear and comprehendible when taken out of context. Ask yourself, "If someone who does not know much about the project reads this task name, will he or she be able to understand the gist of the task?"

This is important because there are possible scenarios when people will see the task name out of the context of your project schedule. For example, if you are using Project Professional in conjunction with Project Server, when resources are assigned tasks, and they go to update their work schedule to include the tasks you have assigned them, the task name appears on its own. If the task name is vague, they will come to you asking for further explanation. You can avoid this by making sure your task names are specific and make sense outside the project schedule.

If you create long and descriptive task names, they are difficult to fit in their cells, and they will most likely get cut off in your Gantt Chart view. The section "Displaying Long Task Names," later in this chapter, explains how to resolve this problem so that people can easily read and understand the task name, no matter what its length is.

When you have completed entering a new task and press Enter on your keyboard, the selection automatically changes to the next row so you can enter another task. However, if you do not want the selection to change when you press Enter, you can turn off this feature by choosing Tools, Options, Edit tab. You need to clear the Move Selection After Enter check box and then click OK.

 caution

Although you can create tasks using the mouse by drawing bars in the timescale side of the Gantt Chart view, this is not a good method for creating tasks. You still have to name the tasks and enter their information. Also, you usually have to adjust your duration unless you are very accurate with the mouse, and if you are using Auto Scheduled mode, you automatically create a date constraint on the task. Either the task is constrained to start no earlier than the date you clicked on if you dragged the mouse to the right, or it is constrained to finish no earlier than the date you clicked on if you dragged the mouse to the left.

Copying Task Names from Another Application

Besides typing task names into the Task Name field directly, an alternative option for entering task names is to copy them from another application and paste them into your task list in Microsoft Project. Perhaps these names already exist in another document, spreadsheet, or database. You might save yourself some time by copying and pasting them rather than retyping them all.

 For details about copying additional task information from another application, see the "Copying Data from Other Applications into Project" section, p. 875, in Chapter 26.

 note

This section describes the process for copying and pasting task names only. There is a way to copy and paste additional task information, such as dates and duration, but it is a more complicated process.

Follow these steps to copy a task name or list of task names from another application:

1. Open Project and the application from which to copy the task names.

2. Select the names you want to copy in the other application, keeping these requirements in mind:

- Each task name must be on a separate row of text if the other application is a word processing document, such as Microsoft Word or Microsoft PowerPoint.

- Each task name must be in a separate cell in a column of entries, and all the names you want to copy must be adjoining, if the other application is a spreadsheet, such as Microsoft Excel.

- The task names must be in a single field of the database if the other application is a database, such as Microsoft Access. Select the cells in that field only. Do not select the records because that would select other fields as well, and Project would not know what to do with the other fields.

3. Use the Copy command (generally located under Edit, Copy) or use the Ctrl+C keyboard combination, which copies the list of names to the Clipboard.

4. In Microsoft Project, select the cell in the Task Name field where you want to place the first name in the list, and use the Paste command (select the Task tab, Clipboard, Paste).

Entering Task Durations

Although it is best to create the entire task list prior to entering durations, the Duration field is extremely important for creating your project schedule. *Duration* is defined in Microsoft Project as the amount of time scheduled on the project calendar to work on a task. In other words, duration is the amount of working time between a task's start and finish dates—the amount of *elapsed* time it will take a resource to complete those hours of work.

Duration is not the amount of work needed to complete a task; rather, it is the amount of time units that are scheduled to work on a task. The time units are defined in the project calendar, such as eight hours for one day of duration. For auto-scheduled tasks, the Duration field is governed by the scheduling algorithm as soon as you enter Work or Resource Names on a task.

What makes Microsoft Project confusing for novices is that it can shorten or lengthen the Duration you enter based on how many resources you add to a task, on the default Task Type, and whether it is effort-driven. You can also start creating tasks in Manually Scheduled mode and change them individually to Auto Scheduled mode and watch the results.

> *Before you get too frustrated about entering estimates into the Duration field and seeing the Duration change when you add resources, **see** Chapter 9, "Understanding Work Formula Basics," **p. 269**.*

Some key things to keep in mind when estimating by duration of a task are as follows:

- Working hours do not have to be continuous, but duration usually is. Microsoft Project assumes that work should be assigned to the first available hours on the calendar, starting with the default of 8:00 a.m. and continuing to the default of 5:00 p.m. on the start date. For instance, Project will initially schedule the work of eight hours for one day, but you can go back later and change the schedule to fit your needs, even assigning work for one hour a day for the eight hours if necessary. If you do, each hour occurs on one day at a time, and the duration for the task will be eight days.

- Duration does not measure total work or effort; it measures only the number of units of time on your calendar that are scheduled. So, a one-day task that has two people working on it for four hours might be the same as one person working for eight hours, or four people working for two hours. Again, the actual duration might be predicated on how you have set up task types, effort, and the number of resources on the task.

- When you are estimating duration, always ask experts, leads, work managers, or the resources themselves to help increase the accuracy of the estimate. Consider past experiences, the skills and experience of your resources, and how many resources you plan to use. If possible, talk to other project managers or look at past projects.

> *For additional information about task types and effort-driven and non-effort-driven scenarios, **see** Chapter 10, "Scheduling Single and Multiple Resource Assignments," p. 301.*

As indicated previously, when you first enter a value in the Duration field on the Task Entry table, Project schedules auto-scheduled tasks to occur as soon as possible. That is, if you define a task's duration as five days, Project schedules that task for the first five working days after the start of the task (at 8:00 a.m. of the start date if that has been defined in the calendar). You can also choose to reschedule the task so it is not continuous (such as one day a week for five weeks).

> *Refer to the "Defining Recurring Tasks" section later in this chapter for more information about task durations.*

Creating Tentative Duration Estimates

If you have previous experiences with tasks similar to the one you are working with currently, take those experiences into account when estimating the duration for the current task. How long did it take last time? How many resources worked on it? Was their skill level comparable to the skill level of the resources you have now?

Gather whatever information you can to postulate the most educated, realistic duration estimate for your task. Keep in mind the number and skill level of resources you might assign to the task and the amount of effort per day they could actually work on the task. For instance, a resource might be available for only four hours of each day (more or less) to work on your task, so the duration might be twice as long as the hours in a day. A task taking 40 hours could take two weeks based on resource availability. This duration estimate will determine the start and finish dates for the task, unless you have already defined those (which is not advised unless those dates are definite).

> *See the "Attaching Notes to Tasks" section later in this chapter for more information on the Notes field.*

 tip

The Notes field can aid you in remembering your thought process as you are creating your duration estimates. If you assign resources to tasks days or weeks after you have entered the duration estimates, it might be difficult to remember how many resources you were thinking about, and who those resources are. Keep track of that kind of information in the Notes field.

As you have seen already, when you create a new auto-scheduled task, Microsoft Project gives it the default duration of one day, followed by a question mark (1 day?). The question mark signifies that the duration estimate is tentative and serves as a good reminder to go back later when you have a more informed idea of the duration to correct it. After you have determined your best estimate for the duration of the task, replace the default duration value with your own, and the question mark will disappear. You can also remove the question mark by double-clicking on the task, and clearing the Estimated field check box in any tab within the Task Information dialog box.

 For details about using the Tasks with Tentative Duration filter, or any other filters, **see** *the "Understanding Filtering and Grouping" section,* **p. 393**, *in Chapter 11.*

 tip

If you want to display all the tasks with tentative duration estimates together, to see which tasks you need more confident estimates on, use the Tasks with Estimated Durations filter (View tab, Data, Filter). Project displays only those tasks with a question mark in the Duration field.

Understanding the Duration Time Units

For the time units of durations, you can use minutes, hours, days (the default), weeks, or months. Microsoft Project automatically applies the default duration time unit even if your organization uses a different unit for duration. To change the default duration time unit from days to something else, select the File tab, Options, Schedule and choose from the drop-down list in the Duration Is Entered In field. The new default time unit also appears in the Duration field every time you create a new task.

⚠ caution

Because months are inconsistent from each other in their length, do not choose months as your default time unit.

No matter what your default time unit is, Project internally converts it into minutes, because all calculations in Project are performed in minutes. One hour is always 60 minutes. Other time unit assumptions are defined in the Schedule tab under Options (File, Options).

The default time unit assumptions are as follows:

- 1 day equals 8 hours.

- 1 week equals 40 hours (five 8-hour days if you are using the default).

- 1 month equals 20 days.

If your organization works five 7-hour days a week, you would want to adjust the definition of a day to be 7 hours, and a week to be 35 hours. The same is true for a company that works four 10-hour days a week. You will not need to change the definition of a week, because the total number of hours is the same as the default 40 hours, but you will need to change a day from 8 to 10 hours. If your organization works under different time units, you want to define those assumptions in your project. To do so, follow these steps:

1. Select the File tab, Options, Schedule.

2. In the Hours per Day field, enter the number of work hours in a day (the default is 8).

3. Enter the number of weekly work hours in the Hours per Week field (Hours per Week = Hours per Day × Days per Week). The default is 40 hours per week.

4. Enter the number of days you want to define in each month in the Days per Month field. The default is 20 days per month.

5. If you want the change to be applied to all subsequent project schedules, select All New Projects from the drop-down next to Calendar Options for This Project. Click OK to save and apply these definitions. If you want the change to be applied only to the current schedule, just click OK.

> *For details about setting up calendars to reflect different hours for work during the week, see the "Defining Calendars" section, p. 144, in Chapter 5.*

> **⚠ caution**
>
> Make sure project and resource calendars also match these daily and weekly work settings.

Using Time Unit Abbreviation

If you prefer, you can enter time units as abbreviations instead of the complete word. You can also abbreviate in the plural form. Refer to the following list for acceptable abbreviations:

- **Minute**—m, min, mins, minute, minutes

- **Hour**—h, hr, hrs, hour, hours

- **Day**—d, dy, dys, day, days

- **Week**—w, wk, wks, week, weeks

- **Month**—mo, mon, mons, month, months

Therefore, to enter "2 weeks," you could type **2w**, **2wk**, **2wks**, **2 week**, or **2 weeks**. No matter which one you choose, Project displays it as "2 wks." You can change the default display to a different spelling of the time unit in the Options dialog box (Tools, Options). In the Edit tab, under the View Options for Time Units section, use the drop-down lists to change the default spellings.

> **⚠ caution**
>
> Minutes and months are easy to confuse because they both start with m. It might be helpful to avoid abbreviating "months" so you do not accidentally define the time unit as "minutes."

> **note**
>
> Years can be abbreviated as y, yr, and yrs. However, years is not a duration time unit; it is used for resource pay rates.

Defining Elapsed Duration

The previous sections discussed time units for *working* time. Additionally, you can schedule an *elapsed* duration amount for a task. Elapsed duration means uninterrupted work on a task. In other words, an elapsed duration entry includes all time, both working and nonworking, continuously.

This is helpful in situations where the task can or must run after working hours. For example, if you are painting a bathroom in your new house, you might include the time the paint needs to dry as a task. If the paint takes 10 hours to dry, you would not want to enter **10 h** in the Duration field, because Project would schedule the paint to finish drying well after it was actually done.

If you were working with the Standard base calendar (eight hours = one day), and you assigned a duration of 10 hours, Project would calculate its finish date to be a day or two later, depending on the task's calculated start time. This is because it would take up an entire eight-hour day, and the remaining two hours would be scheduled the following day to finish the task.

However, you can define the task's duration as 10 elapsed hours, so it would be scheduled to finish exactly 10 hours later.

To do this, enter the letter *e* before the time unit in the Duration field. In this case, you would enter **10 eh**, which stands for 10 elapsed hours. Project would then schedule the task accordingly.

Figure 6.3 displays the task (Task A) that has elapsed duration. The first row (ID number 1) is the task with assigned a duration of seven elapsed days, and the second row (ID number 2) is the task assigned a regular duration of seven days. Notice how the first row is scheduled to finish much sooner than the second row. Because it is assigned an elapsed duration, row number 1 does not have to wait until working time resumes; it is scheduled continuously.

note

Elapsed days are 24 hours, as opposed to the 8 hour default working day. Elapsed weeks are 168 hours (seven 24-hour days), and the elapsed month is 720 hours (thirty 24-hour days). Elapsed month hours will vary, depending on the month. Project adjusts appropriately if your Current System Date is accurate.

Figure 6.3
Use elapsed duration to define tasks that work on continuous time.

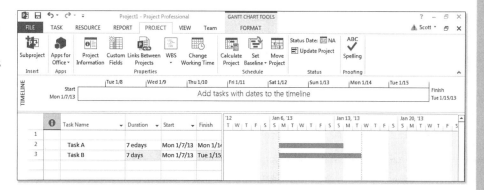

caution

The resource calendar governs when a resource can work. Therefore, if a resource is assigned to a task with elapsed duration, the calendar will not let the resource work outside the defined working time. You must either assign overtime to the resource or modify the resource calendar to complete the task.

Alternatively, you can assign a task calendar to the task and define the working time on the task calendar to coincide with the extended working time for the particular task. Project gives you an option to schedule from the task calendar and ignore the resource calendar on this task, and you should select that option.

Editing Tasks Using the Task Information Dialog Box

The Task Information dialog box enables you to view more fields of task-related information than any view in Microsoft Project. There are several ways to open the Task Information dialog box: Double-click any cell in the task row, right-click any cell in the task row and choose Task Information, or select any cell in the task row and select the Task tab, Information (see Figure 6.4).

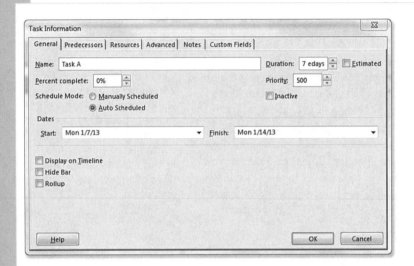

Figure 6.4
You can define and edit all task details in the Task Information dialog box.

The Task Information dialog box is the only single place to edit task information. Most of the fields in the Task Information dialog box are displayed in other views, but no single view contains all the fields found in the Task Information dialog box.

The Task Information dialog box contains six tabs. The following list briefly describes these tabs:

■ **General tab**—Define and edit general task information under the General tab, such as Start and Finish dates and whether the task is manually scheduled or auto-scheduled. Also, adjust the priority (0 is the lowest, 1000 is the highest, and 500 is the default). If a resource is scheduled to work on multiple tasks in a project at once, you can use the Leveling feature in Project. Project will then schedule the resource to work first on the task with a higher priority. You can also define the progress of a task in the Percent Complete field. Select the Inactive option to strike and gray out the task in the task list. Data on inactive tasks is not included in any summary totaling. Finally, select the Display on Timeline option to make the task visible on the timeline (see "Using the Timeline View" later in this chapter for a detailed description of timeline functionality).

 note

The Task Name and Duration fields are displayed on every tab in the Task Information dialog box. Also, next to the Duration field is a check box for estimates. Select it if the duration you entered is estimated, or tentative. Microsoft Project puts a question mark next to your entry to signify that it is tentative.

➡️ *For more details about leveling tasks,* **see** *Chapter 24, "Resolving Resource Allocation Problems,"* **p. 801**.

▪ **Predecessors tab**—Define the task's predecessor tasks in this tab, including the predecessor task's ID number, task name, dependency relationship type, and lead/lag. Predecessor tasks are tasks whose finish or start date determines the finish or start date of another task. Predecessors are particularly important to auto-scheduled tasks.

➡️ *For more details about predecessor/successor dependency relationships,* **see** *the "Linking Tasks" section,* **p. 186***, in Chapter 7.*

▪ **The Resources tab**—Display and assign resources to the tasks in this tab.

➡️ *For more details about assigning resources to tasks,* **see** *Chapter 10, "Scheduling Single and Multiple Resource Assignments,"* **p. 301***.*

▪ **Advanced tab**—Create deadlines and date constraints for the task in this tab. Also, choose the task type, assign calendars and WBS codes, and choose the Earned Value method, all of which are discussed in greater detail throughout this book. If a resource is assigned to the task, you can choose to ignore the resource calendar. Finally, you can mark the task as a milestone (milestones are explained later in this chapter in the section "Defining Milestones"). Note that the Constraint type, Constraint date, Task type, Calendar, Effort Driven, and Scheduling Ignores Resource Calendars are grayed out if the task is in Manually Scheduled mode.

▪ **Notes tab**—Attach a note to the task in this tab. This concept is explained later in this chapter in the section "Attaching Notes to Tasks."

▪ **Custom Fields tab**—Create and define custom fields for the task in this tab.

➡️ *For more details about custom fields,* **see** *"Creating and Customizing Fields"* **p. 745** *in Chapter 22.*

 tip

All six tabs in the Task Information dialog box contain the Help button. This feature comes in handy if you are unsure about the use of a field in that particular tab.

Using the Multiple Task Information Dialog Box

You also have the ability to make the same changes to several tasks at once. From your task list, choose the tasks you want to make the same change to by holding down Ctrl and selecting the tasks. Then, select the Task tab, Properties, Information. The Multiple Task Information dialog box appears, as shown in Figure 6.5.

Any change you make is applied to all selected tasks. For example, the Multiple Task Information box is helpful when you want to inactivate or change the task mode on multiple tasks.

Some tabs or fields will be restricted because you cannot apply certain values to multiple tasks. Those tabs are grayed out, as shown in Figure 6.5.

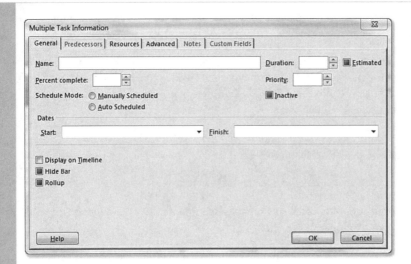

Figure 6.5
Make the same changes to multiple tasks using the Multiple Task Information dialog box.

Manipulating the Task List

No matter how hard you try to avoid it, you will almost always have to make changes to your task list after you have started creating it. Many of these edits can be made by selecting the cell and typing directly into it, or typing in the Edit bar above the Task Entry table if it is displayed (File tab, Options, Display, Entry Bar). If you use the Edit bar, click the check mark to the left of the bar to apply the change, or click the X to cancel it.

You can perform other commands to edit or manipulate your task list to be more accommodating to your project, or to account for changes that will inevitably arise. These commands apply to all views, not just the Gantt Chart view, and are discussed in the following sections.

Displaying Long Task Names

Earlier in this chapter, the section "Creating Task Names" discussed the concepts behind constructing task names so they make sense when taken out of the context of the project schedule. This can make for a longer task name than the original cell space provides for, and you might want to adjust the width of the column to display the entire name.

You can do this with the mouse. At the top of the column, in the cell that contains the column header (in this case, Task Name), place your mouse on the right-side border of the cell (the left border moves the column to the left of it). Your mouse pointer becomes a double-headed left and right arrow with a vertical line down the middle. When you see this arrow, double-click on the column's border. Project automatically adjusts the width to fit the column's longest entry.

Alternatively, when you see the double-headed arrow, you can click and drag the border while holding down the mouse button, and adjust it as much or as little as you want.

 note
This process works not just in the Task Name column, but in any column in the Task Entry table.

Right-clicking in the middle of the column header cell (when you do not see the double-headed arrow) opens up the Field Settings dialog box, as shown in Figure 6.6. In this box, you can define the width numerically, set the field to Wrap text, or click the Best Fit button, which adjusts the width to the longest entry in the column.

Figure 6.6
Adjust the width of a column in the Field Settings dialog box.

Adjusting the Height of Task Rows

Another option for displaying long entries such as task names is adjusting the height of the rows. Like adjusting column width, adjusting row height enables you to display longer entries in the fields. By default, Project adjusts row height to display the entire task name automatically. You can always lower it again to a more suitable height.

Adjusting row height is similar to adjusting column width. Highlight the row you want to adjust by clicking the ID field. Move your mouse to the bottom border of the cell (the top border moves the row above it; see Figure 6.7). A double-headed arrow appears, only this one has arrows pointing up and down and a horizontal bar going through the middle. In the highlighted cell, drag the bottom border down or up until you reach the desired height. The maximum number of lines of text you can define for a row is 20.

You can also adjust the heights of multiple rows simultaneously. Highlight the multiple rows by holding down Ctrl as you click the ID numbers, or select all the rows by clicking in the upper-left cell, above the row numbers and next to the column headings. Then drag the bottom of any of the ID number cells of any of the selected rows to your desired height. All selected rows will become the same height, regardless of their previous height.

Figure 6.7
When you have long task names, it is easy to change the height of a row so the text will wrap around.

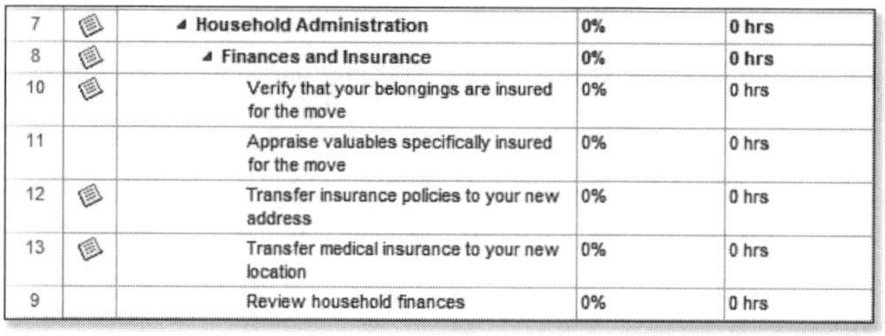

7		◢ **Household Administration**	0%	0 hrs
8		◢ **Finances and Insurance**	0%	0 hrs
10		Verify that your belongings are insured for the move	0%	0 hrs
11		Appraise valuables specifically insured for the move	0%	0 hrs
12		Transfer insurance policies to your new address	0%	0 hrs
13		Transfer medical insurance to your new location	0%	0 hrs
9		Review household finances	0%	0 hrs

Undoing Changes in the Task List

You can access the Multiple Undo feature by clicking the down arrow in the Undo icon on the Quick Access toolbar. (Right-click the Ribbon if the Quick Access Toolbar isn't showing, and select Show Quick Access Toolbar.) From the drop-down list, you can then see all the recent changes you have made, as shown in Figure 6.8. Select any of those, and Microsoft Project undoes that change, and everything that came before it. In addition, the Multiple Undo feature enables you to undo multiple changes at once, as many as you select.

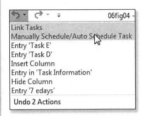

Figure 6.8
Click the arrow in the Undo icon on the Quick Access toolbar to display the multiple undo drop-down list.

You can increase or decrease the number of undo levels available by selecting the File tab, Options, Advanced, Undo levels.

The same concept applies for multiple redos. The Redo icon is just to the right of the Undo icon on the Standard toolbar.

Change Highlighting

Change Highlighting highlights all affected fields when you make a change and will help you understand undo and redo operations. For instance, if you change the duration of the task, Project will highlight the start and finish dates of any tasks that are its predecessors or successors, or its summary tasks, because those fields would be affected by the duration change, as shown in Figure 6.9. Change Highlighting will also be activated if you undo any previously made changes.

11		◢ Preparation	18.3 days?	Wed 1/9/13	Tue 2/5/13	
12		◢ Demolition	13.5 days?	Mon 1/14/13	Thu 1/31/13	
13	▦	Begin Demolition	0 days	Mon 1/14/13	Mon 1/14/13	
14		Empty Cabinets, Shelves, and countertops	10 days	Mon 1/14/13	Fri 1/25/13	13
15		Remove old appliances	0.5 days?	Mon 1/28/13	Mon 1/28/13	14
16		Demolish old cabinets, countertops, and floors	3 days?	Mon 1/28/13	Thu 1/31/13	15
17		Demolition Complete	0 days	Thu 1/31/13	Thu 1/31/13	16
18		◢ Clean up	2.8 days?	Thu 1/31/13	Tue 2/5/13	
19		Begin Clean up	0 days	Thu 1/31/13	Thu 1/31/13	17
20		Dsipose of old materials and appliances	1 day?	Thu 1/31/13	Fri 2/1/13	19
21		Remove floor adhesives and clean room	1.8 days	Fri 2/1/13	Tue 2/5/13	20
22		Clean up complete	0 days	Tue 2/5/13	Tue 2/5/13	21

Figure 6.9
The areas are highlighted because a change in another field affected the highlighted fields. Enable or disable this feature on the Standard toolbar, or select View, Hide/Show Change Highlighting.

Inserting, Deleting, and Clearing

As your project develops, you will have a need to insert, delete, or clear tasks. These are simple revisions made on your task list.

When inserting a new task, keep in mind that new rows are always inserted above the selected row. Therefore, select the row that you want directly under the new task by clicking its ID number. After you've selected that row, press the Insert button on your keyboard, or select Insert, New Task. You can also insert a new task by right-clicking the row where you want to insert a task and then selecting New Task. The blank new row appears above the task, and you can enter the task information.

If you want to insert multiple new tasks in the same location, high-light the number of rows you want to insert and follow the same process. For example, to insert three rows, highlight three exist-ing adjacent rows. The top row will be directly below the newly inserted rows. Press the Insert key, or select Insert, New Task, and three blank new rows appear above the tasks you had selected.

If you select the Task Name cell of an auto-scheduled task and press the Delete key, only the contents of that cell are deleted. Furthermore, a delete smart tag appears (refer to Table 6.1 and see Figure 6.10). Click the smart tag, and you can choose to delete the entire task or only the Task Name field.

 note

Project lets you select mul-tiple nonadjacent rows, but when you insert the new ones, they will be above the highest row. For example, if you select two rows, skip one, select the next row, and then press Insert, you insert three news tasks above the highest task you selected.

Figure 6.10
When you delete a task name, click the delete smart tag to select to delete the task name only or the entire task.

To delete an entire task altogether, select the row header (the task's ID number in many views) to highlight the task and then press the Delete key on your keyboard. You can also delete an entire task by clicking in any cell in the task you want to delete and selecting Edit, Delete Task.

Besides pressing the Delete key, you can delete or clear a task or the contents of a cell by highlighting the cell, selecting the Task tab, Editing, Clear, and then choosing which Clear option you want to apply. You can clear multiple cells in the same column at once by holding down Ctrl and clicking any number of cells, or you can select the entire row by clicking the task ID number. The Clear options are as follows:

 tip

If you accidentally delete anything, just use the Undo command to restore it (Edit, Undo, or the Undo icon on the Standard toolbar).

- **Clear Hyperlinks**—Like the Notes field, the Hyperlinks field is not always displayed. Select this option to clear the field.

- **Notes**—No matter which cell you have selected, choosing the Clear Notes command clears only the notes for that particular task. The Notes field is usually not displayed.

- **Entire Row**—This command clears the entire task. Select any cell in the task row and apply this command to clear the entire task. Unlike the Clear Contents and Clear All commands, the default duration and start and finish fields are not refilled; the entire row is left blank.

- **Clear Formatting**—This command leaves all the content intact, but clears any formatting for the cell(s) you have selected.

- **Clear All**—Choosing All clears all contents of the cell(s). If you have selected the task ID number, and thus the entire row, choosing Clear, All clears all the fields but leaves the task row intact. Automatically, the default duration and start and finish dates are entered.

 note

In Project, you can restore formats that have been cleared, as well as the other cleared items, unless the Undo queue has been purged. There are several actions in Project that purge the undo, after which you cannot restore to the previous action. One of the purging operations is a save.

Copying, Cutting, and Moving Tasks

In Project, you can cut, copy, and move entire tasks or cells within task rows. You might decide to move tasks on your task list so they are listed in a more appropriate order. Or, you might want to copy a task or several tasks and paste them in another project file.

Follow these steps to move a task field, entire task, or group of tasks with the Cut/Copy and Paste method:

1. Decide what you want to cut or copy. To select an entire task, click its ID number, or select any cell in the task row and press Shift+spacebar. To select multiple adjacent tasks, click the first task, hold down Shift, and click the last task. All tasks in between, including the tasks you clicked, will be selected. You can also select single cells, or multiple adjacent cells, using the same method.

 note

In previous versions of Project, your selections had to contain only adjacent cells or rows. If you wanted to cut, copy, or move cells or rows that are not adjoining, you had to cut, copy, or move those cells or rows separately. In Project 2013, you can select nonadjacent rows.

2. Decide whether you want to cut your selection (removing it entirely) or copy it (leaving the original task[s] or cell[s] intact). To cut, you can use any of the following methods: Right-click and select Cut Task (or Cut Cell); choose Edit, Cut Task (or Cut Cell); use the Cut command on the Standard toolbar; or press Ctrl+X. To copy, you can right-click and select Copy Task (or Copy Cell); choose Edit, Copy Task (or Copy Cell); use the Copy command on the Standard toolbar; or press Ctrl+C.

3. Select the task row or cell where you want to put your copied or cut selection(s). If you are relocating multiple tasks or cells, you still select only one row or cell.

4. To paste, use one of the following methods: Right-click and choose Paste; choose Edit, Paste; use the Paste command on the Standard toolbar; or press Ctrl+V. Pasting whole rows inserts new rows and shifts down the existing ones in the targeted area to make room for the new ones. Pasting cells replaces the existing data in the targeted cells, or creates new tasks if the targeted area is blank.

Additionally, you can move a task or multiple tasks using the drag-and-drop method. To do this, follow these steps:

1. Click the Task ID number for the task you want to move. To move multiple tasks, click the ID number of the first one, hold down Shift, and click the ID number of the last one. Remember that for you to move multiple tasks, they must be adjacent.

2. Hover the mouse over the ID number of any of the selected tasks. The mouse pointer becomes a four-headed arrow.

3. Holding down the mouse button, drag the pointer in the direction you want to move it. A shadowed I-beam appears. Release the mouse button when this I-beam is located across the top of the row you want to move the selected task(s) to.

You can also use this procedure to copy and paste the task(s). As you drag the selected task(s), as described in step 3, hold down the Ctrl key.

 caution

If you want to cut, copy, or move an entire task, be sure you either click its ID number or use the Shift+spacebar command when you have a cell highlighted. This ensures that you are selecting all task fields, including those that are not displayed. Otherwise, you might be moving only part of the task fields, because none of the views originally display all task fields.

 tip

After you have cut or copied data, you can paste it as often as you want, as long as it remains on your Clipboard.

 caution

When you move a task using the cut-and-paste method, the old task is being deleted from the list, and a new task is being created. This means that the new task will now have its own unique ID number. This will not affect the task list if you are inserting or deleting other tasks, or moving the task around, but might be important if you compare versions of the project files and cannot understand why there are two different unique ID numbers for what is essentially the same task.

Using the Fill Command

Sometimes, you might have several fields that contain the same value. For example, you might have multiple tasks with the same duration, such as tasks relating to appliance deliveries and installations in your new house. Microsoft Project's Fill command makes it easy to enter these values without having to type in each one.

To use the Fill command, first select the cell that you want to copy and, while holding down the mouse button, drag the mouse pointer up or down through all the cells into which you want to insert the copied value. The original cell (the one with the value to fill into the other cells) should be at the very top or very bottom of the highlighted list. When you have the cells selected, right-click and choose Fill Down to copy the value of the original cell. You can also press Ctrl+D to use the Fill Down command.

If the cells are not adjacent, you can still perform this command. Select the nonadjacent cells by holding down Ctrl and clicking in the cells. When you have them all selected, right-click and choose Fill Down. All the selected cells will now share the value of the original cell.

Another method to fill cells with a copied value is by using the cell's *fill handle*. The fill handle is the small black square in the lower-right corner of the cell. When you hover the mouse pointer over the fill handle, it becomes a plus sign (+). Click the fill handle, and while holding down the mouse button, drag the mouse pointer to other adjacent cells to enter the identical value.

Defining Summary Tasks and Subtasks

In Microsoft Project, there are three kinds of tasks: summary tasks, subtasks, and milestones. Milestones are discussed later in this chapter in the section, "Defining Milestones."

A *summary* task is a major topic or phase in the project. A summary task summarizes the duration, cost, and amount of work that is spent on a major phase in the project. Summary tasks are broken into *subtasks*, which are detail tasks that make up the total work for the summary task. Most tasks in a project are subtasks. Think of summary tasks as the end goal, and subtasks as the steps you must achieve to reach it.

On the timescale side of the Gantt Chart view, auto-scheduled summary tasks are displayed as black bars with upside-down triangles on the ends; auto-scheduled subtasks are the rounder, blue bars (see Figure 6.11). Manually scheduled summary tasks have a blue bar running beneath the end points of the summary task when the manual values match what the scheduling engine would calculate. When the summary task start and end dates differ from the calculated start and end dates, the bar turns red. Manually scheduled subtasks are a lighter blue with blackened, squared ends.

When you have created your task list, you can then outline the lists to reflect summary tasks and subtasks (and milestones). Outlining organizes the tasks into functional groups and is visually quite helpful. Subtasks are indented under summary tasks. When you indent a task, it is called *demoting* the task. Likewise, outdenting a task is called *promoting* it. The theory is that the more a task is outdented, the more significance it holds to the overall project scope, and the more general it is. The more a task is indented, the more detailed it is. These concepts are described in more detail in the following sections.

After you have transformed a task into a summary task, you cannot define its start or finish dates unless it is a manually scheduled task. The summary task's start date is the earliest start date of its subtasks, and its finish date is the latest finish date of its subtasks. Similarly, the total cost and amount of work for a group of subtasks are rolled up and summarized in the Cost and Work fields of their summary task.

 caution

For best results using Project, do not assign resources or work to the summary-level tasks. Instead, create another subtask underneath your summary task and provide the work and resource information there. Summary tasks are there to organize and summarize information. Furthermore, if you do add work and resources to a summary-level task, your work totals for higher summary tasks will probably not add up properly, so it is best to avoid this.

Figure 6.11
Summary tasks and subtasks are displayed in an outline form in the Gantt Chart view. Notice the difference in their placement (indented vs. outdented) in the Task Name column on the Task Entry table side, as well as the taskbars on the timescale side. The arrows on the timescale side represent dependency links.

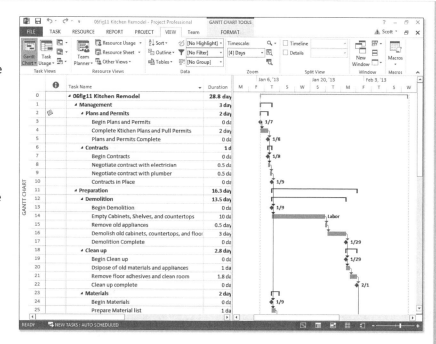

➡ *For more details about the critical path, **see** Chapter 12, "Performing a Schedule Reality Check," on **p. 411**.*

Understanding Duration of Summary Tasks

Just as you cannot modify an auto-scheduled summary task's start or finish dates, you cannot modify its duration. A summary task's duration is the amount of working time between its subtasks' earliest start date and latest finish date.

No matter how its subtasks' durations are displayed, a summary task's duration is always displayed in the default setting for the time units. To change this setting, select the File tab, Options, Schedule and choose the time unit you want in the Duration Is Entered In field. For example, if most subtasks are entered in hours, but the default time unit setting is days, the summary task's Duration field shows the value in days.

Indenting and Outdenting Tasks

Summary tasks can contain subtasks that are also summary tasks to another series of tasks. For example, Planning the Move is the summary task of Calculate Moving Expenses, but Calculate Moving Expenses is the summary task of Calculate Moving Company Fees. As tasks become more and more indented, they become more detailed. Outdented tasks are more general, and rely on the completion of their indented subtasks for their own completion.

Project offers several methods of indenting (demoting) and outdenting (promoting) tasks to define them as summary tasks or subtasks. All of the following methods produce the same result.

First, select the task or tasks you want to indent or outdent, and then do one of the following:

- On the Task tab, use the Indent or Outdent button to change the outline level of the task(s). The Indent button is an arrow pointing to the right, and the Outdent button is an arrow pointing to the left (refer to Figure 6.11).

- Drag the task name to the right or left using the mouse. In the Task Name field, place the mouse over the first few letters of the task name. The mouse pointer will become a double-headed arrow pointing left and right. Drag the pointer to the right to indent or to the left to outdent. If you have selected multiple tasks, they are indented or outdented together.

- Press the key combination Alt+Shift+right arrow to indent, or Alt+Shift+left arrow to outdent.

> **⌘ caution**
>
> All outlining actions you apply to summary tasks are in turn applied to their subtasks. If you indent a summary task, all its subtasks are indented (demoted) even further. Furthermore, if you delete, copy, move, promote, or demote a summary task, all of its subtasks follow the same action. This includes other summary tasks that are subtasks to the summary task you are changing.

If a task is indented and you promote it (outdent it to the left), the tasks below it are affected in one of three ways, as follows:

- If the tasks immediately below the newly promoted task are at its same level of indentation, they become subtasks of the newly promoted task. If you want them to remain at the same level, select them all and promote them simultaneously.

- If the tasks immediately below the newly promoted task are already subtasks, they remain subtasks, but shift to the left as well, following their summary task (remember, an action done to a summary task is in turn done to its subtasks). If a subtask is indented one level more than the newly promoted task, it remains indented one level more by moving with it.

- If the tasks below the newly promoted task are at a higher level of indentation (already farther left than the promoted task), these tasks are unaffected by the promotion.

Alternatively, if a subtask is indented one level to the right of its summary task, and if you promote it, it is no longer a subtask because you promoted it to the same level of indentation as its summary task. The tasks then become equal in terms of their outline level.

Adding a Summary Task

If you want to add a new task into the task list as a summary task, you must enter it just above the task(s) you want it to summarize. If the subtasks are already indented, you can simply outdent the newly inserted task to define it as their summary task. If the subtasks are not indented at all, you must indent all the tasks you want to be subtasks of the newly inserted summary task.

For example, if you have a summary task called Pack Rooms, its subtasks would be all the tasks for packing all the rooms in your old house. After you list them all, you probably would realize that there are many subtasks for packing the rooms of an entire house, and you would want to organize them further by creating summary tasks for each room, such as Pack Kitchen, and so on.

These new summary tasks would be subtasks of Pack Rooms but summary tasks to the original subtasks. You can insert these new summary tasks above the appropriate tasks for packing that particular room, and indent all the applicable subtasks for the newly inserted summary task.

➡ *If the new summary tasks are not in order, you can move them using the methods described in the "Copying, Cutting, and Moving Tasks" section earlier in this chapter.*

Collapsing and Expanding the Outline

When you want to look at the general progress of your project without viewing all the subtask details, Microsoft Project enables you to collapse the outline by hiding all the subtasks and viewing only the summary tasks. Because subtasks solely determine the progress of a summary task, you can quickly examine the overall status of each summary task.

Collapsed tasks are hidden, not deleted. When a summary task is collapsed, nothing about its subtasks is displayed, including the row ID numbers (see Figure 6.12).

Figure 6.12
Collapse or expand the outline or part of the outline using the Outline button on the View tab.

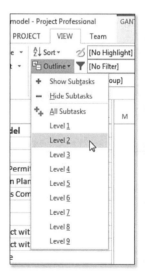

Use the Outline button to display or hide various outline levels. The Outline button is located on the View tab. Click it to display the Outline submenu. On the Outline submenu, select the outline level you want to display. Selecting All Subtasks displays all levels of the outline. Outline Level 1 displays only the top-level tasks (regardless of subtasks), Outline Level 2 displays top-level tasks plus the first level of subtasks, and so on, down to the ninth level.

You can also expand or collapse subtasks for individual summary tasks. Double-click on the summary task's ID number. If the outline is collapsed, it expands to show all its subtasks, and their subtasks. If it is expanded at all, it collapses entirely.

If outline symbols are displayed, summary tasks contain a Hide Subtasks button, which is a minus sign (−), or a Show Subtasks button, which is a plus sign (+), to the left of their name in the Task Name field. If the subtasks are already shown, the Hide Subtasks button is in the field (refer to Figure 6.10). Click it to hide the subtasks. If the subtasks are hidden, the Show Subtasks button is in the field. Click it to show the subtasks.

➡ *For more information about displaying outline symbols, see the "Selecting the Display Options for Outlining" section later in this chapter.*

If these symbols are not displayed in the Task Name field of a summary task, you can use the Hide Subtasks and Show Subtasks buttons, located on the outline submenu.

---

 tip

It is good practice to have a minimum of three outline levels within a project: project level (a project summary task over the entire project; the entire level is only one task row), phase level (summary tasks of the projects' phases), and work level (subtasks). You can, of course, have more levels than this. No matter how many levels you have, the lowest is the work level. It is here, on the work level, that the tasks should be linked and the resources assigned. Linking tasks and assigning resources are discussed later in this book.

Editing Outlined Projects

When you have created outline levels in your project, you still edit tasks in the same way described earlier in this chapter. However, you cannot edit some fields when the task mode is Auto Scheduled, such as the Duration fields for summary tasks (because summary task durations are defined by the start and finish dates of their summary tasks, as described previously in this chapter).

Double-click any nonsummary task to display the Task Information dialog box to make any edits, or use any of the other task-editing options previously discussed in this chapter.

Keep in mind that changes you make to a summary task are also done to its subtasks (such as deleting, copying, cutting, pasting, moving, promoting, or demoting). However, summary tasks have their own Notes field, which you can and should use for notes about the summary task itself.

➡ *See the "Attaching Notes to Tasks" section later in this chapter.*

Selecting the Display Options for Outlining

Microsoft Project automatically indents subtasks under their summary tasks as a means of organizing the task list by outline levels. There are several display options for formatting your outline structure, all located on the Format tab:

- You can choose to display the task outline number next to the name to help distinguish summary tasks from subtasks. Unlike task ID numbers, outline numbers cannot be edited. If the outline number of a summary task is 4, its first subtask is 4.1, its second subtask is 4.2, and so on. If subtask 4.2 has its own subtasks, they would begin with 4.2.1, 4.2.2, and so forth. To display outline numbers, select the Format tab, Outline Number check box.

- As mentioned previously in this chapter, Project by default places Hide Subtasks or Show Subtasks to the left of the summary task name, depending on whether the subtasks are displayed. These symbols not only make it easy to expand or collapse a summary task with one mouse click, they also serve as an indicator that a task is a summary task. If the Show Subtasks symbol is showing, that task has subtasks hidden.

- You can hide summary tasks, displaying only milestones and subtasks. This might be useful for sorting tasks for reports by start date, duration, or alphabetically. Because the summary tasks are not actually assigned resources to work on, they might get in the way and take up space in the reports. To hide summary tasks, select the Format tab and clear the Summary Tasks check box.

- As advised earlier, it is good practice to display an overall summary task for the entire project, called the Project Summary task. Its duration spans from the start of the very first subtask to the finish of the very last one. When this task is displayed, all other tasks are indented at least one level. The task name is the name of the project. Editing the task name changes the project name as well, so the Project Summary task name and project name are always the same. To display the Project Summary task, select the Format tab, Project Summary Task check box.

Using Rollup Taskbars

By default, in the timescale side of the Gantt Chart view, summary taskbars are displayed spanning the entire summary task as black bars with upside-down triangles at the start and finish dates, and subtask taskbars are blue, rounded-edge bars spanning the duration of the particular subtask. Each taskbar is located to the right of its row in the Task Entry table.

However, you can roll up the subtask taskbars to the summary taskbar, which marks each subtask's start and finish on the summary taskbar. This produces a segmented bar that shows the duration of each subtask within the summary taskbar (see Figure 6.13).

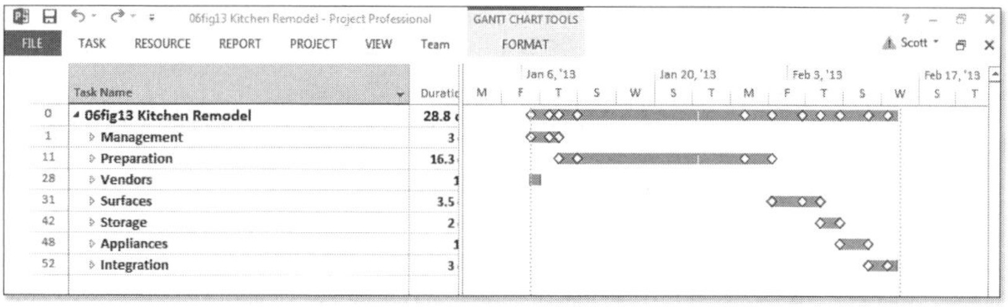

Figure 6.13
A subtask's taskbars are displayed within their summary tasks to show duration within the summary task when you roll up the subtask taskbars.

You can roll up all the subtask taskbars, or roll up some and leave the others alone.

To roll up all taskbars, select the Format tab, Format, Layout to display the Layout dialog box (see Figure 6.14). Or, you can right-click in the bar chart (timescale) area and select Layout. In the Layout dialog box, select the Always Roll Up Gantt Bars box. The rollup bars then appear in front of the summary taskbar.

Also in the Layout dialog box, you can choose to display the rollup taskbars only when their sub-tasks are hidden by checking the Hide Rollup Bars When Summary Expanded box. That way, when the summary task is expanded, you will not see the rollup bars.

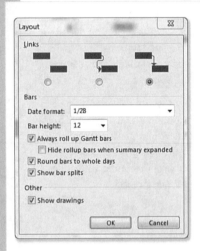

Figure 6.14
Roll up taskbars by using the Layout dialog box.

For the most part, the rollup functionality formerly in the Gantt Chart has been removed in favor of the Timeline view. In previous versions of Project, it was possible to select individual tasks for rollup to summary tasks using the Task Information dialog.

➡ *The Timeline, which is significantly more powerful and flexible, is discussed in the "Using the Timeline View" section later in this chapter.*

Defining Milestones

As in real life, a *milestone* in Project represents a critical landmark, turning point, or decision within your project. In the Move to New House project, a milestone would be the time you signed the papers and got the new house keys, moved completely out of your old house, or any successful completion of a major phase of the move. Milestones come in handy for marking major phases in the project, and you can filter the task list to display only the milestones to quickly see all the important dates a milestone represents.

You can and should create a milestone at a point in a project you want to monitor closely. If, for example, you are re-carpeting your new house before you move in, you might want to enter a milestone when all tasks of that phase are complete. The milestone could be called Re-Carpeting Completed. The duration would be zero, because, similar to a summary task, no actual work is done on a milestone. (Remember, though, summary tasks do have durations; their durations are defined by the total duration of their subtasks.)

The end of each phase of the project, as well as the end of the entire project itself, should be marked with a milestone.

To create a milestone, enter **0** in the Duration field. Project automatically classifies the task as a milestone.

The following list contains examples of when you would want to add a milestone in your project:

- It is beneficial to add a milestone for every crucial deliverable.

- Perhaps you have a client or a project sponsor who wants to see project milestones. If you do, it is recommended that you create two separate types of milestones—ones that are internal to the team, and ones your client or project sponsor would like to see. Separating the two will help both you and the client or sponsor. Your client probably does not want to see every single one of your milestones—just the driving ones that either make or break the project. Similarly, you do not want to limit yourself to only a handful of milestones that do not include intermediate deliverables that you will need to consider.

- There might be specific milestones associated with the billing. If there are, it might be beneficial to include those specific milestones to remind yourself which of your deliverables influence the invoicing.

 tip

Your project should also have a final milestone to close the entire project. This milestone connects your entire schedule together and defines the formal completion of a project. All too often, work on a project finishes, but the project just fizzles out because there is no formal completion to it. A final project milestone prevents this from happening and adds a final element of organization to your project.

There are at least two other ways to create a milestone, as follows:

- Right-click on the Timeline view (View tab, Split View, Timeline) and select Insert Task, Milestone. The task information dialog appears with a Zero duration already entered.

- Select the Task tab and click Milestone. The new task will be inserted with the name <New Milestone>.

Another way to define a milestone is in the Task Information dialog box. Open the Task Information dialog box by double-clicking on the task name, or by any other method described earlier in this chapter. On the Advanced tab, select the Mark Task as Milestone box (or clear it to remove its milestone status) and then click OK.

By default, a milestone is displayed as a diamond on the timescale side of the Gantt Chart view. There is no taskbar to show duration. To change the display of a milestone to something other than the black diamond, select Format, Bar Styles. The Bar Styles dialog box appears (see Figure 6.15). In the Bar Styles dialog box, select Milestone and change its appearance using the drop-down lists at the bottom of the dialog box.

➡️ *For more details about using the Bar Styles dialog box to change how items are displayed in the Gantt Chart view, **see** the "Formatting the Gantt Chart Views" section, p. 583, in Chapter 19.*

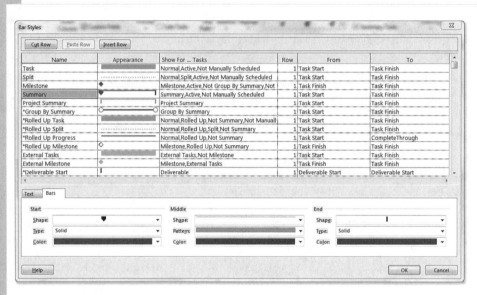

Figure 6.15
Change the display of a milestone in the Bar Styles dialog box. In this example, the summary start point has been changed to the old style.

---

 tip

Although it is possible to mark a task as a milestone that has a duration greater than zero, this is not a good practice because it can be misleading. Instead, apply the duration to the tasks that coincide with the milestone and leave the milestone's duration set at zero.

Attaching Notes to Tasks

When managing a project, it is always good practice to stay as organized as possible. As you get deep into the work of a project, you as the project manager are often juggling several things at once every day. It is easy to say you are going to remember a little detail and quickly forget it in minutes due to another issue that inevitably arises.

Therefore, you should attach notes to tasks in your project to give you the peace of mind of staying on top of things without having to remember every little detail about a task. A note can be a reason why you made a specific decision about a task, the scope of particular item, a reminder of a situation involving the task, an informational message to other users (other project managers or resources) of the project file, any assumptions you have made, or anything else relating to the task.

These notes can be included on printed reports if you want by choosing the File tab, Print, Page Setup, and in the View tab, selecting the Print Notes check box.

Tasks with notes attached display the Task Notes icon in the Indicator field (refer to Table 6.1). If you hover the mouse pointer over the Task Notes icon, it displays the beginning of the note's text.

 tip

Notes are a great way to capture the scope of a task and explain in greater detail the goal of the task. This is also relevant for summary tasks, which have their own Notes field.

Furthermore, you can document the changes made to the scope of a task, its result on the task's duration, and its effect on the overall project.

Typing and Formatting Notes

You can attach notes to tasks in a variety of ways:

- Double-click on the task to open the Task Information dialog box (or use any of the other methods described earlier in this chapter). Then open the Notes tab.

- Right-click a task and click Notes.

At the top of the Notes text box in the Task Information dialog box is a formatting toolbar that provides options to format the note (see Figure 6.16). Hover the mouse over the buttons for a description of what they do.

 tip

You can perform a search of the Notes field to find specific text for a task note in your project. However, Microsoft Project stops the search as soon as it encounters most nonprintable characters, such as the Enter key. To avoid the problem where the Find command stops searching a note when it encounters the Enter key, use Shift+Enter when you want to start a new paragraph when typing your note.

 tip

You can type hundreds of thousands of characters in the notes text box. However, if your note is large, it might be easier to insert a link to an external document rather than type it all out This process is discussed in the next section.

The Notes text box contains many of the text-formatting capabilities of Microsoft Word. Edit your notes as you would a Word document as it supports rich text format.

When you are finished entering your note, click OK.

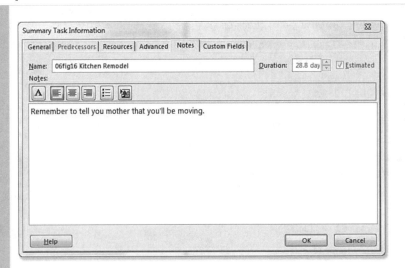

Figure 6.16
Type your note in the Notes text box in the Task Information dialog box, and format the text using the toolbar at the top of the text box.

 tip

Although notes can hold thousands of characters, Microsoft Project can search the Notes field for only the first 255 characters. It also stops when it runs up against a nonprintable character, such as Enter. If you need to make long notes, see "Inserting Objects in Notes," later in this chapter.

Several keys are useful when moving through the Notes text box:

Key	Effect
Home	Moves the cursor to the beginning of the line.
End	Moves the cursor to the end of the line.
Ctrl+Home	Moves to the beginning of the note.
Ctrl+End	Moves to the end of the note.
Ctrl+left arrow	Moves one word to the left.
Ctrl+right arrow	Moves one word to the right.

Inserting Hyperlinks in Notes

You can insert a hyperlink in the Notes text box to link to a website. To do so, type the website address in its full format (for example, http://www.website.com). Alternatively, you can copy and paste the address into the Notes text box. The hyperlink will be displayed underlined and in the color used for hyperlinks on your computer (the default is blue). When you click the hyperlink, the browser is opened to the web page. See the section, "Attaching Hyperlinks to Tasks," later in this chapter, for more information on hyperlinks and tasks.

Inserting Objects in Notes

Another option when adding notes to tasks is inserting data objects from other applications into notes. An *object* is defined as a data file in a format maintained by another application, such as a picture, reference document, spreadsheet, word processing document, presentation, sound and video clip, and so on. You could, for example, insert an Excel spreadsheet and edit that spreadsheet within the note to apply it more directly to the task or project.

You have a choice of inserting the actual object into the note, or inserting just a link to the area where the object resides outside the project. If you insert the actual object, rather than just a link, the size of the project file increases by the size of the object. If you are trying to keep your project file size as small as possible, you should insert the link to the object instead of the object itself.

Inserting the link rather than the object is also beneficial if the object is something that needs to be seen by other people. When you click on the link, Project opens the object, and any edits you make are saved to the object outside Project. The link opens the object with the saved changes the next time you click the link (if you saved your edits properly). This includes changes made by other people. If you insert the actual object, only the edits made within Project are seen when you open the object in Project; if you or other people edit the object outside Project, those changes will not be saved in the note.

Most objects larger than the actual Notes text box can be expanded to display. Therefore, you should insert an icon that, when double-clicked, will open up the actual object.

Follow these steps to insert a data object into a note:

1. Open the Task Information dialog box (double-click the task) for the task and open the Notes tab. Click the Insert Object button on the formatting toolbar at the top of the Notes text box, or right-click in the Notes text box and select Object. This opens the Insert Object dialog box (see Figure 6.17).

2. To insert a blank object that you can design and edit only from within Project, choose Create New. Then choose the application to create the object from in the Object Type list (see Figure 6.18).

3. To insert an object from an outside application that is already saved as a file, choose Create from File. The Object Type field changes to a File field. Type the path and filename in the box, or use the Browse feature to select the file from the directory structure (see Figure 6.18).

   Alternatively, you can create a new file and insert it as an object here. Browse to the folder where the new object is to be stored, right-click over a blank space in the file list, select New, and select the application that will create the file. Replace the default name for the new file with the filename you want to use, and click Insert. When you finish step 6, double-click the object to create its data.

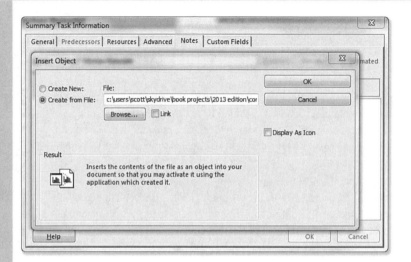

Figure 6.17
Insert objects into notes
by using the Insert Object
dialog box. This example
displays the dialog box
when inserting the object
from an existing file.

4. If you want to insert only a link, select the Link check box. If you want to insert the actual object, clear this box. Refer to the beginning of this section for explanations of the two options.

5. Select Display As Icon to display an icon for the object instead of the object itself. Most of the time, it is best to insert the icon, due to lack of space in the Notes text box. Then you can double-click the icon to open the object.

> ### 🛜 caution
> Although you can set up the Notes field as a column in a table, if you edit the note in the field, be warned that you will lose all of your inserted objects. A warning message reminds you of this if you forget the warning here.

6. Click OK to finish and insert the object in the note.

> ➡️ *For more details about inserting objects in Microsoft Project,* **see** *the "Placing Objects into Project" section,* **p. 888** *in Chapter 26.*

Figure 6.18
Insert objects into notes
in the Insert Object dialog
box. This example is what
the box looks like if you
are creating a new object.

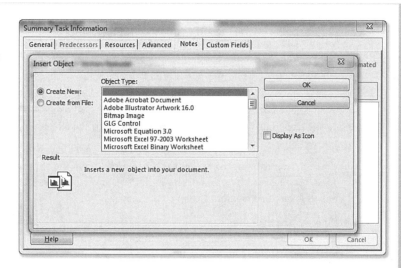

Attaching Notes to the Overall Project

Instead of attaching a note to a particular task, you can attach it to the entire project. Select the File tab, Project Information, Advanced Properties (right pane). In the Summary tab, enter the note in the Comments field. You cannot insert objects here.

For longer, more extensive notes, you should display the project summary task. As described earlier in this chapter, display the project summary task by choosing Tools, Options; on the View tab, select the Show Project Summary Task check box. The project summary task will be listed at the top of the task list.

After the project summary task is displayed, open its Task Information dialog box (double-click the task name, which is also the name of the project). Then, attach a note as you would to any other task (see the previous sections for further explanation).

 caution

If you insert an object in the project summary task, it will be lost if you later attach or edit a note in the Comments field in the Properties dialog box. A warning appears if you make edits in the Comments field and click OK. You can cancel the changes to save your inserted object, or keep the changes and lose the object. You can avoid this problem by creating a milestone task at the top or bottom of the task list strictly for attaching a note with links to important documents or other data objects.

Attaching Hyperlinks to Tasks

Hyperlinks can be a useful tool to gather information not directly contained in your project. Perhaps it is to another project file, another task or resource, or a website. In the moving example, you could link to a moving company website or to a public storage website.

As previously discussed, you can insert a hyperlink to websites in the Notes text box of a task. In addition, you can store hyperlinks for tasks in the Hyperlink field. There are several reasons why using the Hyperlink field is more versatile than using the Notes text box:

- If there is a link in the Hyperlink field, an icon appears in the Indicator field, and you can simply click the icon to open the hyperlink. If it is attached in the Notes text box, you have to open the Task Information dialog box or the Task Form view to access the note that contains the hyperlink. It is more convenient to just click the icon.

- Whereas the hyperlink in the Notes text box can link only to Internet or intranet sites, a link in the Hyperlink field has much more flexibility. You can link to other files on your computer, network, specific locations within files (such as a specific task in another project file or a specific cell in an Excel spreadsheet), file folders, other tasks or resources within your current project, or an email message to a specific person.

- You can browse to find the location you want as a hyperlink when you define it in the Hyperlink field. If it is attached to a note, you must know the URL for the site; you cannot browse.

However, there is one advantage to storing a hyperlink in a note: You can store multiple hyperlinks in a note. You can define only one hyperlink in the Hyperlink field.

As with attaching notes to tasks, there are several ways to attach a hyperlink. You already know about inserting it in the Notes field. To attach a hyperlink directly to a task (without using the Notes field), do one of the following:

- Right-click the task and choose the Hyperlink option.

- Select the task and press Ctrl+K.

Any of these options open the Insert Hyperlink dialog box (see Figure 6.19). The remaining steps are detailed in the next few sections, depending on what you want to do.

Attaching Hyperlinks to Existing Files or Web Pages

To attach a hyperlink to an existing file or web page, follow these steps:

1. Select the task you want to attach the hyperlink to, and open the Insert Hyperlink dialog box by any of the methods described in the previous section. The Insert Hyperlink dialog box is displayed as in Figure 6.19.

2. On the left of the Insert Hyperlinks dialog box, click the Existing File or Web Page option.

Figure 6.19
Locate files or websites to attach to tasks as hyperlinks in the Insert Hyperlink dialog box.

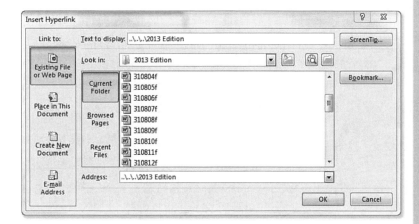

3. If you know the full path and filename, enter it in the Address box at the bottom. If not, you can browse for the address of the existing filename or website. The following is a list of ways the Insert Hyperlink dialog box helps you browse for the address:

   ■ In the Address box, click the arrow to open the drop-down list to choose from the list of recently accessed folders and websites.

   ■ Click Current Folder to browse folders on your computer, starting in the folder listed in the Look In box.

   ■ Click the Browse for File button (icon on the right) to browse for the file using Windows Explorer, starting in the folder listed in the Look In box.

   ■ Click Browsed Pages to choose from the list of recently viewed web pages.

   ■ Click Recent Files to choose from the list of recently opened files.

   ■ Click the Browse the Web button (icon to the left of Browse for File) to search for a website using the Internet.

   ■ If you have chosen a file that supports bookmarks, click the Bookmark button to see a list of bookmarks defined in that file. This causes the hyperlink to go directly to that part of the document when you open the hyperlink.

4. If you want to display the link using custom text (such as a description of the hyperlink rather than its address), change the text in the Text to display box.

5. If you want to customize the Screentip that appears when you hover the mouse pointer over the hyperlink indicator, click the Screentip button.

6. Click OK to save the hyperlink.

You can also create a hyperlink by using the Paste as Hyperlink command:

1. Open your document and select the location you want to link to.

2. Choose some part of the document in that location and select the Copy command. Specific applications require different selections:

   - Microsoft Project requires choosing a cell in a task row.

   - Excel requires choosing a cell or group of cells.

   - Word requires choosing a word or section title.

   - PowerPoint requires choosing a word or title in a slide or the outline.

3. Go back to Microsoft Project and choose a cell in the row for the task you want to hold the link.

4. Select Edit, Paste as Hyperlink, and your link is set.

Attaching Hyperlinks to New Files

You can insert a hyperlink to a file that does not yet exist and create that file simultaneously.

If you want to insert a hyperlink into a document that does not yet exist, follow these steps:

1. Click the Create New Document button in the Insert Hyperlink dialog box.

2. Enter a name in the Name of New Document box and remember to include the file extension, so Microsoft Project knows which application to open when it creates the file. It defaults to the path of the active project file, but you can use Change to pick a different folder.

3. Choose either Edit the New Document Later or Edit the New Document Now.

Attaching Hyperlinks to Tasks or Resources in the Same Project

Perhaps you want to attach a hyperlink to a task to jump to a resource or another task in your project. This can be a helpful shortcut to a related task or resource. You can also specify the view to display when you link to that task or resource. To create this kind of hyperlink, follow these steps:

1. While attaching the hyperlink, you cannot browse for the task or resource. Therefore, find the task or resource and note its ID number.

2. Select the task you want to attach the hyperlink to and open the Insert Hyperlink dialog box (right-click the task, choose Hyperlink, or use any of the other methods previously described).

3. Choose Place in This Document.

4. In the Enter the task or resource ID box, enter the ID number for the task or resource to link to.

5. Select the view you want displayed when you open the hyperlink in the Select a view in this project field. Select a resource view if you are linking to a resource. Otherwise, Microsoft Project just keeps the current task view.

Using Hyperlinks to Create Email Messages

You can use a hyperlink to open Outlook or other email programs to compose an email message. That way, when you open the hyperlink, the email message is addressed and ready to go; you just have to write the content.

To set up an email hyperlink, follow these steps:

1. Right-click the task, select Hyperlink, and then select the E-Mail Address option on the left.

2. Enter the address for your recipient in the E-Mail Address box. You are required to enter an address; however, there is no link to your address book or contacts folder. You can find recently used addresses in the Recently Used E-Mail Addresses box. If you enter something into the Subject box, Microsoft Project uses this text to fill the Subject field every time you open the hyperlink to send a message.

3. Click the OK button to save your changes.

Editing and Deleting Hyperlinks

To edit a hyperlink, select the task and open the Insert Hyperlink dialog box (right-click the task and choose Hyperlink, Edit Hyperlink, or use any of the other methods described earlier). Make your edits in the Insert Hyperlink dialog box.

To delete a hyperlink, click the Remove Link button in the Insert Hyperlink dialog box.

You can also use the Clear command: Select the task first; then select the Task tab, Edit, Clear, Clear Hyperlinks.

Placing Hyperlinks in the Custom Text Fields

As mentioned before, there is only one Hyperlink field for each task. However, 30 custom text fields are available to store additional hyperlinks in. To use these custom fields, you must first display the text field as a column in the Task Entry table:

1. Simply right-click any column header, click Insert Column, and start typing the word **Text**.

2. Choose one of the text custom fields (Text1 through Text30).

3. The new column should be inserted to the left of the column you originally selected. You can then use the field to insert a hyperlink by either directly entering a URL, typing a document path, or using the Ctrl+K option.

Like attaching hyperlinks in the Notes field, there are limitations to storing hyperlinks in text fields. The hyperlink must be the only thing typed in the text field. Also, like attaching to notes, there is no browse feature to help define the hyperlink. You can copy the site and paste it into the text field, however. Also, you must enter the complete URL. For example, www.*website*.com would not work, but http://www.*website*.com would. Be sure to enter the entire address.

Defining Recurring Tasks

Sometimes in your project, you will have *recurring tasks*—tasks that repeat regularly throughout the project. For example, perhaps you have a weekly or monthly meeting scheduled with your lawyer or Home Owner's Association, or perhaps you have regular inspections on the progress of your home. You could set up a recurring task to make your monthly house or utility payments that occur during the life of the project. You might also schedule a weekly project team status meeting using recurring tasks.

Instead of entering the task every week or every month, you only have to enter it once as a recurring task, and Microsoft Project applies it to the entire project schedule.

Creating Recurring Tasks

To create a recurring task, follow these steps:

1. Select the task row below where you want your new task to be inserted. Find the row where you want to insert the recurring task, and click the Task Name field. If the row is blank, the recurring task will be housed in the row when you finish creating it. If the row is occupied, that task will be pushed down to make room for the new recurring task.

2. Select the Task tab, Insert, Task, Recurring Task. This opens the Recurring Task Information dialog box (see Figure 6.20).

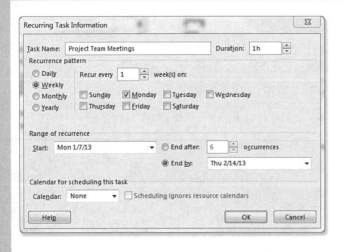

Figure 6.20
Create recurring tasks in the Recurring Task Information dialog box. This example shows a weekly status meeting with your project team every Monday for one hour.

3. Enter the task name and duration information in the Task Name and Duration fields at the top of the Recurring Task dialog box.

4. Choose the recurrence pattern for the recurring task: Daily, Weekly, Monthly, or Yearly. If the task happens every week, choose Weekly. If it happens every day, choose Daily. If a task happens twice a week, you would choose Weekly.

5. Define the frequency of the recurring task within the recurrence pattern. The frequency options vary depending on the recurrence pattern you defined in step 4:

- If you have selected Daily, choose whether the task occurs every day, every other day, and so on, up to every 12th day from the drop-down list. Then, select whether you mean every day or every workday. You define the calendar (which, in turn, defines what workdays are) shortly.

- If you have selected Weekly, choose whether the task occurs every week, every other week, and so on, up to every 12th week from the drop-down list. Then, select the day or days of the week the task occurs.

- If you have selected Monthly, you have two options. Either the task occurs on the same date of every month (such as the 21st of every month) or on the same day of every month (such as the third Monday of every month). If it occurs more than once in a month, you want to define your recurrence pattern as Weekly, and specify the recurring task using a Weekly frequency pattern.

- If you have selected Yearly, you have a similar option to Monthly. Either the task is the same date every year (such as August 21st) or it is the same day every year (such as the third Monday of August).

6. Next, define the date range. Choose when you want the recurring task to start its recurrence pattern in the Start field. Then, define its end. You can enter a specific number of times the task occurs before it ends in the End After field, or enter a specific date it should end by in the End By field. If you choose a specific date in the End By field, Microsoft Project shows the projected number of occurrences in the End After field. However, you cannot edit this number unless you select End After.

By default, the Start and End By fields show the project start and finish dates. If the task is to start occurring sometime after the project starts, enter that date in the Start field. Also, if the task occurs at a specific time, such as a meeting that is always at 2:00 p.m., enter the time in the Start field. To display the time, change the Date Format field to include time, which can be found on the View tab in the Options dialog box (Tools, Options, View tab, Date Format field).

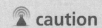

> **caution**
>
> If you enter a finish date for the recurring task that is past the finish date of the project, the duration for the project is extended to the finish date of the recurring task.

7. Choose the calendar to use when scheduling the recurring task in the Calendar field. If you have created base calendars or task calendars, they will be in the drop-down list along with the default base calendars. Selecting None automatically uses the project base calendar.

➡ *For more details about creating and using calendars, **see** the "Defining Calendars" section, **p. 101**, in Chapter 5.*

8. Resources have their own calendars to define their working and nonworking times. If you assign a resource to the recurring task and want Project to ignore their availability defined in their resource calendar, select the Scheduling Ignores Resource Calendars check box. The resource will be assigned to the task regardless of his or her resource calendar.

9. Click OK or press Enter to complete the creation of the recurring task, or click Cancel to exit without creating it.

If the newly created recurring task falls on any nonworking days, Microsoft Project warns you and gives you the following options: Reschedule the affected tasks to the earliest available working time, skip the dates that are affected and not schedule those recurring tasks that fall on nonworking time, or cancel the creation of the recurring task altogether.

When the recurring task is created, it appears on the Task Entry table as a summary task. Its duration begins on the first occurrence and ends on the last occurrence. Rather than a solid taskbar on the timescale, it is displayed as short segments representing the time the task occurs throughout the project (see Figure 6.21).

caution

When you are setting up recurring tasks and you enter a number larger than the calculated default, Project automatically sets up the number of occurrences you enter. However, these later occurrences are beyond the original finish date, and they extend the duration of your project.

	Task Name	Duratio
0	◢ 06fig21 Kitchen Remodel	28.8 c
1	◢ Management	25.13
2	▷ Plans and Permits	2
6	◢ Project Team Meetings	25.13
7	Project Team Meetings 1	
8	Project Team Meetings 2	
9	Project Team Meetings 3	
10	Project Team Meetings 4	
11	Project Team Meetings 5	
12	Project Team Meetings 6	
13	▷ Contracts	
18	▷ Preparation	16.3
35	▷ Vendors	1

Figure 6.21
After a recurring task is created, it is displayed as a summary task, and all the recurrences are rolled up to one row on the Task Entry table. Here, the Project Team Meeting2 recurring task is expanded to show all occurrences.

An icon is displayed in the Indicators column that signifies the recurring task (see Figure 6.21 and Table 6.1). Hover the mouse pointer over the indicator, and the Screentip displays the number of occurrences and the date range for the recurring task.

If the Project Team Status Meeting tasks were collapsed, the task ID numbers would jump several numbers between the recurring task and the task under it (Task ID numbers 7–12 would be missing). This is because each recurrence of the task is assigned its own ID number, but the tasks are rolled up as a summary task and thus not displayed. To display all the recurring tasks on the task entry table, expand the summary task by clicking on the plus sign (+) in the Task Name column (see Figure 6.21) or by using any of the Show Subtasks command methods described earlier in this chapter. Click the minus sign (−) to hide them again, or use any of the Hide Subtasks command methods.

It is possible when setting up a recurring task that Microsoft Project might place the task on a non-workday. If this happens, Project warns you, as shown in Figure 6.22, and then asks you what you want to do:

- Select Yes if you want Project to reschedule the task to the earliest possible working time.

- Select No if you want Project to skip those days and leave the tasks out of the series of recurring tasks.

- Select Cancel to stop creating recurring tasks altogether.

Figure 6.22
When you run into a problem while setting up recurring tasks, Microsoft Project displays a message.

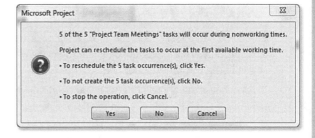

 note

You can link other tasks in the project to individual occurrences of the recurring task without linking all occurrences of the recurring task. To do so, you must display, or show, all the recurring tasks, as described in the preceding paragraph.

➡️ *For more details about linking tasks, **see** the "Linking Tasks" section, **p. 186**, in Chapter 7.*

Editing Recurring Tasks

You can edit recurring tasks by double-clicking the task, thus opening the Recurring Task Information dialog box. Make your changes and click OK. A warning box appears, informing you of the consequences of making your edits (see Figure 6.23). All scheduled occurrences will be deleted, and the recurring task will be rescheduled based on your edits. Click OK if this is okay, or Cancel if it is not, which will not apply your edits.

You can delete a recurring task as you would any other task (click the row ID number, which selects the entire task, and click Delete, or follow any of the other task-deletion methods described earlier in this chapter). You can also delete or edit individual occurrences of the recurring task. Display all the recurring tasks in the Task Entry table and delete or edit as you would any other task.

Figure 6.23
Microsoft Project automatically warns you when it has to delete existing tasks after you change the frequency of your recurring task.

Creating WBS Codes

When you add a task, Microsoft Project will create a default WBS code in the WBS field for each task automatically. These default codes are the same as the outline numbers that Project creates and stores in the Outline Number field.

If you want to show the WBS field, you need to insert the WBS column. You can also see the WBS field using the Task Information dialog box by selecting the Advanced tab. If your client or company requires a specific format for the WBS codes, you can easily edit them in either of these locations, changing the project outline number to your own WBS code. Changing the WBS field, however, will not change the entry in the Outline Number field.

You can easily define the customized format to match your specific WBS code scheme. Project then uses the custom format to set up new default codes for the WBS field, instead of the value in the Outline Number field. Your custom format can include numbers, letters, and symbols, plus ASCII characters.

If you have a custom WBS format defined for another project file, you can copy it right into your current project without having to create it anew. Select the File tab, click on the Organizer button, and then use the Fields tab to copy your custom WBS format from one project file to another. If you want to use it in all files, you can copy it to the Global template.

➡ *For more details about building the WBS, **see** the "Work Breakdown Structure" section, **p. 76**, in Chapter 4.*

The WBS code can be customized to fit an organization's WBS numbering schema or to simplify the display of your project tasks.

➡ *For detailed information and steps on creating WBS codes; inserting, deleting, and moving tasks with custom WBS codes; editing and renumbering custom WBS codes, **see** the "WBS Numbering" section, **p. 80**, in Chapter 4.*

Using Other Views to Create Tasks

The Gantt Chart view is the most commonly used view to create task lists. It displays the Task Entry table and the timescale containing the task's duration bar side by side. However, some people prefer to use different views. The following sections discuss two other popular views for creating a task list: the Task Entry view and the Task Sheet view.

 *For additional information about views, **see** Chapter 11, "Using Standard Views, Tables, Filters, and Groups to Review Your Schedule," **p. 357**.*

 note

Views are just different ways to display the same information in a project. If you change the data in one view, it will be reflected in all the other views.

Using the Task Entry View

The Task Entry view is a slightly more advanced version of the Gantt Chart view. In the Task Entry view, the Gantt Chart view is displayed in the top pane and a Task Form view is displayed in the bottom pane. The Task Form view in the bottom pane shows details for whatever task is selected in the top pane (see Figure 6.24).

Figure 6.24
The Task Entry view combines the Gantt Chart view in the top pane with a Task form, displaying additional details for the selected task, in the bottom pane.

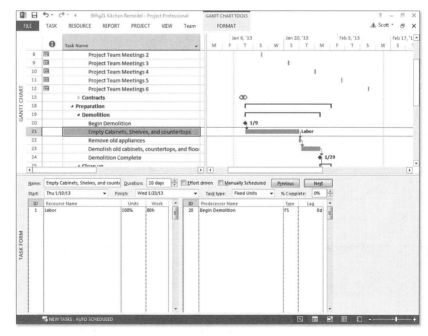

The Task form in the bottom pane is very effective for assigning resources and linking tasks as you are creating a task list, because it is all done on the same screen. It might not be very helpful to have open if you are simply defining basic task information such as task names and durations.

To change from the Gantt Chart view to the Task Entry view, select the Task tab and click Details. Whenever you split the screen when you have a task view displayed, Microsoft Project displays the

Task form in the bottom pane. To take the Task form off the screen, select the Task tab, and click Details again.

You can also right-click over the timescale area and choose Show Split to display the Task form.

Using the Task Sheet View

The Task Sheet view is the Task Entry table. Basically, it is the Gantt Chart view without the timescale side (see Figure 6.25). This view is advantageous because there is more room on your screen to display the columns that might otherwise be hidden by the timescale. It is also a good view to print if you want to show just the task outline and not the timescale graphics. In addition, Task Sheet view might be especially helpful when initially entering tasks. It enables you to concentrate on creating the list of tasks and breaking down the scope of your project and work more efficiently, without additional elements that could be a distraction.

To display the Task Sheet view, select the Task tab, and then click on the Gantt Chart text below the Gantt Chart icon. Select Task Sheet from the list. You can also split the window to display the Task form in the bottom pane (click Details on the Task tab).

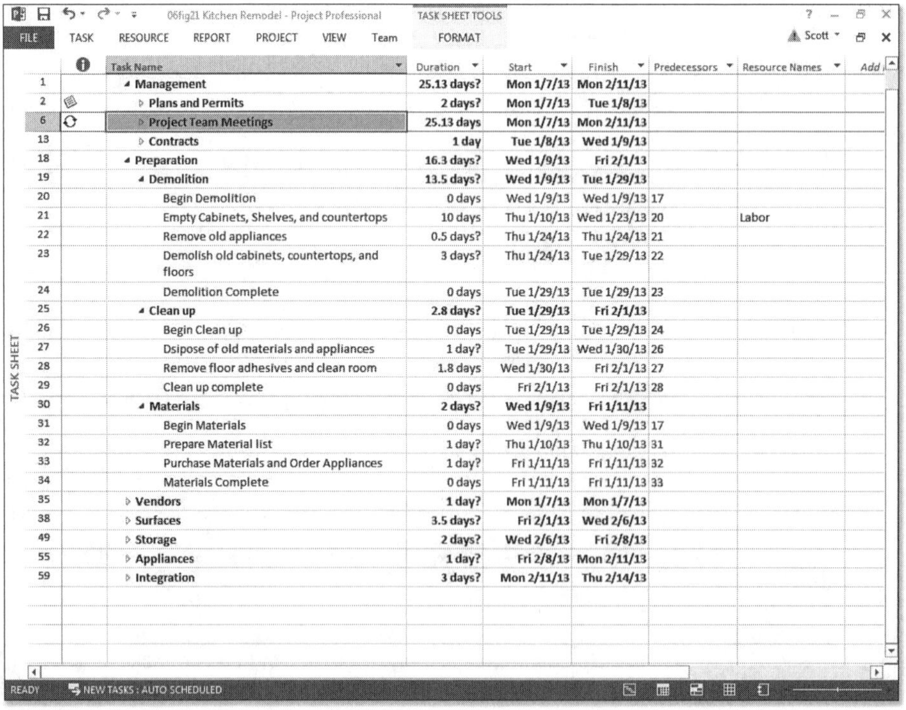

Figure 6.25
The Task Sheet view is the Task Entry table of the Gantt Chart view, and is helpful in displaying additional columns that might have been hidden by the timescale in the Gantt Chart view.

Using the Timeline View

The Timeline enables you to create a single-line, summarized view of your project that can be exported in a variety of ways. Select the View tab and check the box next to Timeline to show the timeline. To hide the Timeline, right-click anywhere on the timeline pane except the timeline graphic itself and deselect Show Timeline (see Figure 6.26).

Figure 6.26
The time-line view showing selected tasks and a callout for the Storage task.

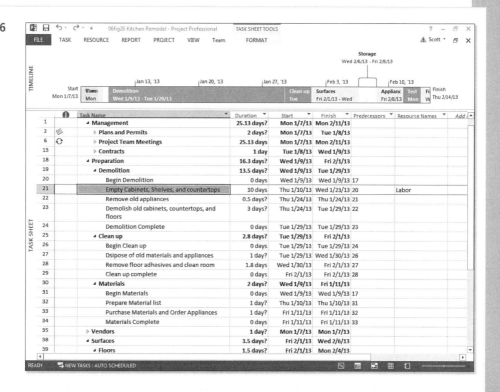

To show a task on the Timeline, select a task and open the Task Information window. Select the General tab and check the box next to Display on Timeline. Alternately, select a task or multiple tasks and select the Task tab and click Add to Timeline.

To insert a task directly on the timeline, right-click the timeline and select Insert Task (this can also be done from the Format tab using the controls in the Insert group). You will have the option of inserting a callout task, a task, or a milestone. Inserting tasks this way creates a new task in the task table. In other words, this is a "real" task, not just something that only appears on the Timeline.

To remove a task from the timeline, right-click the task and select Remove from Timeline.

Tasks can be shifted up or down, but not forward or backward (this would require altering their start and finish dates). They can be shifted off the main bar, at which point they become callout tasks. The callout label can be moved freely anywhere but the main bar. The label remains tethered to the task timeframe by a single line (see Figure 6.27).

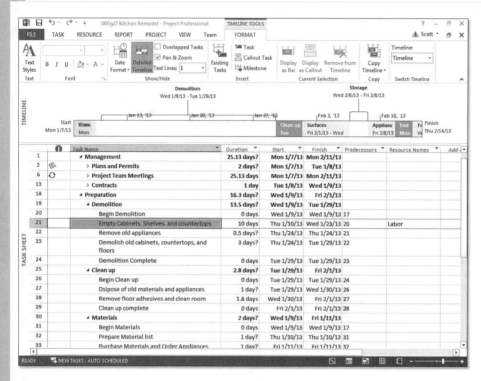

Figure 6.27
The Timeline tools tab, showing tasks both on the timeline and called out.

Finally, right-clicking on a task enables you to directly open the Task Information dialog, create task notes, or jump to the task in your task table.

Because the Format tab is context aware, it presents controls tailored to the timeline when you click anywhere on the Timeline.

The Text Styles group enables you to apply style changes to all things in the Timeline or to only certain types of things. Select the Items to Change drop-down to specify which type of Timeline item text you want to change; then make the change (see Figure 6.28). (You can also reach this control by right-clicking the timeline and selecting Text Styles.)

To use controls in the Font group, select an item or items directly on the Timeline by clicking them. Ctrl+click or use the Windows lasso to select multiple items. This enables the Font group, which works exactly like every other Office application.

To change the task date format, select the Task Date Format on the Format tab. You can also use this control to show or hide the Task dates, the "Today" marker, or the timescale.

Figure 6.28
The text styles dialog is consistent across many
views, with slight modifications.

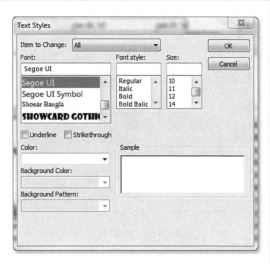

The main difference between the Detailed and Summarized views of the timeline is the lack of labeling. Callouts, task names, and task dates are not included in the summarized timeline.

Overlapped Tasks controls how tasks planned for the same time are displayed. Checking the Overlapped Tasks box stacks simultaneous tasks (see Figure 6.29). Unchecking the box attempts to layer tasks one on top of another (see Figure 6.30). This has obvious limits in legibility.

Figure 6.29
Concurrent
tasks are
stacked on
the time-
line.

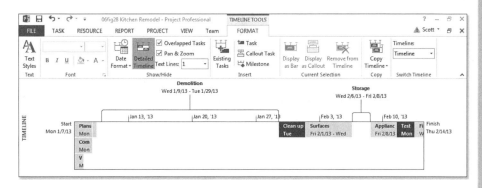

To select tasks for inclusion on the timeline from a compact dialog, select the Existing tasks control. The Add Tasks to Timeline dialog shows a hierarchical pick-list. You can add multiple tasks at once. The other three controls in the Insert group are self-explanatory.

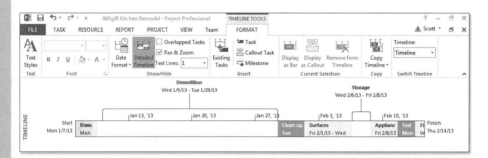

Figure 6.30
Concurrent tasks set to overlap.

Display as Bar and Display as Callout toggle selected task(s) between the two states. Remove from Timeline is self-explanatory.

Finally, the Copy Timeline control adds a copy of the timeline to the clipboard. The difference between the selections is the size of the Timeline image; you can use the clipboard contents in any application.

Consultants' Tips

For the seasoned project management veteran, this chapter might seem obvious, but mastery of the basics is fundamental to success. The greatest cake mix in the world is useless without clear, complete instructions. A project schedule is similar—if the tasks are not clear, or ordered correctly, the project will not turn out well.

Not to endorse any particular product, but Betty Crocker is one of the best project managers in the history of the profession. She can give you a clear, crisp, concise project schedule that is highly successful, highly repeatable, and a hit at the office potluck.

Following the advice in this chapter might not get your name on a baking product box, but it can win you recognition as one of the desirable project managers in your business. Do not shun the basics because you have done this many times before.

DEFINING TASK LOGIC

After you enter project tasks and estimate durations, you must focus on developing the schedule of start and finish dates for project tasks. This chapter focuses on logic: how to link tasks to define the logical sequence of activity, providing Project specific information for calculating a schedule. Besides linking tasks, this chapter explains constraints and discusses performing advanced actions on tasks.

If tasks are not worked on in a logical order, schedules will not make sense and the project will turn into chaos. This chapter helps you avoid that and shows you how to logically link and schedule tasks.

A Microsoft Project schedule depends on a number of factors, including the following:

 tip

Task dependencies can become confusing. Project 2010 introduced the Task Inspector to help clarify dependencies. Project 2013 introduces the Task Path feature, providing a visual way to track dependencies backward through a schedule.

- Whether tasks are auto-scheduled or manually scheduled, or a combination of the two. Because manually scheduled tasks really don't take advantage of the Project scheduling engine, this book assumes for the most part that tasks are auto-scheduled.

- The project schedule either begins on a fixed start date or is calculated to end on a fixed finish date. You control this factor in the Project Information dialog box.

➡ *For more information on defining the start or finish of a project, **see** the "Understanding the Project Information Dialog Box" section in Chapter 5, **p. 92**.*

- Project normally schedules tasks only during the working times defined by the base calendar that you select for the project. Exceptions can occur when you assign resources or attach task calendars to tasks. The resource or task calendars define working time that is different from the project's base calendar.

  ➡ *For guidelines on defining the project base calendar,* **see** *the "Defining Calendars" section in Chapter 5,* **p. 101.**

- The schedule depends heavily on the duration estimates for the individual tasks. The duration of the tasks is one of the driving forces of the schedule. The longer the task duration for any given start date, the later the scheduled finish date for that task.

- The schedule also depends on the logical order, or scheduling sequence, for the tasks. Typically, most tasks have start or finish dates that depend on the start or finish date of some other task. These are called *dependency links*, and this chapter is largely devoted to defining them. These links are ignored when a task is manually scheduled.

- The schedule accommodates any arbitrary limits, or *constraints*, that you might impose on the start or finish dates for individual tasks. Imposing date constraints is covered later in this chapter.

- You can modify the schedule for an individual task by assigning a *task calendar*.

  ➡ *For additional information on assigning task calendars,* **see** *Chapter 5, "Task Calendars,"* **p. 89.**

- By default, a task is scheduled without interruption for its duration, based on the Task, Resource, or Project calendar's defined working time. Nonworking time will also interrupt a task. You can insert one or more interruptions in the work on a task by splitting the task schedule. See the section, "Splitting Tasks," later in this chapter.

- The task schedule also depends on the availability of resources that are assigned to work on the tasks when you level resources to prevent overallocation.

- The schedule is affected if you delay a resource assignment to start after other resources have started or if you contour the daily work assignment for a resource.

  ➡ *For additional information on contouring and delaying resource assignments and the effects they have on the task schedule,* **see** *Chapter 10, "Scheduling Single and Multiple Resource Assignments,"* **p. 301.**

In practice, after you learn to use Project, you will probably outline, link, and impose constraints on the task list as you enter the tasks. The process is divided into separate chapters in this book to focus on all the options and techniques possible for each activity. After you learn it, the process will become second nature.

By far the most important topic in this chapter for you to understand is linking tasks. The sequencing or linking of tasks makes it possible for Project to calculate a schedule when the tasks are in

Auto Scheduled mode—and that is one of the main reasons for using it. This is also what makes it possible for Project to identify the critical tasks—those that must finish on time or might be worthwhile attempting to finish faster when you need to compress the overall duration of the project. Critical tasks are tasks with little to no slack and that directly influence the completion of the project on time. Critical tasks are discussed in more detail throughout this chapter.

Manipulating Your Schedule

Microsoft Project is equipped with two key features for manipulating your schedule: the Multiple Undo/Redo feature and the Change Highlighting feature. These features are particularly useful for "modeling" changes or "what-iffing." They are described in the next two sections.

Using the Multiple Undo and Redo Feature

The Multiple Undo and Redo feature enables you to view all changes you have made and to select any number of them to undo or redo simultaneously. The Multiple Undo and Redo features are located in the Quick Access toolbar by default, as shown in Figure 7.1.

To use the Multiple Undo feature, click on the arrow directly to the right of the Undo button, which opens a drop-down list of your recent actions. When you hover up and down the list of the Multiple Undo button, the changes are highlighted, and if you click on an item, your selection and all of those above it will be undone at once. The undo items are also now shown by "name." For example, if you have switched to the Gantt Chart view, this item appears labeled as View Apply 'Gantt Chart'. If you have changed the duration of a task to two days, for example, it is labeled Entry '2'. The button directly to the right of Multiple Undo is Multiple Redo, and it provides the same options—you can redo any number of changes you removed from the schedule.

Combined with Change Highlighting (discussed in the next section), this is a very powerful feature that enables you to see what happens to your schedule when you make modifications. The combination of these features can also be used for light modeling because you can make a lot of changes and undo them all if the result is unsatisfactory. You are able to observe what happens to your project schedule if those changes were to occur.

Figure 7.1
Use the Multiple Undo and Redo features to undo or redo several items at once.

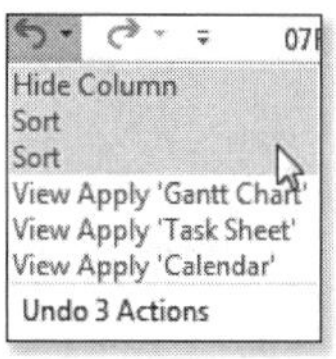

Using Change Highlighting to View Changes

Change Highlighting automatically highlights all tasks affected by a change to another task. For example, if you change the finish date on a task, all its dependent tasks will be highlighted, alerting you that they are affected by the finish date change. Similarly, if you add a task dependency to a task, all tasks that are linked to it will be highlighted to note the change. Figure 7.2 shows the schedule with the change highlighting feature turned on, where changing Task 68 duration affects subsequent tasks plus the summary Tasks 63 and 66.

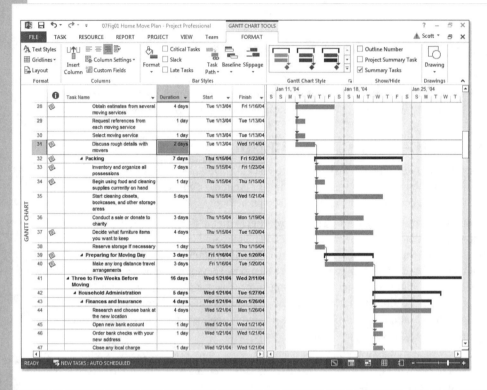

Figure 7.2
Use the Change Highlighting feature to analyze the effects of your changes on your project schedule.

To enable or disable the Change Highlighting feature, add the Display Change Highlighting control to the Quick Access toolbar.

➡️ *For more information on how to customize the Quick Access toolbar,* **see** *Chapter 22, "Customization Almost Beyond Reason: Views, Tables, Filters, Groups, Fields, Toolbars, Menus, and Forms,"* **p. 699.**

Linking Tasks

As you know, projects are made up of tasks. Together, these tasks should represent the entire scope of work that needs to be completed to successfully finish the project. In that sense, all tasks of a project are connected; they all contribute to the successful completion of the project.

However, some tasks are linked to each other in greater detail. There are two types of tasks when working on a project: *summary tasks* and *subtasks*. Summary tasks provide summary information about the tasks that are subordinate to the summary within a project, and the subtasks are the detailed tasks that must be accomplished to complete the summary tasks. For example, if you had a project called Home Move Plan, a summary task would be Packing, and subtasks would be Inventory and Organize All Possessions, Clean Closets and Storage Areas, Conduct a Sale or Make Donations, and so on.

The subtasks are detailed tasks of the summary task, and they can (and should) be logically linked to each other. The total span of time, from the earliest start date to the latest finish date, for all the subtasks is the duration of the summary task. These types of relationships between tasks, and how they apply to Project, are discussed in the following sections.

Understanding Task Relationships

Some tasks in a project often cannot start until one or more other tasks have finished. Usually this is because a task might need to use the output generated by another task. In the example of moving to a new house, you must calculate your expenses before you can determine the best method of moving. Therefore, at the start of the task Determine the Best Method of Moving is determined by, and should be linked to, the finish of the task Calculate Moving Expenses. The link expresses that the schedule for determining the best moving method is dependent on the schedule for calculating your expenses, because you cannot make the decision until you know your moving budget.

A novice scheduler in this moving project might just list the tasks and type in start and finish dates for all the tasks using Manually Scheduled mode. But if the scheduler later finds out that for some reason the Calculate Moving Expenses task will be delayed, he or she will then have to go through the entire project, typing in later start and finish dates for all the tasks that will be affected by the initial delay; an inefficient and error-prone process. When project schedule tasks start or finish dates are manually entered on an auto-scheduled task, a Constrained Task symbol is added to the Indicator column. Constraints are not added to Manually Scheduled tasks.

However, if the auto-scheduled tasks are created in Project and dependency links are defined, the scheduler can simply enter a delayed start date for Calculate Moving Expenses, and Project calculates the new start and finish dates for all the tasks that are dependent, directly or indirectly, on that task. To correct the schedule due to a delay, all the scheduler has to do is modify the task (the start date or the duration), and all the other tasks will be recalculated and those changes highlighted.

 note

The reason you take the time to define links between tasks is so that Project can recalculate the schedule for you quickly when there is a schedule change that affects other tasks.

Defining Dependency Links

Tasks are linked to show a dependency relationship as *predecessor* and *successor* tasks. The predecessor task determines the schedule of the successor, or dependent task. The terms *predecessor* and *successor* are used to refer to the direction of the link and not the position of the tasks. You will see that more sophisticated linking can create a situation where successor tasks begin before predecessor tasks are accomplished, even though the successor tasks depend on the predecessor tasks for completion. See the section, "Choosing the Dependent Tasks," later in this chapter, for an example.

To illustrate usage of the terms *successor* and *predecessor*, suppose you need to schedule the painting of a room. Four tasks are involved: Put on the Protective Tape, Apply the Primer, Apply Paint, and Clean Up. The start of Apply Paint depends on the finish of Apply Primer; therefore, Apply Primer is the predecessor to Apply Paint. Similarly, Apply Paint is the predecessor to Clean Up (because you cannot clean up until you have applied the paint). In theory, Clean Up is the successor to Apply Paint, because you want to clean up after all the painting is done, but realistically you can begin to clean up before completing the Apply Paint task. This variation is discussed in the section, "Allowing for Delays and Overlaps," later in this chapter.

The start date for the successor task should be linked to the finish date for the predecessor. As illustrated in Figure 7.3, Project draws a small arrow from the finish of each predecessor task to the start of its successor task.

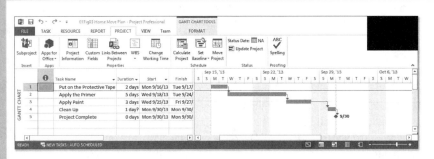

Figure 7.3
Predecessor and successor task relationships are indicated by arrows drawn from the predecessor taskbar's start to the successor taskbar's start.

When you refer to a dependency link, the linked date of the predecessor task (either its start or its finish) is named first, and the linked date of the successor task is named last. In the painting example in Figure 7.3, the dependency relationships for the first three tasks are called *Finish-to-Start links* because the predecessor's finish determines the successor's start. Finish-to-Start is the most common type of link, but there are three other types you can use: Finish-to-Finish, Start-to-Start, and Start-to-Finish. The section, "Defining the Types of Dependency Link Relationships," later in this chapter, describes the use of all four types of links.

By establishing the link in the painting example, you instruct Project to set the start date for Apply Paint based on the scheduled finish date for Apply Primer. Any change that alters the calculated finish date for the predecessor causes Project to also reschedule the start date for the dependent or successor task. If you define task links, Project automatically reschedules dependent tasks when the schedule for the predecessor changes.

When you link two tasks in manual task mode, Project shifts the start date of the successor task to the finish date of the processor task as if the tasks were auto-scheduled. However, changes to the predecessor task will not automatically propagate to the successor. The successor tasks will be highlighted with a dashed "warning" outline, indicating that the task would move if it were auto-scheduled.

➡ *For steps to follow in using leveling delays,* **see** *the "Leveling Delay Effects" section in Chapter 9, p. 294.*

⚠ caution

Do not link two unrelated tasks just to level out the workload for a resource who is assigned to work on both tasks. It is true that the link forces Project to schedule the tasks one after the other, thus allowing the worker to complete one task before starting the next. But if the worker is later removed from working on one of the tasks, there is no way to tell that the link no longer serves a purpose and can be removed (unless you just happen to remember it or create a note on the task), and you will be left with an unnecessary delay that could prolong the finish of your project. The preferred way to deal with this problem is to *delay* one of the tasks by using the Leveling Delay Field.

Defining the Types of Dependency Link Relationships

You can create four types of dependency relationships, depending on whether you use the start dates or finish dates when linking tasks. The name for each dependency type includes a reference to the linked date for the predecessor (either its start date or its finish date), followed by a reference to the linked date for the dependent task (either its start or finish date). Therefore, a Finish-to-Start relationship signifies that the finish date of the predecessor task is used to schedule the start date of the dependent task. The predecessor is referenced first, and then the dependent or successor task is referenced.

Project usually uses two-letter code abbreviations for the four dependency types, as shown in Table 7.1. The first letter in the code refers to the predecessor's start or finish, and the second letter refers to the dependent task. Thus, the code for Finish-to-Start is "FS." The following subsections describe the different dependency types.

Table 7.1   Linking Relationships in Microsoft Project

Code	Dependency Type	Meaning
FS	Finish-to-Start	Predecessor's finish determines successor's start.
SS	Start-to-Start	Predecessor's start determines successor's start.
FF	Finish-to-Finish	Predecessor's finish determines successor's finish.
SF	Start-to-Finish	Predecessor's start determines successor's finish.

By default, when you link tasks, they are defined as a Finish-to-Start relationship. You can change this dependency relationship type in the Task Information dialog box. After you have established the link, open the Task Information dialog box for the successor task by right-clicking on the task and selecting Task Information. Then, on the Predecessors tab, you can change the dependency relationship from the drop-down list in the Type column.

This concept is examined further in the upcoming section, "Creating Links by Using the Task Information Dialog Box."

tip

Be sure you choose correctly; remember that the predecessor comes before the successor in the name. Also remember that Start-to-Finish means the predecessor's start determines the successor's finish.

*For more details about the Task Information dialog box, **see** the "Editing Tasks Using the Task Information Dialog Box" section in Chapter 6, **p. 146**.*

Using the Finish-to-Start Relationship

The Finish-to-Start relationship is the most common of the four types of dependency relationships. The finish date of the predecessor determines the start date of the successor task. For example, framing the walls of a new house should be scheduled to start after the foundation is prepared, with the foundation pouring task acting as the predecessor to the framing task. Referring to the painting example, the links between Tasks 1 and 2 and Tasks 2 and 3 in Figure 7.3 are all Finish-to-Start links.

The linking arrow in the Gantt Chart is drawn from the finish of the predecessor task to the start of the dependent task. The Finish-to-Start dependency relationship is the default relationship created via the Edit, Link Tasks command, or by highlighting the tasks and clicking the Link Tasks button on the Standard toolbar. You must select the predecessor task first and then the successor when highlighting the tasks.

Using the Start-to-Start Relationship

In the Start-to-Start relationship, the start date of the predecessor task determines the start date of the successor task (see the tasks in Figure 7.4). You can schedule the two tasks to start at or near the same time by using this type of relationship.

> ## note
>
> A lag is often associated with Start-to-Start links. The start of the dependent task is delayed until some time after the predecessor task is underway. Lags and leads are discussed later in this chapter.

For example, suppose a company leases new office space and plans to move to the new space when remodeling is completed. As part of the move from one office to the other, several tasks need to be accomplished, such as packing boxes, disconnecting desktop computers, disassembling furniture, and loading the boxes and furniture into the moving truck. Because the movers can start loading the vans shortly after the packing starts (after the first load is ready to move), the start of the Load Trucks task can be linked to the start of the Pack Boxes and Disassemble Furniture task, with a small amount of delay or lag time. The arrow is drawn from the start of the Pack Boxes and Disassemble Furniture task (predecessor) to the start of the Load Trucks task (successor/dependent) with a day of lag time.

Figure 7.4
You can use the Task tab, Schedule, Link Tasks control to link the tasks and change the dependency type to Start-to-Start in the Task Information dialog box.

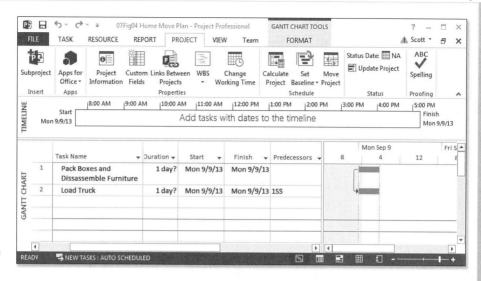

Using the Finish-to-Finish Relationship

In the Finish-to-Finish relationship, the finish date of the predecessor determines the scheduled finish date of the successor task. In other words, you schedule two tasks to finish at or about the same time. For example, when remodeling a kitchen, the delivery of the new kitchen appliances should be completed by the time the cabinets and countertops are installed, so that the new appliances can be installed as soon as the cabinets and countertops are completed (see Figure 7.5).

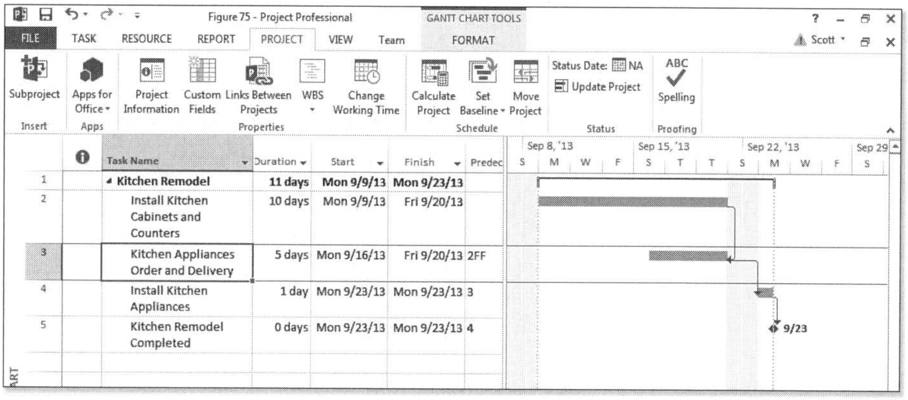

Figure 7.5
Finish-to-Finish relationships entail the predecessor's finish scheduling the successor's finish.

> ### 🔍 note
> The link types Start-to-Start and Finish-to-Finish with leads and lags can be used to schedule tasks to overlap and are commonly used when *fast-tracking* a project—that is, compressing the overall duration of the project by overlapping tasks that are normally scheduled to be completed sequentially.

> ➡️ *For additional information on fast-tracking,* **see** *Chapter 12, "Performing a Schedule Reality Check,"* **p. 411**.

Using the Start-to-Finish Relationship

In the Start-to-Finish relationship, the start date of the predecessor task determines the scheduled finish date of the successor. With this type of relationship, you schedule a task to finish just in time to start a more important task that it supports. This type is most helpful when scheduling from the finish date rather than from the start date.

Here are some examples that illustrate the Start-to-Finish relationship:

- When scheduling the delivery of merchandise to a new store, the grand opening date determines when the deliveries must be scheduled. A delay in construction that pushes back the grand opening leads to the merchandise suppliers having to delay their deliveries.

- *Just-in-time scheduling* in manufacturing is a policy that strives to stock raw materials just in time for the manufacturing process to begin. This policy saves money by not tying up cash in materials' inventories any longer than necessary.

Figure 7.6 illustrates a project where the framing materials (lumber) are to be purchased just in time for framing the walls. The Purchase Lumber task is scheduled to finish just as the Frame Walls task begins. Lumber Purchase and Delivery is dependent on Frame Walls, because you are scheduling the purchasing to be finished just in time for the framing, making Frame Walls its predecessor. If the framing is delayed because of weather, availability of workers, or another reason, the delivery of lumber will be delayed too. The link is a Start-to-Finish link, and the arrow is drawn from the start of the predecessor to the finish of the dependent task. In actual practice, it is rare to see the Start-to-Finish link type used in anything but a project that is scheduled from the end date.

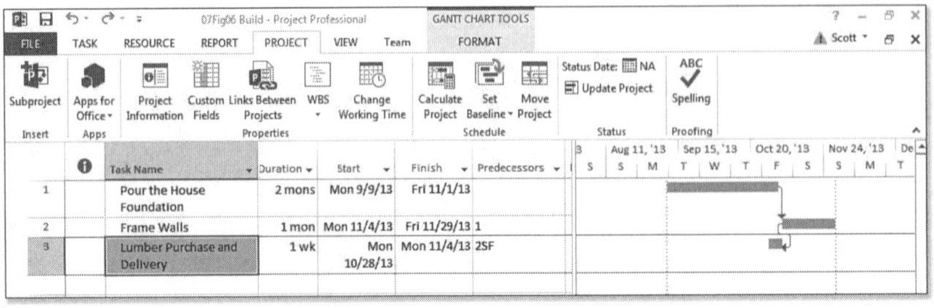

Figure 7.6
Use a Start-to-Finish dependency link for circumstances where you want the successor task to finish just in time for the predecessor to start.

Now, say for example, preparing the foundation has a longer duration than in the original schedule, and that delays the scheduled start for Frame Walls. Automatically, Project delays the dependent task Lumber Purchase and Delivery just enough so that it will still be finished just in time for the new start date of Frame Walls.

That is the difference between setting up the dependency link like the illustration in Figure 7.6 and using a Finish-to-Start dependency relationship. If the predecessor is delayed, the successor is delayed. Otherwise, the Lumber Purchase and Delivery task would have occurred as planned, and you would have a huge pile of lumber sitting around your work site, waiting for the Frame Walls task to begin, rather than have the lumber purchased just in time for the walls to be framed.

Choosing the Dependent Tasks

Deciding which of two tasks is the dependent task (the successor) and which is the predecessor is often obvious. In many cases, as with the building example used earlier, the dependent task requires the output of another task. In such a case, you make the other task its predecessor. Other times, however, it is not so simple.

Consider the following case, in which a person, not a computer, is doing the scheduling.

Katy is an on-the-job trainee for a residential construction project. She is responsible for making sure that lumber and materials are on hand when the foundation is finished and it is time to frame the walls of the new house. Katy must watch the progress on finishing the foundation and call the lumberyard four days before the foundation is finished to schedule the delivery of the lumber. Katy's instructions are to avoid ordering the lumber any earlier than necessary because that would mean paying interest on borrowed money for a longer period of time.

When it is just about time to call the lumberyard, Katy learns that the carpenters are being diverted to another project that has a higher priority, and the framing has been put on hold for a week. Katy's common sense tells her that the lumber order is really linked to the start of the framing, not to the finish of the foundation, and she delays placing the delivery order until two days before the new start date for the framing. Although her instructions were to order the lumber four days before the foundation is finished, these instructions assumed that there would be no gap between working on the foundation and the framing. Because there was a gap, Katy was correct to link her task (ordering lumber) to the framing task.

If you were scheduling this example, you would want to give Project enough information to be able to do what Katy did—delay the start of the lumber order task if the framing task is delayed. To do that, you need to treat the lumber order as a task that is dependent on the start of the framing task.

The decision about which task should be the predecessor and which task should be the dependent, or successor, might depend on which task you have more control over. If you have equal scheduling control over both tasks, make the task that must come first the predecessor and let the later task be the dependent successor. In cases for which the schedule for one task is out of your control, you might want to arbitrarily make the more flexible scheduled task the dependent task—regardless of which task actually must come first in time (like Katy did in the previous example).

Allowing for Delays and Overlaps

Sometimes you might need to schedule a delay between the predecessor and the successor tasks. For instance, in the painting example, you need to allow time for the first coat of paint to dry before you apply the final coat. This kind of delay is known as a *lag* or *lag time* in a task scheduling, and you could add a one-day lag to the Finish-to-Start link between the Apply the Primer and Apply Paint tasks. The successor task's start would lag behind the predecessor's finish in the manner you define.

Other times you might want to allow the dependent task to overlap or start before the predecessor task is finished. You add *lead time* to a link when you want the linked date for the successor task to anticipate the linked date of its predecessor. For example, the Clean-Up crew can begin the Clean-Up task when the painters are close to finishing the Apply Paint task. The successor task's start would lead to the predecessor's finish.

Figure 7.7 shows the painting example again. The first set of tasks has no lead or lag defined, whereas the revised schedule has lead and lag time added to the links. There is a lag added to the link between the primer and paint, because you have to wait for the primer to dry. But there is a lead time between the Apply Paint and the Clean Up task, because you can begin cleaning up before the paint is dry. The lag adds to the overall duration of the painting project, but the lead allows the project to finish faster than it would otherwise.

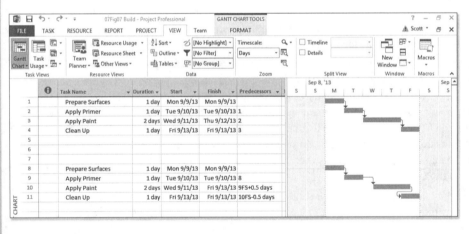

Figure 7.7
Lag and lead times enable you to create a more realistic schedule, and often enable you to finish earlier than expected.

 tip

Identifying task relationships where overlaps such as lead time are possible is one of the best ways to shorten the overall time it takes to finish a project.

For more information on compressing (or crashing) a schedule, **see** Chapter 12, "Performing a Schedule Reality Check," **p. 411**.

Lags and leads can be defined in ordinary duration units or in elapsed duration units. If you want Project to schedule the lag during working time on the calendar, you use ordinary duration units. If Project can use nonworking time also for scheduling the lag, you use elapsed duration units. For example, assume the Apply Primer task finishes on a Friday, the last day of the working week. If the one-day lag for the Apply Paint task was defined as one ordinary day (typically eight hours of working time on a standard calendar), Project would let one day of working time pass before scheduling the start of the Apply Paint task. Because the next working day after Friday is Monday, the successor task would be scheduled for Tuesday. But if the lag was defined as one elapsed day (that is, 24 hours of continuous time), Project would use the weekend days for the lag and the paint would be scheduled for Monday.

Although you usually define lags and leads in fixed time units (such as nine hours or four elapsed days), Project also enables you to define lags and leads as a percentage. With the percentage format, Project makes the length of the lag or the lead a multiple of the length of the predecessor task. For instance, if a predecessor task is scheduled for one day (eight hours), and you define a lag time of 50%, the lag time will be four hours. Using the different methods of entering leads and lags is discussed in the following section.

Entering Leads and Lags

Entering leads and lags is done the same way whether you use the Task Information dialog box mentioned previously or other dialog boxes or forms. When entering lags and leads, bear in mind that both are entered in the same Lag box; there is no separate Lead box. Use positive numbers to represent lag time and negative numbers to represent lead time.

You can enter a lag or lead as a number followed by one of the regular or elapsed time code letters you use for entering duration time: minutes=m or em, hours=h or eh, days=d or ed, weeks=w or ew, and months=mo or emo. Lead time is entered as a negative lag. For example, you enter **4d** to define a four-day lag and **-8h** to define an eight-hour lead. You type **4ed** to schedule a lag of four elapsed days (four full, real-time days, as opposed to four working days, which would not include weekends or holidays). If you type a number without a time unit, Project attaches the default duration unit (which is days by default).

Using Percentage Lags and Leads

You can also express lag or lead time as a percentage of the predecessor's duration. If you want a task to start when its predecessor is within 20% of being finished, you can enter a Finish-to-Start link with a 20% lead, entered as **FS-20%**. Project schedules the task to start so that it overlaps the last 20% of the predecessor task duration. Using percentage lags and leads enables the amount of lag or lead to vary with changes in the duration of the predecessor. Thus, the longer the duration of the predecessor, the more time a percentage lag or lead would entail.

When you use percentage lags and leads, Project uses the start or finish of the predecessor (as specified in the link type) for the starting point, and offsets the start or finish of the successor from that point by the lag percentage multiplied by the duration of the predecessor. For example, if the predecessor has a duration of eight days, a Start-to-Start lag of 25% causes the successor's start to be scheduled two days after the predecessor starts. A Finish-to-Start lead of 75% produces the same start for the successor—as long as the duration of the predecessor remains unchanged. Changes in the duration of the predecessor, however, cause these two links to result in a different start date for the successor.

 tip

If changes in the schedule occur as the project develops, a percentage would likely give you a more preferred successor start date than a time duration, because the time duration might not accurately reflect that changed schedule. Creating this relationship works well in outlining company methods and templates in which the scaling of the project is dependent on the relationship delay or overlap, not a specified duration.

Linking Summary Tasks

As discussed earlier in this chapter, summary tasks roll up the information from the working tasks that are executed to complete the summary tasks. Standard practice is to link subtasks and not to link summary tasks. However, summary tasks can be linked to each other, or to subtasks under other summary tasks. Project will not let you establish an explicit link between a subtask and its summary task because summary tasks are implicitly linked to their own subtasks.

Subtasks are bound to many of the same attributes as their summary tasks. If the summary task is linked to a predecessor, the predecessor relationship dictates when the summary task—and therefore its subtasks—can begin. Likewise, as you see later in this chapter, if the summary task has a date constraint, its subtasks are effectively constrained to that date also. If the summary task has no link or date constraints, its start date is derived from the earliest start date of any of its subtasks, and its finish date is derived from the latest finish date of its subtasks.

 tip

Linking summary tasks is not a good practice. This is because summary tasks do not define the activities where work gets done; they summarize data from the component tasks that are subordinate to the summary. For example, the summary start date is the earliest start date in the summary's subordinate tasks. Planning the Move is a summary task, and Calculate Moving Expenses is one of its subtasks. Links should generally reflect the scheduling requirements of the tasks where work is done.

But there are always exceptions, and Project is flexible. Linking summary tasks might be useful if a summary task represents a self-contained group of tasks that have a logical relationship to subtasks under another summary task. In that case, linking the summary tasks has the advantage of enabling you to change the subtasks within each group without worrying about redefining the link between the summary tasks.

note

If you select all tasks and let Project link the tasks in an outlined project, Project links all tasks at the first outline level to each other, whether they are summary tasks or not. It then links the next level of subtasks within any summary task to each other, and so forth, until all outline levels in all summary tasks are linked at their own levels. All links are the default Finish-to-Start link type. Linking tasks in this manner is not recommended.

If you create a task link that involves a summary task as the dependent (or successor) task, you can only use the link types Finish-to-Start and Start-to-Start. Project does not let you establish the other link types; it does not allow you to link the summary task's finish date as a dependent task. However, if the link involves a summary task as the predecessor to a subtask, you can use any of the four possible link types. These same rules apply in both fixed start-date and fixed finish-date projects.

The following sections describe the various methods of linking tasks. Some processes are more complicated than others, but might provide greater compatibility. It is recommended that you try all the following methods as you read about them, and decide which method you prefer.

Creating Links by Using the Menu or Toolbar

There are several ways to link tasks. One option is to select the tasks and then click the Link Tasks button in the Schedule group on the Task tab. Another way is to select the tasks and press Ctrl+F2. These links are always the default Finish-to-Start links, without lag or lead. You have to edit the links if you want a different link type or if you want to add lag or lead. In Figure 7.8, four tasks are selected and have been linked in series with the Link Tasks button on the Task tab.

Figure 7.8
There are multiple ways to link tasks, and you can link more than two tasks at a time.

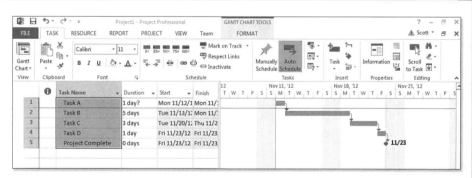

There is no limit to the number of tasks you can select for linking with the Link Tasks tool. You can link just one predecessor and one successor at a time, or you can link all the tasks in the project with the same operation.

If you select adjacent tasks by dragging the mouse pointer or by using the Shift+down arrow or Shift+up arrow key combination, Project links the selected tasks from the top down. In other words, tasks higher on the list (that have lower ID numbers) are predecessors for the tasks below them (that have higher ID numbers). The same concept applies if you select all tasks by clicking one of the column headings, such as Task Name.

If you build the selection by using Ctrl+click (holding down Ctrl and clicking on the tasks you want to link) to add tasks, Project links the tasks in the order in which you added them to the selection. The first selected task is the predecessor to the second, and so forth.

 tip

You have the same options to remove a task link as you have to create links. To remove a link, select the linked tasks and either click the Unlink Tasks tool or press Ctrl+Shift+F2. To remove all links to a task, including all the task's predecessors and successors, select just the task itself and use the Unlink Tasks toolbar button or command.

Creating Links by Using the Task Information Dialog Box

You can use the Predecessors tab of the Task Information dialog box to create and edit a selected task's predecessor links, no matter what view is active (see Figure 7.9). Unlike the Edit, Link Tasks command, the Task Information dialog box enables you to choose the type of link and to enter the lag or lead time.

To create a dependency relationship by using the Task Information dialog box, follow these steps:

1. Select the dependent (the successor) task.

2. Open the Task Information dialog box by clicking the Information button on the Task tab toolbar, or by double-clicking the task.

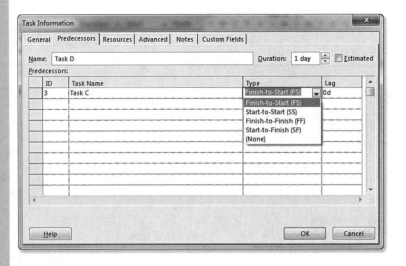

Figure 7.9
The Predecessors tab in the Task Information dialog box enables you to create dependency relationships.

3. Click the Predecessors tab. The Predecessors tab features a table in which you can define predecessors, including the type of link and any lead or lag time (refer to Figure 7.9).

4. Activate the first blank cell under the Task Name field. Choose the name of the task to be the predecessor task from the drop-down list in the field. The drop-down lists the names of all tasks in the project. Project automatically supplies the ID number and the default Finish-to-Start link type, with no lag, unless you choose otherwise.

   Alternatively, if you remember the ID number for the predecessor task, you can enter it in the cell in the ID column. Press Enter to finish the cell entry or select the green check button on the Entry bar. Project automatically supplies the task name for that ID number and supplies the default Finish-to-Start link type, with no lag.

5. Use the drop-down list in the Type column to change the dependency type, if needed.

6. To create lag or lead time, click in the Lag field and type the amount of lag or lead time, followed by a time unit (unless you want to use the default time unit). Use a negative number to specify a lead time.

7. If additional predecessors exist for the task, repeat steps 4 through 6 as needed for each predecessor.

8. To delete a predecessor, select any cell in its row and press the Delete key.

9. Click OK or press Enter to accept the changes.

Creating Links by Using the Task Form View

With a task view such as the Gantt Chart view in the top pane, you can split the window and use the Task Form view in the bottom pane to define the predecessor and successor relationships (see Figure 7.10). To split the window, click the Details button in the Properties group on the Task tab. This is an easy way to define or edit complex dependency relationships. Select a task in the top pane and define its predecessor or successor link in the predecessor or successor details in the bottom pane.

The default display of task details in the Task Form view is to show resources and predecessors. If you want to display both predecessor and successor details, right-click over the Task form and choose Predecessors & Successors, as shown in Figure 7.10. Or you can activate the Task Form view and select the Format tab. Because the Format tab is context dependent, functionally this view serves the same purposes as the Task Information dialog.

If you display the predecessor details, you can define a predecessor for the dependent task by following these steps:

1. Select the dependent task in the top pane or use the Previous and Next buttons in the lower pane to move to the desired task.

2. In the bottom pane, activate the first cell in either the ID or Predecessor Name column.

 note

If you want to enter the successor details in the Task Form view, select the predecessor task in the top pane and use the successor detail fields in the steps that follow instead of the predecessor fields. The link is defined exactly the same in either detail area.

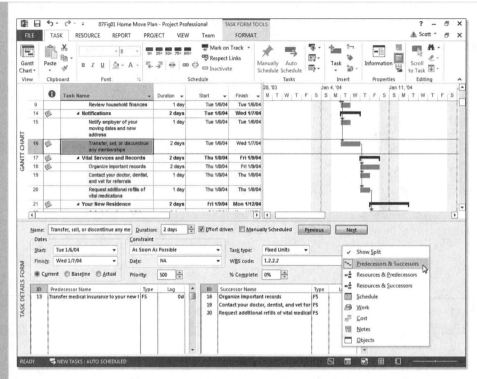

Figure 7.10
Split the window (Task tab, Properties, Details), which opens the Task Form view in the bottom pane, enabling you to define predecessor and successor relationships.

3. If you selected the Predecessor Name field, use the drop-down list of task names to select the name of the task to be the predecessor. The Task Form view still shows the OK button because selecting the task name completes only the cell entry.

   You can also type the predecessor's ID number in the ID field and press Enter to complete the cell entry. Project automatically fills in the predecessor name when you click the OK button to complete the linking definition.

   If you do not know the ID number of the predecessor, you can use the vertical scroll bar in the top pane to view the predecessor task. The ID field remains selected while you scroll the task list. Do not select the predecessor; just view its ID number. Type this number into the ID field. You can then press Enter or click the green check button on the Entry bar to complete the cell entry for the ID number.

4. Select the predecessor's Type field if you want to define a link type other than Finish-to-Start. If you leave the Type field blank, Project supplies the default Finish-to-Start type when you click OK. Type in the two-letter code (FF, FS, SF, or SS) or use the drop-down list to select the code. Press Enter to complete the cell entry in the Type field.

note

The Type field accepts only the two-letter abbreviations for the link types. If you have an AutoCorrect entry for the link type you want to use, Project converts it to the AutoCorrect text when you click OK—and it then rejects the result because it accepts only the abbreviations. There is nothing to do but click Cancel at this point, and then either delete the AutoCorrect definition or edit the link elsewhere (for example, in the Task Information dialog box).

5. Select the Lag field if you want to define a lag or lead time. The default, 0d (zero days, meaning no lag or lead time), is supplied automatically when you click OK if you leave this field blank. You can move the spinner control up to display lags (positive values) or down to display leads (negative values) in the default duration time units or by using a percentage amount.

6. If necessary, add more predecessors on the following rows in the Predecessors table by repeating steps 2–5.

7. To delete a predecessor, click any cell in its row and press the Delete key.

8. Click OK to execute the changes you entered in the Task Form view.

Creating Links by Using the Entry Table

You can create or edit dependency relationships in the Predecessors field on the Entry table (see Figure 7.11). The Entry table is the default table displayed in the Gantt Chart view. To see the Predecessors fields on the table, either move the vertical split bar to the right, or click the right arrow on the horizontal scrollbar at the bottom-left side of the Gantt Chart view.

You can enter the simplest relationship, Finish-to-Start, by just entering the task ID number for the predecessor task in the Predecessors field (or the ID for the successor in the Successors field). The other dependency relationships require a specific pattern of coding.

Assume that you want to make the Pack Rooms task a predecessor with a Start-to-Start link and a one-day lead. The code in the Predecessors column would be 10SS-1d. The explanation for the code is as follows:

- Enter the ID number for the predecessor first (in this case, 10).

- Follow the ID number without any spaces by the abbreviation for the type of link (in this case, SS). If the link is the default FS, you usually do not have to include the abbreviation, except when you want to add a lag or lead. You must add the abbreviation to add a lag or lead.

 tip

One of the most common methods for creating predecessor/successor link relationships is using the Entry table. Furthermore, you can add the Predecessor/Successor column to any table view by selecting a column in the table, clicking Insert Column, and then selecting either Successors or Predecessors.

 note

You can add the Successors field to the table and edit both predecessors and successors for tasks in the table.

- Optionally, you can follow the link type with a plus sign (+) for a lag or a minus sign (−) for a lead. You cannot omit the plus sign with a lag.

- Follow the plus or minus sign with the length of the lag or lead, using duration units (that is, m, h, d, w, or mo), elapsed duration units (that is, em, eh, ed, ew, or emo), or a percentage sign (%). If the current example had a two-day lag, the code would be 10SS+2d. If the lag were two elapsed days, the code would be 10SS+2ed. If a lead were 10%, the code would be 10SS−10%.

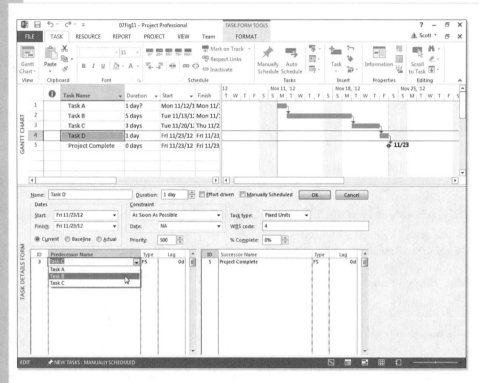

Figure 7.11
You can also use the Predecessors field in the Entry table to add dependency relation-ships.

If a task has more than one predecessor, you separate the predecessor definitions with commas without any spaces. For example, the code 5SS−2d,6,3FS+1d would link the current task to tasks 5, 6, and 3.

 tip

If you do not remember the ID number of the predecessor, leave the cell you are editing selected while you scroll through the task list to find the predecessor task. Do not select the predecessor; just view its ID num-ber. As you start typing, the row for the cell you are editing returns to the screen, and you can finish the link definition.

note

You form codes for the Successors field identically to the way you form codes for the Predecessors field. The only difference is that you begin with the ID number for the successor instead of the predecessor.

Creating Links by Using the Mouse

You can use the mouse to link taskbars on the timescale side of the Gantt Chart view, in the Network Diagram view, or in the Calendar view. You can also use the mouse to edit the linking relationship in the Gantt Chart view or the Network Diagram view.

To link tasks with the mouse in the Gantt Chart view, center the mouse over the predecessor task until the pointer changes into a four-arrow icon. Then click and drag the pointer (which should then turn into a linked-chain icon) over the center of the successor task. Hold the mouse button until Project interprets your action as creating a link. The pointer changes into a linked-chain icon and displays the Finish-to-Start Link information box (see Figure 7.12).

Using the mouse for linking is the most convenient when you can see both tasks you are trying to link onscreen at the same time. If only one taskbar is visible, you have to drag offscreen, and Project begins rapidly scrolling the tasks. You can probably do better with one of the other methods of linking the tasks, as described earlier in this chapter, such as selecting the two tasks (select the predecessor first) and using the Link Tasks tool.

Figure 7.12
Drag the mouse pointer from the predecessor to the successor in the timescale side of the Gantt Chart view to create a dependency link.

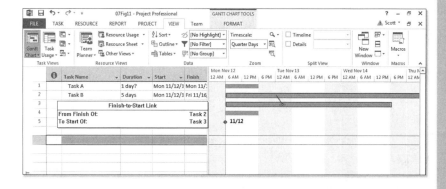

 caution

The mouse pointer is designed to perform a number of actions on tasks, so be careful when creating links by using the mouse. It is easy to accidentally move the task or mark the task as being partially complete. You must watch the shape of the mouse pointer carefully to ensure that you are doing exactly what you intend to do.

tip

If you start using the mouse to link tasks and then want to cancel the linking procedure, simply drag the mouse up to the menu or toolbar area of the Gantt Chart view or the Calendar view and release the button. In the Network Diagram view, you must return the mouse to the task you started with before releasing the mouse button, or you will create a new successor task.

 note

In the Network Diagram and Calendar views, you must drag from the *center* of the predecessor task's box or taskbar, and the pointer is the plain white cross, not the four-arrow shape you look for in the Gantt Chart view. In those views, the four-arrow shape appears when the pointer is over the border of the task box or taskbar, and means that you will move the task if you drag the border. In all cases, make sure that the mouse pointer is the linked-chain shape when you are over the successor task before you release the mouse button.

The dependency type created with the mouse is always a Finish-to-Start relationship. You can change the link type, add a lag or lead, or delete the link by displaying the Task Dependency dialog box with the mouse in the Gantt Chart or Network Diagram view.

To display the Task Dependency dialog box, scroll to display any portion of the linking line between the predecessor and successor tasks. Position the tip of the mouse pointer on the line connecting the tasks whose links you want to edit. A Screentip should appear, with the details of the link. Double-click the linking line, and the Task Dependency dialog box appears, as shown in Figure 7.13. The From task in the dialog box is the predecessor, and the To task is the successor. You can change the dependency type with the drop-down list in the Type field. Choosing None removes the link, as does clicking the Delete button. You can redefine the lag or lead in the Lag field. Click OK to complete the change.

 note

You cannot change the names of the linked tasks in the Task Dependency dialog box, nor can you change which task is the predecessor and which is the successor.

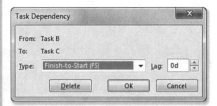

Figure 7.13
Edit the dependency link in the Task Dependency dialog box.

Working with Automatic Linking Options

If you use only simple Finish-to-Start links in a project, Project's Autolink feature (which is enabled by default) can help you maintain the dependency link sequences when you move, delete, or insert tasks within a linked sequence of tasks. However, Autolink works only if the affected links are Finish-to-Start links and are in the middle of the linked sequence.

 tip

Keep in mind that Autolink does not apply to the first or last task in a linked sequence.

When you change the order of tasks, and thus their ID numbers, in a task table (such as the one in the Gantt Chart view), you create a break in the link sequence chain. Autolink repairs the break in the following ways:

- If you cut or delete a task from within a chain of Finish-to-Start linked tasks, Autolink repairs the break in the chain by linking together the former predecessor and successor of the deleted task. In essence, it mends the gap created in the chain by the deletion.

- If you insert a task in a chain of Finish-to-Start linked tasks, Autolink breaks the former link between the tasks. The new task is inserted between the existing tasks, and then the newly inserted task is linked to the task above and below it to keep the linked sequence intact.

- If you move a task from one Finish-to-Start sequence to another, Autolink repairs the chain at the task's old site and inserts the new task into the chain at the new site.

In the Network Diagram and Calendar views, Autolink behaves this way only when you delete a task or insert a new task, because you cannot cut, copy, or move tasks to a different ID order in those views.

 note

If you insert or remove a task from the beginning or end of a linked chain, instead of in the middle of the chain, Autolink does not include the new task in the chain. Inserting a task at the beginning of a series of linked tasks, or after the last task in a linked sequence, does not cause Autolink to extend the chain to include the new task.

To include a task in a sequence, when the task has been added either to the beginning or end of the sequence, you must link the tasks yourself, using one of the previously discussed methods.

By default, Autolink is enabled, but you can disable it by changing the status of the Autolink option. Select the File tab, Options, Schedule. Clear the Autolink Inserted or Moved Tasks check box. To set the option status as a default for all new projects, choose All New Projects from the Scheduling Options for This Project drop-down. Otherwise, the change you make affects only the active project document.

tip

If you have disabled Autolink and need to insert or paste tasks into a Finish-to-Start sequence, you can quickly reestablish the sequence to include new tasks. Select the tasks, starting with the row above the insertion and including the row below the insertion, and use the Unlink Tasks tool to break the original link. Then, with the tasks still selected, use the Link Tasks tool to include the new tasks in the sequence. If there was a lead or lag included in the old link, you need to decide which of the new links should include it.

If you delete or cut tasks from a Finish-to-Start sequence, select the rows above and below the deleted rows and click the Link Tasks tool.

 caution

As convenient as Autolink can be when editing a simple task list, it can cause problems in large or complex projects by creating unintended task links when you insert tasks. You should double-check the links to ensure that they are as you intended for the project. Unintended task links can become a troublesome problem in a project schedule.

If automatic linking is enabled and you rearrange an outline, you should carefully review the links that result each time you move a task or group of tasks in the outline. You might have to edit the links to reflect exactly the relationship you want defined.

 tip

Many project managers leave Autolink disabled because it makes changes without asking for approval. Sometimes they do not notice an unintended change in the linking for their task lists—a problem you should take care to avoid.

Modifying, Reviewing, and Removing Dependency Links

As you develop a project plan, you will inevitably make changes in the task list, and when you do, you will have to adjust the sequence of links you have established. You might want to modify the type of links between tasks, insert lag or lead time, or remove a link entirely. You can modify existing links in the following locations, all of which are described in previous sections of this chapter:

- Select the successor task and modify its predecessor links in the Predecessors tab of the Task Information dialog box.

- Split the window and display the Task Form view in the bottom pane, beneath a task view. With the predecessor and successor details displayed in the Task Form view, select a linked task and modify its links in either the Predecessors or Successors table.

- Double-click a linking line in the Gantt Chart view or Network Diagram view to display the Task Dependency dialog box, where you can modify the link.

If you find that a link between tasks is no longer necessary, or if you prefer to change a link to another task, you have to remove the existing link. Just as you have several ways to create links, you can use many different methods to remove links. You can use the following techniques to remove links:

- You can easily unlink tasks in any of the task views by using the unlink button on the Task tab. Either select the tasks you want to unlink and click the Unlink Tasks button or press Shift+Ctrl+F2. The result depends on the task(s) selected:

  - If you select a single task and then choose Unlink Tasks, Project removes all predecessors and successors for that task.

  - If you select multiple tasks, Project removes all links between any pair of the selected tasks.

  - To remove all links from the project, display any view with a task table and select all tasks by clicking a field name, such as a Task Name, before using Unlink Tasks.

- You can select a successor task and remove its predecessor links by using the Task Information dialog box. For each predecessor listed on the Predecessors tab that you want to remove, click the row for the predecessor and press the Delete key. Clicking OK closes the dialog box and removes those links.

- With a task view in the top pane and the Task form in the bottom pane, you can display the resource and predecessor—or predecessor and successor—details in the bottom pane. Select the task in the top pane. For each predecessor link you want to remove, click its row in the details area and press the Delete key. Click OK to finish the deletion. If you display one of the detail's choices that includes successors, you can select the predecessor task in the top pane and delete the link in the Successors table in the bottom pane.

- In a view that includes a task table, such as the Gantt Chart view, click on the row for the successor task and clear the entry in its Predecessors field by pressing Ctrl+Delete. Remember not to press the Delete key alone because that deletes the entire task!

- You can double-click a linking line in the Gantt Chart or Network Diagram view to display the Task Dependency dialog box and choose Delete to remove the link.

Auditing Task Links

The project schedule is heavily influenced by the linking relationships you establish among tasks. It is easy to accidentally link tasks or break task links, and if you work with Autolink enabled, some changes you have not noticed might have been made. Therefore, you should always review the link relationships carefully before committing to the project schedule. Accidental links can easily distort the finish date of the project.

The Network Diagram view concentrates on the linking relationships by representing each task as a box or node with arrows from predecessor to successor tasks. It is helpful to print the views when using them to review all task links because you see so few tasks on the screen.

➡ *For information about using the Network Diagram view, **see** Chapter 11, "Using Standard Views, Tables, Filters, and Groups to Review Your Schedule," **p. 357**.*

The Gantt Chart view shows the task links as arrows connecting the taskbars, with the arrow always pointing from the predecessor to the successor task. The Gantt Chart view shown earlier in this chapter, with the predecessor and successor details in the Task Form view in the bottom pane, provides a good review of the task links. For the task you have active, the predecessor and successor tasks are listed in the bottom pane, along with any lag or lead associated with the link. Use the Previous and Next buttons in the bottom pane to review the links.

The Relationship Diagram view is perhaps the most useful view for auditing task links (see Figure 7.14). It shows the predecessors and the successors for just the selected task as task nodes, like the Network Diagram view, and is useful for confirming that you have defined the task relationships as you intended. You can display the Relationship Diagram view by itself, but it is most useful when displayed in the bottom pane, beneath another task view in the top pane, such as the Gantt Chart or Network Diagram view. To do this, select the View tab. In the split view group, select the Details check box. In the drop-down next to it, select More Views, Relationship Diagram.

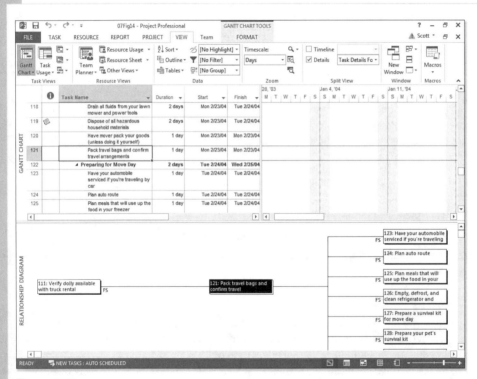

Figure 7.14
The Relationship Diagram view displays the dependency relationships for the task selected. In this case, the window is split, and the task selected in the top pane is displayed in the Relationship Diagram view in the bottom pane.

The task you have selected in the top pane is represented by a box or node in the center of the relationship diagram in the bottom pane, with links to nodes for its predecessors on the left and successors on the right. The type of relationship and any lag or lead is shown next to the linked task nodes. In Figure 7.14, the relationship diagram in the bottom pane makes it clear that Pack Travel Bags and Confirm Travel has multiple successors and one predecessor, and it defines those dependency relationship types.

To display the Relationship Diagram view below the Gantt Chart view, split the window (View tab, Split View, Details) and activate the bottom pane by clicking in it. Choose More Views, and select Relationship Diagram in the More Views box. Then click the Apply button to display the view.

You can select tasks in the top pane to see their predecessors and successors displayed in the bottom pane.

 note

The Relationship Diagram view is a display-only view. You cannot make changes in this view, nor can you print it. You can, however, display the Task Information dialog box for the selected task and make changes there.

 tip

If you select multiple tasks in the top pane, you see only one of the selected tasks in the center of the bottom pane at a time. You can use the horizontal scrollbar in the Relationship Diagram pane to scroll through all the selected tasks. Pressing the Home key displays the view for the first of the selected tasks, and pressing the End key displays the view for the last of the selected tasks. You can use these same techniques to scroll through the tasks if you display the Relationship Diagram view as a full-screen view.

Using the Task Inspector

The Task Inspector is an enhanced version of the Task Drivers feature. It provides detail about why a task is scheduled to start where it is, including any specific predecessor tasks. To open the Task Inspector pane, select the Task tab and click Inspect, Inspect Task. This displays the Task Drivers options in a new pane on the left. The Task Inspector feature displays tasks that are linked to the selected task, as well as their relationship. After the Task Inspector is displayed, you can select any task, and its attributes will be displayed in the Task Inspector pane (see Figure 7.15).

 note

The Task Inspector feature also provides information about how the scheduling engine might reschedule a manually scheduled task and options for repairing scheduling issues if there are any.

tip

The Task Inspector feature is useful when working on projects with complex calendars or a large number of tasks. It is a quick and effective method of reviewing a task's links and progress. In addition, the Task Inspector helps you determine what tasks will be affected if you make any changes to the selected task.

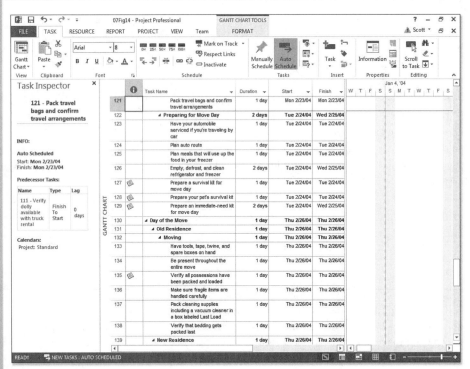

Figure 7.15
Task
Inspector
enables you
to easily
trace rela-
tionships
and depen-
dencies
between
tasks in
your project
schedule.

Using Task Path

Task Path is a new feature for understanding projected task start dates in a properly linked schedule. To use Task Path, go to the Bar Styles group on the Gantt Chart Tools format tab (see Figure 7.16). By default, none of the tasks paths are highlighted. Select a highlighting option and then select a task. The Gantt chart bars colors will change to highlight the task path type you selected.

There are four task path types:

- **Predecessors**—When selected, highlights every preceding linked task.

- **Driving Predecessors**—When selected, highlights tasks that actually affect your selected tasks' predicted start date.

- **Successors**—When selected, highlights linked tasks that follow your selected task.

- **Driven Successors**—When selected, highlights linked tasks whose predicted start dates are affected by your selected task.

Figure 7.16
Task Path adds still
another way to better
understand the Project
predictive engine.

Defining Constraints

If a project has a fixed start date, you probably want Project to schedule tasks as soon as possible after the start of the project to minimize the overall duration of the project. For the same reason, if a project is scheduled from a fixed finish date, you want Project to schedule tasks as late as possible so that they are close to the fixed finish date and keep the duration of the project as short as possible. This assumes that tasks are auto-scheduled; manually scheduled tasks stay exactly where you put them. Or, they don't have start dates at all.

However, there are many circumstances in which a task must be scheduled to start or finish by a specific date. These fixed-date requirements are called *task constraints* in Project. The constraint types are classified as *inflexible* if they present a barrier to an expanding project schedule, and *flexible* if they do not. The As Soon As Possible (ASAP) and As Late As Possible (ALAP) constraints present no barriers in any situation and are always classified as flexible. Inflexible constraints might be due to requirements from outside the project, or they might be the result of temporary deadlines imposed by the project manager. Constraints that are internal to the project might be such things as progress reviews and reevaluations of the schedule as each major phase of the project nears completion. External constraints might be the deadlines specified by customers, contractors, the government, or policies within the organization that are external to the project. The following are some specific examples of task constraints:

- You are planning a Fourth of July fireworks display, and the fireworks need to be delivered a day in advance to have enough setup time. The fireworks delivery task must be completed by July 3rd.

- An alteration facility needs two weeks to alter a bride's dress, so the dress-fitting task must be completed at least two weeks before the wedding date.

- An environmental agency is examining erosion over a specific period of time. The tests must begin on a specific date, so the test preparation task must be completed before the test date.

- Progress reports are due at specific intervals throughout the project. The person in charge of compiling the reports must have them ready on specific dates.

In all cases, either the start or finish date of a task is linked to a specific date in the schedule, and you want Project to take this constraint into consideration when scheduling the task.

Understanding Types of Constraints

Constraints are defined by entries in the Constraint Type and Constraint Date task fields on the Advanced tab in the Task Information dialog box (see Figure 7.17). By default, a new task you create has no constraint date. When you add a task to a project that is scheduled from a fixed start date, Project supplies the default entry As Soon As Possible in the Constraint Type field. This entry means that there are no fixed-date requirements—no constraints—and the task will be scheduled as soon as possible after its predecessor requirements are met. The Constraints Date field for the task is given the default entry NA (the Constraint Date field is not applicable because there are no constraints).

Figure 7.17
On the Advanced tab of the Task Information dialog box, you can set constraint types and constraint dates in the appropriate fields.

If the project is scheduled from a fixed finished date, Project supplies new tasks with the default entry As Late As Possible in the Constraint Type field. This entry also means that there is no constraint, and the task will be scheduled as close to the finish date of the project as possible. Project considers the schedule for successor tasks, which must also finish before the project's finish date, when scheduling the task. Again, the Constraint Date field has the default entry NA.

Besides using the Task Information dialog box, you can insert the Constraint Type and Constraint Date fields as columns in a task table. The Constraint Type field provides a drop-down list of the eight possible constraint types that you can use to define any possible date constraint. These types are described in Table 7.2. Constraint types are usually referred to by the acronym shown in the first column in the table.

Table 7.2 Constraint Types

Acronym	Constraint Type	Description
ASAP	As Soon As Possible	Marks a task as not constrained and not requiring a constraint date. The task will be scheduled as soon as its predecessor requirements are met.
ALAP	As Late As Possible	Delays the task as long as possible, considering the scheduling requirements of its successor task, all of which must finish before the project finish date. This constraint type does not require a constraint date.
SNET	Start No Earlier Than	Means the task must start on or after the defined constraint date.
SNLT	Start No Later Than	Means the task must start on or before the defined constraint date.
FNET	Finish No Earlier Than	Means the task must finish on or after the defined constraint date.
FNLT	Finish No Later Than	Means the task must finish on or before the defined constraint date.
MSO	Must Start On	Means the task must start exactly on the defined constraint date.
MFO	Must Finish On	Means the task must finish exactly on the defined constraint date.

The duration of a sequence of tasks can expand for a variety of reasons. For instance, new tasks might be inserted in the sequence, or existing tasks might experience *duration inflation*—an increase in duration values. In a project with a fixed start date, the expansion of duration pushes tasks to later dates. If the tasks in the sequence have the constraint type ASAP, they can be rescheduled to later dates without limit as the sequence expands. In a project with a fixed finish date, the expansion pushes tasks back to earlier dates. If the tasks in a sequence have the constraint type ALAP, they can be rescheduled to earlier dates without limit as the sequence expands.

 note

The first two constraint types in Table 7.2, ASAP and ALAP, have no associated constraint date. In fact, they are really nonconstraints.

The constraint types are classified as *inflexible* if they present a barrier to an expanding project schedule, and *flexible* if they do not. The ASAP and ALAP constraints present no barriers in any situation and are always classified as flexible.

The last two constraints in Table 7.2, MSO and MFO, are considered inflexible in all circumstances because they can block the expansion of a task sequence. If the linked sequence expands so much that it requires a task with one of these constraints to move beyond an MSO or MFO constraint date, Project cannot honor both the defined links and the defined constraints at the same time because they contradict one another. By default, Project honors the constraint and ignores the dependency link, forcing the constrained task to overlap its linked task in a way that is contrary to the intent of the link. See the section "Deciding to Honor Links or Honor Constraints," later in this chapter, for information about changing this default.

Figure 7.18 illustrates the conflict between a task link and an inflexible constraint. The milestone Product Ready for Delivery must be completed by September 9, 2013. It has a Finish-to-Start link to its predecessor, Prepare for Shipping. The predecessor finishes in time for the milestone to meet its deadline in Scenario A. In Scenario B, however, the predecessor has been delayed because of duration inflation in an earlier task, and now it is impossible to honor both the link and the constraint.

Project enables you to choose to honor the constraint or the link. Honoring the link would push the milestone to a later date. In this example, the milestone has been chosen over the link, and Project schedules the milestone on its constraint date, which requires that it ignore the intent of the link. The predecessor finishes after the milestone's date, causing the linking line to wrap back around as though the link were defined with lead time.

note

Although not a constraint, the Deadline feature discussed later in this section provides a visual indication of a deadline on a task and will alert you to missed deadlines.

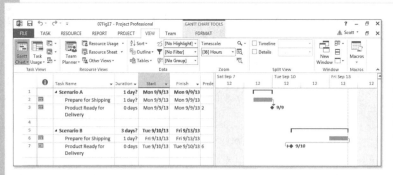

Figure 7.18
Sometimes, you have to choose to honor a constraint or a link, as the two conflict each other. In this example, in Scenario B, the constraint was chosen over the link.

In a fixed start-date project, duration inflation in predecessor tasks tends to push successor tasks to later dates. Constraints that prohibit successor tasks from being rescheduled to later dates are therefore inflexible constraints. Thus, SNLT and FNLT constraint types are called inflexible in fixed start-date projects.

In a fixed finish-date project, duration inflation in successor tasks tends to push predecessor tasks to earlier dates. Constraints that prohibit predecessor tasks from being rescheduled to earlier dates are inflexible constraints. Consequently, the SNET and FNET constraint types are called inflexible in fixed finish-date projects. But the SNLT and FNLT constraints are flexible in fixed finish-date projects.

If you change a fixed start-date project to a fixed finish-date project, SNET and FNET constraints change from flexible to inflexible. Similarly, the flexible SNLT and FNLT constraints in a fixed finish-date project become inflexible if you switch to fixed start-date scheduling. If you change the project scheduling type, you should look for constraints that switched from flexible to inflexible and consider modifying them to avoid potential conflicts as the schedule changes.

note

Although the SNET and FNET constraints are flexible for the expansion of the fixed start-date schedule, they nevertheless create a barrier if you are attempting to compress the project's duration. To shorten the overall project, you must shorten the critical path, and if a task with one of these constraints is on the critical path, it can block your efforts. Although you might shorten the duration of its predecessors, an SNET or FNET task will not move to an earlier date, and the critical path will not be shortened.

Similarly, in fixed finish-date projects, the SNLT and FNLT constraints are called flexible because they do not inhibit the natural expansion of the project. However, they can block compression of the project duration.

 caution

If you change a project from a fixed start date to a fixed finish date, the ASAP constraint type for existing tasks is replaced with ALAP constraints. However, all new tasks are given the new default ALAP constraint type. Likewise, changing a fixed finish-date project to a fixed start-date project leaves the ALAP constraints unchanged, but the new tasks are set to ASAP. Neither of these results affects the duration of the project, but some tasks are scheduled earlier or later than they could possibly be without affecting the start or finish of the project.

One of the most common mistakes made by novice users of Microsoft Project is unintentionally creating a constraint when working with auto-scheduled tasks. Any time you type a date into the Start or Finish field for a task, or drag the taskbar to a new date in the Gantt Chart view, Project creates a constraint to honor that date, unless the task is manually scheduled. When you create a recurring task, Project also creates a constraint for each occurrence.

Fortunately, Project always makes these flexible constraints. Therefore, if you type in the start date for a task in a fixed start-date project, Project changes the constraint type to SNET and places the date in the Constraint Date field. The task is then scheduled to start on the date you typed (even if its predecessors would allow it to be scheduled earlier), but it can be freely moved to later dates if its predecessors experience duration inflation. Similarly, in a fixed finish-date project, the flexible constraints SNLT and FNLT are supplied when you specify start or finish dates for tasks.

When a task has a constraint type other than ASAP or ALAP, Project displays an icon in the Indicators field of the Gantt Chart view. The icon looks like a calendar with either a blue or a red dot in the middle. A blue dot signifies a flexible constraint, and a red dot signifies an inflexible constraint. Table 7.3 summarizes the flexible/inflexible status for the eight constraint types in both fixed start-date and fixed finish-date projects, and describes the indicators you see for them.

 tip

If you decide to permanently change a project from fixed start date to fixed finish date (or vice versa) and want to change all the old default constraints to the new default (such as replacing ASAP with ALAP), you can use Project's Replace command. For example, type **As Soon As Possible** in the Find What box, type **As Late As Possible** in the Replace With box, and select Equals in the Test box.

note

Some constraints also affect the critical path. If you apply a Must Start On or Must Finish On constraint, Project automatically makes the task a critical task. If you are scheduling from a fixed start date, an ALAP constraint makes the task critical. If you are scheduling from a fixed finish date, an ASAP constraint makes the task critical.

Table 7.3   Flexible and Inflexible Constraints and Their Indicators

Constraint Type	Fixed Start Date	Fixed Finish Date
ASAP	Flexible (no indicator)	Flexible (no indicator)
ALAP	Flexible (no indicator)	Flexible (no indicator)
SNET	Flexible (blue dot)	Inflexible (red dot)
FNET	Flexible (blue dot)	Inflexible (red dot)
SNLT	Inflexible (red dot)	Flexible (blue dot)
FNLT	Inflexible (red dot)	Flexible (blue dot)
MFO	Inflexible (red dot)	Inflexible (red dot)
MSO	Inflexible (red dot)	Inflexible (red dot)

Entering Task Constraints

As mentioned previously, if you enter a date in a task's start or finish field or drag the taskbar in the Gantt Chart view, you create a flexible constraint for the task, unless it is a manually scheduled task. You can also create task constraints by using the Schedule Tasks Project Guide or by filling in the Constraint Type and Constraint Date fields in the Task Information dialog box. If you want to create or modify many task constraints, you might want to enter the constraint fields to the Entry table or display the Task Details Form view, which makes the constraint fields available for editing.

 note

No matter which method you use for creating constraints, if you create an inflexible constraint, the Planning Wizard displays a warning. More detailed information about the Planning Wizard's warning is covered at the end of this section.

Creating Constraints in the Task Information Dialog Box

To enter task constraints in the Task Information dialog box, follow these steps:

1. Display the Task Information dialog box by double-clicking the task you want to modify.

2. Select the Advanced tab (see Figure 7.19).

tip

Because creating inflexible constraints can affect a schedule so significantly, it is very important that you document why a constraint has been defined. You should always add an explanation to the Notes field to explain the purpose of the constraint. This is especially important information if you are sharing the project file with colleagues or if someone else takes over the project. It is also a valuable reminder if there is a later conflict that you must resolve.

Consider using the Manually Scheduled task mode if you are unsure whether a constraint is valid. Manually scheduled tasks appear differently on the Gantt Chart, and the scheduling engine is free to calculate what it would do if the task were auto scheduled.

When you type a constraint date, you can also include the time of day with the date. If you do not include the time of day, Project supplies one for you. Using the default values from the Calendar tab of the Options dialog box, Project includes the default start time for all constraint types that restrict the start of a task and the default end time for all constraints that restrict the finish of a task.

Figure 7.19
The Advanced tab of the Task Information dialog box provides fields to create constraints.

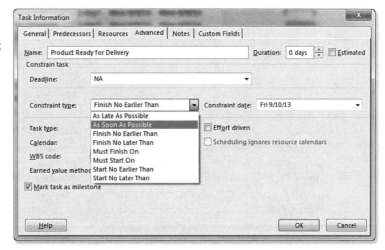

3. In the Constraint Type field, select the constraint type from the drop-down list.

4. For constraints that require a date, which are all the constraints except ASAP and ALAP, enter the constraint date in the Constraint Date box. Enter the time of day if you want a time other than the default start time or default end time.

   If you do not enter a date, Project uses the task's current start or finish date as the constraint date—the start date and time for start date constraints, and the finish date and time for finish date constraints.

5. Select the Notes tab and add a note explaining the reason for the constraint.

6. Click OK to complete the constraint definition.

Creating Constraints in a Task Table

If you need to create or edit a number of constraints, you can display the Constraint Dates table in the Gantt Chart view (see Figure 7.20). This is also a good view to use when reviewing the constraints in a project. To display the Constraint Dates table and create a constraint, follow these steps:

1. Display a task view that includes a table, such as a Gantt Chart.

2. Select the View tab. In the Data group, select the Tables control. Select More Tables to open the More Tables dialog box. In the More Tables dialog box, select Constraint Dates and click Apply.

	Task Name	Duration	Constraint Type	Constraint Date	Add New Colum
1	Task A	1 day?	Must Finish On	Mon 11/12/12	
2	Task B	5 days	As Soon As Possible	NA	
3	Task C	3 days	Start No Earlier Than	Mon 11/19/12	
4	Task D	1 day	Must Finish On	Mon 11/12/12	
5	Project Complete	0 days	As Soon As Possible	NA	

Figure 7.20
The Constraint Dates table enables you to set task constraints in the Constraint Type and Constraint Date fields.

3. On the row for a task you want to constrain, use the drop-down list in the Constraint Type column to choose the type. Press Enter to assign the constraint. As mentioned previously, if you have defined an inflexible constraint, the Planning Wizard makes you confirm that you want to keep the constraint (see Figure 7.21). Project supplies a default date in the Constraint Date column, unless the constraint type is ASAP or ALAP. To do so, Project uses the task's start date and time if the task's start is constrained, and the finish date and time if its finish is constrained. For additional details on the Planning Wizard warning, see "Responding to Warnings from the Planning Wizard," later in this chapter.

4. If appropriate, type a different date or use the drop-down calendar to select one. Enter the time of day if you do not want Project to supply the default time.

 note

To return to the Entry table with its task fields, repeat step 2, but select Entry.

You can add the constrained fields to any task table. See "Creating a Modified Constraint Dates Table," later in this chapter.

Creating Constraints in the Task Details Form

The Task Details form provides easy access to the constraint fields. It is best used in the bottom pane with the Gantt Chart view or another task view in the top pane (see Figure 7.21). To enter task constraints in the Task Details form, follow these steps:

1. Display the Gantt Chart view or other task view in the top pane and split the window (select the Task tab, check the Details box in the Split View group). The Task form is the default selection in the drop-down.

2. Right-click over the Task Details form and choose the Notes details for display so that you can document the reasons for the constraint.

You can select the task to be constrained in the top pane, or use the Previous and Next buttons in the bottom pane to scroll to the task. Then in the bottom pane, select the constraint type from the drop-down list in the Constraint box, and enter the constraint date and time in the Date field.

Figure 7.21
The Task Details Form view in the bottom pane of a split window provides a means for you to define task constraints, as well as to attach notes as to the reason for the constraint.

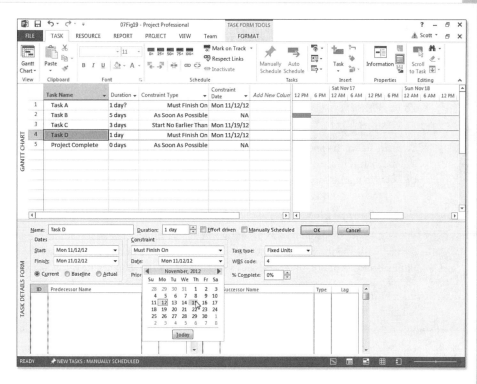

Responding to Warnings from the Planning Wizard

As mentioned previously, if you define an inflexible constraint for a task that has dependency links, you create a potential conflict between the requirements of the constraint and the requirements of the links. When you create an inflexible constraint, the Planning Wizard warns you that your action could create a problem either now or in the future, and it makes you confirm the action. The Planning Wizard displays the dialog box in Figure 7.22 to warn you and gives you three options. You must select the third option to create an inflexible constraint.

Figure 7.22
Whenever you create a conflict by placing a date constraint on a task, Project displays a warning, confirming further actions.

The three options include the following:

- You can select Cancel, which is the default. If you leave the default option selected, you can click either OK or Cancel to cancel the action. Either way, no constraint will be set.

- You can select the second option, Continue, but avoid the conflict by using a Finish No Earlier Than constraint instead. Depending on the type of the constraint originally set, the wording in this option might vary. If you select this option and click OK, Project substitutes the flexible version of the same constraint. For example, if you define an FNLT constraint in a project that is scheduled from a fixed start date, Project offers to change it to an FNET constraint.

- You can select the third option, Continue. A Finish No Later Than constraint is set. The wording in this option might vary, depending on the type of constraint you tried to schedule. You must both select this option and click OK to actually create the constraint you specified.

If you confirm the creation of the inflexible constraint, and the constraint creates and immediate conflict with the task's dependency links, the Planning Wizard displays another warning that requests you to confirm that you want to go ahead and create the conflict (see Figure 7.23).

You must choose whether to cancel, in which case the constraint is not created, or to continue, in which case the constraint is created and the scheduling conflict exists. Again, you must choose the Continue option before you click OK to actually create the constraint.

The Planning Wizard warning in Figure 7.23 is also displayed by another action that causes a constraint date to be in conflict with a dependency link—for example, if you create new links or increase the duration of a predecessor task so much that the constraint date becomes a barrier.

Figure 7.23
The Planning Wizard warns you again if an inflexible constraint is created that interferes with the task's dependency links.

The Planning Wizard warning that a constraint conflict had been identified includes a task ID number to help you troubleshoot the conflict (refer to Figure 7.23). The ID number is usually the ID of the predecessor for the task that has an inflexible constraint. In a fixed finish-date project, it would be the successor task's ID. However, in some instances, the ID number is for the constrained task itself, as in Figure 7.23. Thus, in Figure 7.23, the message identifies Task 2, the task that is being given an inflexible constraint.

For ways to find and resolve constraint conflicts, see the sections, "Finding and Reviewing Tasks That Have Constraints" and "Resolving Conflicts Caused by Constraints," later in this chapter.

> **note**
> Project does not display the second warning if you have deselected the Tasks Will Always Honor Their Constraint Dates check box in the Schedule tab of the Options dialog. More information is discussed in the next section, "Deciding to Honor Links or Honor Constraints."

 caution
If you see this warning from the Planning Wizard and choose to continue and allow the conflict to be created, you should make a note of the task ID number because you will not see this message again and you need to do something to resolve the conflict.

Deciding to Honor Links or Honor Constraints

As mentioned earlier in this chapter, in the section "Understanding Types of Constraints," when you define an inflexible constraint for a task, it might be impossible for Project to honor both the constraint and one or more links that you have defined for the task. When this type of conflict arises, Project's default scheduling method is to honor the constraint definition and ignore the link definition, as shown in Scenario B in Figure 7.18 earlier in this chapter.

When Project honors inflexible constraint dates, the inflexible constraints are called *hard constraints*. You can change Project's default behavior and force it to honor a task's links instead of its constraint. Select the File tab, Options, Schedule tab, and clear the Tasks Will Always Honor Their Constraint Dates check box (see Figure 7.24). note that this is different from the Respect Links button in the Schedule group on the Task tab. The Respect Links button moves a selected task (usually a manually scheduled task) in accordance with any predecessor relationships it has.

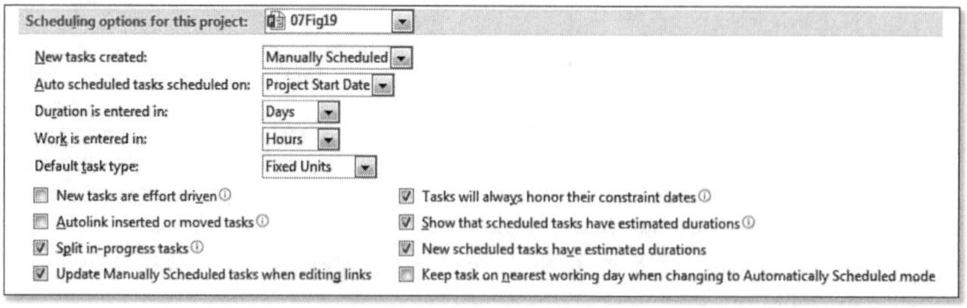

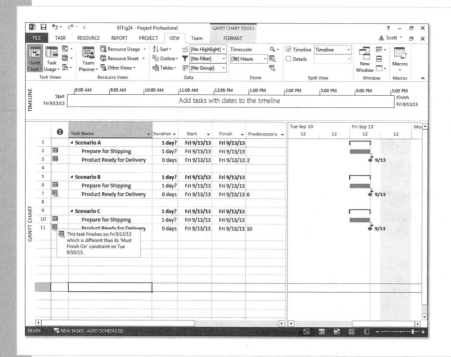

Figure 7.24
Clear the Tasks Will Always Honor Their Constraint Dates box, which tells Project to honor tasks' links instead of constraints.

In Figure 7.25, another set of tasks, Scenario C, is added to those from Figure 7.18 (discussed previously) to show how Project schedules soft constraints to honor their links instead of their constraint dates.

Figure 7.25
In Scenario C, a soft constraint is applied, so Project honors the link rather than the milestone's constraint, and the milestone is scheduled later than its constraint date.

In Scenario A, there is no constraint conflict. In Scenario B, the product ready for delivery milestone is a hard constraint and is scheduled to honor its constraint date. In Scenario C, a soft constraint is scheduled to honor its link. Therefore, it falls three days after the constraint date (in this case, on September 13, 2013).

If you go back into the Options dialog box and select the Tasks Will Always Honor Their Constraint Dates check box again (in other words, turn soft constraints into hard constraints again), the presence of any existing constraint conflicts in the project causes Project to display the warning shown in Figure 7.26. You should make a note of the task identified at the start of the warning message so that you can find the tasks involved in the conflict and resolve the issue.

Figure 7.26
The Planning Wizard warning box appears if you turn soft constraints into hard constraints.

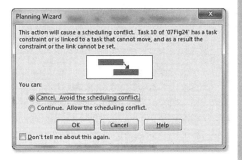

If all the links and constraint definitions are both appropriate and necessary to the project, it is best to use soft constraints (in other words, to have tasks honor their links) for the following reasons:

- **Honoring links is usually most realistic**—The project manager needs to revise the schedule so that the constraints can be met while honoring the links. This requires shortening the duration of the linked sequence of predecessors (or successors, in a fixed finish-date project) that have caused the conflict.

- **Honoring links causes the Missed Constraint indicator to appear in the Indicators column**—This is the only reliable way to find constraint conflicts in a schedule. You can scan the Indicators column to see whether you find tasks that have the indicator and then do something to the schedule to remove the indicator. Honoring constraints, on the other hand, merely causes the linking line to curve around the task that has a conflict, which is visually no different than a link with a lead time.

> *For additional information on techniques and tools you can use to find problem areas in your schedule, **see** Chapter 12, "Performing a Schedule Reality Check," **p. 411.***

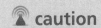
caution

These missed links are difficult to find in the schedule; you have to carefully scan all linking lines in the entire timeline, and often the need for corrective action is overlooked until it's too late.

tip

Based on these two points, it is recommended that you clear the Tasks Will Always Honor Their Constraint Dates check box as described previously and make it the default for all your new projects by clicking the Set as Default button. However, be aware that clearing the check box means that you no longer get the warning shown in Figure 7.22 when you create a conflict between links and constraints. In this case, you have to diligently search for them, as described in the next section.

Finding and Reviewing Tasks That Have Constraints

Just as it is important to double-check the task-sequencing links before committing to a project schedule, you should also review all the task constraints to be sure they are warranted and correctly defined. At the very least, you should attempt to identify any constraint conflicts and resolve them, or your project schedule will be unrealistic.

To review the constraint conflicts, disable the Tasks Will Always Honor Their Constraint Dates option on the Schedule tab of the Options dialog, as described in the previous section. Then, scroll down to the list of tasks in the Gantt Chart view while you watch for the Missed Constraint indicator in the Indicators column. If your project is large, it will be easier if you also filter the task list for constrained tasks, as described next. When you find a task with the Missed Constraint indicator, follow the guidelines outlined in the section, "Resolving Conflicts Caused by Constraints," later in this chapter.

If your project is scheduled from a fixed start date, you can use the Tasks with Fixed Dates filter to display the tasks that have a constraint other than ASAP, for both flexible and inflexible constraint types. This filter also selects tasks that have an actual start date entered; so, if you apply this filter after you start tracking work on the project, it also selects the tasks that have started. However, if you use it during the planning stage of a fixed start-date project, it selects just the tasks that have a nondefault constraint.

To apply the Tasks with Fixed Dates filter, select the View tab, Filter, More Filters, and select Tasks with Fixed Dates from the list of filters. Click Highlight to highlight the selected tasks, or click Apply to hide all but the selected tasks.

Microsoft Project selects all tasks that do not have the constraint type ASAP, as well as those that have a start date entered. Project also displays the summary tasks for the selected tasks, which is helpful for remembering where the task falls in the outline in a large project. You can scroll through the filtered task list to easily review the constrained tasks.

When you are finished using the filter, press the function key F3 to clear the filter, or select No Filter from the drop-down list on the Filter tool.

 tip

A convenient view for reviewing constraints is the Gantt Chart view, with the Task Details Form view and the Notes field in the bottom pane, as described in the section, "Entering Task Constraints," earlier in this chapter.

tip

A practical way to review tasks that have constraints is to display the Constraint Dates table in the Gantt Chart view, as described earlier in the section "Entering Task Constraints." Even better, you can create a customized version of this table that is more useful (see the section "Creating a Modified Constraint Dates Table," later in this chapter). Select the View tab and select Display Auto Filter from the Filter drop-down in the Data group. In the title cell of the Constraint Type column, click the AutoFilter drop-down list arrow. The drop-down list includes the names of all constraint types that appear at least once in that column. Click one of the constraint type names in the list, and Project displays all tasks that have that constraint type, along with their summary tasks.

You can create much more useful filters for finding inflexible constraints, for both fixed start-date and fixed finish-date projects. If you often work with fixed finish-date projects or want to be able to isolate constrained tasks after tracking has begun, or if you want to find scheduling conflicts, these filters are well worth adding to your Global template.

Removing Task Constraints

To remove a task constraint, simply change the constraint type to ASAP (or ALAP in a fixed finish-date project) using one of the methods discussed earlier in this chapter for creating constraints. Setting the task to Manually Scheduled mode will not erase the constraint, although it will render it inactive and uneditable.

To return several tasks to an unconstrained state, follow these steps:

1. Select all the tasks you want to change.

2. Display the Multiple Task Information dialog box by clicking the Task Information tool on the Task tab.

3. Choose the Advanced tab and select As Soon As Possible or As Late As Possible from the Constraint Type drop-down list.

4. Click OK to make the changes in all the selected tasks.

To remove all constraints in the project, select a column heading in the task list table and choose the As Soon As Possible or As Late As Possible constraint type in the Task Information dialog box.

Resolving Conflicts Caused by Constraints

As previously discussed, when you add an inflexible constraint to a linked task or link a task that has an inflexible constraint, the Planning Wizard displays the potential conflict warning shown in Figure 7.22. If Project is honoring task constraints (the default) and the potential conflict becomes a reality, the Planning Wizard gives you the warning shown in Figure 7.23. This can happen when you complete the constraint definition, or the link definition, or it can happen later, as a result of changes in the schedule that push the

 caution

You can discontinue the display of Planning Wizard warnings by selecting the Don't Tell Me About This Again check box. However, you might then be unaware of the conflict. You should leave the Planning Wizard active to warn you about scheduling conflicts.

linked task past its constraint. If Project is not honoring task constraints, you do not get the warning shown in Figure 7.23, but you see the Missed Constraint indicator in the Indicator column.

If you see the Planning Wizard warning and choose to create the constraint conflict, you should make a note of the task ID number in the message because you will not see this warning again. You need to examine that task and the task to which it is linked to find a way to resolve the conflict.

> ### 🄌 tip
>
> When you first open a project document, you can press F9 (the Calculate key) to force Project to display its most recent scheduling error message. The message you see should be similar to the one displayed in Figure 7.26. However, you only see one warning message like Figure 7.26, even if there are several constraint conflicts.

The four fundamental ways to resolve a constraint date scheduling conflict are as follows:

- Reassess the need for the constraint and the conditions that make the constraint necessary. Substitute a flexible constraint, if possible.

- Reevaluate the dependency relationships in the sequence of tasks that are linked to the constrained task. Be certain that all links are necessary and defined to allow maximum overlapping of tasks, using Start-to-Start, Finish-to-Finish, and lead time, where reasonable.

- Change the duration of individual tasks that are in the linked sequence. You can change the duration by entering a number and time unit directly into the Duration field on the Task Value table.

- Change the task mode to Manually Scheduled. This will not eliminate the underlying problem, if there is one, but it will "inactivate" the conflict as far as Project is concerned.

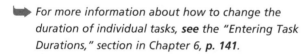 *For more information about how to change the duration of individual tasks, **see** the "Entering Task Durations," section in Chapter 6, **p. 141**.*

You must choose the course of action that makes the most sense in your project. Frequently, a careful review of the tasks, constraints, and task relationships reveals that new definitions are called for. Conditions might have changed since the original definitions were entered, and the definitions might now be more restrictive than they need to be.

> ### tip
>
> Check to see whether a task note exists that might explain the need for the constraint. This might give you some guidance about how to resolve the conflict.

Creating a Modified Constraint Dates Table

It is easier to analyze constraint conflicts if you modify the standard Constraints Dates table to include the Indicators, Predecessors, and Successors fields. The Indicators field enables you to see the Constraint Conflict indicators (if Project is honoring task links instead of constraint dates). The Predecessors field enables you to identify the links that conflict with the constraints in a fixed start-date project, and the Successors field serves the same function in a fixed finish-date project.

To customize the table, follow these steps:

1. In a task view such as the Gantt Chart view, right-click over the Select All cell (the table's upper-left cell over the ID number column) and choose More Tables from the shortcut menu (or select the View tab, Tables, More Tables).

2. In the Tables list in the More Tables dialog box, select Constraint Dates and click the Copy button.

3. In the Name box, change the name for the new table if desired.

4. To insert the Indicators field, click on the row below ID in the Field Name column and click the Insert Row tool to insert a blank row.

5. Select Indicators in the Name column. Press Enter to add the field.

6. Repeat step 5 in the blank rows at the bottom of the list of field names to add the fields Predecessors and Successors. You should change the Align Data entry to Left for both of these fields.

7. Select the Show in Menu check box if you want this table to appear on the menu of table names.

8. Click OK to create the table, and click Apply to display it.

Performing Advanced Actions on Tasks

You can perform several advanced actions on tasks, such as entering task deadlines, filtering for missed deadlines, splitting tasks, and creating task calendars. These actions, and the methodology behind them, are discussed in the following sections.

Entering Deadline Dates

You saw earlier in the chapter that you can define a constraint date for a task when the task must be finished by a certain date. You can also use the Deadline Date field to record a task's finish deadline. The Gantt Chart view shows a deadline marker next to the taskbar, and if the task finish is scheduled after the deadline date, a special icon appears in the Indicators column to alert you that the task finish is scheduled after the deadline date (see Figure 7.27).

 note

If you are highlighting critical tasks, a missed deadline also turns the task into a critical task.

Unlike an inflexible constraint date, there are no conflict error messages or warnings when a deadline is missed. However, you can apply the Tasks with Deadlines filter to select all the tasks that have deadlines defined, and you can check the Indicators column for the Missed Deadline icon. To create a custom filter to select missed deadlines, see the "Filtering for Missed Deadline Dates" section later in this chapter.

Figure 7.27
Notice the downward pointing arrow to the right of Task 1's taskbar, representing the deadline, and the indicator in the Indicators column, signifying that that deadline is scheduled to be missed.

An especially useful application of the Deadline Date field is for tasks that have a constraint date defined for the task start, and also a deadline for the task finish. Because you can have only one constraint date per task, the deadline date enables you to define requirements for both the start and finish of a task.

You can define deadline dates in the Task Information dialog box, or in the Deadline column if you add that field to a table. When you enter a deadline date, you can also enter the time of day. If you fail to enter the time of day, Project supplies the default End Time, as defined on the Calendar tab of the Options dialog box (5:00 p.m., by default).

To define a deadline date in the Task Information dialog box, follow these steps:

1. Select the task and activate the Task Information dialog box by either double-clicking the task or using the Task Information tool.

2. Select the Advanced tab (see Figure 7.28).

3. Type a date, including the time of day if appropriate, in the Deadline field, or activate the drop-down box and choose the date in the Calendar control. To remove a deadline, type NA instead of a date. You can enter a time of day after the date is entered.

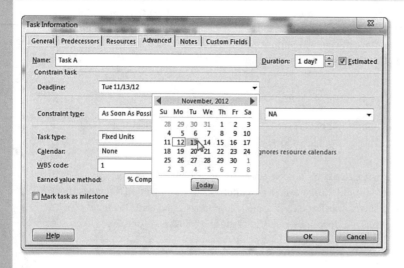

Figure 7.28
You can also set deadlines in the Task Information dialog box.

4. Click OK to complete the definition.

If you want to enter many deadlines, or if you want to review all the deadlines, you might want to add the Deadline field to a task table (refer to Figure 7.27). Click the column heading where you want to insert the field and press the Insert key. Select the Deadline field. You can then enter deadline dates in this column for any task.

Project includes a built-in filter that lets you select the task for which deadlines are defined. You might want to insert the Deadline field in a table to review the deadlines. Otherwise, you have to use the Task Information form for each selected task to see the deadline date.

To apply the filter, select the View tab, Filter, More Filters. Choose the filter named Tasks with Deadlines to hide all but the tasks that have deadlines in the display. If you want to merely highlight the tasks that have deadlines, click the Highlight button instead of the Apply button to display the full task list with tasks that have deadlines highlighted.

> **note**
>
> Project does not provide a filter for *missed deadlines*. See the following section, "Filtering for Missed Deadline Dates."

Filtering for Missed Deadline Dates

The standard Tasks with Deadlines filter selects all tasks with deadline dates, whether the deadlines are missed or not. The deadline is missed when the task's Finish date is later than the date in the task's Deadline field.

To create a filter that selects only missed deadline dates, follow these steps:

1. Select the View tab, Filter, More Filters.

2. Select the Tasks with Deadlines filter name and choose the Copy button.

3. Type Missed Deadline Dates or another suitable name in the Name text box.

4. In the table of criteria, select the first blank cell on the second row (under the column named And/Or) and type **and**.

5. In the Field Name column, type **Finish**.

6. In the Test column, type **is greater than**.

7. In the Value(s) column, type **[Deadline]**.

8. Select the Show in Menu check box if you want this filter on the Filtered For menu.

9. Click OK to complete the filter, and click Apply if you want to apply it immediately.

Splitting Tasks

Normally Project schedules work on a task to continue uninterrupted until the task is complete. If you know that there will be interruptions or periods of inactivity on a task, or if after starting work on the task you find that you must interrupt the work and resume at a later date, you can split the task into two or more scheduled segments.

Several examples of tasks that would be good candidates for task splitting include the following:

- Suppose someone is scheduled to work on a task, but a week-long vacation is planned during the time he or she is scheduled to work on this task. The work on the task is going to stop during the week the person is gone and resume when the person returns. You can incorporate the interruption in the planning stage of the project by splitting the task around the vacation.

- Suppose that a specialized employee is working on a low-priority task when a task with a higher priority requires his or her attention. You can slip the low-priority task and reschedule the remainder of its work after the higher-priority task is complete.

- Suppose work on a task has already begun but nothing has recently been done on the task. The remaining work needs to be rescheduled to start now or in the future. You can split the task at the point where work is completed and reschedule the remaining work to a later date.

 note

A task can have an unlimited number of splits. When you link to a task that is split, the link is to the task. You cannot create a link to a split segment of a task.

The easiest way to split a task is in the Gantt Chart view, where you use the mouse to split a taskbar and drag the right-hand segment to the right to resume at a later date. To split a task in the Gantt Chart view, follow these steps:

1. Activate the Gantt Chart view, and select the task you want to split.

 tip

When using your mouse to create a split task, it is recommended that you modify the timescale of the Gantt Chart to make the action more accurate and easier to perform.

To modify the timescale, right-click on the current timescale in the Gantt Chart and select Timescale. Use the Top Tier, Middle Tier, and Bottom Tier tabs to decrease the default units. For example, you might want to modify the timescale to include only two tiers, Middle and Bottom, where the Middle tier displays days and the Bottom tier displays hours. This is a very detailed timescale and might not work for longer tasks. In this case, you might want to increase the timescale to be able to see the task in its entirety.

2. Select the Split Task tool in the Schedule group on the Task tab on the Standard toolbar or right-click the taskbar and click the Split Task icon from the shortcut menu above the bar. The Split Task information box appears (see Figure 7.29).

3. Position the mouse pointer over the taskbar where you want to split, but do not click yet. As you hover the pointer right and left over the taskbar, the Start date in the Split Task information box tells you the date where the split will occur after you click the mouse.

4. When you locate the correct Start date, you can either click the taskbar or click and drag. The different results are as follows:

   - If you click the taskbar, Project inserts a split in the schedule, starting on the date in the Split Task information box, at the default start time of day (normally 8:00 a.m.). The length of the split or interruption is one unit of the time unit used in the minor scale of the timescale. If the minor scale is days, even if it displays every third day, the split is one day.

Figure 7.29
The Split
Task infor-
mation box
appears
when you
choose to
split a task.

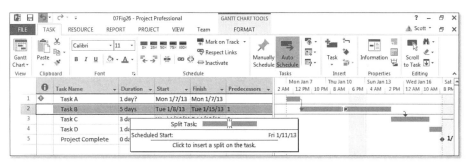

■ If you click and drag, you insert the split as you would by
clicking the taskbar, but you also drag the remainder of the
task on the right to begin on another date, thus modifying the length of the split. As soon as you start dragging,
the Split Task information box is replaced by the Task
Information dialog box, which tells you the start date of the
new segment (that is, that date when the task will resume) and
the finish date for the task. Release the mouse when
your reach the date on which you want the new segment to
start.

 tip

Watch the start and finish
dates in the Split Task information box carefully to determine when this segment of
the split task resumes.

➥ *For additional information on creating splits in tasks
and assignments, **see** the "Splitting Tasks" section in
Chapter 24, **p. 818**.*

After you have split a task, resting the pointer over a split segment
displays the Task information box for just that segment, telling you
the start date, the finish date, and duration for that segment.

Dragging the first segment of a split task moves all segments of
the task together. Holding down the Shift key as you drag a later
segment also moves all segments together.

You can drag any but the first segment to the right or left to
change the start and finish of that segment of the task, as long as
you don't touch another segment of the task.

You can remove a split (that is, rejoin segments of a split task) by
dragging the segment on the right toward the left until it touches
the next segment.

 note

You can also split tasks in
the Task Usage view, and
if resources are assigned
to a task, you can split the
resource assignments to the
task in the Resource Usage
view. If all assignments are
split at the same point, the
task itself is effectively split.

 caution

Do not drag a middle seg-
ment to the right to touch a
later segment. Project often
loses track of part of the task
duration.

To change the duration of a segment, and thus the duration of the
task, drag the right end of the segment to the right or left. The Task information box appears and
shows the effect of the current position of the cursor to the finish and duration. If you are adjusting
the final segment of the split task, the finish and duration are those for the entire task. If you are
adjusting any other segment, the finish and duration are those for that segment.

Consultants' Tips

The Deadline Feature

The Deadline feature is often overlooked because sponsors and even project managers who should know better confuse a deadline with a milestone.

When used in conjunction with a milestone, deadlines provide a visual indication of predicted late delivery. You set the deadline date, and when the task or milestone associated with the deadline passes that date, you get a visual reminder in the Indicator column.

Many people who are slightly familiar with Project confuse a milestone with a deadline. They insist on seeing the black milestone diamond, even though they really want to see the deadline, and whether the planned delivery of the milestone is early or late. You might not want to fight this. Use the Format tab for the Gantt Chart to change the appearance of the Deadline and Milestone indicators.

Scheduling Logic

With all the help from PMI and Microsoft to get your schedule defined and ordered quickly, consider that you are taking the "road less traveled." First, sit down by yourself with an old pad of paper and an antique pencil (#2 or mechanical, your choice). Using these tools, compose the right things to do in the right order to define the high-level network diagram of work necessary to meet the scope of the project. If you do not know the scope, before you try to solve the problem or create a new product, get the scope recorded and agreed upon.

The Manually Scheduled task mode can be very helpful during this stage of your project if pencil and paper aren't appealing. Manually Scheduled mode frees you from Project's schedule calculations, making it much more a sketch pad and less a predictive tool. You can always turn on Auto Scheduled mode when the scope is firm. Be careful, though: Manually scheduled tasks often resemble what you want to see, rather than the truth.

After you have the "big box" work defined, share this information with your team. Did you miss anything big? Is the task list accurate? Is the order logical? Will the scope be achieved if you do what is on the paper? Let your team of experts help you refine the high-level network diagram.

The result of using pencil and paper tools is that you slow down and use all your senses to start the project planning. Going slowly in planning often means you can move more quickly in execution with greater certainty of delivery and success. Just because a tool as sophisticated as Microsoft Office Project is available doesn't mean that you have to or even should start from a blank project. (Get the schedule logic right, and the schedule will be so much more understood and manageable.)

Deadlines Versus Sponsor Schizophrenia

Many project-driven organizations believe that they must schedule using constraints because they face manic and schizophrenic sponsors. The sponsor says, "We have to have it on June 30," so they apply Must Finish On constraints to reinforce the volume managed demands of red-faced sponsors. There are two problems with this seemingly standard project management behavior.

As one who understands scheduling, you should first take the requests and demands and all other information at your disposal, plug it all into the Microsoft Project scheduling engine, and let the real expert crunch the numbers, values, and assumptions and tell both you and the sponsor what is doable. Trust the tool and your expertise to explain to the sponsor that the original values applied to the Triple Constraint are unrealistic, but you have a solution! Trust the tool and your ability!

Also, why use scheduling methods that only cause you pain? Scheduling with constraints out of fear is both uninformed and unwise. This does not mean that you have to schedule without using constraints, but understand that judicious application is prudent and often warranted. The use of constraints needs wise counsel.

Here is an alternative. Use the Deadlines feature. It captures the request from the sponsor (whether sane or not) and allows for the visual representation of the captured promise, but will not upset the scheduling engine from producing the best possible answer, given the planning assumption. Using deadlines is a pain-free way to attempt to appease the sponsor without breaking your schedule against unrealistic constraints. Try diplomacy, but trust in your tools. You just might hear an improvement in the volume of your project meetings.

Connecting Tasks with the Mouse

It can be difficult to precisely control the mouse pointer on very short duration tasks, so use the Zoom In feature to change the timescale and make the Gantt bars longer and easier to manipulate.

For tasks that are not on the same screen, you have several choices. You can use the Zoom Out tool to see more tasks on the screen, you can roll up subtasks between the two tasks, or you can select the first task, hold down Ctrl, and then select the second task. As you have probably learned already, the scroll can become very fast.

Showing Detail in the Gantt Chart

Sometimes you will have complex logic in your project plan. In this situation, the link lines can be confusing rather than clarifying as intended.

On the Format tab, click the Layout button. At the top of that dialog box, you can choose to show no link lines (it just hides the line—it doesn't remove the link). Or, you can choose to have the link connector to the successor task come in at the end of the Gantt bar, instead of at the top, which is the default. Choosing the second option can make the view more complex.

Of course, you can also use the Zoom controls to manage the display, so you can see the link lines as separate lines.

DEFINING PROJECT RESOURCES

Project resources impact how Project calculates a schedule in many ways. Resources can be different kinds, such as "cost" or "work." They can be generic, such as "engineer," or they can be named, such as "John Smith." This chapter covers how to set up the right resources for your schedule.

Understanding How Project Uses Resources and Costs

This chapter focuses on resources: understanding what resources are, how to organize them, and how resource costs are defined and calculated in Microsoft Project. With this foundation, you will be prepared to assign resources and costs to tasks, modify those assignments, and resolve resource allocation conflicts.

Resources are the people, facilities, materials, and equipment assigned to work on a task of a project. Although it is possible to create a schedule in Project without assigning resources to the tasks, it is not recommended. By not assigning resources to tasks, you are assuming that you will have all the necessary resources on hand whenever you need them, and that assumption is dangerously unrealistic. People get sick, go on vacation, or have unique work schedules. Machinery and equipment fail and require downtime for maintenance. Employees who play a crucial role in your project leave the company and new ones in need of training arrive. New facilities are sometimes not ready for occupancy until midway through a project. All these are realistic examples of situations in which a resource that is necessary to complete a task might not be available when Project schedules the task. You can avoid these problems and make a project schedule more realistic by defining and assigning resources to tasks (someone has to do the work!). At the very least, you should assign a person's name to each task he or she is responsible for seeing through to completion.

There are several benefits of including resources in a project schedule, as follows:

■ By including resources in your project schedule, you can create a more valid timeline of activities and support your schedule finish date. Without using resources, you have a checklist of activities to be accomplished and an unsupported timeline.

■ You can communicate assignments to the resources and other project managers through MS Project reports.

> ➥ *For additional information about reports,* ***see*** *Chapter 15, "Using Reports for Tracking and Control,"* ***p. 497***.

■ The working time information for each resource (which is specified using the Resource Calendar) is used by Project to automatically schedule tasks during those times only, creating a more realistic schedule.

■ After you assign resources to all the tasks, Project can help you model your schedule to see the staffing levels required to meet a specified completion date.

■ Every project manager needs to know how much the project will cost, not necessarily in dollars but at least in effort (work). Exempt personnel (salaried) will get paid whether they work on a specific project or not. The cost incurred is opportunity cost of doing another project. If financial cost of a project is required, you can include the cost information for each resource. Project automatically calculates the cost of each resource assignment to individual tasks and sums those costs to show the total cost of each task and the overall cost of the project. These cost calculations can be very helpful in estimating the budget for the project and in capitalizing labor costs on a capital project.

You can define a comprehensive list of resources at the beginning, including resource cost rates and availability information. Later, you will assign these resources to tasks. Alternatively, you can define the resources as you create the tasks, while you are thinking about how the work will be performed. When you assign new resource names to a task, Project adds these names to the list of resources (see Figure 8.1). As you create new resources, you must remember to at some point modify the resource cost rates, availability information, and other fields as necessary.

Figure 8.1
Splitting the view to show both the Gantt Chart and Resource Sheet views enables you to enter more detailed resource information as you create or assign resources to tasks in the Gantt Chart view.

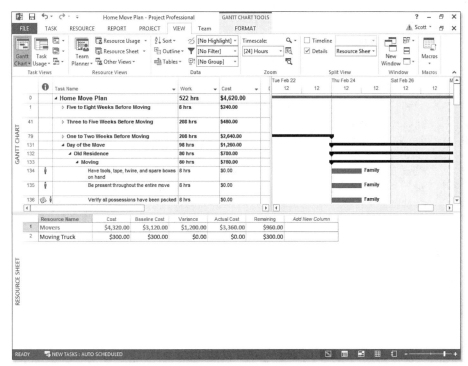

Cost Resources

In addition to commonly known resource types (Work and Material), Project includes cost resources. Cost resources enable you to identify specific project costs across multiple tasks, such as travel expenses, per diem costs, and so on. In addition to being able to identify these resources, you can use cost resources for integration with the accounting systems. Cost resources add another dimension to the cost model of Project, allowing for additional flexibility and traceability of costs.

You can also define Work and Cost resources as budget resources. You assign budget resources on the project summary task, which enables you to allocate the budget on a time-phased basis. You can then compare the planned cost/actual cost/Estimate at Completion (EAC) to the budget on the project.

Defining Resources and Resource Information

Resources are the backbone of a project. Without resources to complete assigned tasks, those tasks would not be completed. Essentially, the cost of a project is a reflection of the sum of all project resources' costs needed to complete each task within the project.

Examples of resources are workers, supervisors, managers, facilities, factories, equipment, travel costs, supplies, and materials.

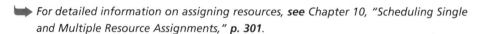 *For detailed information on assigning resources,* **see** *Chapter 10, "Scheduling Single and Multiple Resource Assignments," p. 301.*

Understanding Resource Types

Project includes three types of resources: work, material, and cost. Work resources are resources that are not consumed at the completion of their assigned task and are available to be assigned to future tasks. The ultimate example of a work resource is people. Material resources, on the other hand, are consumed or used up as a task progresses. Ink, gasoline, concrete, and camera film are examples of material resources. Cost resources represent additional costs incurred on a task that used to be hard to track prior to the addition of the Cost resource type in Project. The most common example of a cost resource is travel expenses.

Understanding Budget Resources

In addition to the three resource types, Project includes an option to define the cost or work type as a Budget resource. Budget resources are assigned on the project summary task. Budget Cost and Budget Work are included in baselines, and you can use them as a reference point when creating and tracking your schedule costs/work.

Distinguishing Single and Group Resources

Some resources that you add to a resource list represent individual people or assets. A resource name could be a person's name, for example. Also, you can name a single piece of equipment, a facility, or a raw material as a resource. If you contract out a task to a vendor who is totally responsible for the task, you could simply name the vendor as a resource, even though there might be many individuals on the vendor's team who actually work on the task.

You can also define a resource to represent multiple resources. These could be a group of individual people with similar skills, or multiple pieces of identical equipment. The max units for the resource should be set to the total number of resources available as part of the set. For example, Moving Truck's Max Units of 500% mean you have five trucks included within the resource defined.

With this type of resource, you are not concerned with assigning individual resources by name to a given task. For example, you might define a group of seven engineers as the "Engineers" resource, and the manager of those engineers would dictate which of the seven engineers would work on the task. Similarly, you could define a group of five work trucks as the "Trucks" resource, and assign at 500% to a single task. This would represent in the schedule that the task needs five trucks to accomplish the work within the duration of the task. Another option would be to assign at 100%, and the person in charge of the work trucks would decide which one would be used to complete the task.

caution

Individual members of a group resource cannot be assigned a unique cost rate, and you cannot recognize separate vacation days or other nonworking times for the individuals. All the individuals in a group resource must share a common cost rate and must be scheduled by a single resource calendar that is defined for the group.

Using Generic Resources for Common Skills

In many cases, the project manager does not know the capabilities and skills of many individual resources or does not have the authority to assign individuals by name to a task. Generic resources can be defined as a common skill or capability—for example, you are starting a project that will require carpenters to work on multiple tasks. If you are staffed with three carpenters but are unsure of which one will be the best for a certain task, you could create a generic resource called "Carpenters" and assign it to all the individual tasks. Later, you can substitute the names of the specific carpenters in the appropriate task assignments.

This process gives you the advantage of deducing the total number of carpenters needed to complete the project without assigning individuals to the specific tasks. This is especially relevant when many project managers share the same resources in a shared resource pool. After you have figured out how many carpenters you need, you can see which specific individuals are available and are the best fit for the specific tasks.

 note

Project Professional in conjunction with Project Server enables organizations to define an enterprise level, shared resource pool. The resources in the organization are added to the resource pool, and when a project manager creates a schedule, he or she can add resources to their project directly from the pool. This level of resource sharing also enables you to more accurately track resource availability across the organization. If you are using Project Standard, the resource sharing becomes more difficult and does not include the flexibility available in the enterprise environment.

Using the Resource Sheet View

One of the most effective and commonly used views for manually entering basic resource information is the Resource Sheet view. The Resource Sheet enables you to see many resources on the screen at once. It also shows you a number of important fields for each resource. Indicators notify you when there is critical information in other fields (see Figure 8.2). To display the Resource Sheet view, click the View control on either the Task or Resource tab and choose Resource Sheet. For now, use the Resource tab because that will provide resource-centric functionality.

 tip

The resources defined within the Resource Sheet view detail what resources are available to the specific project you are working on (or to all the projects in the case of shared resources). This view does not specifically define which resources are assigned to tasks, but rather which ones are available to be assigned.

#	ⓘ	Resource Name	Type	Material	Initials	Group	Max.	Std. Rate	Ovt.	Cost/Use	Accrue	Base	Code
1	◈	Movers	Work		M	Cost	0%	$30.00/hr	$0.00/hr	$0.00	Prorated	Standard	
2		Moving Truck	Work		M		100%	150.00/day	$0.00/hr	$0.00	Prorated	Standard	
3	◈	Family	Work		F		100%	$0.00/hr	$0.00/hr	$0.00	Prorated	Standard	
4		Packing Boxes	Material		P			$0.00		$0.00	Prorated		
5		Packing Paper	Material		P			$0.00		$0.00	Prorated		
6		Peanuts	Material		P			$0.00		$0.00	Prorated		
7		Gasoline	Material		G			$0.00		$0.00	Prorated		
8	📝	Truck Insurance	Cost		T						Prorated		

Figure 8.2
The information column includes additional information available about a resource, such as external hyperlinks, notes, and so on.

If your video resolution is 800×600 pixels or less, you will have to scroll to the right to see all the columns of the Resource Sheet. Select a resource and click the Details toggle on the Resource tab. You can see all the fields for the resource that is selected in the top pane (refer to Figure 8.1).

You can also use the Resource Form view to display and edit the Notes field. To display the notes, follow these steps:

1. Activate the Resource Form view by selecting the Resource tab, Properties, and clicking the Details control.

2. Select the Resource form by either right-clicking it and selecting notes or selecting the Format tab for Resource Form Tools (if it says Resource Sheet Tools, this is because the Resource form is not the primary or active window pane) (see Figure 8.3).

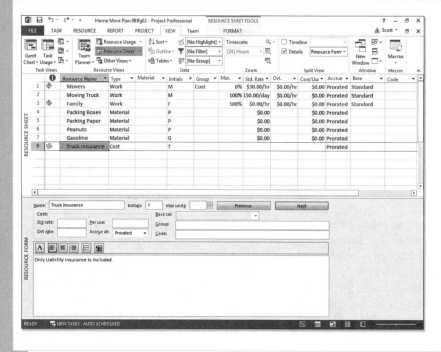

Figure 8.3
In addition to notes, you can select many other details, such as Cost, Schedule, and Work.

To add a resource in the Resource Sheet view, simply select an empty cell in the Resource Name column and type in a descriptive name for the resource. Project will automatically provide default values for a number of fields to the right. Replace the default values or fill in the blanks for the rest of the fields, using the definitions and instructions from the "Using the Resource Fields to Define Resource Details" section later this chapter.

➡️ *For detailed information on resource views,* **see** *Chapter 11, "Using Standard Views, Tables, Filters, and Groups to Review Your Schedule,"* **p. 357**.

Defining Resource Information Using the Resource Information Dialog Box

The Resource Information dialog box contains almost all of the imperative resource definition fields, including several important resource fields that are not available on the Resource Sheet view or the Resource Form view (see Figure 8.4). The additional fields on the Resource Information dialog box supply the following information:

- When the resource is normally available for work (General tab).

- When the normal working times are changed for vacations, illnesses, or other exceptions (Change Working Time option on the General tab).

- Alternative cost rates to use for different types of work and when different cost rates become effective (Costs tab).

- How to communicate electronically with the resource (General tab and Details button).

- Notes about the resource (Notes tab).

- Custom fields defined for the resource such as department, division, skills, and so on (Custom Fields tab).

You can complete the definition of the resource by using the Resource Information dialog box with the Resource Sheet. Enter the resource name in the Resource Sheet. Then use the Resource Information button on the Resource tab (or double-click the resource name) to display the Resource Information dialog box for that resource. Fill in the rest of the fields, and then click OK to return to the Resource Sheet view.

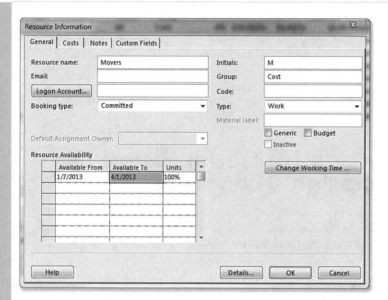

Figure 8.4
The Resource Information box contains the most comprehensive and important details about each resource.

Using the Resource Fields to Define Resource Details

The Resource Sheet view is the simplest, most convenient view for entering and reviewing resource information because it resembles an Excel sheet. To access the Resource Sheet view, select the Resource tab, and in the View group drop-down control, select Resource Sheet. Alternately, the Resource Sheet view can be selected directly from the Quick Launch toolbar. You can use this view in combination with the Resource Information dialog box to enter all the important fields of information that define a resource. Double-click on the resource name to bring up the Resource Information dialog box (refer to Figure 8.4).

When defining a resource, you should provide a resource name and information about the availability and cost of the resource. The following sections list the fields that are commonly used in defining resources. Their order in this chapter coincides with the order of the columns in the Resource Sheet view and the related fields in the Resource Information dialog box.

Using the Resource ID Field

The ID numbers for the resources are the row numbers listed all the way to the left side of the screen in the Resource Sheet view. The ID number does not appear in the Resource Information dialog box. These numbers are fixed; if you move a resource on the list, it automatically acquires the ID number for the row that you moved it to. Like the task ID numbers, you cannot edit this field.

Interpreting the Indicator Field

Indicator icons are helpful in pointing your attention to additional information about the resource. The Indicator field displays icons that show the status of critical fields that might not normally be displayed. For example, the Hyperlink indicator you saw in Figure 8.3 signifies a hyperlink associating the resource with a website or a document file.

The Overallocation indicators mean those resources have been overallocated at some point in the project; they may have been assigned to work on two different tasks at the same time, violating the amount of time they were available to work. The note indicators show that there is text in the Notes field for those resources. Resource Indicators appear only on resource table views such as the Resource Sheet view.

Specifying Resource Names Using the Name Field

You can define a descriptive name for a resource in the Resource Name field. The name can contain any characters except for the square brackets ([ ]) and the Windows separator character, which is, by default, the comma (,) in the United States. Resource names can be up to 255 characters in length. The resource name can be a specific name, such as John Smith, or it can describe a group of resources, such as Movers.

 caution

Be cautious when entering resource names to avoid duplicate ones. If you add a resource name that is a duplicate of another name on the list, Project accepts it and does not warn you that you have duplicate names. Additionally, if you assign a nonunique resource name to a task, Project uses the first resource it finds with that name from the resource list.

 tip

It is helpful to come up with a standard naming convention for resources. Two approaches are commonly used: full first name space full last name (John Smith), and full last name space full first name (Smith John). The format last name comma first name (Smith, John) is not allowed in many language versions because Project uses the comma to separate the resource names when assigning multiple resources to a task. Also with cost or budget resources, it is helpful to prefix or suffix the resource name—for example, Budget Expense, Travel Costs.

Using Resource Type to Categorize Resources

As stated previously, Project distinguishes between work resources (resources that are not consumed after contributing their work to tasks), material resources (resources that are consumed by their assignments), and cost resources (resources that represent additional costs on a project). The cost of work resources is based on the number of hours the resource works on a task and the hourly cost for the resource. The cost of material resources is based on the cost of a unit of the resource and how many units are consumed. The cost of cost resources is an assigned one-time charge. The default resource type is Work, but you can select either Work, Material, or Cost with the drop-down arrow in the Type field.

Work resources units can be formatted as a percentage (the default) or decimal values. Material resources are formatted only as decimal values.

A material resource is said to have a fixed consumption if the amount of the material that is consumed does not depend on the duration of the task. For example, the amount of metal used to build a car's body does not depend on the duration of the task.

A material resource is said to have a variable consumption rate if the amount of the resource consumed varies with the duration of the task. For example, the amount of film consumed when shooting a movie depends on the number of takes a director chooses to shoot the scenes. Project factors the duration of the task when calculating the cost of using a variable-consumption-rate resource.

To tell Project that it should factor duration into the calculated cost for a material resource, you have to attach a time unit abbreviation when you enter the assignment units. For example, to assign five reels of film per hour to a task, you would enter the units as **5/h**.

 caution

Be cautious about changing resource types after they are assigned to tasks. When you assign a resource to a task, its type determines how the assignment affects the schedule for the task. For instance, if it is a work resource, the resource calendar determines when the work can take place. If it is a material or cost resource, there is no resource calendar to consider. Project warns you with a dialog box that the schedule will be affected and that the changes cannot be undone if you try to change the type of resource after it has been assigned.

➡ For details on assigning various resources types to tasks, **see** Chapter 10, "Scheduling Single and Multiple Resource Assignments," **p. 301**.

Using the Material Label to Specify Units of Resource Measure

You use the Material Label field to define the unit of measure for material resources. For example, lbs for pounds, ea for each, bx for box, and gals for gallons are all measuring units. You define the unit cost of the resource using the measuring unit. This field is not available for work or cost resources.

Using the Initials Column to Shorten Resource Names

Sometimes using full names creates clutter and takes up unnecessary space. The Initials field provides a place for a shortened form of the resource name. The abbreviated name can be used in views such as the Gantt Chart and Network Diagram views. After you enter the resource name in a new row, Project automatically provides the first character of the name as the default initial but makes no attempt to keep it unique.

 tip

If you intend to use the initial (or initials) to identify resources in any view, be sure to edit the initial to make it uniquely identify the resource and be meaningful to you.

Using the Group Field to Categorize Resources

The Group field enables you to enter an identifying label or keyword that you can use for organizing (sorting, grouping, or filtering) resources. For example, you could identify all packing materials, such as boxes, tape, wrapping paper, and so on, by entering Packing Materials, all moving personnel by entering Movers, or all pieces of equipment by entering Equipment. You can then use the Resource Group filter to view only the resources that have one of those values in this field.

Many users put skills in a custom text field so they can filter the resource list for resources that have comparable skills. It is also useful to identify the skill level. The most effective method is to combine the skill category with the skill level.

For example, if you adopt the scale 1=Trainee, 2=Semi-Skilled, 3=Skilled, and 4=Expert, any semi-skilled technician could be identified with Technician2. Use commas to separate entries for people who have multiple skills.

 tip

Some users of Project find it helpful to put the name of the department that manages a resource in the Group field.

 note

When applying a filter to locate one keyword in a list in the Group field, you should use the logical test "contains" rather than "equals." See the section "Filtering Resources" later in this chapter for an example of using filters.

 tip

"Group" has a special meaning when Project Professional is associated with an instance of Project Server. Even though this is a default field, in an enterprise environment, it is probably best to use a completely new custom field with a different name.

 tip

In Project Server, skills are defined using enterprise custom fields. Even when you are not using Project Server, you can use resource custom fields to define skill sets. Figure 8.5 illustrates a skill implemented in a custom field. note that each level of the outline gets more specific about the skill of the resource. This enables you to find an engineer, a mechanical engineer, or specifically an advanced mechanical engineer based on the level of specificity you request when searching the Skill field.

➡ *For additional information on customizing custom fields, **see** Chapter 22, "Customization Almost Beyond Reason: Views, Tables, Filters, Groups, Fields, Toolbars, Menus, and Forms," **p. 699**.*

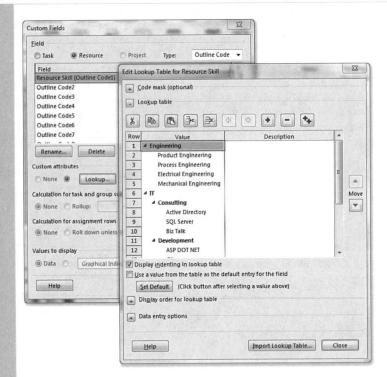

Figure 8.5
You can define resource skill sets using the Custom Fields Lookup Table option.

Using the Max Units and Resource Availability Table to Specify Resource Availability

Use the Max Units field to enter the maximum number of units that can currently be assigned to tasks at any one time. Project uses the Max Units field to determine when the resource is overallocated (when more units of the resource have been assigned than are available) and when leveling resources.

For instance, suppose that Greg's Max Units field shows 80%. That means that Greg is available to spend up to 80% of his working time on tasks in your project. If you assign Greg to spend 30% of his time on one task and 60% of his time on another task, and if the scheduled dates for those two tasks overlap, you will have assigned 90% of Greg's time during the period of the overlap. Because this is more than the Max Units of 80%, Project calculates that the resource is overallocated; the resource name turns red in the Resource Sheet view and displays a symbol in the Indicator field to flag the overallocated resource.

You can format the Max Units field as a percentage or as a decimal. The default is the percentage format. You can change the format for the Max Units field in the Options dialog box by following these steps:

1. On the File tab, select Options.

2. In the Options dialog box, select the Schedule tab.

3. Use the drop-down list in the Show Assignment Units as A box and select either Percentage or Decimal.

Project applies a default Max Units of 100% (or 1 in decimal format) when you create a resource. However, you can change the value to anything between 0% and 6,000,000,000% (between 0 and 60,000,000 in decimal format). For a single-unit resource, the default value of 100% means that this resource is available to work 100% of the hours on its calendar on this project. It can also signify that the resource is fully dedicated (100%) to complete the assigned task during the defined period. If you are grouping resources into a group resource, you enter a greater value than 100%. Thus, if you have two full-time movers in a Movers resource, you can enter 200% (or 2 in decimal format).

 note

There is no Max Units value for material or cost resources. Project assumes that you will acquire as many units as you have assigned.

A resource may have some variability concerning its actual availability. For instance, sometimes a resource is not hired until after the project starts, so up until that date, its Max Units remains 0%. On the reverse side, a resource might leave the company before the project is completed, so after his or her last day with the company, the Max Units field will be 0%. At all other times, the resource availability may vary from 0 to 100% for very specific reasons during very specific times.

You might also intend to add more units of the resource over the duration of the project. In this case, you need to record the dates when the additional units would come on board using the Resource Availability table.

You can find the Resource Availability table on the General tab of the Resource Information dialog box. Use this table to define the time periods and the max units for each time period (refer to Figure 8.4). The default values for both the Available From and Available To columns in the Resource Availability table are NA (not applicable), and the default value in the Units (Max Units) field is 100%. The NA value means from the earliest possible date (Jan. 1, 1984) and latest available date (Dec. 31, 2049), respectively. Figure 8.6 shows that the Movers resource will not start work until 1/7/2013, even though the project starts earlier, and will be available until 4/1/2013 per the contract agreement, even though the project still continues after 4/1.

The Max Units field on the Resource Sheet view and on the Resource Form view displays the Units value from the Resource Availability table for the current date. The current date is normally the computer's current date, but it can be any date you choose to enter into the Current Date field in the Project Information dialog box. If you look at the Max Units field for Movers on the Resource Sheet view on any date prior to 1/7/2013, the value will be 0%, because the movers are unavailable to work on the project before 1/7/2013 according to the Available From column. After 1/7/2013, it will be 100%.

When Project examines this schedule to see if the Movers resource is overallocated, it shows the overallocated indicator if the total assignments for the Movers resource exceed 100% on any date outside the date range of 1/7/2013–4/1/2013.

To change the Resource Availability table for a resource, follow these steps:

1. In a view that shows resource names, such as the Resource Sheet view, select the resource and click the Resource Information button on the Resource tab of the Ribbon. You can also simply double-click the resource name.

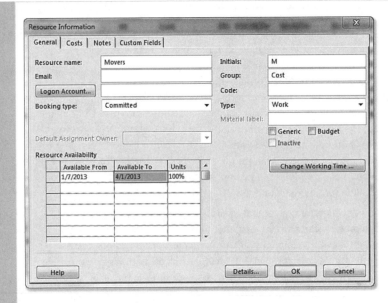

Figure 8.6
The Resource Information dialog box's Resource Availability table is used to track the changes in resource availability down to specific date ranges and units.

2. Click the General tab, if it is not displayed.

3. Click the cell for the date you want to change under the Available From or Available To column. You can either type in the date or use the drop-down arrow to select the date.

4. Enter the max units for that row's date range in the Units column.

5. After all entries are completed, click OK to save the changes. Or you can click Cancel to close the dialog box without saving any changes.

 tip

Be sure that the dates in the Resource Availability table are in sequential order and that you leave no gaps in the dates from one row to the next. If you have an Available From date that is more than one day later than the Available To date on the previous row, Project assumes the resource is unavailable between those dates and uses 0% as the Max Units value for the dates in the gap.

caution

When entering dates in the Available From and Available To columns, be aware that those dates are fixed unless you change them. If a resource's availability dates change, be sure to correct the changes in the Resource Availability table.

note

The Resource Availability table is not available for material resources, which are assumed to be always available to the project.

Selecting Resource Calendar to Specify Resource Base Availability

In addition to Max Units and the Resource Availability table, Project uses resource base calendars to specify resource availability. One of the project's base calendars is designated to define the normal working days and hours for the resource.

To select a specific resource calendar, use the drop-down arrows to display a list of all the base calendars that have been defined and select the one that most closely fits the resource. The resource calendar inherits all the chosen base calendars' values: the working days and hours, as well as the individually marked nonworking days and hours that are defined in the base calendar. The default base calendar is Standard.

 tip

You might want to create a special base calendar if you have more than one named resource with the same set of exceptions to one of the standard base calendars. Otherwise, you will have to mark the same exceptions in each of the resource calendars. For example, if several resources will be assigned to work on a project on a night shift and they all have the same basic schedule on night work hours, you can save time by creating a base calendar for night shift work and then using that base calendar for all resources with these hours. Instead of customizing each night shift worker's resource calendar, you can define the hours only once and apply the base calendar wherever necessary.

If you create additional base calendars in your project that resources or tasks are linked to, remember to make company-wide changes in working days and hours to all base calendars. For example, if your company decides to make the day after Thanksgiving a holiday, you need to edit each base calendar used by resources or tasks to apply the holiday to all schedules.

 For details on creating the base calendar, **see** *Chapter 5, "Setting Up Project for Your Use," **p. 89**.*

Specifying the Resource Working Time

As previously mentioned, a resource calendar is based on one of the base calendars, and it inherits the base calendar's normal working times per week, as well as all the holidays or other exceptions to the normal working times. You can enter exceptions to working time on the base calendar for a resource by using the resource calendar. To modify the working time for the resource on a particular day, follow these steps:

1. In the Resource Information dialog box, select the General tab if it's not already selected.

2. On the General tab, click the Change Working Time button.

3. Ensure that the Work Weeks tab is selected and then select a date on the calendar.

4. Click the Details button and enter the working time hours for the resource in the resulting dialog box, as shown in Figure 8.7.

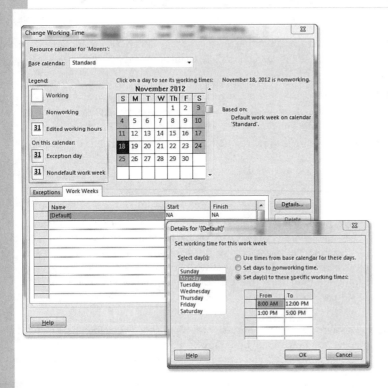

Figure 8.7
You can use the Details dialog box to specify any working hours deviations from the standard resource calendar.

To create an exception, follow these steps:

1. In the Resource Information dialog box, select the General tab if it's not already selected.

2. On the General tab, click the Change Working Time button.

3. On the Exceptions tab, enter the name of the exception and then enter the exception start and end dates.

4. Click the Details button and ensure that the Nonworking option is selected.

For example, in Figure 8.8, the resource calendar for Movers shows that they will not be available to work February 11–15 because they have scheduled vacation during that time.

Figure 8.8
Use the Exceptions tab and the Details button to specify exceptions to the standard calendar, and the specific times resource will not be available.

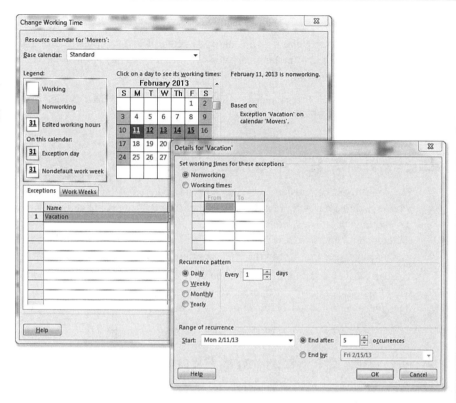

Follow these additional steps to edit a resource calendar:

1. Select the resource in a resource view or on the Assign Resources dialog box and double-click the resource name to display the Resource Information dialog box. Click the Change Working Time button to display the resource calendar and time fields.

2. Use the Base Calendar drop-down list to select the base calendar for the resource.

3. To give the resource time off on dates that are normal working dates on the base calendar, select the dates on the calendar and click the Details button. Select the Set Days to Nonworking Time option.

4. Similarly, to schedule a resource for work on dates that are normally nonworking dates, select the dates (they are shaded before you select them), click the Details button, and select the Set Day(s) to These Specific

> **note**
>
> You can edit a resource calendar from the Change Working Time dialog box, although you cannot change the name of the base calendar the resource calendar is linked to from there. Select the Project tab, Change Working Time to display the Change Working Time dialog box, and then use the drop-down list in the For box to select the resource name.

Working Times option. In the Working Times table, specify the From and To hours the resource will be available to work on that day.

5. Modify the hours of work on any date as needed. The date appears with a diagonal shading pattern to indicate that the hours are nonstandard for that day of the week, and the date is underlined to show that it is an exception to the base calendar.

6. Click OK to save your changes in the resource calendar, or click Cancel to abandon the changes without saving them.

Defining Resource Costs

There are three cost measures you can associate with a resource. The Standard Rate is used for work completed during normal working hours. The Overtime Rate is used for work completed during overtime hours. Cost Per Use is a special, one-time cost per assignment that is independent from the number of hours worked. Each of these cost measures has a default rate that you can define in the Resource Sheet view or in the Resource Information dialog box.

You can create four additional sets of the three rates in the Resource Information dialog box if you want to charge different rates for different kinds of work. You can also define time periods when the rates will change. These features are covered in the section "Understanding the Cost Rate Tables" later in this chapter.

Applying the Standard Rate to a Resource

You use the Standard Rate field to show the current default cost of each unit of the resource assigned to a task:

- For work resources, the standard rate is the amount to charge per time unit of normal working time for the resource. Enter the rate as a number, followed by a forward slash (/) and one of the following units or its abbreviation: minute (m), hour (h), day (d), week (w), month (mo), or year (y). Project assumes an hourly rate if you type just a number without a time unit. For example, you can type **900/w** for $900 per week, **46000/y** for $46,000 per year, or just **18.7** for $18.70 per hour. Suppose you were to rent a moving truck for $100 per day. You could create a resource named Moving Truck and enter the standard rate **100/d**.

- For material resources, the standard rate is the amount to charge tasks per unit of the resource consumed. The unit is defined in the Material Label field. There is no time unit attached to the dollar amount. Enter the standard rate as an amount, with no time unit, and it is understood to be the amount per unit of the resource. For example, if you include gas as a material resource for the moving truck, its material label might be gallons (which is already defined in the Material Label field) and the standard rate might be 3.00, which means $3.00 per gallon.

- Cost resources use a flat charge amount assigned to it and do not have either units or standard rate.

If the standard rate is entered with a time unit, the rate is converted to an hourly rate and is applied to the number of hours of work it takes to complete the task. For annual rates, the hourly rate is calculated by assuming there are 52 weeks in a year, and the number of hours per week is that which is defined on the Calendar tab of the Options dialog box. For the standard workweek of 40 hours, the annual rate is divided by 2,080 (52 weeks × 40 hours) to get an hourly rate. For monthly rates, the hourly rate is calculated using the Calendar tabs' definitions for days in a month and hours in a day (Hourly Rate in a Month = Monthly Rate / (Days in Month × Hours in Day)).

When you want to charge more or less than the default rate, you can define four more rates in addition to the default standard rate that can be used for assignments. See the section "Understanding the Cost Rate Tables" later in this chapter for details.

---

 tip

Although the standard rate is frequently the hourly or salaried rate for a resource, organizations often define the standard rate as the billed-at rate. When the standard rate is defined as the billed-at rate, a project plan serves as a budget estimate for the work to be performed under contract.

Often, a project plan demonstrates to the client early in the proposal stage that client requirements are understood and acknowledged and gives the client important confidence. Expectations are set for the project in the early stages of planning, as opposed to being unpleasantly discovered during project execution. Estimates of cost and work are based on defined work rather than ballpark estimates.

Applying the Overtime Rate to a Resource

Project uses the entry in the Overtime Rate field when calculating the cost and actual cost of overtime hours that you schedule for a work resource. There is no overtime rate for material and cost resources. The default overtime rate is zero (0.00), so for salaried employees you can leave the zero value if these resources are not paid extra for their overtime hours. If the rate for overtime work is the same as the regular rate and you intend to collect actual overtime work, you must enter that amount again in the Overtime Rate field, or overtime hours will be charged at the zero default rate.

 note

Overtime work can be scheduled using the resource or task usage views by displaying the overtime work column. Overtime work can only be scheduled and actual overtime collected at the assignment level.

Resources that are paid by the hour often receive a higher wage when working overtime. Be sure to enter this amount in the Overtime Rate field.

As with the standard rate, you can define four additional overtime rates for each resource and use them for special tasks. See the section "Understanding the Cost Rate Tables" later in this chapter.

---

 note

You can set the default values for the standard and overtime rates for all new resources in the Options dialog box. Choose Tools, Options, and then click the General tab. Enter an amount per time unit in both the Default Standard Rate and the Default Overtime Rate fields. All resources added from that point on initially show these default rates.

Applying the Cost Per Use to a Resource

The Cost Per Use field is titled "Cost/Use" in the Resource Sheet view and "Per Use Cost" in the Resource Information dialog box. This field contains any cost that is to be charged once for each 100% of a unit of a resource that is assigned to a task, regardless of the duration of the assignment. In other words, the amount entered in the Cost Per Use field will be charged every time the resource is assigned to a task.

For example, if you rent a piece of equipment by the hour but also have to pay a flat charge of $400 for having it delivered to the work site, you could enter the delivery charge as a Cost Per Use cost. Keep in mind, however, that if you assign the equipment to more than one task, the $400 will be charged for each assignment. Therefore, you should always be careful when using the Cost Per Use field with work resources, because the amount entered in that field will be charged once for each 100% of the resource that is assigned to any task.

 tip

Be sure to take advantage of the Cost Per Use field when you are laying out your project plans. One example of this would be a required trip charge for deploying a resource. Perhaps a plumber charges $50 to examine a plumbing problem, regardless of the number of hours spent and the materials necessary to fix the problem. The Cost Per Use field enables you to assign flat-rate costs to various tasks.

Understanding the Cost Rate Tables

The Costs tab of the Resource Information dialog box contains five Cost Rate tables—Tables A through E—which show the default cost rates (Table A) plus four other levels of cost that you can define for different types of assignments. For example, a Plumber resource's Table A would contain its default rates, which might be for new commercial plumbing assignments. Table B might contain the rates for new residential plumbing assignments, Table C might show rates for modifying commercial plumbing, and Table D might contain the rates for modifying residential plumbing. You can select the rate to apply to an assignment in the Assignment Information dialog box.

 tip

You cannot change the labels on the five cost tabs to something more descriptive than A–E, so you should use the resource Notes field (in the Resource Information dialog box) to document what each rate is to be used for.

Figure 8.9 shows Cost Rate Table B for Movers. This table defines the default cost rates to use for the Movers' assignments.

The entry in the first cell in the Effective Date column is always two dashes, signifying that there is no set start date for that level of rates. To enter additional levels for subsequent dates, enter the change date in the Effective Date column and then enter the values for the Standard Rate, Overtime Rate, and Per Use Cost columns. Movers will receive a raise of 20% to both the standard and overtime rates on 2/14/2013 (refer to Figure 8.9). You can enter up to 25 dated rate changes in each of the five tabs.

You can also allow for changes over time in these rates. For example, if you assume that inflation will cause your costs to increase by 5% per year, you could show different rates for each of the years during which the project lasts.

Figure 8.9
Use the Cost Tables to specify various cost rates for each resource.

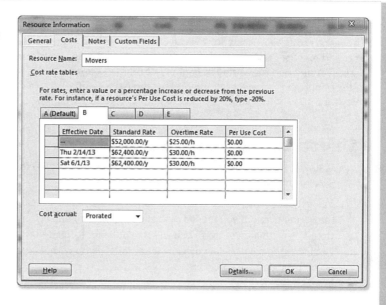

If you want Project to calculate a percentage increase or decrease in one of the rates, enter the plus or minus percentage with a percent sign (%), and when you leave the cell, Project applies that increase to the value in the cell just above it, displaying the calculated result instead of the percentage you entered (see Figure 8.10).

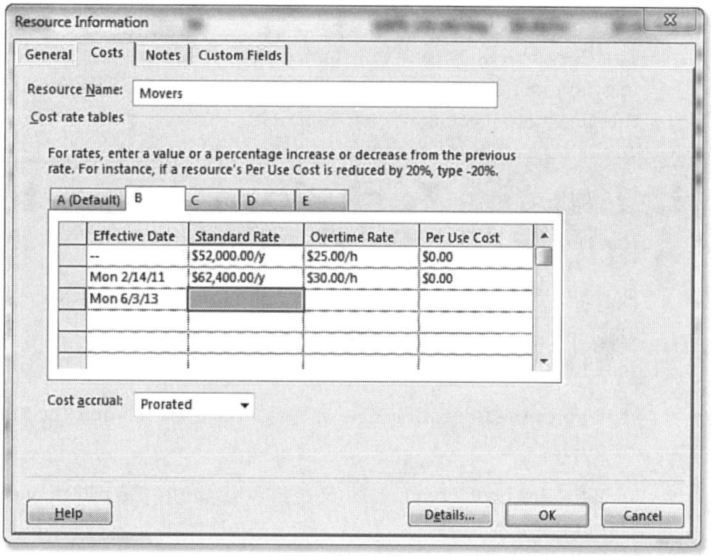

Figure 8.10
Enter the 5% raise increase in a new row of the Cost Table B Standard Rate field and click the Tab button on your keyboard to have project automatically calculate the dollar value.

tip

The various cost tables allow for the use of a resource that might be billed at different rates for various services and functions within the project. For example, suppose one of your resources is a bilingual writer who is billed at one rate for writing in English but charges a different rate for writing in Russian. By factoring in the resource's competency in using each language, a different rate can be charged for utilizing the same resource with various skill sets within the same project.

Selecting the Cost Accrual Type

The Cost Accrual field determines when costs are recognized for standard and overtime costs. You can choose one of three options: Start, End, or Prorated.

The default accrual method is Prorated, which means that planned cost is distributed equally across the duration, and if you mark a task at 15% complete, the actual costs for all assigned resources would be estimated to be 15% of the scheduled or estimated cost of those assignments. This method is the most widely used because it keeps up with the pace of the project, allowing the cost to coincide with task progress.

If you choose Start as the accrual method, total planned costs are shown on the task start date; then, as soon as you indicate that work on a task has started, Project considers the entire standard and overtime costs of the assignment as the actual cost. In other words, after a task has begun, the entire cost is incurred and recognized as if the task were complete.

If you choose End, Project postpones recognition of the actual cost until you enter a finish date and the assignment is 100% complete.

The Cost Accrual setting only matters when you are printing interim reports and when you are working on a task assignment that has started but is not finished.

 note

Only the standard and overtime rates are affected by the accrual method you choose. The Cost Per Use value is always accrued at the start of an assignment, no matter which accrual method you choose for the resource.

Using the Task Form View to Add Additional Resources

One of the most popular views for assigning resources is the Gantt Chart view with the Task Form view in the bottom pane. You can also add resources in that view by using the resource details in the lower pane. To add resources in the Task Form view, follow these steps:

1. Display the Gantt Chart view. Select the Task tab and click the Details control in the Properties group.

2. If the resource details are not displayed in the Task Form view, click anywhere in the lower pane to activate it and then select the Format tab. Select Resources and Predecessors (see Figure 8.11).

3. In the top pane, select a task.

4. Click in the Resource Names column in the Task Form view, where you can select an existing resource to assign to the task, or you can type in the name of a new resource to assign to the task. In Figure 8.11, Gasoline is being typed in as an additional resource. If you type in a new name and click OK, Project provides the default values for the Assignment Units and Work because you did not. (Resources are not created automatically unless you check Automatically Add New Resources and Tasks under the *I* tab, Options, Advanced is checked.)

5. Double-click the resource name to display the Resource Information dialog box, where you can fill in the rest of the fields that define the resource.

Figure 8.11
The split-screen Gantt Chart and Task Information view is one of the most convenient views for assigning resources to a task.

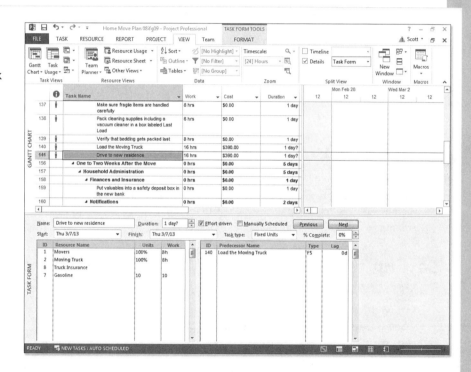

➡️ *For additional details on using views, **see** Chapter 11, "Using Standard Views, Tables, Filters, and Groups to Review Your Schedule," **p. 357**.*

Understanding Resource Constraints

To complete the resource definition process, resource constraints need to be completed. There are few definable resource constraints but many different constraining factors on a resource. Human resources might be constrained due to scheduling conflicts, overallocation, availability, physical location, or controlled budgets. Other resources such as machinery might be constrained due to condition, compatibility, or failure. These and other resource constraining factors can create serious headaches for project managers and are often the root cause for task or project failures. Using Project can help avoid these headaches and manage resource constraining factors with more control.

By using Project, you can create a profile for a resource that will help you manage your project from start to finish. You have, at your fingertips, all the attributes of a resource that could potentially lead to problems or constraints. For example, Mary Powell is a resource you need for a specific task, but when assigning her to a task, you realize there is a conflict. Perhaps she is on vacation, or lives in another city, or only works part time, or has already been assigned to tasks and is unavailable during the time you have allotted for completing the task.

As a project manager, you have to analyze the risks involved with changing your plan and predict all the various outcomes. Maybe another resource can perform the task you want to assign to Mary Powell, or maybe you can move the task to a later date when she is available to work on it. You need to weigh the risks and ask yourself: "If I wait until Mary is available to start this task, what will be the consequences? Is it worth the risk, or should I assign another resource to the task?"

If you have another resource that is capable and available, chances are you should assign the task to the other resource. But if Mary Powell is the only qualified resource to complete the task, it is worth the wait. Resource and risk management are significantly aided by Project.

Working with Resources

As you are undoubtedly aware by now, Project offers several options when categorizing, organizing, and working with resources. Depending on your project, some methods will be of more use to you than others. The following pages discuss these different methods and will give you a greater understanding of working with resources in Project.

Setting the Automatically Add New Resources and Tasks Option

Setting the Automatically Add New Resources and Tasks option determines how Project reacts when you assign a resource to a task that is not currently in your resource list.

When you assign a resource name to a task, Project checks the resource list for the name you have entered. By default, if Project does not find the resource, it adds it to the resource list without asking your permission. This causes problems if you did not intend to add a new resource, but rather typed in the wrong or misspelled resource name accidentally.

This feature can be dangerous because it enables you to accidentally create multiple resource names for the same resource. For example, suppose you have created a list of resources that includes Matt, Maria, and Charles. As you are assigning resources to tasks, you type in Marie instead of Maria as a typo. A new resource, Marie, is added to the list of resources, so you

 caution

All resource fields for the new name receive default values, and you must remember to update those fields later. You can end up with miscalculations in your costs if you neglect to go back and fill in the data for the new resource, because the default cost rates are usually zero (and by now you must know that is inaccurate!).

then have Matt, Maria, Charles, and Marie. You end up not having a comprehensive list of the assignments for Maria, because they are split between the Maria and Marie resources.

However, if the Automatically Add New Resources and Tasks option (in the File tab, Options, Advanced) is disabled, Project prompts you to choose whether it should add the new resource to the resource list. If you did in fact type in a wrong or misspelled resource name, disabling this feature allows you to double-check your possible error.

In Figure 8.12, the resource name Bill Kirk was accidentally typed in an assignment, and Project prompts you to decide whether this is a new resource you want added to the list. If you confirm that you want to add the resource, the resource is added, and you must remember to define the rest of the resource fields. In this example, you would select the No button to avoid adding a misspelled version of Bill Kirk's name to the resource list.

Figure 8.12
Disabling the Automatically Add New Resources and Tasks option enables you to avoid accidentally creating erroneous resources.

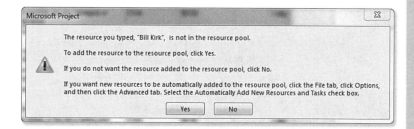

➥ *For detailed information on how resource assignments work,* **see** *Chapter 9, "Understanding Work Formula Basics,"* **p. 269**.

 tip

It is a good idea to disable the Automatically Add New Resources and Tasks option to avoid the possibility of creating new resources unintentionally. If you are going to leave the option enabled, you should avoid typographical errors by always using the pick list of resource names that is available when you assign a resource to a task.

To disable or enable the Automatically Add New Resources and Tasks option, select the File tab, Options, Advanced, General Options for this project. Clear the check box Automatically Add New Resources and Tasks to disable the feature, or select the check box to enable the feature.

Sorting Resources

The resource names in the Resource Sheet view are normally listed according to ID number, which initially reflects the order in which you enter the resources. Project enables you to temporarily sort the resource list for analysis purposes. Also, after you sort the resource list, you can permanently change the row ID numbers to match the new order.

note

Permanently changing the ID numbers does not change the unique ID that is assigned when you add a resource.

 caution

Never cut and paste to change the order of the resource rows if you have already assigned resources to tasks. Cutting deletes the original resource, and its assignments are deleted also. Therefore, the new resource you paste in will have a new unique ID and no assignments.

For instance, after entering all the resources, you could permanently sort the list so that all the work resources are listed first in alphabetical order by name and the material resources are listed below in order by name (see Figure 8.13). Or, if you have used generic resource names, you might sort the list to show the generic names first and then the actual names.

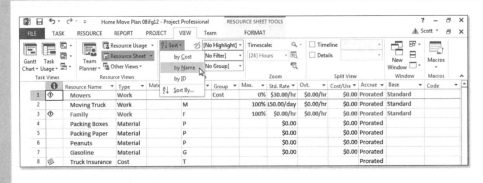

Figure 8.13
By using Sort, you can sort the list of resources by up to three columns at once.

Another useful application of sorting is to see which resources add the most cost to the project. In this case, you apply the Cost table to the Resource Sheet view, to show the cost of all the task assignments for each resource. Then you could sort the resource list by the Total Cost field, in descending order (see Figure 8.14).

You can sort a table by up to three fields at a time. Each of those fields can be sorted in ascending or descending order. For example, to produce the sort of order shown in Figure 8.13, you would sort first on the resource's Type field, in descending order, to put work resources before material resources alphabetically. Next you would sort by the Resource Name field in ascending order to list the names in alphabetical order.

To sort resources, select the View tab, Sort to display the Sort submenu. Sorting by cost, name, or ID is done so often that these

 note

If you sort the resource table by the Standard Rate field, Project sorts the work resources that have been defined with annual cost rates using the hourly equivalent of the annual amount, based on 52 weeks of 40 hours each.

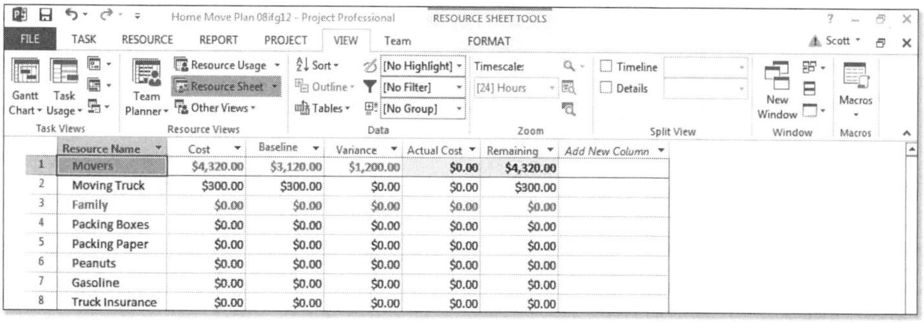

Figure 8.14
Applying the cost sort enables you to view the resources in your project that have the most impact on cost.

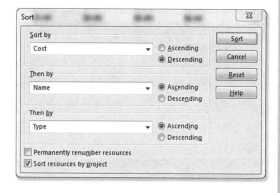

options appear on the submenu. Cost sorts in descending order, but both Name and Type sort in ascending order by default. These three choices use the current settings at the bottom of the Sort dialog box.

If you choose Sort By at the bottom of the Sort submenu, Project displays the Sort dialog box, where you can define up to three fields to use for sorting, and each can be sorted in either ascending or descending order, as shown in Figure 8.15.

Figure 8.15
Use the Sort dialog box to customize the current view.

To produce the sort order by Type and then by Name, as you saw illustrated in Figure 8.13, follow these steps:

1. Display the Resource Sheet view by selecting it from the Quick launch.

2. Select the View tab, Sort, Sort By to display the Sort dialog box.

3. You can sort a maximum of three fields, using the Sort By, Then By, and Then By fields. Enter the first sort fields in the Sort By box. Use the drop-down arrow to display the list of fields. Type the first letter of the field name (in this case, *T*), and Project highlights the first field that begins with that letter. Scroll down and select the Type field.

4. Click the Ascending button if you want the field sorted in normal order. In this example, you click the Descending button to list work before material resources.

5. In the first Then By box, select the Name field.

6. Select Ascending to sort the names in normal order.

7. Select the Permanently Renumber Resources check box if you want Project to change all ID numbers to match the new sort order. See the following Caution box if you elect to fill this check box.

 caution

If you fill the Permanently Renumber Resources check box in a sort operation, as soon as the sort is completed, you should immediately open the Sort dialog box again, click the Reset button, and then click Sort. The Reset button disables the Permanently Renumber Resources option and sets the sort key to ID, and does not interfere with the initial sort you just completed. If you do not take this extra step, the Permanently Renumber check box remains filled, and every future sorting using the Sort submenu renumbers your resources until you clear the box. Also, future sorting of tasks permanently renumbers the tasks.

If you decide to cancel a sort operation and you have already filled the Permanently Renumber Resources check box, be sure to clear the check box (or click the Reset button, which also clears it) before clicking the Cancel button.

8. If you have combined several project files into a consolidated display, you can select the Sort Resources By Project box to keep the resources for each project together and sort them within that grouping.

9. When all settings are ready, click the Sort button to execute the sort and close the dialog box. Or, click the Cancel button to close the dialog box without sorting the resources.

 tip

If you have done a custom sort previously in the same session and used three sort keys, click the Reset button to clear the extra (second and third) sort keys if you no longer need them.

 note

You can undo a sort operation, even after you permanently renumber the resources. However, you must undo the sort operation before you make any other changes. Just as a precaution, it is wise to save a copy of the file before permanently renumbering the resources, just in case you want to undo it later.

You can put the rows back into the order in which they were originally entered by sorting the Unique ID field. This action puts the rows back in their original order.

To return the list to the ID order, you can either press Shift+F3 (which cancels the current sort order) or choose Project, Sort, ID from the menu.

tip

Press Ctrl+Shift+F3 to reapply the last sort instructions. This is in case you have sorted the resource list in a special order and have made changes that might make the order of the resources no longer fit the sort order you defined. For example, if you sorted by resource type and cost and then you make task assignments or change some resource cost rates, the list might no longer be in descending cost order within each type. You can press Ctrl+Shift+F3 to sort by type and cost again.

note

If you frequently use a custom sort order and would like to place it on the Sort submenu, you can create a macro and customize the Sort menu to include that sort order.

➡ For information on customizing the menus, **see** Chapter 22, "Customization Almost Beyond Reason: Views, Tables, Filters, Groups, Fields, Toolbars, Menus, and Forms," **p. 699**.

Grouping Resources

You can sort tasks or resources into groups, based on the entries in one or more of the fields, by using the Group By command. For example, you could group resources by resource types (see Figure 8.16) or by entries in the Group field.

➡ For detailed information on the Group By command, **see** the "Creating Custom Groups" section on **p. 741** in Chapter 22.

Figure 8.16
Use the Group By command to sort the resources and organize them into logical groups to simplify the resource views.

Resource Name ▼	Cost ▼	Baseline ▼	Variance ▼	Actual Cost ▼	Remaining ▼	Add New Column ▼
▲ **Type: Work**	**$4,620.00**	**$3,420.00**	**$1,200.00**	**$0.00**	**$4,620.00**	
1 Movers	$4,320.00	$3,120.00	$1,200.00	$0.00	$4,320.00	
2 Moving Truck	$300.00	$300.00	$0.00	$0.00	$300.00	
3 Family	$0.00	$0.00	$0.00	$0.00	$0.00	
▲ **Type: Material**	**$0.00**	**$0.00**	**$0.00**	**$0.00**	**$0.00**	
7 Gasoline	$0.00	$0.00	$0.00	$0.00	$0.00	
4 Packing Boxes	$0.00	$0.00	$0.00	$0.00	$0.00	
5 Packing Paper	$0.00	$0.00	$0.00	$0.00	$0.00	
6 Peanuts	$0.00	$0.00	$0.00	$0.00	$0.00	
▲ **Type: Cost**	**$0.00**	**$0.00**	**$0.00**	**$0.00**	**$0.00**	
8 Truck Insuranc	$0.00	$0.00	$0.00	$0.00	$0.00	

A difference between sorting and grouping is that in grouping, a Group By record is inserted at the start of each group. Project calculates totals for any numeric fields in this record for the records grouped beneath it. In Figure 8.16, the cost table has been applied and the fields show various measurements of the cost of assignments for the resources. You can see that the total cost of assignments for work resources is $4620.00, whereas the total cost of assignments for material resources is zero. The inserted grouping rows have no resource ID or row number, and they disappear when you remove the grouping.

 note

Project displays the resource list in outline format by outline code number if you define a custom outline code for resources and use that field for the Group By order.

 tip

If you create a custom outline code for resources—perhaps outlining them geographically by divisions, cities, departments, and job codes—you will find that grouping on that outline field produces a hierarchical outline with rolled-up costs that can be very useful.

If you use a custom text field to identify resource skills, you can insert the Work column in the table and then group by the skills and by start dates to see the total amount of work needed for each skill per week or month. If you insert the Peak column (which shows the maximum number of units assigned for a resource at any moment during a given time period), you could forecast the number of units of a skill that are needed per time period.

To group resource records on the resource type as in Figure 8.16, select the View tab and choose More Groups from the Group By drop-down. Select Work vs. Material Resources. To remove the grouping, choose Project, Group By, No Group, or press Shift+F3.

You can change the sort order while the resources are grouped. The sort settings are applied within each group. In other words, resources do not move to a different group as a result of the new sort order. The resource list shown previously in Figure 8.15 is sorted by cost, in descending order. You can also apply filters while the resources are grouped, which is discussed in the next section.

Filtering Resources

Use filters to select all the resources that meet some condition that you specify. For example, you might want to select all your material resources. This condition—that the resource type must be Material—is called the filter criterion. Project has a built-in filter named the Resources–Material filter that implements this criterion for you, as shown in Figure 8.17.

 tip

Filtering for specific resources is a great way to isolate only the resources that meet specific criteria that you have defined and to temporarily omit the other ones. By doing so, you can save a lot of time by applying a single change that affects an entire group of resources instead of having to change each one independently.

Figure 8.17
When the filter is applied, the resources that do not satisfy the selected criteria are hidden from the current view.

After Project selects the resources that meet the criteria, it normally changes the display to show only the selected resources, temporarily hiding all those that do not meet the criteria. However, you can also choose to use a highlight filter, and Project simply highlights the selected resources, without hiding all the others. In Figure 8.18, the Resources–Material highlight is applied as yellow fill for each row.

Figure 8.18
The highlighter enables you to continue to display all available resources but highlight the resources that meet the filter criteria.

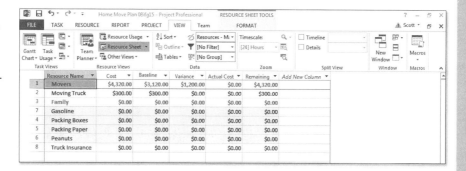

For information on how to customize the highlight filter, **see** Chapter 22, "Customization Almost Beyond Reason: Views, Tables, Filters, Groups, Fields, Toolbars, Menus, and Forms," **p. 699**.

When you finish using the filtered display, you must apply either the [No filter] or [No Highlight] options to return to the normal display, or simply press the F3 key.

Another useful filter for reviewing how you categorized your resources is the Group filter. You can quickly filter the list to show all the resources that have a specific keyword if you have entered keywords in the Group field. For example, if you entered department names in the Group field, you could filter the list for "Design" to identify all the resources that are managed by the Design department. If you used job titles, you could use the filter to isolate resources who might qualify for a certain resource assignment.

Project lets you filter the list of resources to be displayed in the Assign Resources dialog box. This dialog box is especially useful for substituting one resource for another. Usually, you want to substitute resources that have the same skill set. If you use a custom text field to enter skill keywords, you can filter the resource list to see all resources that might be appropriate substitutes. If you include a comma-separated list of multiple skills, you need to define a special filter for this purpose.

You can use filters to quickly check the status of resources after work on the project has begun to see at a glance where problems might lie. The following partial filter listing illustrates how useful filters can be in managing a project and enables you to identify specific categories of resources:

- Use the Overallocated Resource filter to focus on resources that are assigned to more work than they can possibly finish in the scheduled time period.

- Use the Cost Overbudget filter to find resources whose scheduled costs are more than you had budgeted.

- Use the Work Complete filter to find resources that have finished all their work.

- Use the Slipping Assignments filter to see which resources are taking longer than planned to finish their assignments.

- Use the Resource/Assignments with Overtime filter to see which resources have been assigned overtime work.

 *For a complete list of the built-in filters and how to use them, **see** Chapter 11, "Using Standard Views, Tables, Filters, and Groups to Review Your Schedule," **p. 357**.*

 *For instruction on creating your own custom filters, **see** Chapter 22, "Customization Almost Beyond Reason: Views, Tables, Filters, Groups, Fields, Toolbars, Menus, and Forms," **p. 699**.*

You can apply a filter by selecting the View tab. For example, if you want to display only material resources in a resource view, you would follow these steps:

1. Display one of the resource views that has a table of resources in the top pane.

2. Click the Filter drop-down to display the drop-down list of resource filters, and then click Resources–Material.

Project hides everything but the resources that have Material in the resource's Type field.

tip

Project also lets you use the Assign Resources dialog box to do availability-based scheduling. Highlight a task and check the Available to Work check box, and Project will show you only resources that have a specified amount of availability during the time a task is scheduled. This technique is extremely helpful when trying to find the right people to work on a schedule that has inflexible dates.

note

You can apply filters only to full-screen views or views that are in the top pane of a combination view. The bottom-pane views are already filtered for the task or resource that is selected in the top pane. Thus, you cannot apply filters to views in the bottom pane.

tip

To use a filter that is on the menu as a highlight filter, use the Highlight drop-down.

If you have applied a filter and then made changes that might alter which resources are selected by the filter, use Ctrl+F3 to reapply the filter.

Consultants' Tips

Make sure you have a solid understanding of resource types and apply those accordingly in your project schedule. The cost resource adds another dimension to the capabilities of Project and improves your ability to model a project accurately. You should become comfortable with it and the other resource types. Learn how to use them in the right context to improve your accuracy in predicting time and cost.

Use the Budget resource type to include your capital project budget, if you have one that you must maintain and meet. Even though you will baseline your project to capture your planned values, the Budget resource can help you maintain a comparison value to compare to your baseline, ensuring that you did not exceed it in your planning. This feature also becomes important if your planned budget is less than your capital budget, in which case you might have a budget reserve that you can use later in the tracking phase if the project begins to slip.

Keep the resource calendars and availability contouring simple. As you have seen, Project has tremendous capability to model resources—and consequently to generate possibly excessive complexity. Use only the data fields required, and remember that any data included needs to be maintained. For example, if you create a separate resource calendar for a resource, you will need to maintain it throughout the life of the project, so make sure that it is going to be worthwhile to do that. Contouring is an effective way to model and predict resource usage, but it can be difficult to maintain the precision and accuracy in a real-world project. Keep the level of detail appropriate to the accuracy required for your project.

Use the Resource Availability Available From date to indicate when the resource became available to your project. This can give you time-phased staffing levels and eliminate confusion when looking back at how resources were applied to your project.

UNDERSTANDING WORK FORMULA BASICS

Welcome to the most critical chapter in this book. If you read nothing else in this book, you should read this chapter and, at the very least, this introduction. Microsoft Project is at heart a scheduling engine. A scheduling engine is a tool that helps you "model" the actions you need to perform to achieve a goal. This "model" enables you to plan actions prior to making them. Planning is important for understanding ALL of what must be done and WHEN it must be done, but after you begin the process of fulfilling the plan, the "model" underneath must be able to adjust when real life collides with the beautiful vision of "what will happen"; otherwise, the plan will be useless immediately.

With the introduction of Manually Scheduled mode, it is possible to create tasks and assignments that do not take advantage of Project's scheduling capability (hence the designation "Manually Scheduled"). Throughout this book, we call attention to the differences this task mode makes. This chapter, however, is focused on using the scheduling engine to its fullest. Therefore, Manually Scheduled mode is covered sparingly.

Understanding Task Levels

Project models the actions you need to perform (that is, *tasks*, sometimes called *activities*). Each task can be performed by one person or many. One person's contribution to the fulfillment of a task is called an *assignment*. Project must correctly model the different kinds of assignments a person might be asked to do AND how a set of assignments contributes to the achievement of a task.

This is the foundation of auto-scheduling in Project. On the foundation is built layer upon layer of further logic to handle additional needs. Think of it as an inverted pyramid. Knowledge of the bottom-most level is a key component to understanding all the higher levels. The pyramid has the following levels, and each higher level requires another layer of modeling logic to be provided by Project (see Figure 9.1):

- **Program**—The impact of projects upon each other.

- **Project**—The impact of tasks upon each other.

- **Task**—How the set of individual resource contributions (assignments) interplay to achieve an activity (or action) to be performed.

- **Assignment**—How one person fulfills his portion or contribution to the achievement of a task. For purposes of this discussion, assignments will be performed only by people and no other resource type (material, cost, or budget).

This simple list is of course complicated by actual implementation: Individual calendars vary, people seldom work on only one project a time, project resources come and go, some resources are more productive than others, and so on.

Work, Duration, and Units

Project models all of these, but the first thing that must be understood, the base of the inverted pyramid upon which all else is built, is the assignment—a single person's contribution to the completion of a task. In everyday real life, many things affect how the performed assignments are completed. Modeling this is the real purpose of the work formula, and it is not as simple as you might think.

Figure 9.1
The inverted pyramid represents the levels of modeling logic involved in achieving a realistic output: your project schedule.

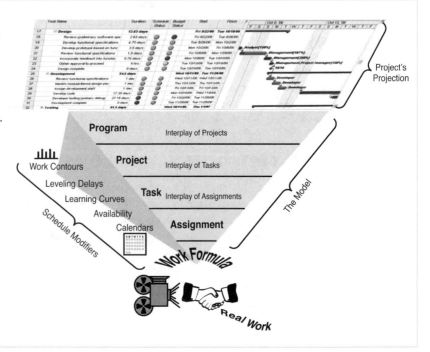

The formula itself is as follows:

Work = Duration × Units

If a resource works for five days at 100% of his eight work hours per day, he has an assignment that will be completed in 40 hours: 5 days × (100% of 8 hrs/day) = 40 hours of effort. Simple. The formula also reflects that if a resource works 125% of his workday (or 10 hours), he would work 50 hours. But remember, Project at this level is modeling the activity that must be completed (the result of the effort), not the effort to achieve it. The result of the effort is the work to be performed where "work" is used as a noun—or call it the "job." So, if it would take a resource 40 hours to complete the assignment, and the resource chooses to work 10 hours per day, those two values (Units and Work) are held constant and the third one (Duration) is solved for by the formula.

Used this way, the activity is correctly modeled as having a duration of four days instead of five days. This is an example of how the formula is used. Two of the three variables are held constant, and the formula is used to "solve" for the third.

Tasks with Multiple Assignments

The next level up in the pyramid is about how multiple assignments (multiple resources) work together to achieve the task, which again comes down to the type of work the task is intended to model. It could be that the task is "eat a 100-foot-long hot dog"; the more people you add to the task, the faster the hot dog is eaten. Or, it could be that the task is like a meeting—no matter how many people you put on it, they are all still there for the hour-long duration of the meeting, so the work effort grows with each person added. All of this is modeled in Project. Real life continues to impact this scenario through the scheduling of the work produced over time. The meeting lasts longer if you break for lunch in the middle. The hot dog takes longer to eat if the people are available only during lunch hour, or if some of the people can stay only for 10 minutes, but others can stay for an hour.

The next level up in the inverted pyramid represents the modeling of the impact tasks have on each other. The hot dog must be cooked before it can be eaten. The meeting attendees must read the document that is the topic of the meeting prior to having the meeting, and so on.

The program level adds additional modeling complexity in regard to rollups, prioritization, external links, program phases, cross-program leveling, and so on.

For the purposes of this chapter, the levels are referred to as the assignment level, task level, and project level. Duration, units, and work are the three key variables in the formula. The results of the formula are used by higher modeling layers in the inverted pyramid, and when all of this is applied to a schedule, additional real-life impacts come into play as well (Resource calendars and availability, learning curves, and so on). These real-life impacts here are called *schedule modifiers*, as they modify how the result of the formula is applied to a calendar.

This is an introduction to the complexity that Project must model. The rest of this chapter drills into each of these areas again and provides more depth.

Understanding Resource and Task Assignments

This chapter and Chapter 10, "Scheduling Single and Multiple Resource Assignments," are the key components in the Project scheduling engine, or as one consultant put it, "This is where the rubber hits the road." This chapter helps you gain an understanding of the background behind resource scheduling and the calculations that Project makes when you assign one or more resources to a task. You also look at the work formula and the behavior that the combination of task types (from Chapter 8, "Defining Project Resources") and the work formula drives. Project makes calculations while you are editing resource assignments. Not understanding why it is making these changes might cause frustration, as even minor changes might have a much larger impact than you ever expected. This chapter helps you understand why Project makes those changes and how to interpret and even predict those changes, thus preventing frustration and getting the outcome you expect.

In Chapter 10, you see how the basic formula adapts for single-resource or multiple-resource assignments, complex calendar requirements, and the specific scheduling requirements of your project.

You also learn how the task types affect the work formula. To understand the work formula, you must have a strong grasp of the different task types and understand their relationship and how they work together.

 tip

The majority of this chapter discusses the work formula. It is composed of three basic variables: the *duration* of a task (D), the amount of effort or *work* (W) required, and the amount of resources or *units* (U) that perform the work. It is important to understand that you can control *two* of the three variables; the remaining variable will be calculated by the work formula. Understanding this fundamental principle makes the rest of this chapter much easier to understand and your scheduling efforts much less frustrating.

For information on task relationships, **see** Chapter 7, "Defining Task Logic," **p. 183**.

Reviewing the Essential Components of Work Resource Assignments

A work resource is anyone or anything that does "work," such as an employee or the backhoe that the employee is using. When a work resource is assigned to a task, Project completes the work formula and schedules the resource for a specific time period, based on the dates established when the task was entered into the schedule. The time period is determined by a variety of factors, including calendars, task types, preset start and finish dates, duration, work, and links to other tasks.

When you are assigning resources to tasks, you must keep several key factors in mind. Each of these factors is discussed in more detail in other sections of the book. See the "Schedule Modifiers That Affect the Complexity of the Scheduling Engine" section later in the chapter for the list of schedule modifiers that influence the behavior of the work formula.

After work resources have been assigned to tasks, Project calculates the schedule assignment, taking into consideration the schedule modifiers listed in the section, "Schedule Modifiers That Affect the Complexity of the Scheduling Engine." You can then modify this schedule to suit any specific requirements or needs you might have.

➡ *For more information on how to adjust schedules in a variety of ways,* **see** *Chapter 10, "Scheduling Single and Multiple Resource Assignments,"* **p. 301***.*

Understanding the Resource Assignment Fields

When a resource is assigned to a task, you must, at the very least, identify the resource; Project provides default values for the other essential assignment fields. You can also assign the number of resource units to the task and the amount of work that the assignment will require. Figure 9.2 shows where the fields are to enter this information.

Figure 9.2
The bottom pane of the combination Gantt Chart view enables you to enter multiple resources and various resource assignment attributes.

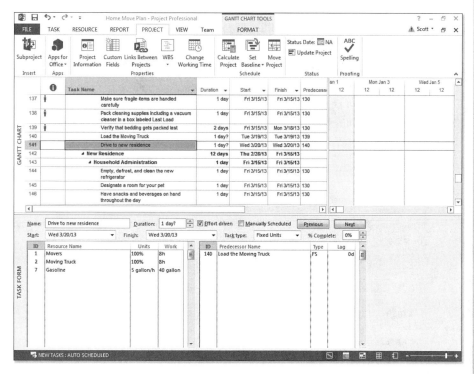

Assigning a Resource to a Task

To assign a resource to a task, you have to identify the resource by either its name or its ID number. In most cases, the Resource Name field has a drop-down list of the names that have already been defined in the resource sheet. You can also add a new resource name, and Project adds that name to the resource sheet as it assigns the name to the task.

 caution

As mentioned in Chapter 8, you should have Project alert you before a new name is added to the resource sheet. This prevents the name from being mistyped. If you do enter a resource that is mistyped, Project creates a new variation of the same resource in the sheet, but with a different spelling. This can cause the workload of the correctly spelled resource to be misrepresented because it does not include the assignments incorrectly given to the misspelled resource.

➡ *For details on how to change the option for Project to automatically add new resources,* **see** *the "Setting the Automatically Add New Resources and Tasks Option" section,* **p. 258**, *in Chapter 8.*

Understanding the Assignment Units Field

Assignment units, often simply labeled *units*, define how much of a resource is assigned to an individual task. You can see the Assignment Units field in Figure 9.2 earlier in the chapter.

Project shows units for work resources in both the Max Units and Assignment Units fields as percentages, but you can change these to a decimal format. Although the percentage format can be advantageous when assigning individual people resources, it becomes very confusing when you are working with group resources.

➡ *For additional information on group resources,* **see** *Chapter 8, "Defining Project Resources,"* **p. 235**.

To select the format for the resource Units field, perform the following actions:

1. Select the File tab, Options, Schedule, Schedule.

2. In the Show Assignment Units as A field, select Decimal or Percentage.

3. This setting affects the display for all work resources.

The easiest way to understand how to assign work resources is to think about the way you spend your day. If Jenny, the graphic artist, is needed all day working on one project, you need to set her Assignment Units field at 100%, so Project schedules her for 100% of her time. If Dan, the attorney, is needed only for part of the day, to review the contracts, set his Assignment Units field at 10% because he will probably spend the rest of his day working on other assignments. When using named resources such as people, it is easy to think in percentages of their days.

If, however, you are working with several named resources, such as a group of computer programmers or a fleet of delivery trucks, it is often more intuitive and logical to use the decimal point format in the Assignment Units field. Instead of using 500% to represent the five computer programmers you have working on a project, it makes more sense to use 5.0 in the decimal format, or instead of having 1600% of your truck fleet working, you have 16.0 trucks on the road. The flip side to this is that it does not make sense to have Dan the attorney working .25 units; instead, it is much more intuitive for him to be working 25% of his day on something. Just use your logical judgment when deciding whether to use the decimal or the percentage format.

Using the percentage format, however, helps to explain the way that Project uses the Assignment Units field. Project uses this field to calculate how many hours of work it will schedule for the resource per hour of working time on the calendar. For instance, if you have two mechanics, Scott and Mike, but they are set up as one work resource, you expect one hour of effort from each of them during every hour of time they spend on the project. That is what happens if you assign units equal to 200%; Project assigns two hours of effort for every hour of working time on the calendar until the task is complete.

When using a work resource that is actually a team of individuals—such as a group of computer programmers or several drivers for your fleet of trucks—you must remember that a 100% entry into the Assignment Units field will not represent all of your individuals. Project schedules only one hour of effort for every hour of working time on the calendar until the task is complete. If there are five individuals on your team, you must enter 500% into the Assignment Units field to represent all five of them. A 500% entry tells Project to schedule five hours of effort for every one hour of working time on the calendar, until the task is complete.

 For additional details on assigning multiple resources, see Chapter 10, "Scheduling Single and Multiple Resource Assignments," p. 301.

 note

You can also contour the work to assign a resource to exact expectations of actual work in a given day or work period. Resource contours are discussed in more detail later in this chapter.

Percent Allocation is a time-phased field and can be viewed in the task or resource usage views.

 note

For the purpose of this chapter, it is important to remember that units can be assigned in percentages of any amount.

 note

Remember that Project takes any entry into the Assignment Units field and schedules it down to the minute across the specified or calculated duration. If you were to enter 25%, it would in fact represent two hours out of an eight-hour workday. However, Project schedules 15 minutes for work for each hour in the eight-hour day, which totals two hours. In most cases, the resource, or employee, will realistically sit down and complete all the work in two hours, in one sitting, rather than working for just 15 minutes an hour every hour on the project. If you are concerned only about the overall time (in this case, two hours and not the exact amount of time the resource is actually spending during each hour), you can just ignore the difference between the way that Project schedules time and the way the work is actually performed. If you want the schedule to reflect that the resource worked full time for two hours continuously and then was idle for the rest of the task, you can enter the Assignment Units field at 100% and then change the duration to .25 days.

The default Units value for work resources is usually 100% (or 1.0 in the decimal format). However, if the Max Units value is set at less than 100%, the default Units value reflects that change. You can set the Max Units number at anything between 0% and 6,000,000,000% (or 0.0 to 60,000,000 in the decimal format).

---

 note

When assigning a resource to a task, Project sets the assignment units to the lesser of the value of the Max Units for the resource or 100% unless you set the Units value. Project does not enforce a maximum number of available units when you make resource assignments. You can assign more units than the Max Units value when you are planning a project. When the maximum units for any resource are exceeded within any duration unit, you get an overallocated special indicator for those resource names in the Resource Sheet or the Resource Usage view.

You can enter fractions of a percentage into the Assignment Units field, but they are automatically rounded up to the nearest whole number. Project uses fractional percents in the calculations, but it will not display them.

Material resources are always formatted as a decimal. If you miss entering the assigned units, it defaults to 1, followed by the material label defined for the resource. If you defined the material resource of dirt with the Yd label (for cubic yard), the default units supplied by Project will be 1 Yd, which means the task will consume 1 cubic yard of dirt.

When you enter a numeral into the Units column for a material resource, it is called a *fixed consumption rate*. The amount is considered to be fixed and independent of the task duration. Using our current example, Project figures 1 yard of material for the task, and if the task duration changes, the consumption rate will not.

 note

If you enter something that Project does not understand, such as *yards* instead of *Yd*, it shows you the warning (see Figure 9.3). This warning is to let you know that what you entered is not a valid Units value. Simply enter a numeric value and let Project provide the correct label.

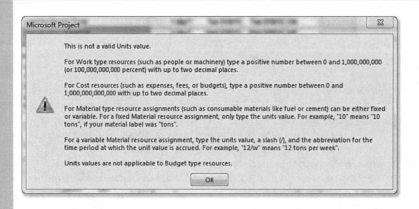

Figure 9.3
Click OK in the warning window and let Project figure out the units for the selected resource.

If you want to assign material resource units that have a variable consumption rate, where the amount of material resource depends on the duration of the task, you simply enter the units, followed by a forward slash (/). For instance, if you have a backhoe that uses 10 gallons of gas an hour, you can enter either **10/h** or **10 gal/h**. Project then calculates the consumption of 10 gallons of fuel per hour for every hour of working time on the calendar until the task is complete.

Assigning the Work

Work resources spend hours of time working on a task, and you can measure their contributions in hours, days, or some other kind of time unit. It is this unit of the work resources that gives a task duration in the first place, as well as the time it takes to finish the work on a task. In fact, when you estimate the duration of a task, you should be thinking about how long it will take the work resource to complete the work, or how long it takes an employee to do a task. Material resources do not expend effort, however; they are simply used up by a task. That is why you measure them as units consumed. Although both work and material resources are displayed in the Work field, Project ignores values for material resources and just calculates the hours for the work resources when figuring total work.

In the case of work resources, the term *work*, sometimes called *effort*, measures the time required by a resource on a task. Project displays work in hours, by default, but you can change the default to any standard time unit, such as minutes, days, weeks, or months. To change the time unit used to display work, follow these steps:

1. Select the File tab, Options.

2. Click the Schedule tab and select the time unit in the *Work Is Entered In* list box.

Work can be entered by the user, but Project completes it automatically when a resource is assigned if nothing is entered (assuming tasks are auto-scheduled). You can also enter work by using any time unit, regardless of the unit used to display work, as long as you follow your entry with the time unit label.

If a work resource is scheduled for full time on a task that has a duration of one week, that resource is assigned for 40 hours of work. However, if the resource is assigned to the task only half time (that is, units is equal to 50%), it is assigned to 20 hours of work during the week. If two resource units work full time all week (or 200%), there are 80 hours of work or effort. Other things being equal, the following holds true:

- The longer the duration of the task, the more work is scheduled.

- The larger the resource units assigned, the more work is scheduled.

The amount of work that Project schedules for the resource is tied to the duration of the task and the number of units assigned to the task. This relationship is defined more precisely in the next section, "Understanding the Work Formula."

In the case of material resources, the Work field shows the total number of physical units consumed in completing the task. If you enter the units, Project completes the work units for you. For fixed-rate consumption assignments, the Work field acts the same as the Units field. If you assign 10 gallons (10 gal) of fuel, the Work field shows 10 gallons. If you assign 10 gallons per day (10 gal/d), however, Project calculates 50 gallons in the Work field for a week-long task.

Assigning the Duration

The Duration field that Project uses in the scheduling engine refers to the duration of an assignment as the number of days covered by spreading the work from the start date forward across the available work hours *as determined by the combined Project, Resource, and Task calendars.*

 note

Note that the finish date is calculated differently!

The finish date is calculated on an assignment basis by spreading the work from the start date forward across the available work hours *as determined by the hours per day setting* (select the File tab, Options, Schedule). The Gantt bar always displays start date to finish date.

The Task-Level Duration and Finish fields are calculated from merging the assignment day coverage (using Start and Duration fields) and the latest assignment finish date.

The Duration calculation at the task level is based on the set of assignments for the task. If there are no assignments, for the purpose of calculating the Duration field only, a single assignment will be assumed (using 100% units and the Project and Task calendars).

 tip

The fact that the finish date is calculated differently than duration can lead to confusion. See the section, "The Difference Between Calendar Duration and Actual Assignment Duration," under the "Consultants' Tips" at the end of this chapter for more information.

Understanding the Work Formula

The work formula consists of three variables: work, duration, and units. The work formula is calculated only when the task is in Auto Scheduled mode. In Manually Scheduled mode, it is possible to enter an amount for work without having a resource assigned.

The calculating formula works as follows:

Duration × Units = Work

In symbols, it is represented like this:

D × U = W

You multiply the task duration (D) by the assigned units (U) to calculate work (W).

 note

These formulas do not apply to material resources that have fixed consumption rates. For those resources, the value in the Work field is identical to the value in the Units field. The formulas do apply, however, to resources with variable consumption rates. These formulas were developed and implemented before the material resource type was introduced, and so the following makes more sense if you think in terms of work resources.

Simple algebra can be used to reformulate this equation to calculate values for duration when work and units are given:

Duration = Work / Units *or* D = W / U

The same applies to when duration and work are given, and you need to calculate units:

Units = Work / Duration *or* U = W / D

Project uses assignment units as a multiplier to calculate how work must be scheduled, and understanding this formula is very important and can save you a headache down the road.

 note

Even though duration can be displayed in minutes, hours, days, weeks, or months, Project converts the duration to minutes when calculating work and then displays it in the default units for work, which is usually the hour.

An example of this formula works like this: If you assign two movers (200%) to work on a task with a duration of four hours, Project schedules two hours of work for each of the four hours duration; total work equals eight hours.

 note

In former versions of Project, work always equaled duration multiplied by (assignment) units. It is now possible to enter a value in the Work field that does not equal duration multiplied by units, even when the task mode is Auto Scheduled. Project retains the original value entered in the Units field.

At this time, we recommend avoiding manually editing the Work field for auto-scheduled tasks with assignments that have anything other than a flat contour. After you've edited the Work field, there are many permutations of schedule problems that manifest in various subtle and blatant ways. Editing the Assignments Unit field maintains the integrity of the work equation. Fortunately, editing the Assignments field forces Project to recalculate work and duration correctly.

The Peak Units field, which is used in resource overallocation views, usually indicates that something is wrong. Unfortunately, Peak Units is not a reliable replacement for what was formerly the Units field when an assignment is contoured. For example, in the case of an assignment with a front-loaded contour, it is possible that neither the Peak Units nor the Assignment Unit fields accurately reflect the Units value.

Applying the Work Formula in New Assignments

Before you assign resources to a task, the auto-scheduled task has duration (one day by default or entered value) but usually does not have a Work value unless entered, because in the work formula, units = 0, and therefore work = 0. When you create the resource assignments, Project calculates the work and sums that value into the task's Work field. In some cases, the work called for in an assignment cannot be completed within the initial duration estimate for the task, and Project might have to change the task duration to accommodate the needs of the assignments. If the task has multiple resources assigned and some of those assignments take longer to complete than others, the task duration is calculated to be at least as long as the longest assignment. However, if the task is a fixed-duration task, Project cannot recalculate the duration. See "Setting the Task Type," later in this chapter, for more information on this topic.

To help you understand how Project calculates the changes brought about by assigning resources, the simplest case will be examined first, where you assign a single resource in an initial task. Subsequently, Project's response to changes in existing assignments will be explored.

It is best to experiment with each of the three different cases to have a better understanding of how the work formula operates. Remember, the better grasp you have of this information, the easier it will be later on:

1. Select Gantt Chart view from the Task tab.

2. Toggle Details on by clicking the Details control on the Task tab. This opens a split window in the bottom pane.

3. Right-click the Task Form view and choose Resources and Predecessors from the Detail list.

4. The Assignment Units and Work fields appear next to the resource name in the resource details (see Figure 9.4).

5. Enter different values for units and work until you feel comfortable predicting the outcome when you create an assignment.

For the work formula to operate properly, Project defaults all new auto-scheduled task durations to one day. The duration for a task is already defined before you assign the first resource to the task. Thus, task duration is already established. Project handles your entries when assigning the initial resource slightly differently for work and material resources, so they need to be considered separately.

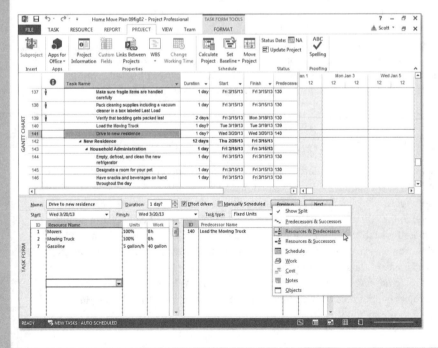

Figure 9.4
Customizing and combining views enables you to maximize the use of the screen and see exactly the fields you need.

The following examples show what happens for an initial assignment of a work resource. The distinctions are based on task type and which fields you fill in: Units only, Work only, or both Units and Work. Each example assumes that the task has a duration of 1 day and that days and weeks are defined to be 8 hours and 40 hours, respectively. It is also assumed that the task type used is fixed units. To verify your settings and ensure that they meet the assumptions described here, follow these steps:

1. Select the File tab, Options, Schedule.

2. In the Schedule tab, verify the Hours per Day, Hours per Week, and Days per Month settings.

3. Click OK to close the Options dialog box.

There is more information on other task types later in the chapter.

Project responds to entries when creating a work resource assignment as follows:

If you enter the resource name when creating the assignment and do not provide the values for units or work, Project assumes that you want the default units (the lesser of Max Units or 100%) and calculates the work from the duration and units. It will do this for either manually scheduled or auto-scheduled tasks. For example, if you assign a work resource to a one-day task without specifying the units, Project supplies 100% to the Units field and calculates eight hours for the Work field (see Figure 9.5).

Figure 9.5
Duration × Units = Work. Therefore, 8h × 100% = 8 hours.

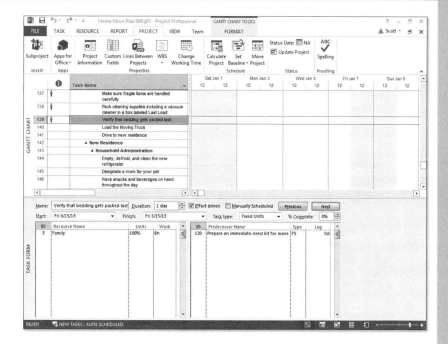

If you enter the Units value, Project uses that value with the duration to calculate the work. For example, if you assign a resource to a one-day task and enter **50%** in the Units field, Project calculates the Work value (see Figure 9.6). Again, it will do this for tasks in either task mode.

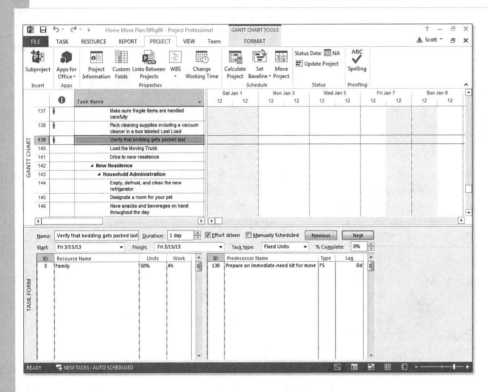

Figure 9.6
Duration
× Units
= Work.
Therefore,
8h × 50% =
4 hours.

The task duration, however, is still one day.

If you enter the Work value but do not supply the units, Project assumes that you want the default units (the lesser of Max Units or 100%) and calculates a new value for the duration, based on the specified work and the assumed value for units. For example, if you assign a resource to a one-day auto-scheduled task and enter **16h** in the Work field but leave the Units field blank, Project calculates a new Duration value (see Figure 9.7) because it takes more than one day for a single resource unit to complete 16 hours of work.

If you enter both the Units and Work values, Project recalculates the existing auto-scheduled task duration, using the new entries. For example, if you assign Units the value **200%** and Work the value **32h**, Project calculates a new task duration by using this variation of the work formula (see Figure 9.8).

Figure 9.7
Duration × Units = Work. Duration × 100% = 16 hours. Therefore, Duration = 16h / 100% = 16 hours (that is, 2 days).

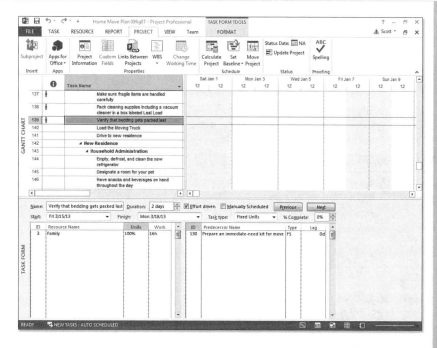

Figure 9.8
Duration × Units = Work. Duration × 200% = 32 hours. Therefore, Duration = 32h / 200% = 16 hours (that is, 2 days).

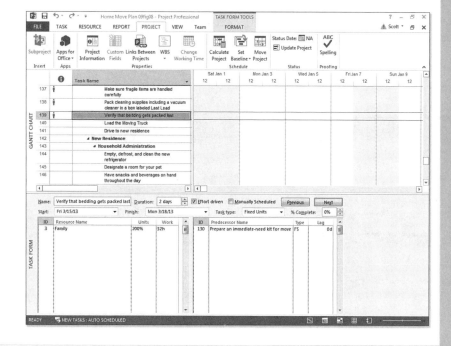

When the resource is a material resource, there are fewer alternatives to consider than with work resources. Similarly, assume that the task is a one-day task. This time, however, the resource is the material resource Packing Peanuts, and its label is cubic feet. As you might remember for material resources, the Units field is always displayed in decimal format. Project's response to your entries when creating a material resource assignment is as follows:

- If you just enter the material resource name but do not provide either the Units value or the Work value of the assignment, Project assumes that the Units value is 1 and calculates all the work to be 1 cubic foot. For example, if you assign the Packing Peanuts resource to a one-day task without specifying the units, Project supplies 1 cubic foot to both the Units and Work fields (see Figure 9.9).

- If you enter the Units value as a number (in other words, as a fixed consumption rate), Project enters that value into both the Units and the Work fields. For example, if you assign the Packing Boxes resource to a one-day task and enter 30 in the Units field, Project supplies 30 boxes to both the Units and Work fields (see Figure 9.10).

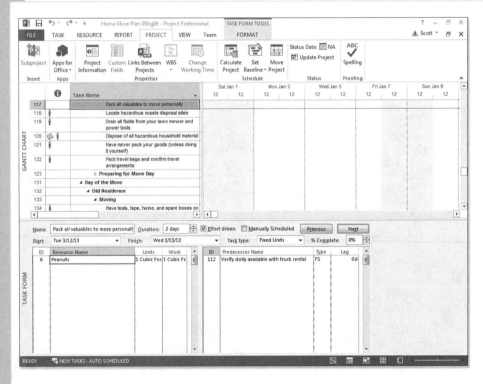

Figure 9.9
Duration × Units = Work. Therefore, 1 × 1 cubic foot = 1.

Figure 9.10
Duration
× Units =
Work. 1 day
× 30 boxes
= Work.
Therefore,
Work = 30
boxes.

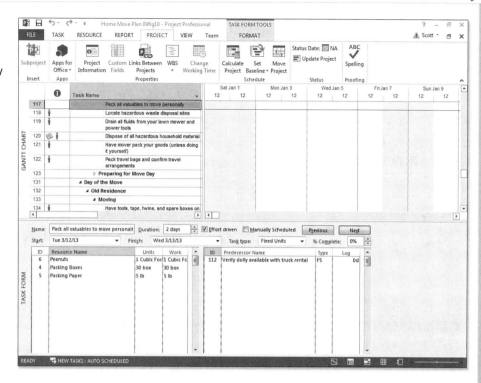

- If you enter the Units value as a variable consumption rate, Project uses that rate with the task duration to calculate the Work field. For example, if you enter **5 / h** in the Units field for gasoline, Project converts that to 5 / hour and multiplies that value by the duration (1 day, 8 hours) to calculate the Work field entry of 40 (see Figure 9.11).

- If you enter the Work value of **5 lbs** for Packing Paper but do not supply the units, Project assumes that the amount you entered has a fixed consumption rate and puts that amount in both the Units and Work fields (see Figure 9.12).

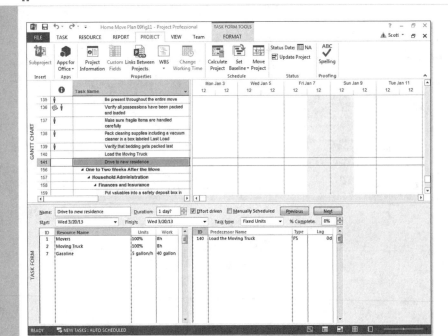

Figure 9.11
Duration × Units = Work. 1 day (8 hours) × (5 gallons/hour) = Work. Therefore, Work = 8 × 5 = 40.

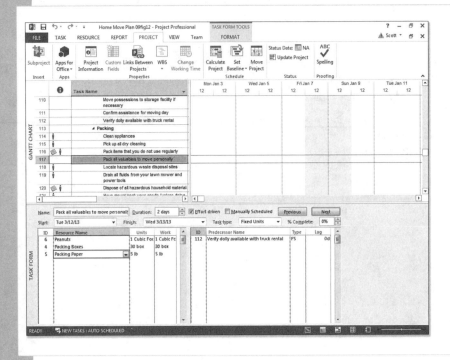

Figure 9.12
Work / Duration = Units. 5 lbs / 1 day = Units. Therefore, Units = 5 / 1 = 5 lbs.

- If you enter a variable consumption rate of **5/h** (5 gallons per hour) for gasoline in the Units field and also enter **200** in the Work field, Project recalculates the duration of auto-scheduled tasks so that the consumption rate yields the total units in the Work field (see Figure 9.13).

Figure 9.13
Duration
× Units
= Work.
Duration
× (5 gal/h)
= 200.
Therefore,
Duration
= 200 / 5 =
40 hours,
which is 5
days.

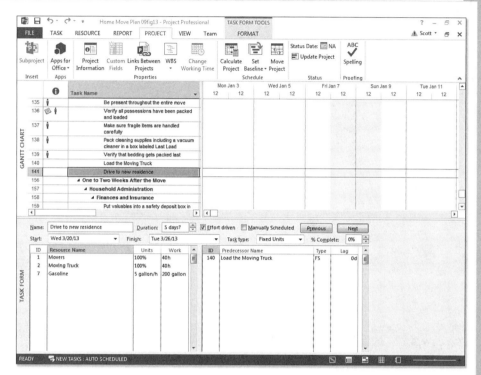

Using the Task Form View

An advantage of using the Task Form view to create assignments is that the initial assignment can include all resources that are to be assigned to the task, and you can specify units or work for each assignment. Other methods of assigning resources require you to complete each assignment individually or do not let you regulate both units and work, so the Task Form view might become your preferred entry method. As you see in Chapter 10, individually assigning multiple resources to a task creates additional variations on how Project calculates the task work and duration.

To create multiple assignments with the initial assignment, you can simply enter multiple rows in the Resource Details table before you click OK. Project then calculates each of the assignments individually, using the principles outlined previously and using the existing task duration in each calculation.

For example, in Figure 9.14, two task forms are shown (select the Task tab, View, View control, and select the Task form). The top form shows the initial assignment being created, and the bottom form shows the results after the OK button has been clicked. The task is a 0.5-day task; two movers are assigned and one moving truck. The task also consumes 5 gallons per hour for gasoline.

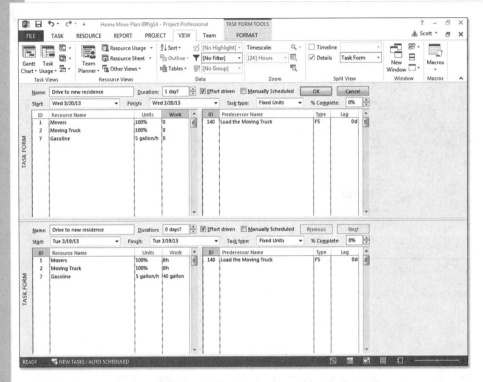

Figure 9.14
List all your resources first and then click OK.

Applying the Work Formula in Changes to Existing Assignments

In the examples so far in this chapter, it might seem as though Project is free to recalculate any of the three variables in the work formula (except when the Work value is manually entered on a task with a contoured assignment, as discussed previously in this chapter). However, in the next section, you see that one of the three variables in the equation is always fixed for a task, which also means it is fixed for any assignments to that task. Project chooses not to allow you to change the fixed value when it has to recalculate the work equation for an assignment.

For example, by default, tasks are created as Fixed Units tasks, as indicated by the underline in the following formula:

$$D \times \underline{U} = W$$

If you change the duration, Project has to leave the units unchanged and must recalculate the work, or if you change the work, Project must recalculate the duration. You can define which variable is fixed for a task and is therefore fixed for all of that task's assignment calculations. This is how you control how Project responds when you make changes in assignments.

Selecting Task Settings

Now that you have a grasp of the work formula, this section discusses the three types of tasks, as defined in the Task Type field: Fixed Units, Fixed Work, and Fixed Duration. Sometimes the task will fall easily into one of the three categories. Perhaps the task duration is set by the client, and you must work within that timeframe. You could define the task as a Fixed Duration task to keep Project from changing the duration. Or, perhaps you have a contract to provide a fixed amount of work for the client, in which case you could define the task as a Fixed Work task so Project will not change the amount of work scheduled.

You can make changes to the Task Type field to control how Project responds to an assignment change on an auto-scheduled task. If you wanted to increase the duration of a task, but keep the amount of work constant, you can make a Fixed Work task and then change the duration. Figure 9.15 provides a model for illustrating how the work formula is affected by the task type.

The work formula can be thought of as a triangle with three sides: duration, units, and work. In the work formula, one variable is always fixed by the task type, and the user has two remaining variables to modify. When a user modifies one variable by decreasing or increasing its value (lengthening or shortening one side of the triangle), Project recalculates the free range variable that is not fixed (the free side of the triangle is resized to ensure that the triangle remains geometrically intact).

This model provides an easy way to visualize the work formula as you cannot resize one side of a triangle and expect the other two sides to remain unchanged; the triangle shape will not be maintained. For example, in Figure 9.15, when you have a Fixed Duration task, the Duration side of the triangle remains unchanged and true to the original size. If the user increases the units by lengthening the Units side of the triangle, the Work side automatically resizes to maintain the triangle shape. Similarly, when the user increases units on a Fixed Duration task type, the work is recalculated by Project to maintain the mathematical proportion.

Table 9.1 helps to summarize which variable Project recalculates when a value changes in an existing assignment. The table assumes that your initial change is an increase in the respective variables, indicated by the plus signs in the column. If your initial change is a decrease, simply reverse the plus and minus signs for the columns to the right.

 note

When using the task types, remember that Fixed Units will always be Project's default type. You can change the default type in the schedule options so that any new task created uses the specified task type. To do so, select Tools, Options, Schedule Tab, and select the Default task type that you want Project to apply to all tasks.

 note

Also note that "Fixed" does *not* mean "will not change." For example, the duration of a "fixed duration" task can be changed by the user or by adding actuals. Use the Manually Scheduled task mode if you really do not want task values to change without your manual interaction.

Figure 9.15
Using the different task types, one variable is always fixed by the specified task type, the second one is specified by the user, and the third one is a free range variable calculated by Project based on the changes the user made to the second variable.

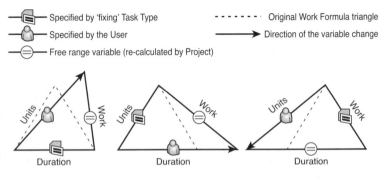

The first column lists the task type. The three columns to the right show which variable Project recalculates as a result. The up or down arrow indicates the direction of the resulting change. An underline in the formula is used to indicate which is the fixed variable (set by the Task Type applied). This enables you to follow the logic of the changes. In the first row, an increase in duration for a Fixed Units task leads to an increase in work, but for a Fixed Work task, it leads to a decrease in peak units.

Table 9.1 Task Type and Work Formula Calculations as They Apply to Auto-Scheduled Tasks

	Variable Calculated If You Change:		
Task Type	**Units**	**Duration**	**Work**
Fixed Units $D \times U = W$	Duration	Work	Duration
Fixed Duration $D \times U = W$	Work	Peak Units	Peak Units
Fixed Work $D \times U = W$	Duration	Peak Units	Duration

If the initial change is to the fixed variable itself, the rule is a little more complicated. Remember that duration is a task variable and that units and work are assignment variables. When you change one of the assignment variables, such as units or work, and it is a fixed variable, Project leaves the other assignment variables alone and changes task duration. When duration is fixed and you change it, Project leaves the assignment work unchanged and adjusts the units.

Suppose you want to force Project to calculate the number of resource units you need to assign when you know the duration of the task and the amount of work you want done. As an example, you can make the task a fixed duration and enter the amount of work. Project has to calculate the necessary units to keep the work formula in balance.

Setting the Task Type

You can define the task's type in the Task Information dialog box and in the Task Form view, or you can add the Task Type field to any task table. Figure 9.16 shows the Task Type field in the Task Information dialog box and on the Task Form view.

Figure 9.16
Both
the Task
Form view
and Task
Information
dialog box
enable you
to set the
task type
one task at
a time.

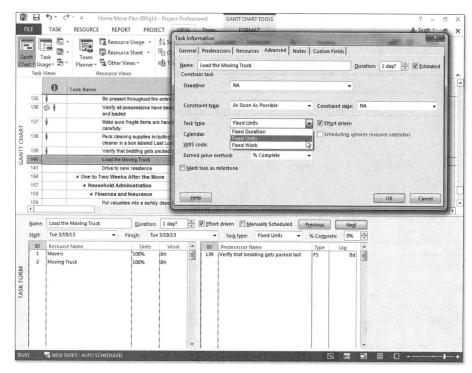

As mentioned earlier in this chapter, the default task type in Project is Fixed Units, not Effort Driven. You can change the default type for new tasks in a project by selecting the File tab, Options, Schedule. Set the Default Task Type field value (see Figure 9.17).

It is helpful to add the Type and Task Mode columns in the Gantt Chart view for recognition of task types to understand the rules about how the work formula is calculated. Project responds in the following ways when you create a new assignment for a task. As mentioned earlier, Project still calculates values even for manually scheduled tasks. However, the Units field retains its initial value no matter what changes are made; consequently, the Peak units field shows the correct value for flat-contoured tasks.

- If you enter a value in units and leave the Work field blank, Project calculates the unknown work, because both units and duration have been given values. This is true no matter what the task type or task mode—Project assumes that you have an eight-hour duration, even in a manually scheduled task with no duration entered.

- If you enter the value in work and leave the units blank, units won't change, but peak units will. Project's calculation depends on the task type:

  If the task is not a Fixed Duration task, Project adjusts the Duration value. It assumes that the Units value is the default and calculates the Duration value that is necessary for the resource to complete the amount of work you assigned.

  However, if the task is a Fixed Duration task, Project cannot change the Duration entry, and it calculates the peak units needed to complete the Work value you entered and places that value in the Peak Units field.

- If you entered values in both the Units and Work fields, Project again bases its calculations on the task type:

  If the task is not a Fixed Duration task, Project adjusts the Duration value to accommodate the Work and Units values you entered.

  If the task is a Fixed Duration task, Project keeps the work amount you entered and calculates a new Peak Units value that can do the specific work in a given (fixed) duration.

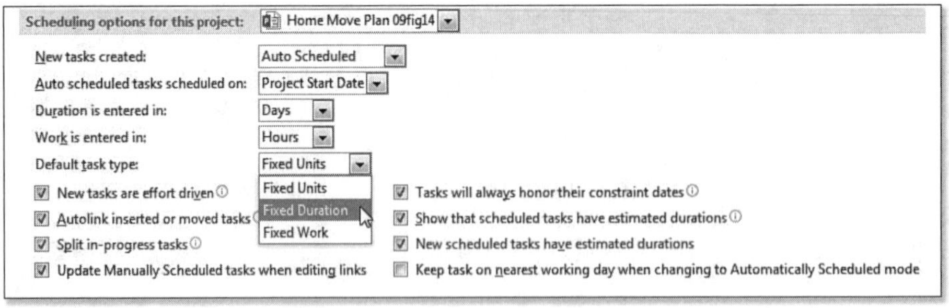

Figure 9.17
Use Default Task Type to set the task type for all tasks in your project.

Schedule Modifiers That Affect the Complexity of the Scheduling Engine

In addition to the work formula itself, there are several schedule modifiers that affect the calculations of the scheduling engine and, therefore, the result shown in your project schedule. Schedule modifiers are additional Project functions that, when used, can change the way Project schedules the tasks and assignments within your project. In addition to the function-related schedule modifiers described in this section, behavioral schedule modifiers can influence the scheduling as well. The behavioral schedule modifiers include learning curves, change of project teams, increase of the scope of work, and many others.

It is important to recognize that scheduling is driven not only by the formula, but by other constraints you define within the assignments, tasks, and project.

Ta

oject applies scheduling algorithms to your
lencies and constraints and allow empty
ot. You should use care when mixing task
d when doing so.

Pr
W

Assignment to Start

edules that resource's work to start on
onstant and uninterrupted assignment rate

*s that can be used to modify this default
and Multiple Resource Assignments,"*

S

tting a no-work period for the resource in
tion crew digging up and fixing a section
perator during the digging and burying
u could therefore split the assignment for

f the inverted pyramid, the Task level,
task (refer to Figure 9.1).

*signments, **see** Chapter 10, "Scheduling
. 301.*

S

ork for one specific resource, which allows
human resource is needed to inspect
ase, you can schedule a delay into that
assigned hours as the task reaches its

*ys, **see** Chapter 10, "Scheduling Single
and Multiple Resource Assignments," **p. 301.***

Leveling Delay Effects

The Leveling Delay field is a Project field that enables you to specify the amount of delay for the assignment of a resource. This field can be found in several views and windows in Project. For example, you can see it within the Task Entry view (select the Task tab and click the Details toggle, opening the Task form in the bottom of the split. Right-click the Task form and select Schedule).

If the schedule has an *overallocated* resource, meaning that there are more units of the resource assigned to the task than the maximum units of resources available, you can add a *leveling delay*. This is a delay similar to the scheduled delay mentioned previously, but serves a different purpose. A scheduled delay will likely remain indefinitely; that's the way the task should normally be scheduled. A leveling delay might become unnecessary if there are other ways to eliminate the overallocation—for example, if another resource is substituted for the overallocated resource to reduce the workload and eliminate the overallocation.

A leveling delay is a way for you to postpone the start of the assignment for a particular resource on a task and to create a model that is closer to the real-life scenarios that fit into this model. For example, if you have Task A and you assign Jim and Karen to it, Task A is scheduled to start on 01/10/2013 and to last for five days. You know that Jim will be unavailable to begin working on it until 01/11/2013 because he is tied up on another project. In this case, you can schedule a leveling delay of one day for Jim, allowing him to begin his assignment on 1/11 when he is available, instead of overallocating him by double-booking his time on 1/10.

The consequences of scheduling a leveling delay are that the assignment will not begin when originally planned and that duration might increase if the resource with the leveling delay is the driver resource. In this case, it causes the task to slip.

The leveling delay schedule modifier affects the scheduling engine at the second level of the inverted pyramid, the Task level, which represents the interplay of assignments within the task (refer to Figure 9.1).

 note

The Leveling Delay field is used by Project when the automatic leveling function is run by the user (select the Resource to see the Level group). In this case, if you have manually entered a value in the Leveling Delay field, it will get overwritten by Project. However, if you do not use the built-in Project leveling feature and level your resources manually instead, the Leveling Delay field can be used with no problems.

It is important to remember the effects that the leveling delay has on scheduling when you add it to resources within your project.

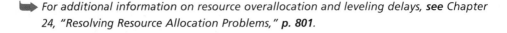 *For additional information on resource overallocation and leveling delays, **see** Chapter 24, "Resolving Resource Allocation Problems," **p. 801**.*

Work Contour Effects

Work contours are predefined patterns for scheduling work that is spread over the duration of the assignment. Work contours enable you to distribute the work based on the pattern in which the work will be done. You can contour the work assigned to each period of the task manually, overwriting the default flat distribution of the work that is normally scheduled. This creates a period of high activity and another period of low activity for the task during the assignment. If you needed someone to work on a task, for instance, but need him or her to work only part time during the first two weeks and full time during the second two weeks, you could use this option.

You can also use Project's predefined work contours (distribution of work on a task), which automatically change the amount of work assigned to different times of the task. For instance, you could use the *front-loaded* contour to schedule full-time work at the beginning of the task, which then contours down to part time as the task wraps up.

Work contours help accommodate scenarios where the amount of work done on a task is not constant throughout the duration of the task. For example, if you have resources transitioning from one task to another, the transition might not be as clean as finishing the first task and then beginning to work on the second one. In many real-life cases, the resource starts on the second task, coming up to speed and getting familiar with the task, while still finishing the last touches on the first task. Another scenario might be that you have tasks that are more labor intensive in the beginning than at the end. For example, you might have a developer working on a piece of code, so he or she spends a lot of time in the beginning designing the code architecture and writing the code, and less time at the end, which involves fixing some minor bugs and other code maintenance.

Work contours affect the scheduling engine at the first level of the inverted pyramid, at the individual task assignment (refer to Figure 9.1).

It is important to remember the effects that work contours have on the resource assignments within your schedule to ensure that the scheduling model you are trying to portray is indeed the correct one.

➡ *For additional information about work contours,* **see** *Chapter 10, "Scheduling Single and Multiple Resource Assignments,"* **p. 301**.

Resource Availability Effects

Resource availability is defined by the percentage of time (or units) a resource is available to be scheduled for work. Resource availability is impacted by the calendars (Project, Task, and Resource). The remaining resource availability is influenced by the interplay of projects within the organization, where the remaining availability is equal to total availability minus the work already assigned to that resource on other projects or tasks.

A resource might be unavailable because he or she has requested vacation during the week that you want to assign them to your project for work. Or, a resource might be unavailable because he or she is working full time on another project in your organization. If you do not take this schedule modifier into consideration, you might schedule a resource to work on a task when he or she is unavailable, therefore delaying the planned start of the task, and potentially, your entire project.

You must be aware of this schedule modifier when scheduling the work in your project because it affects the scheduling level, starting at the Task level and all the way up to the program (refer to Figure 9.1).

> For additional information about the resource availability and how it affects the scheduling within your project, **see** Chapter 10, "Scheduling Single and Multiple Resource Assignments," **p. 301**.

Calendar Effects

Project contains three types of calendars: Project, Task, and Resource. Each of these calendars is used to define the standard working times specific to the project, a task, or a resource. Calendars are also used to define any exceptions that might influence how the work is scheduled within your project. For example, if resources work four 10-hour days (Monday through Thursday) on your project each week, you must modify the Project calendar to reflect the change. Otherwise, Project schedules the tasks to get executed Monday through Friday, which are the default working times. This can, in turn, affect the duration of tasks and the completion date for your assignments, tasks, and your project.

Project schedules work only during the dates and times that are identified as working time according to the Project and Resource calendar. In other words, it will not schedule work during weekends, vacations, or any other time that has been marked as nonworking on the Project or Resource calendar. This means that the assignment changes to show the available working times according to the schedule.

When a Task calendar is attached to the task, Project, by default, schedules work only during times that are working times for both the Task calendar and the Resource calendar. You can, however, disregard the Resource calendar and simply schedule work for the resource whenever the task is scheduled. Be cautious when you choose to ignore the Resource calendar and schedule the work based on the Task calendar, as you might be ignoring important exceptions to the availability of the resource.

The amount of work scheduled for any given day is the number of working hours as defined for that day by the relevant calendar, multiplied by the number of resource units assigned to the task. Therefore, if you have two resources scheduled for 8 hours that day, the total amount of work is 16 hours.

Calendars affect the scheduling engine at each level of the inverted pyramid, and it is important to keep them in mind when creating your project schedule.

> For additional information about calendars, **see** Chapter 5, "Setting Up Project for Your Use," **p. 89**.

Effort-Driven Task Effects

An effort-driven task is a special type of task that enables you to have fixed work on a task, when you assign additional resources to it, so the work on the task becomes shared (distributed) between the resources. As a matter of fact, effort-driven means that the task is fixed work type. For instance, if you have two movers unloading a moving truck, the original assignment is for 200% units (two people). However, if you changed that to 400% (add two more movers), because the work is fixed, Project cuts the duration in half.

The effort-driven option for tasks also modifies the work formula—in addition to having one variable fixed by the task type, work is now fixed because the task is effort-driven.

The effort-driven option affects the scheduling engine at the Task level, represented by the interplay of assignments within that task.

> ➤ *For additional information about effort-driven tasks, **see** Chapter 10, "Scheduling Single and Multiple Resource Assignments," **p. 301.***

Effects of Using Driver Resources

Driver resources are the resources whose assignment(s) drive the task end date. In some cases, you might have multiple resources assigned to a task, which do not begin the work on the task at the same time. The resources whose assignments last until the end of the task, determining the task end date, are referred to as the driver resources. Because driver resources have direct impact on the task end date, it is important to take them into consideration when creating your project schedule.

Driver resources affect the scheduling engine at the Task level of the inverted pyramid (refer to Figure 9.1).

> ➤ *For additional information about driver resources, **see** Chapter 10, "Scheduling Single and Multiple Resource Assignments," **p. 301.***

Consultants' Tips

80/20: Using Task Modes

Although this chapter and most of this book assume that tasks are auto-scheduled, there are many good reasons to use the Manually Scheduled mode. The most obvious—that Project stops making unexpected changes—is probably the weakest. The changes Project makes to a well-formed schedule are actually the most valuable feedback that Project provides.

However, there are stages in the life cycle of a project where it is legitimately easier to work with manually scheduled tasks, particularly when it is too early to know key pieces of information, such as what the duration of a task might be. There are also tasks, such as Level of Effort tasks, that probably should not be part of Project's scheduling considerations at any point in the life cycle of a project.

Before mixing task modes in a single schedule, consider carefully how you intend to identify and manage tasks in each mode, and what the conditions are for moving a task from Manually Scheduled mode to Auto Scheduled mode. Manually Scheduled mode enables you to deceive yourself accidentally. Project is at its most useful when it tells you the truth about the future, based on your scheduling assumptions.

Work Formula Factors

As detailed previously in this chapter, the work formula consists of three variables: the duration of a task (D), the amount of effort or work (W) required, and the amount of resources or units (U) that perform the work. It is important to remember that you can control two out of the three variables; the remaining, free-range variable, gets calculated by the work formula. Remember that in addition to the work formula, Project's scheduling engine contains many different schedule modifiers that also affect the way your project is scheduled. The modifiers include work contours, leveling delays, scheduled delays, resource availability, calendars, task types, effort-driven assignments, and many others.

80/20: Using Task Types

Remember to change the Project default task type of Fixed Units, Effort Driven when scheduling tasks within your project, if you have different constraints. If the amount of work you schedule on a task cannot be changed, you might want to set the task type to be Fixed Work. Similarly, if your duration cannot be changed due to the project requirements, using the Fixed Duration task type will work best for you.

Determine and set the default options for your project before creating tasks.

Use standard naming conventions for task names to make it easier to set and check task types. You can use "Meeting" in tasks and ensure that the task type is set to Fixed Duration and *not* Effort Driven. Or, use "SS" as a suffix for "Steady State" tasks.

Use Fixed Units *not* Effort Driven for "Steady State" type tasks (those tasks that you want to retain a fixed assignment level for the duration of the task). You might want a "Project Management" task and assign a project manager at 25%. Based on the actual work rate, the duration expands or contracts and will need to be adjusted.

Analyze the real-life constraints that have an effect on your schedule and configure your Project schedule accordingly to more closely mimic real-life work scenarios. When getting used to working with the work formula, it is a good idea to use the split screen option described earlier in this chapter. Apply one change at a time (to work, unit, or duration as appropriate) and watch how it changes your schedule until you have mastered the formula.

80/20: Using Effort-Driven Task Types

Remember that effort-driven means that the work you assign to the task is shared (or distributed) between the resources on that task. Set this option for tasks where resources truly share the work and the task gets completed faster if more resources are assigned. Also remember that the effort-driven setting changes the operation of the work formula, but only when you change the task's assigned units by adding or removing a resource.

The Difference Between Calendar Duration and Actual Assignment Duration

You might run into a scenario where the task duration in the Duration field of the Gantt Chart view might not match the duration of the Gantt bar for that task. This situation is possible if your project or task calendar working times do not match your default Hours per Day (set under Tools, Options, Calendar tab, Hours per Day). If you make a change in the Project calendar, remember to make the change in the Hours per Day option, and vice versa.

For example, in a project using the Standard Project calendar (working times of Monday through Friday, eight hours per day) and the default Hours per Day option (eight hours per day), do the following:

1. Create a task (Fixed Units type is the default), do not assign a resource to it, and enter 10 days in the Duration field.

2. Modify the Hours per Day to 20 (select Tools, Options, Calendar tab) and make no changes to the Project calendar.

The Duration field changes to show four days because that is how long it would take to complete the assignment using the 20 hours per day now set in the Hours per Day field on the Options dialog box.

The Gantt bar duration still shows 10 days because it uses work settings from the project calendar, which have not changed and are still based on eight hours per work day. Also note that the Finish field shows the same finish date as the Gantt bar because it uses the same calculation as the Gantt bar. This means that when you are dealing with task or assignment duration, you should focus on Task Start + Duration, rather than involving the Finish field.

Summary tasks maintain the inconsistency with the Gantt bar length being calculated from the earliest start to the latest finish, whereas the Duration field on the Summary line reflects the merged durations as calculated from Task Start + Duration.

SCHEDULING SINGLE AND MULTIPLE RESOURCE ASSIGNMENTS

In Chapter 7, "Defining Task Logic," you learned how to create tasks. In Chapter 8, "Defining Project Resources," you learned how to create resources. In Chapter 9, "Understanding Work Formula Basics," the work formula was introduced. In this chapter, you learn how to combine resources and tasks using the work formula to create assignments that make sense for your project.

In essence, you have no real "work" to model until you have something that needs to be done (a task) assigned to one or more people who will do the work (resources). Work just does not exist without this mapping. In other words, the basic work formula that you learned in Chapter 9 does not apply until you have created an assignment. This chapter is all about creating those assignments and mapping the tasks or activities (that you need to complete) with the resources (that will accomplish them).

 note

The addition of Manually Scheduled task mode turns off Project's schedule calculation engine. For the sake of brevity, most of this chapter assumes tasks are auto-scheduled. Manually scheduled tasks are essentially the same as auto-scheduled tasks, only much more work has to be done "manually."

The chapter itself is organized in four broad groups, as follows:

- First you are introduced to the screens and views that enable you to map resources to tasks. The different areas/mechanisms through which assignments are created and maintained are highlighted.

- The second grouping focuses on initial creation of the assignments, first looking at the simplest case (one resource to one task) and then looking at the differences when mapping multiple resources to a task.

- The third grouping in this chapter is on assignment maintenance and the details of updating existing assignments that you have already created.

- The last grouping in this chapter goes into more specific information on how to achieve the modeling you want through a series of "how-to" descriptions.

Mechanisms: Methods for Adding Resources

This section focuses on the mechanisms (views, screens, dialog boxes, tables, and so on) available to you to add resources to tasks, thereby creating assignments. Step-by-step guidance is provided for simple assignment creation techniques. The in-depth details around what you are actually accomplishing are provided in the next section.

The primary mechanisms discussed are as follows:

- Assign Resources dialog box

- Team Planner view

- Task Entry view

- Task Information dialog box

- Task table

- Assignment Information dialog box

- Task and Resource Usage views

 note

Some of the mechanisms focus on tables available in multiple views.

The Task and Resource Usage views are covered in the third grouping in this chapter regarding the updating and maintenance of existing assignments.

Adding Resources Using the Assign Resources Dialog Box

The Assign Resources dialog box is the most common and the preferred way to assign resources. It is easy to remember because of the friendly People-in-Profile icon that opens the dialog box.

Follow these steps to change assignments using the Task Information dialog box:

1. In a Task view (use the Gantt Chart view for simplicity), select the task to which you want to add a resource.

2. Select the Resource tab, Assignments, Assign Resources.

3. The Assign Resources dialog box opens with the name of the task selected and a list of possible resources. Filter the list as needed to find the resources you want. If you do not see any resources in the list, it is likely that you have a filter specified in the filter section of the dialog or

you have not created any resources. In the latter case, go ahead and type the resource name directly into the list. This is a fast way to create the resource (see "Config: Turn Off Automatic Resource Creation" in the "Consultants' Tips" section later in the chapter).

4. Select a resource by clicking (or Ctrl+clicking to select multiple resources) the resource Name field and click the Assign button.

5. The resource(s) are assigned to the task at the default Unit value (see the "Consultants' Tips" section at the end of the chapter) and moved to the top of the dialog list with a check mark to the left to indicate they are assigned.

6. Remove resources mistakenly assigned to the task by clicking the Remove button (which is not grayed out and is available when an already assigned resource is selected).

7. Modify the Units and Cost fields as appropriate.

 tip

Creating resources in anything other than the Resource Sheet view or the Assign Resources dialog box is generally not a good practice (it is too easy to add the same person twice because you cannot easily see the full list of resources to keep from creating multiple entries for the same resource). See "Config: Turn Off Automatic Resource Creation" in the "Consultants' Tips" section.

Adding Resources by Using Drag-and-Drop

With the Assign Resources dialog box, you can create an assignment by dragging a resource name to a task. The advantage to using the drag-and-drop method is that you do not have to preselect the task for which a resource should be assigned. Microsoft Project, however, automatically assigns the default units (usually 100%).

To assign resources to the task by using the drag-and-drop method, follow these steps:

1. Display the Assign Resources dialog box by selecting the Resource tab, Assignments, Assign Resources.

2. Select the resource by clicking the Name field.

3. Click or hover over the gray cell just to the left of the resource name. The Assign Resources graphic appears just below the mouse pointer. You can see the pointer and graphic in Figure 10.1, where Movers is being assigned to a task.

4. Hold down the mouse button and a plus sign appears next to the pointer graphic. Now drag the mouse pointer to the task for which the resource should be assigned.

5. When the task is highlighted, release the mouse button and assign the resource.

 tip

To assign multiple resources to a task by using the drag-and-drop method, hold down the Ctrl key while selecting the resource names in the Assign Resources dialog box. When you click on any of the gray cells and drag the mouse pointer to the task, all selected resources are assigned at once.

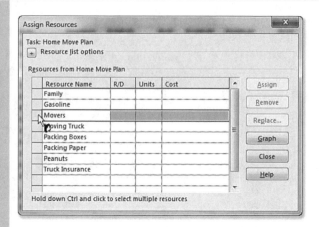

Figure 10.1
Assign resources to tasks by using the drag-and-drop method in the Assign Resources dialog box.

Assigning Resources with the Team Planner View

The Team Planner view, as shown in Figure 10.2, takes a graphical, resource-centric approach to creating assignments.

The Team Planner is split into four separate panes. The panes to the left are lists—resources are listed on top and unassigned tasks are listed on the bottom. Both panes to the right are time-phased, like the Gantt Chart.

Resource assignments are made by dragging tasks between resource rows. Unassigned tasks from the bottom pane can be dragged to the appropriate resource on the top pane. Assignment dates are resources that can be changed by dragging tasks in the top pane. Resource overallocations are represented by default as red-highlighted Gantt bars.

The behavior of manually scheduled and auto-scheduled tasks in the Team Planner view appears to be similar. However, changing assignment start dates by dragging auto-scheduled tasks creates constraints that effectively disable the Project scheduling engine.

As the name suggests, the Team Planner can be extraordinarily effective when you need to plan the efforts of a team. This is a resource-centric approach, where keeping resources busy and preventing overutilization are primary concerns. In this scenario, most tasks should probably remain manually scheduled, allowing managers and planners to use the graphical indicators of the Team Planner to highlight resource bottlenecks or idle time. In this scenario, you should sparingly use task dependencies, if you use them at all.

Of course, you can also use the Team Planner for managing resources on a project. If the project has a well-formed network, the drag-and-drop graphical capabilities of the Team Planner can make assigning resource quicker, and the Team Planner can be useful in early planning stages.

Figure 10.2
The Team
Planner is
a graphi-
cal tool for
planning
and man-
aging the
activities of
a team.

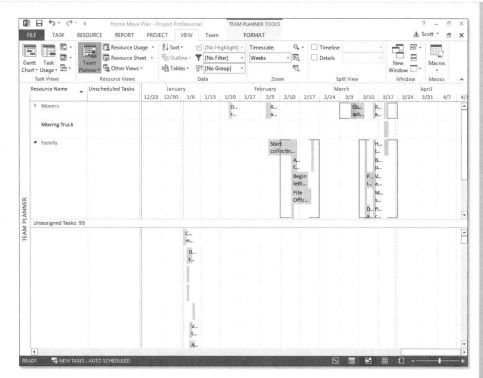

Assigning Resources with the Task Entry View

The Task Entry view, with the Gantt Chart view in the top pane and the Task Form view in the bottom pane, is one of the best combination views for assigning resources. The default (and most commonly used) form in the bottom pane is the Resources and Predecessors form. To see a list of other
forms, just right-click in the background color of the form for a list
and choose the one you want. (The Resources Schedule form is
particularly good for understanding scheduling lags in assignments
within tasks.) The Resources and Predecessors form is a
convenient place for assigning resources because it enables you to
enter resource units, work, or both, for each resource assignment.

Display the Task Entry view by selecting the Task tab, View, More
Views, Task Entry. You have to scroll down to find the view. The
Gantt Chart view then is displayed in the top pane and the Task
Form view in the bottom pane with eight possible sets of details.
You can right-click over the form, and select the detail forms you
want to use. For assigning resources, you should use either the
default Resources and Predecessors form or the Work form, as
shown in Figure 10.3.

 tip

If you are using the Task
Entry view (or any method
other than the Assign
Resources dialog methods),
you can use the Assign
Resources dialog box (at the
same time) to review and find
the best resources and make
the initial assignment. You
can then use the Task form to
easily modify the assignment.

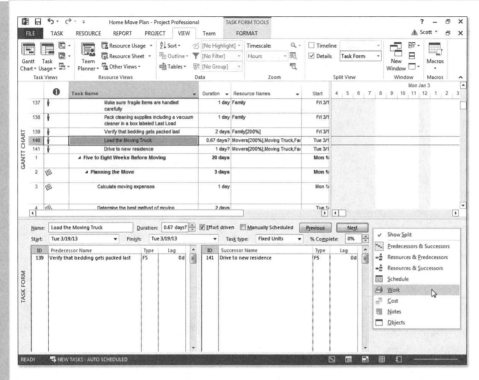

Figure 10.3
Right-click in the bottom pane of the Task Entry view to choose from the list of detail forms to display in the bottom pane.

For additional information on using views and tables, **see** Chapter 11, "Using Standard Views, Tables, Filters, and Groups to Review Your Schedule," **p. 357**.

Assigning Resources Using the Task Information Dialog Box

You can use the Resources tab on the Task Information dialog box to add, change, or delete the resource assignment information for a selected task. As with the Assign Resources dialog box, you can use the Units field of the Task Information dialog box to enter a work value rather than a unit value by using a numeral followed by a time unit. Be careful, however: Entering work in this way preserves the duration of the task. Microsoft Project calculates (and then displays) the units that would produce that much work while keeping the duration of the task the same. This is NOT the same behavior as entering Work in a Work field (which, in the default task type of Fixed Units, holds 100% Units constant and extends the duration of the task).

Follow these steps to change assignments using the Task Information dialog box (see Figure 10.4):

1. Select the task for which you want to add or change a resource assignment.

2. Display the Task Information dialog box by selecting the Task tab, Properties, Information.

3. Select the Advanced tab and review the selections for the Task Type and Effort Driven fields. Be sure these are appropriate for the change you intended to implement.

4. Select the Resources tab to assign or view the resource information for the selected task.

Figure 10.4
Change assignment information on the Resources tab of the Task Information dialog box.

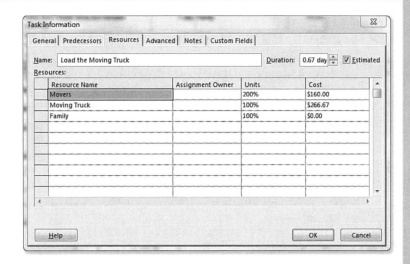

5. In the Resource Name box, edit an existing entry or choose a blank row to add a new resource. To add or change the resource, select a resource from the drop-down list in the field. You can create nonexistent resources by typing the name in directly unless the default option Automatically Add New Resources and Tasks has been cleared (File tab, Options, Advanced, General Options for This Project).

6. Type the unit assignment for the resource in the Units field. If you leave the Units field empty, Project supplies the default value, the lesser of 100% or the Max Units value for the resource. You can modify an existing assignment by entering a work amount followed by a time unit in the Units field. If you enter a work amount, Project adjusts the assigned units, not the duration of the task.

7. To add more resources to the selected task, click the next Resource Name field and repeat the preceding steps.

8. After you have completed all the resource assignments for the task, click OK.

If you use the Ctrl key or drag across multiple rows to select more than one task before opening the Task Information dialog box, Project displays the Multiple Task Information dialog box so that any resource you select is automatically assigned to all selected tasks. The dialog box will not display any existing assignments on the tasks (you cannot edit these using the Multiple Task Information dialog box). The resource assignment entries you make in the Multiple Task Information dialog box are added to existing resource assignments for the selected tasks.

note

You cannot change existing resource assignments for multiple tasks by using the Multiple Task Information dialog box.

Assigning Resources with the Task Table

You can use the Resource Name field on the Task table to assign resources to a task, but you should be aware of some potential problems before you use this method. You can edit the field in two ways: via direct typing or via a pull-down list function that displays all the resources from the Resource Sheet view. Use of the pull-down is the recommended method because you will be selecting an existing resource from the resource sheet and will not be able to automatically create a new resource if you accidentally misspell the name. You can enter only one resource at a time using the pull-down list. If you choose to type directly, you can type ResourceName1, ResourceName2, and so on, and each resource will be assigned to the task at 100% Units or their Max Unit setting from the Resource Sheet view (whichever is less). Note that if a resource is assigned at 100% units, the entry reverts to the name without square brackets. To enter varying unit values while you type requires the following syntax:

> ResourceName1[Units],ResourceName2[Units],ResourceName3[Units]...

When you are entering data using this format, note that the Units value is placed in square brackets and follows immediately after the resource name, without an intervening space. Unit values of the lesser of 100% or the resource's Max Units value (from the Resource Sheet view) do not need to be specified. The Resource Name field entry for the Load the Moving Truck task might be as follows:

> Movers[200%],Moving Truck[1],Family

Figure 10.5 shows this assignment. Because of the width of the Resource Names column, other columns and the Gantt Chart view are hidden in the figure.

 note

If you want to import a list of tasks with resource assignments, you must have the Resource Name field format in the source data to identify the resource assignments.

➡ *For information about importing data,* **see** *Chapter 25, "Exporting and Importing Project Data,"* **p. 835**.

Follow these steps to assign resources to tasks in the Resource Names field:

1. View a Task table like the one in the Gantt Chart view.

2. If the Resource Names column is not displayed, after you scroll through the columns, right-click the column header before which you would like to insert the Resource Names column and choose Insert Column. Select the Resource Names column to add it to the current table. Alternatively, you can select the View tab, Data, Tables to select any table that includes a Resource Names column, such as the Entry table.

3. Select the Resource Names cell for the task to which you want to assign resources.

Figure 10.5
Use resources created in the Resource sheet to assign resources at their Max Units setting.

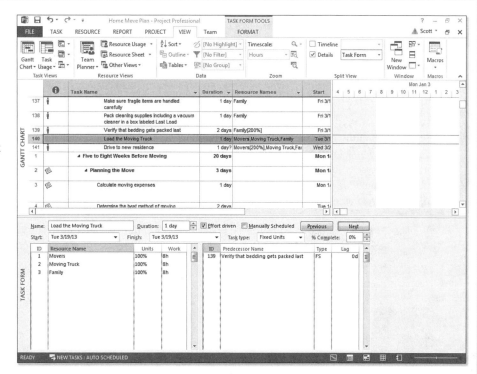

4. Enter the resource name. You can select the name(s) from the drop-down resource pick list, which appears in the cell when the Resource Names column is active.

5. If the number of units required is not 100% (or the resource Max Units from the Resource Sheet, if less than 100%), enter the units, enclosed in square brackets, immediately after the name in the edit bar.

6. Press Enter or select any other cell to complete the resource assignment.

Creation: Assigning a Single Resource

Now that you have seen methods for making resource assignments, it is time to review how Project uses the information to schedule work. This section focuses on the initial creation of an assignment accomplished the first time you map one resource to a task. It is helpful to treat the mapping of a single resource to a single task separately from mapping multiple resources to a task because it teaches you what is going on without adding in the complexities of how multiple resources interplay within a task. This section walks through the process to assign one resource to one task to build a framework for the more complex discussion in the following section.

Assigning a Resource Using the Assign Resources Dialog Box

The previous section demonstrated many possible ways to add a resource to a task. Although any of the methods will work, this section uses only one: the Assign Resources dialog box.

When a resource is assigned to an auto-scheduled task, Project schedules that resource's work to start on the same date as the task and to continue working at a constant and uninterrupted assignment rate until all the work is scheduled.

The creation of the first assignment on a task establishes an initial schedule for work to be done. Certainly the task mode is the most significant determinant of behavior, but assuming the task mode is auto-scheduled, the task types, work values, and calendars have an impact on the assignment. Manipulations of load, interrelationships with other assignments, and manipulations of a task to "model" real work performance can be done after initial assignment creation.

> ➡ *See the "Contouring Resource Usage" section later in this chapter for details on advanced scheduling techniques that can be used to modify this default approach, p. 339.*

To add a resource assignment to a selected task or group of tasks, follow these steps:

1. Select the task or tasks to which you want the resource assigned.

2. Display the Assign Resources dialog box by selecting the Resource tab, Assignments, Assign Resources.

3. Select the resource name from the Resource Name list or type the name for a new resource.

4. Different resource types require different uses of the Units field when you are assigning them:

   ■ If the resource is a work resource, the Units field determines the percent of a full work day to allocate for that resource. 100% would be full allocation of a single resource. (See the "Consultants' Tips" section at the end of the chapter for how to determine the default Units value used.) If you want to assign a different number of units, select the Units cell to the right of the resource name and enter the new value.

   ■ If the resource is a material resource, enter the number of units to be consumed by the task in the Units cell. If you just enter a numeral, Project schedules that total number of material units to be consumed by the task, no matter what the duration is. If you enter a number with a time period appended (for example, 2/d), Project schedules that number to be consumed per time period for the duration of the task.

   ■ If the resource is a cost resource, do not bother with the units. Enter the cost of the resource. The cost accrues over the timeframe of the task using the accrual type defined on the Resource Sheet in the Accrual Type field (prorated, start, end).

 tip

For work resources, the units should be no greater than the maximum units available for the resource at the time the task is scheduled. If you do not know the max units available, double-click the resource name to see the Resource Information dialog box. The Resource Availability table in that dialog box shows the maximum units for different time periods.

5. Click the Assign button or press Enter to assign the Resources and Unit or Cost information to the selected tasks.

6. Select either Request or Demand in the R/D field. A resource that is *demanded* cannot be replaced using the Resource Substitution Wizard. A *requested* resource is free to be replaced. *Requested* is the default used if the field is left blank.

 note

The R/D field is not of any particular value if Project Professional is used without Project Server or if the Resource Substitution Wizard is not used.

 note

Project Professional carries an additional attribute (settable from the Resource Sheet) that enables you to mark each resource in a project as soft-booked or not. When soft-booked resources are assigned to a task, they are considered tentative placeholders, and the assignment will not reduce the global (across all projects) availability of the resource.

Changing Resource Assignments

When using the Assign Resources dialog box to change resource assignments, Project displays a SmartTag to let you choose how it should calculate changes in the schedule (see Figure 10.6). The SmartTag feature compensates for the limited control you have over the variables when you modify an assignment in the Assign Resources dialog box. For example, if you change the units assigned, Project immediately changes the task duration, unless it is a fixed-duration task. However, you can use the SmartTag to have Project put duration back where it was and change the work instead.

Figure 10.6
Increasing the Movers units from 2 to 3 creates a conflict, so Project provides options for adjusting the schedule given the unit change.

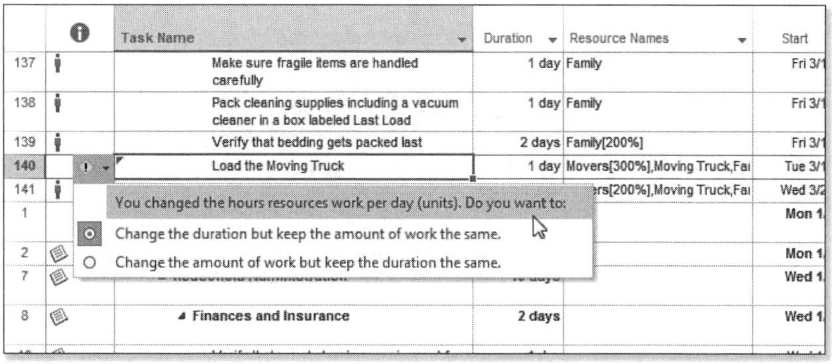

	ⓘ	Task Name	Duration	Resource Names	Start
137	👤	Make sure fragile items are handled carefully	1 day	Family	Fri 3/1
138	👤	Pack cleaning supplies including a vacuum cleaner in a box labeled Last Load	1 day	Family	Fri 3/1
139	👤	Verify that bedding gets packed last	2 days	Family[200%]	Fri 3/1
140		Load the Moving Truck	1 day	Movers[300%],Moving Truck,Fai	Tue 3/1
141	👤			rs[200%],Moving Truck,Fai	Wed 3/2

You changed the hours resources work per day (units). Do you want to:

○ Change the duration but keep the amount of work the same.

○ Change the amount of work but keep the duration the same.

1					Mon 1,
2					Mon 1,
7					Wed 1,
8		◢ Finances and Insurance	2 days		Wed 1,

When you change the assignment, a small green triangle appears in the top-left corner of the Task Name cell. If you select the cell or even move the mouse over that cell, an active button appears, and you can click it to display the calculation options. SmartTags stay visible only as long as you can undo an action.

For example, if you change the units for an assignment, the SmartTag lets you choose to have either work or duration change as a result. If you assign an additional resource to a task or remove an existing resource, the SmartTag lets you choose to change duration (keeping work and units unchanged), change work (keeping duration and units constant), or change units (keeping work and duration constant).

 note

SmartTags are triggered by assignment changes made in the Assign Resources dialog box and in cells in tables. They are not triggered when you make changes by using the Task Form view or the Task Information dialog box, because in those venues, you can control all the scheduling variables before you click OK.

Creation: Assigning Multiple Resources

The last section discussed how to create a single resource assignment within a task. When you add more than one resource to a task, many aspects of a task can be intuitively treated as the aggregation of the information from each individual resource assignment. However, some impacts are less intuitive. This section discusses the less intuitive complexities involved with multiple resources associated with an auto-scheduled task.

The three task level impacts of multiple resources that are the least intuitive are as follows:

- Impacts to overall task duration

- How total task work is impacted by the addition of multiple resources, and how work is distributed across resources (the Effort Driven flag)

- Understanding how multiple resources interact to affect the finish date of a task (the concept of Driver Resources)

Calculating Task Duration with Multiple Resources

The Project definition of *task duration* is the number of active working time periods on the calendar required to complete a task. When multiple resources are assigned to a task, some of them might not be scheduled for the entire task duration. Individual schedules for some resources can be modified to delay an assignment or to split the assignment with a period of inactivity.

For example, Carrie and Nick are both assigned five days to prepare for an upcoming sales conference. The task duration is five days if both Carrie and Nick do their work during the same time periods. However, suppose that Nick is taking two vacation days when the task starts, so Carrie starts working on the task alone. Nick starts working on the task two days later than Carrie does. Then, they work together for three days, and Carrie completes her part of the task. Nick still has two days of work to do.

The task duration is the number of time periods during which anyone is working on the task. Because Carrie has an earlier start date and Nick has a later finish date, the duration is extended. In this case, the task duration is actually seven days—the two days when Carrie worked alone, three days when they worked together on the task, and two days when Nick returned to work alone, after Carrie had completed her part (see Figure 10.7).

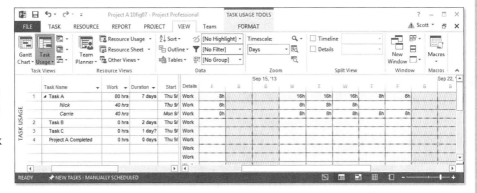

Figure 10.7 The Task Usage view is displayed, and the time-phased work details show the precise work schedule of both Carrie and Nick.

You can see in Figure 10.7 that Nick and Carrie work independently some days and together some days. If you count the number of days in the task row, where total work (across all assignments) is greater than 0, you can see that there are seven such days. That is what determines the task duration of seven days.

Understanding Effort-Driven Tasks

As mentioned previously, if a task is set as Fixed Work, you can increase the number of units assigned to the task and Project reduces the duration of the task, leaving the work amount unchanged. The addition of named resources to a task is another way to change the duration of a task. For instance, if you have three movers unloading a moving truck, the original assignment is for 300% units (three people). If you change the number of units to 600% on a Fixed Work task (that is, add three more movers), Project cuts the duration in half.

The same is true when you increase named resources assigned to a task because it is the same as adding units. Instead of a resource named Moving Truck Personnel, you might have Tim, Melissa, and Mike, and you want to add Gary, Chris, and Pam. Just as when you added units to the Moving Truck Personnel resource, you should expect Project to cut the duration in half.

This is an example of an *effort-driven* task calculation. When you want the amount of work for the whole task to be fixed and you add resources to the assignment list on a Fixed Unit task, Project is allowed to reduce the workload for the resources already assigned to the task. This also works if you have to remove a resource from the assignment list, freeing up work that must be redistributed to the resources remaining on the task's assignment list.

note

There are two things to remember when using effort-driven tasks. First, adding resources to effort-driven tasks never affects work. The task work will be redistributed and either Duration or Units changes (depending on task type). Second, effort-driven tasks assume that the resources are interchangeable (there are no distinctions where one resource might be more efficient than another). If you add more people who are trained to load and unload moving trucks, you can honestly expect the duration to be cut in half, just like the schedule says. However, if you added three people who are trained to be cashiers, and the task is Fixed Units, the resulting reduction of duration might not be achieved in reality. (Subsequent sections of this chapter provide you with techniques to change this default distribution model.)

When you add resources to an effort-driven task, Project guards the total work and the task type (Fixed Duration, Fixed Units) and reduces the remaining free variable (either Duration or Units). If a task is shown as effort-driven and the task type is Fixed Work, Units is held fixed and Duration is used as the free variable. (In essence, you are holding the same variable constant, leaving two possible free variables.)

There are many different ways to model work, and the work formula is sophisticated enough to adapt, but it can be confusing. The order in which you choose to model the work dictates how Project works. For example, suppose you decide to add David to the task of unloading the truck at the grocery store. David is not there to help unload the truck; instead, he is there to track the inventory as it comes off the truck. This is not the same work, but rather a parallel task activity. You can create a new task for David or you can add David's work into the total work being done on the task. If you choose to use the latter option, you must change the task to non-effort-driven, add David as a resource, and then change the task back to effort-driven. This enables you to assign him to the task without affecting the amount of work assigned to others on the task. The order of your manipulation controls the impact.

 note

When you set a task as a Fixed Work task, it automatically becomes an effort-driven task because effort-driven means "fixed work." Project fills in the Effort Driven check box and then dims it so that it cannot be cleared.

Project, by default, makes all new tasks effort-driven, but not all tasks you add might be effort-driven tasks. Consider each resource to be sure that it is calculated properly by Project. The Effort Driven field is a check box found on the Task Information dialog box and on the Task Form view and can be cleared to turn it off.

The effort-driven status of a task has no effect on calculations when you are first assigning resources (the initial assignment), because no work has been defined for the task until the first work assignment. So, if you are using the Task Form view and create a list of multiple resource names with assignments before clicking OK (in effect, creating all the assignments at once), Project treats them all as the initial assignment and calculates the hours of work for each of the work resources and the sum as the total work

 note

Adding or removing material or cost resources will not affect effort-driven calculations because the work value for them is not effort hours but rather a consumption rate or a cost.

amount for the task. This works only if you enter them all before clicking OK. If you click OK for each, only the first assignment counts as the initial assignment and the effort-driven state in combination with task type drives the rest of the calculations.

You can change the default effort-driven status for new tasks by performing the following steps:

1. Select the File tab, Options, Schedule, Scheduling Options for this project.

2. Clear (or check) the New Tasks Are Effort Driven check box.

Revising Effort-Driven Tasks

After the initial assignment of resources to a task, if you add or remove some of the work resources, Project automatically figures the effort-driven status of the task in its calculations. If Effort Driven is on, as it is by default, Project redistributes the work for the task across the revised work resource list, prorating the work for each resource, according to its share of the total number of work resource units assigned to the task.

When you increase resources for an effort-driven task, Project reapportions the work amount among the existing resources. It will do this in proportion to the resources' share of the total work units assigned. For example, Drew and Scott are assigned a five-day (40-hour) effort-driven task. You can see in Figure 10.8 an example of the table portion of a Task Usage view, showing three numbered tasks and their resource assignments indented beneath them.

Task A shows the original assignment of Drew and Scott. The total work is 60 hours, and because it is an effort-driven task, the work remains fixed if you add or subtract resources.

Figure 10.8
The original task assignment (effort-driven) shows both Drew and Scott performing 30 hours of work each, totaling 60 hours.

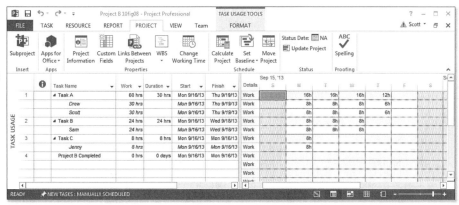

Figure 10.9 shows an example of what happens when Kim is assigned to the task at 50% units. Because Task A is effort-driven, total work remains unchanged, at 60 hours. In the Assignment Units column is the sum of the units assigned, 250%. The custom column Share of Units shows that Kim contributes 20% of the total units (50% / 250%), and Scott and Drew each contribute 40% of

the total (100% / 250%). This shows how Project calculates the work assignment for each resource. Project assigns Kim 20% of the total work for the task, which is 12 hours, whereas Scott and Drew are each assigned 24 hours. Each of these new work assignments can be completed in three days, so the duration changes from five days to three days.

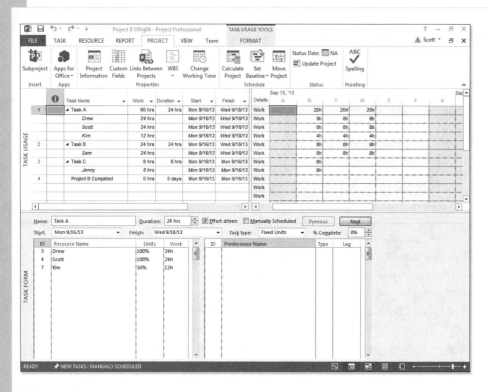

Figure 10.9
Kim's assignment to an effort-driven task has not changed the total amount of work, but has shortened the overall task duration to three days.

If Drew were removed from the assignment, the changes would be reversed. Without Drew's assignment, Kim would contribute one-third of the units and Scott would contribute two-thirds. Kim would be assigned one-third of the total 60 hours (20 hours), whereas Scott would be assigned two-thirds (40 hours).

If you disable the Effort Driven field, by clearing the check box in the Options dialog box, Project assumes that the work of a newly assigned resource is *in addition* to the existing work of all other named resources. The assignments of the existing resources are not changed.

If you remove a named resource from a task, with the Effort Driven check box not selected, Project reduces the total work for the task by the amount of that resource's work assignment, and will not recalculate other resource assignments.

note

The Effort Driven setting regulates calculations only when you add or subtract from the list of assigned resources on a task. If you change the duration of an effort-driven Fixed Unit task, Project will not keep the work of the assigned resources the same, but changes their work to fit the new duration. If the effort-driven task is a Fixed Work task, Project would change the Unit values of the assignments instead of the Durations.

When changing the number of assigned resources, you must consider whether you want the total work to change and then change the Effort Driven status for the task as appropriate. You will do this when you build a list of assigned resources one at a time. For example, suppose you create a task for 30 hours of work unloading a truck and you have already assigned shipping workers. Now you want to assign the pallet jacks they will be using. If the duration, work, and units for the workers' assignment are based on the assumption that they will have pallet jacks to work with, you need to clear the Effort Driven check box before adding the pallet jacks. After the pallet jacks are added, you can turn Effort Driven back on for future calculations.

Understanding the Driver Resource Concept

Chapter 9 explored how various changes in assignments produce changes in both the assignments and the task duration. Understanding the concept of the driver resource helps you understand these changes even better.

The term *driver resource* is used to identify resources whose assignments determine the duration or finish date of the task. The driver resources and the time-phased work as rolled up from the set of assignments associated with a task define how the task Work (for a Fixed Unit task) or Units (for a Fixed Work task) will be impacted when you edit the duration of the task. For simplicity, only the Fixed Work task type is used in the following discussions.

It is not uncommon to have a resource that adds only some minor finishing touches to a task—a small amount of work scheduled right at the end of a task. Unfortunately, you cannot schedule one assignment to start "as late as possible" while the other resource starts when the task begins in Project. You can, however, delay an individual resource assignment so that it finishes at the same time the task finishes, making that resource the *driver* for the task. Any increase in the amount of time scheduled for the driver resource delays the finish of the task, unless you offset the increase by reducing the amount of delay. As mentioned earlier, using the Team Planner to alter assignment start dates automatically creates this effect.

As discussed previously, the significance of the driver resource concept is that increasing the duration of a driver resource assignment affects the task duration, but modest increases in the duration of a nondriver resource have no effect. As we see in more detail in Table 10.1, increasing the duration of the task changes the work by increasing the work assigned to the driver resources (Fixed Unit task). Decreasing the duration of the task reduces the work and might include driver resources or nondriver resources. When duration is shortened, nondriver resources might become drivers.

Figure 10.10 shows the driver resource concept. Jenny, Brian, and Chris are assigned to Task A with differing work amounts, as shown in the Work column. The custom column, Assignment Duration, shows how long it will take each of them to complete the assigned work, given the assignment units. Brian and Chris both require four days, but Jenny can finish in one day. The task duration is four days, and Brian and Chris are both driver resources.

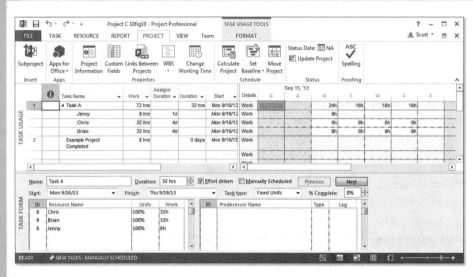

Figure 10.10
Brian and Chris represent driver resources as their assignments are as long as the task duration, whereas Jenny is a nondriver resource with an assignment of only one day.

In this example, a change in the assigned work or units for Brian or Chris would affect the duration of the task. For example, if you increased Brian's workload to 50 hours, he would need a longer time to finish, and the task duration would also have to increase. However, an increase in Jenny's workload, up to a point, would not affect the duration of the task:

- You could increase the work assigned to Jenny from 8 hours to 32 hours, without needing to increase the task's duration.

- You could also change Jenny's units from 100% to as low as 25% before it would affect her ability to complete her assignment in the current duration.

- You could reduce the task duration from four days down to one day without affecting Jenny's assignment, if she worked eight hours at 100% effort. Jenny would become a driver resource.

> **note**
>
> Note that in Figure 10.10, Jenny is assigned full time for one day, but because she only has eight hours of work, she finishes her assignment before the task finishes. If she were assigned eight hours at 25% units, it would take her all four days to complete the task, putting in two hours each day. In that case, she would also be a driver resource.

Figure 10.11 provides an example setup for use with Table 10.1. Two of the resources have a delayed start on the task. This is a planning scenario, and so the Assignment Delay field is used to delay the assignments. An equivalent time-phased work profile can occur naturally when you are maintaining an active project's status and you enter zero actual hours for two of the resources on the first day and eight actual hours for the third resource on the first day.

Figure 10.11
The
Example
Fixed Unit
task whose
work and
duration
will be
manipu-
lated using
Table 10.1.

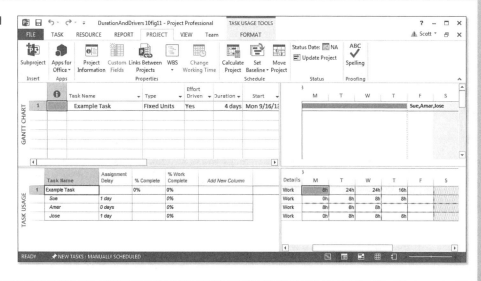

Table 10.1 Microsoft Project Duration and Driver Resources

Task Name	Type	Effort Driven	Duration	Work	Sep 15, '13
1 Example Task	Fixed Units	Yes	2.33 days	32 hrs	Sue,Amar,Jose

Task Name	Assignment Delay	% Complete	% Work Complete	Add New Column	Details	Sep 15, '13
1 Example Task		0%	0%		Work	8h 18.67h 5.33h
Sue	1 day		0%		Work	0h 8h 2.67h
Amar	0 days		0%		Work	8h 2.67h
Jose	1 day		0%		Work	0h 8h 2.67h

> A decrease in task work is distributed across the assignments by their commitment of units (all 100% here).

Task Name	Type	Effort Driven	Duration	Work	Sep 15, '13
1 Example Task	Fixed Units	Yes	3.67 days	64 hrs	Sue,Amar,Jose

Task Name	Assignment Delay	% Complete	% Work Complete	Add New Column	Details	Sep 15, '13
1 Example Task		0%	0%		Work	8h 24h 21.33h 10.67h
Sue	1 day		0%		Work	0h 8h 5.33h
Amar	0 days		0%		Work	8h 8h 5.33h
Jose	1 day		0%		Work	0h 8h 8h 5.33h

> An increase in task work is evenly distributed across the assignments by their commitment of units (all 100% here).

A decrease in duration of one day reduces the task work by the sum of the hours trimmed off when the last working day is trimmed from the task. (Note: Only two resources are affected.)

A decrease in duration of two days reduces the task work by the sum of hours trimmed off when the last two working days are removed from the task. (Note: All three resources are affected, disproportionately.)

An increase in duration of two days increases the task work only by the extended assignment work from the "Driver Resources."

As you can see from Table 10.1, the Driver Resources primary impact is when the task duration is extended. In all other cases, the profile of time-phased hours across the assignments composing the task and the change of duration (as associated with the current finish of the task) determine the remaining impacts.

Maintenance: Modifying Existing Resource Assignments

The prior sections were really about task/assignment creation and introduced the impacts that modeled work has on a task at the assignment level.

This section takes everything a step further to the actual maintenance of existing resource assignments. These are the tools you need to model the reality of work on an ongoing basis.

The views most used here reflect the maintenance aspect of your job. Task Usage and Resource Usage views are key elements. This section introduces these views and goes through some of the maintenance concepts.

The section following this focuses even more on how to achieve some of the common modeling results you want.

Modifying Resource Assignments

Remember that Project takes any entry into the Assignment Units field that is less than 100% and schedules it down to the minute. If you were to enter **25%** on a Fixed Units or Fixed Work task (the default is Fixed Units), it would in fact represent two hours out of an eight-hour workday. However, Project actually schedules 15 minutes of work for each hour in the eight-hour day, which totals two hours. In most cases, the resource or employee realistically sits down and completes all the work in two hours, in one sitting, rather than work for just 15 minutes an hour, every hour, on the project. If you are concerned only about the overall time (in this case, two hours) and not the exact amount of time the resource is actually spending during each hour, you can just ignore the difference between the way Project schedules time and the way the work is actually being done. If you want the schedule to reflect that the resource worked full time for two hours and then was idle for the rest of the task, you can enter **100%** in the Assignment Units field and then change the work to only two hours or manually contour the work to be two hours.

A slight twist on this is when you are actually trying to schedule tasks WITHIN a day. In this case, it is better to set the duration of the task to two hours BEFORE you assign the resource. Then it will be a task with two hours duration and two hours work (at 100% Units). You can even designate the Task Start Date down to the hour of the day. To do this, you must set the Date format on the View tab of the Options dialog box (on the Tools menu) to a format that allows entry of Date and Time.

In prior versions of Project, there were some instances where you wanted to set the Assignment Units field to zero. If this field is set to zero, Project calculates work as zero, and accordingly, sets the cost of the work to zero also. This was simplified in Microsoft Project 2007 by the addition of the cost resource. If you had a situation where a contractor would be working on a task and would complete it for a fixed fee, you could create a cost resource representing the contractor and enter the fixed fee into the Cost field on the Resources tab of the Task Information dialog box (see "Assigning Fixed Costs and Fixed Contract Fees" later in this chapter for additional discussion).

 note

Project does not enforce the maximum number of available units when you make resource assignments. You can assign more units than the Max Units value when you are planning a project, but when you exceed the maximum for any resource, in the Resource Sheet and Resource Usage views, the Resource Name turns red and a special warning indicator is displayed in the Indicator Column.

 caution

You can enter fractions of a percentage into the Assignment Units field, but they will automatically be rounded up to the nearest whole number. Project uses fractional percents in the calculations, but it will not display them.

Material resources are always formatted as a decimal. If you miss entering the assigned units, it defaults to 1, followed by the material label defined for the resource. If you define the material resource of dirt as Yd (for cubic yard), the default units supplied by Project will be 1 Yd, which means the task consumes one cubic yard of dirt.

When you enter a numeral into the Units column for a material resource, it is called a *fixed consumption rate*. The amount is considered to be fixed and independent of the task duration. Using our current example, Project figures one yard of material for the task, and if the task duration changes, the consumption rate will not.

 note

If you enter something that Project does not understand, such as *yards* instead of *Yd*, Project shows you a warning. This warning lets you know that it is not a valid Units value. Simply enter a numeric value and let Project provide the correct label.

If you want to assign material resource units that have a variable consumption rate, where the amount of material resources depends on the duration of the task, you simply enter the units, followed by a forward slash (/). For instance, if you have a backhoe that uses 10 gallons of gas an hour, you can enter either **10/h** or **10 gal/h**. Project then calculates the consumption of 10 gallons of fuel per hour for every hour of working time on the calendar until the task is complete.

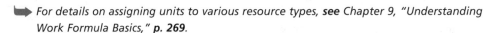
For details on assigning units to various resource types, **see** *Chapter 9, "Understanding Work Formula Basics,"* **p. 269**.

Entering the Assignment Values

Assignment values for resources can be entered in a variety of ways; one of the most commonly used methods is the Task form because it enables you to view all needed resource attributes and easily select as many resources as you need for a task. One of the easiest ways to display the form is to go to the Task Entry view (mentioned earlier). On the Task tab, select Views, More Views and scroll down to click the Task Entry view. This form can also be displayed from any split screen view with tasks in the upper pane. Right-click on the background in the lower pane and select Resources and Predecessors.

Assuming you are using the Task Entry view, follow these steps to assign resources using the Task Form view in the bottom pane:

1. Select the task in the top pane of the Gantt Chart view.

2. In the bottom pane, select the Task Type field to be sure that it is set appropriately to manage the calculations for the assignments you are about to enter. If you are adding work resources and you want to make sure the duration does not change, make the task "fixed-duration" for this assignment, and then return it to its prior setting after completing the assignment.

3. If you are adding new work resource names to an existing list of resource name assignments, select the Effort Driven field for its appropriateness. This also works when deleting existing resource names. If the changes you are about to enter alter the total work associated with the task, clear the Effort Driven check box. However, if changes simply redistribute the existing total work among the resources assigned to the task, leave the field selected.

4. Select the Resource Name field and identify the resource by selecting the name from the drop-down list. You can also type the name, but you must be careful to spell it correctly, so that Project does not create a new resource for the misspelled name.

5. If you leave the Units field blank, Project assigns the default (the lesser of 100% or Max Units for the resource). If you want to specify the units for the assignment, select the Units field and enter the units you want to assign, as follows:

   ■ For work resources, type a Units value as a percentage (for example, 200%) unless you have chosen to use a decimal format for units (for example, 2).

   ■ For material resources that have a fixed consumption rate, type a decimal number that represents the total units to be consumed by the task. For example, if 20 gallons of fuel are to be assigned, enter **20**. Project replaces this entry with 20 plus the material label.

   ■ For material resources that have a variable consumption rate, type the number of units as a decimal, followed by a slash and a time unit to indicate a rate of consumption. To assign 20 gallons of fuel per week, enter **20/wk**. Project replaces this entry with 20 gallons/week.

   ■ Cost resources, such as insurance on a (rented) moving truck, are not measured in units. Their cost is not even specified on the resource sheet. Their cost is specified when you assign the resource to a task (in the Task Entry pane, you change the form to the Resource Cost form to see the Resource Cost field). The cost is accrued across the duration of the assigned Tasks and is identified in the Resource Sheet by specifying the Accrual Type (Prorated, Start, or End).

6. If you leave the Work field blank, Project calculates the work based on the task duration and the assigned (or default) units. If you want to specify the amount of work for the assignment, select the Work field and type the work amount. For work resources, work must be entered with a number plus the unit of measure: m (minute), h (hour), d (day), w (week), or mo (month). For material resources, enter a decimal value. Project uses this value as the fixed consumption rate for the task.

 tip

PMI suggests that tasks should be sized so that the work associated with them is estimated to take no more than 80 hours of effort and no fewer than 8 hours. This is for purposes of managing the activity. The larger the task, the more room for error on both the original estimate and the progress status gathered. The suggested maximum is also why it is suggested to have at least biweekly, but preferably weekly, project status meetings. At the other end of the spectrum, most project managers would not be interested in micromanaging activities that take fewer than eight hours of work. The actual maximum/minimum effort ranges you should use for your task decomposition and how frequent your status meetings should be will be determined by the kind of work you are doing and how early you want to be able to correct the impacts of flawed estimates or delays.

 note

Remember that if you enter both units and work when you assign the first resource, Project recalculates the duration. However, with fixed-duration tasks, Project keeps the duration and work and recalculates the units.

If you are assigning multiple resources, follow these steps:

1. Enter additional resources in the next rows of the Resource Name column before you click OK. For instance, Figure 10.12 shows the resources to be assigned to the task Load the Moving Truck.

2. After all resource assignments are made for the task, click OK and Project calculates the fields that were left blank.

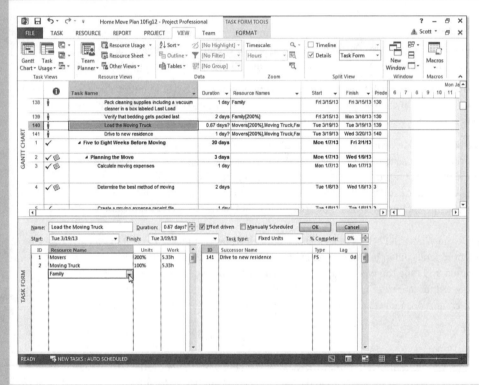

Figure 10.12
The movers are assigned at 200% to indicate two people performing the job, the moving truck has consumption rate of $50/hour, and the family will get assigned the default units of 100% once the OK button is clicked.

When you click OK, Project calculates the values for the fields that you did not fill in, in accordance with the principles discussed in Chapter 9 (see Figure 10.13).

Figure
10.13
Resources
are now
showing
calculated
units and
work.

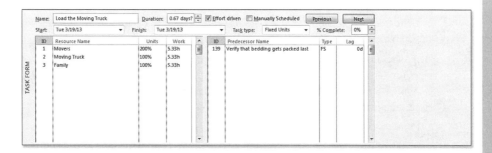

Assigning Resources with the Task Usage View

Everything you accomplished in the previous section with the Gantt Chart view in the top pane can be done with the Task Usage view in the top pane. You can think of the Task Usage view as a less graphical, more detailed version of the Team Planner. You can do the following:

- Display the Assignment Information dialog box, where you can apply work contours and different Cost Rate tables to an assignment and where you can write commentary notes about the assignment.

- View the *time-phased* work schedule. The time-phased view shows work broken down into specific time periods.

- Display the number of time-phased work and cost measures.

- Edit many of the time-phased values directly in the grid cells. You could, for instance, reapportion work among the time periods or create and fine-tune splits or delays in an individual assignment.

Figure 10.14 shows the Task Usage view in the top pane and the Task Form view in the bottom pane.

To display the Task Usage view, select the Task tab, Views, Task Usage.

The table area of the Task Usage view displays all the tasks in the project, using by default the Usage table. Indented under each task are rows for that task's assignments. You can hide or show the assignments by using the outline icon on the left of the task name. The Work field for the task is the sum of the Work field values for the assigned resources.

The right side of the view is a timescale grid of cells that show time-phased assignment details. In Figure 10.14, the work details are displayed in the grid. This is the default assignment detail, but you can display other details if desired. Work detail is the most useful for creating and editing assignments. The value in the Work field for each resource in the table on the left is the sum of the time-phased values displayed in the cells on that row in the timescale.

Modifying Work Schedules with the Task Usage View

As mentioned before, you can use the Task Usage view to customize the amount of work scheduled for each period and to slip and delay task assignments.

To change the amount of work scheduled for any given time period in the Task Usage view, simply select the time-phased cell, type a new value, and either press Enter or select another cell. When you type a value for a work resource, Project assumes that the unit is hours unless you provide a different time measurement unit.

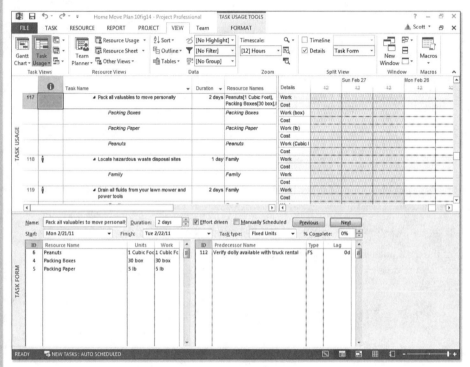

Figure 10.14
Split the window to display the Task Usage view in the top pane and the Task Form view in the bottom pane.

---

 note

If you type a value with a time unit that is not hours, Project converts the value to hours in the display. For example, if the timescale unit is days (that is, each cell is one day) and you type one week, Project displays 40h (40 hours) in that cell. If the assignment unit is 100%, this is too many hours for that one day. This example also serves to warn you that you should not enter a work value that represents more hours than are available for that time period.

There are several different techniques for editing the cells in the time-phase grid:

- If you select a cell or group of consecutive cells in a row, you can use Ctrl+C to copy these values or Ctrl+X to cut those values from the grid. You can then select a cell at a new location and use Ctrl+V to paste the values into the cell at that location. If you choose to cut cells, the cells then display 0h.

- If you select a cell or group of consecutive cells in a row, you can drag the border around the selection to a new location and drop the cells into that new location. The original location cells display 0h.

- If you select a cell or group of consecutive cells in a row, you can drag a copy to a new location by holding down the Ctrl key as you drag the selection border to the new location. The caution about dropping cells on nonworking days applies here also.

- The bottom-right corner of the cell selection border displays a small black square, which is called the *fill handle.* You can drag this handle to bordering cells in the same row to copy the value in the selection into those cells.

- If you select a cell or group of consecutive cells in a row, you can press the Insert key to insert nonworking time (0h) in place of the selection, pushing the selected values to the right. Thus, you effectively introduce a split.

- If you select a cell or group of consecutive cells in a row, you can press the Delete key to remove that work from the assignment. After clearing the cells you had selected, Project shifts to the left any cells on the right that contain work, to fill in the space you deleted.

For example, if you want to increase the work and duration of an assignment, you can select the last cell in the assignment and drag its fill handle to the right to fill as many additional work periods as you choose. If you want to introduce a split in an assignment, you can select the cells where the slip is to occur and press the Insert key. To remove the split, you can select the cells that display 0h and press the Delete key.

If you modify a time-phased cell on the task work row, the new value is apportioned among all the work resource assignments that had work scheduled for that time period. The relative proportions of the total work for each resource are kept the same. If you modified a time-phased cell on an assignment row, the new values change the sum in the row for the task.

When you complete a cell modification, Project immediately recalculates the task and assignments as follows:

- If you modified a cell on the task row, the changes are applied to all assignments that were scheduled during that time period.

- If you modified a cell on a row for a work resource, Project updates the summary value for that time period on the task row.

- The Work column entries for assignments in the table on the left are updated. These are the totals for all time periods for each assignment.

- The Work column entry for the task in the table on the left is updated. This is the total for all assignments for all time periods.

- The duration for the task is updated. If you have not changed the number of time periods in which work is scheduled, there is no change in the duration.

Follow these steps to introduce a split in a task or in an individual assignment using the Task Usage view:

1. Display the Task Usage view in the top pane. You can type changes into time-phased cells in the bottom pane, but you cannot use drag-and-drop techniques in that pane.

2. Select the cell or cells that currently have work in them where you want to insert the split. If you select cells on the task row, the split is applied to all the resource assignments for the task. If you select cells on an assignment row, only that assignment is affected.

3. Press the Insert key. Project shifts the work values to the right, leaving the selected cells with no scheduled work during that period.

To delay an assignment, you could select the cell for the beginning of the assignment and press the Insert key repeatedly until the work is moved to the date when you want it to start. You could, on the other hand, select all the work cells for the assignment and drag the selection to the period where you want the work to be scheduled.

In Figure 10.15, the usage of the material resource Drafting Paper is shown to be delayed until 9/16/13. Originally, Project had distributed the one roll of paper evenly over the task duration (0.04 rolls per day). To create a delayed usage as in Figure 10.15, you would have to delete all the fractional units and type in the new usage, as shown in the figure (0.1 rolls per day beginning on 9/16/13). The quick way to remove all the fractional units is to type **0** in the Work column on the left. Then select the time-phased cell for the date where you want to schedule the usage (9/16/13) and type in the value.

caution

Be careful when using these editing techniques when you have a project with a fixed finish date. The results are not the same as for a fixed-start-date project and therefore are likely to cause you to lose a lot of time trying to correct the changes.

 tip

Drag-and-drop can be difficult to use if the destination is offscreen, because when you drag past the last visible cells, the screen scrolls rapidly. In these instances, it is easier to cut the selection, scroll to the destination, and paste. Alternatively, you can make an entry in the last cell of the selection and drag back (to the left).

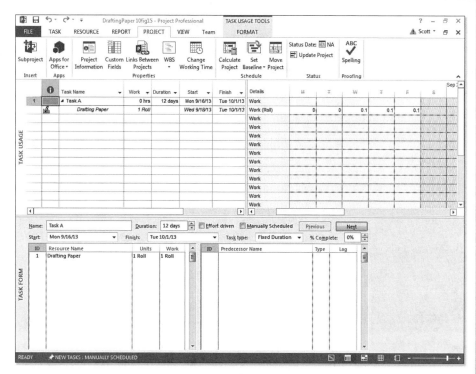

Figure 10.15
The use of the Drafting Paper material resource is delayed until after the task has started.

Using the Assignment Information Dialog Box

You can display the Assignment Information dialog box by selecting an assignment row in either the Task Usage view or the Resource Usage view and then clicking the Format tab, Assignment, Assignment Information button, or double-clicking the assignment row.

Figure 10.16 shows the Assignment Information dialog box for the Load the Moving Truck delayed assignment from the previous example. As you can see, the dialog box provides several fields that you have already worked with on forms and tables, including Work, Units, and Start and Finish. The Cost field is a read-only total cost for the assignment. You can also change the name of the assigned resource here, but there is no drop-down list to choose the resource, so you must know how to spell the name, or you might end up creating a new resource out of a typographical error.

There are three fields in the Assignment Information dialog box you will not find on any other standard view or dialog box in Project, as follows:

- **The Work Contour field on the General tab**—This field enables you to choose from a set of predefined work contours. A *contour* is a planned pattern of scheduled work that is spread over the duration of an assignment, a distribution function in mathematical terms. For example, the Front Loaded contour schedules a lot of work per day at the start of the assignment and the daily work tapers off toward the end of the assignment. The default contour is Flat, which means the resource is scheduled to work the same number of hours each day, as called for by the assigned units and the hours available on the resource calendar. Thus, the workload is the same every day unless the calendar has varying amounts of working time. If you have edited the assignment or applied one of the other contours, you can return the assignment to the standard schedule by applying the Flat contour. The only other way to access and select the predefined contours is to display the Work Contour field as a column in the table in the Task Usage or Resource Usage view.

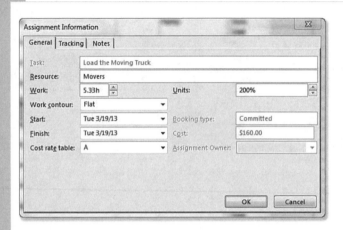

Figure 10.16
The Assignment Information dialog box shows only one resource at a time for the resource you selected.

- **The Cost Rate Table field on the General tab**—This field enables you to select one of the five different Cost Rate tables as the standard and overtime rates for the assignment. The default assignment is Table A. The Cost Rate Table field can also be displayed as a column in the table.

- **The Notes field on the Notes tab**—This field enables you to record notes about an assignment. For instance, you should record why you delayed an assignment or chose a different Cost Rate table. You could also embed links to other documents such as job specifications, cost worksheets, or websites.

The Tracking tab has fields you can use to monitor work progress and record when work starts, how much work has been done so far, and when work is completed.

➡ *For additional information about using these fields,* **see** *Chapter 13, "Tracking Your Project Progress," **p. 431**.*

Scheduling a Late Start for an Assignment

It is possible to assign a resource to a task whose work is not expected to be started until after some work on the task has been completed by others. Suppose that a team is assigned to design a new accessory to its main product and it needs to be able to consult with an expert concerning the design. The consultant's assignment to the design task can be delayed so that it starts after the task has been worked on long enough for the team to understand what it needs to ask the consultant. In addition, another member of the team is a draftsman whose only job is to prepare a drawing of the design, something that cannot be finished until after the design is finished. His assignment must also be delayed.

In Figure 10.17, Brent and Jim are assigned full time to a five-day task, but the consultant and draftsman each have only four hours of work assigned. As explained later, Task 1 represents the way Project assigns the work, whereas Task 2 shows how individual assignments can be delayed.

Figure 10.17 Task 2 schedules the consultant to perform his or her work two days after the team has begun its work. The draftsman is scheduled to begin three days after work has begun.

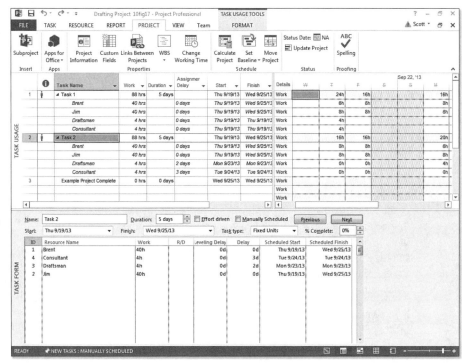

Figure 10.17 displays a Task Usage view, with the time-phased assignment details in the grid on the right, just like the Resource Usage views. The names of the assigned resources are indented under the task names, and the assignment values are rolled up or summed on the row for the task. The Work column in the table on the left shows, for each row, the total of the time-phased work details in the grid.

Task 1 shows how Project, by default, schedules the hours for all assignments at the start of the task (September 19th). Task 2 shows the delayed hours for the consultant (September 24th) and the draftsman (September 23rd).

The bottom pane shows the Task Form view, with the Resource Schedule details table at the bottom. The column titled Delay shows the amount of an assignment delay. The Start and Finish fields show the scheduled dates for the assignment.

Since the Leveling Delay column in the Task form is a different kind of delay, it is explained in Chapter 24, "Resolving Resource Allocation Problems," p. 801.

You can create an assignment delay in several different ways, as follows:

- You can enter the amount of the delay in the Delay column in the resource schedule details of the Task Form view (refer to Figure 10.17). The Delay field is also available in the schedule details on the Resource Form view. If you enter a value in the Delay field, Project automatically calculates the delayed dates for the Start and Finish fields.

- You can enter a delay start date in the Start field to the right of the Delay field. Project automatically calculates the value for the Delay field as well as the new finish date.

- If you add the Assignment Delay column to the Task Usage view, you can enter the delay or the start date for the assignment on the row for the assignment.

- You can also create a delay for an assignment by editing the time-phased work details in the grid in the Task Usage view or the Resource Usage view. You can simply select the cells that contain the hours of work you want to delay and drag them to a later date. You can use the mouse to drag the consultant's four hours of work from September 20 to September 23. Project then calculates the values for the Assignment Delay, Start, and Finish fields.

- If you double-click anywhere in an assignment row in either the Task Usage or the Resource Usage view, or if you select a cell on that row and click the Assignment Information tool in the Standard toolbar, Project displays the Assignment Information dialog box for that assignment (see Figure 10.18). You can enter a delayed start date in the Start box or use the calendar control to the right of the field to select a start date. Although the Delay field does not appear on the Assignment Information dialog box, its value is recalculated if you enter a new date in the Start field.

   See the "Forward-Scheduling Versus Backward-Scheduling" section in "Consultants' Tips" at the end of this chapter, p. 356.

 note

The default entry in the Delay field is 0d, which means no delay. The Delay field is never blank. You can remove the delay by entering zero into the Delay field. However, you cannot erase an entry and leave the field blank.

note

If you enter a date into the Finish field to the right of the Delay field in the Task Form view, Project does not calculate a delay for the start date. Instead, it recalculates the amount of work that is completed between the (unchanged) start of the assignment and the new finish date you just entered.

note

You can enter negative amounts in the assignment Delay field only if the project is scheduled from a fixed finish date. You can enter positive amounts only if the project is scheduled from a fixed start date.

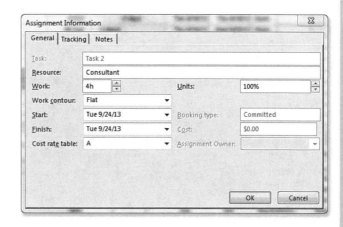

Figure 10.18
The Assignment Information dialog box displays all information about the selected assignment.

Splitting a Task Assignment

Splitting an assignment means that you schedule an interruption in the work. Many conditions might require you to split an assignment, such as a timing conflict for a resource or a required delay after work has begun. There are two basic methods for splitting, as follows:

- You can split the task, and Project automatically splits each resource assignment for the task, with zero work scheduled during the period of the split.

- You can split the individual resource assignment by introducing one or more periods of zero work in the middle of the assignment.

If you introduce a split in an individual resource assignment, Project does not show the split in the task unless it is the only resource assignment for the task, or unless you introduce the same split in all the assigned resources.

You can see in Figure 10.19 the three tasks that both Kim and Dan are assigned. The view has the Gantt Chart view in the top pane and the Task Usage in the bottom.

Dan has a one-day split on the following Thursday, in his assignment to Task B. However, the Gantt bar for the task in the top pane of Figure 10.19 is not split, because Kim is assigned to the task and continues to work on those days, while Dan works on another task.

Removing Resource Assignments from One or More Tasks

As the work on a project moves forward, there will be times when the resources that were planned to be used on tasks are not going to be used. Follow these steps to remove a resource assignment from one or more selected tasks:

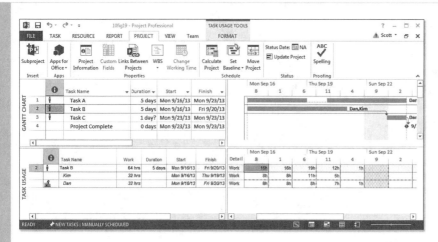

Figure 10.19
Note how Task B does not contain a split even though Dan's work for Thursday is set to 0; this is because Kim continues to work on the task without interruptions, so there is never a period of inactivity on the task.

1. Select the task or tasks in the view that has the resource assignments you want to remove.

2. Display the Assign Resources dialog box, shown in Figure 10.20, by selecting the Resource tab, Assignments, Assign Resources.

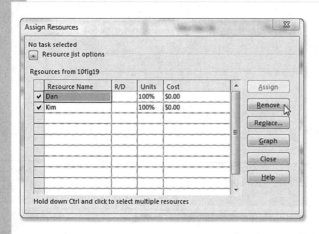

Figure 10.20
Remove a resource assignment using the Remove button in the Assign Resources dialog box.

3. Select the resource you want to remove from the assignment by clicking the row for that resource. Use Ctrl+click to select multiple resources for removal.

 note
Resources assigned to the selected task are identified by check marks to the left of the resource name. If a check mark is gray instead of black, your task selection in the view includes some tasks that have that resource assigned and some that do not.

4. Click the Remove button. The resources selected in the Assign Resources dialog box are removed from any assignments they might have with the tasks selected in the underlying view.

Replacing a Resource on an Assignment

You can use the Assign Resources dialog box to replace one resource with another, to change the assigned units for a resource, or to change the amount of work assigned to a resource. Each assignment should be modified individually, and you can use different techniques depending on what you want to modify.

Follow these steps to replace an assigned resource with another resource name:

1. Select the task. You can select multiple tasks by using the Ctrl key if you want to make an identical assignment change in all of them.

2. Display the Assign Resources dialog box by selecting the Resource tab, Assignments, Assign Resources.

3. Select the resource name to be replaced.

4. Click the Replace button. Project now displays the Replace Resources dialog box over the Assign Resources dialog box. In Figure 10.21, only the Replace Resource dialog box is shown.

5. Select the new resource name.

6. Select the Units field for the selected resource and a new value if you do not want to use the same Units value.

7. Click OK or press Enter.

Figure 10.21
Replace resources in the Replace Resource dialog box; access by clicking the Replace button in the Assign Resources dialog box.

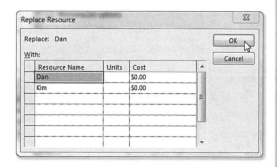

 note

If you have filtered the list of resource names, the list in the Replace Resource dialog box will be filtered also.

To replace the number of units in a resource assignment, you simply edit the entry in the Units field. You select a different cell or press Enter to complete the change. You can then use the SmartTag to override Project's default calculation.

To replace the amount of work assigned to a resource, you should select the cells for the units and type a work amount (a number followed by a time unit abbreviation). Project divides the task duration by the work amount you entered and assigns the resulting units. You can use the SmartTag to override Project's default calculation.

How-To's: Modifying Resource Assignments

This section provides more individual scenario-level guidance on how to achieve the work modeling results you want. The section is loosely ordered from the more general/common situation to the more esoteric.

Key parts to this section are as follows:

- Graphing resource availability

- Scheduling resources for a specific amount of work

- Contouring resource usage

- Selecting a predefined contour using the Assignment Information dialog box

- Using overtime to shorten duration

- Selecting a Cost Rate table for an assignment

- Assigning fixed cost and fixed contract fees

- Scheduling with task calendars

- Adding delay to an assignment

Graphing Resource Availability

Suppose that you want a specific resource to work on a task, but the resource does not have available work hours during the time the task is currently scheduled. One of the possible solutions could be to reschedule the task to a time when the resource has enough work time available.

With Project, there are two ways of using graphs to determine resource availability. The first is by using the Team Planner (Resource tab, View, Team Planner).

The Team Planner is not, strictly speaking, a graph: It is a drag-and-drop hybrid Gantt Chart that depicts resource over- and underallocation in a graphical environment. Resource overallocations are, by default, depicted as stacked Gantt bars with red highlighting.

You can adjust assignment start dates by simply dragging the Gantt bars until the red highlights disappear. In Figure 10.22, Kim is over-allocated across two tasks on Monday, Tuesday, and Wednesday, Dan is overallocated a week later.

Figure 10.22
The Team
Planner
makes over-
allocations
obvious.

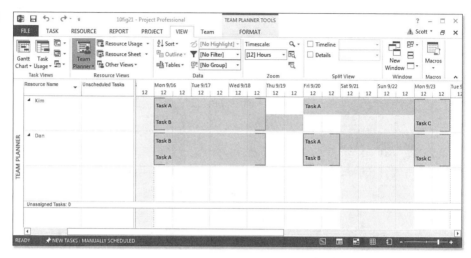

Alternatively, you can do this by selecting the resource in the Assign Resources dialog box and then clicking on the Graphs button to display timeline graphs and accompanying data tables. The timeline graphs and data tables show information about the selected resource's availability and currently assigned work. You can choose from 10 different graphs by using the Format tab, Data, Graph. Two examples include the following:

■ **The Remaining Availability graph**—You can choose the Remaining Availability graph to see the remaining available working time along a timeline (see Figure 10.23). You can zoom in and out on the timeline to look at the data by hours, days, weeks, months, and so on. If you have selected multiple resources, the date for each is color-coded, and check boxes in the graph legend let you temporarily remove and restore the individual resources in the display.

■ **The Work graph**—The Work graph looks similar to the Remaining Availability graph, but it shows already assigned work. You can zoom the timeline, and multiple resources are color-coded and can be removed and restored from the graph (see Figure 10.24).

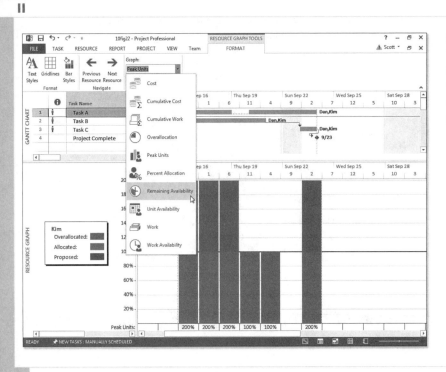

Figure 10.23
The Graphs window enables you to select one out of the 10 available graphs.

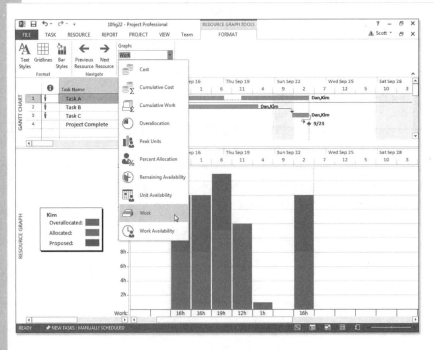

Figure 10.24
You can use the Work graph to review resource availability versus the amount of work the resource is assigned, not only for the selected task, but for other tasks in the project.

Scheduling Resources for a Specific Amount of Work

For work resources, you can also use the Assign Resources dialog box to calculate the number of units needed to complete a specific amount of work within the task's current duration. In the Assign Resources dialog box, enter a work amount in the Units column (a number followed by a time unit, such as **40h** for 40 hours). Project then calculates the number of units needed to do that much work, within the current duration for the task. *This procedure does not work if the task is effort-driven and this is the first assignment of the resource to the task.* You can use this technique to recalculate an existing working resource assignment, even if the task is effort-driven.

Follow these steps to assign resources by using the work amount:

1. Select the task or tasks to which you want the resource assigned.

2. Display the Assign Resources dialog box by selecting the Resource tab, Assignments, Assign Resources.

3. Select the resource name from the Name list.

4. Select the Units field and type the work amount followed by the unit it is measured in: m (minute), h (hour), d (day), w (week), or mo (month).

5. Select a different cell, click the Assign button, or press Enter to have Project calculate the units and assign the resource to the selected tasks.

Contouring Resource Usage

The default resource work pattern is known as the *flat pattern*. In the flat pattern, Project schedules a resource's work to begin when the task begins and to continue working at a constant and uninterrupted rate until either all of the remaining work from the Task is allocated on the assignment or until the Task finish date is reached. This means Project uses the same (specified) units every day until the assigned work is complete.

On some occasions, you might want a resource to put greater effort into a task at the outset, and then taper off the daily effort until the task is finished. If that's what you hope to accomplish, you want to assign more units and hours for the days at the beginning of the task and then use a reduced number of units and hours each day to complete the task. This is known as *front loading* the work on the task.

Other times, you might want to *back load* the work by starting with a small number of hours and assignment units up front and then increasing the work as the task nears completion. Different scheduling patterns such as these are available in Project as *work contours*. The default is a flat contour pattern, but you can have Project change an assignment schedule by applying one of seven different predefined work contours. You can also create your own contour by editing the time-phased values in the Usage View grid.

To change the scheduling pattern, you can display either the Task Usage view or the Resource Usage view. The Resource Usage view is similar to the Task Usage view in that it displays all the resources with their assignments indented beneath them and provides assignment details for each period in the timescale in the grid of cells. You can use either of these views to apply contoured assignments, by either applying one of the built-in contours or by editing the work assigned in any given time period in the grid.

To illustrate contouring, suppose that Ben is assigned to Task A, which is estimated to take 40 hours to complete. In the beginning, he needs to concentrate completely on the task, but after it is underway, he can spend more time on other tasks. You could schedule his assignment like the "before and after" example in the Task Usage view in Figure 10.25. Task A shows the standard assignment schedule.

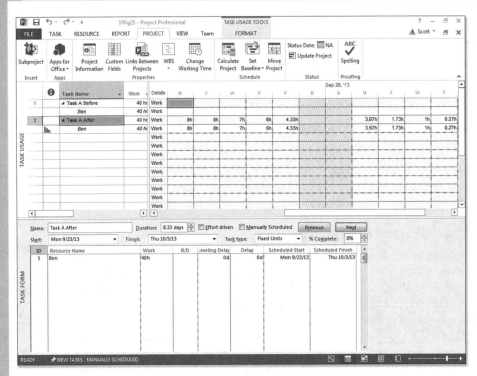

Figure 10.25
Because the front-loaded contour was applied to Task A After, the amount of hours Ben works each day gradually decreases.

Task A After shows Ben's assignment schedule after the front-loaded contour is applied. You can see the icon in the Indicator column that flags this assignment as having a front-loaded contour. Ben's assignment starts at 100% but soon drops to lower and lower levels, until all the work is finished. As a result of this lowering of levels, the hours of work scheduled for each day become less and less; Ben will still do 40 hours of work, but now it takes more days to complete the work. Notice that the duration for Task A After is 8.33 days, instead of 5 days.

In Figure 10.26, you can see the Resource Usage view of Ben's front-loaded task. The main record is now the resource Ben instead of the task, but indented under it is the same assignment record, now labeled with the associated task name. The details in the grid are the same as those for Task A After in Figure 10.25.

The bottom pane of Figure 10.26 shows the Resource Graph view. This view displays a histogram (a vertical bar chart) to give a graphical image of the resource assignment detail that you select. In this case, the peak units detail is graphed and illustrates very nicely the declining nature of the front-loaded work contour. This graph, in fact, is the source of the image that is used in the indicator for front-loaded contours.

Figure 10.26 Ben's decreasing work concept of the front-loaded contour is perfectly demonstrated in the Resource Graph view in the bottom pane.

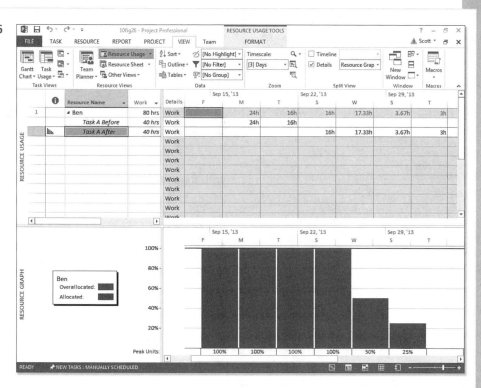

Project has eight predefined work contour patterns that you can apply to a resource assignment. These are in addition to the Flat pattern, which is the default, and used when Project first calculates an assignment. The contour patterns are described in Table 10.2.

Table 10.2 Microsoft Project Work Contours

Contour Icon	Contour Name	Contour Description
	Flat	This is the pattern that Project uses in the initial assignment calculation. All work is assigned as soon as the task starts, and it continues until the assignment is complete. There is no indicator icon for this pattern.

Contour Icon	Contour Name	Contour Description
	Back Loaded	The daily workload starts light and builds until the end of the task.
	Front Loaded	The heaviest daily load is the beginning of the task and tapers off continuously until the end of the task.
	Double Peak	The daily workload starts low, builds to an early peak, drops off, builds to another peak, and then tapers off to the end of the task.
	Early Peak	The daily workload starts light, builds rapidly to a peak, and then tapers off until the end of the task.
	Late Peak	The daily workload starts light, builds slowly to a peak near the end of the task, and then drops off somewhat at the end.
	Bell	The daily workload starts light, builds to a peak in the middle of the assignment, and then tapers off until the end of the assignment.
	Turtle	The daily workload starts somewhat light, builds rapidly to a plateau, remains there for most of the rest of the assignment, and then drops back to a somewhat light level at the end.
	Edited	This pattern does not illustrate a predefined contour; rather, it illustrates the fact that you can edit the work assignments to produce your own work pattern. The indicator, with a pencil in the bar chart, shows that the work assignment has been manually edited. Note that you can only edit the Work cells; you cannot edit the Peak Units values directly.

Figure 10.27 shows the different contour types in an actual calculation by Project.

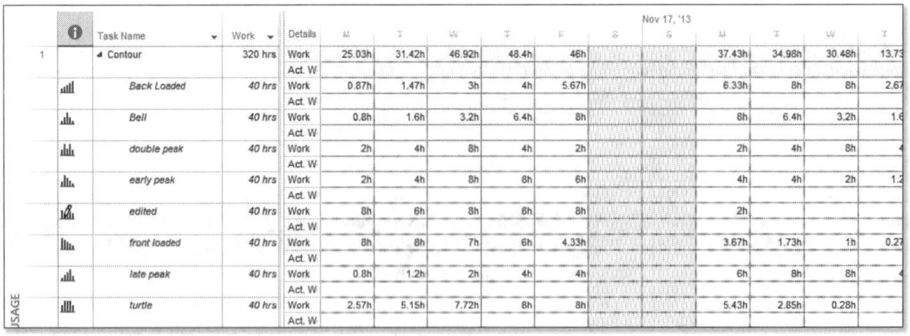

	Task Name	Work	Details	M	T	W	T	F	S	S (Nov 17, '13)	M	T	W	T
1	Contour	320 hrs	Work	25.03h	31.42h	46.92h	48.4h	46h			37.43h	34.98h	30.48h	13.73
			Act. W											
	Back Loaded	40 hrs	Work	0.87h	1.47h	3h	4h	5.67h			6.33h	8h	8h	2.67
			Act. W											
	Bell	40 hrs	Work	0.8h	1.6h	3.2h	6.4h	8h			8h	6.4h	3.2h	1.6
			Act. W											
	double peak	40 hrs	Work	2h	4h	8h	4h	2h			2h	4h	8h	4
			Act. W											
	early peak	40 hrs	Work	2h	4h	8h	8h	6h			4h	4h	2h	1.2
			Act. W											
	edited	40 hrs	Work	8h	6h	8h	8h	8h			2h			
			Act. W											
	front loaded	40 hrs	Work	8h	8h	7h	6h	4.33h			3.67h	1.73h	1h	0.27
			Act. W											
	late peak	40 hrs	Work	0.8h	1.2h	2h	4h	4h			6h	8h	8h	4
			Act. W											
	turtle	40 hrs	Work	2.57h	5.15h	7.72h	8h	8h			5.43h	2.85h	0.28h	
			Act. W											

Figure 10.27 This illustration shows the different contour types for a 40-hour assignment.

In the time-phase details on the right, you can see the work and peak units for each day. Claire is assigned 100% to the task for all five days; 100% of her time is allocated to the task.

Rows 2 through 8 show how Project would schedule the work if one of the predefined contours were applied. The total work remains 40 hours in all cases, as shown in the Work column. The work assignments for each day vary, depending on the contour pattern, as do the peak units.

All the contours reduce the unit assignment during different days in the assignment. The choice of which days determines the pattern that is the source of the different contour names. Because there is less work scheduled on some of the days, the total assignment necessitates that it will take longer to complete. Notice that the duration of the task is extended when the contours are applied. Instead of the task being completed in five days, work must continue into additional days.

 tip

Beware of scheduling back-loaded work effort on a task. This should be done only with careful consideration as you are also back-loading all the risk around the task. Back-loaded tasks have little chance of correction for underestimation. By the time you become aware that the effort estimate was flawed, you are at the end of the task and missing the targeted completion date is likely. In addition, if the contour expectations are communicated to the resource, you also take the risk of being impacted by basic human nature—via procrastination.

The Contoured row in Figure 10.27 is not a predefined contour pattern. It is the name Project applies when the user edits the work details for an assignment. In this case, the resource is scheduled to work 10 hours on Monday and 6 the next day. Manual edits are done in either the Task Usage or Resource Usage view, where you can edit the assigned hours in the work details cells. In either case, you are forcing a custom contour through the edit actions.

To apply a predefined contour to an assignment, see the steps in the next section.

 note

If overtime hours are assigned to a task when you apply a contour, Project spreads out the overtime evenly, over the duration of the assignment, no matter which contour is applied.

 tip

If you want to add a resource with a contoured assignment to an existing task that has other resources already assigned and you do not want the task duration or the other resource schedules to change, make the task a Fixed Duration task and disable Effort Driven before assigning the contour. You can later return the task to its previous task type and effort-driven status. Project applies the contour but has to stop scheduling hours when it reaches the end of the task duration. As a result, the new resource has a lower total amount of work than it initially did. You will undoubtedly have to manually edit the work assignment values to get the results you want.

Selecting a Predefined Contour Using the Assignment Information Dialog Box

By default, the work that Project schedules for an assignment is evenly distributed across available time periods of the assignment (that is, the flat contour). As you have already seen, you can edit the assignments in individual time periods to customize the schedule. You can also choose one of eight predefined contour patterns for Project to apply to an individual assignment.

For example, if a resource schedule needs to show a lot of hours up front, with a tapering off toward the end, you could assign the front-loaded contour to the assignment, and Project changes the work in the individual periods to reflect that pattern.

Follow these steps to select a contour for an assignment:

1. Select the assignment in the Task Usage view or the Resource Usage view.

2. Display the assignment Information dialog box by clicking the Assignment Information tool or by double-clicking the assignment row.

3. On the General tab, use the drop-down list in the Work Contour field to select one of the predefined contours (see Figure 10.28).

4. Click OK to have Project calculate the new assignment pattern.

> **tip**
>
> If you change the work contour, it is a good idea to document why you made the choices you made in the assignment Notes field. You can click on the Notes tab in the Assignment Information dialog box and enter supporting documentation about an assignment, including links to external documents such as job specifications or standards.

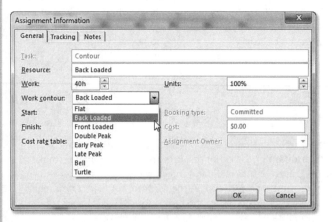

Figure 10.28
You can change the work contour in the Assignment Information dialog box.

Using Overtime to Shorten Duration

Another way to reduce the duration of a task is by scheduling some of a resource's time as overtime. *Overtime work* means work scheduled outside the resource's normal working hours. For Project, that means work scheduled during nonworking time on the resource calendar. Assigning overtime does not reduce the total amount of work for an assignment; instead, the amount scheduled during regular working time is reduced by the amount of the overtime. Project schedules the overtime work by spreading it out evenly over the duration of the assignment. Later, when you enter actual work completed, you can specify exactly how many hours of overtime were completed in any given time period.

Project also charges the resource's overtime rate for overtime work, so costs might rise, depending on your entry in the Overtime Rate field. The cost of the overtime hours is calculated by using the overtime rate that you defined in the Resource Information dialog box for the period in which the work took place.

 tip

Planned overtime can come in handy when you have to plan a midproject correction to get back on track, but you should avoid it in most other cases. It leaves little time for corrective action should an activity slip. Excessive consecutive overtime can take a heavy toll on productivity and performance and therefore quality. Remember, resources are people too.

Scheduled weekend tasks often carry high impact and risk as weekend activities typically consist of tasks that would interrupt or delay many other activities if performed during the week. So, make sure you have a good backup plan or solid resources if you do schedule for a weekend.

Example 1: Suppose that Eric has been assigned full time (100% units) to upgrade the office's computer system, a task scheduled to take 60 hours of work with a duration of 7.5 days to complete (see Task A in Figure 10.29). Eric is scheduled to start on a Monday and finish at midday on Wednesday the following week. The cost of the task is $1,500 (based on Eric's standard rate of $25/hour).

The assignment details in Figure 10.29 have been augmented to show not only work, which is the total work per time period, but also the regular work and overtime work components of total work, as well as the cost of the assignment. The Regular Work, Overtime Work, and Cost columns have been added. These columns and the Work column show the task totals for the corresponding time-phased details in the grid.

For Task A (No Overtime), the total work is 60 hours, which is the sum of the work hours in the grid. You can see the total work for each day is made up of regular work only. The duration of Task A is 7.5 days, and that is due to the fact that there are seven full days of work and one half-day of four hours. The total cost of the task is $1,500, which is the sum of the daily Cost values in the grid.

Task A (With Overtime) in Figure 10.29 shows what would happen if Eric's manager decided that she needed the task completed in no more than five days, and authorizes 20 hours of overtime work for Eric. Eric still spends a total of 60 hours on the task, but 20 hours are overtime hours and only 40 hours are regular working time. Eric now does 12 hours of work per day—8 hours of regular work plus 4 hours of overtime. All 60 hours of work are completed in just five days; thus, the task duration is five days. The cost for each day is $340. This is figured at $200 standard-rate hours (8 hours at $25/hour), plus $140 of overtime-rate hours (4 hours at $35/hour). Note that if Eric's overtime rate had been at the default zero, the daily cost for the task would have actually fallen to $200 (the cost of the regular work hours).

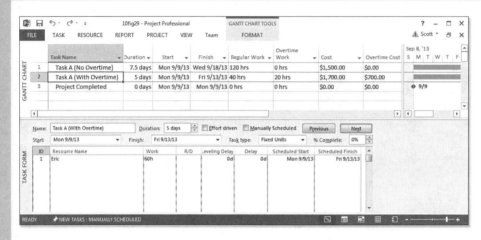

Figure 10.29
Eric will finish faster in Task A (With Overtime) but the task costs more than if he worked regular hours with no overtime assigned.

 note

Overtime work that is scheduled by Project cannot be adjusted manually, meaning you cannot edit the cells in the grid to change the number of overtime hours scheduled on a particular day. However, when you are tracking progress on a task, you can add Actual Overtime Work to the details in the grid, and enter the amount of actual overtime work in each time period to show exactly when the overtime work was performed.

The bottom pane in Figure 10.29 shows the Task Form view with the resource work details displayed at the bottom. Because Task A (With Overtime) is selected in the top pane, the details show the values with overtime assigned. Note that the Overtime Work field displays 20 hours. The Work field shows the total work, 60 hours, which includes overtime.

 tip

Another way to schedule more work during a specific time is to change the resource calendar and increase the working time hours for that time period. You can edit the resource calendar and change nonworking days or hours into working time. Note that Project charges the standard rate for work scheduled during the regular working time hours. This is not a good solution if you must actually pay the resource an overtime rate that differs from the standard rate. However, if pay difference is not an issue, editing the calendar gives you the ability to state explicitly when the extra work time takes place. The drawback in this situation is that if you are to reassign the resource to different tasks, or if the task gets rescheduled to a different date range, you no longer need the extra working time. Project uses the time for other assignments unless you remember to remove the extra working time from the calendar.

You can view scheduled overtime in the Task Usage and Resource Usage views, but you cannot enter overtime in those views unless you add a column to the table for the Overtime Work field. The Overtime Work field appears in three views for you to view and edit, as follows:

- The Task Form view, with the resource work details table displayed at the bottom of the form

- The Task Details Form view, with the resource work details table displayed at the bottom of the form

- The Resource Form view, with the work details table displayed at the bottom of the form

Follow these steps to enter overtime in the Task Form view:

1. Choose a task view such as the Gantt Chart view from the View menu for the top pane.

2. Select the task for which you want to schedule overtime.

3. Display the Task Form view in the bottom pane by selecting the View tab, Split View, Details, Task form.

4. In the bottom pane, right-click the form and select Work from the shortcut menu to display the Work fields in the entry table (see Figure 10.30).

5. Select the Overtime Work field and enter the amount of work that you are scheduling in overtime. Enter a number followed by a time unit abbreviation (m, h, d, w, or mo) and then press Enter. Do not reduce the entry in the Work field. That field's entry must show the *total* amount of work to be done, including both the regular work and the overtime work.

6. Click OK.

In Example 2, in Figure 10.30, overtime has been entered for Linda Elliot's assignment to the Create Advertising Plan task. The total workload for this assignment is 120 hours, which was originally scheduled to take three weeks, but after recording 40 hours of overtime, the regular hours are only 80 and the task duration is reduced to two weeks. Usually, overtime is scheduled for just this reason—to reduce the calendar time required to complete a task.

 note

If you assign all the work to be done in overtime, Project reduces the duration of the task to zero and automatically flags the task as a milestone. You can remove the Milestone flag by opening the Task Information dialog box and clearing the Mark Task as Milestone check box on the Advanced tab. The milestone symbol no longer appears in the Gantt Chart view for the task, although its duration is still zero.

 tip

To remove overtime work, you must reset the Overtime Work field to zero; it cannot be cleared.

note

If you want to eliminate overtime, you must enter 0 in the Overtime field. This field must contain a value, so it cannot be left empty.

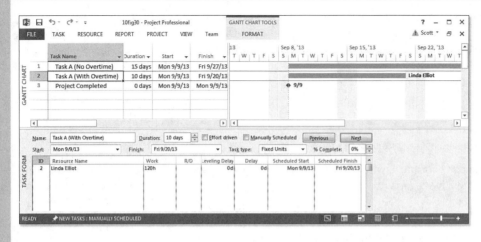

Figure 10.30
In the first task, no overtime is assigned. Forty hours of overtime is assigned in the second task, which is identical to the first, but will finish one week faster.

Selecting a Cost Rate Table for an Assignment

One of the important features in Project is the ability to define and specify different sets of standard and overtime cost rates for a resource so that work on assignments can be charged at different rates for different types of work. For example, a consulting firm might assign a seasoned consultant to highly technical cases at higher rates than it would use for the other more mundane tasks.

You set which Cost Rate table to use for an assignment only in the Task Usage view or the Resource Usage view. In either of these views, you can either add the Cost Rate Table field directly to the view (for easy visibility and access on each assignment row) or use the Assignment Information dialog box. If you are using the Assignment Information dialog box (brought up by double-clicking an assignment), you see the pull-down to specify the Cost Rate table on the General tab. When you see the field (in either the view itself or the Assignment Information dialog box), choose one of the lettered cost tables in the drop-down list in the field to assign that cost table's standard, overtime, and per-use rates to the assignment.

The Cost Rate table for a resource can have different rates for different time periods (to accommodate salary raises, and so on). If there are dated changes in the rates, Project applies the rates that are defined in the table for the dates in which the task is also scheduled.

 *For information on how to define the Cost Rate table entries for a resource, **see** Chapter 8, "Defining Project Resources," **p. 235**.*

🔍 note

You can edit the Cost Rate table only in the Resource Information dialog box. First, display a view with fields for resources, and then either double-click a resource name or click the Resource tab, Properties, Information to display the Resource Information dialog box. Click the Costs tab to display the five Cost Rate tables, A through E.

Assigning Fixed Costs and Fixed Contract Fees

Some tasks might have costs that are not linked to a particular resource that you have named and are not affected by the task duration. This type of cost is treated as a *fixed cost* in Project, and it is entered on the Task level (not the Assignment level) in the Fixed Cost column of the Cost table on a task view such as the Gantt Chart view. Project adds the fixed cost amount to the total of the resource costs and displays the sum in the Cost (Total Cost) columns of various views.

You can also have a cost associated with a resource but not affected by the task duration or any variations in work for the resource. For instance, the resource might be a contractor or vendor who is to deliver the completed task at a fixed cost. In these cases, you should list the contractor or vendor as a resource and enter the cost as part of the assignment information on the Task Form view. If you were to simply add this cost to the task fixed cost, you would lose the relationship of the cost with that specific resource.

To display the Fixed Cost field, display a task view such as the Gantt Chart view in the top pane. To display the Cost table, right-click over the Select All button, the blank area just above the row numbers, and choose Cost (see Figure 10.31).

note

You can associate fixed cost with summary tasks as well as with normal tasks. Because the field might be used for summary task fixed costs, Project does not roll up the Fixed Cost field to summary tasks. In other words, although the fixed cost is included in the Total Cost column, you cannot see a total for all fixed costs.

tip

You should document any fixed-cost amounts in the task's Notes field so that you and others always know what the cost represents.

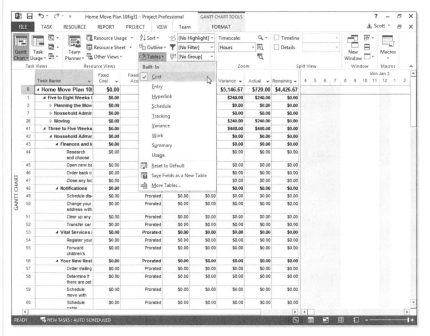

Figure 10.31
The Cost table displays the various costs for the project, such as Fixed, Total, Baseline, Accrual, and so on.

In Figure 10.32, the resource cost details for Task A are displayed in the Task Form view in the bottom pane. The sum of those costs is $3,300. In the top pane, the $1,000 entry in the Fixed Cost column is added to the resource costs to create the value in the Total Cost column.

tip

You can also apply the Cost table to any task view by selecting the View tab, Data, Tables, Cost.

If a resource assigned to a task is working for a fixed fee (say, a contractor or vendor on an outsourced task), you want that cost to remain fixed no matter what happens to the task duration. You do not need Project to track the hours of work for the resource because those hours are important to the contractor or vendor, but not to you. Your cost is not affected if the job takes more work or money than estimated, as long as it is completed on time.

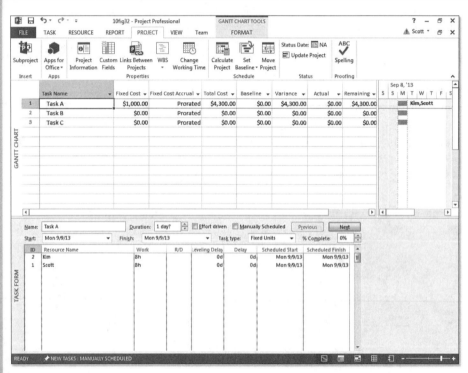

Figure 10.32
The total cost for the task is equal to resource cost ($1,300 + $2,000 = $3,300) plus the fixed cost ($1,000) for the final value of $4,300.

 note

If you enter an amount in the Total Cost (Cost) field to overwrite the calculated value displayed there, Project treats this as the sum of the calculated resource costs and a new fixed cost amount. It then changes the entry in the Fixed Cost column to support this interpretation.

Using the cost resource, you can go to the resource sheet and create a new resource with the same name as the vendor. Select Cost as the Type for the resource and select End for the Accrue At field (specifying that you will not pay them until the task is complete). You now have a cost resource, representing the vendor. You can apply this resource to any task and provide a fixed fee contract cost for that specific task. You enter the Cost value when you assign the resource, by entering a Cost value instead of a Units value. The contract cost will be scheduled to accrue on the last day of the task. If the task moves in time or extends in duration, the cost accrual date changes with it, always accruing on the last day of the task (see Figure 10.33).

Figure 10.33
By using a cost resource, you can create a Fixed-Fee Contract task. Create the task, assign the cost resource, and enter the contract fee.

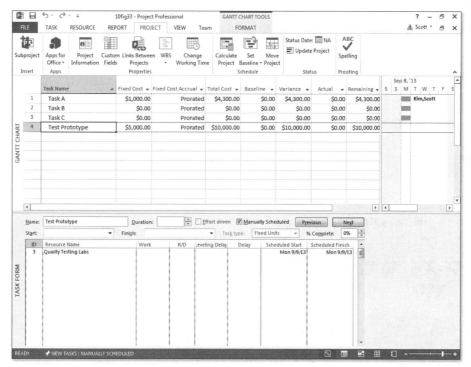

Scheduling with Task Calendars

If a task has its own special calendar assigned to it, by default Project schedules work for the resources only when the working times for both the task calendar and the resource calendar intersect. Project displays the Assigned Calendar indicator for the task (see Figure 10.34).

This option is useful when there are special nonworking times associated with the task (therefore impacting ALL resources on the task). Adding these nonworking times to each resource calendar could cause errors with the scheduling of those resources on other tasks. For example, equipment maintenance might make the company's bulldozers unavailable for two hours every week. You could create an Equipment Maintenance base calendar to define those nonworking hours and assign it to a task. The alternative, adding the nonworking times for this resource to the calendars for all the other resources assigned to the task would interfere with scheduling the other resources for other tasks.

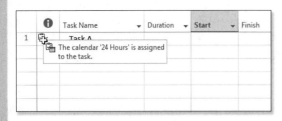

Figure 10.34
The Assigned Calendar indicator identifies tasks using task calendars.

Another use for task calendars is scheduling a task during normally nonworking time. For example, if you wanted to schedule the upgrade for a network server on a weekend to minimize user inconvenience, you could create a task calendar (and assign it to the task) that has working time only on the days and hours when you want the task scheduled. You would then tell project to ignore the resource calendars on the task.

To assign a calendar to a task, you need to create the special base calendar first, selecting the Project tab, Properties, Change Working Time. Then, select the task and display the Task Information dialog box. On the Advanced tab, you display the drop-down list of base calendars in the Calendar box and select the appropriate calendar (see Figure 10.35).

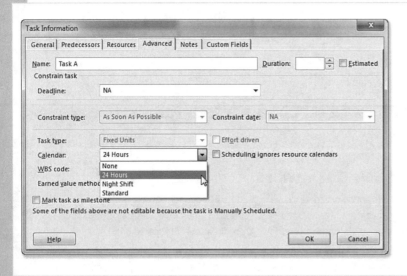

Figure 10.35
Assign a calendar to a task on the Advanced tab of the Task Information dialog box.

If you want Project to ignore the resource calendar working times, you need to select the Scheduling Ignores Resources Calendars check box. After that box is selected, the number of hours of work scheduled for a resource on any given day depends on the units assigned and the work hours defined on the task calendar, not on the resource calendar. You must verify that the resources can meet this schedule.

For example, Eric gets assigned to the network server task scheduled for a Saturday, using the task calendar that specifies only weekend days as working time. Eric's resource calendar is based on the standard calendar that specifies that weekend days are nonworking time. In this case, there is insufficient intersecting working time for both the task calendar and the resource calendar to be honored.

If the task and resource calendars do not intersect for enough hours to complete the task, Project displays a warning to alert you that there are insufficient intersecting working times (see Figure 10.36). You then need to modify one of the calendars to tell Project to ignore the resource calendar.

Figure 10.36
Project displays this warning when resource and task calendars do not share enough common working time to complete the task as scheduled.

Adding Delay to an Assignment

When you assign a resource to a task, Project schedules the work to start when the task starts. Sometimes, however, one or more of the resources assigned to a task might be allowed to delay starting until after the task is partly completed by other resources.

For example, if you assign a marketing manager, an engineer, and a draftsman to draw up a preliminary design for a product, the draftsman's work on the task does not really start until some design details have already been proposed. To accurately schedule the draftsman's work, Project needs to delay the start of the draftsman's scheduled work to some time after the task starts.

Project provides an Assignment Delay field, which you can use to force a delay in the scheduled work for a resource beyond the start of the task. If you want to enter a value in the Delay field on the Task form, you need to display the resource schedule details, where the Delay field is available for editing.

 note

You can get the Delay field by replacing the Task Form view with the Resource Form view and displaying the schedule details, which is just like the resource schedule details on the Task Form view. You can also enter delays on the Task Usage and Resource Usage views. The Task Usage view is discussed in the section "Modifying Work Schedules with the Task Usage View" earlier in this chapter.

➥ *For more information on the Resource Usage view, **see** Chapter 24, "Resolving Resource Allocation Problems," **p. 801**.*

Figure 10.37 shows the Task Form view with the resource schedule details displayed. The Prototype Design task is selected, and the assigned resources are listed in the assignment details. The Draftsman resource is scheduled to work only 16 hours, which is less than the hours for the other work resource.

You can also see in Figure 10.37 that Project has scheduled the Draftsman resource to begin 18 days after the task's start, which is 9/9/2013. Because of the task split, the difference between the start and finish dates is more than the task duration. In reality, the draftsman is expected to execute his assignment in the last two days of the task, 9/26/2013 and 9/27/2013, after the other resource has completed most of his or her work.

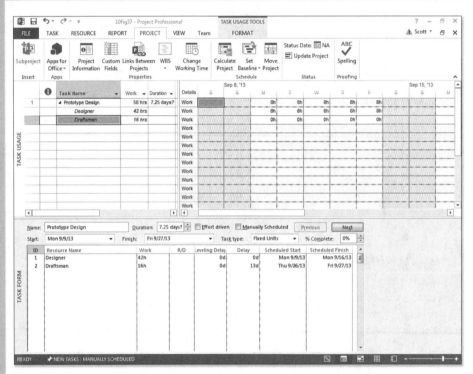

Figure 10.37
The Task Form view with the resource schedule details displayed.

You can create a delay in the Task Form view by entering the amount of the delay in the Delay field or by entering the start date for the assignment. Because of the task split, it is easier to create this particular delay by entering the start date for the draftsman assignment (9/26/13) than to try and calculate the amount of the delay.

In Figure 10.37, the date 9/26/13 was entered in the Assignment Start field for the Draftsman resource, and Project has calculated the delay and the assignment finish to be 9/27/13. Of course, if the delay causes the draftsman's assignment to finish after all the other assignments are finished, it also delays the finish of the task and increases the task's duration.

Follow these steps to enter a delay in an assignment:

1. Display the Task Form view or Task Details Form view in the bottom pane of the Task view.

2. Activate the form in the bottom pane and display the schedule details by right-clicking and choosing Schedule.

3. Select the task for the assignment in the top pane.

4. Select the cell in the Delay field for the resource name you want to delay, and then enter a delay value. Use a number followed by the measurement units for the delay (minutes, hours, days, weeks, or months). You could also enter a delayed start date for the assignment in the start field, as an alternative, and then Project calculates the amount of delay.

5. Click OK to complete the entry.

To remove a delay for an assignment, you enter **0** in the Delay field in place of any existing value and click OK. Project removes the delay, and the assignment start date will match the task start date.

> ### caution
>
> As noted earlier in the chapter, you can create a delay by either entering the Delay value or entering a new date in the Start field. You should not, however, attempt to enter a delayed date in the Finish date column because Project does not treat that as a delaying tactic. Instead, Project treats it as extending the assignment, and it recalculates the Work value of the assignment.

Consultants' Tips

This chapter includes only a portion of the possibilities that Project provides for manipulating your project's resources. As you experiment, you might find many other methods that work well for you. Whatever choices you make, remember to use the Notes tab of the Resource Information dialog box to document an assignment or special contours that you choose. You can type and format the note's text just as you do the text of task notes and resource notes. You can insert documents into the notes or insert links to documents that are stored outside the Project file. You can also insert hyperlinks to websites.

Make Judicious Use of the Team Planner and Manually Scheduled Tasks

With the introduction of the Team Planner and especially Manually Scheduled task mode in Project 2010, many formerly iron-clad rules and methods for using Project changed.

The Team Planner is a powerful tool that only sometimes supersedes older Project usage methods. Consider using it when using resources effectively is your primary concern. Use it less when predicting a project's finish date based on a solid network diagram is most important.

Manually Scheduled task mode breaks many of the calculations and data relationships discussed in this chapter. This provides greater flexibility at the expense of undercutting Project's predictive engine. Consider using Manually Scheduled mode more heavily during project planning, and for ongoing tasks that only loosely fit within a project schedule.

80/20: Use the Task Entry View for Resource Entry and Modifying Assignments

In addition, use the Assign Resources dialog box to find resources to assign to the task (it has the best filtering capabilities and enables you to see all the resources). Use both the Task Entry view and the Assign Resources dialog box for the best results.

Depth: Calculation of the Default Units Value Used When Assigning a Resource

When you assign a resource to a task, an assignment is created. If you do not specify the Units value to the Resource when you create the assignment, a calculated default value is used. The rule behind this is simple but not necessarily intuitive. The value used is the lesser of 100%, or the Max Units field set on the resource in the Resource Sheet. If Yvonne has her Max Units set to 125%, when she is assigned to a task (without specifying her units), 100% will be the value used. If her Max Units had been set to 75%, then 75% would have been used.

Config: Turn Off Automatic Resource Creation

By default, resources are automatically created if you type the resource name into any of the fields, forms, or views that enable you to specify a resource. This is a source of a serious potential problem. Typing errors can leave you with two or more resource entries all representing the same real person. Frequent checking of the Resource Sheet view is necessary to keep the subtle issues caused by this from creeping in. As an alternative, you can turn off the ability to automatically create resources when typing. Go to the File tab, Options, Advanced, General Options for this Project and clear the Automatically Add New Resources and Tasks option.

Forward-Scheduling Versus Backward-Scheduling

The discussion in this chapter is presented in terms of forward-scheduled projects—projects with fixed start dates and dynamic, calculated finish dates. Project can be set to backward-scheduling mode through the Project Information dialog box opened from the Project menu. Setting the Schedule From pull-down to Project Finish Date effectively reverses all the scheduling logic in Project to drive from the finish date backward to calculate the start dates of assignments, tasks, and, therefore, of the whole project. If you see calculations behaving oddly in all areas of Project, check this setting!

As mentioned earlier, project managers are sometimes tempted to use this option because there is a hard project deadline. This is generally a mistake. Scheduling backward is only effective when a project's start date is flexible—and the optimal start date has not already passed.

USING STANDARD VIEWS, TABLES, FILTERS, AND GROUPS TO REVIEW YOUR SCHEDULE

Views, tables, filters, and groups provide an efficient way to review your project information and display precisely the details you are looking for. Views are not reports, which are generally created for either end-users or analysis. Views in Project are used for data entry and modification, as well as analysis.

The previous chapters of the book discussed some view and table basics to define your project's tasks and resources as well as to assign resources to tasks. This chapter explores in detail all other views you can utilize to efficiently review your project schedule and focus on the information you need.

 tip

Reports and Visual Reports in Project 2013 provide many additional options for analysis sponsor or team reporting. The techniques and tools described in this chapter are primarily for the project manager who needs to work actively within the project schedule.

What Can I View Using Microsoft Project?

Microsoft Project includes information about the following entities:

- **Tasks**—Project activities and their relationships with one another

- **Resources**—People and materials assigned to the tasks within a project schedule

In addition, each entity has three dimensions of project data that can be applied to it, as shown in Figure 11.1:

- **Cost**—Costs associated with tasks and resources in your project

- **Schedule (Duration)**—The length of a task and the time it takes to complete

- **Effort (Work)**—The amount of work completed, number of effort hours remaining and worked, and general progress of your project's schedule

Figure 11.1
Cost, Duration, and Work represent the three main dimensions for tasks and resources, and they influence the formula used to calculate work in Project.

Tasks that are manually scheduled still have the same three dimensions, only some or all of them can remain blank. Moreover, they can be in disagreement with each other. Changing a task to Auto Scheduled mode will resolve dimension disagreements between cost, schedule, and effort, providing a more objective picture of how long a task is likely to take or cost.

When using views and tables to display entity information, you will find that some views and tables are more appropriate for displaying information than others. Choosing the right view not only depends on the common usages of the view, but also knowing yourself and the best ways you absorb information. For example, if you are a person who works a lot with calendars, Calendar format might be more meaningful to you than something displayed in a spreadsheet. Similarly, if you are a visual person, the graphical representation of information might be the most useful.

The "Viewing Strategies" section of this chapter discusses some general strategies for choosing the appropriate views based on the task at hand.

Viewing Strategies

This section provides a light high-level overview of strategies you need to consider when selecting the appropriate view to review your schedule.

Strategies on Using Views

Views are logical organizations of data displayed on the screen. Project provides many built-in standard views that you can use "as is," or customize and combine with other views and tables to create more personalized and practical data displays.

You can organize views by the entity type they display: either task or resource. They show information about one or the other, but never both at the same time.

With the Ribbon, you can access views in many different ways. Although the Ribbon organizes views into logical groups and tabs, it's mostly possible to get to any view from anywhere. You can access views by selecting from the Gantt control in the View group on the Task tab, as shown in Figure 11.2, which displays some of the most commonly used views in Project. To display additional views, select the View tab, Task Views or Resource Views, Other Views, More Views, as shown in Figure 11.3.

Figure 11.2
Accessing commonly used views in Project.

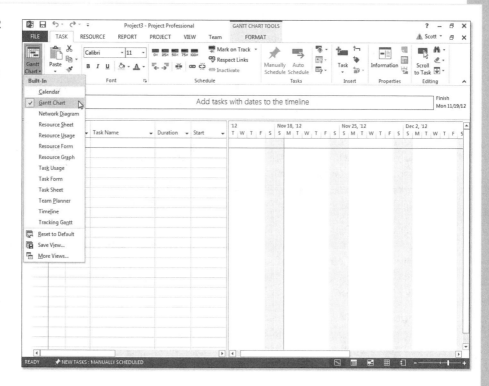

Figure 11.3
Accessing all Project views.

Views can be organized into four main categories, as follows:

- **Graphical views**—As the name suggests, these views show a graphical representation of information. For example, the Team Planner shows resource demand and overallocations as a series of colored bars. Most graphical views, except for the Network Diagram, are particularly good at displaying time-phased task and resource information. Graphical views can also help you visualize your project schedule information much better. This can be especially useful to more visually oriented people. Table 11.1 details the views included within this type.

For example, reviewing the Gantt Chart or the timeline provides a high-level view of all tasks and milestones within your project over time. That allows for two-dimensional data display, but lacks the amount of detail you could get if you were to combine it with something like a Task Sheet view, providing for a third dimension—the drill-down.

 note

All Gantt Chart-type views are variations of the standard Gantt Chart view and differ by the formatting of the Gantt Chart itself and the table combination selected to complement it.

- **Sheet views**—These views are similar to an Excel presentation of data and allow for large amounts of information to be logically grouped and displayed on the screen. The Sheet views are especially useful when entering task- or resource-related information. Table 11.1 details the views included within this type.

Sheet views might not be the best choice to view timeline data because they make it hard to view where all the tasks in your schedule fall relative to time, but they can be a great way to view multiline, large-volume data. You can customize sheet views to include helpful visual cues, such as graphical indicators to provide schedule and cost status of each individual task and of the entire project.

- **Form views**—These are views displayed in a two-pane format that enable you to easily see information about a particular item, such as a task or a resource, by showing you one item at a time. Isolating each item helps drill into its details and declutter your screen. However, Form views fail when you need to compare data. Table 11.1 details the views included within this type.

■ **Combination views**—Combination views make use of several views to bring together types of information that usually are not contained in one view, but that complement each other. Table 11.1 details the views included within this type.

Combination views are more complex and create multidimensional representation of entities. They enable you to mix time-phased, detail, and graphical information all on one screen. This can be a great tool when performing analysis or reviewing several aspects of your projects at once. As useful as combination views are, they can be too complex for simple jobs, such as entering task, resource, or cost information. They can also clutter the screen and distract you from concentrating on the details you need.

Table 11.1 summarizes the four view types and the predefined views by the entity they relate to—task or resource. Views marked with an asterisk are the most commonly used views and are displayed in the View menu. You can access the rest of the views by clicking More Views on the Views menu.

Table 11.1 Standard Views by Type and Entity

View Category	Task View	Resource Views
Graphical views	Calendar*	Resource Graph*
	Gantt Chart*	
	Network Diagram*	
	Tracking Gantt*	
	Bar Rollup	
	Descriptive Network	Diagram
	Detail Gantt	
	Leveling Gantt	
	Milestone Rollup	
	Multiple Baseline Rollup	
	Relationship Diagram	
	Team Planner	
	Timeline	
Sheet views	Task Usage*	Resource Sheet*
	Task Sheet	Resource Usage*
Form views	Task Details Form	Resource Form
	Task Form	Resource Name Form
	Task Name Form	
Combination views	Task Entry	Resource Allocation

In addition to the predefined Project views, you can customize or create new views.

➡ *For detailed information on customizing views,* **see** *Chapter 22, "Customization Almost Beyond Reason: Views, Tables, Filters, Groups, Fields, Toolbars, Menus, and Forms,"* **p. 699**.

Detailed information about each view is provided later in this chapter.

Strategies for Using Tables

Tables are the backbone of Project. They are logical combinations of data in the context of task and resource information. Tables consist of columns and, similarly to views, can be altered to display only the needed information. They are filtered based on and controlled by the type of view selected. For example, if a Gantt Chart view is selected, the tables displayed will all relate to the task entity. With the introduction of the Ribbon, you can access and change tables in many ways. One way is by selecting the View tab, Data, Tables, which displays a list of tables that complement the views you can see in the View menu, as shown in Figure 11.4.

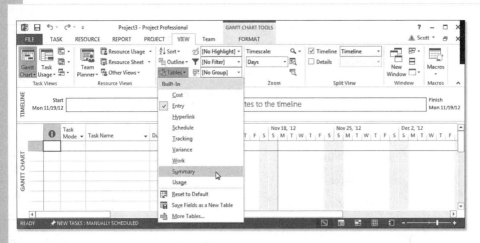

Figure 11.4
Accessing commonly used tables in Project.

You can access additional views for both task and resource entities by selecting the View tab, Data, Tables, More Tables. When you access the More Tables window, you can choose the entity to display by selecting the Task or Resource option button (see Figure 11.5). In addition to the predefined Project tables, you can customize or create new ones.

➡ *For detailed information on customizing tables,* **see** *Chapter 22, " Customization Almost Beyond Reason: Views, Tables, Filters, Groups, Fields, Toolbars, Menus, and Forms,"* **p. 699**.

Figure 11.5
Accessing all Project views by entity.

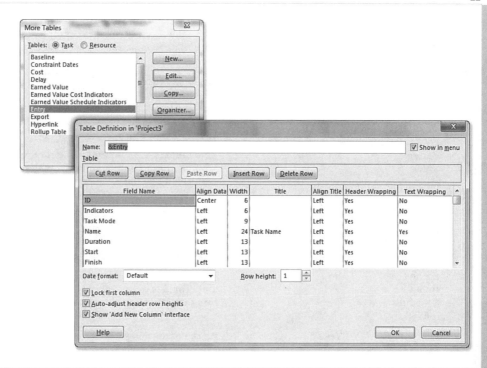

Task Tables

Task tables enable you to view various information about tasks (activities) in your schedule. Task tables have several dimensions, such as cost, work, and schedule, as was shown in Figure 11.1. The combination of those three dimensions encapsulates all available standard views.

Table 11.2 details the task entity standard views available in Project.

Table 11.2 Standard Task Tables

Table Name	Commonly Used	Table Application
Cost	Yes	This table shows the cost variation between the values you planned and the current ones. It contains the standard columns (such as Fixed Cost, Actual Cost, Total Cost, Baseline, Variance, and so on) for viewing various cost data and is a great tool for comparison.
Baseline	No	The Baseline table provides a snapshot of project schedule information when it was frozen at the end of the planning phase. Baseline is used to compare your project progress to the plan for improvement and risk mitigation.

Table Name	Commonly Used	Table Application
Constraint Dates	No	This table is an excellent tool for locating tasks with applied constraints, whether those were intentional or accidental.
Delay	No	The Delay table displays the leveling delay field, which you can use to see the delays that have been applied to your schedule either by you or by Project. This is the default table for the Detail and Leveling Gantt views.
Earned Value	No	This table is used for analyzing progress on your x project based on the work planned and work performed by your resources. It is used to determine whether the task will meet its target budget or exceed it.
Earned Value Cost Indicators	No	This table is based on the Earned Value table and provides additional calculations of variances and factors that affect earned value on your project.
Earned Value Schedule Indicators	No	This table is related to the Earned Value table and provides details about schedule-related factors that affect earned value on your project.
Entry	Yes	As the name suggests, this table is particularly useful for entering task-related information in the planning project phase. This table is displayed by default with the Gantt Chart view.
Export	No	The Export table provides an easy and efficient way of exporting your project details to another application.
Hyperlink	Yes	This table displays hyperlinks to other files that are not necessary project files. It provides an easy way to manage your external links.
Rollup Table	No	The Rollup table enables you to control the placement of the task name text for the rollup bar. This is the default table for the Rollup views.
Schedule	Yes	Including slack in your project can make the difference in meeting your deadline or performing a heroic effort to barely finish when needed. A Schedule table enables you to view the slack you have and adjust your schedule accordingly.
Summary	Yes	The Summary table is a great way to get a quick glance at high-level information about your project schedule, from basic task information to progress.

Table Name	Commonly Used	Table Application
Tracking	Yes	One of the project management objectives is to consistently update the progress of your schedule and reevaluate the effect it has on your scope, schedule, and cost status. Use the Tracking table to update your project schedule progress.
Usage	Yes	You can use the Usage table to view progress information for each task in your schedule. Usage is the default table displayed with the Task Usage view.
Variance	Yes	In addition to tracking progress, it is important to regularly reevaluate your schedule and analyze any deviations from the original plan. A variance table enables you to compare your estimates with your actuals and includes precalculated variance fields.
Work	Yes	The Work table displays information about planned and actual work on a particular task. It is an efficient way to analyze your project schedule for tasks requiring additional effort than originally planned.

 note

Several task views within Project do not utilize tables as their display mechanism; therefore, when they are selected, you cannot choose a table to apply to these views. These include Calendar, Network Diagram, Descriptive Network Diagram, Relationship Diagram, Resource Form, Resource Graph, Resource Name Form, Task Details Form, Task Form, and Task Name Form.

Resource Tables

Resource tables enable you to view various information about resources (people or materials) in your schedule. Resource tables have several dimensions, such as cost, work, and schedule, as shown previously in Figure 11.1. The combination of those three dimensions encapsulates all available standard resource views. Resource tables are available for selection when a resource view is selected. Table 11.3 details the predefined standard task tables in Project.

Table 11.3 Standard Resource Tables

Table Name	Commonly Used	Table Application
Cost	Yes	The Cost table displays cost information related to each resource. You can use this view to analyze which resources are the most expensive and which ones are over or under budget.

Table Name	Commonly Used	Table Application
Earned Value	No	The Earned Value table compares budgeted work and cost to the planned work and cost. This is an analysis view and provides recalculated fields for how much the work performed by your resource is actually costing.
Entry	Yes	The Entry table displays the general resource information and is recommended to be used during the planning phase of the project to record your project resource data. This is the default table used in the Resource Sheet view.
Entry – Material Resources	No	This view is commonly used during the planning phase of the project to enter information about material resources (instruments, machinery, hardware, and so on) needed for the project.
Entry – Work Resources	No	This view is commonly used during the planning phase of the project to enter information about work (people) resources needed for the project.
Export	No	The Export view is used to export resource information to another application for distribution, further analysis, or history-archiving purposes.
Hyperlink	No	This table provides information about external links to the files linked to your project.
Summary	Yes	The Summary view contains high-level information about your project resources.
Usage	Yes	The Usage view displays data about the amount of resources used by your project. The Usage view is a great tool for analyzing which resources are over- or underutilized.
Work	Yes	The Work table is used for displaying resource progress on tasks they are assigned to and comparing the current information to the planned fields.

 note

Several resource views within Project do not utilize tables as their display mechanism; therefore, when they are selected, you cannot choose a table to apply to these views. These include the Team Planner, Resource Graph, Resource form, and Resource Name form.

Understanding Standard Views

To efficiently use views, it is important to gain a thorough understanding of the different view types and the details displayed in them.

Calendar View

The Calendar view is just what it sounds like: a calendar representation of project schedule tasks. The Calendar view displays information by week or month, or allows for a custom selection of the period to display. The information shown by default in the Calendar view includes every task in the currently opened project schedule, displaying task name, task duration, and task type (milestones are displayed using a black bubble with white text), as shown in Figure 11.6.

Figure 11.6
Calendar view displays project schedule tasks in a familiar calendar format for reviewing and printing the project schedule.

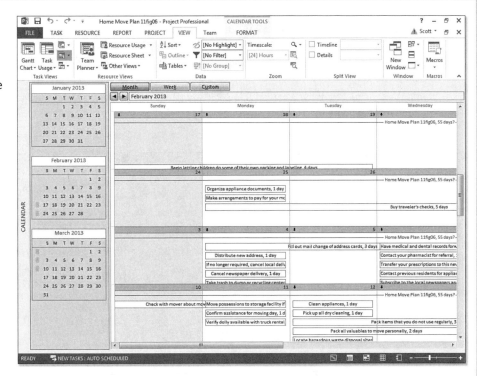

Calendar view is particularly friendly because it is probably the most familiar visualization of time-phased information everyone has used in the past. However, Calendar view can be limiting because it can only display up to a certain level of detail for each task before getting too cluttered and unusable.

The most common use of this view is to review your project schedule and to possibly print it to keep by your desk as another calendar to abide to.

caution

Even though it is possible, it is not recommended to use the Calendar view for editing information. Many details are hidden from the calendar and, therefore, can lead to the wrong adjustment decisions. In addition, creating new tasks using this view adds constraints to the task, which can be dangerous because you might not even be aware of them.

To simplify a complex Calendar view, it is also recommended that you use various filters to reduce the amount of data shown in the calendar. For example, if you are trying to get an idea of when the major deliverables for your project are, create milestone tasks for completion of each deliverable and then filter the Calendar view to display only milestone tasks. Another helpful filtering option is to display only the critical path tasks.

From the Calendar view, you can double-click any particular task to view the Task Information box, which provides you with all task-related information you want to know, as shown in Figure 11.7.

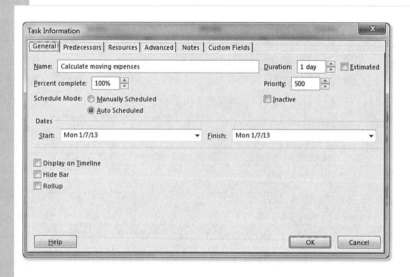

Figure 11.7
Even though the Calendar view is not the best option for viewing task details, you can easily access the Task Information box by double-clicking any task within the calendar.

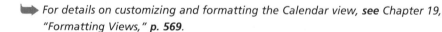 For details on customizing and formatting the Calendar view, **see** Chapter 19, "Formatting Views," **p. 569**.

 tip

If you are trying to locate a particular task using the Calendar view, you can use the Go To option and search for the particular task.

Gantt Chart Views

The Gantt Chart view is by default the first view you see when initially opening Project. This view consists of two main parts: the Task Sheet table and the Gantt Chart graphical view (see Figure 11.8). The Gantt Chart is, and always has been, one of the most popular project management views. The Gantt Chart is a great view to review your project schedule prior to moving into the execution and control phases by analyzing task dependencies, resource assignments, and milestone tasks in a view that adds the perspective of time.

Figure 11.8
The Gantt Chart view combines the time-phased summary-level information and the detailed drill down into project schedule details with the Task Sheet table to provide an informative display of your project schedule.

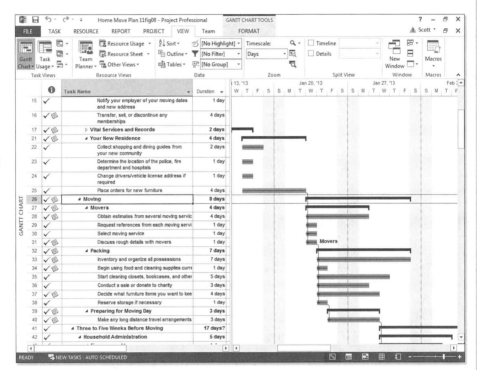

The chart part of the view contains several different types of bars. The solid black bar spanning a large portion of time represents a summary-level task.

Milestone tasks are shown in the shape of a diamond and include the date in MM/DD format. The length of each bar is determined by the duration of the task. It is also possible for a task to be split, which is illustrated with a dotted line connecting the parts of the split task. Arrows are used to visualize the predecessor/successor relationships between tasks. The Gantt Chart also includes the names of the resources above the task they are assigned to. See Figure 11.9 for a visual representation of the various task information in the Gantt Chart.

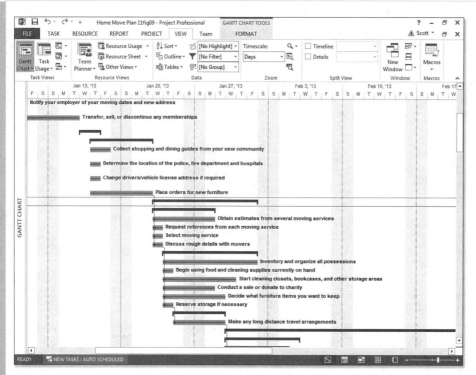

Figure 11.9
In addition to the default types of information, you can customize the data and its visual representation on the Gantt Chart.

The Gantt Chart view is a multipurpose view and can be useful at the different phases of the project. For example, you can use the Task Sheet view portion of the Gantt Chart view for task entry during the planning phase. The Gantt Chart will be automatically updated and will visually display the information you are adding to your project.

The options and choices for formatting the Gantt Chart view are extensive.

➡ *For detailed information on formatting and customizing the Gantt Chart view,* **see** *Chapter 22, "Customization Almost Beyond Reason: Views, Tables, Filters, Groups, Fields, Toolbars, Menus, and Forms,"* **p. 699**.

The Gantt Chart view also has many predefined variations that are all customizations of the original Gantt Chart and were each designed for concentrating on a different view of project data. These variations are discussed in more detail in the following sections.

Detail Gantt View

The Detail Gantt view shows the same information as the regular Gantt Chart, but in addition, it shows where delays have been created as a result of leveling, either by automatic Project or manual leveling using the leveling delay field. The Detail Gantt view does not show the task history of scheduling prior to leveling, but it does include the slack amount at the right side of the slack bar (see Figure 11.10).

➤ *For detailed information on leveling your project schedule,* ***see*** *Chapter 24, "Resolving Resource Allocation Problems,"* ***p. 801.***

Figure 11.10
The Detail Gantt chart highlights critical path tasks in red and also adds an additional column of Leveling Delay to the standard Gantt Chart view.

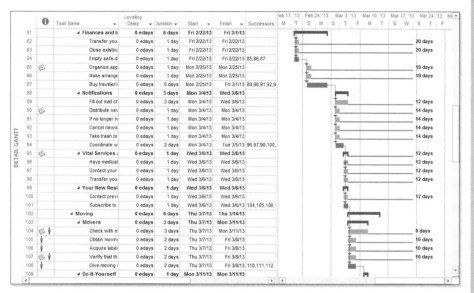

The Detail Gantt can be used for reviewing your project scheduling after it has been leveled to analyze the changes made to the project schedule.

Leveling Gantt View

The Leveling Gantt view is similar to the Detail Gantt chart in that it displays delays. It can be used for both viewing the leveling effects on the project schedule and scheduling a delay on a task if resources or materials are not available for the task in time. The Gantt Chart part of the Leveling view remains nearly unchanged from the standard Gantt, but in addition, it displays a narrow line in front of the tasks, tracing from the initial task schedule date to the new start date based on the delay (see Figure 11.11).

To the right of each task bar is another narrow line that demonstrates free slack. Free slack represents the amount of time a task can be delayed without delaying its successor tasks.

➤ *For detailed information on leveling your project schedule,* ***see*** *Chapter 24, "Resolving Resource Allocation Problems,"* ***p. 801.***

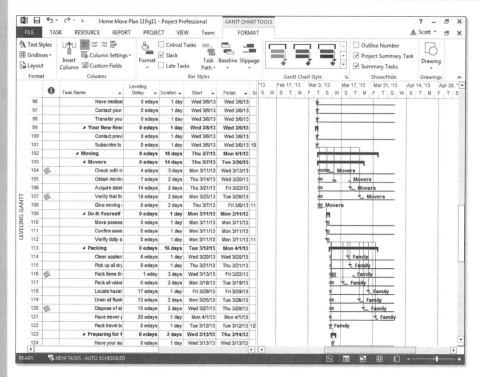

Figure 11.11
The Leveling Gantt view visually shows slack, free slack, and schedule changes due to the leveling of the project schedule.

Multiple Baselines Gantt View

The Multiple Baselines Gantt view is generally a view used during the execution and control phases of the project. It is used to compare multiple baselines and evaluate the evolution of the project schedule. The baseline process generally directly relates to the changes in the project scope.

Baseline view can be used to analyze the effect a new baseline has on the schedule and review the scope and contract information to ensure that the project does not contain scope creep (slow escalation of scope due to the changes from the client or project sponsors).

The Multiple Baselines Gantt view does not show any additional columns within the Task Sheet part of the view, but it does demonstrate, usually by using a different color, the migration of the project schedule (see Figure 11.12).

Figure
11.12
The
Multiple
Baselines
Gantt view
displays
all saved
baselines
in a graph-
ical format
within
the Gantt
Chart
itself.

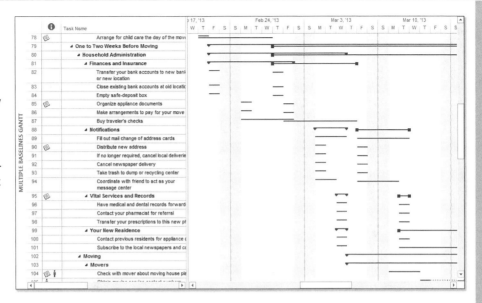

Team Planner View

The Team Planner was a significant new addition to Project in Team Planner is designed from a resource-planning perspective. Its primary purpose is to easily make maximum use of resources without overallocating them. Between the Team Planner view and manually scheduling, for the first time users of Project need to understand very little or nothing about project management to get good results. All a resource manager needs to do is add resources via the resource sheet and tasks via the task sheet. The Team Planner provides a visual and detailed tool for making sure resources are assigned to tasks (see Figure 11.13).

Although you can use the Team Planner view with tasks that are auto-scheduled, using the Team Planner with tasks that are manually scheduled provides the most flexibility. Most people with a resource planning-orientation will find it easier to understand Manually Scheduled task mode.

- Unassigned tasks are presented in the lower pane.

- Resources are listed in the upper pane.

- You can drag unassigned tasks from the lower pane to the appropriate starting time in the time-phased view to the right of the resource list.

- Overallocations are emphasized graphically in several different ways, as shown in Figure 11.14.

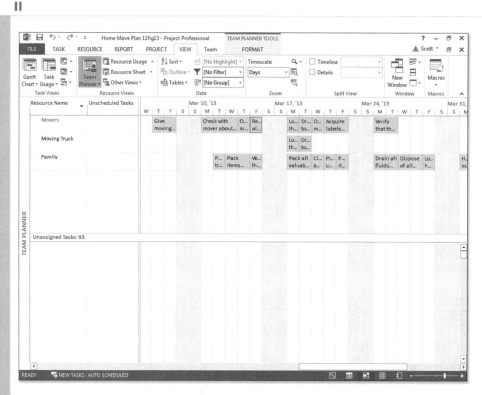

Figure 11.13
Non-project managers can use the Team Planner for resource planning.

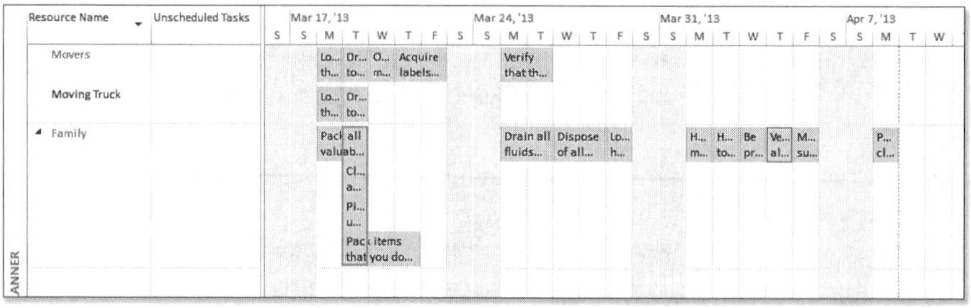

Figure 11.14
Overallocations are represented by double-stacked bars and red highlighting.

Like all views in Project, the Format tab is context-sensitive. You can control the format, styles, and visible elements of the Team Planner using the Format tab. The Schedule group has one control: Prevent Overallocations. Toggling Prevent Overallocations on causes Project to automatically reschedule tasks for that resource to the nearest available timeslot (see Figure 11.15).

Figure 11.15 The Format tab for the Team Planner view enables you to turn Prevent Over-allocations on or off.

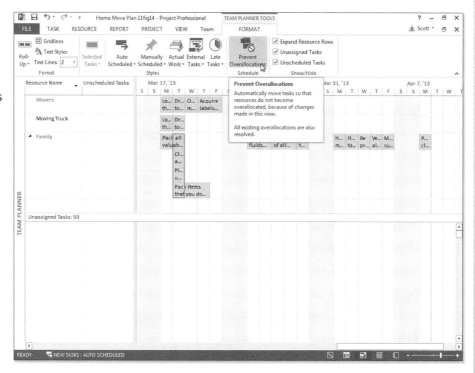

Network Diagram View

The Network Diagram view, also referred to as *Program Evaluation and Review Technique (PERT)*, is a logic diagram that graphically represents relationships between tasks. You can view the Network Diagram as a type of flowchart, where the main objects are tasks (including milestones and summary tasks), and the lines between tasks represent predecessor/successor relationships.

The Network Diagram view is also structured to show the critical path tasks, displayed in red, while regular tasks are blue, the project summary tasks are black with white text, and milestones are in the shape of hexagons (see Figure 11.16).

You can use this view for viewing all of your project tasks and detecting any tasks currently not linked within your project schedule. This application is particularly useful if your schedule is large and contains many tasks. Often it is hard to notice such detail in a list view.

Another common use for the view is to communicate project information to the project team by printing it out and displaying it on a wall. This provides an everyday visual cue and enables the project team to view the schedule as a whole, as well as the specific tasks within it.

> **caution**
>
> The Network Diagram, can be awkward for modifying a project schedule and moving tasks around. Even if the view is zoomed out, sometimes it is not feasible to display the entire project schedule in a Network Diagram format on a computer screen. Modifying and moving tasks in this view can cause problems.

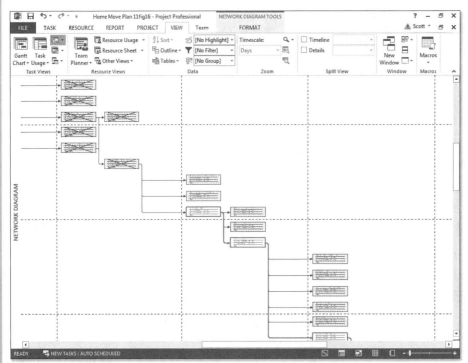

Figure 11.16
To navigate the Network Diagram view, use the scrollbars to move vertically and horizontally around the view and use Zoom In/Zoom Out features to increase/decrease the level of detail visible.

If you are really looking to modify tasks in this view, you can double-click a particular task within the Network Diagram to view the Task Information box. This provides all the task-related information, and you can safely change it.

Network Diagram also is not time-phased, so it is hard to picture the timeline of the project against a time window. However, you can modify the order of tasks according to time periods by selecting the Format tab.

Descriptive Network Diagram Views

The Descriptive Network Diagram view is a variation of the Network Diagram view. Similarly, it concentrates on demonstrating tasks relationships. However, the boxes representing tasks contain more detailed information (see Figure 11.17).

Figure 11.17
Apply additional filters to the Descriptive Network Diagram view to simplify the view and sort out the unnecessary information.

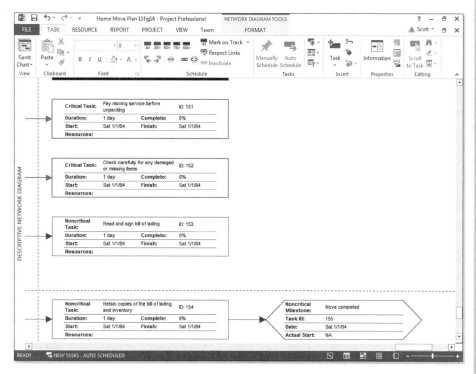

Task Usage View

The Task Usage view is used during the execution and control phases of the project. It presents actual task information by showing the amount of work scheduled and performed on a particular task.

Task Usage view is time-phased and enables you to customize the frequency at which the data is displayed—daily, weekly, quarterly, and so on.

This view is especially helpful when checking resource assignments and the scheduled work for a particular task (see Figure 11.18).

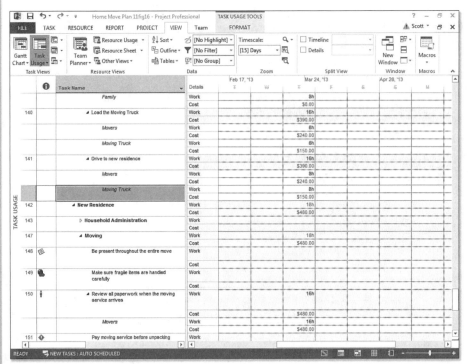

Figure 11.18
Providing additional information, such as Resource Availability and Actual Work, can expand the use of the Task Usage view.

Tracking Gantt View

The Tracking Gantt view is used primarily during the Execution and Control phases of a project. It uses the standard Gantt Chart view for its bases, but differs in displaying baseline information in addition to the current project schedule view (see Figure 11.19).

The Tracking Gantt view displays progress information in two ways:

- By showing solid color on the scheduled taskbar, where the Gantt Chart shows a black progress line

- By showing the percent complete value on the right side of each bar

Resource Graph View

The Resource Graph view is used to display resource allocation and overallocation time-phased information in a bar chart format. It performs nearly the same function as the Team Planner view. The Resource Graph view is often used in combination views, with the top pane showing the Gantt Chart or a similar detail view. It not only shows which resources are overallocated and when, but it also specifies by how much, based on their availability during that period (see Figure 11.20).

Figure 11.19
Tracking Gantt is
one of the most
powerful views
used by project
managers because
it not only shows
task scheduled
dates, but also
includes baseline
information.

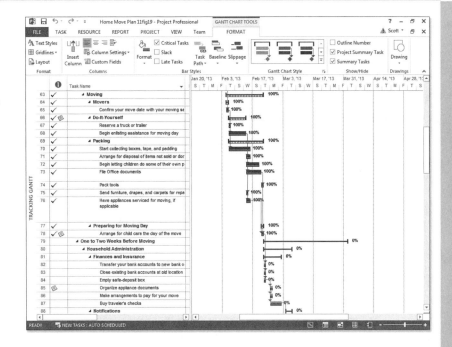

Figure 11.20
The Resource
Graph is some-
times referred
to as *Resource
Histogram* because
it provides great
historical and
upcoming resource
allocation informa-
tion.

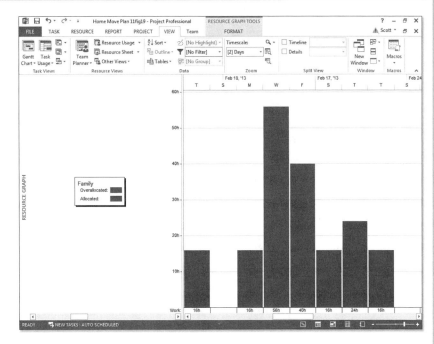

tip

You can use the Resource Graph throughout the project life, but it is especially beneficial during planning because it can help detect and resolve resource allocations early. In many cases, the Team Planner view can be used for the same purpose.

Resource Sheet View

The Resource Sheet view is a list view that is used to display detailed resource information. Being a list view and providing a fair amount of detail, Resource Sheet view is beneficial to use during the planning phase of the project to enter project resource information. Each row of the view is dedicated to a resource (see Figure 11.21). It also contains visual cues, such as the Indicators column that alerts you to which resources are overallocated. You can heavily modify the Resource Sheet view by selecting one of many different tables that can be applied to it. In addition, you can customize the view even further by adding more columns.

➡ *For detailed information on customizing views,* **see** *Chapter 22, " Customization Almost Beyond Reason: Views, Tables, Filters, Groups, Fields, Toolbars, Menus, and Forms," **p. 699**.*

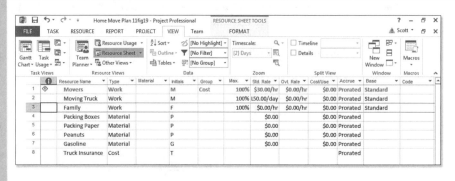

Figure 11.21
The Resource Sheet view can be combined with other views, such as the Resource Graph, to add the time-phased dimension.

Resource Usage View

Resource Usage view is a resource allocation and overallocation sheet view. It is similar to the Team Planner, but more appropriate for a project manager than a resource planner. You can view the information displayed in the Resource Usage view based on a different timescale. Columns displayed include hours of work, hours of overallocated work, cost, available time, and other details.

The information in the Resource Usage view is grouped by resource, displaying all the tasks a resource is responsible for underneath its name. You can use the symbol similar to the outline symbol to hide and display particular tasks for a resource.

For example, tasks for Family have been hidden. The plus symbol next to the name indicates that not all information is currently displayed (see Figure 11.22).

Figure 11.22
The Resource Usage view is used to resolve resource over-allocations and detect when resources require lev-eling.

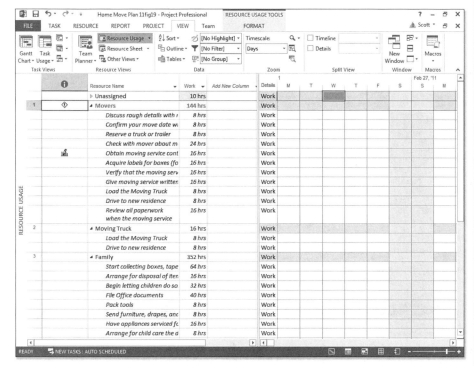

Resource Usage view also helps detect resources that need to be leveled. These resources contain a diamond with an exclamation point in the Indicators column.

Combining the Resource Usage view with a Gantt Chart creates a powerful combination with the task- and resource-level information and is useful for reviewing the schedule.

Bar Rollup View

The Bar Rollup view is part of the collection of views that represent grouped information. This view displays the task information that has been rolled up onto collapsed summary views. The bar rollup view uses colored boxes on the summary taskbar for each rolled-up task.

When any task other than the milestone is rolled up, the summary taskbar resembles more of a regular task than a summary task. The Bar Rollup is useful for highlighting certain tasks when task details are not displayed (see Figure 11.23).

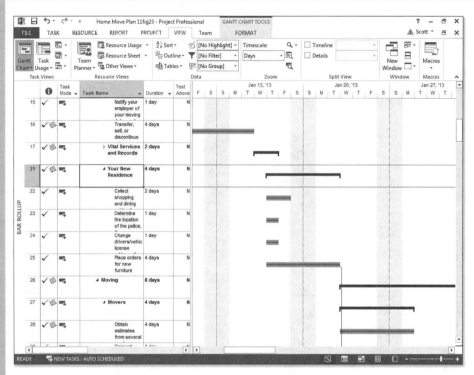

Figure 11.23
The Bar Rollup view helps emphasize task details within the collapsed outline.

Milestone and Milestone Date Rollup Views

The Milestone and Milestone Date Rollup views are part of the collection of views that represent grouped data. As the name suggests, these views roll up only the milestones within the project schedule.

The Milestone Rollup view is similar to the Bar Rollup because it rolls up only the milestones themselves and excludes the dates. The main purpose of this view is to provide a summary display with only specific types of tasks—milestones.

The Milestone Date Rollup view rolls up both the milestones and their dates to the summary-level tasks. The dates are displayed directly in the Gantt, eliminating the necessity to have to print the sheet view along with the Gantt to have complete information about a milestone. The milestone names appear above the summary taskbar, and the date is displayed below it (see Figure 11.24). The diamonds represent milestone tasks only in this view.

**Figure
11.24
The
Milestone
Date Rollup
view rolls
up mile-
stone name
and date
information
within the
Gantt.**

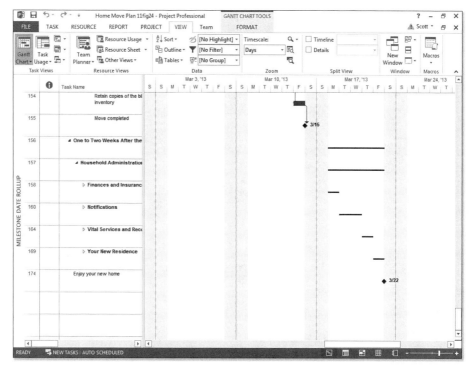

Relationship Diagram View

The Relationship Diagram view is another view from the Graphical Views category that displays
task-related information and is a special type of Network Diagram view. Similar to the Network
Diagram, the Relationship Diagram view graphically displays task relationships within your project
schedule. The Relationship Diagram is generally displayed in the bottom part of the task split view
and shows immediate predecessors and successors for the task selected in the top frame.

 note

You cannot apply any filters to the Relationship Diagram view because the view is already automatically
filtered by Project based on the task selected in the top part of the view.

This view is especially useful during the planning phase of a project to ensure that all tasks are
properly linked within your project schedule. The Relationship Diagram also displays the type of
relationships between the tasks to provide even more detail (see Figure 11.25).

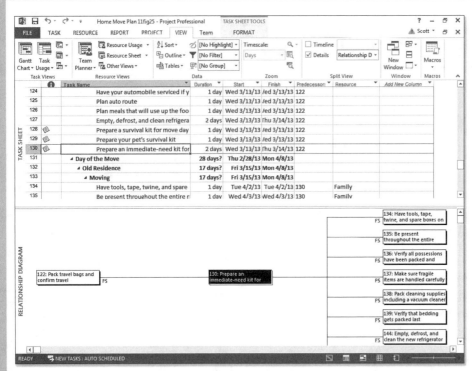

Figure 11.25
The Relationship Diagram view helps you ensure that every task within your project schedule is linked and verify that a correct relationship type has been established.

Resource Allocation View

The Resource Allocation view is displayed for the Resource entity and is a combination view. Again, it is similar to the Team Planner view—which is preferable is a matter of choice and audience. Resource Allocation view combines the power of the detail in the Resource Usage view and the graphical, time-phased representation of a Leveling Gantt.

As the name suggests, this view is intended for resolving resource overallocations. The Resource Usage part of the view helps you determine which resources are overallocated or require leveling, during what timeframe, and to what extent. You can then use the Leveling Gantt to identify the tasks assigned to the overloaded resource. This combination creates a complete scenario of the current situation, which will help you then determine the appropriate plan of action to resolve the overallocation (see Figure 11.26).

Resource and Resource Name Form Views

The Resource and Resource Name Form views are variations of one another and display information in a form. The only difference between these views is the amount of detail they include. Resource Form views are often used at the bottom of a combination view, such as the one in Figure 11.27, and enable you to view the detailed resource information based on one task at a time.

Figure 11.26
The Resource Allocation view is a powerful tool in analyzing resource overal-location problems by looking at both resources and tasks assigned to the resources.

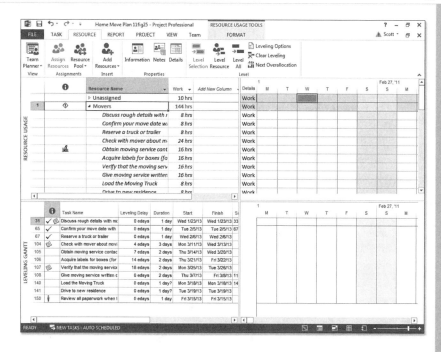

Figure 11.27
The Resource Form view can be com-bined with any other resource view for an additional level of detail that provides a drill-down to the resource attributes.

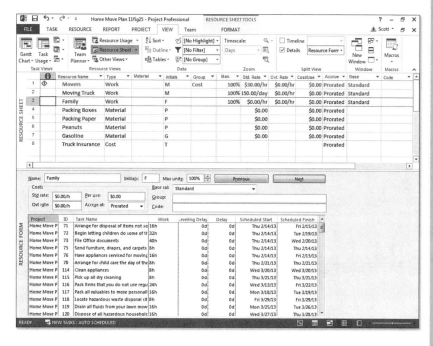

The Resource Form view is opened by default when a resource view with a split frame is displayed. It contains the same information as the Resource Sheet view. When you select a resource in the Resource Sheet view, the Resource Form view is automatically filtered to display the details about the selected resource. The bottom part of the Resource Form view can be formatted to display tasks assigned to the resource. To customize the bottom part of the Resource Form, select Format, Details or right-click within the form view itself.

The Resource Name Form view acts identically to the Resource Form view, but displays only the resource name in the top portion of the view. You can customize the bottom part of the view similarly to the Resource Form view by selecting Format, Details.

Task, Task Detail, and Task Name Form Views

Task Form views, similarly to the Resource Form views, present detailed information based only on one task at a time. The Task Form views are generally used at the bottom of a combination view to provide additional drill-down into selected tasks. To display the Task Form view at the bottom of another view, select Window, Split. Click in the bottom part of the screen and from the View menu, select the particular Task Form view to display (see Figure 11.28).

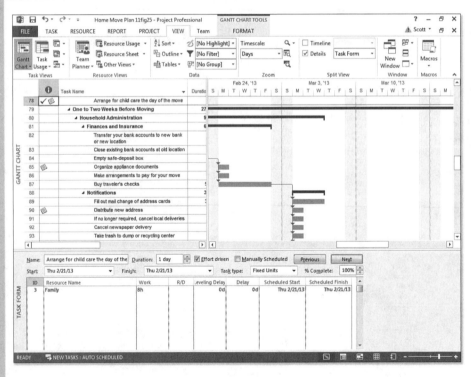

Figure 11.28
Task Form views help to easily and efficiently display task details for one particular task at a time.

You can customize the level of detail displayed in a Task Form view by selecting Format, Details or by right-clicking within the view itself. This will show all available fields that can be added to the view for more information.

In addition to adding the Task Form view to a combination view, you can also view it independently and navigate between the tasks by clicking the Previous and Next buttons in the top-right corner.

The Task Details view is a variation of a Task Form view that includes additional details about the task, such as Current, Baseline, and Actual dates. You can also use this view to display the constraints on tasks. If you are using a split view, the default Task Form view is probably displayed in the bottom pane. To switch to the Task Detail Form view, click in the bottom pane and then select View, More Views, and Task Detail Form.

The Task Name Form view displays only the name of the task in the top portion of the form. Similar to the Task Form and Task Details Form views, the Task Name Form provides formatting options and the ability to add more fields to be displayed in the view. This view is especially useful in a combination view and enables you to compress the amount of data displayed in it, thus decluttering the screen.

Task Entry View

The Task Entry view is a combination view that combines the power of the Task Sheet, Gantt Chart, and Task Form views. The Task Entry view provides the three dimensions to your project schedule: the Task Sheet view displays the high-level task details and is easy to read; the Gantt Chart view adds the time dimensions, displaying the time-phased data; and the Task Form view displays the drill-down into the task details, as shown in Figure 11.29.

 tip

The Task Entry view is the most comprehensive task view you can display in Project and is great for combining all task-related information on one screen.

Figure 11.29
The Task Entry view is a combination view providing summary-level, graphical representation, and task detail information on one screen.

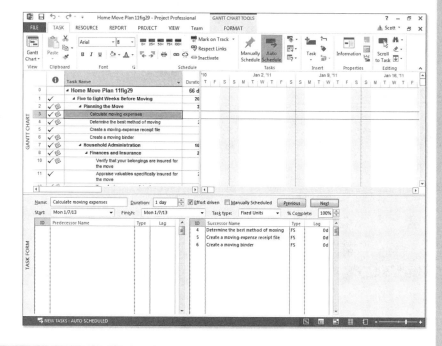

Task Sheet View

The Task Sheet view is a list view that provides a linear display, reminiscent of the Excel sheet, and is great for entering task information during the planning phase of a project. The Task Entry does not provide time-phased information about the tasks, except for start and end dates.

The Task Sheet view can be used standalone or in a combination view to display all tasks in a project schedule as rows with columns of information details. The Task Sheet view uses tables to designate which columns are displayed in the view. You can modify the columns you see by relating them to specific information you are trying to view (see Figure 11.30). For example, if you are trying to review task-related costs within the Task Sheet view, select the Cost table from the View menu. If you are interested in viewing task work information, select the Work table, and so on.

When the Entry table is applied to the Task Sheet view, it actually becomes the Task Entry view used during planning to create the initial project schedule.

 tip

In addition to the columns displayed in the Task Sheet view, you can add more columns, such as Cost, Baseline, and so on. To do so, right-click on a column and select Insert Column Option. In the Column Definition window, select the column to add and click OK.

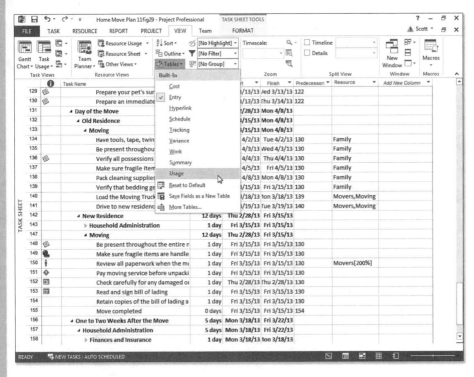

Figure 11.30
The Task Sheet view is a simple way to display task details in a list format, but you can customize it to include visual cues, such as Status Indicators and Information icons.

Understanding Standard Tables

Now that you have seen all the different views that can be used to display data within Project, this section discusses the details of the standard tables. Tables are used to determine the fields of information displayed within views and are crucial to efficiently reviewing the information. As previously discussed, you can divide tables into task and resource information tables. The specific table types within these categories are discussed in the following sections.

Task Tables

Task tables are used to display task-specific information. Task tables use the three dimensions of project data (cost, schedule, and work; refer to Figure 11.1) to provide a complete picture of each task within your project schedule. The various types of task tables are discussed next.

Cost Table

The purpose of the Cost table is to view task-specific cost information. The Cost table displays not only the actual and planned cost data for each task, but also includes the baseline cost and variance information.

You can apply the Cost table to a combination Gantt Chart and Resource Form view to display schedule, cost, and resource information on one screen, which can be beneficial for reviewing your schedule.

Delay Table

The Delay table is intended to provide the leveling delay information. You can use this table in the Leveling Gantt Chart view, and the table enables you to view and easily modify the task delay information.

Entry Table

The Entry table enables viewing the general task information and is a great way to enter initial project schedule data.

Schedule Table

The Schedule table provides schedule-related task details, such as start, finish, and slack. The Schedule table is a great way to perform analysis of the project schedule while updating the slack available on a task. You can easily see the effect the slack has on the start and finish dates. You can also combine the Schedule table with a Gantt Chart view to see the slack effect in a graphical view.

Summary Table

The Summary table does just that—summarizes task data used for tracking task progress. It includes the start and end dates for each task, duration, percentage complete, cost, and work. This task table incorporates all three dimensions of project information and enables you to view it all on one page.

Export Table

The Export table is used for exporting data to another application. It is a common practice to include all available column information in a view like this one. Following those practices, the Export view incorporates all task columns available in Project Standard.

 note

This view contains the most comprehensive set of information about tasks, but can be hard to use to review it on a computer screen because the information area is too broad.

Hyperlink Table

The Hyperlink table exposes all external hyperlinks linked to tasks. This table can be efficiently used for both entry and review of the task hyperlinks.

Rollup Table

The Rollup table is used in the Rollup Data view and rolls up task information to the summary level.

Constraint Dates Table

The Constraint Dates table displays the constraint details for each task within the project schedule. This table is especially useful for reviewing your schedule to ensure it does not contain any unnecessary constraints.

Earned Value

The Earned Value table displays the standard precalculated fields used to calculate the value produced by executing the project. Even though Earned Value can be a great way to analyze how a project is performing and assess your budget, schedule, and scope problems, for this to be meaningful, the Earned Value table must contain the most up-to-date, accurate actual information.

 *For detailed information on using Earned Value and Work Breakdown Structure on your project,* **see** *Chapter 4, "Getting Started After the Business Initiative Is Approved," **p. 71**.*

Earned Value Cost Indicators Table

The Earned Value Cost Indicators table is a variation of the Earned Value table that displays only the cost fields of the Earned Value, excluding the Schedule Variance and other schedule-related fields.

Baseline Table

The Baseline table concentrates on displaying all available baselines side by side, allowing you to compare and analyze the progress, effects, and the evolution of your schedule since the planning phase.

Tracking Table

The Tracking table is used during the execution and control phases of the project and provides progress and status information related to each task.

Usage Table

The Usage table is generally used in combination with other views and provides the standard task information, such as start and end dates, duration, and work.

Resource Tables

Resource tables are used to display resource-specific information. Resource tables use the three dimensions of project data (cost, schedule, and work; refer to Figure 11.1) to provide a complete picture of each resource within your project schedule.

Entry Table

The Entry table is a simple way to enter your resource information using a list during the planning phase of your project. The entry table provides many different columns of fields and allows for easy viewing, but it does not enable you to view time-phased resource information. After the Entry Table is populated, you can utilize other views to see time-phased resource data.

Entry – Material Resources Table

The Entry – Material Resources table is a filtered entry table that includes only resources of the Material type (hardware, tools, machinery, and so on). This entry table enables you to quickly and efficiently add all material resources to your project.

Entry – Work Resources Table

The Entry – Work Resources table is a filtered entry table that includes only resources of the Work type (that is, people). This entry table enables you to quickly and efficiently add work resources required for your project.

Entry – Cost Resources Table

The Entry – Cost Resources table is a filtered entry table that includes only resources of the Cost type (airplane tickets, lodging, and so on). This entry table enables you to quickly and efficiently add cost resources required for your project schedule.

Export Table

The Export table is used for exporting data to another application. It is a common practice to include all available column information in a view like this one. Following those practices, the Export view incorporates all resource columns available in Project.

> **note**
>
> This view contains comprehensive information about resources, but can be hard to efficiently use for reviewing resources on a computer screen because the information area is too broad.

Hyperlink Table

The Hyperlink table exposes all external hyperlinks linked to resources within Project. This table can be efficiently used for both entry and review of the resource hyperlinks.

Summary Table

The Summary table does just that—summarizes resource data used for tracking task progress. It includes the start and end dates for each task, duration, percentage complete, cost, and work. This task view incorporates all three dimensions of project information and enables you to view it all on one page.

Work Table

The Work table displays all the work dimension resource-related information, organized by resource. You can use the Work table to view the amount of work, overtime, baseline, remaining, and actual work performed by the resource. You can combine the Work table with several views, such as the Resource Overallocation, to determine which resources have scheduled overtime or are overallocated.

Usage Table

The Usage table displays the use of a resource on your project. This table provides a one-to-one relationship between the resource and the work scheduled for the project.

Cost Table

The Cost table displays all cost information about the resources in your schedule. You can use this view to analyze the scheduled and actual costs for a particular resource, the budget remaining to spend on that resource, the baseline cost, and the current variance. You can use this table to analyze and reevaluate your planning process and resource and budget allocation.

Earned Value Table

The Earned Value table for resources enables you to tie the Earned Value variances and indicators to a specific resource. Even though Earned Value can be a great way to analyze how a project is performing and to assess your budget, schedule, and scope problems, for this to be meaningful, the Earned Value table must contain the most up-to-date, accurate actual information. It is especially hard to include such information about your resources, as an organization's financial system often contains the most up-to-date, valuable data. But, if you commit to attaining Earned Value and keeping your financial and project information synced up, this view can help you improve your projects in the future and prevent scope creep and other problems associated with scope from occurring.

> ➥ *For detailed information on using Earned Value and Work Breakdown Structure on your project, **see** Chapter 4, "Getting Started After the Business Initiative Is Approved," **p. 71**.*

Understanding Filtering and Grouping

In addition to views and tables, you can break down the information displayed in Project using filters and logically combine the information using groups. When you properly utilize these features, they can add a lot of value to how effectively you can view your project data and locate the exact information you need.

Exploring Filters in Microsoft Project

You can apply filters to all views, except for the Relationship Diagram, which is limited to the information it displays and, therefore, does not require filtering.

Project provides built-in filters, which are available under the View tab, Data, Filter, as shown in Figure 11.31. These filters are predefined and include the commonly used columns by which to filter the view or table. Project provides different options for standard filters based on the entity to which the view or table relates, such as a task or resource.

Figure 11.31
Selecting a standard filter to apply to the current view.

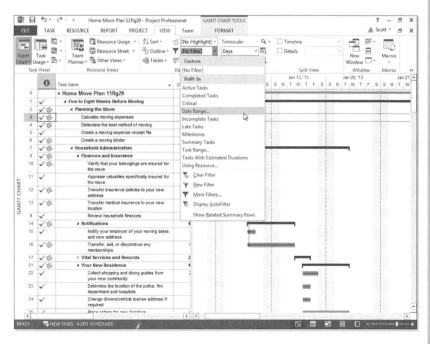

Filters can also be accessed from the down arrow on column headings, as in Figure 11.32, if the Display AutoFilter control is toggled on (View tab, Data, Filter, Display AutoFilter).

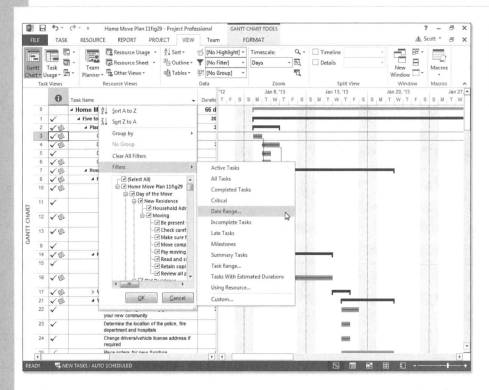

Figure 11.32
Selecting an
AutoFilter to
apply to the
current view
with a table.

 note

The AutoFilter can be applied only to tables because it requires the current view to contain columns to filter by.

 note

When you are using combination views with a split screen, the view on the bottom part of the page cannot have any filters applied to it because it is automatically being filtered by Project based on what is selected in the top part of the view.

When a filter is applied to the view, only tasks or resources that meet the specified criteria are displayed. All other tasks or resources are temporarily hidden and can be viewed again once the filter is removed.

Filters can also be subdivided into two categories:

- **Calculated**—These filters are used to compare a value you provide with values available for a particular field in the Project database. Calculated filters can also be used to compare two values, such as baseline cost and actual cost. Calculated fields do not require you to use only values from the Project database. You can, for example, compare the task start date to a value you provide and view only the tasks that start on that date.

- **Interactive**—These filters require user collaboration in the form of providing a comparison value to apply to the filter. For example, using the Resource Sheet view, you can filter only for resources that are part of a particular group (department), such as Marketing.

In addition to simple filtering, Project includes composite filters that use multiple conditions in combinations to filter for a task or resource. When using composite filters, you can either include or exclude particular criteria:

- **Inclusive**—This test uses the AND condition and requires that all tests must be true for it to return a value.

- **Exclusive**—This test uses the OR condition and requires at least one condition to be met to meet the filtering criteria.

In addition to the commonly used filters that are displayed directly under the View tab, Data, Filter menu, Project includes other filters that can be accessed by selecting More Filters from the menu. In the same way tables and views can be applied to the two main entities in Project, filters are grouped by tasks and resources as well.

Using Standard Filters

Standard filters are provided to define the commonly used and recommended filters for the user. When you use standard filters, several rules must be met:

- Filters can be applied only to the view of the same entity as the filter. For example, task filters can be applied only to task views and resource filters to resource views.

- The Highlight filter can be applied only to a list view because it requires column/row information to apply the highlighting. For example, you will not be able to apply a filter to any of the form views.

- When a filter is applied, it compares the provided criteria to all resources or tasks available in the Project database. To apply more than one criteria at a time, you must edit a standard filter or create a new one.

 tip

Color highlighting may be used in cases where the filter does not suppress the items that do not meet the filter criteria. For detailed information on how to change the filter highlighting and customize filters, see Chapter 22.

 note

Any filter provided in the list that includes ellipses (...) at the end of its name is an interactive filter.

Table 11.4 provides the list of primary task filters included in Project. There are 45 task filters in total, any of which can be selected by clicking Filter, More Filters.

Table 11.4 Primary Task Filters of Microsoft Project

Task Filter Name	Commonly Used	Purpose
All Tasks	Yes	Displays all tasks within your project schedule.
Active Tasks	Yes	Displays only started but incomplete tasks.
Completed Tasks	Yes	Displays only the completed tasks (that is, tasks with the %Complete field equal to 110%).
Critical	Yes	Displays only tasks that are part of the critical path for the project.
Date Range...	Yes	Displays tasks that are planned to start or finish within the specified date range. This is an interactive filter and requires the user to enter the values to filter for.
Incomplete Tasks	Yes	Displays all tasks that have not yet been completed. It tests for the %Complete field to be less than 100%.
Late Tasks	Yes	Displays all tasks that are projected to be late based on deadline.
Milestones	Yes	Displays only tasks that are milestones.
Summary Tasks	Yes	Displays only summary-level tasks.
Task Range...	Yes	Displays all tasks whose ID is within the specified range. This is an interactive filter and requires the user to enter the values to filter for.
Tasks with Estimated Durations	Yes	Displays tasks whose duration has not been finalized and still contain a question mark (?) next to them.
Using Resource...	Yes	Displays tasks that have the specified resource assigned to them. This is an interactive filter and requires the user to enter the values to filter for.

Table 11.5 provides a list of primary resource filters included in Project. There are 25 resource filters in total, any of which can be selected by clicking Filter, More Filters.

Table 11.5 Primary Microsoft Project Resource Filters

Resource Filter Name	Commonly Used	Purpose
All Resources	Yes	Displays all resources in the Project database.

Resource Filter Name	Commonly Used	Purpose
Budget Resources	Yes	Displays only the budget type resources.
Cost Overbudget	Yes	Displays only resources whose actual cost is larger than the baseline.
Group...	Yes	Displays resources that belong to the specified group. This is an interactive filter and requires the user to enter the values to filter for.
Non-Budget Resources	Yes	Displays all non-budget resources—that is, resources with the type material or work only.
Overallocated Resources	Yes	Displays resources who are assigned to a task for too many hours during any timeframe of the project.
Resource Range...	Yes	Displays a resource whose ID is in the specified range. This is an interactive filter and requires the user to enter the values to filter for.
Resources-Cost	Yes	Displays only resources with type cost. These resources include additional costs on the project, such as airplane tickets and hotel room charges for travel required for execution of the project.
Resources-Material	Yes	Displays only resources whose type is material. These resources include hardware, machinery, instruments, and so on needed for the project execution.
Resources-Work	Yes	Displays only resources whose type is work. These resources are people who have been assigned to complete activities within the project.
Work Overbudget	Yes	Displays resources with overbudget work, calculated by comparing scheduled work to the baseline work.

Using AutoFilters

AutoFilters are a filter type that allows the user to select any columns to filter by. It also enables more than one selection simultaneously.

When AutoFilter is toggled on (View tab, Data, Filter, Display AutoFilter), a drop-down list appears above each column in the current view, enabling you to filter by a specific value selected in the drop-down, as shown earlier in Figure 11.32.

Depending on the view and the columns displayed in the view, some of them include special values within the AutoFilter. For example, the Gantt Chart view with the Task Entry table contains Today, Tomorrow, This Week, Next Week, This Month, and Next Month options for the Start and End Date columns.

You can customize the AutoFilter by selecting the Custom option from the drop-down list. This enables you to create two exclusive or inclusive conditions. You can also save the custom filter to use it in the future without having to re-create it. To save the custom filter, click the Save button, provide a meaningful name for your custom filter, and click OK, as shown in Figure 11.33.

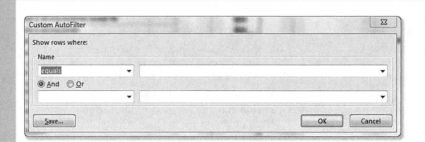

Figure 11.33
Creating a custom filter from the AutoFilter.

Exploring Standard Groups

In addition to using filters, you can group information in views and tables into logical categories to perform further analysis or to organize large quantities of data for easier comprehension using groups. In addition to creating categories of data, grouping also enables you to calculate subtotals, which are numeric values based on the grouped information. Whenever a new grouping strategy is applied, the outline of tasks or resources in the view is temporarily rearranged, according to the criteria specified in the Group By condition.

To better control the subgrouping structure of your new outline, grouping also enables you to include value intervals for the Group By fields.

You can access groups by selecting the View tab, Data, Group By, as shown in Figure 11.34.

Like the rest of the viewing mechanisms within Project, Group By is divided into the entity types it can be applied to—either task or resource.

Table 11.6 provides a list of predefined and commonly used task Group By options.

Figure 11.34
Group By options change based on the view you have selected. For example, when Gantt Chart is selected, you can group by various task properties, such as whether the task is critical.

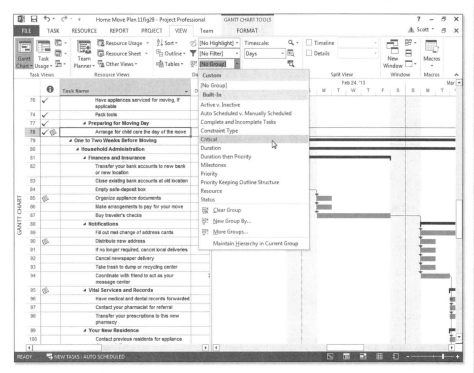

Table 11.6   Standard Microsoft Project Task Group By Options

Group By Option Name	Commonly Used	Purpose
No Group	Yes	Displays all tasks without applying any grouping condition.
Active v. Inactive	Yes	Groups tasks into two categories—first, active tasks; second, inactive tasks.
Auto Scheduled v. Manually Scheduled	Yes	Groups tasks into two categories—first, auto-scheduled tasks; second, manually scheduled tasks.
Complete and Incomplete Tasks	Yes	Groups tasks into two categories—first, completed tasks; second, incomplete tasks.
Constraint Type	Yes	Groups tasks into categories by the constraint type applied to the task. The groups are listed in alphabetical order.

Group By Option Name	Commonly Used	Purpose
Critical	Yes	Groups tasks into two categories—critical and noncritical. The noncritical tasks group is displayed first.
Duration	Yes	Groups tasks into categories by their duration. The number of categories depends on the number of unique Duration field values.
Duration Then Priority	Yes	Groups tasks first by duration and then within each duration grouping by priority, with the lowest one first.
Milestones	Yes	Groups tasks into two categories—milestone and regular tasks. The regular tasks group is displayed first.
Priority	Yes	Groups tasks by their priority, using intervals of 100.
Priority Keeping Outline Structure	Yes	Groups tasks by their priority, using intervals of 100, while maintaining the outline structure.
Resource	Yes	Groups tasks by resource.
Status	Yes	Groups tasks by status.

Table 11.7 provides a list of predefined and commonly used resource Group By options.

Table 11.7 Standard Microsoft Project Resource Group By Options

Group By Option Name	Commonly Used	Purpose
No Group	Yes	Displays resources without applying any grouping conditions.
Assignments Keeping Outline Structure	Yes	Groups resources by resource assignments, while maintaining the original outline structure.
Complete and Incomplete Resources	Yes	Groups resources into two categories—the ones assigned to completed tasks and the others to the tasks that have not been completed yet. The incomplete tasks group is displayed first.
Resource Group	Yes	Groups resources by resource group and subtotals the values based on the Group field entries within the Resource Sheet view.

Group By Option Name	Commonly Used	Purpose
Resource Type	Yes	Groups resources by resource type, based on the number of resource types present. At maximum, there are three categories: Work, Material, and Cost, displayed in that order, with Work always being first.
Standard Rate	Yes	Groups resources by resource pay scale.
Work v. Material Resources	Yes	Groups resources by type, work, or material.

Combining Views, Tables, Filters, and Groups to Review Project Schedule Details

This section of the chapter explores some specific examples and viewing strategies you can apply when reviewing your schedule during your project's planning phase. The examples provided here represent the common usage scenarios employed by project managers when reviewing their project schedule. This section is also intended to serve as an initial checklist for reviewing your project schedule, but you should consider other checks, specific to you and your project, because this list is not all-inclusive.

Does My Schedule Contain the Needed Milestones?

Accurately identifying and listing required milestones can be crucial to a project's success. Milestones not only ensure that there is an expected deliverable at the end of each step of the project, but they also help ensure that your schedule is organized correctly. There are several things you should evaluate when deciding what types of milestones you need to include in your schedule, as follows:

- Do you have crucial deliverables in your project? If you do, then it is beneficial to add a milestone for each one of those deliverables.

- Do you have a client or a project sponsor who wants to see project milestones? If so, then it is recommended that you create two separate types of milestones—internal to the team and ones your client or project sponsor would like to see. Separating the two will help both you and the client/sponsor. Your client/sponsor probably does not want to see every single one of your milestones, just the crucial ones that either make or break the project. Similarly, you do not want to limit yourself to only a handful of milestones that do not include intermediate deliverables that you will need to consider.

- Does your project have a final project milestone that connects your entire schedule together and defines a formal completion?

- Are there specific milestones associated with the billing? If there are, it may be beneficial to include those specific milestones to remind yourself which of your deliverables influence the invoicing.

After you have answered these questions for your project, there are some techniques and view combinations you can apply to your project schedule to ensure it contains the necessary milestones, as follows:

- **Formatting text styles**—You can format the text styles to highlight the milestones to make them more visible and noticeable. To do so, select the Format tab, Format, Text Styles, and then in Item to Change, select Milestone Tasks. Modify the style options, such as font color, size, italic, bold, and so on. Figure 11.35 shows an example of using different text styles.

Figure 11.35
Milestone tasks will stand out in the schedule and are easy to notice because they are in blue italics.

- **Creating a custom field to filter by**—Using the custom fields in Project, you can create a custom text field that provides various categories for milestones, which you can then use to filter or group by. Figure 11.36 shows an example of grouping by the custom field Milestone Type, where the Milestone Type column has been added to the Gantt Chart view and then a custom group is applied to group by it.

 tip
One of the easiest ways to customize any of the views or tables is to provide additional columns by right-clicking on the column area and selecting Insert Column. This enables you to view not only other fields within Project, but also the custom ones you have added.

Figure 11.36 Grouping by the Milestone Type custom field enables you to easily assess whether your project contains the needed milestones.

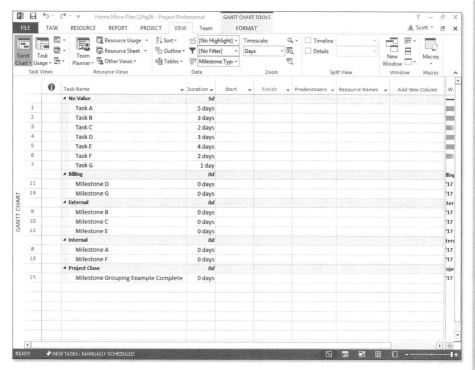

Do I Know My Critical Path?

When reviewing your schedule, it is important to review your critical path tasks. These are the tasks that have no slack, and if they slip, they will dramatically affect your entire project schedule.

You can apply several techniques to your project schedule to ensure that you know your critical path tasks and that they are easy to see, as follows:

- **Formatting text styles**—You can format the text styles to highlight the critical path tasks to make them more visible and noticeable. To do so, select the Format tab, Format, Text Styles, and then in Item to Change, select Critical Tasks. Modify the style options, such as font color, size, italic, bold, and so on. Figure 11.37 shows an example of using different text styles.

- **Displaying the Total Slack column**—By definition, critical path tasks are tasks whose total slack is equal to zero. By displaying the Total Slack column, you can easily locate the critical path tasks because their Total Slack value is zero, as shown in Figure 11.38.

tip

To view the Total Slack column, just apply the Tracking Gantt view.

- **Grouping critical and noncritical tasks**—You can apply the Group By, Critical predefined group to the Gantt Chart view, which clearly separates critical from noncritical tasks, as shown in Figure 11.38.

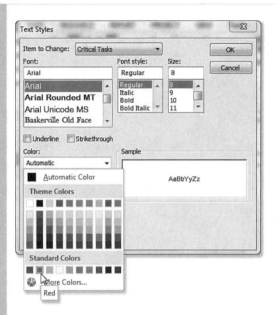

Figure 11.37
Highlighting critical path tasks in red within the Gantt Chart view helps you easily distinguish the tasks that drive your project schedule.

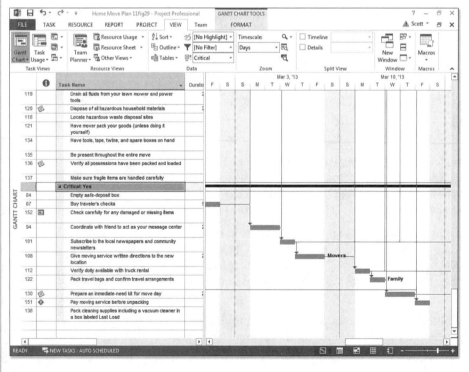

Figure 11.38
Grouping the tasks by type is one of the easiest views to visually separate them and ensure you know what your critical path is.

- **Filtering for critical path tasks**—You can apply the Filter By, Critical predefined filter to the Gantt Chart view to view only the critical path tasks.

Are My Tasks Linked?

One of the easiest things to miss can be a task that gets added at the last minute and does not get linked with the rest of the schedule. If that happens, that can have really bad consequences when you cannot view its impact on your project. One of the most important aspects of the schedule to review is that all of your tasks are not only linked, but have the correct relationships with one another.

The following are just several techniques and views you can use to ensure that task relationships are properly defined within your project schedule:

- **Combining Gantt Chart and Relationship Diagram views**—This enables you to view the relationship of each task within your schedule. When you select the task in the Gantt Chart, the bottom part of the screen (the Relationship Diagram view) will filter to display the predecessors and successors of the selected task, as shown in Figure 11.39.

Figure 11.39 Combining the Gantt Chart and Relationship Diagram views enables you to easily see the relationships between tasks in your project schedule.

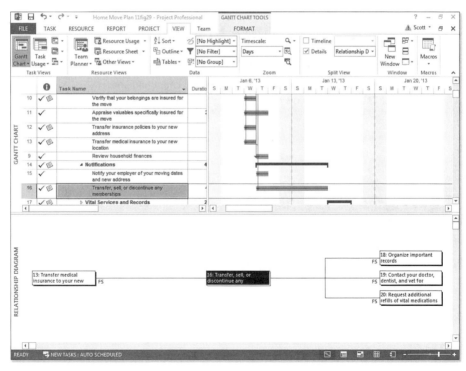

- **Displaying the Task Entry view**—This view is particularly helpful when ensuring that task relationships are correct and all tasks within your project are linked. The Task Entry view shows the Task Entry table with a Gantt Chart and the Task Form view at the bottom. The Gantt Chart can be of great help in identifying which tasks have not been linked into the rest of the schedule. Similarly, the Task Form displays predecessors for each task, so if there are none, you need to make sure you intended that task to not have any.

- **Displaying the Predecessor/Successor column**—This enables you to view both the predecessors and successors for each task. The non-summary-level tasks that have no predecessors or successors should be of concern to you and are a good idea to double-check. To add the Predecessors and Successors column, right-click and select Insert Column.

> **tip**
>
> To display predecessors and successors in the Task Form view, right-click in the view and select Predecessors & Successors. This changes the view and displays predecessors in the right table and successors in the left one.

Does My Schedule Contain Constraints?

Project schedules that contain constraints can be a little dangerous because, a lot of the time, those are constraints you are unaware of. Before finalizing and baselining your project schedule, it is a good idea to double-check that the constraints you do have in your schedule are intentional.

One of the easiest ways to find out what types of constraints are set on various tasks is by displaying the Constraint Type column within any of the task views, as shown in Figure 11.40.

> **note**
>
> When task constraints are applied, special symbols appear in the Indicators column of the Gantt Chart. You can hover over each icon to see the name of the constraint applied.

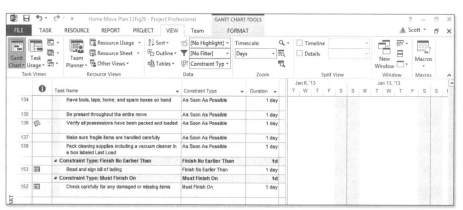

Figure 11.40
Displaying the constraint column and grouping/filtering by Constraint Type is an easy way to verify task constraints.

Are All Needed Task Details Included?

Another detail to verify in your project schedule is that you have included the necessary attributes and details for each task.

To review the details of your tasks, use the Detail Gantt combination view and apply the Task Form view on the bottom You can change the detail displayed in the Task Form view by right-clicking and selecting a different option to display.

Making Sure There Is Flexibility in the Schedule

When scheduling your project tasks, it is important to include enough flexibility in your schedule so that if it were to slip, the final completion date would not change.

One of the task attributes that defines the schedule flexibility is how much slack each task in your project schedule has. It is also important to know which tasks have the most slack because those can be easily delayed, if needed, without affecting the final project completion date.

In addition to possibly affecting the project completion date, schedule flexibility influences project risks. For example, if you have a schedule delay risk associated with Task A, and Task A has a week lag time, the risk severity and priority are minimized because of the extra time built into the schedule.

The Detail Gantt Chart view enables you to view the lag on each task. In addition, you can then filter or group your tasks by the amount of lag they have.

Are My Resources Overallocated?

One of the most important things to review in your schedule prior to baselining is whether any of your resources are overallocated.

You can use the Team Planner, or you can combine the Resource Usage view on the top and the Resource Graph on the bottom. This enables you to not only view which resources are overallocated and by how much, but also which days and which tasks contribute to the overallocation, as shown in Figure 11.41.

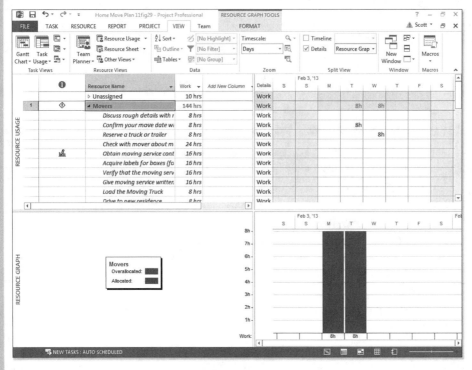

Figure 11.41
The Resource Graph and Resource Usage views enable you to view all your resource allocations and drill into the task level.

Is My Schedule Baselined?

As an official completion of the planning phase, your project schedule must be baselined.

➡️ *For details on baselining your schedule, see Chapter 12, "Performing a Schedule Reality Check," p. 411.*

To view the current baseline information, you can apply the Multiple Baselines view. You can also modify the Gantt Chart view and display additional columns, such as any of the baseline columns. These include Budget Cost, Budget Work, Cost, Deliverable Finish, Deliverable Start, Duration, Finish, Start, and Work.

How Do I Communicate the Tasks?

Project provides some convenient ways to communicate your project schedule to your team, as follows:

- **Calendar view**—This is an easy and familiar-to-everyone way to display the project schedule. You can customize the Calendar view to display tasks for a specific resource and then print that view either to a printer or a PDF.

- **Network Diagram view**—This is one of the older, more common ways of presenting your project schedule to the rest of the team. The Network Diagram view can be more complex because it most often does not fit nicely on the page, so printing or exporting it can be complicated. The Network Diagram view, however, clearly and consecutively presents your project schedule and the needed information within it.

- **Resource Usage view**—This view is grouped by the resource, displaying all the tasks assigned to the resource under the resources' name. Columns displayed include hours of work, hours of overallocated work, cost, availability, and other details.

- **Gantt Chart view**—The old and reliable Gantt Chart, with the appropriate filtering, sorting, and grouping, is a great way to show your team members their assigned tasks along with the time-phased data shown in the Gantt section.

 tip

It is not considered a best practice to let other people (other project managers, team members, sponsors, and so on) access your project schedule directly. So, it is recommended that you not just send the file as a method of sharing the information. Your project schedule file is a controlled environment, and any potential changes can jeopardize it.

How Do I Present My Project Schedule to the Project Sponsors?

It is generally not a good idea to distribute a Project file as-is and expect your sponsors to appreciate it. For the detail-loving sponsor:

- **Export the project schedule to Excel**—To export your project schedule data to an Excel workbook, select Save As in the File menu and then, under the file type, select Excel Workbook.

  *For additional information on exporting to other file formats, such as Excel, XML, CSV, and so on, **see** Chapter 25, "Exporting and Importing Project Data," **p. 835**.*

- **Create a Visual Report using Excel or Visio**—Visual Reports enables you to create Excel- or Visio-based reports that display any type or detail level of data contained in the Project database. Visual Reports can be an effective way to create custom information displays for communicating your project schedule information.

  *For additional information on creating and working with Visual Reports, **see** Chapter 21, "Reports Part II: Visual Reports," **p. 653**.*

- **Create a Report using the new Report functionality**—Project 2013 provides a new highly flexible mechanism for building reports that replaces the old reporting functionality.

  *For additional information on creating and working with reports, **see** Chapter 20, "Reports Part I: 2013 Reports," **p. 625**.*

Consultants' Tips

Stop Expecting Your Resources and Sponsors to Look at the Same Views You Do

Between Visual Reports and the new Reporting functionality in Project 2013, there are few reasons to show anyone printed or exported views from Project. The reports project stakeholders need—reports that are clear and useful—can and should be built using the new tools.

Use the Team Planner When Resource Planning Is Your Main Goal

Combined with manual scheduling, the Team Planner (available in Project Professional) is a powerful Project 2010 addition that enables people with no project management interest or expertise to graphically plan the activities of a team. First, you should create the team using the Resource Sheet view. Then create manually scheduled tasks using the Task sheet view. Finally, use the Team Planner view to assign tasks to resources, clear up resource bottlenecks, and identify resource downtime. Add new tasks and resources as needed.

Keep It Simple

There is often a tendency for people to want to create views that contain a lot of information—so much information, as a matter of fact, that it becomes difficult to understand. Before you spend a lot of time designing a new Project view, get a good understanding of the views available to you and how they might be easily modified. For example, in a Resource Usage or Task Usage view, right-clicking in the grid on the right side of the screen gives you a number of options to add more information to the view.

Remember that views are there to assist you in providing the most efficient, useful, and effective display of the information, so a minimalist approach is often the favorable one.

Easy Way to Not Accidentally Type in Actuals When Using Resource or Task Usage Views

In either of those views, right-click in the data grid and then select Detail Styles from the menu that pops up. On the right side of the Detail Styles dialog, in the Show These Fields box, select All Assignment Rows and then click Hide. This prevents entry of data in the default Work rows. To add actuals, select Actual Work from the Available fields section and click Show. You can configure each type of data with different colors to make it easier to manage the process of entering data.

PERFORMING A SCHEDULE REALITY CHECK

Schedules are literally an attempt to predict the future. Fortunately, there are several ways Microsoft Project can help verify that a schedule really does constitute a "best guess," and not sheer fantasy. This chapter highlights methods and tools that can be used to ideally make the predictions in a schedule more likely to be true, or at least highlight the risks and assumptions that underpin it.

Auditing the Schedule for Reasonableness

Before you are ready to call your project planning phase complete, it is important to review your project schedule and ensure that it is ready for execution. This chapter provides some important questions that you need to ask yourself, as well as some good reality checks to ensure that you are truly ready to execute what you planned.

During the planning phase, you have created your task schedule, defined the task relationships and dependencies, and assigned all necessary resources. Hopefully you have set most or all tasks to Auto-Scheduled mode. This chapter provides guidance for reviewing your schedule and making the necessary adjustments. The more time you spend making sure your project is complete and realistic while you plan, the more problems you can avoid during the execution.

Many organizations require that you capture a baseline of your schedule at the end of the planning phase. You should capture a baseline of the entire project after you are satisfied that your schedule is a realistic structure for work activities. The baseline enables you to later assess the performance of the project compared to the plan as you execute the details of the project. Make sure you check your organization's policies to determine when a baseline capture is required.

Looking for Logic Errors

Logic errors in a project occur when, for example, you forget a task or summary task while setting up your project, or schedule your tasks in the wrong order. It can be difficult to judge your own schedule as the errors might be harder to notice because of how familiar you are with it.

However, you can do some initial logic checks by answering the following questions:

- **Is all required work included in the schedule?** To answer this question, review your project scope statement and your Work Breakdown Structure (WBS) to ensure that your schedule captures the full scope of your project and all work has been included.

- **Does the organization of the schedule achieve the project's Measure of Success?** When starting up any project, you define the Measure of Success, which is your metric for what it really means for your project to have successfully achieved everything you planned for it to achieve. The tasks and milestones you have defined in your schedule must represent the Measure of Success you have defined.

- **Does the schedule include all and only necessary deliverables and tasks that achieve the work in the WBS?** It is important to recognize all of the project deliverables that support the Measure of Success you have defined. It is also important to remember that a successful project schedule should not include extraneous deliverables that might seem like they are needed, but are really not part of your project scope.

  For example, you have a house remodeling project in which you set out to replace the floors throughout the entire house. The tasks to purchase the materials, hire the contractors, and replace the flooring in each room of the house are all part of your scope. But the natural human thinking may lead you to consider that while you are replacing the floors, you might as well replace the doors on the interior of the house, even though it is not part of the original plan.

  Following this way of thinking, you can end up remodeling your entire house, even though your initial intent was to only replace the flooring. This is called *scope creep* and can be a dangerous scenario for any project, because scope creep is often responsible for projects finishing over budget and behind schedule. Even though the example described here may be an exaggerated one, situations similar to this occur and can lead to serious problems.

- **Are the tasks scheduled to occur in the correct order?** The order of tasks can be as essential as the tasks themselves. It is important to remember that not only should tasks occur in chronological order, but you should also allow for enough slack in tasks with the most risk. For example, adopting a new technology can be a risky task because you may encounter unforeseen problems, so scheduling those tasks earlier can be beneficial and can help you avoid delays later in the project. In addition, you must ensure that each task has all of its prerequisites met. For example, you would not schedule movers to come in and load the moving truck before you have packed your belongings. Similar logic should apply to all of the tasks in your project.

note

A good practice for determining logic errors is to have a trusted associate or your project team look at the project for you. Make sure the reviewer understands that he or she is just looking for your logic errors by reviewing your scope, tasks, task arrangement, and planning logic. It is possible your associate will want to change your schedule because he or she might have done things differently in another project. Everyone has his or her own way of doing things, and just like everything else in Project, there is more than one way to achieve the same result. In this case, ask the people reviewing your schedule to concentrate on your logic without focusing on trying to improve your project using his or her own standards. However, be open to the criticism, too; that is one of the best ways to learn.

Schedule Estimation Methods

Schedule estimation errors are the second type of error you need to check against when reviewing your project schedule. Estimation errors are caused by mistakes in setting your task durations, work, and budget. There are several ways to help you resolve estimation errors.

To discover estimation errors, you need to ask yourself the following questions:

- **Are tasks, work, and duration estimates viable?** Make sure that your work and duration estimates are realistic for all tasks. Many people underestimate, which leads to additional work, time, and in turn budget increases. Similarly, overestimating the work and duration is also undesirable because you might not be able to meet your project requirements. Ideally, your estimates should attempt to reflect the reality as closely as possible. For tips on achieving this, see the section "Are You a Pessimistic or an Optimistic Estimator?" at the end of the chapter.

- **Are budget estimates viable?** Budget estimates are also an important aspect of project planning. Ensuring that the budget you have allocated for your project is met and not exceeded can be the deciding point between success and failure. Ensure that the initial budget estimates you have are realistic and meet your project requirements.

To better understand estimation errors, it is important to review the three main estimation methods—analogous, expert judgment, and parametric duration.

Analogous Estimation Method

Analogous duration estimates simply ask the question, "What was the duration the last time we did this?" If you have been following the project management best practice of recording lessons learned at the end of each project, you have proof, which increases in accuracy with every project you complete. You can use the past performance as an estimation comparison if your previous project is similar to your current scope.

The advantage to analogous estimates is that they focus on system-level activities, such as integration, documentation, configuration management, and others. They also require minimal project detail and are usually faster and easier to develop; plus your information is readily accessible in previous Project schedules.

The downside to analogous duration estimates is that if you do not have any previous information, you have no detailed basis for justifying your estimates. Also, because it focuses on the system level, it can be hard to identify lower-level problems that can raise costs.

Program Evaluation and Review Technique (PERT)

Expert judgment is a great tool to use when hard data is scarce. Former versions of Project included a Program Evaluation and Review Technique (PERT) analysis tool. PERT uses a network diagram analysis technique to create three estimates: Optimistic, Expected, and Pessimistic. These three estimates are then combined to estimate an activity's duration, using a weighted statistical average of the three values. The statistical technique considers: 1 part Optimistic, 4 parts Expected, and 1 part Pessimistic, all divided by 6 parts. This method yields a weighted average duration for a given task.

 note

Unfortunately, PERT analysis is supported only with a combination of custom fields and custom code or with third-party products. Consequently, discussing these things is outside the scope of this book.

Parametric Duration Estimation Method

Finally, the parametric duration estimates are simply mathematical models used when estimating task durations. If you had a machine that produced a product at a rate of 10 units per hour and you needed to make 200 units, you are looking at 20 hours. This process produces exact estimates, but your estimate can change if you add another machine, increase the productivity, or decrease the duration of the task. Many different industries already have standard calculations, devised from years of experience, that can be used for this type of estimating.

Looking for Technique Errors

Technique errors are problems such as data omissions or mistakes made while putting a schedule together. Here are some of the most common technique errors:

- Missing data
- Data where there should be blanks
- Misspellings
- Duplications
- Incorrect variables

To prevent or detect technique errors, audit your tasks, resources, schedule, and calendars.

Auditing Tasks for Technique Errors

When auditing your tasks for technique errors, check for the common problems related directly to the individual tasks:

- **Do all tasks have at least one predecessor and successor?** If you do not verify this, you might end up with "dangling" tasks. These are tasks that do not explicitly drive from the beginning or to the end (measurable definition of success) of your schedule. This can cause problems for the following reasons:

  - You might have tasks in your schedule that are extraneous or unnecessary. You might also have forgotten important relationships between tasks; this situation can cause your schedule to reflect incorrect dates.

  - There are exceptions when it is acceptable to have tasks with no predecessors or successors—for example, recurring meetings and ongoing tasks, such as project management. It also might be okay for tasks to have no resources assigned, although this situation needs to be reviewed. For example, a task that is outside the control of the project might be added to represent the elapsed time. Consider leaving these tasks in Manually Scheduled mode. The default group Auto Scheduled vs. Manual Scheduled (View tab, Data, Group) will make it easy to separate the two types of tasks.

- **Do all tasks have resources assigned?** Milestones and summary tasks are exceptions. If tasks do not have resources assigned, who is going to complete those tasks? This can be a problem because if no one is assigned to complete a certain task, the work will not be accomplished and your project potentially can be delayed. In addition to this, you should ask yourself whether you have enough resources or too many resources.

- **Are there any unnecessary task constraints?** Task constraints are based on the logic of the workflow and natural deadlines, such as the start date of a trade show, the favorable season for climbing in Nepal, the availability of launch pads, and so on. However, if you incorrectly schedule your tasks, Project can insert constraints, so make sure you are aware and agree with all constraints in your project.

- **Are the tasks the appropriate size?** This is a personal measure: How large or small do you want tasks to be? Is two days too small; is four weeks too large? Only you can decide. The task size depends on the purpose of the project schedule. If the purpose is to calculate the overall duration of the project for a rough estimate based on the achievement network at the top level, task sizes of two weeks or more are acceptable. However, it might be more helpful to your team to have tasks broken down into smaller parts to create a well-defined list of deliverables and the actions that need to be performed to achieve them. Here are additional considerations for task sizes:

  - Is the schedule used for execution?

  - How often is progress monitored?

  - What is the experience level of the people doing the work?

 note

Remember, the more detailed the schedule is, the more work it will be to maintain as the project progresses. Many project managers make the mistake of building overly elaborate, highly detailed schedules only to find that maintaining them takes far more time than it's worth. In these situations, Project often unfairly shoulders the blame for being "too complicated," when in fact it's the schedule detail itself that exceeds the bounds of usefulness.

Auditing Resources for Technique Errors

Problems relating to resources are important. If your resources are not available, are overallocated, or are assigned to incorrect tasks, you will have problems. To audit your project resources, review the following common problems:

- **Does your project contain duplicate resources?** Have you used two or more names for the same person? This can happen easily when multiple individual resources are assigned to multiple tasks in a schedule. If work is assigned to duplicate resources, you might have created overallocation for the actual individual resource.

- **Does your project schedule contain generic resources?** This scenario can occur if you, for example, have assigned a task to "System Engineer" because you are not sure about the specific individual resource available for this task assignment, but you know the skill set required to complete the task. Until the individual resource is determined, uncertainty can exist in your schedule. What if this person is assigned to a higher-priority task in another project in the meantime; who will be responsible for the task in your schedule? As a final step in verifying your schedule, ensure that all generic resources have been replaced with the real ones.

- **Are any of the resources in your project schedule overallocated (or underallocated)?** This is a situation where a resource is scheduled to perform more work during a workday than he or she can accomplish. As a result:

  - The overallocated resource can fall behind on his or her work, affecting the schedule. If the resource is working on critical path tasks, this might cause the entire project finish date to slip.

  - The overallocated resource might become unhappy or burnt out.

- **Are any resources scheduled for overtime?** How would you define overtime? When is it appropriate to use and not use overtime? When does overtime become a problem? Based on previous experience, take into consideration the following:

  - Extended periods of overtime for many weeks tend to burn people out.

  - Scheduling overtime creates a more optimistic view of the project completion date than might be warranted.

Auditing the Schedule for Technique Errors

When auditing your project schedule for technique errors, concentrate on the following questions:

- **Is your schedule up to date?** Verify that your project reflects the latest contract changes and that the scope of the project has not changed since the last time the schedule was updated.

- **Is your schedule the appropriate size?** Does it include all of the necessary deliverables and milestones?

- **Is your schedule baselined?** Baselining enables you to finalize the project estimates and designates the end of the planning phase. If you neglect to baseline your schedule, Project will not have any base values to compare your actuals to, making reporting and analysis difficult.

- **Are all milestones entered correctly?** Ensure that all tasks you intended to be milestones have a duration of 0. In addition, milestones represent the mark for starting or completing something, so ensure that your milestones are linked to the correct tasks.

- **Are project costs specified in the schedule?** To effectively track your project budget, ensure that it reflects the most up-to-date cost rates for your resources. Having erroneous costs in your project can cause problems during analysis.

Auditing Calendars for Technique Errors

Correctly defined calendars are fundamental and an important component of your project schedule. When auditing calendars, address the following common problem areas:

- **Are corporate holidays defined in the project calendars?** If holidays are not defined in the resource calendars, Project will schedule work during those days. This can cause problems because work will be scheduled when resources are not available, which guarantees the tasks to slip. In addition, this creates a more optimistic view of the project completion date than might be warranted.

- **Are vacation days defined in the resource calendars?** If vacation days are not specified in the resource calendars, work will be scheduled during those days. This can cause problems because work will be scheduled when resources are not available, which guarantees the tasks to slip. In addition, this creates a more optimistic view of the project completion date than might be warranted.

- **Is the working-day length set correctly?** Scheduling eight working hours per day might be unrealistic. Very few days are that productive, especially over a long period of time, because of other obligations, such as meetings, email, and so on. Take this fact into consideration when scheduling working time in your project calendar.

Reviewing the Big Picture: Critical Path Analysis

Critical path can be defined as the longest path through your project and determines the finish date for the project as a whole. Tasks that are on the critical path contain no slack, so if these tasks slip, a delay will result in the chain of tasks within your project. It is important to review your project's critical path because it determines whether your project can be completed on schedule.

Not knowing your critical path and what you can do to reduce it can cause problems, such as the following:

- The overall project schedule might be extended unnecessarily.

- As the project manager, you need to monitor the schedule to guard against slippage. If tasks are not on the critical path, improving the speed of delivering them will not change the project end date.

- The critical path can and does change quickly during the life of a project. As the project manager, you must continuously monitor the amount of slack available for tasks so that unexpected problems do not arise.

- Your sponsor or client might be willing to shorten the schedule by using different task scheduling techniques or spending more money. You need to be able to identify these opportunities to your sponsor or client.

What Is My Current Critical Path?

The critical path is the longest path of linked tasks in the project and includes all tasks that impact the overall project end date if any of them are delayed. Some tasks have slack and, therefore, are not considered critical. Free slack is the amount of time a task can be delayed without delaying any successor tasks. Total slack is the amount of time a task can be delayed without delaying the finish date of the project. In addition to critical tasks, your project contains the near-critical tasks, tasks that are considered high risk and can potentially become critical.

 tip

If a near-critical task slips, it can jeopardize your critical path. This scenario is often overlooked, but when reviewing your critical path, pay attention to the tasks that can *become* critical if project conditions change.

You can use Project to help you distinguish your critical path by applying a different text style to these tasks using the Text Styles tool. To do so, select the Format tab, Format, Text Styles. In the Text Styles dialog box under Item to Change, select Critical Tasks. Select a distinct font style, color, background color, and so on to help you visually distinguish critical tasks, as shown in Figure 12.1.

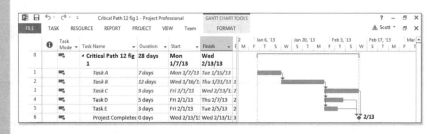

Figure 12.1
The critical-path tasks are styled in red, bold, italic font to help easily distinguish them from the rest of the schedule.

By default, Project critical tasks are tasks with total slack less than or equal to 0. You can change the tolerance level and set the total slack to a different number you feel more comfortable with. To do so, open the Options dialog box by selecting the File tab, Options, Advanced, Calculation Options for This Project and change the number displayed in the Tasks Are Critical If Slack Is Less Than or Equal To option to, say, 4 days. As a result, additional tasks that are near-critical are then added and become part of the critical path, as shown in Figure 12.2.

Figure 12.2
Task D is a near-critical task because its Total Slack is greater than 0, but it is part of the critical path because the tolerance has been changed to 4 days.

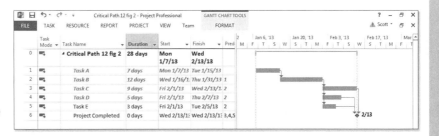

> **⚡ caution**
>
> Be aware of the impact of manually scheduled tasks on the critical path. A manually scheduled task scheduled to finish last on the project will always be "The" critical path. A manually scheduled task with a duration that extends beyond the end of the project but without a specified end date will wipe out critical path calculations completely. Always be sure your manually scheduled tasks are scheduled to finish before at least one auto-scheduled task to eliminate these issues. If manually scheduled tasks should be included in the critical path calculation, it's a strong indication that their task mode should be changed to Auto Scheduled.

You can display the Total Slack column in your current view to help you distinguish between the true critical tasks and the near-critical ones. To do so, click the column header, right-click, and then select Insert Column. In the Column Definition window, select Total Slack under Field Name and then click OK. Tasks whose Total Slack is less than or equal to 0 are your critical tasks, and tasks with slack greater than 0 that are still marked as part of your critical path are the near-critical ones.

How Can I Reduce the Duration of My Critical Path?

You will encounter situations when you need to reduce your project's total duration. Here are two established methods for reducing your schedule duration and therefore the critical path:

- **Crashing**—This common project management term refers to a method used to decrease the duration of an activity by assigning more resources. The distinguishing point of crashing when compared to the second method (fast tracking) is that crashing employs changes to resources to reduce the critical path. Be cautious because when you add more resources, you also add more cost, so be aware of the tradeoff conditions when using this method.

- **Fast tracking**—This common method is used to reduce your project's critical path duration by shortening a sequence or path of activities via overlapping or accomplishing activities in parallel. The fast-tracking method takes advantage of changes made to the activities schedule to reduce the critical path. This method might increase the quality risks to your project because activities are started before the original intended sequence.

Both of these methods achieve the same result but have different effects on your project.

When decreasing the critical path duration, you do have to be aware of the effects this has on the rest of your project attributes, such as scope, cost, and quality. All these variables are interdependent, so when you change one variable, one of the other variables has to change for the project to maintain balance. For example, if you crash your project schedule by adding additional resources to the project, your project cost will increase to accommodate for the pay of the added resources. Similarly, if you use the fast-tracking method and break a critical task into smaller tasks worked on by different resources, the quality of the project may suffer because the work is being divided between a lot of different people.

Strategies for Crashing the Schedule

As was mentioned in the previous section, crashing the schedule is a technique used to help you reduce your critical path by making changes to the way the resources are scheduled in your project. This section discusses methods you can use to crash your project schedule.

Assigning Additional Resources

The first method for crashing your project schedule is to assign additional resources to the critical path tasks. Adding resources will in turn decrease the duration, thus shortening the critical path. When using this method, be aware of the effects it has on the rest of your project. If you have unlimited use of resources, this method can be a great way to reduce the critical path without it having any effect on your overall project. However, if you have to pay for the additional resources you add, you are increasing the overall cost of your project, which can put your project over budget. Carefully weigh your options to make sure that the tradeoffs you are making are worth it.

Scheduling Overtime

Another way to crash your schedule is to arrange overtime for the resources already assigned to the critical path tasks. This option can work well, but you must ensure that the resources are available to work overtime and that the amount of overtime is reasonable and not going to burn out your resources. You can schedule overtime by modifying the task's calendar to schedule resources to work, for example, on Saturdays. Besides having negative effects on your resources, this method can also influence other aspects of your project, such as budget, if your resources are contracted to be paid overtime.

Strategies for Fast Tracking the Schedule

As mentioned previously, fast tracking is a technique used to reduce your project's critical path duration by making changes to the way tasks are scheduled within your project. This section discusses methods you can use to fast track your schedule.

Parallel Scheduling

The first option is to revise the task dependencies to allow more parallel scheduling. This overlaps the activities within your schedule to shorten the overall critical path duration. There are times when this option is not feasible because the critical path tasks have Start-to-Finish relationships, and one cannot be started until the previous one is fully completed. In addition, this can have an effect on your project resources. For example, if you have the same resource working on the two tasks that you schedule to be performed in parallel, either the resource will be unable to complete his or her assignments or he or she will have to work overtime. This, in turn, can have an effect on your budget, if this resource gets paid an additional rate for the overtime hours. Make sure you evaluate the consequences of parallel scheduling and ensure that this will not cause further problems within your project.

Decomposing Tasks

The second option for fast tracking is to break critical tasks into smaller tasks that can be worked on simultaneously by different resources. The tradeoff of using this method is that it can potentially decrease the quality of work being performed on the tasks because you have many different people performing separate parts of the task. This can cause inconsistencies in the final product. In addition, ensure that the resources are available to perform the work that you schedule to prevent having resource-overallocation problems in the future.

Changing the Scope of Your Project

Changing the scope of your project is really a third technique that does not fit under either crashing or fast tracking the schedule, but it does enable you to reduce the length of your critical path. This option, however, generally requires the involvement of your project sponsors in that you must receive their approval. This option is commonly used on product development projects. For example, if the goal of a project is to release software as soon as possible, you may need to remove some of the features from the original design to have the project finish on time. The removed features can then be released as a patch later in the product life cycle or moved to a consecutive phase of the product release.

Reviewing the Project-Level Statistics

As part of your schedule reality check, you can ignore the old Project Statistics window. It's still there, under Product Information in the File tab. However, the reports under the Report tab, like the Project Overview report and others, are far more useful and flexible:

1. Select the Report tab.

2. Under the Dashboard item, select Project Overview.

3. Alternately, select any report under the In Progress menu.

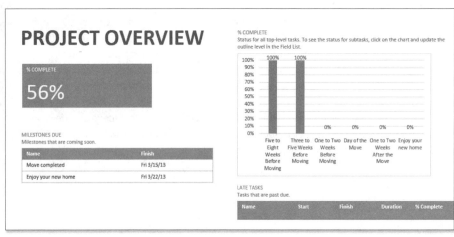

Figure 12.3
Use the new reports to review high-level summary information about your project.

Methods of Examining Your Schedule

Take advantage of the tools included in Project to help you examine various aspects of your project. You can use groups, filters, and views to review the parts of your project, as follows:

- **Groups**—A useful feature for organizing items in your schedule based on predefined criteria. To apply groups, select the View tab, Group By.

- **Filters**—Enables you to limit what information is displayed in the current view based on the criteria you select. To view all available filters for the selected view, select the View tab, Filter, More Filters.

- **Views**—Collections of data that are used to present a certain type of information in a particular way. In addition to the Gantt Chart view, the Resource Usage, Task Usage, and Team Planner views are useful views for analyzing and finding potential problems with your schedule.

- Task Usage view shows you each task you have entered into the schedule, with resource assignment information grouped directly under each task. Although not recommended, you can review the assignments, when they are scheduled for work, and, if necessary, edit the time-phased resource work data cells. After you edit the work, you may restrict Project's capability of leveling and moving the resource assignment work.

- Resource Usage view displays a resource's scheduled work for your project. This can be useful to get an overall picture of which tasks are assigned to each resource, as they are grouped by resource name. This can be an easy way to determine which tasks have no resources assigned to them. In addition, this view is helpful in reviewing the resource allocations where overloaded resources are highlighted in the color red. You might want to change the timescale to view the allocation on a week-by-week or month-by-month view. To do so, use Format, Timescale to change the formatting settings for the timescale or use the Zoom buttons on the Standard toolbar.

- The Team Planner view can be extremely useful for finding potential problems. You can think of it as a kind of alternate or enhanced Resource Usage view. Unassigned tasks are shown graphically in the lower pane. Unscheduled tasks—a feature of the Manually Scheduled task mode—are listed in the left pane. Overallocations "pile up" graphically in the top-right pane and are highlighted in red. As with the Resource usage view, it is possible to change the timescale or use the zoom controls.

> For additional information about using groups, filters, and views to review your schedule, **see** Chapter 11, "Using Standard Views, Tables, Filters, and Groups to Review Your Schedule," **p. 357**.

Strategies for Analyzing Costs

In addition to schedule and resources, cost plays a significant role in each project. Often when reviewing your final project schedule, it is important to review the project costs and attempt to reduce them as much as possible. Reducing costs can provide you with more leverage during the project execution because if your original estimate is lower than the capital budget you have for the project, you can use the difference to correct problems that arise throughout execution.

Budget resources enable you to add another resource to the project summary-level task, also known as task number zero, within your project to capture the capital budget. You can use it to compare your baseline and actual total project budget to.

> For additional information about budget resources, **see** Chapter 8, "Defining Project Resources," **p. 235**.

You can use the following two techniques to reduce the cost in your project schedule:

- Reduce resource costs.

- Decrease project scope.

Reviewing the Cost Table

Project provides many different ways to review your project costs. One of the ways is to display the Resource Sheet view (select the View tab, Resource Sheet) and apply the Cost table (select the View tab, Tables, Cost). This view displays all resources in your project and their costs. To make this view even more useful, you can use sorting, filtering, and grouping to help you identify various cost categories.

For example, you can group your resources by type and then sort the list in descending order, so that the most expensive resources in each category are displayed at the top of the list. To do so, follow these steps:

1. Select the View tab, Group By, Resource Type.

2. Select the View tab, Sort, By Cost. This sorts the list of resources in descending order, with the most expensive resource at the top, as shown in Figure 12.4.

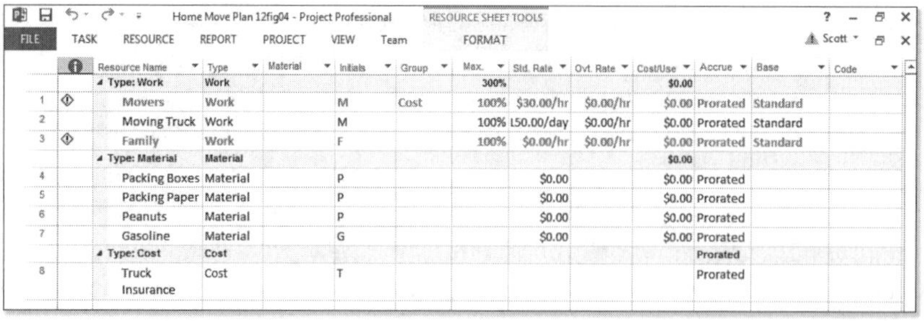

Figure 12.4
Use the Resource Sheet Cost table, grouped by resource type and sorted by cost, to review your most expensive resources in each resource category.

➡️ *For additional information about using groups, filters, and views to review your project costs,* **see** *Chapter 11, "Using Standard Views, Tables, Filters, and Groups to Review Your Schedule," **p. 424**.*

Reducing the Cost of Work

One way to reduce the cost of your project is reduce the cost of work. This can be accomplished by using less-expensive resources, for example. Here are some points to keep in mind:

■ If you have contractors assigned to perform some of the tasks in your project, you can replace them with employees, which are generally cheaper to use. If you decide to do this, ensure that internal resources are available for work and that you will not cause any resource overallocations.

■ If you have material resources in your project, you can try to find a better deal or a cheaper source for purchasing them. Similarly, you can shop around for a better deal on the cost of services as well. Maybe it is cheaper to rent equipment instead of buying it. Look for alternatives to reduce the cost of these resource types and take into account special promotions and so on.

Finalizing the Schedule

After you have reviewed your schedule yourself, but before you are ready to baseline it and move into execution, it is important that you perform several last steps in the project management process. Here are some things you should do before baselining your schedule:

■ **Get feedback from other people**—After performing all the schedule checks yourself, it is always a good idea to get someone else to review the schedule as well. You might be so intimately familiar with the project by the time you review it that it is possible that you will not notice some mistakes you made.

■ **Receive stakeholder approval**—Even if you have not made any drastic changes to the project schedule, it is always important to ensure that your project stakeholders approve the

> **tip**
> As a best practice, always have a "second pair of eyes." Use reports to gather feedback and not views unless you are working with a skilled Project user.

current plan. The best way to get approval is to hold a review session with project stakeholders prior to the project kickoff. During this session, you can discuss the changes and tradeoffs you made, bring up any outstanding issues with the contract, and discuss project risks.

- **Receive project team and organization buy-in**—After you receive your stakeholders' approval to go ahead with the project, it is important that you meet with the parties involved in the project from your organization. This includes not only your project team, but also resource managers and other people who can have potential influence or impact on your project.

- **Secure the resources**—Ensure that the resources you scheduled to work on your project are available and there is no resource overallocation.

- **Prepare for the kickoff**—After you have gotten approval from project stakeholders and sponsors and have received buy-in from the project team and your organization, you should prepare to hold a kickoff meeting, in which you bring together everyone who will be participating in the project execution. It is important that you discuss the scope of the project, highlight major deliverables and their deadlines, discuss major project milestones, and review the consequences of those milestones not being met. In addition, you should set forth the expectations of each project participant, so that everyone is aware of his or her responsibilities.

Baselining the Schedule

One of the last steps in preparing your project for execution is baselining it. A baseline represents a snapshot of all the planned data as it was outlined within the contract and approved by project stakeholders. Project includes 11 baselines you can use to track authorized changes made to the project planned data. In addition, the baseline plays an important role in the tracking and analysis of your project schedule. Project uses the baseline values to derive variances in cost and schedule while comparing them to the actual data you record.

A baseline, according to the PMI's *PMBOK Guide*, is defined as "the original plan, plus or minus approved changes."

➡ *For more on PMI and the PMBOK Guide,* **see** *the "Exploring Project Management Industry Standards" section on* **p. 58** *of Chapter 3.*

Baselining copies several key data types in your schedule and saves them for future reference and analysis. These data types include all tasks, start and finish dates, durations, costs, assigned work, budget cost, budget work, fixed cost, accrued cost, deliverable start, and deliverable finish.

Saving Your Project Baseline

You can set the project baseline by performing the following steps:

1. Open the Set Baseline dialog box by selecting the Project tab, Schedule, Set Baseline, Set Baseline.

2. In the Set Baseline dialog box, you can select to either save the entire project baseline or save the interim plan. Select the appropriate options and click OK, as shown in Figure 12.5.

Figure 12.5
Use the Set Baseline dialog box to select the baselining options for your project and to set the baseline.

---

 note

Although Project records task splits, there is no explicit data field to show the split conditions. However, you can view these task splits in addition to the milestones and tasks that the baseline records using the Gantt Chart. In addition, task splits appear as time periods with zero hours of work in the time-phased data of the Usage views. The overall task duration shows the accumulated working periods disregarding the split sections.

When Project records a baseline, it saves the current schedule for all tasks, plus the start and finish date, duration, costs, assigned work, budget cost, budget work, fixed cost, accrued cost, deliverable start, and deliverable finish.

> *For additional information about the new baseline fields in Project,* **see** *Chapter 13, "Tracking Your Project Progress," **p. 431**.*

You can save up to 11 different baselines. The first time you save a baseline, Project records it in the default baseline, named Baseline. If you create additional baselines after that, Project names them Baseline 1, Baseline 2, and so on. Project records the same fields for each baseline, so that you can compare them later. You can use additional baselines to track additional authorized changes to the project after the execution has started. Often the changes reflected in the following baselines reflect change requests that are amendments to the original contract. This enables you to keep track of all changes, including the original plan that your project goes through.

The process of revising your project schedule is known as *rebaselining*. If you do rebaseline, you should save the current baseline to one of the other available baselines and then set the new current baseline from your project schedule. To do so, select Tools, Tracking, Set Baseline, which opens the Set Baseline dialog box. The Set Baseline dialog box provides four different options, as follows:

- **Set Baseline**—This is the default selection when you open the Set Baseline dialog box. It saves the date from the current schedule into the baseline default setting. You can, however, select the down arrow to choose another baseline to save to.

- **Set Interim Plan**—This option is used for copying data from one version to another. For example, if you wanted to save the current default baseline to Baseline 1, you could select Baseline in the Copy text box and Baseline 1 in the Into text box.

- **For**—This option enables you to choose whether the baseline you are saving is for the entire project or for selected tasks only.

- **Roll Up Baselines**—This option is available only when you choose the For Selected Tasks option. When a baseline is saved, Project, by default, does not update that baseline for a summary task when a subtask is added, deleted, or modified. The two options under Roll Up Baselines enable you to choose to roll up the baseline changes for subtasks into their parent summary tasks. Select the To All Summary Tasks option, which includes the rebaselined subtask.

If you want to update only the selected summary tasks, choose those summary tasks along with the subtask(s) that you want to rebaseline (use Ctrl+click to add more than one subtask). Then choose From Subtasks into Selected Summary Task(s). You can click the Set as Default button to make your selection the default for either or both of these options on all new projects.

> **caution**
> The Multiple Undo feature of Project enables you to undo the setting of a baseline. However, be cautious because some actions in Project, such as a Save operation, will clear the Undo list, after which you will no longer be able to undo the changes you have made.

The already-used baselines have the "last saved" date next to the baseline version name. If you attempt to save your current baseline to the already-used baseline version, Project displays an overwrite warning message, as shown in Figure 12.6. If you are still in the process of making changes to the original project schedule plan, you can safely overwrite the baseline. However, if you are executing the project, it is recommended that you save your data to the next available baseline version.

It is a project management best practice to save the baseline after the project has been approved and before it has started execution. Also, the original approved baseline should always remain unchanged.

Figure 12.6
Be careful when overwriting an already existing baseline. If you are sure that you want to overwrite the previously saved baseline, select Yes in the warning box shown here.

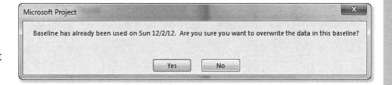

Consultants' Tips

Are You a Pessimistic or an Optimistic Estimator?

Most people tend to either be pessimistic or optimistic in their work estimates, and this is an important factor to recognize and take into account when planning a project. It is imperative not only for the estimates you create yourself, but also for the estimates your team provides to you. After you learn the nature of your team (or your own nature), future estimating will become a better predictor of reality, making your work and duration estimates more viable.

One way to determine the nature of your team is by figuring out the "reality ratio." The reality ratio shows you how much off someone's original estimate was from the actual execution, and you can calculate it from past projects. For example, you have a resource who estimates that it will take 30 hours to complete a certain type of task.

After the project is completed, the actual work for that task is 45 hours, which means that the original estimate the resource gave you was optimistic. The reality ratio in this case is 1.5 (that is, 45 / 30 = 1.5). The next time, the same resource gives you an estimate for the same type of task or project, you can use the reality ratio to adjust that estimate, which will make the estimate more realistic and thus reduce the number of estimation errors in your schedule.

If you do feel that you need to adjust a resource's original estimate, make sure to discuss the changes you want to make with the resource and ensure that you are both in agreement with the change.

Schedule Problems Checklist

Table 12.1 provides some high-level questions that you need to answer as part of the schedule reality check process. This ensures that your schedule does not contain any obvious mistakes and that you are ready to move into the Execution and Control phases.

Table 12.1 Schedule Problems Checklist

Question	Explanation/Example
Tasks	
Do the tasks in your project schedule accomplish all of the work you defined in your WBS and encompass the entire scope of your project?	Your organization should have a method to capture the business objectives with project scope and budget statements. A business plan is an example that can be used to determine whether the schedule tasks perform all of the required scope.
Are all tasks in your project of appropriate size?	Are you required to follow project management best practices or other established standards for the length of tasks. For example, your tasks may be no less than a week in hours of duration and no larger than two weeks.

Question	Explanation/Example
Do any tasks have fixed costs associated with them?	Some tasks may also have accrual at the beginning or end of the task activity.
Do tasks in your schedule have constraints? Are those constraint dates set in the future?	You may want to consider creating special milestones that precede a series of work activities. Use these milestones to set constraints such as Start No Earlier Than.
Does your schedule contain any auto-scheduled "dangling" tasks?	Dangling tasks are tasks that have no successors/predecessors and, therefore, are not connected with the rest of your project schedule.
Are the task-naming conventions consistent and do they meet your project requirements (if there were any)?	Task names should reflect a deliverable item that can be clearly measured. A task name like "Research" is ambiguous and cannot be clearly measured. Using a task name like "Write Research Report" enables you to clearly measure success regarding the completion of the task.
Resources	
Does your resource pool contain duplicate Resource Name entries?	For example, "Mary Smith" and "M Smith" might actually refer to the exact same person, but Project does not "know" this distinction.
Have you replaced all generic resources with actual resource names?	Project schedule templates often have generic resources on task assignments. Make sure you substitute the generic resources for named resources before you begin tracking schedule progress.
Do all of your resources have cost information associated with them?	Check your organization's policies before assigning cost data to resources. Some organizations forbid the use of detailed resource costs.
Are any of your resources overallocated?	Always determine whether resources are overloaded. If you ignore overload conditions, you dramatically increase your risk of project failure.
Which of your resources are scheduled for overtime, and was this intentional?	Analyze the workload conditions to ensure that you have not accidentally overlooked overtime situations.
Schedule	
Are all of the tasks in your schedule baselined?	You need some basis of comparison when you execute the schedule details. Baselines are a convenient way to compare performance to the original plan.

Question	Explanation/Example
Does your project include correct and necessary milestones?	Use milestones as success markers within the life cycle phases of the project.
Does your schedule reflect the latest scope information?	Check the business plan and change control logs to make sure the schedule reflects the full scope.
Calendar	
Does your project calendar include the accepted holiday information?	In addition to standard accepted holidays, also check for special "all company" events that should be included within the calendars.
Do your resource calendars correctly reflect the vacations and other non-working days for your project resources?	You need a general policy for maintaining resource calendars to reflect varying conditions throughout the the year.
Does your calendar include the correct working day length throughout?	You may also decide to use part-time, 24-hour, or other calendar variations as needed to reflect resources or project working conditions.

Avoiding the "While You Are Here" Syndrome

When creating your project schedule, avoid the "while you are here" syndrome—that is, do not add extra task activities that do not contribute to the measure of success of your project. The project manager must constantly monitor approved project scope and avoid unintentional scope creep by adding new tasks, even though those activities seem to be a logical progression of work. This syndrome is a common project manager trap that is responsible for many projects finishing over budget and behind schedule.

Deleting Baselined Tasks

Even baselined tasks can be deleted. In a sense, the baselined task still exists in the baseline record, but its loss can only be inferred—there is no "baseline view" that shows only the baselined data. This can be troublesome if the baseline is being used for audit purposes. In cases where the project schedule needs to have an auditable baseline, consider creating a baseline copy of the Project file and *compare projects* instead of trying to make the baseline functionality serve this purpose.

13

TRACKING YOUR PROJECT PROGRESS

You have probably created a project schedule, assigned resources to tasks, captured baseline information, and then convinced yourself the schedule is ready to move into the execution life cycle phase. Now you want to track progress and compare project performance to your original plans. This chapter helps you do the following:

- Understand how to interpret progress compared to baseline data.

- Use Project functions to enter actual progress.

- Understand how key Project calculations work within the tool.

Overview of Tracking

So you are finished creating your schedule. You have entered all the resources, assignments, and tasks; set the predecessors and successors; made sure that everything was correct; and set the initial baseline. You are ready to start using your project schedule, so now what? Although this is a common stopping place for many project managers, it is not using Project to its fullest potential. It would be like making a big print out of the schedule, hanging it up on the wall for everyone to admire, and assuming that everything goes just as you planned. You made a perfect plan, so everything should work perfectly, right?

*For more information on how to set the initial baseline, **see** the "Baselining the Schedule" section of Chapter 12, **p. 425**.*

This chapter explores how to use Project to track the progress of your schedule against the baseline and also spot scheduling issues if conditions deviate from your original plan. Your ability to identify and address problems early on will keep your project on track. There are several ways that Project helps you to manage your project:

 note

This chapter assumes tasks are in Auto Scheduled mode. For tasks in Manually Scheduled mode, the Project scheduling engine still makes the calculations described here, but they are not displayed in the schedule.

- You can open a view with your initial baseline to review the values that have been set. Remember, a baseline is a record of the project that you can use for comparison later on. The intent of a baseline is to establish a framework to measure schedule variance as you move through project life cycles. You can use various features to clearly see how variations from your original plan might create high-risk conditions to the overall success of the project.

- You can use several data-editing methods to enter and record information of what has actually happened during the execution phase of the project. This is called *tracking* in Project.

- As you enter tracking information, Project replaces scheduled items, such as start and finish dates or costs, with the actual dates or costs. It also recalculates entries such as task or assignment duration and adjusts resource workload.

- Finally, Project helps you snapshot incremental progress conditions to help you analyze overall performance during interim life cycles or at the end of the project. This type of analysis can help you, and your organization, better understand how well you perform when compared to initial project scope and estimates.

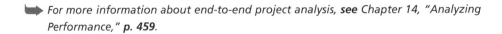

➡ *For more information about end-to-end project analysis,* **see** *Chapter 14, "Analyzing Performance,"* **p. 459.**

Working with Project Baselines

The key thing to remember when preparing to baseline your project is that neither the project nor the baseline is sacred. As much as you might like to think that your project is perfect, conditions will change—usually things outside your control. It is because of these changes that you need to baseline; using the baseline helps you to track these changes. Although you should always make sure to keep a copy of your original baseline, as you make changes to the project, you can use one of the additional 10 baselines to keep track of the changes.

According to PMI's *PMBOK Guide*, a baseline is defined as "the original plan, plus or minus approved changes." Setting a baseline enables you to use variance and earned value analysis to later understand how the work is performed and whether the project is proceeding according to plan.

➡ *For more information on the PMI and the PMBOK Guide,* **see** *the "Exploring Project Management Industry Standards" section on* **p. 58** *in Chapter 3.*

For additional information on saving your baseline, **see** Chapter 12, "Performing a Schedule Reality Check," **p. 411**.

Viewing Baselines

Project provides several methods to view baseline and tracking data. Each task and resources assignment contains many types of information such as task name, duration, work, cost, start and finish dates, and so forth. When you select the Project tab, Schedule, Set Baseline, Project copies key parts of the task and assignment data into special baseline fields.

Project has several predefined combinations of view, table, groups, and filter settings to let you review task and assignment baseline data. You can also create and store your own combinations of views and tables that show you information in a familiar format. For instance, you can do the following:

- Use the default views and tables to see baseline columns with additional columns you need.

- Activate filters and groups to show important baseline and tracking data based on task completion status, assigned resources, and so forth.

Consider using the following helpful viewing combinations to review baseline and tracking information:

- View the default Tracking Gantt with the Baseline table to see baseline columns with Gantt bar overlay showing plan versus baseline duration.

- View the Detailed Gantt with Delay table to see task slippage and free slack.

- View the Multiple Baseline Gantt if you are comparing several baselines side-by-side.

- View the default Tracking Gantt with the Variance table to show differences between the baseline and your current progress conditions.

- View the default Tracking Gantt with the Tracking table to see the data field where you can enter progress information, such as actual start, % Complete, actual work, and so forth.

- Select the View tab and then Group by Complete and Incomplete Tasks.

Figure 13.1 illustrates the combination of Tracking Gantt with the Baseline table. You can add your own data columns, such as work, % Complete, physical % complete, and so forth to suit your needs. Notice how any task that does not have baseline data will show "NA" in the data field and also show missing bars within the Tracking Gantt view. Also notice how the baseline Gantt bars might be shifted to the past or future, compared to the current task start and finish dates.

 tip

Remember that your current view of your project's schedule data can be modified in a variety of ways, including the More Views selection underneath the Gantt Chart or Task Usage controls or the Filter, Group By, and Tables controls on the View tab. These tricks enable you to organize information and also see settings or options that might be hidden.

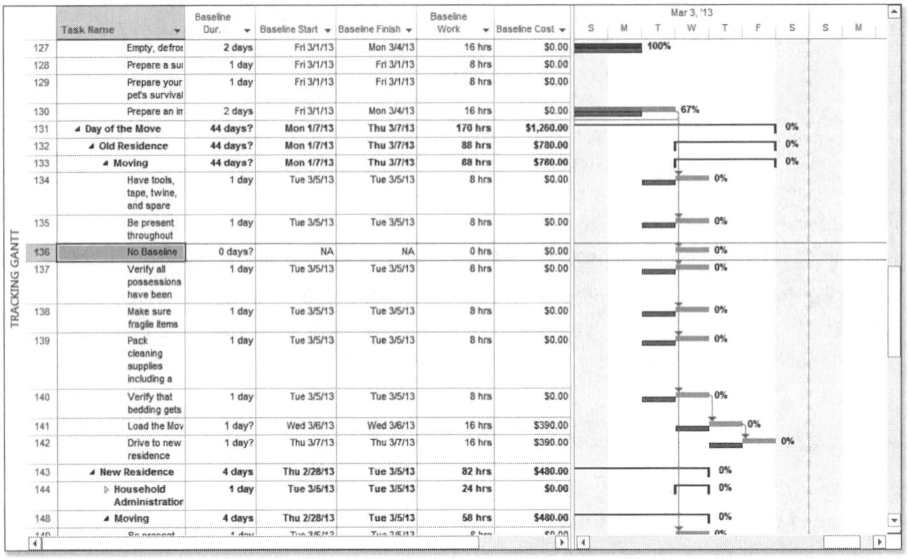

Figure 13.1
Use View and Table combinations to see baseline data.

Using Usage Views to Show Time-Phased Details

Project has powerful viewing and editing functions that are enabled when you decide to use special display formats called Usage views. You can access Usage views in many ways through the Ribbon, but they are always under the View controls in the View groups on the Task, Resource, and View tabs. There are three major view types that show time-phased, sometimes also known as time-scaled, data details of resource assignments. You should become thoroughly familiar with the Usage views so that you can take advantage of several powerful features to view and edit data.

The Task Usage view displays tasks with each resource assigned within individual rows below the task. The Resource Usage view simply inverts the data, showing resources with a list of task assignments for each resource.

> As detailed in Chapter 11, "Using Standard Views, Tables, Filters, and Groups to Review Your Schedule," the Team Planner provides similar functionality, but does it graphically, **p. 373**.

You can arrange the left half of a Usage view to show numerous data columns based on the table that you select, or you can insert any combination of task and assignment columns you need. The right half of the screen shows a detailed breakdown of the assignment data, such as Work, Cost, Baseline Work, and so on. Figure 13.2 shows a typical layout of a Task Usage view with the Baseline Table showing the columns on the left side and time-phased details on the right.

Figure 13.2
The Usage
views show
time-phased
details.

	Task Name	Act. Start	Act. Finish	% Comp.	Phys. % Comp.	Act. Dur.	Rem. Dur.	Details		Feb 17, '13			Mar 24, '13	
									M	T	W	T	F	
133	◢ Moving	NA	NA	0%	0%	0 days	3 days?	Work				80h		
								Cost				$780.00		
134	▷ Have tools,	NA	NA	0%	0%	0 days	1 day	Work				8h		
								Cost				$0.00		
135	▷ Be pres-	NA	NA	0%	0%	0 days	1 day	Work				8h		
								Cost				$0.00		
136	▷ Verify all	NA	NA	0%	0%	0 days	1 day	Work				8h		
								Cost				$0.00		
137	▷ Make su	NA	NA	0%	0%	0 days	1 day	Work				8h		
								Cost				$0.00		
138	◢ Pack cle	NA	NA	0%	0%	0 days	1 day	Work				8h		
								Cost				$0.00		
	Far	NA	NA					Work				8h		
								Cost				$0.00		
139	◢ Verify th	NA	NA	0%	0%	0 days	1 day	Work				8h		
								Cost				$0.00		
	Far	NA	NA					Work				8h		
								Cost				$0.00		
140	◢ Load the	NA	NA	0%	0%	0 days	1 day?	Work				16h		
								Cost				$390.00		
	Mo	NA	NA					Work				8h		
								Cost				$240.00		
	Mo	NA	NA					Work				8h		
								Cost				$150.00		
141	◢ Drive to	NA	NA	0%	0%	0 days	1 day?	Work				16h		
								Cost				$390.00		
	Mo	NA	NA					Work				8h		
								Cost				$240.00		
	Mo	NA	NA					Work				8h		
								Cost				$150.00		
	Ga	NA	NA					Work				10		
								Cost				$0.00		

TASK USAGE

You can see tasks with assigned resources listed below each task as you inspect the left side of the screen. Each task and resource assignment row on the left side of the screen can have one or more time-phased detailed row on the right side of the display. You can right-click within the right-side data display to show more rows, and also include other hidden rows if you select the Detail Styles menu item.

 tip

You can right-click the calendar header of a Usage view to adjust the display characteristics, such as zoom factor and timescale column headers.

The time-phased data rows on the right side of the Usage view display show the internal details for each task and resource assignment. You can zoom into a level of detail that shows date and time information to 15-minute increments for each hour in each day. You can also zoom out to show data in a year-by-year rollup.

You can directly edit many time-phased data fields on the right side of the Usage view. Those fields are usually displayed with a white background. The numbers you enter are internally distributed between the task start and finish period for the selected cell according to factors such as task and resource calendars. Therefore, you need to be cautious when directly editing data in the time-phased fields.

You should also be aware that most time-phased data fields immediately roll up to the associated tasks or summary task items and might also change the column data on the left side of the Usage view. However, some time-phased fields do not immediately roll up as you alter the time-phased data. Baseline data fields are an example of data that does not immediately roll up when you change the time-phased data.

Time-phased baseline data is copied from planning data fields when you set the baseline using the Set Baseline control on the Project tab. Taking a baseline essentially performs a general copy and paste operation from planning data into the time-phased baseline rows.

Some time-phased data fields, such as Cost, might be derived or calculated from other conditions such as individual resource settings. You cannot directly edit the derived fields in the time-phased fields, even though the data cells might have a white background. Those data fields are calculated by factors such as resource cost per hour, or cost per use settings.

You also need to be careful when editing Task Usage time-phased data within the task rows, generally shown with a yellow background. You can directly edit some of those time-phased data fields, such as Work. Data you enter within a task row cell will be distributed, also called rolled down, to the resources assignments for that task. This type of edit can also transfer directly to the data columns on the left side of the display.

 note

Create some simple schedule examples with resource assignments that you can use to experiment with Task and Resource Usage views. Watch how edits made in the left side of the display propagate to the right side time-phased data and vice versa. Then watch what happens to time-phased data when you perform functions such as setting a baseline.

➡ *For additional information about using groups, filters, and views to review your schedule, **see** Chapter 11, "Using Standard Views, Tables, Filters, and Groups to Review Your Schedule," **p. 357**.*

Tracking Your Project's Performance and Costs

The key to tracking progress of your project is the feedback that you get from your resources about their progress and then entering that information into your project. If you are using Microsoft Project Server, you can set up Project to automatically request progress updates from the team. Employees and other resources receive a timesheet-style form to fill out and submit; then after review, you can update your project automatically.

 note

In theory, having resources enter task status directly in to the project schedule through Project Server is a great, work-saving idea. In practice, as the project manager, you should expect a *steep* learning curve and a lot of additional work in the short run.

Understanding Fields Used in Updating the Project Schedule

As you begin building your schedule, you enter information into the appropriate fields: Actual Start Date, Actual Finish Date, Actual Task Duration, % Complete, % Work Complete, and so forth. Plus, as you include resources, Project calculates amounts of work, overtime work, and cost for these resources. Project recalculates your resource workload as you work with and change task conditions such as the starting date or duration during the planning phase. You can plan that you are going to start on a specific date, that it is going to take a specific amount of time, and that you will be finished on that date, but this is just guesswork until the tasks within the project are completed.

Tracking is entering your results into the "Actual" assignment fields, such as Actual Start, Actual Finish, Actual Work, and Actual Cost. The various task and assignment data fields are interrelated, so you need to understand those relationships before you enter tracking data.

The term "tracking" is what happens as you manually enter task and assignment actual data or if you use the Project Update control on the Project tab. For example, when you enter the Actual Start date, Project replaces the planned start with your new entry. This might now affect successor tasks, if you start early or late, and Project calculates the changes your actual start date makes to the schedule.

Two things happen in Project when you enter an actual start date:

- The entry you made in the Actual Start field is copied into the (scheduled) Start field, and Project recalculates the schedule for any successor tasks. Any other dates that are affected are highlighted with the change highlighting color control within the menu sequence Format, Text Styles, Changed Cells Background Color. This helps you to see whether you need to make any changes down the road to the schedule, based on your early or late start.

- Project sets the Start field as fixed, meaning that it cannot be recalculated. So after you enter the Actual Start date, Microsoft Project will not change the value. However, you can manually edit that date if conditions require a change.

The same type of reaction occurs when you enter an Actual Finish date, except that Project also marks the % Complete schedule field as 100% complete for the affected tasks. You should be aware that Project also updates other fields, such as Actual Duration, Actual Work, and so forth when you enter the Actual Finish date. Now your baseline is the only record of your originally scheduled project, so you can compare actual data to baseline data variances to see what went right and what did not.

There are several different ways of entering the actual values into your project. The following methods are listed in order from least exact to most precise, assuming that all data provided is valid. The method you choose depends on your need for precision and the expectations for reporting and lessons learned analysis:

- Update the % Complete task field to a fraction between zero and 100% without worrying about any of the actual schedule dates, work, cost, and so forth. Although this is the fastest technique to update tasks, it is also the least accurate because this method assumes actual task activities occurred exactly as planned. This method gives you no information about how well you estimated or any information for future comparisons.

- Record when a task is started and finished, but do not include how much actual work or actual cost was involved. Microsoft Project assumes the work, cost, and other planned data occurred as originally planned when you enter actual date information. This will at least give you some idea for planning completion dates in the future.

- Record when a task starts, and then periodically enter estimates, such as Remaining Work and Remaining Duration, when you enter % Complete. This helps you spot tasks that are not making headway as planned and helps you make adjustments to get things back on track.

- Ask resources how much actual work they did during each time period and enter it. This method allows the most information about progress and performance, but also takes up the most time because the data must be entered manually.

- Use Project Server to request timesheet reports, and then have Project Professional automatically update the fields from the data submitted. This takes much less time and is the one of the best ways to track your schedule progress.

 tip

Project uses the term % Complete to mean the percentage complete along the start through finish time-line—that is, duration. You should use the phrase "% Duration Complete" whenever you consider the meaning of the % Complete field.

You might also want to search the Internet for timesheet entry tools that enable your team members to provide actual work information. Some tools enable the project manager to post actual work, cost, and so on into task data fields. Microsoft Project Server provides robust schedule tracking and reporting functionality.

If the task is in Auto Scheduled mode, the scheduling engine makes changes automatically. It is important that you understand the potential impact of the method you choose for project status updates. Which method you choose depends on how precisely you need to track progress and how much time you can spend tracking your progress. You need to understand how the various fields interact so you should experiment with various methods and techniques before establishing a general schedule updating policy within your organization. You learn more about these data fields in the following sections.

Entering Tracking Information at the Task Level

This section covers how to use tracking fields at the task level to update task status. This is how you would manually enter progress, if you choose to use this method.

This section looks at the following task-tracking fields:

- Actual Start

- Actual Finish

- % Complete

- Actual Duration

- Remaining Duration

- Actual Work

- % Work Complete

- Remaining Work

- Time-Phased Work

You can view and edit most of these fields on the task by using the Gantt Chart view with the Tracking table columns showing (see Figure 13.3). To display the Tracking table in a task view, select the View tab, Tables, Tracking. To display the Work table in a task view, select the View tab, Tables, Work. You can edit the % Work Complete and Remaining Work fields, and you can enter time-phased work in the time-phased grid on the Task Usage view.

 See the "Using Microsoft Project's Facilities for Updating Tasks" section later in this chapter on **p. 455** to find out how to open forms that make these fields available.

🔍 **note**

Keep in mind that Project's Auto Scheduled mode employs different calculations for the "work" fields and the "% Complete" fields. By default, the %Work Complete for resource assignments and % Complete task fields are coupled such that an edit to either field updates the other field. You can decouple these two fields by selecting the File tab, Options, Schedule, and then clearing the Updating Tasks Status Updates Resource Status check box. This means that it is possible to complete 100% of the work on a task and yet the % Complete for the duration field is not at 100%, but you then must manage each field individually for every task in the schedule.

Figure 13.3
The task Tracking table gives you access to many of the fields needed for tracking progress at the task level.

	Task Name	Act. Start	Act. Finish	% Comp.	Phys. % Comp.	Act. Dur.	Rem. Dur.	Act. Cost				Mar 3, '13					
0	◢ Project 13fig03	Mon 1/7/13	NA	85%	0%	.56 days	.44 days?	$3,360.00									
1	▷ Five to Eight Weeks Before	Mon 1/7/13	Mon 1/28/13	100%	0%	16 days	0 days	$240.00									
41	▷ Three to Five Weeks Before	Thu 1/24/13	Fri 2/15/13	100%	0%	17 days	0 days?	$480.00									
79	▷ One to Two Weeks Before Moving	Mon 2/18/13	NA	98%	0%	11.79 days	0.21 days	$2,640.00				98%					
131	◢ Day of the Move	NA	NA	0%	0%	0 days	7 days?	$0.00							0%		
132	◢ Old Residenc	NA	NA	0%	0%	0 days	3 days?	$0.00							0%		
133	◢ Moving	NA	NA	0%	0%	0 days	3 days?	$0.00							0%		
134	Have tools, tape,	NA	NA	0%	0%	0 days	1 day	$0.00				0%					
135	Be present	NA	NA	0%	0%	0 days	1 day	$0.00				0%					
136	Verify all possess	NA	NA	0%	0%	0 days	1 day	$0.00				0%					
137	Make sure	NA	NA	0%	0%	0 days	1 day	$0.00				0%					
138	Pack cleaning supplies including	NA	NA	0%	0%	0 days	1 day	$0.00				0%					
139	Verify that	NA	NA	0%	0%	0 days	1 day	$0.00				0%					
140	Load the	NA	NA	0%	0%	0 days	1 day?	$0.00					0%				
141	Drive to new	NA	NA	0%	0%	0 days	1 day?	$0.00					0%				
142	◢ New Residen	NA	NA	0%	0%	0 days	5 days	$0.00						0%			
143	▷ Household Administr	NA	NA	0%	0%	0 days	1 day	$0.00						0%			

TRACKING GANTT

---

 note

The Task Type conditions you select from the Task Information settings can affect all the tracking fields. Fixed Work, Fixed Duration, and Fixed Units tasks behave differently to data edit changes, so make sure you consider the task type settings as you update tracking data.

Editing the Task Actual Start Date

Project uses "NA" for the Actual Start date field value until you enter an Actual Start date or modify the % Complete field. Then, the date you enter or the planned start date replaces the NA. Moreover, the *planned* (not actual) finish date will shift using the planned duration to account for any difference between actual start and what was the planned start. Finally, any resource assignments to tasks with the same scheduled Start date as the task will be assigned the Actual Start date of that task. Project then recalculates all assignments to that task and might also impact successor tasks and assignments.

 tip

Make sure you enter the Actual Start date if the task does not begin on the scheduled Start date, before editing any of the other fields used for tracking progress. You might see unexpected results if you edit another field prior to entering the Actual Start date.

However, if the Actual Start date contains "NA" and you edit certain fields, such as % Complete, Actual Work, and so on, Project will presume that the original planned Start date should be used as the Actual Start date.

Editing the Task Actual Finish Date

Just like the Actual Start date, the Actual Finish date contains "NA" in the entry until you edit information, indicating the task is complete. If you do not provide an explicit Finish Date, presume the task is finished just as scheduled. If you enter an Actual Finish date, on the other hand, several data conditions might change on your schedule:

- Project replaces the scheduled Finish date with the Actual Finish date.

- If you have not indicated the task has started, all progress fields that still show NA will be replaced with the scheduled entry and the task will be marked as 100% complete. Be careful if you enter an Actual Finish date that is later than the scheduled Finish date. In this case, Project increases the values in various data fields, such as task duration, costs, work, and other entries therein.

- Based on the Actual Start and Actual Finish dates, Project calculates the Actual Duration and changes the scheduled Duration to the same value, and then changes the Remaining Duration to zero.

- Both % Complete and % Work Complete will be changed to 100% for the task and all assignments.

- The Actual Work and Actual Cost values for the task and assignments will be calculated, whereas Remaining Work and Remaining Cost will be set to zero.

- If the tasks were on the critical path, they will be changed to noncritical, and preceding linked tasks might also be set to noncritical.

In summary, if you enter an Actual Finish date, Project assumes you are finished with the task and calculates all the unspecified actual values for tasks and assignments. You should experiment with examples so you can learn how Project behaves in different situations.

Editing Task % Complete (Percentage Complete)

You can edit the task % Complete field to indicate that a task has started or finished, so you need to become familiar with the behavior of Project when you perform edits. Whenever you see the % Complete field, you should always mentally replace that name with the phrase "%Duration Complete," so that you recognize the meaning of this field. Therefore, task % Complete provides a method to track how much of the planned task duration, between the start and finish dates, has been finished.

Project assumes that the task % Complete is zero until a task update has been entered—for example, Actual Work, Actual Duration, and so on. % Complete is then calculated with the following general formulas and rules:

> % Complete = 100 × (Actual Duration / Duration) Duration = Actual Duration + Remaining Duration

You can either enter the percentage complete yourself or let Project handle the calculations by just entering the Actual Duration, the Remaining Duration, or any other field that calculates Actual Duration as greater than zero.

Several changes can occur when you edit the % Complete field:

- When the Actual Start field is still NA, Project replaces it with the scheduled Start date.

- An entry of 100% causes Project to use the scheduled Finish date to set the Actual Finish date.

- Actual Duration is set equal to % Complete × Duration, whereas Remaining Duration is set equal to Duration – Actual Duration.

- % Work Complete is set equal to 100 × Actual Work / Work when the default menu Tools, Options, Calculation tab, Task Status Updates Resource Status check box is selected.

- Actual Cost and Actual Work are set the same as the scheduled time-phased work and cost for the time period set by Actual Duration.

- Remaining Work is set equal to the Work – Actual Work.

Editing Task Actual Duration

This field enables you to display and enter the amount of task duration that has been used so far in the project. If you enter a value less than the total scheduled duration, Project presumes everything is on schedule and makes the following calculations:

- The Actual Start field will be replaced with the scheduled Start date if Actual Start field is still NA.

- Remaining Duration is replaced by Duration – Actual Duration, while % Complete is calculated as 100 × Actual Duration / Duration.

- Finally, Actual Cost and Actual Work are set the same as the scheduled time-phased work and cost scheduled for that duration.

If, on the other hand, you enter a value for Actual Duration that is longer than the scheduled Duration, Project presumes the task is finished and took longer than scheduled and calculates the following:

- % Complete is set to 100%, while Remaining Duration is set to 0.

- Actual Finish is changed to match the longer duration.

- The scheduled Duration and scheduled Finish are set to match the Actual Duration and new Actual Finish.

- If the task type has been set to Fixed Units or Fixed Duration, any assignment scheduled to end when the task ends has its Actual Finish changed to match the task Actual Finish field. The Actual Work, Work, Actual Cost, and Cost fields for the aforementioned assignments are increased by the same proportion as the duration has been changed.

- If the task type is Fixed Work, Actual Cost and Actual Work are then set to equal the scheduled Cost and Work. Any assignments scheduled to finish when the task finishes get the same Actual Finish as the task. The Actual Cost and Actual Work fields are changed to the same as their scheduled Cost and Work fields.

- Any assignments that were scheduled to finish before the task is finished are presumed to have finished on time, and their scheduled Cost and Work fields are copied into the Actual Cost and Actual Work fields.

Editing Task Remaining Duration

The Remaining Duration field is closely coupled with the task Duration and Finish date fields. If the Actual Start field contains NA, any editing done to the Remaining Duration field might have a direct effect on the other tracking fields. The task Finish date and Duration will change if you alter the Remaining Duration data before the Actual Start date has been declared. Furthermore, other calculated fields like Cost will be changed as the task duration is recomputed.

If the Actual Start field has an entry, and you alter the Remaining Duration, the following behavior occurs:

- A reduction in the Remaining Duration to a nonzero value results in a change to the task Duration and a recalculation of Finish date, Cost, Work, and so forth. If Remaining Duration is reduced to zero, Project changes the Actual Finish to the scheduled Start date, changes the task to 100% complete, sets the task Duration to zero, and recalculates other fields accordingly. This type of edit also marks the task as a milestone.

- An increase in value in Remaining Duration, after the task has started, means that Project presumes the scheduled Duration has increased and calculates new values for scheduled Cost, Finish, Work, Remaining Cost, Remaining Work, % Complete, and so forth.

Editing Task Actual Work

The task Actual Work field shows the amount of work that has been completed by the resource or resources assigned to the task. The field is zero until tracking begins. If you enter any amount in the task Actual Work field, this entry is distributed between the resources according to their individual calendars. If the Actual Start date has not been declared, the actual work data distribution begins on the planned start date for each resource.

For instance, Eric and Stacey are full-time workers and scheduled to start task work on the same day; their work is distributed as 30 hours and 10 hours, respectively. If you enter 20 hours in the task Actual Work field, Project records 10 hours of Actual Work for Eric and 10 hours of Actual Work for Stacey. Eric will have 20 hours of remaining work, whereas Stacey has zero remaining work. The task is not yet complete because Eric's work is not complete.

Just like when entering Actual Duration, if you enter a value greater than the scheduled Work value, Project assumes that the task is finished and recalculates data fields, such as Actual Start as scheduled (if it is NA), Actual Duration and Actual Finish commensurate with the added work, % Complete and % Work Complete are set to 100%, and Remaining Duration is set to zero.

> **note**
>
> The calendar conditions for the project, tasks, and resources can also affect the end result of Actual Work edits. Task Actual Work data are distributed differently when you have a mix of full-time and part-time resources. Make sure you experiment with variations so you can understand the tool behavior when you edit Actual Work.

Editing Task % Work Complete

When you edit the % Work Complete field when the Actual Start field is NA, Project presumes that the task has started and sets Actual Work as a result. Project then calculates Actual Work by multiplying % Work Complete by Work for the task. This assumes that the work scheduled was completed up through the amount of Actual Work, which determines Actual Duration. After that, % Complete is calculated by dividing Actual Duration by Duration. Actual Cost is then updated with the amount of cost scheduled for Actual Work.

Editing Task Remaining Work

You can use the Remaining Work field to indicate the amount of work to be completed in the future. If the Actual Start date is NA, your edits to Remaining Work do not affect any of the other tracking fields, but your edits can impact the task duration and finish date. Your edits also change conditions, such as scheduled Work, Cost, Duration, and so on.

For example, if you have a task that has started and accumulated an amount of Actual Work, Project automatically calculates the Remaining Work for the remaining duration of the task. If you decrease that Remaining Work value, you are indicating that there is less work to do to finish that task. Project might in turn recalculate conditions, such as % Work Complete, % Complete, Duration, Remaining Duration, Cost, and so on.

If you increase Remaining Work, however, it means that the total work requirements for the task have increased, and Project recalculates scheduled Work, Duration, Finish, % Complete, % Work Complete, Cost, Remaining Duration, and so forth.

Editing Task Time-Phased Actual Work

If you open the Task Usage view, you can edit Actual Work and Actual Overtime Work for the periods in which they were performed. If you want to look at the time-phased Actual Work field, right-click in the grid on the right and select Actual Work. To record Actual Overtime work, right-click again and choose Detail Styles. Double-click Actual Overtime Work in the list on the left to place it in the list on the right, and then click OK.

Every cell in the grid is a time period, and any edits to a cell are distributed between the beginning and ending dates for that cell. So, if the bottom tier in the timescale displays weeks, and you enter 8 hours in a week that contains a 1-day holiday, Project distributes 2 hours of work in each of the remaining 4 days of the week. If you want to place all 8 hours in 1 day, zoom in to display 1-day intervals in the timescale.

If the task Actual Start is NA, the Actual Start will be established on the date of the cell period where you enter Actual Work.

If the entered Actual Work is less than the scheduled Work for that cell, remaining work is rescheduled into the future, after the planned end date for the task, therefore extending the task duration. If Actual Work is greater than scheduled Work for that cell, the extra work is subtracted from the remaining cells in the task, and the duration shrinks.

 tip

If you skip any time-phased periods between your data edits for Actual Work, those periods get zero time-phased task Actual Work, and the zeros roll down to time-phased assignment Actual Work. Work scheduled for those zeroed days will be rescheduled at the end of the task, therefore extending the duration.

Entering Tracking Information at the Assignment Level

The preceding sections of this chapter help you better understand how Microsoft Project behaves when you enter tracking data for tasks. Those sections also help you understand some of the tracking conditions regarding resource assignments on tasks.

This section discusses how Project calculates task progress when you enter tracking data for individual resources assigned to tasks. You need to understand a distinction between task-level data fields compared to similar data fields for resource assignments on tasks, before you begin studying the following details.

You already know there are many task-level tracking fields with familiar names, such as Actual Work, Remaining Work, and so on. You will now learn that there are related tracking fields for each resource assigned to a task. The data details for these assignment-level fields are actually different, even though they are spelled the same. You will also notice that task-level and assignment-level data cells are strongly associated, so edits to a specific data cell might change the associated data.

You will use the Task Usage or Resource Usage views to see and edit assignment-level data fields. Remember, these usage views have two major sections: the left and right sides of the screen. The left side contains Table columns that are associated with the time-phased period cells on the right side of the screen. You can use mouse right-click actions to add columns as desired on the left side and also add rows on the right side.

 tip

This might seem confusing at first, but there is an easy way to remember the distinction: Any view showing a task row contains task-level tracking data cells, whereas resource rows contain data cells directly related to the specific resource. This is specifically true when you open a Usage view. Refer to Figure 13.2 for an illustration of a Usage view.

Editing Assignment Actual Start

Just as with task Actual Start, editing assignment Actual Start causes Project to change the assignment's scheduled Start to match the assignment's Actual Start. In addition, Project recalculates the assignment scheduled Finish date according to factors such as the resource duration and calendar settings.

If the task has a single resource assignment and the task Actual Start is NA when you edit the assignment, Project sets the task Actual Start equal to the resource assignment Actual Start.

One of three actions occurs if multiple resources are assigned to a task, as follows:

- If the assignment Actual Start is the same as the task scheduled Start, the task Actual Start will be set to the task scheduled Start.

- If the assignment Actual Start is later than the task scheduled Start, the task Actual Start is set to the task scheduled Start. The task schedule finish might be delayed if the late assignment start is the critical resource on the task.

- If the assignment Actual Start is earlier than it was scheduled to start, and earlier than the task scheduled Start date, the task Actual Start is changed to the assignment Actual Start. The task and assignment finish dates might also be changed per the overall duration settings.

Editing Assignment Actual Finish

Edit changes to the assignment actual finish have similar behavior to edits to the task Actual Finish. If the assignment Actual Start displays NA when you edit assignment Actual Finish, Project presumes the assignment started on schedule and ended on the edited finish date. If the new Actual Finish date is different from the scheduled Finish date, Project changes Cost and Work accordingly.

If it is the only assignment for the task, the task- and assignment-tracking fields will be identical after the recalculations, except possibly Actual Cost, which might include some task fixed cost.

If the task has multiple assignments, editing Actual Finish for one assignment causes Project to recalculate the task Actual Work, Actual Cost, Actual Duration, % Complete, % Work Complete, Remaining Duration, Remaining Work, and Remaining Cost fields.

 tip

The task type determines how work and duration are recalculated, as you can see in "Editing Task Actual Duration."

Editing Assignment Actual Work

If either the task or assignment Actual Start reads NA, any edits to the assignment Actual Work field cause Project to set the assignment and task Actual Start dates to the assignment and task scheduled Actual Start dates. Project also recalculates both the assignment and task % Work Complete, Remaining Work, Actual Cost, Remaining Cost, and so on.

Editing Assignment % Work Complete

You might decide to track progress by updating the assignment-level %Work Complete for each resource on a task. Use the Task Usage view with the Work table to edit the assignment % Work Complete field.

If the assignment has not been started, any edits to this field cause Project to set the assignment Actual Start date equal to the scheduled Start date. Project also sets the task Actual Start date to the task scheduled Start date, if that was NA. The assignment Actual Finish date is set to the scheduled Finish date if the edited value of % Work Complete is set at 100% and all resource assignments are also 100% complete.

Project recalculates the assignment and task Actual Work, Remaining Work, % Work Complete, Actual Cost, and Remaining Cost fields. The task Actual Duration, % Complete, and Remaining Duration fields are updated as well.

 note

The task Actual Duration is determined by taking the task Actual Work, which is the sum of all assignments' Actual Work, and calculating how long it would have taken to complete that amount of work if all the assignments (not just the ones that show work complete) had completed work as scheduled. Then, % Complete and Remaining Duration are both calculated by using the value for Actual Duration.

Editing Assignment Remaining Work

Your resources might provide periodic estimates of remaining work to be performed for scheduled tasks. You can use the assignment Remaining Work field to capture those estimates. This field is also found on the Task Usage view with the Work table. Editing this field is similar to editing the Remaining Work field for tasks. If the assignment is not started, edits to Remaining Work change the scheduled Work for the assignment and thus change the scheduled Finish for the assignment. Make sure you review the task type when editing assignment-level Remaining Work fields because the calculated results are different based on the task type settings.

Edits to an already started assignment that *reduce* Remaining Work lead to increases in assignment % Work Completed. This causes a ripple effect as described in the earlier section on edits to assignment Actual Work.

Edits to an already started assignment that *increase* Remaining Work redefine the total scheduled Work for the assignment and lead to recalculated values for the tracking fields, such as assignment scheduled Finish date, scheduled Cost, and % Work Complete. These new values mean recalculated values for the related task fields as well.

Editing Assignment Time-Phased Work

If you provide resources with timecards that enable the resources to fill in the amount of actual work completed, and optimally the amount of overtime work as well, updating a project with these timecards produces edits to the assignment time-phased fields Actual Work and Actual Overtime Work. Such edits mean recalculated values for assignment Actual Work, Remaining Work, % Work Complete, Actual Cost, and Remaining Cost. Those, in turn, mean recalculations for task-tracking fields, which you read about in "Editing Assignment Actual Work," earlier in this chapter.

You might recall that each cell in the time-phased cells is for specific time periods, and any edits to the cell are distributed equally between the beginning and ending dates for the cell period. If the edited cell is the first actual work recorded (meaning the assignment Actual Start was NA), Actual Start for the assignment is set to the begin date for the cell you edited. If no more remaining work exists after the edit, assigned Actual Finish is set to the end date for the cell.

If the task type is Fixed Units or Fixed Work, and the entered Actual Work is less than scheduled Work for the cell you are editing, remaining work for the cell is rescheduled after the end date for the assignment. If the entered Actual Work is greater than the scheduled Work for that cell, any remaining work is moved to reduce the assignment finish date. If the task type is Fixed Duration, any differences between the scheduled and actual work for the period are divided equally among the remaining time periods in the assignment.

 tip

If you skip any periods when entering Actual Work, the skipped periods will fill with zero time-phased Actual Work. Any work scheduled for these skipped periods is rescheduled at the end of the assignment, unless the task type is Fixed Duration, in which case the work for the assignments is reduced.

Understanding the Calculation Options That Affect Tracking

Project provides you with several options that control default conditions used to calculate task and assignment results. You learn more about those options in this section.

Looking back at "Entering Tracking Information at the Task Level" and "Entering Tracking Information at the Assignment Level," the descriptions of edits to task- and assignment-tracking fields assume that default calculation options are enabled. Specifically, the edits to task status are also applied to assignments, and actual costs are calculated by Project. This section takes a look at the impact of those options on tracking calculations if you disable these defaults, as well as other options that are disabled by default.

To disable or enable those options, use select Options on the File tab. There are calculation settings in both the Schedule and Advanced sections (see Figures 13.4 and 13.5). In either case, you can apply these changes specifically to this project or to all new projects by using the section drop-down.

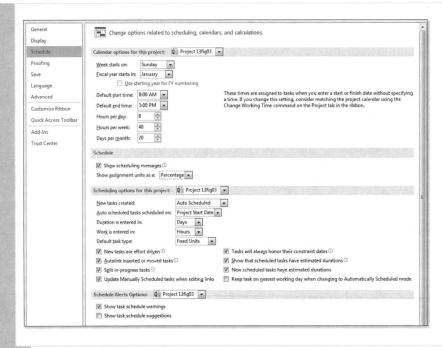

Figure 13.4
Between the Schedule tab and the Advanced tab (Figure 13.5), you can see all the different Calculation options available to you that can affect tracking.

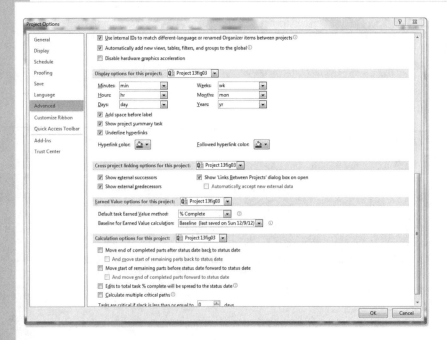

Figure 13.5
Between the Advanced tab and the Schedule tab (Figure 13.4), you can see all the different Calculation options available to you that can affect tracking.

Using the Updating Task Status Updates Resource Status Option

If you enable the option Updating Task Status Updates Resource Status (which is the default setting), edits to the task % Complete cause Project to calculate Actual Work and % Work Complete at both the task and assignment levels. The link behavior is reciprocal; any edits to assignment Actual Work causes Project to recalculate task Actual Duration, % Complete, and Remaining Duration.

If you *disable* Updating Task Status Updates Resource Status, the following conditions take effect:

 caution

There is an exception to the last point on the preceding list. If you reset each assignment's Actual Work to zero, Project resets task % Complete to 0%, which means you lose any manual edits to the % Complete field. This does not happen if you reset the task Actual Work to zero.

Also, setting assignment or task % Complete to 100% has the opposite effect of setting % Work Complete to 100% when Updating Task Status Updates Resource Status is turned off. This is the more common occurrence that users run into, and they do not understand why they have actual work on a task when the option is disabled.

- Edits to task % Complete affect only task Actual Duration and Remaining Duration. Actual Work, % Work Complete, and Remaining Work remain unaffected at both the task and assignment levels.

- Task Actual Work continues to be the rolled-up sum of assignment Actual Work. Edits at the task level to Actual Work, % Work Complete, and Remaining Work still roll down to assignments. Edits to those fields at the assignment level still roll up to the task.

- Edits to Actual Work, % Work Complete, or Remaining Work do not affect task % Complete, Actual Duration, or Remaining Duration.

If you are working with Updating Task Status Updates Resource Status disabled and then change your mind and decide to return to working with the setting enabled, Project does not recalculate previously edited work- and duration-tracking fields to align their values. Rather, it waits until you edit either a task duration–tracking field (Actual Duration, % Complete, or Remaining Duration) or a work-tracking field at either the assignment or task level (Actual Work, % Work Complete, or Remaining Work).

If your first edit is to a duration-tracking field, Project recalculates all the other duration-tracking fields and then recalculates all the work-tracking fields using the new Actual Duration. If your first edit is a work-tracking field, Project recalculates all the task assignment work-tracking fields and then recalculates the duration-tracking fields based on your edits to actual work.

➡️ *For additional information on earned value analysis,* **see** *the "Analyzing Performance with Earned Value Analysis" section on* **p. 474** *in Chapter 14.*

tip

One of the tricks you can use by disabling Updating Task Status Updates Resource Status is to compel Project to calculate earned value fields using % Work Complete values instead of % Complete. To do this, save the file and perform the following steps with a copy of the file, so you can delete it when finished:

1. With the Updating Task Status Updates Resource Status disabled, and both % Complete and % Work Complete displayed as columns in the task table, choose the column for % Work Complete and use Ctrl+C to copy the information.

2. Select the column for % Complete and use Ctrl+V to paste the information into that column.

You can then conduct your analysis of earned value knowing that the earned value calculations are much closer, though not identical, to those you could get by using a traditional method of calculating earned value.

Using the Actual Costs Are Always Calculated by Project Option

When the option Actual Costs Are Always Calculated by Project is enabled (which is the default setting), Project calculates Actual Cost as you track progress on the task by adding accrued Fixed Cost to the sum of Actual Costs for all assignments.

Here is the formula for this behavior:

Assignment Actual Cost = (Actual Work × Cost Rate) + (Actual Overtime Work × Overtime Cost Rate) + Cost Per Use

The cost rate and overtime cost rate are taken from the cost rate table, defined for the resources assigned to the task.

When the Actual Costs Are Always Calculated by Project option (in the scheduling section of the Options) is enabled, you cannot edit Actual Cost at the assignment or task level until the task is 100% complete. However, when the task is complete, you can edit the task Actual Cost field, the assignment Actual Cost field, and the task or assignment time-phased Actual Cost field. The Remaining Cost field is always a calculated field and cannot be edited.

The effects of editing the actual cost fields after the task is completed, when Actual Cost has been calculated by Project, are listed here:

- Edits to assignment Actual Cost roll up to the task Actual Cost. As with other "Actual" fields, the value in Actual Cost is copied to the scheduled Cost field.

- Edits to the assignment time-phased Actual Cost also roll up to the task time-phased Actual Cost and then to task Actual Cost.

- The task Actual Cost field sums the rolled-up assignment Actual Cost field entries, so edits into the task Actual Cost field are *not* rolled down to the assignments. Instead, they are presumed to be actual fixed cost adjustments, and the difference between the edited value and the sum for the assignments is added to Fixed Cost, which is then added to the total in the Cost field. The end result is that the Cost field is equal to the Actual Cost field.

Therefore, increasing task Actual Cost by $100 will cause the Fixed Cost field (and also the Cost field) to rise by $100. Decreasing the Actual Cost field by $100 causes the Fixed Cost field to fall by the same, and could result in a negative value.

- Any edits to the task time-phased Actual Cost field are distributed among assignments for that same time period in proportion to their share of existing Actual Cost for that time period. Project also recalculates assignment Actual Cost for each assignment and rolls up the total to the task Actual Cost field. Therefore, edits to task time-phased Actual Cost do not lead to a change in Fixed Costs, like direct edits to task Actual Cost will.

You can view the Actual Fixed Cost in the time-phased Actual Fixed Cost field. The time-phased Actual Fixed Cost field is a calculated field only, so you cannot edit actual fixed cost in the time-phased cells.

The Cost field initially shows the estimated cost of completing a task or assignment. It is actually calculated as the estimated cost of work that remains to be finished, plus the actual cost already recorded. Before the task begins, the Cost field shows the same value as the Remaining Cost field, which you can see if you display the Cost table.

As you record work that is completed, the remaining cost normally falls and is replaced by the actual cost of the completed work. If Project is not calculating Actual Cost, however, the effect on the Cost field when recording actual work is that Cost falls until you enter the Actual Cost field information yourself. Marking a task at 100% without entering Actual Cost causes the Cost field to fall to zero.

Editing the Actual Cost field, however, causes the Cost field to rise by the same amount as the Actual Cost field. Unlike when Project is calculating actual cost, edits to the Actual Cost field never change the Fixed Cost field.

You are still unable to overwrite Project's "scheduled" costs for an assignment, because they continue to be calculated based on resource work and cost rates plus cost per use.

If you edit the Actual Cost fields when Actual Cost is not calculated by Project, the following happens:

- Edits to assignment Actual Cost or assignment time-phased Actual Cost roll up to the task Actual Cost and task time-phased Actual Cost and are also added to the assignment Cost.

- Edits to task Actual Cost roll down to the assignments and are distributed among the assignments in proportion to the Remaining Cost for the assignments, not counting Remaining Overtime Cost.

- Edits to task time-phased Actual Cost roll down to the assignments in the same time period, also in proportion to Remaining Cost, as shown in the time-phased Cost field.

 tip

If you disable the Actual Costs Are Always Calculated by Project option, you are able to enter your own actual costs. In fact, you *have* to enter those values because Project will no longer automatically calculate the field based on work completed.

When you enable the Actual Costs Are Always Calculated by Project option after it has been disabled, Project immediately overwrites any manually entered Actual Cost values with the calculated Actual Cost, based on Work and % Complete.

If Actual Costs Are Always Calculated by Project is disabled, the Edits to Total Actual Cost Will Be Spread to the Status Date suboption becomes available. The Edits to Total Actual Cost Will Be Spread to the Status Date option directs how Project distributes the time-phased values when you edit the assignment or task Actual Cost field yourself. Normally, Actual Cost edits are distributed from the start of the assignment or task, as planned in the scheduled cost distribution.

If you enable Edits to Total Actual Cost Will Be Spread to the Status Date and then edit the task Actual Cost, the increase or decrease in task Actual Cost is distributed equally over the empty time-phased cells, starting after the last period in which time-phased Actual Cost was recorded up through the Status date (or Current Date if the Status date is undefined). Using the Edits to Total Actual Cost Will Be Spread to the Status Date option will smooth out the time-phased Actual Cost fields.

 tip

Although disabling the option Actual Costs Are Always Calculated by Project might give you more ability to match accounting costs in your project plan, it means a lot more work for you and hides the cost implications of the schedule.

 tip

To define your status date, choose Project, Project Information and fill in the Status Date field.

Using the Edits to Total Task Percentage Complete Will Be Spread to the Status Date Option

The Edits to the Total Task % Complete Will Be Spread to the Status Date option (in the Advanced section of Options) is disabled by default. The Edits to Total Task % Complete Will Be Spread to the Status Date option affects only how time-phased % Complete is distributed when you edit the task % Complete field. Distribution of the time-phased % Complete field affects earned value calculations and how progress lines are displayed. It has no impact on how time-phased actual work is actually distributed among the time periods.

> ➡ *For more information on progress lines,* **see** *the "Using Progress Lines" section on* **p. 462** *in Chapter 14.*

When Edits to Total Task % Complete Will Be Spread to the Status Date is disabled, any edits you make to the task % Complete field cause the amount of task Actual Work to be calculated and the time-phased Actual Work to be distributed from the start of the task, as scheduled for all assignments, until the Actual Work is accounted for. The time-phased % Complete field shows the percentage of total work completed in each time period, with the entries added up to the edited amount for % Complete.

When Edits to Total Task % Complete Will Be Spread to the Status Date is enabled, the time-phased Actual Work is distributed the same, but the time-phased % Complete field is equally distributed among the time periods from the last recorded time-phased % Complete value to the Status Date (or the Current Date if no Status Date is defined). This will smooth out the increments in earned value over time instead of causing discrete jumps. This option must also be enabled if you want progress lines to connect to tasks that have actual work completed ahead of schedule.

Options to Reschedule Parts of Partially Completed Tasks

This section discusses the Calculations options shown in Figures 13.4 and 13.5 (File tab, Options, and either Schedule or Advanced). Because tasks are rarely completed exactly on schedule, you often have tasks that should have been completed when you enter tracking information, but that still have incomplete work.

You can set the Status Date from the Project tab to any date you want, often different than the current date. The status date affects calculation and earned value results. As you can see in Figure 13.6, the current status date is set to the 23rd, meaning tasks A and B are behind schedule.

Task A was scheduled to be completed by the status date, but only three days of actual duration were reported for the status update. This remaining work needs to be completed but is scheduled for days that are in the past. You need to move the incomplete part of Task A to start after the Status date.

Figure 13.6
You should reschedule unfinished work that is overdue to a more reasonable start date.

You can use the options described in this section to automatically reschedule parts of a task like those in this example. Note that each of these options functions only at the moment you enter a change to a task. These options will not impact tasks where you have entered tracking information before turning on the reschedule options.

 note

The Split In-Progress Tasks check box, found on the Schedule tab of the Options dialog box, must be enabled (which is the default) for the following rescheduling options to work.

Using the Move End of Completed Parts After Status Date Back to Status Date Option

If the Move End of Completed Parts After Status Date Back to Status Date option (in the Advanced section of Options) is enabled (it is disabled by default) when you record the Actual Work, Project moves the completed part of the task to the status date so that the task resumes on the status date. The rescheduled part of the task is shown as Task B in Figure 13.7. This option setting saves you the trouble of remembering to enter the actual start date for tasks that start early.

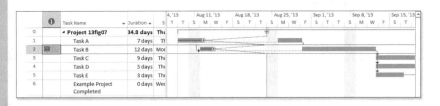

Figure 13.7
To correct your schedule, Project can automatically reschedule sections of partially completed tasks.

---

 tip

The Move End of Completed Parts After Status Date Back to Status Date feature might also produce a task split. Drag the right-hand section to the left or right to reschedule the split portion of remaining work.

The And Move Start of Remaining Parts Back to Status Date suboption is disabled by default and becomes available only when the Move End of Completed Parts After Status Date Back to Status Date option is enabled. This option moves task split conditions to the Status date.

Using the Move Start of Remaining Parts Before Status Date Forward to Status Date Option

The option Move Start of Remaining Parts Before Status Date Forward to Status Date (in the Advanced section of Options, disabled by default) automatically reschedules any unfinished work that was scheduled before the status date to start on the status date. That enables you to move the rescheduled part to a later date, if you set the Project Information Status date to a future period.

You can see that Task A, in Figure 13.7, started on schedule but still has unfinished work as of the status date. If this option had been enabled when the actual duration was entered, Project would have entered the scheduled Start in the Actual Start field and automatically rescheduled the remaining duration to start on the status date, as shown in Task A. If work will not resume right away, you can drag the remaining duration farther to the right to the date when you want to resume scheduled work.

 tip

You can reschedule the unfinished work, even if the option was not enabled, by clicking on the unfinished section of the task bar in Task A and dragging it to the right to reschedule. Microsoft Project splits the task automatically at the end of the duration.

When you enable Move Start of Remaining Parts Before Status Date Forward to Status Date, the suboption And Move End of Completed Parts Forward to Status Date becomes available.

When this option is enabled, Project moves the completed section of the task to join the unfinished section at the status date.

Using Microsoft Project's Facilities for Updating Tasks

Project enables you to select several views and forms to assist with recording your tracking. Here are some of the more common and frequently used options.

General Shortcuts

There are several shortcuts that you can use while working with the Tracking Toolbar, as follows:

- **Quartile Percentage**—Use these buttons to set the % Complete for selected tasks. They are in the Schedule group on the Task tab. You can also access them by right-clicking on a Gantt bar.

- **Mark on Track**—This button is used to set the selected task's Actual Start to its scheduled Start, and to record Actual Duration complete through the Status Date (or Current Date if Status Date is undefined). This is also in the Schedule group on the Task tab.

- **Reschedule Work**—This button is used to reschedule incomplete work to start on the Status Date (or Current Date if Status Date is undefined) for the selected task. It is not on the Ribbon or in the Quick Access toolbar by default, so it has to be added.

- **Add Progress Line**—Right-click on the Gantt Chart and select Display in the Current Progress Line Group. Peaks are drawn from the line to the left for any task that should be but is not finished as of the progress date line. Use this to find tasks that might be missing their tracking information or that need to be rescheduled.

> *For more information on progress lines, see Chapter 14, "Analyzing Performance," p. 459.*

- **Update Tasks**—This button displays the Update Tasks form for any tasks you select. See the section, "Update Tasks Form," for more details on how to use this form.

> **🔍 note**
>
> Remember, these buttons affect only the task or tasks you have selected. If a button does not work right the first time, make sure you have selected the right task.

Update Tasks Form

You can enter task-level tracking information for one or more selected tasks by using the Update Tasks form, which you can see in Figure 13.8. You can open this form by selecting the Task tab, Schedule, Mark on Track, clicking the down arrow next to Mark on Track, and selecting Update Tasks.

You might find it convenient to use the Update Tasks form instead of editing data in a view that contains the Tracking table. You can edit task data in the Update Tasks form and then click OK to have Project update the cells and recalculate the updates in a single action.

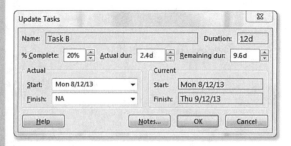

Figure 13.8
Use the Update Tasks form to view and edit any actual records for a selected task.

Update Project Form

You can use the Update Project form to enter tracking information for all tasks scheduled throughout the project or a group of selected tasks. Select the Project tab and click Update Project to display the form shown in Figure 13.9.

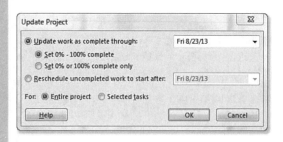

Figure 13.9
You can update your project quickly using the Update Project form.

You can perform two tracking functions with the Update Project form: You can update work as complete through the status date (or current date if status date is not set), or you can reschedule uncompleted work to start on the date you choose. Both of these options, by default, apply to all tasks in the project, or at least those tasks you have selected.

Using the Update Work as Complete Through Option

Use the Update Work as Complete Through option to update all scheduled work as completed up through the specified date. By default, the status date you defined appears in the date box. The current date appears if you have not defined a status date. If you edit the Date box, any new date you enter will become the project's status date.

If you use this option, Project sets the Actual Start date equal to the scheduled Start date, for all tasks that were scheduled to start before the status date. It also sets the Actual Finish date to the scheduled Finish date for tasks that were scheduled to finish before the status date.

If you choose to use the default suboption Set 0% – 100% Complete, Project sets the Actual Duration to complete through the selected date and calculates % Complete. If you choose the Set 0% or 100%

Complete Only suboption, tasks that were scheduled to finish on or before the selected date are also marked 100% complete. Those not marked complete are left with 0% in the % Complete field.

The Entire Project button is selected by default, and all changes will be applied to all tasks in the project. Choose the Selected Tasks button when you want changes to be applied only to selected tasks. You need to select the tasks you want before displaying the form, and then click the Selected Tasks option on the form.

Using the Reschedule Uncompleted Work to Start After Option

Your organization's tracking standards might require you to use the Reschedule Uncompleted Work to Start After option to move incomplete work to resume after a selected date. Use the date drop-down to set the date threshold to reschedule remaining work. The date box shows the current date (or status date, if defined) by default. Editing this date does not reset the project status date. When you click OK, Project reschedules any uncompleted work for tasks that have started to the date entered in the second date box.

 note

Remember that you have to select your tasks first before you can use the Selected Task option on the Update Project form.

If a task has not started, but should, Project reschedules the entire task by giving it a Start No Earlier Than constraint for the date shown in the second date box. If this happens, a Planning Wizard dialog box alerts you to any constraints so you can look at the tasks individually for possible rescheduling (see Figure 13.10).

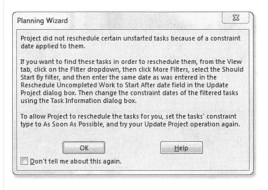

Figure 13.10
This Planning Wizard informs you when there is a task with a constraint on it that needs to be rescheduled.

You need to deal with this Planning Wizard by rescheduling the constraint task manually. You can identify the tasks by applying the Should Start By task filter, as suggested by the dialog box. Choose Project, Filtered For, More Filters, select Should Start By, and click Apply to enact this filter. This is an interactive filter, and it will ask you to supply the start-by date (the date by which tasks should have started). Enter the current date or the status date if it is defined because that is the date that was used in the Update Project command. The filter then finds all tasks not started but that have scheduled start dates that are before the date you have entered.

If you select a constrained task and open its Task Information dialog box, you can reschedule its constraints. Change the Constraint Type setting on the Advanced tab to Start No Earlier Than, and enter the rescheduled date into the Constraint Date box. To remove all constraints and run the Update Project reschedule command again, you need to select all the constraint tasks, click the Task Information button to show the Multiple Task Information dialog box, and then change the Constraint Type to As Soon as Possible and click OK.

Consultants' Tips

Always Keep the Original Baseline

When working with baselines, it is important that you keep the original baseline for future comparisons. When you are finished setting your schedule, save the original baseline in the primary baseline (Baseline without a number) and also as Baseline 1. The primary baseline can then be used as the "current" baseline information, and Baseline 1 (the "original" baseline) is never changed.

Regular Statusing of Team Assignments

Proper statusing of team assignments in a project is critical to using Project as a management tool. Although there are several ways to do this, from setting finish dates to setting % percent complete, you can get the most benefit from the tool if you establish a regular statusing cycle of weekly or bi-weekly updates. During these updates, get your project team together and get information on what started during the reporting period, what the progress is in terms of either percentage complete or effort spent, and what their estimate is of work or time to complete the remaining work on the task.

With this information, you can always have a clear picture of whether your project is performing to plan and whether your commitments will be met. For example, you can use the first half of the meeting to go through the current tasks in the project and update them in real time. Then, use the second half of the meeting to discuss the impact of this update to the critical deliverables of the project, cover any issues that need to be addressed, and set new objectives for the next cycle.

In theory, Microsoft Project Server makes this process easier by providing a simple way to use statusing forms to enter progress information. In practice, having resources status their tasks through Project Server is a challenge that should not be taken lightly. Process and scheduling maturity should be at relatively high levels before attempting this.

14

ANALYZING PERFORMANCE

As a project manager, planning the project is only one phase of your overall objective. In fact, the process model supported by Project Management Institute (PMI) begins with initiation, followed by planning, executing, controlling, and closing the project. This is an excellent model to emulate to obtain the greatest success rate for managing your project. This chapter focuses on the controlling aspect of project management.

Every plan is obsolete the minute it's finished. A project plan is never more than the best estimate of how the project will proceed as estimated by the project manager(s) and other project stakeholders. Projects rarely take less of anything than you originally thought; usually they take more of everything. It is your responsibility as a project manager not only to keep track of a project's progress, but to react and adapt accordingly when things change.

Often it is necessary to backtrack when following the PMI process model referenced previously. If, during the control-

 note

The questions "How are things going?" and "How are we doing?" become crucial to managing the progress of a project. Ask early and ask often. Continuously monitor the progress from the project's start date. The more on top of the situation you are, the more prepared you will be to make necessary adjustments to the plan.

ling phase, you need to make adjustments, your course of action might require you to go back to the planning phase, and continue to move forward from there. Do not get discouraged if this happens more than once; it might seem like you have made a mistake, but in reality you are a better project manager for making the adjustments than ignoring the need for them. Clients might be unhappy if the project has gone off schedule or off budget, but they will be much more appreciative to find out as it is happening (and that it is being accounted for) rather than at the end of the project.

This chapter focuses on different practices and procedures for analyzing the performance of your project.

Reviewing the Current Status of a Project

Several features within Microsoft Project aid in reviewing and analyzing a project's current status. Views, reports, and filters, as well as status fields and progress lines, are all helpful analyzing tools. The next several sections discuss these and other methods for analyzing a project's current status.

 For more information about capturing baselines, **see** *the "Saving Your Project Baseline," section in Chapter 12,* **p. 425***.*

 note

Capturing the baseline of your project is crucial to analyzing its progress. A baseline is more or less a snapshot of your project at any given time. That way, you have something to compare the project's current status to.

Reviewing the Status Via the Current Schedule

The first step in analyzing a project's current status is to review the current schedule. Specifically, you are looking for tasks that are behind schedule. There are multiple ways of doing this. The Status and Status Indicator fields are immediate gauges of whether a task is behind schedule. Also, you can insert a progress line into the Gantt Chart view to display the information graphically. In addition, you can apply filters to find tasks that are behind schedule. All of these processes are described in the next three sections.

Status and Status Indicator Fields

The Status and Status Indicator fields are excellent quick references as to a task's progress. These fields label the task as Complete, On Schedule, Late, or Future (for a task that has yet to begin). The Status Date in the Project Information dialog box is used as a reference point for the status indication. In other words, Project compares the task's % Complete value (duration percentage complete) to the Status date, is able to calculate the progress based on that value, and labels the task based on that calculation.

Insert the Status and Status Indicator fields into a table by right-clicking on a column, choosing Insert Column, and selecting Status or Status Indicator from the list. The column will be inserted where you selected, and all columns move to the right to make room for it (except those already on its left, which stay put).

Assume that a task has a scheduled duration of three weeks and is scheduled to start on September 9, 2013. Project would calculate its finish date to be September 27, 2013. Project calculates the status of the task based on its % Complete versus its scheduled finish date. Therefore, if you entered a Status date of September 25, 2013, and entered the % Complete as 60%, the Status and Status Indicator fields would show the task's status to be Late, because the task should be more than 60% complete by September 25. If, however, the task was 60% complete and the Status date was September 12, 2013, the Status and Status Indicators fields would show the task as On Schedule, because it is on pace to finish on or before the scheduled finish date (see Figure 14.1).

The Status and Status Indicator columns primarily display the same information. The Status column displays the information in words (Complete, On Schedule, Late, or Future), whereas the Status Indicator field displays the graphical indicator (see Table 14.1).

To enter a Status date, select the Project tab and use the Status Date control to enter a date in the Status Date field. Project uses this date on which to base its calculations. If no Status date is entered, the Current Date is used to calculate the status of a task. You can also enter **NA** in the Status Date field to bypass the status date and use the current date.

> **tip**
>
> For this information to be accurate, you must enter an accurate % Complete value in the Task Information dialog box (right-click on a task and choose Task Information).

Figure 14.1 shows the Gantt Chart view with the Status and Status Indicator fields displayed. Notice the different values in the two fields. The Status Date is set for September 20, 2013, and is represented on the timescale as a black vertical dashed line.

Figure 14.1
The Status and Status Indicator fields display status information for a task's progress.

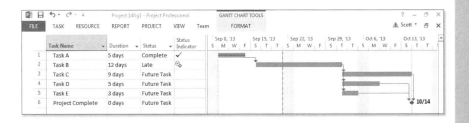

> **note**
>
> The status indicators are determined by the task status relative to the status or current date. It does not use the baseline values in the criteria to determine task status.
>
> The values displayed in the Status and Status Indicator fields are useless if you have not accurately updated the progress of the task. If a task is 50% complete, but the % Complete field in the Task Information dialog box is not updated, you should update it with actual work or % complete as accurately as possible before noting the values in the Status and Status Indicator fields.

Table 14.1 Status Labels, Status Indicators, and Their Meanings

Status Label	Status Indicator	Meaning
Complete	✓	The task is 100% complete.
On Schedule	☑✓	The task is not yet complete, but all work that is scheduled for completion by the Status date is complete. The task is on pace to finish on or before the scheduled finish date.

Status Label	Status Indicator	Meaning
Late	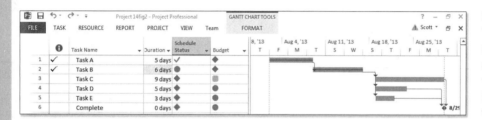	Not all work scheduled to be completed by the Status date is complete. The task is on pace to finish later than its scheduled finish date.
Future	(No indicator)	The task is not scheduled to start until after the Status date. This Status value has no indicator.

As an alternative to inserting the Status and Status Indicator fields, you can create custom fields that use a formula to determine the status of a task. You can also apply a graphical indicator to be displayed in the custom field that indicates a task's status. For example, the custom field could display the colors of a stoplight (red, yellow, and green) to indicate whether a task is late (red), in danger of being late, (yellow), or on time or early (green), as shown in Figure 14.2.

Figure 14.2 The custom schedule and budget fields have been added to provide a quick at-a-glance status of your project.

For more information about creating custom fields with formulas and graphical indicators, **see** the "Creating and Customizing Fields," section in Chapter 22, **p. 745**.

Using Progress Lines

The Status and Status Indicator fields are good references for a task's progress on the Task Entry table side of the Gantt Chart view. This section discusses *progress lines*, which are graphical indicators of a task's progress on the timescale side. Progress lines are vertical lines on the timescale that spike out to the left and right to quickly call your attention to tasks that are ahead or behind schedule. They are customizable in their format and appearance.

You can choose to display a progress line at the current date, status date, or any other date of interest to you. The line appears centered over the date you choose. You can also set up a progress line at specific intervals within the project schedule. For every incomplete taskbar that the progress line runs through (excluding completed tasks or tasks whose start date is later than the progress line date), it spikes out to the left or right, depending on the task's progress. If the task is ahead of schedule, the progress line spikes out to the right; if it is behind schedule, it spikes out to the left. This is, of course, very dependent on the % Complete field in the Task Information dialog box.

The spike connects to the point on the taskbar that represents the task's percentage complete for its duration. In other words, if the task is 50% complete, the spike from the progress line connects to the middle of the taskbar.

Figure 14.3 shows a progress line and several tasks. Notice how it spikes to the left for tasks that are behind schedule (late). For tasks that are on schedule, the line simply runs down the middle, as it does for completed tasks or tasks that begin after the progress line date and have not started yet (because progress lines call attention only to tasks that are ahead of or behind schedule).

 tip

To get the best usage of a progress line, be sure to update the progress for all tasks as accurately as possible by the tracking method used. Otherwise, the progress line(s) will not be accurate.

Figure 14.3
A progress line is a visual indicator of tasks that are off schedule.

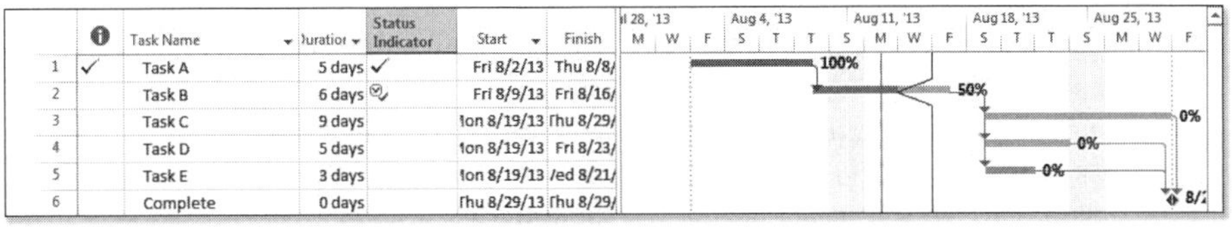

	0	Task Name	Duration	Status Indicator	Start	Finish
1	✓	Task A	5 days	✓	Fri 8/2/13	Thu 8/8/
2		Task B	6 days		Fri 8/9/13	Fri 8/16/
3		Task C	9 days		Mon 8/19/13	Thu 8/29/
4		Task D	5 days		Mon 8/19/13	Fri 8/23/
5		Task E	3 days		Mon 8/19/13	Wed 8/21/
6		Complete	0 days		Thu 8/29/13	Thu 8/29/

There are a few ways to display a progress line. One is to right-click on the graphical side of the Gantt Chart view and select Progress Lines. Another is to select the Format tab for the Gantt chart and select Progress lines from under the Gridlines drop-down. Both methods open the Progress Lines dialog box, as shown in Figure 14.4.

Figure 14.4
Define where and how often a progress line is displayed on the Dates and Intervals tab of the Progress Lines dialog box.

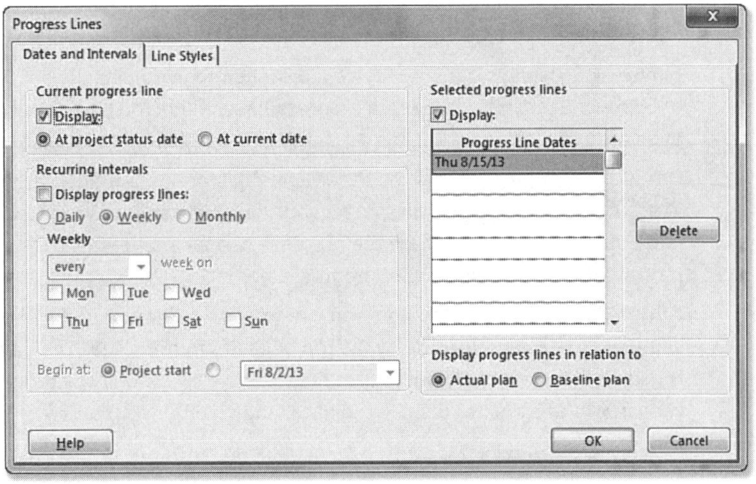

At the top of the Dates and Intervals tab of the Progress Lines dialog box, you can select Always Display Current Progress Line and choose whether you want the progress line on the status date or on the current date.

You can select a date other than the current or status date by selecting the Display Selected Progress Lines check box. Choose a date from the drop-down calendar in the Progress Line Dates field(s). You can enter multiple dates to display multiple progress lines, or delete a date by selecting it and clicking the Delete button. You can also temporarily hide the progress lines by clearing the Display Selected Progress Lines check box. This hides the progress lines but keeps the date list, so the next time you open the Progress Lines dialog box, you simply have to select that check box to display them again.

As mentioned before, you can display progress lines at specific intervals. This might be helpful to analyze the pattern of deviation or progress over the course of your project. Select the Display Progress Lines at Recurring Intervals check box and define whether you want the progress line displayed daily, weekly, or monthly. Then, set the recurrence pattern. Your options are different depending on your interval selection (Daily, Weekly, or Monthly). By default, these recurring progress lines begin at the start of the project, but you can change them to begin on a specific date by selecting the date from the Begin At field at the bottom.

At the bottom-right corner of the Progress Lines dialog box is an option to display the progress lines in relation to the actual plan or the baseline plan. By default, Actual Plan is selected, meaning the progress lines are displayed in relation to the current schedule, including start and finish dates. If you choose Baseline Plan, the progress line is drawn to the date that represents the percent complete as applied to the baseline schedule. The progress line is drawn to the baseline bars if the Gantt Chart view displays baseline bars; if not, it is drawn on the calculated date anyway, even if the date does not fall on a scheduled taskbar.

 tip

After you have displayed a progress line, you can double-click the line itself to open up the Progress Lines dialog box and modify the display.

Figure 14.5 displays the Line Styles tab of the Progress Lines dialog box. On this tab, you have multiple options for setting how the progress lines will be displayed, including types, colors, shapes, and the date display.

Choose the Progress Line Type based on which of the four illustrations is most appealing to you. Then, in the Line Style fields, you can opt for different line types (solid, dashed, and so on), colors, point shapes (the point where the progress line meets the taskbar), and the point color for the current progress line and all other progress lines.

At the bottom of the dialog box, you can select the Show Date for Each Progress Line check box if you want to display the date at the top of each progress line. This might be helpful if your timescale is zoomed in a way that makes it difficult to see the date of the progress line. Next to that, you can choose which format to display the date, and change the font if you want.

When you are satisfied with your selections on both tabs of the Progress Lines dialog box, click OK to display the progress lines as you have defined them, or click Cancel to exit the dialog box without applying anything.

Figure 14.5
Format the look of prog-
ress lines in the Line
Styles tab of the Progress
Lines dialog box.

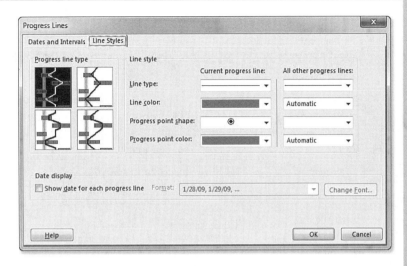

Filtering for Slipping Tasks

Filtering is another quick way to identify tasks that are not on schedule. Two built-in filters are good for this purpose: the Slipping Tasks filter for a task table, and the Slipping Assignments filter for a resource table.

In Project, a task is *slipping* when it is not complete, and its scheduled finish date is later than its baseline finish date. Therefore, if you have not yet captured the baseline for a task, the task will not be selected by the filter, even if it is behind schedule.

➡ *For more information about capturing baselines,* **see** *the "Saving Your Project Baseline" section on* **p. 425** *in Chapter 12.*

To apply the Slipping Task filter to the Gantt Chart view (or any view with a task table), select View tab, Data, Filter (Filters Gallery), More Filters. Click Apply to apply the filter or Highlight to show all tasks but highlight those that meet the filter requirements (the slipping tasks).

Follow the same procedure for the Slipping Assignments filter, although it can only be applied to a resource table.

If you apply the Slipping Task filter to the Task Usage view, both the slipping assignments and their tasks are displayed. This enables you to determine the specific assignments that are causing tasks to slip. Similarly, if you apply the Slipping Assignments filter to the Resource Usage view, the slipping assignments are grouped by resource, and you are able to see whether certain resources have a significant amount of slipping assignments.

Reviewing the Status Via the Project Plan

So far, this chapter has described ways to pinpoint tasks that are off schedule (ahead or behind). But identifying these tasks is only part of the analyzing process; you must also know the implications of making changes to the schedule to account for the slipping tasks. The next several sections examine the impact of schedule changes to the overall project.

Defining Variance Fields and Percentage Complete Fields

Variance in Project is defined as the difference between the actual value and the baseline. The related fields are Duration, Work, Cost, Start Date, and Finish Date. Thus, Project automatically calculates field values for Duration Variance, Work Variance, Cost Variance, Start Variance, and Finish Variance. To get these values, Project performs a simple subtraction calculation. For example:

Duration Variance = Duration − Baseline (Planned) Duration.

The same formula is applied to the other four variance fields.

If the result is zero, there is no variance, and your project is executing as planned. However, changes in the schedule produce nonzero results, either positive or negative. If a positive number is produced, the current value is greater than the baseline, which generally is unfavorable because the task is taking longer, starting or finishing later, taking more effort, or costing more than originally planned. On the reverse side, if a negative number is produced, the task is ahead of schedule, taking less effort, or costing less money than originally planned, which is a good thing!

You can display any of the five variance fields in any task table. Insert one by right-clicking on the column heading where you want it, choosing Insert Column, and choosing from the drop-down list in the Field Name field.

Until you enter actual values to track a task's progress, variances are calculated using the estimated values of the current schedule. Therefore, to display an accurate variance value, you must not only have captured your baseline, you must also enter actual values for a task. This can be done on most Tracking views, or on a task table such as the Task Entry table on the Gantt Chart. When these values are entered, the variance will reflect the difference between the planned value versus the actual value.

 note

Like many topics covered so far in this chapter, this formula relies heavily on the assumption that you have captured the baseline. Note that *which* baseline is used for comparison is determined by the Baseline for Earned Value Calculation option under File tab, Options, Advanced, Earned Value Options.

 tip

Notice that you cannot change the value in a variance field; all calculations are done internally.

Similar to the variance fields are the percentage complete fields. The difference between these fields and variance fields is that variance fields compare scheduled and baseline values, whereas percentage complete fields compare scheduled and actual values.

The two percentage complete fields are % Complete and Work % Complete. % Complete measures the percentage of the duration complete, and Work % Complete measures the percentage of work complete. These values are not necessarily the same; you could have a % Complete of 20% but a larger Work % Complete value because multiple resources have worked on the task during that duration.

These fields can also be displayed and defined in a number of ways. You can insert a column in any task table (both fields are at the top on the drop-down list in the Field Name field in the Insert Column dialog box) or Tracking view. Also, you can enter the % Complete in the Task Information dialog box (right-click on a task and choose Task Information).

Reviewing Status at the Project Level: Using the Project Overview

Project is equipped with several features that enable you to quickly view the overall progress of a project. The Project Overview Report and the Slipping Tasks report both provide excellent references to the health of the project.

You can access the Project Overview report by selecting Report tab, Dashboards, Project Overview. Figure 14.6 displays an example of the Project Overview report for a simple project where the current date is 9/10/13, and one task has already fallen behind.

Figure 14.6
The Project
Overview
Report pro-
vides useful
at-a-glance
informa-
tion.

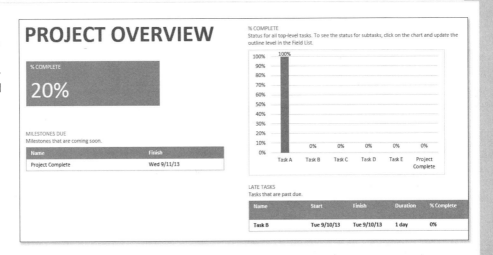

As you can see, the Project Overview reports shows the percentage of the project completed, milestones that are due, progress against top-level tasks, and late tasks all in one place. The Project Overview reports can of course be customized extensively.

> ➡ *For more information about customizing reports,* **see** *Chapter 20, "Reports Part I: 2013 Reports" p. 625.*

Another quick reference screen to the overall progress of a project that relies on baseline data is the Project Slipping Tasks report.

To view the Project Slipping Tasks report, select Report tab, In Progress, Slipping tasks.

The Slipping Tasks report in Figure 14.7 shows at a glance what state your project is in as compared with your current baseline. The graph shows both how much work remains to be done according to plan (Remaining Cumulative work) and how much Actual work remains to be done. The table on the right shows tasks that the Project Scheduling engine predicts will be late.

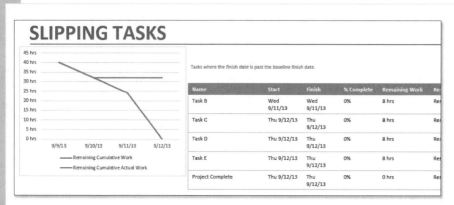

Figure 14.7
The Slipping Tasks report shows the state of your project as compared to your baseline in a summarized and customizable view.

Reviewing Status at the Project Level: Using the Project Summary Task

The project summary task provides yet another way to view most of the project information. There are two ways to display the project summary task:

1. If you are on a view displaying a task table, select Format tab, Show/Hide, Project Summary Task.

2. Select File tab, Options, Display options, Show Project Summary Task.

The project summary task appears at the top of any task table with an ID number 0 (zero).

The project summary task does not display all the project summary data on the same screen. In fact, you have to apply different tables to see the full range of summary data, or insert additional columns or fields to view all the information, such as some of the variance fields.

 tip

As mentioned earlier in this book, it is a good practice to include the project summary task in your task list. That way, you have a summary task that encompasses the entire project, rather than several smaller summary tasks.

 caution

You might be tempted to create your own project summary task by inserting a task with the project name at the top of the task list and indenting (demoting) all other tasks. This method is not recommended because you would be duplicating information that already exists.

With your project summary task inserted, you can view various tables to view both specific (individual task) information as well as general (project summary task) information for different aspects of your project. For example, to view the Cost table, select the View tab, Data, Tables, and then choose Cost from the list. You can follow the same procedure to view the Work table or any other table of interest to you. Additionally, these tables are all customizable to fit your specific needs.

> ➡ *For more information about customizing tables,* ***see*** *the "Creating and Customizing Tables" section on* ***p. 700*** *in Chapter 22.*

After reviewing specific aspects of your project, you can also collapse the tasks to review specific outline levels. If you have inserted a project summary task, it is the highest outline level by itself. The next level will be Outline Level 1 (because the project summary task is on its own level, think of it as Outline Level 0). Outline Level 1 generally consists of the phases of the project, usually made up of summary tasks, but subtasks might be included as well.

To display specific outline levels, use the Outline button on the View tab. When you click it, a drop-down list appears (see Figure 14.8). Select any of the outline levels from that list.

Figure 14.8
The Outline drop-down list is a quick and easy way to select a specific outline level.

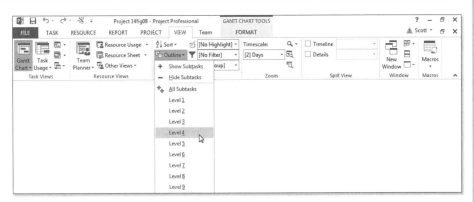

Alternatively, you can apply the Top Level Tasks filter to any task table to display the top outline level.

You can apply filters or use the Show button using different tables (Cost, Work, and so on) to more specifically analyze different aspects of your project.

Reviewing Status at the Task Level

It is good practice to analyze variances as often as you record actual values. The reason you record actual values in the first place is to track progress on your project; therefore, it is not very productive to enter actual values if you do not pay attention to the significance of those values to your project's progress.

You can examine variances by using a variety of views, filters, and reports. Although you can apply these tools to the overall project or any phase in the project, this section looks at analyzing variances occurring at the individual task level.

> **note**
>
> Even if the actual values differ only slightly from the baseline, those differences can add up quickly, and if you do not monitor them regularly, they can make for an unpleasant surprise when you finally do get around to analyzing them.

The AutoFilter feature is a great tool to analyze variances. Remember that a positive number in the Variance field is unfavorable, meaning the actual value is greater than the baseline value. In other words, the actual value is later, longer, requires more work, or is more expensive than the planned baseline (depending on if you are looking at schedule, duration, work, or cost).

To use the AutoFilter, first apply the table you want to analyze (such as Cost, Work, Variance, and so on). In the Variance column, open the drop-down list and choose Filters, Greater Than. Enter a 0 in the form shown in Figure 14.9. Project filters for all variance values greater than zero (and thus, unfavorably off the baseline plan). A funnel icon appears, indicating that this table is filtered based on values in the funnel-marked column.

> **note**
>
> The AutoFilter test for positive variance values assumes that the baseline was captured for all tasks; therefore, if the baseline was not captured, all the variances will be positive and the test is pointless.

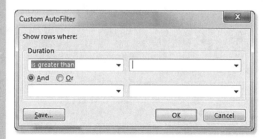

Figure 14.9
Create a custom filter test for the AutoFilter feature in the Custom AutoFilter dialog box.

Reviewing Task Start and Finish Date Variances

A date variance occurs whenever the current start or finish date estimates differ from the baseline dates. There are a number of reasons as to why this happens:

- The task began or finished at a different time than originally planned, so you entered the actual start or finish date as a different value than the baseline date.

- A predecessor task was delayed or finished earlier than planned, which in turn forced a successor task to be rescheduled accordingly.

- The task's duration and dates changed because you recorded more or less work than originally planned.

- You adjusted a task relationship, which altered the start or finish date.

Add the start variance and finish variance to review and analyze.

*For more information about revising your schedule to get back on track, **see** Chapter 16, "Revising the Schedule," **p. 527**.*

Reviewing Task Cost Variances

Cost variances become unfavorable when the current cost estimates are higher than the baseline estimates. Cost variances can happen for a number of reasons, and are not necessarily connected to the schedule. For example, a task can start and finish on time, but still have an unfavorable cost variance. If you assigned a resource when planning the project, but for some reason had to use a different resource with a higher cost rate, your cost variance might be affected unfavorably.

Apply the Cost Overbudget filter to the Cost table to filter for tasks with unfavorable cost variances. This filter tests for tasks that have captured baselines, and whose current estimated cost is higher than the baseline cost. You can apply the filter when viewing another table, but the Cost table enables you to see the actual values.

*For more information about creating views, **see** the "Creating and Customizing Views" section on **p. 708** in Chapter 22.*

tip

Resource competency is not taken into account automatically in Project; assigning a more expensive resource will not shorten the duration of a task. When revising the duration, you should take into consideration the competency of the resource and make changes if necessary.

Reviewing Task Work Variances

As with other fields discussed so far in this chapter, work variances are unfavorable if the Variance value is a positive number. This means that the resource will have to apply more work to complete the task than originally anticipated. The easiest way to view work variances is to apply the Work table (select the View tab, Data, Tables, Work). The work variance values are displayed in the Variance column (see Figure 14.10).

tip

You might want to create a custom view that applies the Cost Overbudget filter to the Cost table. That way, you have to apply only that view, rather than apply both the table and the view; it saves you a step.

To quickly display all tasks that have an unfavorable work variance, apply the Work Overbudget filter. This filter behaves a lot like the Cost Overbudget filter, selecting tasks whose current work estimates are larger than the baseline values. Because this filter uses the Actual Work values when testing instead of the Work values, it does not account for tasks that have not started. These tasks still might have an unfavorable work variance, even though they have yet to begin. However, you can customize the filter to include these tasks by following these steps:

1. Select the View tab, Data, Filter (Filter Gallery), More Filters, and choose Work Overbudget.

2. Click Copy.

GANTT CHART

	Task Name	Work	Baseline	Variance	Actual	Remaining	% W. Comp.	Add New Column	Dec 23, '12 F T S	Jan 20, '13 W S	Feb 17, '13 T M F
63	◢ Moving	208 hrs	208 hrs	0 hrs	208 hrs	0 hrs	100%				
64	◢ Movers	8 hrs	8 hrs	0 hrs	8 hrs	0 hrs	100%				
65	Confirm your move date	8 hrs	8 hrs	0 hrs	8 hrs	0 hrs	100%		Movers		
66	◢ Do-It-Yourself	8 hrs	8 hrs	0 hrs	8 hrs	0 hrs	100%				
67	Reserve a tru	8 hrs	8 hrs	0 hrs	8 hrs	0 hrs	100%		Movers		
68	Begin enlistin	0 hrs	0 hrs	0 hrs	0 hrs	0 hrs	100%				
69	◢ Packing	184 hrs	184 hrs	0 hrs	184 hrs	0 hrs	100%				
70	Start collectin	64 hrs	64 hrs	0 hrs	64 hrs	0 hrs	100%		Family		
71	Arrange for disposal of	16 hrs	16 hrs	0 hrs	16 hrs	0 hrs	100%		Family		
72	Begin letting children do	32 hrs	32 hrs	0 hrs	32 hrs	0 hrs	100%		Family		
73	File Office do	40 hrs	40 hrs	0 hrs	40 hrs	0 hrs	100%		Family		
75	Send furniture,	8 hrs	8 hrs	0 hrs	8 hrs	0 hrs	100%		Family		
76	Have appliances	16 hrs	16 hrs	0 hrs	16 hrs	0 hrs	100%		Family		
74	Pack tools	8 hrs	8 hrs	0 hrs	8 hrs	0 hrs	100%		Family		
77	◢ Preparing for I	8 hrs	8 hrs	0 hrs	8 hrs	0 hrs	100%				
78	Arrange for c	8 hrs	8 hrs	0 hrs	8 hrs	0 hrs	100%		Family		
79	◢ One to Two Weeks E	208 hrs	208 hrs	0 hrs	0 hrs	208 hrs	0%				
80	◢ Household Admir	8 hrs	8 hrs	0 hrs	0 hrs	8 hrs	0%				
81	◢ Finances and I	0 hrs	0 hrs	0 hrs	0 hrs	0 hrs	0%				
82	Transfer your bank	0 hrs	0 hrs	0 hrs	0 hrs	0 hrs	0%				
83	Close existing	0 hrs	0 hrs	0 hrs	0 hrs	0 hrs	0%				
84	Empty safe-d	0 hrs	0 hrs	0 hrs	0 hrs	0 hrs	0%				
85	Organize app	0 hrs	0 hrs	0 hrs	0 hrs	0 hrs	0%				
86	Make arrange	0 hrs	0 hrs	0 hrs	0 hrs	0 hrs	0%				
87	Buy traveler's	0 hrs	0 hrs	0 hrs	0 hrs	0 hrs	0%				

Figure 14.10
View work variances by applying the Work table.

3. Give the filter a unique name, such as **Work Overbudget (revised for Work)**. Because you are copying the Work Overbudget filter instead of editing it, the original Work Overbudget remains intact.

4. In the first row under Field Name, change Actual Work to **Work**.

5. Click Save to finish the filter definition.

6. Click Apply to apply the filter, Highlight to show all tasks but highlight those selected by the filter, or Close to close the dialog box without applying the filter. The filter will now be in the More Filters list.

Reviewing Status at the Resource Level

The previous sections described methods used to analyze variance for tasks. The methods are similar for analyzing variance and progress for resources.

As with tasks, Project saves the baseline date, work, and cost values for each assignment. The work and cost baseline values are the total baseline values for all of a particular resource's combined task assignments. Likewise, the resource's currently scheduled work and cost values, as well as actual work and actual cost values, are the total combined values for all task assignments for the resource (see the next section, "Reviewing Status at the Assignment Level," for information about analyzing variances for individual assignments). Therefore, the variance values are determined by comparing the total scheduled and total baseline values.

When analyzing resource variances, it is possible that certain resources are responsible for task variances. You might notice a pattern, caused by one of the following reasons:

- Tasks were assigned to resources whose skill level was not capable of completing the tasks within the planned duration.

- Resources arrived later than anticipated to work on the project, thus delaying all the start dates for their tasks.

- When planning the project, you underestimated (or overestimated) the amount of work for tasks assigned to a resource or resource group.

- A resource was overallocated and was not able to apply the percentage of time to the project you originally planned for.

- The original cost of a resource was underestimated or overestimated, or a different resource was later assigned to the task(s) that had a higher or lower cost than the original resource.

- A particular resource or resource group consistently had slipping tasks.

- A resource simply was not applying the appropriate effort needed to complete tasks on time and on budget.

Table 14.2 shows the tables and filters you can apply to show resource variances. Apply these tables and filters to the Resource Sheet view to identify the resource names selected by the filter, or apply them to the Resource Usage view to see specifically which assignments are contributing to the resource variances. Applying these tables and filters is a quicker way to analyze variances than the methods described for analyzing task variances.

Table 14.2   Suggested Tables and Filters for Resource Variance Analysis

Table	Filter	Displays
Cost	Cost Overbudget	Resources whose current estimated cost is greater than the originally estimated baseline cost.
Entry	Slipping Assignments	Resource assignments whose current estimated finish date is later than the planned baseline finish date.
Entry	Should Finish By (interactive filter)	Resource assignments that should have finished by the date you specified.
Entry	Should Start By (interactive filter)	Resource assignments that should have started by the date you specified.
Work	Work Overbudget	Resources whose current estimated work is greater than the originally estimated baseline work. The Work Overbudget filter uses work instead of actual work; you can edit the filter to use actual work if you prefer.

➡ *For more information about using interactive filters,* **see** *the "Using Interactive Filters" section on* **p. 737** *in Chapter 22.*

➡️ *For more information about editing filters,* **see** *the "Creating and Customizing Filters" section on* **p. 729** *in Chapter 22.*

Reviewing Status at the Assignment Level

As previously discussed, baseline assignment values for work and cost are combined and rolled up to the resource or task level. You can view individual assignment details by displaying either the Resource Usage or Task Usage views and applying the appropriate table (or inserting appropriate columns). The Task Usage view displays both the current estimates and the baseline estimates; they also display variance values for these fields. However, resource assignments do not have the start and finish variance fields available; only the work and cost variance values are displayed in the Resource Usage view.

To display assignment level details, select the View tab and choose either Task Usage or Resource Usage. You can then display the Cost, Work, or Variance tables to see assignment variances. Choose the View tab, Data, Tables, and select the appropriate table to display. To see various time-phased baseline values for each assignment, right-click on the grid under the timescale and choose the appropriate value from the shortcut list. You might have to widen the row label's column to display the entire value name; drag the right boundary of the Details column header field.

Analyzing Performance with Earned Value Analysis

So far, this chapter has discussed using variances as a means of analyzing progress on a project. However, variances are all measured in different units: dollar amounts (cost variances), hours (work variances), and time units (date variances). Variances also do not measure whether productivity is at the levels you planned for in the baseline; in other words, variances do not tell you the output per dollar cost, and whether there is enough money left in the project's budget to continue the project and finish as planned.

Earned value analysis evaluates work and cost performance. You can compare the value of the work completed with the cost of completing it. The primary purpose of earned value analysis is to try to measure the value you have earned based on the work that was planned and what was actually performed. These predictions are based on an estimated strategy, such as an educated estimate, a wild guess, scientific predictions, and so on. No matter how you end up with these estimates, you are going to capture them in a baseline at some point. So, earned value analysis compares how you are doing along the timeline of your estimates, and whether your project is likely to be on track with those estimates or if there are variances.

The reason you are looking for variances is to try to predict the future. You are trying to assess the likelihood of achieving your estimates by comparing your progress to them. Evaluation of the past performance is critical and used to determine the cost and schedule performance index, which in turn is used to forecast the future performance. The future is where all the value is—all your effort and costs you have yet to expend.

Earned value analysis measures performance—or productivity—of a project as of a specific date (the status date, or current date if a status date is not identified). If a project is not producing the output per dollar cost that you had originally planned for, earned value analysis will detect the setback and call your attention to it.

Earned value analysis is based on earned money, because it is an accounting term. If you have $100, and you got your work done using only $80, you made a profit. Or, if you spent $150 to get the work done, you lost money. The other side of earned value analysis is work performance. If you have 100 hours worth of work (forget about cost for a minute), and you finish it in 80 hours, you have 20 hours profit of work remaining, or 20 hours of resource availability that you did not have when that work began.

On the other hand, assume that you have 100 hours allotted to complete the work but know now it will take 200. Of course, the extra work chews up cost, but even worse, it uses resources and time. Earned value analysis predicts the future using a cost component and a schedule component to find your risk profile (low or high) for the remainder of the project.

 note

The accuracy of earned value measurements is dependent on the accuracy of your tracking methodology. You must record actual start and finish dates, actual cost, and actual work, and you must reschedule work that was not completed on time and completed work that was scheduled after the status date.

➡ *For more information about earned value and how it relates to Work Breakdown Structure (WBS),* **see** *Chapter 4, "Getting Started After the Business Initiative Is Approved,"* **p. 71**.

Understanding Earned Value Measurements

To comprehend how earned value analysis works in Project, you must first understand its core measurements. Project tasks generate value as work is accomplished, and that value must be at least equal to the project's baseline cost of the work scheduled. If the two values are equal, the task is progressing as expected. Thus, the baseline cost of project tasks acts as a measure of the project's productive output.

Earned value analysis in Project lets you look at today or look to the past for synchronization points. Earned value analysis produces a quality measure if the following are true:

- You have reasonable estimates of the work to be done, broken down into your task list.

  ➡ *For additional information on using the WBS,* **see** *Chapter 4, "Getting Started After the Business Initiative Is Approved,"* **p. 71**.

- The baseline estimates for cost and effort for your tasks and resources were derived using a reasonable methodology.

- You are collecting tracking data in a reasonable way and can depend on the data.

 tip

Using the Work Breakdown Structure (WBS) not only helps you logically split up your work, but also helps you better control scope and better estimate the work to be done.

The word *reasonable* is mentioned throughout the preceding list because all these factors contribute to quality of the EV measure.

Three core measurements are involved with earned value analysis, summarized in the following list. Note that Project fields for Earned Value often have two names, which reflects a transition in the Earned Value world itself:

- **Planned value**—Planned value (PV) is the amount of baseline cost scheduled to be spent on work on the progress up to the status date. The field name for planned value in Project is both Budgeted Cost of Work Scheduled (BCWS) and Planned Value (PV). When you see PV or BCWS anywhere in Project, it is referring to the planned value. The PV or BCWS value is calculated as soon as the baseline is saved. It is the cumulative sum of all baseline costs up to and including the status date.

 tip

If you need to add Planned Value to a table or a view, look for the BCWS field. Or use the default Earned Value tables.

- **Earned value**—Earned value is the value of completed work expressed in terms of the budget assigned to that work. The field name for earned value in Microsoft Project is both Earned Value (EV) and Budgeted Cost of Work Performed (BCWP). When you see BCWP anywhere in Project, it is referring to the earned value.

  Earned value is calculated by the portion of a task or assignment that has been completed. For tasks, the calculation is done based on the percentage of duration complete (the % Complete field). For assignments, the calculation is done based on the percentage of work complete (the Work % Complete field). The percentage complete is based on the current schedule, and not on the baseline amount of duration or work.

 tip

If you need to add Earned Value to a table or a view, look for the BCWP field, or use the default Earned Value tables.

Also, note that % Complete as calculated by Project is not ANSI compliant. Use Physical % Complete instead.

- **Actual cost**—Actual cost is the actual cost of work completed as of the status date. The field name in Project is ACWP, which stands for *Actual Cost of Work Performed*. Actual costs and planned costs might differ for several reasons. For example, resource cost rates might have increased since the baseline was captured, or more expensive resources might have been reassigned to the tasks.

Differences in Earned Value and Planned Value

Earned value and planned value are the same if work on a task has been completed as scheduled up to the status date. However, differences can arise due to several reasons. For example, assume a task was originally scheduled for 8 hours and to cost $500 (the planned value). If your resources have completed 5 of those hours, but the task's duration has changed to 10 hours, the duration is 50% complete (5 hours out of 10, not 5 hours out of 8), and the earned value is $250. Because the scheduled duration increased after the baseline was captured, the actual work generated a smaller value than planned (5/10 or 50%, instead of 5/8 or 63%).

Another example is if overtime was used but not scheduled, then more work was completed than scheduled, and earned value is greater than planned value (it cost more to complete the task than planned due to overtime work). Also, if a resource has been reassigned to a higher-priority task or project, the earned value is less than the planned value, because, as of that status date, less work has been done to the task or project than planned.

An Alternate Explanation

Here is another way to think about earned value analysis: Resources create, or "earn," the value delivered by a project as they work on it. Therefore, "earned value" of any assignment, task, or project is the portion of planned value associated with completed work at any moment in the project's life cycle.

For example, you might have a project with a baseline cost of $200,000. This is the planned value for the project ($200,000), comprised of the baseline costs for all tasks and assignments. Now, on any specific date, you might find that 50% of all scheduled work for the project is complete; therefore, the earned value for the project as of that specific date is 50%, or $100,000. Perhaps the baseline schedule defined the project to be 40% complete on that date. The planned value for that date would be $80,000, and the project would be earning value at a faster rate than planned.

Suppose even further that the actual cost at that specific date is $90,000, meaning you have spent more on your project than you originally budgeted to spend. In other words, the actual cost ($90,000) is greater than the planned value ($80,000) on that specific date. So the question becomes: "Do I have enough money left in the budget to finish the project?" It is likely that you do, because the earned value of what has been produced thus far ($100,000) is greater than both the planned value ($80,000) and the actual cost ($90,000). Because the productivity is greater than you planned for, the project will likely finish on time (or early) and under budget. Then you can pat yourself on the back!

 note

These core measurements (planned value, earned value, and actual cost) help you analyze progress better than simply analyzing variances. Earned value analysis creates earned value variances and productivity indexes that you can use to predict when the project will finish and the total cost upon completion.

In the previous example, and in the summary of the core measurements, a specific synchronization date, or status date, was mentioned. Earned value analysis uses this status date as a point of reference. By default, this date is the current date, taken from your computer's system date. This provides for the most accurate, up-to-date measurements. However, you must remember to track your progress so it is up to date. If you last updated tracking information a week ago, but use today's date for the earned value calculations, Project would not have any actual work and cost to compensate for the planned work and cost from the past week. Therefore, the status date for earned value measurements should be the date you last updated your actual values. Set the status date in the Project Information dialog box (Project tab, Properties, Project Information).

In Project, the three core calculations are performed at the assignment, task, and summary task levels. Calculations at the summary task level are rolled-up sums for their subtasks. At the task level, planned value (PV or BCWS) and actual cost (ACWP) are rolled up into combined sums for the assignments. Earned value (EV or BCWP) calculations are performed using the % Complete (duration percentage complete) value for the task level and the % Work Complete value for the assignment level. This might result in a difference between the earned value of a task and the rolled-up earned value of its assignments.

Earned Value Examples

Consider the following example and figures. Because this subject is advanced material, the details involved will be simple values to ensure that the concept is correctly conveyed and understood.

Task 1 is scheduled to last five days (January 7, 2013, through January 12, 2013). The status date is set to Thursday, January 11, four days into the five-day task, and you can assume it is also the current date. Ryan is the lone resource assigned 100% to the task (five days, or 40 hours). Ryan's standard rate is $10 an hour; therefore, the planned value for the task is $400. No work has been recorded yet on the task. Figure 14.11 illustrates this information.

 tip

Much of the following information is summed up in the upcoming section, "Summary of Using Earned Value Analysis in Project." It might be useful to read that section before reading this one.

Figure 14.11
Notice the Planned Value field (PV or BCWS) has an entry of $320 (calculated through the status date, not the finish date), but the Earned Value (EV or BCWP) and Actual Cost (ACWP) fields have an entry of zero because no work has been recorded.

In Figure 14.11, the top pane displays the Tracking Gantt Chart view with several Earned Value fields inserted into the table (right-click on a column header and insert the column to display these fields). The bottom pane displays the Task Usage view with the Earned Value table applied. The top row is the information for Task 1, and the bottom row is the information for Ryan (in italic).

To save screen space, some of the column headers have been abbreviated (for example, Planned Value – BCWS has been abbreviated to just BCWS). On the right side of the bottom pane, several fields have been inserted.

To re-create this, right-click on any of the fields under the Details column heading and choose Detail Styles. The Detail Styles dialog box appears, as shown in Figure 14.12. Choose the desired field from the Available Fields column, and click the Show button to move the field to the Show These Fields column. The table then displays the field(s) you select in the order they are listed in the Show These Fields column.

In the top pane in Figure 14.11 are two taskbars: The bottom is the baseline taskbar, and the top is the scheduled taskbar. The baseline taskbar, as well as the value for the BCWS field, are automatically displayed in the Tracking Gantt Chart view when you capture the baseline. 0% is next to the scheduled taskbar because no work has been recorded yet, which is also the reason the Earned Value and Actual Cost (ACWP) fields show zero as their entry.

Figure 14.12
Select detail fields to display in the Detail Styles dialog box by highlighting them in the Available Fields column and clicking the Show button.

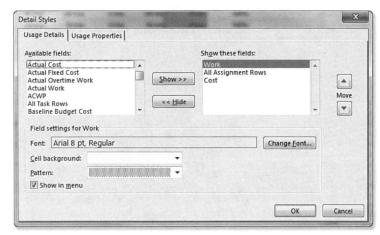

In the lower half of the screen of Figure 14.13, the Task Usage view displays time-phased details for the task. Notice how the planned value (PV or BCWS) is calculated for each day up to and including the status date, and is cumulative. This calculation is performed instantly when the baseline is captured.

Now, assume that at the end of the fourth day of the task (the status and current date), you discover Ryan has only worked three days on the task instead of four, so you enter **60** in the % Complete field, because Ryan has worked 60% of the scheduled duration (three days out of five). Figure 14.13 illustrates the results.

Notice how on Day 4, no actual work or actual cost is displayed in the details side of the bottom pane. This is because Project automatically calculates these values based on the entry of 60% in the % Complete field. 60% is equivalent to three days in this task; therefore, only three days of actual work are recorded.

The Earned Value field is marked as $240, because Ryan has earned $240 by doing three days of work at his rate of $10 an hour. Compare this to the planned value of $320, and you see that Ryan has not earned as much as planned in the baseline, because he did not work according to the schedule.

> **note**
>
> To display details for the task in the bottom pane, as shown in Figure 14.11, you must have the task selected in the top pane. If you have a field selected that is not in the task row in the top pane, the bottom pane will not display the details for the task.

Using Earned Value Schedule Indicators

Project provides tables to help you analyze progress using earned value. You can apply the Earned Value Schedule Indicators table to deduce whether your project is earning value at the planned rate.

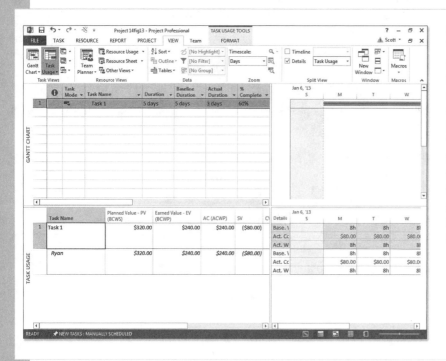

Figure 14.13
The Earned Value and Actual Cost (ACWP) fields have values now that actual work has been recorded. The Change Highlighting feature is enabled to point out the effects of entering 60% in the % Complete field.

Figure 14.14 illustrates the Earned Value Schedule Indicators table as applied to both panes in the example of Ryan and Task 1. Again, some column headings have been abbreviated to save screen space, and the Detail Styles dialog box has been used to display specific detail fields on the timescale side of the Task Usage view (right side, bottom pane).

Three important indicator fields are displayed on this table:

- **SV (Schedule Variance)**—This field displays the difference between planned value and earned value, calculated by subtracting planned value from earned value (EV − PV). In this example, ($80.00) is displayed. The parentheses indicate a negative number, because the earned value is less than the planned value. Therefore, the project has earned $80 less than what was planned for by this point because less work has been done than planned (hence the name *schedule variance*).

> **note**
>
> If the number was positive, the earned value would be greater than originally planned for by this point in the project, which is good news for you.

- **SV% (Schedule Variance percentage)**—This field displays the value of the schedule variance as a percentage. It is calculated by dividing schedule variance by the planned value (SV / PV). In this case, it is −$80 / $320, which equates to −25%. In other words, the earned value is 25% less than the planned value.

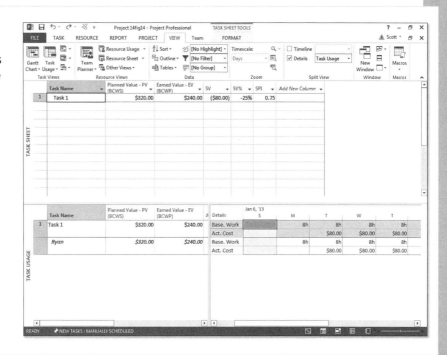

Figure 14.14
The Earned Value Schedule Indicators table helps you see the rate at which your project is earning value as compared to the planned rate.

Negative numbers such as this one indicate that something is keeping the work from being completed as scheduled, and because you are the project manager, this should signify to you that the matter is in need of investigation. Perhaps you need to assign additional resources. On the other side, a positive number might indicate that you are ahead of schedule, and you might be able to reassign some of the resources to other tasks that are slipping for them to catch up.

- **SPI (Schedule Performance Index)**—This field displays the ratio of earned value to planned value (EV / PV). In this case, the value is 0.75 ($240 / $320). In other words, the task is earning $0.75 for every $1 of value that was planned to earn, or is .75 as productive as originally planned. Obviously, this is unfavorable. Anything greater than 1.0 in this field would be favorable, and anything less than 1.0 provides the same indications to you as the project manager to fix the slipping task (in this case), assignment, or project.

You can also use the SPI to estimate the project or task's finish date. Divide the remaining duration by the SPI. You can insert the Remaining Duration column into the table as you wish. For example, in this case, you would divide 16 hours (remaining duration) by .75 (SPI), which equals 21.3 hours. Therefore, at this rate, it will take 21.3 more hours to complete the task, or 45.3 hours total. This is 5.3 hours (close to a full day) behind schedule if the progress rate continues to stay the same.

So far in this example, the earned value (BCWP) and the actual cost (ACWP) have been the same. They would change, however, if Ryan was moved off the task and another resource was reassigned to the task. Say, for instance, Chris is the new resource, but his rate is 50% more than Ryan's at $15 an hour. This will boost actual cost.

note

SV% and SPI are not calculated at the assignment level.

Figure 14.15 shows the calculations after Chris has replaced Ryan to work 100% on Task 1. The % Complete (60%) remains the same. Like the previous examples, column headings have been abbreviated to save screen space, and the Detail Styles dialog box has been used to display specific detail fields in the timescale side of the Task Usage view (right side, bottom pane).

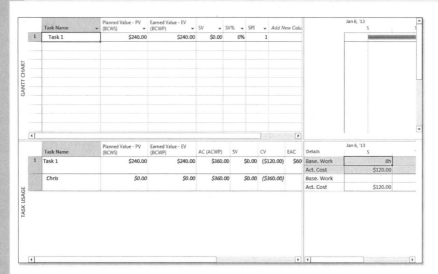

Figure 14.15
When the Earned Value (BCWP) and Actual Cost (ACWP) fields differ, you can compare the two to see whether you spent more than you earned.

Although the planned value (BCWS) and earned value (BCWP) are the same no matter which resource is used to work on the task, clearly the actual cost is different because Chris costs more than Ryan. Because Chris costs $120 a day and Ryan costs $80 a day, the actual cost increases by $40 a day, while the earned value remains the same. If this trend continues, you will be well over budget when the task or project concludes.

Again, there is a table to help indicate cost variance—the Earned Value Cost Indicators table. Figure 14.16 illustrates the Earned Value Cost Indicators table applied to the same example, with Chris working on the task instead of Ryan. As usual, the column headings have been abbreviated to save screen space and the Detail Styles dialog box has been used to display specific daily information on the timescale side of the Task Usage view.

➡ *For more information about editing and saving tables, **see** the "Creating and Customizing Tables" section on **p. 700** in Chapter 22.*

Figure 14.16
The Earned Value Cost Indicators table helps to summarize the cost versus earned value thus far.

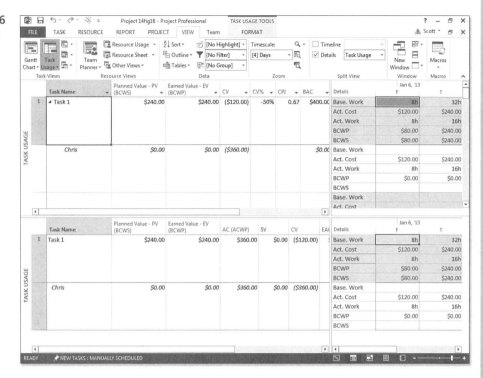

 note

By default, the Earned Value Cost Indicators table does not include the Actual Cost (ACWP) field. It might be helpful to insert this field, as in Figure 14.16. Choose the column where you want to insert it and right-click on the column header. Choose Insert Column from the list, select ACWP from the drop-down list under Field Name, and click OK. You might also want to save this modification so all future uses of this table will include the ACWP column.

The cost indicators found in this table are defined in the following list:

- **CV (Cost Variance)**—This field displays the difference between earned value and actual cost, calculated by subtracting actual cost from earned value (EV – ACWP). In this example, the cost variance is –$120, shown in parentheses as ($120.00), meaning the actual cost was $120 more than the earned value of the work (as of the status date). Again, this is an unfavorable result; the value of the work is lower than the cost of producing it. In other words, you are spending more than the work is worth. If the cost variance is a positive number, it is viewed as a favorable result.

- **CV% (Cost Variance percentage)**—This field displays the value of the cost variance in terms of percent. It is calculated by dividing cost variance by the earned value (CV / EV). In this example, the value is −50%, meaning you spent 50% more than you planned so far. This is primarily because Chris is a much more expensive resource than Ryan. At this rate, you will not have enough money left in the budget to complete the remaining work.

- **CPI (Cost Performance Index)**—This field displays the ratio of earned value to actual cost (EV / ACWP) for the actual work complete through the status date. CPI tells you how much cost value you earn for every dollar spent. In this case, the value is 0.67 ($240 / $360). In other words, the task is earning $0.67 of cost value for every $1 spent, about two-thirds as profitable as originally planned. Obviously this also is unfavorable, and the significant difference has much to do with Chris being a more expensive resource that Ryan, as well as being behind schedule. Anything greater than 1.0 in this field would be favorable, and anything less than 1.0 is not.

> 🔍 **note**
>
> CV% and CPI are not calculated at the assignment level.

This field is used to calculate the Estimate at Completion (EAC) field, which is discussed later in this section.

The Earned Value Cost Indicators table includes additional fields to the right of the three fields just described. You might have to scroll to the right on the table to see them, but they are displayed in Figure 14.16.

- **BAC (Budget at Completion)**—This is the Baseline Cost field, displayed in this table as BAC. It represents the total planned value for the completed task.

- **EAC (Estimate at Completion)**—Earlier versions of Project used to equate this field to the estimated total cost. Since Project 2002, however, EAC is a calculated estimate of what the total cost will be when the task is completed if the CPI rate of performance remains constant through the end. In other words, the EAC calculation takes the actual cost as of the status date and adds an estimated remaining cost based on the CPI.

  The formula used to calculate this estimate is ACWP + (BAC − EV) / CPI. Project begins by subtracting the earned value (EV) from the budget at completion (BAC) to get the remaining value yet to be produced. Next, that remaining value to be earned (BAC − EV) is divided by the CPI. CPI tells you the value you are currently earning for each dollar spent; therefore, dividing the remaining value to be earned by the value you are earning for each dollar gives you the number of actual dollars you need to spend to produce the remaining value to be earned. Add that value (the amount you need to spend to produce the remaining value to be earned) to the money you have already spent (actual cost, or ACWP), and you have an estimated total cost at completion. In this case, it would be approximately $600, which is $200 more than planned.

  Of course, the EAC will change over time as your CPI rate changes, but it is an estimate for the current status date.

- **VAC (Variance at Completion)**—VAC is the difference between the total baseline cost (BAC) and the estimated total cost (EAC), calculated by subtracting the total estimated cost at completion from the total planned value (BAC − EAC). If the VAC is a positive number, the cost estimate is lower than budgeted cost. If it is negative, like the example in Figure 14.14, the current cost rate is greater than the budgeted cost, and the project will complete over budget if the pattern continues. As a reminder, negative numbers are shown in parentheses.

- **TCPI (To Complete Performance Index)**—TCPI is the ratio of the value of remaining work to the budgeted funds remaining to be spent, as of the status date. The calculation uses this formula:

$$(BAC - EV) / (BAC - ACWP)$$

In other words, the value of remaining work is divided by the budgeted funds remaining to be spent.

The TCPI formula calculates the value each dollar remaining in the budget must earn to stay within the budget. Each remaining dollar spent must earn the TCPI value to stay within budget. In this example, each dollar spent must earn $4 to stay within the planned budget. Most of this discrepancy is due to using a resource that cost 50% more than planned, but it also has to do with being behind schedule.

If you are currently over budget as of the status date, the TCPI will be greater than 1.0 in order to catch up. You will likely have to increase productivity or reduce the cost of work. If the TCPI is less than 1.0, you are under budget and have the opportunity to increase the scope or quality of work, or save the money to use elsewhere in the project or in another project.

 tip

Experience shows that clients are most appreciative when you deliver what is expected, not more and especially not less. In other words, even favorable variances are sometimes viewed as poor project management, simply because variances of any sort indicate a difference between estimated and actual values, and thus disprove your ability to accurately plan.

It is wise to plan exactly as you see fit based on experience and research. Trying to impress your client with a low budget or quick schedule will only end up hurting you in the end when you cannot deliver the end result within the planned baseline. On the other side, do not cushion your estimates so your project finishes earlier or under the budget you planned. You might do this to look like an overachiever as a project manager, but finishing early only leaves your resources with nothing to do until their next project assignments begin, which have been scheduled to start according to your finish date estimates. Think of when an airplane arrives early—it has to simply sit on the runway and wait until its assigned gate is clear before the passengers can exit the plane. That particular flight might be early, but it still has to operate in sync with every other airport factor.

Controlling the Calculation of Earned Value

As mentioned previously, Project calculates earned value at the task level using the duration percentage complete (the % Complete field). You have the option to use Physical % Complete instead. This might be more beneficial when calculating earned value for tasks that involve the production of physical units of output or the processing of physical units of input (tasks that produce or receive physical materials). This is because work on a task might not produce materials as consistently as duration uses time; duration is linear, but production levels vary. In other words, a task that takes 10 days to produce a certain number of material items might start slow, but after a few days, as the resources get more accustomed to the work, their productivity increases. Calculating earned value using Physical % Complete might, therefore, be more accurate because it measures the amount of materials produced at the status date, not the amount of time used.

To change the earned value calculation method, open the Task Information dialog box (double-click on a task), select the Advanced tab, and choose from the drop-down list in the Earned Value Method field at the bottom of the box. If you choose Physical % Complete, that field will be included on the Tracking table, and you can enter values there.

In Figure 14.17, the Earned Value table is displayed with the Earned Value Method and the Physical % Complete fields inserted. The two tasks are identical to convey the difference between the two earned value methods. Each version of the task is scheduled for 10 days, and the duration percentage complete is 50% (5 days into the task). However, only 25% of the work has been completed. You can see the difference in the earned value depending on which earned value method you select. Task 1 calculates the earned value using the duration percentage complete, and Task 2 uses the Physical % Complete value.

Figure 14.17
Notice the earned value difference if you use % Complete versus Physical % Complete.

You can also change the default calculation from % Complete to Physical %, as shown in Figure 14.18. Complete if you feel that is more beneficial to your project. Select the File tab, Options, Advanced. Scroll to the Earned Value options for this project section. Underneath it is the Baseline for Earned Value Calculations field. Remember, Project enables you to save a total of 11 baselines—the default baseline plus 10 additional baselines (Baseline 1 through Baseline 10). Select which baseline to use to calculate the earned value. For example, if a project schedule has been heavily revised since the original baseline was captured, you might want to use the revised baseline instead of the original.

 note

Changing the baseline in the Earned Value dialog box affects earned value only; the duration, work, cost, start, and finish variances still use the standard baseline fields.

Similarly, changing the Default Task Earned Value Method setting affects tasks that are inserted after the default is changed.

Figure 14.18
You can change the earned value method and the baseline used for calculating the earned value in the Earned Value section of the Advanced tab.

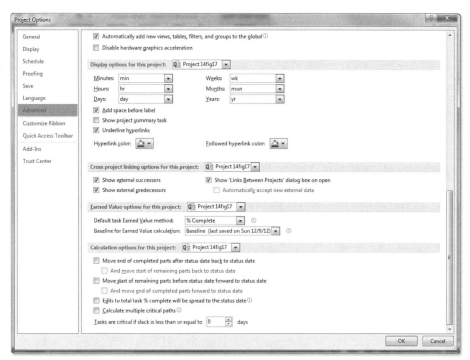

Summary of Using Earned Value Analysis in Project

As previously stated, earned value analysis is an effective means of analyzing progress in your project. Its usage is best summarized as follows.

There are four basic steps you must follow to use earned value analysis in Project:

1. Use the Work Breakdown Structure (WBS) technique to plan your work. You must also ensure that the resources used have a cost rate.

2. Capture the baseline for the project. You can capture up to 11 different baselines.

3. Update the project with the latest tracking information. Be thorough in your tracking methodology, as it will improve the accuracy and significance of earned value measurements.

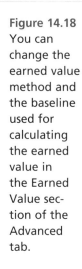 *For more information about tracking your project,* **see** *Chapter 13, "Tracking Your Project Progress,"* **p. 431.**

4. Set the status date to the date you collect actuals and enter tracking information.

When using earned value analysis, the Gantt Chart view is the most common view to display, although other views can be applied that are helpful, such as the Tracking Gantt Chart view. After the view is displayed, you can use three different tables to analyze the earned value calculations.

To apply any of the following three tables, choose View, Table, and select More Tables. In the resulting More Tables dialog box, select one of the following tables:

note

The fields in the following tables and their abbreviations are described in greater detail in the previous section, "Understanding Earned Value Measurements."

- **Earned Value**—This table, shown in Figure 14.19, displays the three core calculations: Planned Value (PV or BCWS), Earned Value (EV or BCWP), and Actual Cost (ACWP). The Earned Value table also displays the Earned Value Schedule Variance (SV), the Earned Value Cost Variances (CV), the Estimate at Completion (EAC), the Budget at Completion (BAC), and the Variance at Completion (VAC). Basically, this table displays all the fields necessary for using earned value analysis. You might have to scroll to the right or move the vertical divider bar to view all columns together.

	Task Name	Planned Value - PV	Earned Value - EV	AC (ACWP)	SV	CV	EAC	BAC	VAC	Add N
1	Task A	$0.00	$0.00	$0.00	$0.00	$0.00	$0.00	$0.00	$0.00	
2	Task B	$0.00	$0.00	$0.00	$0.00	$0.00	$0.00	$0.00	$0.00	
3	Task C	$0.00	$0.00	$0.00	$0.00	$0.00	$0.00	$0.00	$0.00	
4	Task D	$0.00	$0.00	$0.00	$0.00	$0.00	$0.00	$0.00	$0.00	
5	Task E	$0.00	$0.00	$0.00	$0.00	$0.00	$0.00	$0.00	$0.00	
6	Complete	$0.00	$0.00	$0.00	$0.00	$0.00	$0.00	$0.00	$0.00	

Figure 14.19
The Earned Value table displays the earned value calculations.

- **Earned Value Cost Indicators**—This table, shown in Figure 14.20, summarizes the effectiveness of cost thus far in the project in producing the planned value. The Earned Value Cost Indicators table displays Planned Value (PV or BCWS) and Earned Value (EV or BCWP), as well as Earned Value cost variance fields: Cost Variance (CV), Cost Variance percentage (CV%), and Cost Performance Index (CPI). It also displays the estimated final cost fields: Budget at Completion (BAC), Estimate at Completion (EAC), Variance at Completion (VAC), and To Complete Performance Index (TCPI). It might also be helpful to insert the Actual Cost (ACWP) column into the table.

	Task Name	Planned Value - PV (BCWS)	Earned Value - EV (BCWP)	CV	CV%	CPI	BAC	EAC	VAC	TCPI
0	◢ Project 14fig20	$57,600.00	$40,000.00	$0.00	0%	1	$80,000.00	$80,000.00	$0.00	1
1	Task A	$28,800.00	$24,000.00	$0.00	0%	1	$40,000.00	$40,000.00	$0.00	1
2	Task B	$28,800.00	$16,000.00	$0.00	0%	1	$40,000.00	$40,000.00	$0.00	1

Figure 14.20
The Earned Value Cost Indicators table summarizes the effectiveness of cost as of the status date.

■ **Earned Value Schedule Indicators**—This table, shown in Figure 14.21, displays the Planned Value (PV or BCWS) and Earned Value (EV or BCWP) columns, as well as the schedule variance and indicator calculations: Schedule Variance (SV), Schedule Variance percentage (SV%), and Schedule Performance Index (SPI).

Figure 14.21
The Earned Value Schedule Indicators focus on schedule variance as of the status date.

	Task Name	Planned Value - PV (BCWS)	Earned Value - EV (BCWP)	SV	SV%	SPI	Add New Column
0	◢ **Project 14fig21**	**$57,600.00**	**$40,000.00**	**($17,600.00)**	**-31%**	**0.69**	
1	Task A	$28,800.00	$24,000.00	($4,800.00)	-17%	0.83	
2	Task B	$28,800.00	$16,000.00	($12,800.00)	-44%	0.56	

Earned Value Report

Project 2013 ships with a new Earned Value report out of the box.

The Earned Value report provides the visual representation of what is known as the S-curves for at-a-glance earned value analysis. Figure 14.22 displays a modified Earned Value Over Time report that provides the Earned Value graph. You can use the PivotTable tab below the chart to expand or compress the level of detail you see, which is also reflected on the graph above. You can also use the PivotTable Field List to add additional fields to be displayed in the report.

The Earned Value report enables you to easily compare Actual Cost of Work Performed (ACWS), Planned Value (BCWS), and Earned Value (BCWP). It also provides two more graphs comparing Cost Variance to Schedule Variance, and CPI and SPI. In Figure 14.22, you can see that the project, which is only halfway through its planned duration, is already doing badly in every area and will certainly be over budget and late.

➡️ *For additional information on the Earned Value report, **see** Chapter 15, "Using Reports for Tracking and Control," **p. 497**.*

➡️ *For additional information on customizing and working with reports, **see** Chapter 20, "Reports Part I: 2013 Reports," **p. 625**.*

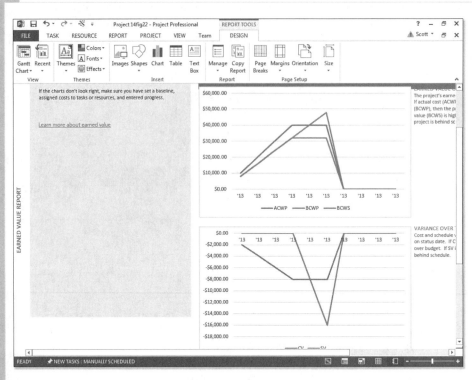

Figure 14.22
The Earned Value report enables you to graphically present the information and provides at-a-glance status to you and your project sponsors.

Using Analysis Views and Reports

Project comes equipped with dozens of views and reports that you can use for analyzing your project. All of these views and reports are customizable in varying degrees to mold them into exactly what you need.

➡ For more information about customizing views, **see** the "Creating and Customizing Views" section on **p. 708** in Chapter 22.

➡ For more information about customizing reports, **see** the "Customizing Reports" section on **p. 646** in Chapter 20.

As the project manager, your primary responsibility is to make sure the project runs as close to the project plan as possible. This responsibility involves a lot of constant analysis. After the project begins to slip, you must fix it right away; the problem certainly will not fix itself and will only get worse over time.

Analysis Views

The views that are found in Project serve many purposes. Some views are designed for project data entry, and other views are designed for project data analysis. This section discusses the various views found in Project that can be used for project analysis. Each of these views is customizable and printable.

➡ *For more information about customizing views, **see** the "Creating and Customizing Views" section on **p. 708** in Chapter 22.*

➡ *For more information about printing views, **see** the "Printing Views" section on **p. 715** in Chapter 22.*

Tracking Gantt View

The tracking views and tables in Project are typically very good for project analysis. The Tracking Gantt view is similar to the Gantt Chart view, but the timescale side also shows tracking information such as percentage complete. It also color-codes the taskbars. Tasks that are complete have a blue taskbar, and uncompleted tasks have a red taskbar.

The progress on a task is also illustrated within the taskbar, and the overall progress on a project is illustrated under the project summary taskbar (if the project summary taskbar is not displayed, you can display it by selecting Tools, Options, and on the View tab, selecting the Show Project Summary Task check box). Below each taskbar is the taskbar for the baseline duration, so you can compare the baseline and actual duration side by side. Figure 14.23 shows how the Tracking Gantt view displays taskbars.

By default, the Entry table is applied to the Tracking Gantt view, but there are several other tables you can apply that will be useful for analyzing the project.

Figure 14.23
The Tracking Gantt view shows progress in the taskbars on the timescale side.

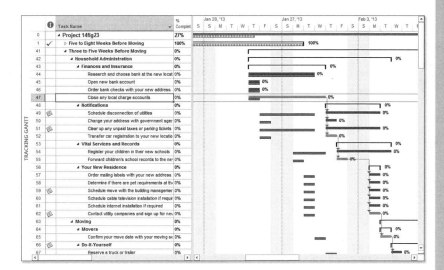

When you apply the Tracking table to the Tracking Gantt view, you combine the tracking timescale with the tracking information, all on one screen. That way, you are able to clearly view your tasks' progress on the timescale side, as well as the following columns of information: Actual Start, Actual Finish, % Complete, Physical % Complete, Actual Duration, Remaining Duration, Actual Cost, and Actual Work. To apply the Tracking table, first display the Tracking Gantt view (Task tab, Views, Gantt Chart, Tracking Gantt); then select the View tab, Data, Tables, Tracking. The Tracking table is applied to the illustration in Figure 14.23.

 note

Although this section describes various tables applied to the Tracking Gantt view for analysis, these tables can be applied to most views in Project. The Tracking Gantt view is used in this discussion because its timescale side aids tremendously in analyzing progress for individual tasks as well as the entire project.

The columns of information found in the Tracking table are all practical for project analysis. These fields display a lot of actual information—that is, what is actually happening in each task, such as when it started or finished, how long it took, how much duration is remaining, how much it costs, and so on. Of course, to fully analyze this information, you must compare it to what was planned. That way, you have an idea of what has actually happened versus what was supposed to happen. If there is a lot of variance, you likely need to make some changes in the execution of your project.

The Baseline table provides several columns of information that display the baseline values for the project: Baseline Duration, Baseline Start, Baseline Finish, Baseline Work, and Baseline Cost. To display the Baseline table, select the View tab, Data, Tables, More Tables, Baseline.

Now, rather than actual information, you are viewing what was planned. Then, you can compare the baseline values with the actual values. There are two primary means of doing this using the two tables discussed thus far applied to the Tracking Gantt view. The first is to print two versions of the Tracking Gantt view—one with the Baseline table applied and one with the Tracking table applied.

➡ *For more information about printing views,* **see** *the "Printing Views" section on p. 715 in Chapter 22.*

The second option is to insert baseline information into the Tracking table, or insert actual (Tracking) information into the Baseline table. To insert a column into a table, right-click on the column heading where you want the new column inserted and choose Insert Column. Choose the column name you want to insert from the Field Name drop-down list in the Insert Column dialog box and click OK. The new column appears where you right-clicked, and all other columns shift to the right. Repeat this process until you have inserted all the columns of information you want to view.

Using the Variance Table

Another helpful table to apply to the Tracking Gantt view to aid in project analysis is the Variance table. To display the Variance table, select the View tab, Data, Tables, Variance. The Variance table is especially useful for analyzing a project's schedule because it summarizes the differences between the Baseline and Tracking (actual) tables for you. This table displays Start and Finish dates, Baseline Start and Baseline Finish dates, and Start Variance and Finish Variance dates. That way, you can examine each task's start and finish dates as compared to what was planned and whether there is any variance. If desired, you can insert more columns of information, such as duration information, to further analyze the schedule.

Using the Work Table

The Work table is perhaps the most accommodating table to apply to the Tracking Gantt view for project scope analysis. Project scope is essentially the work that needs be done to accomplish the goal(s) of the project. Therefore, analyzing work on a project is vital to analyzing scope. To apply the Work table, select the View tab, Data, Tables, Work. The Work table displays Work, Baseline (baseline work), Variance (work variance), Actual (actual work), Remaining (remaining work), and Work % Complete. You can evaluate each task or the project as a whole, and see how many work hours were planned, how many were actually performed, any variance between the plan and the actual values, and so on.

Using the Earned Value Table

The Earned Value table is yet another useful table to apply to the Tracking Gantt view for project analysis. This particular table is best suited for analyzing project budget. The Earned Value table is discussed earlier in this chapter in the sections, "Summary of Using Earned Value Analysis in Project" and "Understanding Earned Value Measurements."

 note

As mentioned previously, any and all of the tables described in this section are customizable. Furthermore, any of the columns of information found in these tables can be inserted into any other table. If you want to combine information from two tables, you can insert the column using the right-click Insert Column command.

Resource Allocation View

Although the Tracking Gantt view and subsequent tables discussed in the previous section are all good for analyzing project tasks, schedule, budget, and scope, the Resource Allocation table is helpful for analyzing your resource workload. To display the Resource Allocation view, select the Resource tab, View, Team Planner, More Views, Resource Allocation.

The Resource Allocation view is a split window. The top pane is the Resource Usage view, which lists the resources and their assigned tasks, and the number of hours each resource is scheduled to work (total as well as per task). The bottom pane by default is the Leveling Gantt view, but you should change it to the Resource Graph view. Change the bottom pane to the Resource Graph view by clicking in the bottom pane to select it, and then select the View tab, Split view, Details, Resource Graph. The screen now displays a split window: the Resource Usage view on top and the Resource Graph on the bottom, as shown in Figure 14.24.

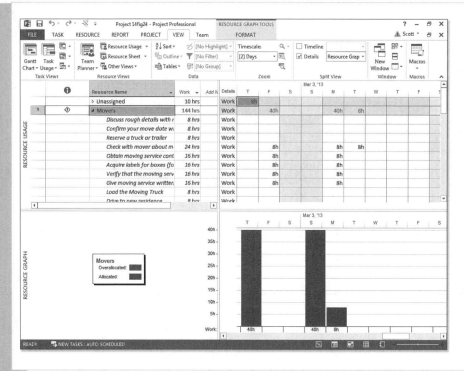

Figure 14.24
The Resource Allocation view with the Resource Graph in the bottom of the split window provides a clear view of which resources are overloaded with work and which are not.

As indicated in Figure 14.24, the bottom pane (Resource Graph) provides a detailed illustration of the workload assigned to the selected resource in the top pane. In this case, the Movers are overallocated; they are assigned more hours of work than are in a normal working day. On the bottom pane of the Resource Allocation view, the bar graph represents the hours per day they are scheduled to work. Notice that on Friday March 1st, they are scheduled to work 40 hours. Because a normal working day is 8 hours, the remaining 32 hours are shown in red on the bar graph as overallocated.

> *For additional information on resource overallocations and techniques for resolving them, **see** Chapter 24, "Resolving Resource Allocation Problems," **p. 801**.*

The Resource Allocation view is a great way to view all your resources simultaneously, and see whether their working hours and assignments are spread evenly across the board. It is also a great view to examine to see whether you can reassign certain assignments to other resources that might not have as large of a workload as some of your overallocated resources.

Analysis Reports

Project contains several basic and visual reports to aid in project analysis. These reports offer many options for analyzing project schedule, budget, and scope—the three main components of project analysis. As mentioned previously, all of these reports are customizable and intended for many different audiences. These reports are described in detail in other chapters of the book.

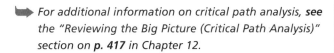 *For more information about using the visual reports for project analysis, **see** "Using Visual Reports" on **p. 510** in Chapter 15.*

Analyzing the Critical Path

Critical tasks drive the project; if they are delayed, the project's finish date will be delayed. Therefore, when you are analyzing performance on a project, it is most efficient to first analyze the progress of the tasks within the critical path. If you can restore the slipping critical tasks, it is likely that you will reestablish the project to its planned schedule or within its planned budget.

One way to quickly analyze the critical path is to apply a filter for critical tasks to a table that displays the analysis fields discussed throughout this chapter, such as any of the earned value tables or variance tables. Apply the critical tasks filter by selecting the View tab, Data, Filter, Critical; then examine which critical tasks are slipping and why. If they are over budget, maybe you need to cut back on resources working on the critical tasks to save money. If they are behind schedule, maybe you need to increase the number of resources, or increase the amount of work to get caught up.

 note

When the overall project is slipping, it is good practice to concentrate first on fixing the critical path. This will certainly improve the project's progress, and likely bring it back up to speed.

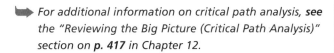 *For additional information on critical path analysis, **see** the "Reviewing the Big Picture (Critical Path Analysis)" section on **p. 417** in Chapter 12.*

Consultants' Tips

Project Performance Analysis Prerequisites

Proper analysis requires:

- Spending a good amount of time planning out the work and breaking it down using the Work Breakdown Structure (WBS) technique to ensure that the full project scope has been captured.

- Ensuring that the cost data in your project schedule is accurate and matches the financial data against which contract invoicing will be performed.

- Ensuring that after you have completed planning, you save the baseline of the project for comparison.

- If you make any subsequent changes to the project schedule planned values, ensuring that the appropriate change request is followed. Resave another baseline to capture your project plan changing.

- Using the most accurate information and updating your project progress regularly to ensure that the performance analysis you perform is based on the latest actual data.

Project Performance Analysis Areas

When analyzing your project performance, include the following:

- **Scope**—Ensure that the project still is within scope by reviewing the task list and scope statements.

- **Budget**—Analyze views and reports described in this chapter to ensure that the budget variance in your schedule is under control and that you notice if the project budget begins to slip.

- **Schedule**—Analyze views and reports described in this chapter to ensure that the project is still scheduled to finish on time. Use any schedule variances you see as a red flag that the project schedule is deviating from the original plan. You can then use additional reports and views to drill in further to determine the source of the problem, so that it can be resolved. This will help you bring the immediate problem under control and mitigate future risks.

Additionally, you may want to analyze these areas:

- **Work**—Analyze the work fields, such as Planned Work, Actual Work, Baseline Work, and Work Variance, to ensure that the work being performed is in line with the original plan.

- **Resources**—Analyze the resource allocation and resource performance to ensure that the resources are performing the work as scheduled. This can help you determine whether your resource productivity is good enough. You can potentially replace them with other resources that would perform better. Resource views can also help you determine whether any resources are overallocated and resolve the problem by either redistributing work better, assigning additional resources, or delaying overlapping tasks.

Project Performance Analysis Options

Project provides several tools to help you analyze your project performance, as follows:

- Use the Project Overview Report to view high-level statistics about your project.

- Use the existing views, such as Tracking Gantt, Earned Value, and many others, as well as customized views achieved by adding more columns.

- Use reports to view additional data, such the Earned Value report and the Earned Value Over Time visual report.

No matter what technique you use, just remember that analyzing and tracking your project progress is as important as planning it. The more often you review the progress and performance, the more aware you will be of any problems that can potentially arise, and the more prepared you will be to address them and still have your project finish within scope, budget, and schedule.

15

USING REPORTS FOR TRACKING AND CONTROL

This chapter provides background and real-world examples of reporting capabilities available in Project. This chapter focuses on reporting using standard reports and covers only basic capabilities. It is a good starting point, but most projects need some customization for their specific needs. Customization is not covered in this chapter.

This chapter has two halves: one covering reports and the other covering visual reports. There is a significant amount of overlapping functionality between the two, but don't let that bother you. Use visual reports when you really want to get your data into Excel or Visio and work with it from there. Otherwise, reports should work well.

Using Reports

The reports that come standard in Project can be used in various ways by the project manager for tracking and controlling a project. A total of 16 reports come with Project, and each is accessed through the View Reports group on the Report tab. To access these reports, select the Report tab, as shown in Figure 15.1.

> **note**
>
> Confusingly, Project comes with two kinds of reports: reports and visual reports. With Project 2013, visual reports are being repositioned as an export tool, useful for moving Project data into either Visio or Excel.

To open a specific report, click a category control in the View Reports group and select it.

You can also navigate through each of the reports by selecting More Reports at the bottom of each category control. Regardless of which category you select, More Reports always shows the same dialog box, giving you access to all the reports, as shown in Figure 15.2.

Figure 15.1
The Report tab is the primary report navigation mechanism.

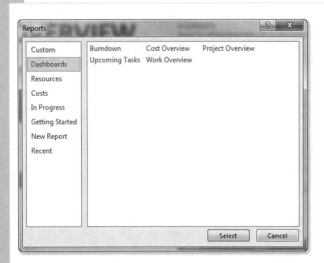

Figure 15.2
The Reports dialog box lists all Project reports found in Project.

Each of these reports is heavily customizable. Also, you have the option to design a new report from scratch if none of the existing reports satisfies your requirements. Customizing existing reports and creating new ones are excellent methods for constructing a report that contains exactly the columns of information you want to display.

➡ *Before working extensively with reports, read the information about customizing existing basic reports and creating new ones included in Chapter 20, "Reports Part I: 2013 Reports," p. 625. Chapter 20 also includes complete tables listing the basic reports found in each category.*

The first part of this chapter focuses on using the existing reports for tracking and controlling your project, and later the chapter focuses on using visual reports for the same purpose.

 tip

Take advantage of the customization options available for each report. You can reformat the heading text to make the report more visually appealing, add or take away various columns of information and other details found in the report, change the sort order for the items in the report, rename the report, modify the time period of information to display in the report, and so on.

The data contained in the reports can be advantageous for different purposes and different audiences. Some reports might be beneficial for project analysis, some might be useful for status reports for the project sponsor, and some might be useful for status meetings with your project team. The next several sections are organized by the basic reports' functionality with examples of who might find them useful and why.

 For more information about common interaction within each report, **see** the "Using the Common Customization Controls" section on **p. 649** in Chapter 20.

> **note**
This chapter provides insight regarding which standard reports are most useful for certain situations. It is advised that you read through Chapter 20, along with this chapter. Chapter 20 discusses how you can modify each report, change the page setup and print options you have available, and other options to make reports suitable for your audience.

Reports and the Iron Triangle

Project reports should help you balance the demands of schedule, scope, and cost. As the project manager, your main focus is to keep the project moving forward as close to its estimates as possible. Reports fall broadly into the three categories of the Iron triangle:

- Reports that deal with when things are being done or not done (schedule)

- Reports that deal with what tasks cost

- Reports that the project manager uses to report on those things to stakeholders, which help to manage scope

Using Reports for Analyzing the Project Schedule

To be honest, almost every single report or feature in Project in some way involves the schedule. However, when analyzing a project schedule, you are looking at how work is being completed on tasks compared to how it was planned and captured in the baseline. You do not want to see a lot of schedule variance, and you definitely do not want to see a lot of slipping tasks—especially slipping tasks in the critical path.

 For more information about accurately tracking your tasks' progress, **see** the "Entering Tracking Information at the Task Level" section on **p. 438** in Chapter 13.

The Upcoming Tasks report presents a high-level opportunity to gut-check your projects progress. Generally, project managers know what tasks should be coming in the next seven days. If the Upcoming Tasks report does not jibe with your expectations, you either have a problem with your schedule (always possible) or you

> **note**
The accuracy of these analysis reports (and most reports in Project, for that matter) obviously depends heavily on the accuracy of your tracking. Project does not know when or if a task has been completed unless you mark it as complete. Experienced project managers take the effort required to keep tasks up-to-date into account when they are building the schedule they will be reporting against.

have a problem with your project's progress. The Upcoming Tasks report is under the Dashboards category control on the Report tab and is shown in Figure 15.3.

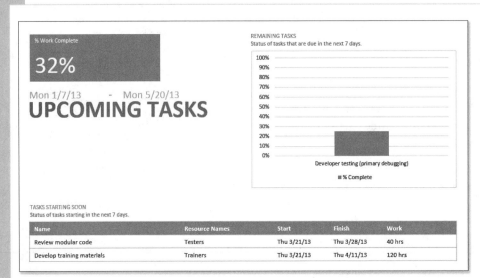

Figure 15.3
If your Upcoming Tasks report doesn't show you what you think it should, you should be alarmed.

The Critical Tasks report displays all tasks that affect the project finish date. If tasks on the critical path slip, the project finish date will likely be delayed. Making your team aware of the critical path tasks might help to avoid having any of the critical tasks slip, because your team will be more familiar with which tasks drive the project and their significance to an on-time project completion.

To display the Critical Tasks report, select it from the In Progress category control on the Report tab (see Figure 15.4).

Late Tasks Report   The Late Tasks reports is easy to confuse with the Slipping Tasks report. The key to understanding it, as with all reports, is to understand the filter. The filter is simply "Status equals late." Unlike the Slipping Tasks report, this filter does not rely on the baseline. If your task is late according to the last status date you entered in Project, then it is reported as late.

What this means is this report can change wildly depending on minor changes in your schedule. Nonetheless, there are many project managers who never take a baseline, or who rely on their schedule to always be their single best guess as to when tasks will be completed. In this case, the Slipping Tasks report is useless, and the Late Tasks report is the best choice.

> 🔍 **note**
> The filters used for all these reports are the same filters you can find on the View tab under Filter, More Filters. This means that, yes, you can change the Upcoming Tasks report to show whatever timeframe you want.

> 〰️ **tip**
> Resist the urge to modify the default reports and filters. Make a copy or start from scratch.

Figure 15.4
The Critical
Tasks
report lists
all tasks in
the critical
path.

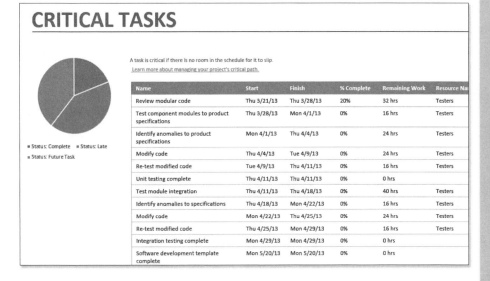

CRITICAL TASKS

A task is critical if there is no room in the schedule for it to slip.
Learn more about managing your project's critical path.

Name	Start	Finish	% Complete	Remaining Work	Resource Na
Review modular code	Thu 3/21/13	Thu 3/28/13	20%	32 hrs	Testers
Test component modules to product specifications	Thu 3/28/13	Mon 4/1/13	0%	16 hrs	Testers
Identify anomalies to product specifications	Mon 4/1/13	Thu 4/4/13	0%	24 hrs	Testers
Modify code	Thu 4/4/13	Tue 4/9/13	0%	24 hrs	Testers
Re-test modified code	Tue 4/9/13	Thu 4/11/13	0%	16 hrs	Testers
Unit testing complete	Thu 4/11/13	Thu 4/11/13	0%	0 hrs	
Test module integration	Thu 4/11/13	Thu 4/18/13	0%	40 hrs	Testers
Identify anomalies to specifications	Thu 4/18/13	Mon 4/22/13	0%	16 hrs	Testers
Modify code	Mon 4/22/13	Thu 4/25/13	0%	24 hrs	Testers
Re-test modified code	Thu 4/25/13	Mon 4/29/13	0%	16 hrs	Testers
Integration testing complete	Mon 4/29/13	Mon 4/29/13	0%	0 hrs	
Software development template complete	Mon 5/20/13	Mon 5/20/13	0%	0 hrs	

- Status: Complete - Status: Late
- Status: Future Task

To display the Late Tasks report (see Figure 15.5), select it from the In Progress category control on the Report tab.

Figure 15.5
The Late
Tasks
report is
for you if
you don't
use a base-
line.

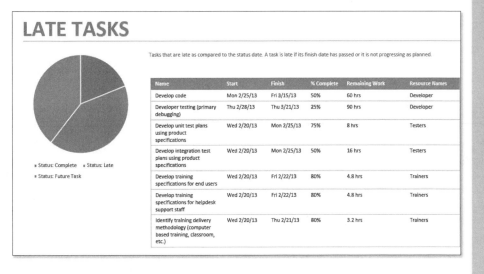

LATE TASKS

Tasks that are late as compared to the status date. A task is late if its finish date has passed or it is not progressing as planned.

Name	Start	Finish	% Complete	Remaining Work	Resource Names
Develop code	Mon 2/25/13	Fri 3/15/13	50%	60 hrs	Developer
Developer testing (primary debugging)	Thu 2/28/13	Thu 3/21/13	25%	90 hrs	Developer
Develop unit test plans using product specifications	Wed 2/20/13	Mon 2/25/13	75%	8 hrs	Testers
Develop integration test plans using product specifications	Wed 2/20/13	Mon 2/25/13	50%	16 hrs	Testers
Develop training specifications for end users	Wed 2/20/13	Fri 2/22/13	80%	4.8 hrs	Trainers
Develop training specifications for helpdesk support staff	Wed 2/20/13	Fri 2/22/13	80%	4.8 hrs	Trainers
Identify training delivery methodology (computer based training, classroom, etc.)	Wed 2/20/13	Thu 2/21/13	80%	3.2 hrs	Trainers

- Status: Complete - Status: Late
- Status: Future Task

Milestone Report If you've done a good job specifying your milestones, this report is beautiful in its simplicity. Significant projects can contain a daunting number of tasks; specifying your milestones with this report in mind can save you a lot of trouble. Milestones are not just concrete outputs; if they are used to define the completion of every work package, they both force you to build a well-formed schedule and reward you with improved schedule transparency.

➡ *For more information about creating milestones, including a list of when to create a milestone, **see** the "Defining Milestones" section on **p. 160** in Chapter 6.*

Milestones reports also include the summary tasks in the project. You can opt to not show summary tasks by editing the report using the Task Report definition dialog box.

To display the Milestone report, select it from the In Progress category control on the Report tab. The Milestone report is displayed, as shown in Figure 15.6.

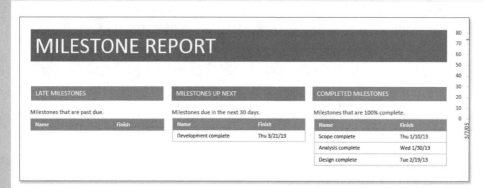

Figure 15.6
The Milestone report lists all project milestones and their finish dates.

Slipping Tasks Report   As stated earlier, unlike the Late Tasks report, the Slipping Tasks report takes the baseline into account. Tasks on this report's projected finish date are later than their base-lined finish date. The problem with this should be immediately obvious: Shortly after your baseline is taken, it's likely almost every task in your schedule will end up on this report.

There are a couple ways to make this report a bit more reasonable and useful. Both involve chang-ing the filter. The first is to use a Finish comparison that isn't a simple Greater Than Baseline Finish. The second is to compare it to any of the subsequent baselines you might take to track your sched-ule. Either way, a minor bit of work can make this report useful.

To display the Slipping Tasks report, select it from the In Progress category control on the Report tab. The Slipping Tasks report is displayed, as shown in Figure 15.7.

Using Reports for Analyzing the Project Budget

You can use several reports to aid in analyzing your project's budget. Most of the relevant reports are located under the Costs category control on the Report tab.

The Cash Flow Report   The Cash Flow report depends on a baseline and shows both project level information and task level information. Across the top it shows the total baseline cost for the project, as well as actual cost to date. By default, it shows all tasks and their costs, but as with each report the filter can be modified.

Figure 15.7
On a normal project, the Slipping Tasks report will have a lot of tasks to display.

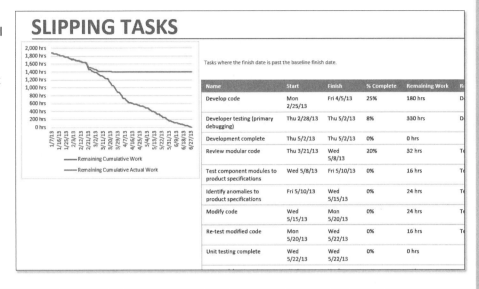

➡️ *For more information about customizing a report's time unit, **see** Chapter 20, Reports Part I: 2013 Reports, on **p. 625.***

To display the Cash Flow report, select it from the Costs category control on the Report tab. The Cash Flow report is displayed, as shown in Figure 15.8.

Figure 15.8
The Cash Flow report relies on a baseline and Earned Value Analysis to assess your project's cash state.

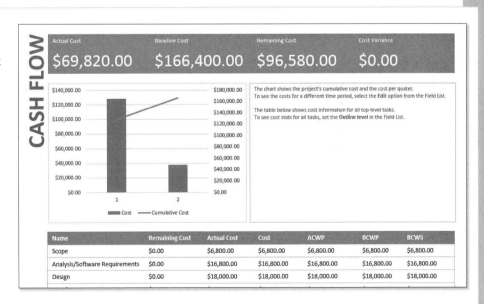

Cost Overruns Report   The Cost Overruns report is fundamentally a backward-looking report that calls your attention to tasks that simply cost more than you thought they would. It also relies on a baseline.

This report should be used when, for example, you are asked exactly why the project went over budget and you are looking for the culprit. It can be used to reset expectations for what the project's likely total cost will be.

To display the Cost Overruns report, select it from the Costs category control on the Report tab. The Cost Overruns report is displayed, as shown in Figure 15.9.

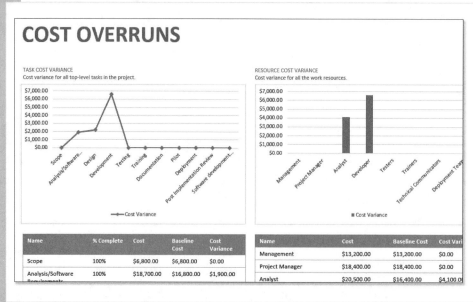

Figure 15.9
The Cost Overruns report helps you find out why your project is over budget already.

Earned Value Report   The Earned Value report is a powerful predictive tool if used properly. It is worth noting again that this report is useless unless you have captured your baseline and tracked all project data accurately. It is also important that a correct WBS be in place and under change control; otherwise, the earned value statistics will be misleading. Finally, it is worth noting that Project does not fully support the ANSI Earned Value Management System standard.

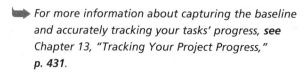 *For more information about capturing the baseline and accurately tracking your tasks' progress, **see** Chapter 13, "Tracking Your Project Progress," p. 431.*

 tip

Many reports depend on the use of the baseline fields for comparison. If you have not set a project baseline or have added tasks after the baseline was set, your reports will not have comparison data available.

To display the Earned Value report, select it from the Costs category control on the Report tab. The Earned Value report is displayed, as shown in Figure 15.10.

Figure 15.10
The Earned Value report shows three basic graphs of Earned Value data.

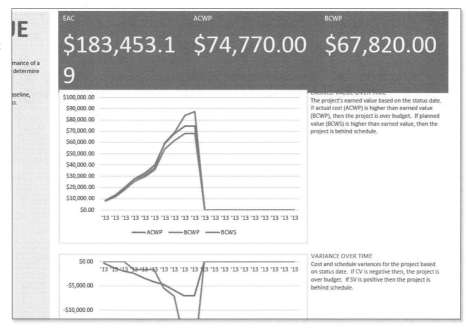

Table 15.1 lists all the column headings in the Earned Value report. Because most of these fields are abbreviated, their full name is written out in the table, along with a brief definition.

Table 15.1 Earned Value Report Column Information

Abbreviation	Full Name	Brief Definition
PV (BCWS)	Planned Value (Budgeted Cost of Work Scheduled)	Amount of cost of scheduled work, captured in the baseline
EV (BCWP)	Earned Value (Budgeted Cost of Work Performed)	The percentage of Planned Value earned by the amount of actual work completed
AC (ACWP)	Actual Cost (Actual Cost of Work Performed)	The actual cost of work completed
SV	Schedule Variance	The difference between the Planned Value and the Earned Value (EV–PV)

Abbreviation	Full Name	Brief Definition
CV	Cost Variance	The difference between Earned Value and Actual Cost (EV–AC)
EAC	Estimated At Completion	The estimated total cost for the task when it is completed
BAC	Budget At Completion	The total Planned Value for the task when it is completed
VAC	Variance At Completion	The difference between the total baseline (planned) cost and the estimated total cost (BAC–EAC)

➥ *For a more detailed explanation of earned value analysis, including more detailed definitions of the fields listed in Table 15.1, **see** the "Analyzing Performance with Earned Value Analysis" section on **p. 474** in Chapter 14.*

If you have captured your baseline and tracked your progress accurately, the Earned Value report provides a helpful reference to how each task in your project is earning value as compared to what was planned.

Resource Cost Overview Report   The Resource Cost Overview report is probably more interesting as an indication of what can be done. Few project managers are interested in a pie chart showing types of resource cost based on whether they are "work" or "material." However, it might be useful, for example, to see a pie chart showing the costs of design, development, and test. Moreover, the cost details table on the lower left provides a handy means of quickly verifying what the most expensive resources on the project are.

 tip

For complex projects, the use of filters and views might make analysis of task and resource data easier than using reports.

To display the Resource Cost Overview report, select it from the Costs category control on the Report tab. The Resource Cost Overview report is displayed, as shown in Figure 15.11.

Task Cost Overview   Finally, the Task Cost Overview report is similar to the Resource Cost Overview report, only it pertains to tasks. Due to the nature of tasks, this report is much more predictive and can actually be used to ascertain and correct problems before they would be identified otherwise.

The Cost Status panel shows a nice, top-level task graph indicating not only how much has been spent for each task, but how that compares to the baseline.

The Cost Distribution panel is useful at a high level if you know where your project should be. If, for example, you think your project is 3.4 complete and this report shows that you are only 1.4 complete, you either have a problem with your schedule, your project, or both.

The Cost Details panel provides detailed table data in support of the two graphs and might clarify what why the graphs are indicating a problem.

To display the Task Cost Overview report, select it from the Costs category control on the Report tab. The Task Cost Overview report is displayed, as shown in Figure 15.12.

Figure 15.11
The Resource Cost Overview report can be used to verify your intuition about which resources are costing your project the most.

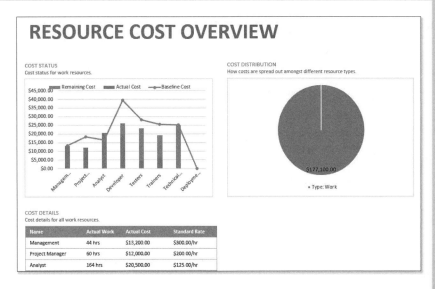

Figure 15.12
The Task Cost Overview report indicates which tasks are running over budget.

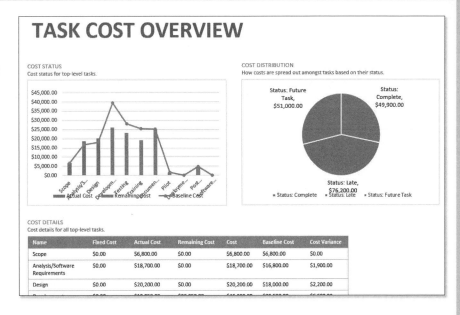

➡ *For more information about using filters and views for data analysis,* ***see*** *Chapter 11, "Using Standard Views, Tables, Filters, and Groups to Review Your Schedule,"* ***p. 357***.

➡ *For more information about customizing filters and views,* ***see*** *Chapter 22, "Customization Almost Beyond Reason: Views, Tables, Filters, Groups, Fields, Toolbars, Menus, and Forms,"* ***p. 699***.

Using Reports for the Project Sponsor

The project sponsor or other project stakeholders are primarily interested in how the project is doing overall: trends, whether it will finish on time, within budget, and whether the project deliverables will be completed as defined in the project scope. Project sponsors should not be expected to review detail reports regarding the entire project. They hired or appointed you as the project manager so they would not have to worry about tracking and controlling the project's details. Therefore, the basic reports typically presented to project sponsors show the three main areas they are concerned with: schedule, budget, and scope. They want to know how things are going as compared to the plan: What is working, what is not working, and what your plan is to bring unsuccessful areas of the project back to the level of success you planned for.

The best project sponsors use reports to understand the status of your project and monitor trends. They typically get more involved only when asked to support your decisions or to help when you need executive support to resolve problems.

The Overview reports category contains two reports that might be of significant interest to your project sponsor, described in the following sections.

Project Overview Report

The Project Overview report is a great snapshot of where the project is as of the current date. A project sponsor would benefit from periodically viewing the Project Overview report. On a single page, it shows the total percent complete, Milestones due to be completed soon, percent complete for all top-level tasks, and tasks that are past due.

➡ *For more information about modifying reports,* ***see*** *Chapter 20, "Reports Part I: 2013 Reports,"* ***p. 625***.

To display the Project Overview report, select the Project Overview report from the Dashboards control (Report tab, View Reports Group). The Project Overview report is displayed, as shown in Figure 15.13.

 note

Out of all the reports, the Project Overview report is probably the one you will want to change. Every project sponsor is different, and it's your responsibility to be sure your communication serves the best interest of the project. Some project sponsors simply do not know how to respond constructively to things like "late tasks," even though late tasks are a perfectly normal part of every project.

Figure 15.13
Some project sponsors will appreciate the Project Overview report because it shows a nice overview of the project's current status.

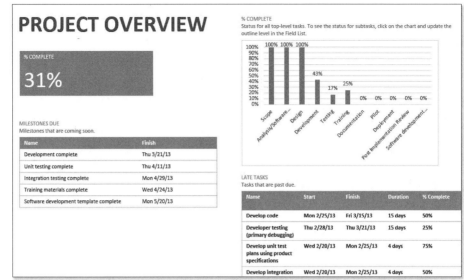

Milestone Report

The project sponsor probably does not want to see the status of each task on a project, especially if the project involves a long task list. Instead, he or she can view the planned schedule for delivery of major components in the project.

The Milestone report is a good report to share with the project sponsor because it lists each milestone you define in the project schedule. A milestone should be created for the completion of deliverables and major phases within the project.

➡️ *For more information about creating milestones, including a list of when to create a milestone, **see** the "Defining Milestones" section on **p. 160** in Chapter 6.*

The milestone and finish date are displayed in the report in one of three columns: Late Milestones, Milestones Up Next, or Completed Milestones. As always, understanding precisely what appears in each of these columns is a matter of opening the filter and editing it to see exactly what the filter criteria is (see Figure 15.14).

To view the Milestone report, select it from the In Progress category control in the View Reports group on the Reports tab. The Milestone report is displayed, as shown in Figure 15.15.

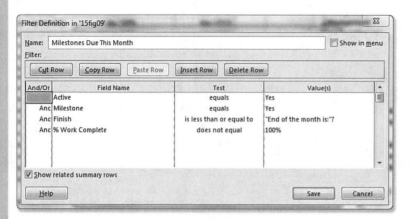

Figure 15.14
This is the exact criteria for Milestones Due This month.

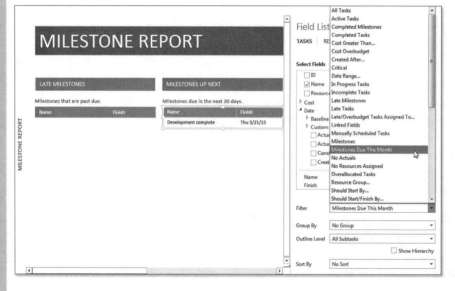

Figure 15.15
The Milestone report lists all project milestones and their start and finish dates, which might be of significant interest to the project sponsor. In this case, the Milestones Due this Month field is selected, the Field List is expanded, and the default filter is highlighted.

Using Visual Reports

Visual reports are visual representations of project data. Visual reports are created using either Microsoft Excel or Microsoft Visio. The data is compiled into charts or graphs in each report, most of which offer three-dimensional functionality. All visual reports are customizable both in their appearance and in their content. You also have the ability to create a new template for a visual report if none of the existing templates meets your requirements.

➡️ *For more information about Project's visual reports, including a table listing all existing visual report templates and which type they are (Excel or Visio), **see** Chapter 21, "Reports Part II: Visual Reports," p. 653.*

see Chapter 21, "Reports Part II: Visual Reports," p. 653.

 note

Microsoft Excel must be installed for Excel-based Visual Reports to work, and likewise for Visio-based Visual Reports.

Visual reports are excellent tools for tracking and controlling your project. Like reports, visual reports provide detailed information about a particular aspect of your project. They are also helpful to print and distribute to your project sponsor, team, or other project stakeholders. Visual reports display the data in attractive charts, graphs, or other customizable formats, making them more exciting and more visually appealing than the basic reports.

 tip

Reports are incredibly flexible, but visual reports go a step further. Visual reports are useful when you really need the full flexibility of Visio or Excel to analyze or visualize your project data. Also, you might not be free to suddenly decree a new reporting format because you've upgraded to Project 2013. Visual reports is a means to continue presenting data in a way your project stakeholders expect to see it.

To access the templates for visual reports, open the Visual Reports – Create Report dialog box by selecting the Report tab, Export, Visual Reports. The Visual Reports – Create Report dialog box appears, as shown in Figure 15.16.

Figure 15.16
The existing templates for the visual reports are divided into seven categories (tabs) in the Visual Reports – Create Report dialog box.

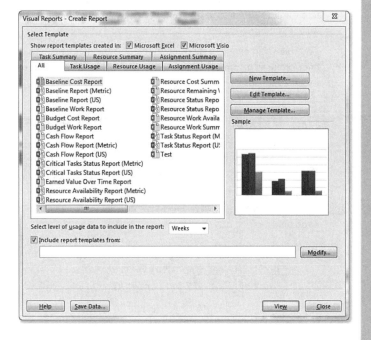

Seven tabs house the existing visual report templates found in the Visual Reports – Create Report dialog box:

- All
- Task Usage
- Resource Usage
- Assignment Usage
- Task Summary
- Resource Summary
- Assignment Summary

You can choose to display visual reports created in either Excel or Visio by selecting the box next to either program at the top of the dialog box. If you check Excel, only the Excel visual reports are listed. By default, both Excel and Visio are selected.

You can also define the time period that the data is displayed in by selecting Days, Weeks, Months, Quarters, or Years from the drop-down list in the Select Level of Usage Data to Include in the Report field, located near the bottom of the dialog box (refer to Figure 15.16).

Visual reports are Online Analytical Processing (OLAP) reports. OLAP databases are also known as *OLAP cubes* because they include several dimensions such as projects, tasks, resources, and time, with summarized data such as work, cost, and availability. Therefore, the visual reports in Project take various dimensions and create a three-dimensional cube, enabling you to slice into the data and analyze it based on more than one factor. Rather than an X,Y comparison, visual reports provide an X,Y,Z comparison.

The following sections discuss which of the existing visual reports are best suited for tracking and controlling your project. They are broken up by their audience: visual reports for project analysis, project sponsors, and the project team.

Using Visual Reports for Project Analysis

Like reports, the visual reports in Project can aid tremendously in analyzing your project. Visual report templates exist in Project that help you analyze the project schedule and budget. With the help of these reports, you can clearly identify problem areas in your project and make the necessary adjustments to get things back on track.

> 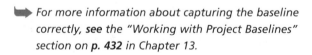 For more information about capturing the baseline correctly, **see** the "Working with Project Baselines" section on **p. 432** in Chapter 13.

> For more information about accurately tracking your project's progress, **see** the "Tracking Your Project's Performance and Costs" section on **p. 436** in Chapter 13.

caution

As noted earlier, it is important that you have captured your baseline correctly, and that you have accurately recorded your tracking information. If not, your analysis will be inaccurate, because your data is not current.

Using the Visual Reports for Analyzing the Project Schedule

A handful of visual reports in Project come in handy when you analyze your project schedule. The main focus in analyzing your project schedule is to see how your resources are working as compared to what was planned. Are they finishing on time? Are they finishing early or late consistently? What you are hoping to see is very little deviation from the baseline schedule in either direction, because that means you planned accurately in terms of your scheduling and duration or work estimates. As with most other reports, it is important that your baseline was captured correctly and you have consistently updated your tracking information.

Baseline Work Report   The Baseline Work report is found in the All tab as well as the Assignment Usage tab of the Visual Reports – Create Report dialog box. It displays Baseline Work, Work (planned work), and Actual Work for each task. Like many other visual reports, you can drill down into this report to display data at the project level, the phase level (summary tasks), or the task level. Generally, your Baseline Work and Work values will be the same or similar if you captured the scope of work correctly.

Like the other reports, you can add other fields into the Baseline Work report to further aid in analyzing your schedule. Add fields in the PivotChart Fields list, which appears on the right side of the graph when you click in it.

Figure 15.17 shows an example of a modified Baseline Work report. The data is displayed at the summary task level. To display individual task data, simply expand the summary tasks listed in the PivotTable underneath the graph.

Figure 15.17
The Baseline Work report shows planned and baseline work compared to actual work values for each task.

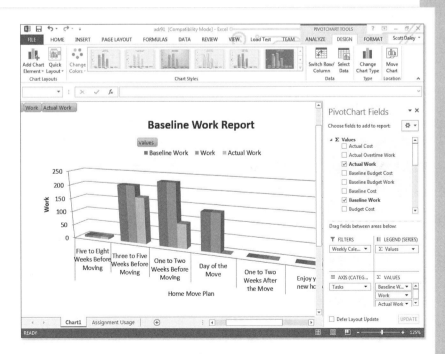

Resource Work Availability Report   The Resource Work Availability report is found on the Resource Usage tab or the All tab of the Visual Reports – Create Report dialog box. It shows the amount of Work Availability (total amount of working time for all resources), Planned Work, and Remaining Availability for all resources combined over time. By default, the report data is displayed in quarters, but you can break it down into weeks if you like; Figure 15.18 shows the second quarter of 2011 (Q1) drilled down into weeks.

This report might be beneficial when analyzing your schedule to see whether your resources have more availability in certain weeks than others, and if so, you can assign more work to make up for any possible slipping tasks that you have and use the available time to catch up.

Figure 15.18 shows an example of a customized Resource Work Availability report. Modifications made to this report are done by collapsing or expanding the time dimension fields in the pivot table below the graph.

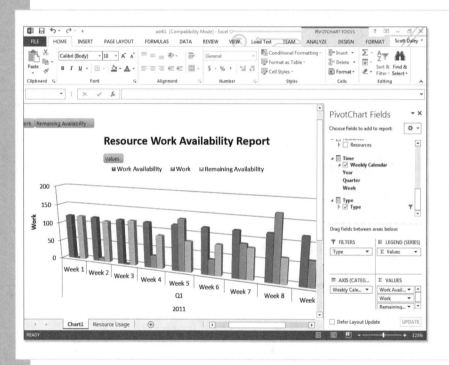

Figure 15.18
The Resource Work Availability report shows total planned work and work availability values for your resources over time. If there are times when you see more availability, you might want to schedule any makeup work during those times.

Resource Work Summary Report   The Resource Work Summary report is found on the Resource Usage tab, as well as the All tab on the Visual Reports – Create Report dialog box. It is similar to the Resource Work Availability report in that it lists Work Availability, Planned Work, and Remaining Availability. However, this report lists the data for each resource rather than total amounts over time. In addition, the Actual Work field is included, enabling you to see the actual work performed by each resource compared to the planned work. This can be helpful for analyzing each resource's performance compared to what was expected as defined in the baseline schedule. You can also analyze each resource's workload side by side.

Figure 15.19 displays an illustration of a customized Resource Work Summary report. As always, you can modify the fields listed in the report, as well as the actual appearance of the data.

Figure 15.19
The Resource Work Summary report shows planned and actual work data, as well as remaining availability, for each resource in your project.

Using the Visual Reports for Analyzing the Project Budget

Analyzing your budget on a consistent basis is an important aspect of project management. You want to make sure the actual cost of the project is aligned with the baseline, that the project is earning value at the expected rate, and that your overall project is staying within its budget. Project comes equipped with a number of visual reports to help you maintain an accurate budget analysis. Monitoring your budget closely and fixing any problems as soon as they arise will help you be more successful in properly managing your project's budget.

Budget Cost Report   The Budget Cost report should be used to analyze your budget. This report is found on the Assignment Usage tab, as well as the All tab of the Visual Reports – Create Report dialog box. The Budget Cost report shows Budget Cost, Baseline Cost, Cost (planned cost), and Actual Cost as a bar graph over time. As with the other visual reports, you can add more fields

 note

Three reports are helpful in analyzing project budget: the Baseline Cost report, the Cash Flow report, and the Earned Value Over Time report. These reports are discussed in the section, "Using Visual Reports for the Project Sponsor."

to the graph in the PivotChart Fields list, or define different units of time on the PivotTable (years, quarters, weeks, and so on). With this report, you can quickly examine your actual cost as compared to your different planned and scheduled cost values side by side.

Figure 15.20 shows a customized Budget Cost report.

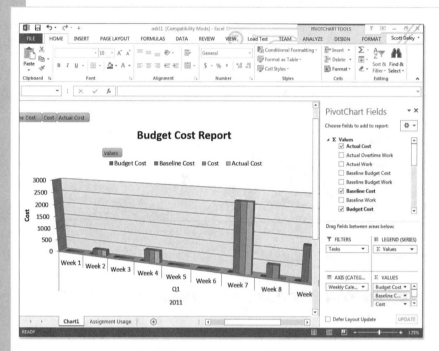

Figure 15.20
The Budget Cost report shows actual cost next to the planned and scheduled cost values.

Resource Cost Summary Report The Resource Cost Summary report is found on the Resource Usage tab, as well as the All tab of the Visual Reports – Create Report dialog box. This is an Excel report that displays a pie chart showing the division of cost among the three resource types: work, material, and cost. If you only have one or two of the resource types in your project, only data for those types is displayed. To further aid in analyzing a project's budget, you can add the Actual Cost field, or other helpful budget analysis fields, in the PivotChart Fields List. Also, you can display data for all resources, or choose certain resources to analyze. The PivotChart Fields list is used to define which resources to display data for.

Figure 15.21 shows an example of a customized Resource Cost Summary report. Notice how most of the cost is to work resources, and because no material resources have been assigned to tasks, there is no data on this report for material resources. Cost resources represent only a small fraction of the total resource cost.

Figure 15.21
The Resource Cost Summary report shows planned cost data for each of the three resource types, enabling you to quickly view which resource types are costing the most, and by how much.

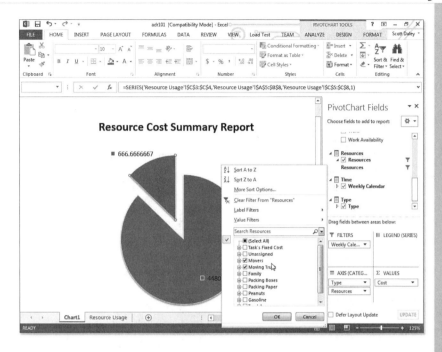

Using Visual Reports for the Project Sponsor

As mentioned earlier in this chapter, a project sponsor is generally not as concerned with project details as he or she is with the overall big picture. Therefore, the visual reports to share with project sponsors should include overall project information—how the project is doing as compared to the baseline.

Baseline Cost Report

The first report to discuss is the Baseline Cost report. This report is the first report listed in the All tab of the Visual Reports – Create Report dialog box. It is also found under the Assignment Usage tab. To access the Baseline Cost report, double-click it, or click it once and then click the View button.

The Baseline Cost report shows a project's baseline cost, planned cost, and actual cost, displayed in a bar graph. When you set your baseline, the Cost (planned cost) and Baseline Cost values start out the same. The Cost field might fluctuate as progress is reported but is typically expected to stay close to the baseline if problems have not occurred. As your project moves through its life cycle, you can analyze Actual Cost values against the Cost and Baseline Cost values. Projects that are in control are typically expected to have Actual Cost values within 10% (plus or minus) of the Cost or Baseline Cost values.

To view this data as text, click the Assignment Usage tab at the bottom of the screen. This displays the Excel spreadsheet that the graph represents visually. You can choose to expand or collapse some of the information, and the graph reflects those changes. For example, the data is first displayed at the project level. There are three bars total (Cost, Actual Cost, and Baseline Cost) for the entire project. If you expand the data on the Assignment Usage tab to show project phases (summary tasks), the bar graph shows the three cost values for each phase rather than the entire project. You can then expand each phase to the task level, and the graph shows the cost values for each task.

Alternatively, you can double-click on the legend underneath each bar on the Chart tab (the graph), and the bar automatically expands. Or, you can right-click on a gridline in the graph and choose Format Axis, and define the level of data to display (project level, summary/phase level, or task level) in the Format Axis dialog box.

 caution

Expanding the data too much can cause the units underneath the graph to mix together and overlap, making it difficult to read. To fix it, right-click on the unit text and select Format Axis, Alignment, Text Direction. From there, you can rotate the text 270 degrees, so the text is displayed vertically instead of horizontally.

Also, you can include additional fields in the report by clicking on the spreadsheet. The PivotChart Fields list appears on the right side of the screen, and you can select boxes next to fields you want included in the report, and clear boxes for fields you do not want included in the report. Then, click the Chart tab to return to the graph to view your changes.

Figure 15.22 shows an example of a customized Baseline Cost report. The report has been modified; the graph is copied and pasted above the PivotTable. Also, the PivotChart Fields list is displayed on the right, where you can insert other fields to include in the report. The appearance of the graph itself has been altered to look more three-dimensional.

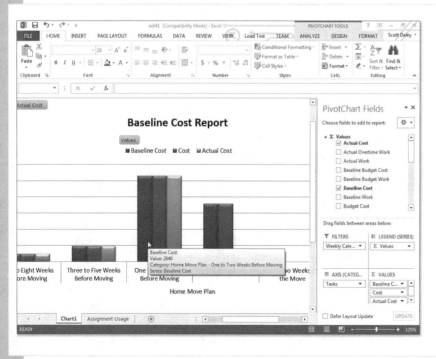

Figure 15.22
The Baseline Cost report shows a project's Baseline Cost, Cost (planned cost), and Actual Cost fields, which the project sponsor would be especially interested in.

Figure 15.23 shows the same Baseline Cost report, only in this example, all the tasks have been rolled up in the PivotTable to display only project summary information.

Figure 15.23
This example of a Baseline Cost report displays only project summary information, rather than data at the task level, as defined in the PivotTable underneath the graph.

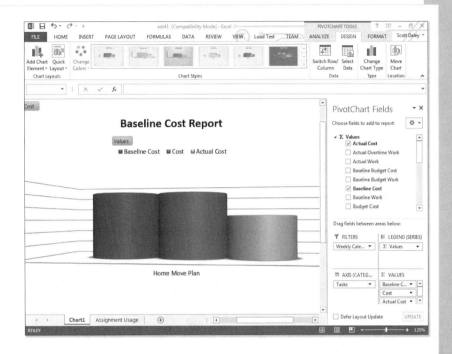

Cash Flow Report

The Cash Flow report can be found on the All tab or on the Task Usage tab of the Visual Reports – Create Report dialog box. This report displays cost (planned cost) and cumulative cost data over time. The project sponsor might be inclined to view this report because it shows a bar representing planned cost as well as the total cumulative planned cost up to that point, so you get an idea of what was expected to be spent during each particular time period, as well as the total amount for the project up through that time period.

Figure 15.24 provides an example of a customized Cash Flow report. The report has been modified; the cumulative cost data is by default displayed as a line, but has been changed to be represented as a bar. Also, the bars are three-dimensional. Actual Cost data has been inserted as well.

As with the Baseline Cost report, you can drill down into the data in the PivotTable on the task usage tab, and the graph displays data that reflects the PivotTable.

 tip

You might want to add the Actual Cost field into the Cash Flow report, as in Figure 15.24. That way, you can compare what you spent with what you planned to spend in each time period. To insert the Actual Cost field into the report, select the Actual Cost check box in the PivotChart Fields list.

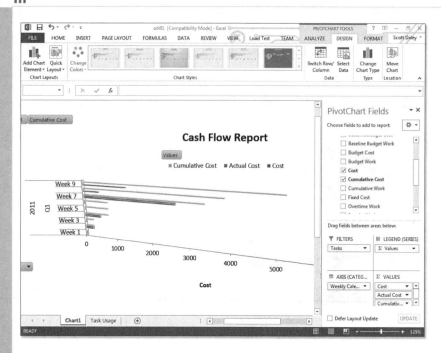

Figure 15.24
The Cash Flow report shows planned cost per time unit, as well as cumulative planned cost up through each particular time period.

Earned Value Over Time Report

The Earned Value Over Time report is found on the All tab and the Assignment Usage tab of the Visual Reports – Create Report dialog box. This report compares planned value, earned value, and actual cost as a line graph. This might be important to a project sponsor for a visual representation of what value was planned, what value was earned, and what was spent to achieve the earned value. Because the graph is represented over time, it is easy to look back and see where the earned value measurements were at some point in the past, as well as examine the pattern over the course of your project.

> ➡ *For a more detailed explanation of earned value analysis, **see** the "Analyzing Performance with Earned Value Analysis" section on **p. 474** in Chapter 14.*

Figures 15.25 and 15.26 show an example of a customized Earned Value Over Time report. Figure 15.25 displays the PivotTable, and Figure 15.26 shows the resulting graph that is based on the information defined in the PivotTable. As with the other illustrations in this section, this example has been customized to appear more visually attractive and represent the data more clearly.

Figure 15.25
Create the level of
data displayed in
the Earned Value
Over Time graph
by defining it in
the PivotTable. The
resulting graph is
displayed in Figure
15.26.

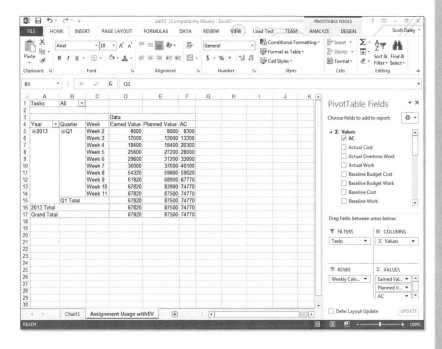

Figure 15.26
The Earned Value
Over Time report
shows earned
value as compared
to planned value
and actual cost.

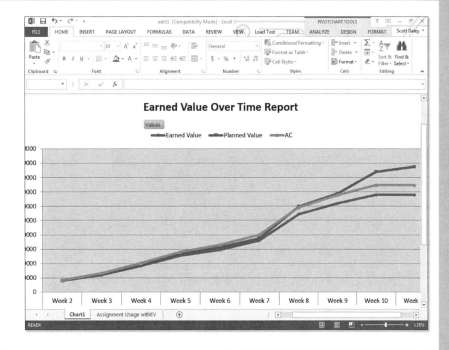

Critical Task Status Report

Critical tasks are those tasks whose finish dates affect the overall project finish date. If critical tasks are behind, it is likely that the project will finish late unless the problem is fixed. Therefore, a project sponsor might be interested in seeing the Critical Task Status report. This report gives the project sponsor an idea of whether the project is running on time, early, or late.

The Critical Task Status report can be found on the All tab, as well as the Task Status tab of the Visual Reports – Create Report dialog box. This is a Visio report that displays the critical tasks in a diagram. Each critical task's work, remaining work, and percentage complete values are shown. You need to have Microsoft Office Visio 2007 or later installed for this report to function.

Figure 15.27 shows an example of a Critical Task Status report.

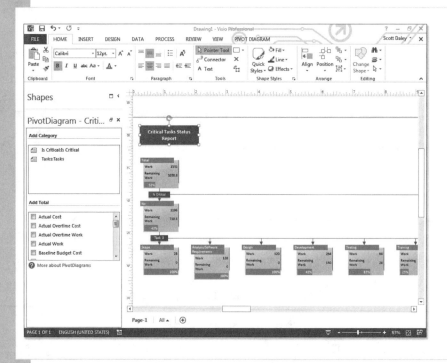

Figure 15.27
Project sponsors might want to see the Critical Task Status report, which can be modified to indicate the status of each critical task.

Custom Project Summary Report for the Project Sponsor

Project does not come equipped with an existing *visual report* that summarizes the important information of a project, like the Project Overview report does. Nonetheless, sometimes your project sponsors will want to see a project summary presented in Excel or Visio.

You will need to create this visual report because it does not exist as a template in Project's visual reports. Your summary visual report should include more information than found in the Project Overview report: cost, work, and schedule information, all listed on the same report with baseline, actual, and variance values.

➡ *For more information about creating new visual reports,* **see** *the "Reporting Capabilities" section on* **p. 665** *in Chapter 21.*

Using Visual Reports for the Project Team

Although the project sponsor benefits more from overall project reports, your project team relies on specific, detailed reports about each phase of the project or their general assignments. Because team members are involved with the project on a daily basis, project overview reports that do not include specific detailed information do not encourage the team members to concentrate on their daily work. Instead, use the visual reports to break down work on a daily or weekly basis, giving the team members several small goals to achieve each day or week, rather than the overall big picture.

As a project manager, you must ensure that your team members stay current with their assignments and perform at the level they are expected to perform. Use a visual report to illustrate the team's performance as compared to the project plan, which can serve as visual evidence of whether a team or team member is up to speed. Create a bar graph in a visual report that displays actual progress with baseline plans for work, schedule, and possibly for cost. A visual report might get your point across more effectively than just telling your team what is going on. Talk to your team, and back up your points with a visual report.

> **tip**
>
> Remember, communication is important to managing a successful project. Each team communicates differently; experiment and find the method of communication that works best for you and your team, and be consistent in maintaining it. Be sure you are available to answer any questions that arise as work on a project progresses.

Resource Remaining Work Report

The Resource Remaining Work report might be helpful for status meetings with your project team. This report displays each resource's actual work completed and remaining work, according to the amount of work planned for each resource. It provides a quick look at a resource's progress, as well as what still needs to be completed in terms of work. You can customize this report to also include Baseline Work or other fields that might be helpful in reviewing work for your project team. By default, the report lists data for all resources, but you can opt to include only certain resources, or even a single resource. These definitions are made in the PivotChart Fields list (see Figure 15.28).

The Resource Remaining Work report is found on the All tab, as well as the Resource Summary tab of the Visual Reports – Create Report dialog box.

Custom Visual Reports for the Project Team

Project provides multiple ways to present the same data so you can communicate with your team the best way possible. For example, you might want to create a to-do list for each resource, created in Visio as a timeline diagram that would be beneficial for the resource to keep in her office or working area. That way, the resource not only has a list of task assignments that include all the necessary task information, he or she also has reports organized chronologically. You can create a to-do list for each resource that spans the entire project lifetime, as well as smaller to-do lists that span each day, week, or other time period throughout the project.

Consultants' Tips

Using Project's native reporting functionality is usually a better way to communicate with project stakeholders than sharing entire project files or Gantt Charts.

When to Use Reports

The new reports in Project 2013 are flexible and nice to look at. Unless you really need to get your project data out into Visio or Excel, these should be your go-to reporting mechanism.

Occasionally you may find you are still printing out the Gantt Chart view or other views because Project views are still data-rich and very flexible. However, most of the time views are better consumed by people who can actually use Project. Reports are for people that want to know a *little* about what's going on, but not as much as you do.

When to Use Visual Reports

Visual reports are very useful when you either have stakeholders that expect project data in Excel or Visio, or when you simply have to have the increased flexibility of working in Excel or Visio. There is a lot of overlap in the functionality of reports and visual reports, but in the end, like anything, using the right tool for the job produces better results.

Customize the Out-of-the-Box Reports for Your Project Needs

You can create an almost endless set of variations of reports and analytical capabilities using the customization options for both the reports and visual reports. You should discuss a small set of reports with your project sponsor in the early stages of developing your project so that you can set them up for regular reporting.

Read Chapters 20 and 21 to learn about the vast array of reporting customization options.

16

REVISING THE SCHEDULE

This chapter provides some insight into options that project managers should consider when there are signs of trouble. Depending on how the project plan and schedule were put together, you can consider alternatives to help get things back on track.

When Things Don't Go According to Plan

A project schedule provides a roadmap, but it is not infallible; it is based on accumulated knowledge and best guesses, and it makes a set of assumptions that do not always work out. For example, if the schedule was put together without any weighted estimates for effort or budget, the chance for meeting the exact date and budget is approximately 50%. To increase those odds, you need to use more sophisticated estimation methods.

➥ For additional information on estimation methods, *see* the "Schedule Estimation Methods" section on *p. 413* of Chapter 12.

There are hundreds, if not thousands, of possible reasons that things do not go according to plan during project execution. The primary component is that projects rely on human resources to get work done, and human resources are not completely predictable. The best that a project manager can do is set up a robust and flexible plan, be steadfast in monitoring all components of the project, and react as quickly as possible when the situation changes. Critical path analysis is an essential component of this analysis.

Critical Path Changes

Critical path analysis is one of the best tools available for analysis of a project schedule. When you monitor the critical path, you will notice changes to the tasks that show up on the critical path and possibly to the amount of lag time that is available on some important tasks. This is the normal process that takes place as work is accomplished on the project; some tasks take longer than planned or start later than planned, whereas others may actually happen more quickly than expected.

 tip

Most task variances are subtle and not a cause for alarm as long as they do not continue to get further behind with each reporting cycle.

For additional information on how to set up critical path analysis, **see** the "Reviewing the Big Picture (Critical Path Analysis)" section on **p. 417** of Chapter 12.

When a schedule changes dramatically, the entire schedule needs to be reviewed carefully to understand the implications of the changes. In most cases, it is because work has been slipping and has impacted the project schedule finish date. The slip often comes as a surprise to a busy project manager who does not have the time to monitor every task in the project. When the work is late enough to change the critical path, other factors may be in play that make the situation even worse. To avoid this surprise, the project manager should also be monitoring tasks with a small amount of slack time because they have the potential to quickly become part of the critical path.

To analyze the "near-critical path" tasks, use the Total Slack field in a view or create a custom view or report that will help you monitor the amount of float time available. You should analyze tasks that have less than a specified amount of slack time to ensure that they will not be a problem. You can create additional views to show tasks that are slipping or late. Figure 16.1 provides an example of a custom view that helps the project manager analyze the "near-critical path" as well as the critical path. The near-critical tasks for this view were defined to include tasks with slack of three days or less (this can be changed: File tab, Options, Advanced, Calculation options for this project).

For additional information about customizing views, **see** Chapter 22, "Customization Almost Beyond Reason: Views, Tables, Filters, Groups, Fields, Toolbars, Menus, and Forms," **p. 699**.

Figure 16.1
This view
is filtered
to show
only "criti-
cal" tasks
defined
in project
options as
three days
or less.

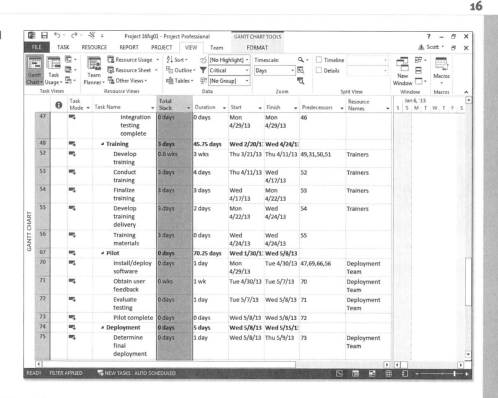

What Can Go Wrong

The following is a set of items that might cause your project to run off course. There are no silver bullets to solve these problems, but there are some things that you can do to minimize their impact or at least help you determine how to recover:

- **Inaccurate estimates**—A common contributor to schedules that go awry is a set of activities with inaccurate estimates. Unless the organization has a solid history of good estimates, there is often little to go on for predicting the effort involved in a new project.

- **Resource issues**—There is always a fair amount of competition for experienced resources because inexperienced resources do not work as efficiently. Illness, job changes, and myriad other issues might cause problems with human resources. Most organizations have more requests for work than they have the ability to do, and the tendency is to take on more than is possible. Key resources are often asked to juggle multiple projects, so their attention is divided.

- **Budget issues**—Budget cuts, cost overruns, and higher costs for resources are just a few of the problems you might encounter.

- **Scope changes**—Scope creep (or fuzzy requirements) is one of the key causes of failure in project management. A large portion of schedule slippage and cost overruns is directly related to changes in the scope of the project after cost and time commitments have been made.

■ **Risks, issues, and so on**—Natural disasters, labor strikes, regulatory requirements, and many other things that you are not able to predict can have an impact on the best of plans. You can have contingency plans for many of these issues, but even that is not always enough.

Prevention and Avoidance

Prevention and avoidance are obviously the preferred methods of dealing with adversity. You can find advice throughout this book to help you:

■ Improved estimation (see Chapter 12, "Performing a Schedule Reality Check")

■ Improved scope definition (see Chapter 4, "Getting Started After the Business Initiative Is Approved")

■ Improved resource management (see Chapter 9, "Understanding Work Formula Basics," and Chapter 10, "Scheduling Single and Multiple Resource Assignments")

■ Improved risk management and contingency planning (see Chapter 4 and Chapter 12)

In addition, Microsoft Project has some features to help you avoid problems and ways to determine what to do when a problem occurs.

You can use the Multiple Undo feature and the Task Driver pane for what-if analysis. Make a set of changes to your project using these features and see what the ripple effect is. You can reduce effort or remove a resource, push out a set of tasks, and a variety of other things. With Project, you have the ability to see how your changes make an impact on the project, and then you can undo these changes one by one.

 tip

It is recommended that you save a version of your project first so that you have a separate version for this activity. If you are using Project Professional with Project Server, you can save several versions to the server as well.

When Recovery Is the Only Option

If your project is in trouble or you can see that it is heading that way, proactive management is your best bet to limit the extent of the problems and get back on track. When dealing with your Project schedule, remember that you have control of only two of the three key components: scope, cost, and time.

Go back and review the Measure of Success that you established to remind the team of which component is the most critical for your project. If quality and accuracy are most important, you might need to let the timeline slip to maintain the quality. If being "first to market" is key to success, you need to look at reducing scope or possibly increasing the budget to bring the project in on time (see Figure 16.2).

Whatever you decide, you will need to make tradeoffs, and you will need the support of your stakeholders and your team to accomplish this. The use of several "what-if" scenarios will help your team visualize the options.

Figure 16.2
You can control only two of these three key components.

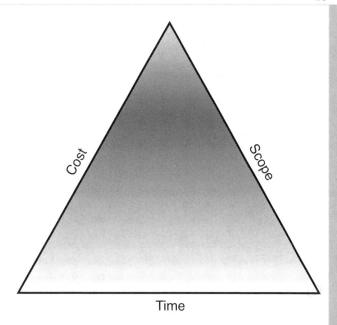

Reducing Project Scope

Reducing scope to meet either budget or timeline requirements means that you must reduce functionality or potentially lower the quality for the finished product.

To remove functionality, review the project schedule to see whether there are tasks (or preferably entire work packages) that you can remove from the scope without serious impact to other components of the schedule. If the schedule was put together using a WBS approach, it will be easier to find sets of functionality that you can isolate and remove. This is the preferred solution because it has the least impact on quality.

➥ *For additional information about the WBS,* ***see*** *the "Work Breakdown Structure" section on* ***p. 76*** *in Chapter 4.*

If functionality cannot be completely removed, perhaps a substitute can be put in place that takes less time to build. In a manufacturing situation, substitution of a prebuilt part for a custom-made component might solve the problem. This solution might increase project cost, but it would reduce the scope so that the project could come in on time.

The last choice would be to reduce the effort associated with tasks so that the final deliverable takes less time to produce. For example, software projects that are running behind schedule often reduce the amount of time available for the final system test, thereby increasing the risk that the quality of the product will be lower than planned.

caution

Arbitrarily reducing task time to suit deadlines will almost never produce good results. A better solution would be removing a portion of the functionality for later delivery because the long-term effect of poor quality has a much larger impact.

Reducing Project Cost

Reducing project costs might be necessary because the project is going over budget or because of outside factors such as an organizational budget cut. The reason for the reduction is extremely important in determining which options the project team should take. The team should first attempt to reduce the project cost without causing an impact to the timeline or the scope and quality of the project. There are several options to review:

- Substitute less-expensive resources or subcontract a portion of the project to an outside resource that is less expensive. The potential impacts of this option are to the timeline (less experienced or outside resources may require more time to perform the work) and to the quality (again, less experience may result in more errors).

- Review all fixed costs for supplies and for subcontracts to see whether other products can be substituted, costs can be trimmed by using other vendors, or contracts can be renegotiated.

- Review any contingency funding or reserve set-aside for possible use. This option adds risk to the project but may be a point for negotiation with stakeholders in the future.

- Negotiate changes in scope or timeline.

Reducing Scheduled Duration

As with the scope and budget components discussed previously, a reduction in the duration of the project comes with some tradeoffs. Because you are working inside a sophisticated scheduling engine, however, more options are available inside the tool to help you solve this problem.

As discussed in many of the earlier chapters of this book, Project uses several things to determine the total duration of your project. These include the relationships between tasks, calendars, resources, and the amount of work required to produce the deliverables:

- **Task relationships**—When schedules are initially built, the relationships between tasks are often set up as Finish-to-Start. In reality, tasks might not need to be related, or they can overlap so that one task does not have to be completely finished before the successor can begin. If different resources are required for the tasks (and the resources can be made available), a change in these relationships can speed things up significantly. To accomplish this, change the lag on the task from zero to a negative number.

■ **Resource changes**—Many options are available to reduce the duration of a schedule by adding and substituting resources. Review the schedule to determine which resources are the most critical on the project because they have the greatest impact on the overall schedule duration. Key resources are often used in multiple projects and can only devote a small percentage of their time to one.

■ **Calendars and resource allocation**—Scheduling overtime can be a short-term fix to a schedule problem. If the amount of time needed is extensive, however, overtime might not solve the problem. Look for other resources that are not overallocated to support some of the work to be done.

■ **Work**—Reducing scope or the amount of effort required to complete certain tasks will have a positive impact on the schedule duration. It is easy to reduce the work in Project by changing or eliminating tasks, so you must be careful to make sure that the new estimates are realistic. You do not want to repeat the same exercise in a week because the estimates were too optimistic.

 note

Note that this change reduces the total schedule duration only if the task is on the critical path, so you should focus on critical-path activities when using this approach (see Figure 16.3).

tip

If other resources can perform some of their work or if the key resource can increase the percentage of commitment to your project, the timeline can be improved.

Figure 16.3 Negative lag on critical-path tasks can reduce the project duration.

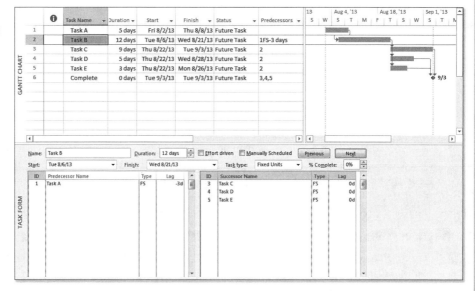

 note

If you need to reduce your schedule duration, also look at any recurring tasks that you have in your project. Often, recurring tasks or ongoing tasks (such as project management) will end up on your critical path and negatively impact the timeline.

Rebaselining Strategies

In several earlier chapters, we discussed the concepts of baselines and change control. At some point in your project, you need to decide whether your project has changed enough that you need to reset the baseline and start fresh.

In general, it is recommended that the original baseline be kept and that new tasks (and some modified tasks) are baselined using the Save Baseline, For: Selected Tasks option. If your project scope has changed significantly, it might make sense to reset the baseline so that the baseline data is useful for comparison purposes.

If your project is under formal change control, there will be a process to follow to determine when a new baseline is required.

 tip

Use one of the 10 available baselines to store a copy of your original baseline so that it is available for historical reference. After it is stored in Baseline 10, for example, you can then reset the primary baseline and move forward.

Consultants' Tips

Regularly Review Your Project Schedule

No matter what changes have impacted your project and what adjustments have been made, you need to regularly review your entire plan and schedule with both your team and your stakeholders. Surprises are not a good thing in the project management business, and timely preparation of the stakeholders will help you when there is a significant change in plans. If you monitor the schedule carefully and are always accurate in what is going on, you build credibility and you have more support when problems arise.

Perform Risk Management and Contingency Planning

Risk management and contingency planning are important activities in planning for success. When you determine that there are risks in your project, make sure that the mitigation plans make it into your project schedule. If the risk does not occur and you do not need to do mitigation, you will be in a position to remove work from your schedule rather than add to it.

Make Your Project Estimates as Realistic as Possible

Try not to be too optimistic in your estimates. Things can and will go wrong, so use the "most likely" or "most pessimistic" estimates for the work packages that are difficult and critical to your project success. This builds some contingency time into your schedules that you will probably need. You want your team to work with the shorter estimates as their goal, so make sure they have the incentive to go for the optimistic version while you plan for the worst.

Pay close attention to both the critical and the near-critical path of your project. This is one of the best early-warning systems you can have to minimize or mitigate the things that can go wrong.

CLOSING THE PROJECT

One of the most important steps in project management is often over-looked: closing a project. Often, project managers or teams do not take the time to officially close their projects for numerous reasons. Some people believe that after work on a project is completed, the project is finished. Or, perhaps they have another project to start and feel their time would be better spent by just diving into the next project. All too often, work on a project finishes, but the project itself just trails away, because it was not properly closed.

At the end of any project, the team should be able to look back and judge its success against the criteria that were set at the beginning of the project. Correctly set up projects have clear measures of success. Microsoft Project has many built-in capabilities to help you with the evaluation. If the project schedule was structured correctly, baselined, and work/costs were tracked accurately, you can use Earned Value tracking and many other features to measure your project's success. These do need to be set up at the beginning of the project, but you need to have the end game in mind when you begin.

Aside from formally completing all contract conditions and deliverables produced by the project, closing the project has several other benefits. You can perform a "lessons learned" analysis of the project, in which you and your team analyze what did and did not go well during the various phases of working on the project, and retain that information to improve work on future projects. This also gives members of the team an opportunity to provide insight to their individual experience with the project, and share final data and other statistical or completion information. Keep in mind, however, that the lessons learned session should not focus on individuals, because that often leads to placing blame. Rather, team members should reflect on what they thought worked well and what did not, and more specifically, on what can be done differently next time to improve the project.

This chapter examines the importance and methodology of closing a project.

Project Close Process Group

The objective of the Project Close process group is to collect all deliverables and relevant artifacts produced by the project, and coordinate their acceptance by the client. If there are any contractual signoffs or stipulations, be sure those are resolved. Also, all tasks within the project schedule should be labeled as Complete. If, for any reason, a task has not been completed, you should attach a note explaining why, as well as what the expectations are for the unfinished task(s).

The Project Close process group has two major steps: closing the project itself and closing the contract. Both of these steps break down into more specific actions, which are listed in this section and described in greater detail in this chapter.

The following is a checklist of what to do to properly close a project. It is based on information provided by the *PMBOK*, Fifth Edition (ANSI/PMI) and the best practices based on years of experience:

- **Obtain formal acceptance of the project**—This includes official signoff from the project sponsor and/or client to ensure that the contract conditions have been met. Some organizations have formal signoff documentation that needs to be completed by both parties, but it can be as simple as having a verbal acceptance.

- **Conduct a lessons learned session**—This includes a formal or informal meeting with the project team to discuss problems and successes as well as what can be done next time to prevent or mitigate the problems.

- **Organize and archive project files**—This includes the official close of the project schedule and archival of its files. During this part of the process, all project deliverables and other artifacts should be archived and moved to a designated location in accordance with the organization's operating procedure standards.

- **Celebrate success of the project**—It is important to acknowledge the completion of the project and celebrate its completion with the project team.

- **Transition to the operational phase of the product or system life cycle**—This includes the handling of project deliverables, as well as the support of a product or a system, if such was produced as a result of the project.

Closing the Contractual Agreement

Closing the contractual agreement is the most important step in the Project Close process group. The following list provides steps for properly closing any contractual agreement. It is also from the PMI's *PMBOK*, Fifth Edition (ANSI/PMI):

- Provide formal written notice that the contract has been accepted.

- Conduct a procurement audit; implement warranty phase, if needed.

- Create a contract file to be included with final archived project files.

When closing a project, it is important that you verify that all contractual obligations have been met, resolve any open items, and document the successful completion accordingly. Be sure to forward this documentation to all relevant parties.

Several things were recommended in the earlier chapters of this book to help you create a project with a successful end in mind. If you followed those recommendations, you now have three components to guide your evaluation of the project:

- Measure of Success (MOS)

- Work Breakdown Structure (WBS)

- Definition of Deliverables (DOD)

> *For more information about establishing these components, **see** Chapter 4, "Getting Started After the Business Initiative Is Approved," **p. 71**.*

Measure of Success

The Measure of Success that was created during the project initiation provides quantifiable criteria for measuring the project success. How do you know that your project met all required criteria? How do you know if you were successful?

You should revisit the MOS criteria at the project's close and determine whether your project was in fact successful. In some cases, the MOS cannot be evaluated completely until a longer period of time has passed because the product or service has not been available for enough time to allow an evaluation. If that is the case, the project manager should establish a date when the final measurements will be taken.

Work Breakdown Structure

Before you begin creating tasks in the schedule, you decomposed your project into a set of work packages that defined what would be accomplished during the project. During project closure, the WBS should be evaluated to determine whether all work packages were completed as planned or whether appropriate change control was in place so that changes to the original plan were documented and approved. The WBS is a key factor in scope control and the management of stakeholder expectations.

Definition of Deliverables

One important question to ask as the project manager is "How do I know when my project is finished?" You must instill quantifiable measures and explicit criteria that declare, "I am finished with the project when X, Y, and Z happen." Teams that are comfortable with the use of WBS will identify these measurements in the WBS dictionary. If you did not use a WBS dictionary, you should at least have a set of deliverables defined for the components in your WBS.

As the project manager, you defined the criteria for the deliverables with your team after the WBS was decomposed into work packages. You can now review the deliverables to see whether they are in compliance with the plan. Here are some factors included when reviewing the deliverables to determine the completion of a project:

- **Fulfillment of the contract**—All contract deliverables and conditions have been met.

- **Completion of the entire project scope**—All work defined for the project has been completed.

- **Completion of all invoicing**—Final invoicing has been submitted and/or received and no outstanding balances remain on either party's side.

- **Review of all tasks**—All tasks, summary tasks, and milestones in the project should be marked as 100% complete with no remaining work. If this is not the case, an explanation should be made for any variances.

By reviewing your project from each of these perspectives, you can be sure the project really is finished, eliminating the potential for surprise later.

Implementing Project Close Custom Fields

As mentioned in many earlier chapters, the use of custom fields can help you maintain the status of tasks or project phases. After you reach Project Close, it is time to perform a final review of the phases and tasks to ensure that all of them have been marked as complete.

➥ *For more information about creating custom fields,* **see** *the "Creating and Customizing Fields" section on* **p. 745** *in Chapter 22.*

In addition to the Phase custom field, you can create a Phase State custom field that provides an at-a-glance look at the state of the phase (open or closed). This gives you the ability to check the status of the project quickly by maintaining the status of each phase. It could have three values:

- Not Started

- In Progress

- Complete

Therefore, you can define which phase a task or summary task is in with the Phase custom field, and what the status is in the Phase Status custom field. You can, for example, have a summary task in the Close phase, with its status defined as In Progress.

To provide you even more insight into the state of your project, you can also create Budget and Schedule Status custom fields. These custom fields can be defined to display graphical color indicators that help you determine whether your project is Under Budget, On Budget, or Over Budget.

Similarly, you can create a field for Schedule Status to help you determine whether your project is Behind Schedule, On Schedule, or Ahead of Schedule. These status fields can help you throughout the life of the project and will provide an easy method to review the deliverables and see which contract terms have or have not been met.

 *For more information about creating custom fields, **see** the "Creating and Customizing Fields" section on **p. 745** in Chapter 22.*

Performing Final Reporting

Creation of project closure reports is an important step to obtain formal acceptance of the project and to conduct lessons learned. Final reporting provides you with documentation as to how the project performed overall, as well as a documented explanation of any variances within the project. It may also be a requirement from your project sponsor to see the final statistics on the project, in which case running the correct reports can be an easy way to meet that requirement.

Project supplies you with several different options for final reporting. You can compare your end results to the baseline plan, as well as perform final reporting on the critical path and the project's deliverables. You can also perform status reporting, where you can look at the project's status as of any given date, which is defined in the Status Date field in the Project Information dialog box.

The first screen to examine is the Tracking Gantt view (Task tab, View, Gantt Chart, Tracking Gantt). You will want to modify the view to display baseline values versus actual values, as well as variance values. To modify the view in this manner, follow these steps:

1. Right-click on the column header in the table where you want to insert this information.

2. Select the field you want to insert.

Repeat this process until you have inserted all the columns you want to include.

 *For more information about modifying views, **see** the "Creating and Customizing Views" section on **p. 708** in Chapter 22.*

 *For more information about variance and actual values versus baseline values, **see** the "Reviewing the Status Via the Project Plan" section on **p. 465** in Chapter 14.*

> **tip**
> Defining the Phase custom field for every task may become tiresome. You can define this custom field at the summary task level.

> **note**
> Helpful columns to insert on this view are Actual Duration and Duration Variance. In addition, you might want to add Baseline Work, Actual Work, Baseline Start, Actual Start, Baseline Finish, Actual Finish, Baseline Cost, and Actual Cost. Your choice should not be limited to just the columns mentioned here, but driven by the requirements you have to meet in your reports.

> **tip**
> By applying the Critical tasks filter to the Tracking Gantt view, you can see your project's critical path performance.

If you apply the Critical task filter to this view, it will show you variance for the critical path at the summary task and subtasks level (depending on whether your outline is collapsed). To apply the Critical tasks filter, select Project, Filtered For and then choose Critical.

Cost Overruns Report

Assuming you managed a normal project, the Cost Overruns report is a helpful report to examine as well, even though it might be uncomfortable. This report contains summary information for task and resource cost variance. And of course, it can be modified to include more:

1. Open the Reports dialog box by selecting the Report tab.

2. Under Costs, select Cost Overruns, as shown in Figure 17.1.

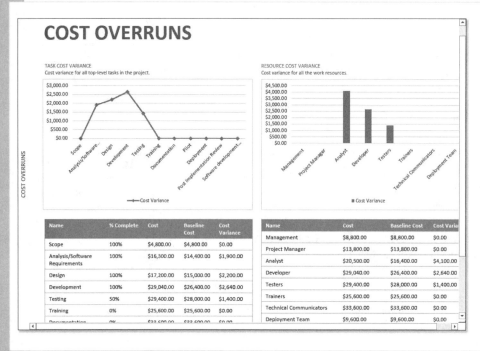

Figure 17.1
The Cost Overruns report can be a useful, if uncomfortable, closing document.

Additional Out-of-the-Box Closing Reports

Project comes out of the box with several additional reports you might find helpful for final reporting. Top-Level Tasks, Critical Tasks, and Milestone reports can all be useful. These can all be found under the Report tab.

Another option for final reporting is to create a custom report. This can be done by selecting the Report Tab, New Report. This opens the template options for the new reports, as shown in Figure 17.2.

For additional information on modifying reports, **see** "Reports Part I: 2013 Reports," p. 625.

Figure 17.2
Use the
new
Reports
Templates
to create
new reports
as needed.

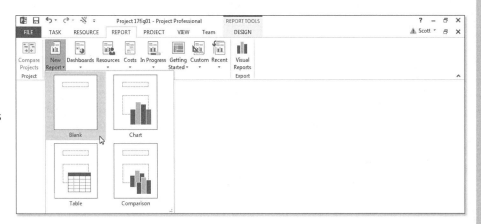

Resource Usage view is helpful for final reporting. Display the Resource Usage view and insert all baseline and actual data by right-clicking on the grid in the right pane and selecting the additional items you want to display, or by inserting the desired columns in the left pane. Then, you will be able to see whether the schedule plan was achieved, which resources performed according to the plan, which resources were consistent, and whether the plan was accurate. If there is a significant amount of resources with schedule and work variances, it is likely that the schedule and work estimates were off.

Finally, the Earned Value report can be created to determine the project results. Earned Value is a valuable method for calculating the variances in your planned and actual costs to determine whether the project brought value. You can find the Earned Value report in two different locations, as follows:

- **Using reports**—Select the Report tab, Costs, and then select Earned Value Report.

- **Using visual reports**—Select the Report tab, Visual Reports, Assignment Usage tab, and then select Earned Value Over Time Report.

Using visual reports provides you with more options, such as graphically displaying your project results in a chart. Visual reports are also highly customizable, so you can create the final project report containing any and all information you need.

> *For more information about customizing visual reports, **see** Chapter 21, "Reports Part II: Visual Reports," **p. 653**.*

> *For additional information about Earned Value and its importance in the project, **see** the "Analyzing Performance with Earned Value Analysis" section on **p. 474** in Chapter 14.*

Performing final reporting is a necessary segue into the next step in the Project Close phase: performing a project retrospective.

Performing a Project Retrospective: Lessons Learned

Like any major accomplishment in life, there are always lessons to be learned at the completion of a project. Performing a "lessons learned" (or a retrospective) is an important step in the Project Close phase because it enables you to take the necessary time to review the actions and events that impacted the project—especially those events that were not planned. This not only helps you and your project team uncover those details, but can also help you prevent them or mitigate them more efficiently in future projects.

Here are some questions to ask when performing a lessons learned, or retrospective:

- What went well, and why?

- What could be improved upon, and how?

- What were the major events that were not planned? Why did they happen?

- What were the causes of variances, either favorable or unfavorable?

- What action was taken when unplanned situations arose? Was it effective?

- What was the most challenging aspect of the project, for both you and for the project team?

- What was the most enjoyable aspect of the project, for both you and for the project team?

One idea to keep in mind while performing a project retrospective is to not put too much emphasis on the negative parts of the project. The negative points are important to discuss, but this is not supposed to turn into a blaming session and make you and your team feel bad. If the project finished late or over budget, try not to get discouraged. Rather, figure out what went wrong, talk about the issues with the people involved with the project, and keep in mind that similar projects in the future will go more smoothly because the project team will have more experience to work with.

It is important to determine when and why negative aspects occurred—not to assign blame, but to learn from them and figure out how to avoid similar problems in the future. Perhaps a particular resource naturally excelled in a certain area of the project; you would want to assign similar tasks to that resource in the future or at least provide cross-training if this was a skills problem. Also consider the opposite situation: if a particular resource struggled with an assignment. Was this a skills mismatch, and would additional training help for the next project?

In any project, there will always be successes to celebrate as well as unsuccessful aspects you wish you could do over again; that is the nature of a project. Retrospective sessions should provide valuable lessons of what to do and what not to do, and those lessons should be used by not only you, but by other project managers, team members, and stakeholders for all future projects.

 note

It is safe to say that the greatest amount of frustration project teams face is schedule related because most schedule errors are errors in scope control and estimation, not in execution. The retrospective can help determine where and why variances occurred, and prepare you to make much more accurate estimates for your future projects.

Project provides quantitative data to support the lessons learned sessions, not only in the reporting described in the previous section, but also in the various views, tables, and filters you can apply. Determine what kind of data you want, and use the features within Project to locate that data.

The Tracking Gantt Chart view is helpful to compare how the project was executed compared to how it was planned. Also, filter for tasks or phases in the project that have a lot of variance, and try to deduce why variance occurred so often in that particular aspect. It is helpful to use the reporting methods previously described and meet with your team, stakeholders, or clients to review. That way, everyone involved will learn from the retrospective session, not just you.

You can display the Task Usage view and insert the actual value and variance fields to show the estimated time and the actual time worked on each task. Tasks with large variances between actual work and planned work usually indicate that resources applied additional effort to complete the tasks on schedule, meaning that your planned duration values for those tasks were not accurate.

Finally, when performing a retrospective, be sure to examine the general process that was used between team members:

- Was the effort and quality delivered by the resources consistent throughout the project?

- Was the communication used within the team, as well as the communication with clients, effective and productive?

- Was everyone on the same page, or were resources or clients sometimes left in the dark about certain aspects of the project?

Remember that throughout this process, it is important to focus on events, and not people's mistakes. Collect and document the lessons learned, and implement any approved solutions in the future. It is also important to focus on positive aspects and make sure that they will also be able to be replicated on future projects.

Archiving Your Schedule

At the completion of a project, it is important to archive your schedule for future reference. Perhaps you need to revisit a task or phase down the road to see how you handled a certain situation, or your client needs further clarification on an aspect of a completed project. It is also possible that you want to create a template from the project you just completed to be used for future projects of the same type. If nothing else, you owe it to yourself and your team to properly save, store, and archive all of the hard work that was exerted into the project. It is also possible that your organization has standards for archiving your files that you must abide by.

As a project manager, you should think of each completed project as a learning tool. Performing a project retrospective, as discussed in the previous section, provides lessons and insight to apply to all your future projects. Perhaps you learned that certain techniques or resources do or do not work well for you. Let your experience guide you. You have heard the phrase "Practice makes perfect." Well, nobody is perfect, but practice and experience will make you better, and you would be wise to take that into consideration.

Archiving your schedule can be especially important if the recently completed project is a type of project you work on often. If the project was especially successful, you should make it into a template—a guide or model on which to base future same-type projects. That way, you will not have to re-create the project information over and over again. Save the template into a unique folder for quick and easy reference, and let your hard work and success carry through into your next project(s).

To convert your project schedule into a template, follow these steps:

1. Open the project file you want to save as a template.

2. Select the File tab, Save As, to open the Save As page.

3. Click on Computer. In the File Name field in the Save As dialog box, type in the name you want to save the template as (see Figure 17.3).

4. In the Save As Type field at the bottom of the Save As dialog box, choose Project Template from the drop-down list. This changes the filename from an .mpp file extension to an .mpt extension. You will not lose the original (.mpp) project file; it remains where you saved it originally, and the template is saved in your Microsoft Templates folder (see Figure 17.3).

5. Click the Save button, which opens the Save As Template dialog box (see Figure 17.4).

6. The Save As Template provides you with options of items *not* to include in the template. Select any item you do not want to be included. Generally, you would not want to include actuals, baseline, and other tracking data. That data will be replaced with data from future projects; it is unique to the completed project, and now that it is a template, the project details are unnecessary. You may, however, want to include your planning estimates.

7. Click the Save button. The newly created template will be saved in your Microsoft Templates folder.

➡ *For additional information about templates, **see** Chapter 18, "Managing Project Files Locally and in the Cloud," **p. 549**.*

After you have saved the file as a template, it may be helpful to review and edit it to ensure that no other schedule information should not be included in the template.

Use the following list to guide you as you review the template:

- Tasks should not have a constraint attached to them other than As Soon As Possible or As Late As Possible. Use the icons in the Indicator column, or display the Constraints table to a task view to verify that no other constraints are applied to the tasks.

 tip

Remember, you are saving your project as a starting point for future projects. If you keep too much information, you'll run the risk of making your life harder, not easier.

- Display the Resource Sheet view. If there are any resources in the template, you might want to remove them or replace them with generic resources. This will help you or other project managers make the correct resource assignments, as well as ensure that resources are not automatically assigned to the same tasks.

Figure 17.3
Name the template file and choose Template from the Save As Type field drop-down list.

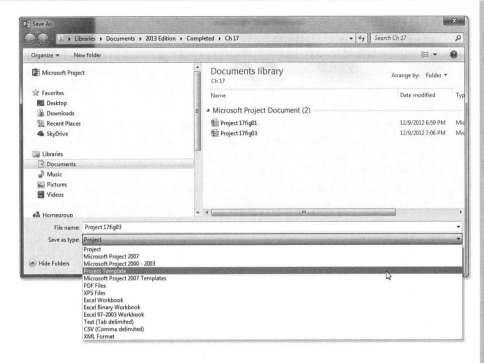

Figure 17.4
In the Save As Template dialog box, select the items you do not want to be included in the template.

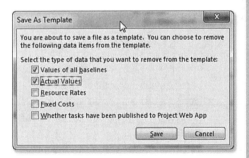

- Review the project plan's logic (its WBS organization and its predecessor/successor dependency relationships). Does the WBS use a noun-based structure that is decomposed into work packages? Are the dependency relationships valid for the template?

- Review task durations compared to work. Do the planned and actual values match, or are they close? If they do match, or are close, you might want to leave the planned values in because they were accurate estimates. If they are not close, you need to adjust the planned values based on the retrospective (described in the previous section).

When you are finished reviewing and modifying the template, click File, Save.

Celebrating Your Project Results

When a project is officially closed, do not skip out on celebrating your results. Hard work deserves to be recognized and celebrated, and closing a project is no exception. Plan to get together with your team, as well as other stakeholders in the project, and put the final stamp on the project with a party!

All too often, team members finish their work on a project and are assigned to work on other tasks for another project. After the project they initially worked on closes, they often do not know about it because they are already immersed in something else. Take the time to invite these hard-working resources to a function of some sort, whether it is in your office or an outside location. Acknowledge the successes of the project, and make sure everyone knows that the project is finished, and that they are officially free of responsibilities to it. Share the final reporting data with everyone, and be sure to also let them know about the lessons learned, so they can retain that information and become more efficient in the future.

Celebrating the project should be done even when a project was not totally successful. You should always make it a point to bring closure to the project for everyone involved with it, and focus on the positive areas of the project. Let the final interaction with the project be a constructive one for team members; they will feel much better about a project that might have been stressful for them, and leaving it on a good note will do well for you as a project manager when they are assigned to work on future projects with you.

A celebration is healthy for a team. It promotes team unity and brings a little light-heartedness at the end of what might have been a difficult stretch of work. People thrive off being rewarded for their efforts and love to experience a sense of accomplishment. Taking an hour or two to celebrate a project's success will go a long way—especially if you serve food and drinks!

Consultants' Tips

Everyone can cite reports about how few projects are considered to be successful (with success being defined as achieving the stated schedule, cost, and quality objectives), and the reasons for having a less-successful project are varied and also well documented. The project manager's role is to watch for challenges (issues and risks), detect them, address them, and then learn from them. That does not mean the issues will not happen again; it just means you will be better prepared to meet the challenges presented.

It is always good to approach the lessons learned sessions with enthusiasm. It is a chance to recognize the team's accomplishments with the stakeholders present, and it is a chance for everyone to learn. As long as everyone put their best effort into the work, there should be no hesitation about participating in a retrospective.

A lessons learned session that is supported by clear and objective data helps the stakeholders and the project team to focus on events and not on people. Showing a Tracking Gantt Chart that displays a lot of slipping tasks might not seem like a good decision, until you point out that the critical path was managed well. The data that Project supplies, in the form of Gantt Charts and reports, provides the visual focus to the story of the project told during the retrospective session.

The visual data needs to be backed up by facts, of course, including approved changes and major risk and issue events. It is often up to the project manager to apply his or her best skills in diplomacy to describe some events, but it cannot be stressed enough that lessons learned cannot focus on people in anything but a positive way. If a specific resource just did not perform his or her assignment, most of the project team members are probably already aware of that, and there is no need to focus on it. If a stakeholder micromanaged people and caused delays, you want to discuss the communication process issues, not the people issues.

And finally, you want to celebrate the project's completion. The retrospective brings closure to the project and, on some projects, marks the transition of people to other projects or to other organizations. Schedule an event to occur shortly after the lessons learned session and make sure everyone who was involved in the project is invited. Go and have fun, because your next project starts soon!

MANAGING PROJECT FILES LOCALLY AND IN THE CLOUD

With Office 2013, Microsoft has increased your options for where you save your files. As an Office 2013 product, Project is no different. Saving files remotely is now an expectation, not an exception. In some cases, this makes your life easier. In others, it adds some complexity to what was a simple, established process.

Project files are similar to any other Office file. People tend to start with the last best version of a project similar to the new one they are starting. This often leads to a pluralization of idiosyncratic and quirky approaches to managing similar projects—projects that would really benefit from some cross-group standardization.

 note

Although Project Professional is now much more seamlessly integrated with SharePoint, that topic falls outside the scope of this book.

Project provides an enormous amount of flexibility. It also provides mechanisms, such as templates, for standardizing project management practices across a small group of project managers. This chapter describes both. Larger groups of project managers should strongly consider the enterprise capability of Project Server.

Saving and Protecting Project Files

When working with Project, you will want to know how to manipulate its important files and how file information is organized within the tool. This chapter explores how to manipulate project files, save and protect your work, create and use templates, and employ the Organizer feature to save and share common custom objects such as fields, calendars, or views in the Global.mpt file for yourself or others within your organization.

Working with the Organizer and the Global File

You can save project files in many different formats when you are working with a group of people and sharing your files. Some of these options include Excel and XML. When sharing your project file, it is important to protect the data within it and limit the control other people have over it. You might also create or need a custom object such as a calendar or view.

The following sections discuss the options you have when saving, protecting, and sharing your project files.

Designating the Default Save Location and Format

When you are using Project and save your project, it is saved to the default location—My Documents with the extension .mpp. However, you can modify the default location for storing your project files, as well as their type, by using the Project Options window. In addition, you can also designate the default save location for the user-defined templates that you create yourself.

To change the default save location for your files, follow these steps:

1. Open Project Options by selecting the File tab, Options.

2. In Project Options, select the Save tab (see Figure 18.1).

3. To modify the default save type for the projects you create, select the Save Files in This Format drop-down list and choose between the four available options:

   - **Project(*.mpp)**—The default Project file type and the recommended option.

   - **Microsoft Project 2007(*.mpp)**—Saves the Project file to be compatible with Microsoft Office Project 2007.

   - **Microsoft Project 2000–2003(*.mpp)**—Saves the Project file to be compatible with Microsoft Office Project 2000, 2002, or 2003.

   - **Template(*.mpt)**—The template file type; used to designate template files within Project.

4. To modify the default location for saving regular project files or templates, change the Default File location. Browse to the new designated location and click OK to save your changes (refer back to Figure 18.1).

Figure 18.1
The Save tab of the Project Options dialog box enables you to set options for saving your project files, including the default file type, location, and Auto Save options.

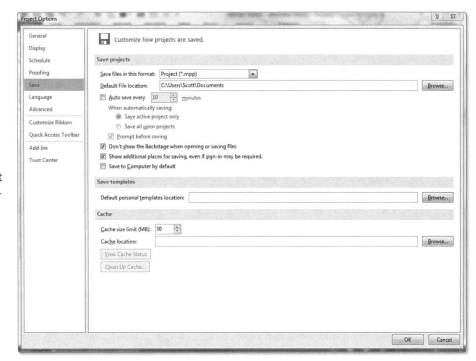

 tip
You should designate a new location for your project files under the My Documents folder on your computer. This will help you organize your files into one central location and keep them separate from other documents on your computer. Similarly, it is recommended to create a User Templates folder somewhere under My Documents as well. This designates a single location for all of your Project templates and makes locating them much easier. If your organization has standards for organizing your personal files on your computer, this is a great place to integrate those standards and create additional folders to accommodate your project and template files. If your organization is sharing project templates, you could change the file location to the network drive where you all share your project templates. You need to make sure that no one changes the location of the network drive without informing all project managers using the templates if you decide to do this.

5. You can also set the frequency that Project automatically saves your project file. To do so, select the Auto Save Every check box under the Save Projects section and then enter the number of minutes in the minutes box. This option also enables you to select what kind of projects you want Auto Save to apply to, as well as whether you want to be prompted each time there is an automatic save (refer back to Figure 18.1).

6. Click OK to save your changes or click Cancel to exit without saving.

Version Compatibility

Project 2013 is backward compatible, meaning you can open files that have been created in previous versions of the tool. However, some restrictions apply. For example, if a particular feature has been removed or modified from a previous version, modifications to the project file regarding that feature might not carry over into the new version. In particular, Manual Task mode was introduced in Project 2010. If you save a project file into an earlier version, your manual tasks will all have been changed to auto-scheduled, with unpredictable results.

Even though Project is backward compatible, the same theory does not work when opening project files created in 2010 using the previous versions of the tool. Microsoft Office Project 2000, 2002, 2003, 2007, and 2010 do share the same file type for project files (.mpp). However, you have to specifically save the project file from Project to the lower version of Microsoft Project for the files to be readable by the earlier versions.

 note

Microsoft Office Project 2000, 2002, and 2003 also had the capability to save project files to be compatible with Microsoft Project 98. However, this hasn't applied since Project 2007.

To save a Project 2013 file to be compatible with one of the previous versions of Microsoft Project (except Project 98), select File, Save As, Computer, Browse; in the Save as Type drop-down box, select one of the other options, as shown in Figure 18.2.

➡ *For additional information about version compatibility,* **see** *the "Exchanging Project Files Across Microsoft Project Versions" section on* **p. 836** *in Chapter 25.*

Saving a File

When saving a Project 2013 file, you can select the File tab, Save As. From here, if you have associated your version of Project Professional with a SharePoint site, or with a SkyDrive, you can save directly to those locations. You can add other web locations, or you can click on Computer, Browse to save locally, which opens the Save As dialog box (refer back to Figure 18.2).

In the File Name box, enter a descriptive filename. This name will be used when printing reports, displaying your file, and any other viewing of your project, so ensure that the name conveys the purpose of the project.

The Save as Type drop-down box provides several options for the file types, as described in Table 18.1.

 tip

You can also save your project file by using the Ctrl+S keyboard combination. This option works only if the project has not been previously saved. If the file has been previously saved, your latest changes will be saved to the previously designated location.

 caution

The project filename can be up to 200 characters in length, including spaces. Certain characters are not accepted for the filename. These include the following:

/ ? \ : * " < > |

Figure 18.2
Project 2013 is compatible with Microsoft Project versions 2000–2010, and you can save the file down to those versions to ensure that they can be opened. The Save As dialog box enables you to select filename, location, and file type for saving your project file.

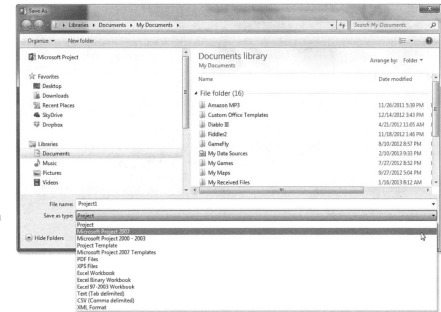

Table 18.1 Project Supported Save File Types

File Type	Extension	Description
Project	.mpp	The standard file type for individual project files for Microsoft Project 2013.
Microsoft Project 2007	.mpp	The standard file type for individual project files for Microsoft Project 2007.
Microsoft Project 2000–2003	.mpp	The standard file type for individual project files compatible with Microsoft Office Project 2000, 2002, and 2003.
Project Template	.mpt	A special type of project file containing a group of tasks or resources to be used as a starting point for creating project schedules of similar type in Microsoft Project 2013. The templates will not be compatible with previous versions of Microsoft Project.
Microsoft Project 2007 Templates	.mpt	A special type of project file containing a group of tasks or resources to be used as a starting point for creating project schedules of similar type in Microsoft Project 2007. The templates will not be compatible with other versions of Microsoft Project.
PDF Files	.pdf	Adobe Acrobat standard pdf files.
XPS Files	.xps	A Microsoft alternative to Adobe Acrobat files.

File Type	Extension	Description
Excel Workbook	.xlxs	The file format used to export project data to Microsoft Office Excel. When you save a project file using this format, the Export Wizard is launched, enabling you to select the types of data (Task, Resource, or Assignment) and fields within those data types to be included in the Excel spreadsheet.
Excel Binary Workbook	.xlsb	The file format used to store Excel files in binary. Excel might be able to open particularly large files saved in this format more quickly.
Excel 97–2003	.xls	The file format used to export project data to Microsoft Office Excel 1997–2003. When you save a project file using this format, the Export Wizard is launched, enabling you to select the types of data (Task, Resource, or Assignment) and fields within those data types to be included in the Excel spreadsheet.
Text (tab delimited)	.txt	The file type used to export project data into a tab-delimited text file. This format can be useful if you are planning on importing it into another system, such as a database, that you can then use to model the data. When this file type is used, an Export Wizard is launched, enabling you to select the data types (Task, Resource, or Assignment) and the fields within those data types to be included.
CSV (comma delimited)	.csv	CSV stands for Comma Separated Values and represents a format commonly used by many databases, where each record is a single line and each field in the record is separated by a comma. This type of file format can be then imported into an external database system, as well as Excel. When this file type is applied, an Export Wizard is launched that enables you to select the data types (Task, Resource, or Assignment) and the fields within those data types to be included.
XML Format	.xml	XML stands for Extensible Markup Language and is a widely used file format for manipulating data. XML is used for document creation and was developed to replace HTML, as it is more versatile and provides better document structure. When you save your project file in this format, the entire project information is exported, including all project details and statistics, calendars, tasks, resources, and assignments. Each part of the data is located on its own node, with the subvalues indented in the leaves below it. You can use this file type to export your project data to be used in any other external system for viewing or analysis.

Your Account

Under File, Account you see your connected services, as shown in Figure 18.3. In the example shown, the copy of Project Professional is associated both with a SharePoint Site and the author's personal SkyDrive through his Live account. Accounts can be added, switched, and dissociated from a particular installation of Project Professional from this page. As of this writing, Microsoft is pushing hard to develop a compelling "Cloud" story for all its major products. Some of this is working well, and some of it is more aspirational than truly user-driven. Project Server still provides the most compelling solution for publishing projects, although Project Server itself is rapidly evolving.

Figure 18.3
Use the Account page under the File tab to control your external connections.

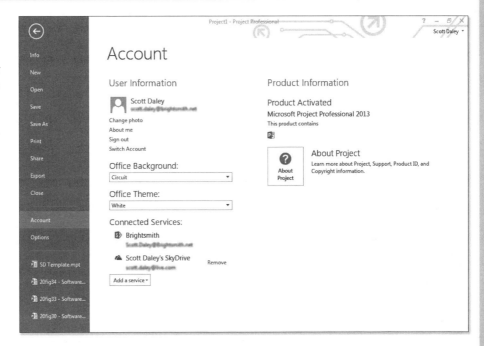

Providing Security for Saved Files

When sharing project files among multiple people, it is important that you protect the highly sensitive data and the data you do not want other people to change.

You can use the password-protect feature by following these steps:

1. Launch the Save As dialog box by selecting the File tab, Save As, Browse.

2. In the bottom-left corner of the Save As dialog box, select the Tools drop-down and choose General Options (see Figure 18.4).

3. The Save Options dialog box includes the following options:

- **Always Create Backup**—You can create a backup of a previous version of a file every time you save the file. This option is useful because it prevents you from overwriting the previous file version, enabling you to always roll back.

- **Protection Password**—You can password-protect the file by creating a password. If you apply this option, anyone attempting to open the file will be unable to, unless she knows the password.

- **Write Reservation Password**—You can write-protect the file, which allows any user to open a read-only copy of the file, but to save any changes to it, the user must know the password. Although this does not prevent users from saving their changes under a different project name, it does give you control over who can change your project file.

- **Read-Only Recommended**—You can also save the project file with the warning that lets other users know that you prefer them opening the file in a read-only mode, forcing them to save any changes they make to a different filename and preventing potentially unwanted changes or loss of data.

4. Click OK to save your changes or click Cancel to exit without saving.

Figure 18.4
Use the Save Options dialog box to protect your project file.

Password-Protecting a File

To password-protect a file, you can enter a password (up to 17 characters) in the Protection Password field of the Save Options dialog box. The password you create is case sensitive and supports all text characters, including symbols, numbers, and spaces. When you click OK, a confirmation is displayed requesting you to reenter the password. Click OK to save your changes.

Every time you or anybody else opens your project file, the password must be entered to view the file. If the password does not match the password you entered in the Save Options dialog box, a warning is displayed, requesting that you or the other user try again. There is no limit to how many attempts a user can make for entering the password.

To remove a password from a password-protected file, follow these steps:

1. After opening the protected file using the password, select the File tab, Save As, Browse from the main menu.

2. In the Save As dialog box, select Tools, General Options.

3. In the Save Options dialog box, simply erase all characters in the Protection Password box and click OK to save your changes.

Saving a Read-Only File

Read-only files can be a great way to protect your project data from being edited by other people. It does not mean that others cannot make any changes to the file, however. They will just be unable to save it to the same project filename.

The Write Reservation Password feature enables you to do just that. If you enter a write reservation password, when the project file is opened, a warning is displayed, stating that the file is write reserved (see Figure 18.5). If the user provides the correct password, he or she is able to view the project in regular mode and make changes to it under the same project name. In addition, if the user does not know the password, he or she has the ability to open the file in read-only mode.

Read-only mode prevents the user from making changes to the project file under the same name. However, the user can save the file under a different name to include the changes.

Saving the file with a write reservation password ensures that only the users authorized to make changes to the project file can make any direct changes.

Figure 18.5
The write reservation password warning is displayed when a user attempts to open the write reservation protected project file.

To remove the write reservation password after opening the protected file using the password, open the Save Options dialog box (select the File tab, Save As, Browse, Tools, General Options), clear the text in the Write Reservation Password field, and then click OK.

Saving a File as Read-Only Recommended

The Read-Only Recommended feature does not prevent users from opening the project file in read-write mode. It only warns them of the preference you have added, and gives them a choice to accept it or bypass it. This option is not very effective at protecting your project file from being modified by other users.

Using the Always Create Backup Option

The option for creating a backup file is activated by selecting the Always Create Backup check box in the Save Options dialog box (select the File tab, Save As, Computer, Browse, Tools, General Options). When you select this option, each time any user saves changes to the file, the original file is saved with the original name and the .bak extension. The active version of the file is then saved under the original project name with the .mpp extension. This option enables you to still access the previous version of your file, without overwriting the data.

Saving the Workspace

A workspace in Project is a pointer to all currently opened project files, although a separate copy of each file is not created in the workspace. This feature is very useful when working on multiple files. For example, if you have two projects open and leave the office to go home, you can save your entire workspace to reopen it where you left off in the morning.

This feature can also be useful to capture the files that you work with regularly, bypassing the need for you to open each project separately each time you work. Project does not let you select multiple files using the Open dialog box; therefore, creating a workspace is a great workaround for this issue.

To save a workspace, the Save Workspace command has to be added to the Quick Launch bar. Select Save Workspace, and in the Save As dialog box, enter the name for the workspace and its location (by default, Resume.mpw displays). The workspace file will be saved with the .mpw extension. Microsoft Project prompts you to save changes to each file that was modified during that session.

 note

The fact that Microsoft has chosen to leave the Save Workspace command off the ribbon is probably an indication that this method of sharing data across projects is not part of Project's extended future.

 note

If you are saving a file that you just created and have not saved yet, you are prompted to include it in the workspace. New project files that are empty are not added to the workspace.

Project Safe Mode

Project supports a safe mode feature that is enabled when your system experiences instability, such as Registry corruption or an unexpected crash. This allows Project to continue working on your project files in a safe mode, with some of the features disabled. To start in safe mode, open Project with the Ctrl key pressed.

 caution

Continuing to work in an unstable environment can be risky. When instability occurs, save your work, close all open files, close all open applications, and restart Windows.

Creating and Using Project Templates

In this section, you learn how to create and reuse project templates.

A *template* is a project that has been specially designated to be used more than once by you or others. When you save a template file correctly, it has the file extension of .mpt rather than the .mpp extension that reflects a normal project file. A template has special characteristics, one being that it is saved into a special location reserved for templates.

Templates are especially useful for establishing consistent and repeated activities in a project so you do not have to start a project from scratch. For example, if you were in construction, you might be building condominiums, and each condo project requires similar activities. You could set up the project once with all of the tasks already entered, and save it as a template to be used over and over for each condo project. As another example, suppose you are working on a major acquisition project; you can easily make a template that has custom fields that can be used by both the buyer and the seller. Project templates do not have to be detailed or include all project information. Instead, project templates need to contain the common and repeatable project details that you can easily modify to fit to the new project you are creating.

A template can help you to set standards for projects within your organization, especially if the project structure and setup can be reused by several different project managers. A template enables you to reuse common tasks, project information, customized fields, calendars, and notes in a template project. It also lets you set up shared standard resources and equipment lists.

When you are building a template, you should strive for minimum threshold, not maximum. Build the template so that the basics are included, but let your project managers add their own tasks when they create their projects. If you have a template where project managers seem to be removing tasks over and over again, then those tasks do not belong in a template. Estimated durations can be included to establish standards. In the construction project example, it might be useful to include a task for wiring the condominiums and provide an estimated duration that represents the standard that you want to maintain.

Finally, you should try to include task relationships when designing a template. The closer the template reflects the actual activities and sequence of work performed on projects, the easier it is going to be for project managers to use the template, which makes them more productive. The purpose of building a template is to make it as useful as possible, so you can save time in the future.

Creating a New Project Template

When you have a project you want to use as a template, or have entered all of the project template details in a new project file, you can now save it as a template so that it will be available to be used in the future.

Follow these steps to save a project as a template:

1. From the main menu, select the File tab, Save As, computer, Browse.

2. In the File Name field, enter the name of your template. Try to provide as descriptive a name as possible, which enables you to easily tell what the project template contains. You might even want to include Template at the end of the name for easy identification.

3. In the Save as Type drop-down box, select Template (which you can see is a .mpt file). After you select the Template file type, Project automatically changes the location to the Templates folder.

4. Click the Save button.

5. In the Save As Template dialog box, select the values you want to be excluded from your template, as follows (see Figure 18.6). It is good practice to always select all the fields in the Save As Template dialog box, unless you have very good reason to include the values described in your template. If you leave the check boxes cleared and use this file as a template, every project based on the template will have the values left in the template:

caution

Do not change this location if you want to use the process "Opening a Template File to Create a New Project" described later. This template location will sync up with the file location you left as default or changed as described in "Designating the Default Save Location and Format" earlier in the chapter.

- **Values of All Baselines**—Select this box to remove any baselines that might have been set in the project (which you would have set using Tools, Tracking, Set Baseline).

- **Actual Values**—Select this box to remove any actual values from the template. Selecting this item removes data in the Actual Work, Actual Duration, Actual Cost, as well as other actual data fields.

- **Resource Rates**—Select this box to remove any rates on resources that might be on the Resource Sheet or assigned tasks in the project. If you have added resources and their rates to this project, leaving this option cleared saves that resource information on the project schedules based on this template.

caution

You might want to leave this option cleared if you are using generic resources to calculate an estimated budget for the project using the template. Be cautious if you decide to leave resource rates in the template. Resource rates do change and will need to be modified. If you fail to modify the rates, you risk having an inaccurate project budget.

- **Fixed Costs**—Select this box to remove any fixed costs in the project template. In some templates, you might want to leave fixed costs in the template, although you should review the template occasionally to see if the fixed costs should be modified. For instance, there may be a fixed cost for inspections for the condo project template. You might want to leave the fixed costs in the template for others to use.

- **Whether Tasks Have Been Published to Project Web App**—Select this box to remove the designation that specifies whether the project has been saved to Project Server and, therefore, has dependencies with it. Project Server is the enterprise-wide edition of Project, and if you are using the Standard edition of Project, you will most likely want to select this item for exclusion.

6. After you have made the desired selections, click the Save button to save your project as a template.

Figure 18.6
The Save As Template dialog box enables you to choose what project data to exclude from the template.

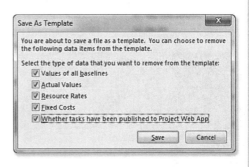

---

 tip

It is important to note that you can save any project as a template, even one you have created as a regular project—even if it has already been completed. The options described in step 5 are particularly useful if you are using an old project as a template. These options enable you to exclude the actual values, baselines, and other project-specific information that you do not necessarily want in your template. However, you still want to be cautious of any other data you could save in a template. For instance, you may also have included hyperlinks in the file you are saving as the template, and those hyperlinks will be irrelevant for future projects using the template.

Modifying Existing Template Files

Project provides no direct option to open an existing .mpt file. Therefore, to make changes to an existing project template file, you must open a copy of the template, make the desired changes, and resave it under the default name and .mpt extension. You must make sure to select the Project Template file type in the Save As dialog box; otherwise, a regular project file will be created by default. If you perform this action correctly, you see a message saying the filename already exists. When the template file is resaved, it overwrites the original copy, creating a more up-to-date one you modified.

Opening a Template File to Create a New Project

If you created a new template following the instructions in the previous section, and if you used the Project default location, that template will be available as one of the templates available when you create a new project, as shown in Figure 18.7. When you open a template file, you are opening a copy of the template file, not the original template file itself.

To create a new project based on a template, follow these steps:

1. Open Project.

2. In the main menu, select the File tab, New.

3. In the New Project pane, you see options to create a new project from Excel, SharePoint Tasks List, and many of the standard default project templates. Select New from existing project (see

Figure 18.7). This opens a standard file browser; change the filter in the lower-right corner to Project Templates to see only Project template files.

Figure 18.7
You can use the New Project pane to access the predefined project templates.

4. Select the template you want to use and click OK. One of the first things you should do in the new project is select the Project tab, Properties, Project Information and change the Start Date to the relevant start date of your project.

5. Templates retain all the old dates that were saved in the original template. Select the Project tab, Schedule, Move Project to update all tasks and deadlines to match your new project start date.

Working with the Organizer and the Global File

When you modify an object in your project file, such as the Standard Task Calendar, or create a new custom view or report, they are only available and saved within the currently opened project file. Project provides the Organizer feature, which enables you to manage and reuse custom or modified objects. The Organizer is used to copy modified or custom objects from one project file to another or to Global.mpt.

To access the Organizer, select the File tab, Organizer (see Figure 18.8).

Figure 18.8
The Organizer feature enables you to access items that can be customized and shared in Project.

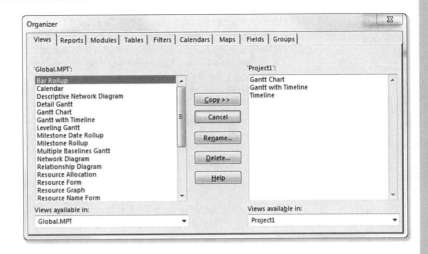

You can also access the Organizer by using one of many different options:

- From the File tab, Info, click Organizer

- While on any report, from the Report Tools tab, click Manager, Organizer

- Accessing the More Views dialog box by selecting the View tab, Task Views or Resource Views, Other Views, More Views, Organizer

- Accessing the More Tables dialog box by selecting the View tab, Data, Tables, More Tables, Organizer

- Accessing the More Filters dialog box by selecting the View tab, Data, Filter, More Filters, Organizer

- Accessing the More Groups dialog box by selecting the View tab, Data, Group by, More Groups, Organizer

Table 18.2 lists objects contained within the Organizer.

Table 18.2 Organizer Objects

Type	Description
Views	Views are tables and charts that are used to organize, categorize, and display project data. Views are used to view two main categories of data within project: tasks and resources. Project provides three different types of views: charts or graphs, sheets, and forms. You can customize views to create new views to fit your needs. For additional information about customizing views, see "Creating and Customizing Views" in Chapter 22, p. 708.
Reports	Reports are predefined, printable representations of project information. You can customize reports so that they best fit your needs. For additional information about customizing reports, see "Customizing Reports and Creating Reports" in Chapter 20, pp. 646–647.
Modules	Modules represent macros that you create within Project. Project uses Visual Basic to create macros. Forms are dialog boxes designed to enable you to enter specific data for a selected task or resource. You can customize forms to best fit your needs.
Tables	Tables are collections of fields, organized by rows and columns, reminiscent of a spreadsheet. Tables are used in many views, either by themselves or in conjunction with charts or graphs. You can customize tables to best fit your needs. For additional information about customizing tables, see "Creating and Customizing Tables" in Chapter 22, p. 700.
Filters	Filters are used to highlight or isolate specific information in the view based on the specified criteria. Project supports two types of filters: task and resource. You can customize filters to best fit your needs. For additional information about customizing filters, see "Creating and Customizing Filters" in Chapter 22, p. 729.
Calendars	Calendars are used for specifying date exceptions and details to be used within the project schedule. Project contains three types of calendars: project, task, and resource. You can customize calendars to best fit your needs. For additional information about calendars, see "Defining Calendars" in Chapter 5, p. 101.
Maps	Maps are used to track data exported to other programs. They are also used in the Export Wizard when saving project data to Excel or other export formats. For additional information about maps, see "Exchanging Project Data with Other Applications" in Chapter 25, p. 837.
Fields	Fields are columns or boxes that contain a specific type of information about a task, resource, or assignment. You can create custom fields to best fit your needs. For additional information about customizing fields, see "Creating and Customizing Fields" in Chapter 22, p. 745.
Groups	Groups are tools to organize and summarize the display of project information. Project supports two types of groups: task and resource. You can customize groups to best fit your needs. For additional information about customizing groups, see "Creating Custom Groups" in Chapter 22, p. 741.

Global.mpt File

Global.mpt is a special type of file in Project that is a part of every new or existing project file. All projects inherit all the features of the Global.mpt. The first time you launch Project, a copy of the Global.mpt file is created and becomes the active Global.mpt file. A backup of the Global.mpt is also created, called Globalbackup.mpt. The Global contains all the default objects that Project comes with, such as the Gantt Chart view or the standard calendar (see the list of objects in Table 18.2). It also contains the default selections in the Tools, Options dialog box. For instance, if you change the Default task type from Fixed Units to Fixed Duration in the Schedule tab of Tools, Options, and click the Set as Default on the screen, you have changed the Global.mpt. Whenever you make changes to the Global.mpt file, you affect all new project files created from that point forward. Global.mpt is stored in the default location under C:\Users\<user name>\AppData\Roaming\Microsoft\MS Project\15\1033 directory.

When you open Global.mpt, you see the Organizer, but it will not act as a normal project file.

There are two ways you could share the objects of the Global.mpt from your desktop with others: Send your Global.mpt to them to copy and use, or send a project with the custom objects you have built. They can open the file on their desktop and move the custom objects into their own Global.mpt using the Organizer.

Manipulating Objects Using the Organizer

You can use the Organizer to copy, rename, and delete objects in Project. Rather than opening the Global.mpt file directly, you can move custom fields or changes to default objects within any project file to the Global.mpt using the Organizer. The following sections explore the details of each one of these actions.

Using the Organizer to Copy Objects

To open an object by using the Organizer, open the file that contains the custom object and follow these steps:

1. To display the Organizer, select the File tab, Organizer. Note that if you are copying an object to a file other than Global.mpt, make sure that both the source and the target files are open.

2. Select the tab that contains the object you want to copy. Figure 18.9 shows the Fields tab selected. The fields that have been used, modified, or newly created are listed on the right. The fields that would currently be included in the Global.mpt file are listed on the left.

3. Use the Custom Fields Available In drop-down box on the left to specify the target file to have the selected object copied into.

4. Use the Custom Fields Available In drop-down on the right to specify the source file to copy the selected object from.

5. Use the Task or Resource radio button to specify the type of field you want to copy.

6. Select the field you want to copy from your source file (on the right).

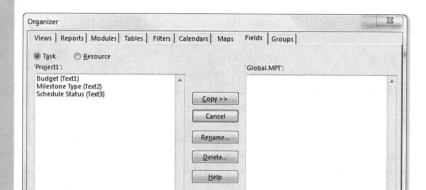

Figure 18.9
You can use the Organizer dialog box to copy an object from one project file to another.

 tip

You can copy multiple objects at once by selecting the first one and holding down the Shift key to select a range of objects. You can also select objects that are contained in the list out of order by holding down the Ctrl key and selecting each one.

7. Click the Copy button to copy the field. If a field with the same name already exists in the target file, Project displays a confirmation to replace the former field with a new one (see Figure 18.10).

Figure 18.10
Project displays a warning if you attempt to copy an object with a name that already exists within the target file.

8. Click the Yes button to replace the field in the target file with the one from the source file. You can also click Cancel from the warning dialog box and then click the Rename button in the Organizer to provide another name that is currently not being used for the field being copied to the target file.

9. Click the Close button to close the Organizer dialog box and save your changes.

tip

If you accidentally overwrite an object, you can restore it by copying it from the Global.mpt file, as long as the object in the Global.mpt file has not previously been customized. You might want to make a backup copy of the Global.mpt before making major changes so that you can copy the original object to replace the edited one.

 note

If the item you are copying is currently visible in Project and you are copying the item from a file into the currently active project, you get a message saying you cannot perform the copy.

Using the Organizer to Rename Objects

In addition to copying objects, you can also use the Organizer to rename existing ones.

To rename an object using the Organizer, follow these steps:

1. Open the Organizer by selecting the File tab, Organizer.

2. Select the tab for the object you want to rename.

3. In the Global.mpt file that you want to reflect the change, select the object to rename.

4. Click the Rename button.

5. Provide the new name and click OK to save your changes.

6. Click Close to exit the Organizer window.

 note

Objects in the Global.mpt file are not automatically updated. So, for your changes to be reflected in the new project files, the custom object must be copied in the Global.mpt. Any existing projects that contain the object must be manually updated as well.

Using the Organizer to Delete Objects

You can use the Organizer to permanently delete objects. Note that you cannot delete objects currently in use. To do so, follow these steps:

1. Open the Organizer by selecting the File tab, Organizer.

2. Select the tab that contains the object you want to delete.

3. In the Global.mpt file that contains the object, select the object to delete.

4. Click the Delete button. A confirmation box appears. Click Yes to confirm object deletion.

5. Click the Close button to exit the Organizer window.

Consultants' Tips

Global.mpt

When working with Project, remember that there are underlying influences to how your project file looks and behaves. The Global.mpt file is the default template (not to be confused with project templates you create for building new projects) on which all new project files are based. Global.mpt contains all default and custom project information, such as fields, views, filters, reports, and so on.

In addition, make sure that you make a copy of the Global.mpt prior to making any changes to it, such as deleting objects, and so on. This is a good practice to ensure that you never lose data and can revert to the original if you have to.

Using the Organizer

Learn how to use the Organizer to copy favorite custom views for use in other projects. You or your organization may create a view that lets you see common project tracking information, such as % Complete and Actual Work. You can use the view for all of your projects by copying it into Global.mpt, and then you can use your file so others can copy the view into their Global.mpt. Using the Organizer is a powerful tool for creating common and standard processes within an organization.

Protecting Your Project Files When Sharing

When sharing your project files among several people, it is important to protect your file from being edited without your knowledge. To protect your file, use either the Protection Password, Write Reservation Password, or Read-Only Recommended option.

Basic Steps for Starting a Project

Whenever you start a project, either from a template or blank project, always begin with the same steps:

1. Set the project start date. If you are using the template, your project will use the start date the template has when it was saved, so it is unlikely you want that date to be your start date.

2. Set the project properties. This includes setting the project calendar. In addition, set the calendar in the Gantt section, unless you are using the Standard calendar in both.

3. Display the project summary task (Task 0).

Use Templates and Keep Them Simple

When creating templates, it is best to keep the project schedule as simple as possible. The more details you specify and create, the harder they may be to manage and edit in the future. Consider putting only generic information into your template and then customizing it for each project accordingly.

FORMATTING VIEWS

Microsoft Project provides many "preformatted" views that you can use to look at project information. These views are organized into Gantt or graphical views, Usage or sheet views, and forms for task data entry. For instance, the Gantt views show schedule, tracking, and cost information in a combination view made up of a table of data items and the graphical schedule display with preset graphical formatting. Usage views are also combination views made up of a table of data items and a time-phased display of values, including work and costs. You can modify and customize all three category formats to meet individual requirements. This includes tables, Gantt styles, fonts, colors, and timescales. This chapter focuses on the various formatting features available for views.

You can use the Format commands to change the current view, and the new format remains for all future displays of that view. If, for instance, you change the timescale on the Gantt Chart to show days instead of weeks, that format change would be displayed until you modify it again. The Format Change is specific to the current view only. If you were to display another view that uses a timescale, however, that timescale would be based on changes you made the last time you displayed that view, not the changes you made to the previous view.

Sorting the Tasks or Resources in a View

Sorting can be a fast and easy way to find specific information, especially for views that show tasks or resources using the table or list layout. You can also sort the order in which tasks and resources appear in form views as you scroll using the Next and Previous buttons. The only view you cannot sort displayed items in is the Relationship Diagram view.

You can use sorting to set up lists by several different predefined fields, as well as up to three columns or fields of your choice. Your predefined fields change from view to view; for instance, when using a resource view, your predefined fields are By Cost, By Name, and By ID. In task views, you can find By Start Date, By Finish Date, By Priority, By Cost, and By ID. If you want to sort through the entries in a view, select the View tab, Data, Sort. A menu with the predefined sort fields opens, as shown in Figure 19.1. When you select one of these, your tasks or resources will be sorted by the field you selected into ascending order immediately. If you choose the Sort By option, the Sort dialog box opens to offer you more choices, as shown in Figure 19.2.

Figure 19.1
You can sort your tasks or resources using this cascading sort list.

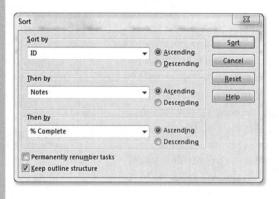

Figure 19.2
The Sort dialog box gives you many different options for sorting your tasks or resources.

Selecting the Sort Keys

With the Sort dialog box, you can use the drop-down list in the Sort By area to choose which sort field you want to use; then you can sort it in ascending or descending order by selecting the appropriate button. You can then sort further by using up to two additional Then By sort field areas.

Besides sorting by the predetermined fields, you can sort using custom fields, such as the Work Breakdown Structure codes you might have created. If you are using a custom field that has been renamed, both the generic field and the alias for it will show up in the sort key lists.

You can also use any of the columns in the table view as the sort by field. From any view that displays a table in it, click the down arrow next to the column name to sort by that field. This opens a sort, group, and filter control. The sort options change depending on whether the column is Alpha,

Numeric, or a date. Double-click the top of the ID number column to return to ID number ordering. You have fewer options for sorting this way than you do when using the Sort dialog box.

Selecting the Sort Operation

You should always save your project file before you sort. You should also choose to keep tasks under their summary tasks, and sort them within their summary tasks, by selecting the Keep Outline Structure check box. Clearing this check box results in all tasks being sorted throughout the project.

While in resource views, you can sort your resources by their assigned projects (by selecting the Sort Resources by Project check box). This option is useful when using a pool of resources that are spread across several projects.

 For additional information about resources, ***see*** *Chapter 8, "Defining Project Resources," **p. 235**.*

To sort a list after specifying its criteria, click the Sort button. If you want to return your sort to Project's standard sort (by ID numbers), use the Reset button.

---

 caution

Although you can undo a sort, keep in mind that if the sorted tasks or resources are permanently renumbered (by selecting the Permanently Renumber Tasks or Permanently Renumber Resources check box in the Sort dialog box, depending on your active view), they will be given new ID numbers.

If you have filters and macros set on tasks by their ID numbers, the Permanently Renumber Tasks/Resources check box will change everything. The only way to recover from this is to reopen a previously saved project file.

Formatting Text Styles for Categories of Tasks and Resources

Many of the views in Project enable you to set special formatting options to display text, such as changing font, type size, style, and color to help you display your data. You could, for instance, set all your critical tasks to display in red, or set apart your milestones by displaying them in italic. The Format tab is context-dependent. It changes depending on which view is currently active. You can open the Text Styles dialog box by going to the Format tab, Format, Text Styles, as shown in Figure 19.3.

---

caution

After you have made changes to the formatting of text, you cannot undo or reset those changes without going in and manually restoring the text to its original formatting.

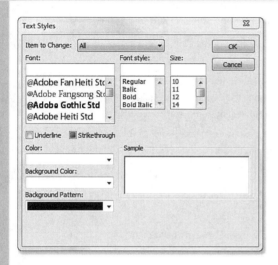

Selecting an Item to Change

When you click on the Item to Change drop-down list, you find several different categories to choose from. If a task or resource belongs to two or more categories, some of the items take priority over others. The hierarchy of the Item to Change list, in descending order of priority, is as follows:

- Highlighted tasks

- Marked tasks

- Summary tasks

- Milestone tasks

- Critical tasks

For instance, if a milestone is also a critical task, that task's display is controlled by the text format for milestones. If the same task is also selected by a highlight filter, it displays the task using the Highlight task format, instead of the Milestone or Critical task formatting.

You can highlight a series of tasks when you need to make them stand out for any reason. The first step is to open the list of filters, under the View tab, Data, Highlight. This gives you a short list of built-in Highlight filters; select one, and the highlight will be applied. To see the entire list, select More Highlight Filters under the drop-down list. This brings up a list of all the filters you can choose from, as shown in Figure 19.4. Choose which filter you want to use, and then select the Highlight button instead of the Apply button. For instance, you could select Incomplete Tasks and click Highlight, and those tasks now stand out in bold, blue font. To turn off highlighting, go back to the View tab, Data, Highlight and select Clear Highlight.

The benefit to using highlighting instead of applying a filter is that highlighting just changes the text format of your tasks, instead of rearranging or hiding them. Project has a default format already set in the Text Styles dialog. This format can be changed and saved as the default.

Milestone tasks have a logical value of Yes in the Milestone field. When you set a task to zero duration, it automatically becomes a milestone (with a value of Yes in the Milestone field). You can also designate a task as a milestone by opening the Task Information dialog box, selecting the Advanced tab, and clicking the Mark Task as Milestone check box.

You can change all of your tasks quickly and easily by selecting the All item in the Item to Change drop-down list in the Text Styles dialog box. Simply select All and make the formatting text changes you want. This will, however, override all other changes you have already made to specific tasks.

 tip

You can manually select tasks using the Marked field. You can use this to select tasks of interest without having to define a filter or custom field by marking them as Yes.

Figure 19.4 Using the Highlight option can make it easy for you to find tasks that meet specific qualifications quickly and easily.

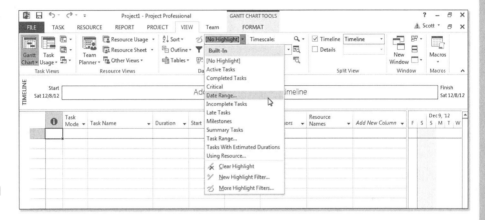

The items after All in the Item to Change list are specific to either tasks or resources, depending on the view you have open at the time. If the Gantt Chart view is your active view, the first items are for tasks. Here are the text style items available for the Gantt Chart view:

- All
- Row & Column Titles
- Critical Tasks
- External Tasks
- Highlighted Tasks
- Marked Tasks
- Noncritical Tasks
- Milestone Tasks
- Summary Tasks

- Top, Middle, and Bottom Timescale Tier

- Bar Text – Left

- Bar Text – Right

- Bar Text – Top

- Bar Text – Bottom

- Bar Text – Inside

- Changed Cells

- Inactive Tasks

If you were using the Resource Usage view, on the other hand, your list would look like this:

- All

- Allocated Resources

- Overallocated Resources

- Highlighted Resources

- Row & Column Titles

- Assignment Row

- Middle, Bottom, and Top Timescale Tiers

- Changed Cells

- Inactive Tasks

Changing the Style of Text Displays

When you open the Text Styles dialog box (by selecting the Format tab, Format, Text Styles), notice that it is similar to text formatting dialog boxes in other Microsoft applications, such as Word. The Text Styles dialog box enables you to change the assigned font, font formatting (that is, regular, bold, italic, and bold italic), font size, color, and background color. You can also select the Underline check box for underlining text. To revert back to the default text style, click the Reset button.

 note

You can use the Color drop-down list to change the color of your text. If you do not have a color printer, all text prints as black with grayscale shading. You can select the Clear Color option to make text transparent, although the item's row still appears on the screen and paper. Even if you do not use a color printer, colored text can really make certain tasks or resources stand out when displayed onscreen.

Formatting Font for Selected Text

Besides changing categories of styles, you can also change selected text items. Open the Font dialog box using the Format controls in the Font Group on the Task tab to change any text you have selected. The changes to text you make using the Font controls are the same as changes you make using the Text Styles dialog box, except that they affect only preselected text. If you want to make just one specific task stand out, select that task, select the Task tab, and make the changes you need, such as making the text bold or changing the text color to red, to make it really stand out.

A fast way to copy formatting from one set of text to another is to use the Format Painter button in the Clipboard section on the Task tab. Select the text, either a task or resource, that has the format you want to copy, and then click the Format Painter button. Your mouse changes to a cross with a paintbrush attached. Choose the text to which you want to apply the formatting, and then release the mouse button. If you want to change more than one set of text, you can click and drag your mouse to select multiple sets.

 note

The main difference between using the Text Styles dialog box and the Font controls is that with the Font dialog box, you are making changes only to specific selected text, whereas with the Text Styles dialog box, you are changing categories of tasks or resources. If you made a change to a task with the Font dialog box, for instance, it affects only that task. However, if you change all of your incomplete tasks using the Text Styles dialog box, any future tasks you enter that are incomplete will have the same formatting.

Formatting Gridlines

Gridlines are the guides on tables and timescales, and are usually added by default. They are the lines drawn between the rows and columns of a table, between column titles and between the units of a timescale. Gridlines can be added to views, such as adding a Project Status date line in the Gantt Chart view.

You can make changes to gridlines for your current view by selecting the Format tab, Format, Gridlines, which opens the Gridlines dialog box, as shown in Figure 19.5. You can also open the Gridlines dialog box by moving your mouse to any blank area of the Gantt Chart view and right-clicking, and then selecting the Gridlines option that appears on the shortcut menu.

Different options appear in this dialog box depending on which view you are using. Figure 19.5 shows the Gridlines dialog box for the Gantt Chart view. Figure 19.6 shows some of the common gridlines you could use; those not shown by default on the Gantt Chart view are marked with an asterisk.

To change a gridline, select your choice from the Line to Change list. You can see which gridlines are in use if they have anything entered in the Normal, Type box. If there is nothing there, these are not default gridlines.

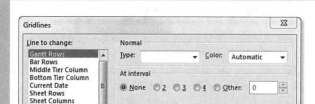

Figure 19.5
Changing the look of the gridlines is easy using the Gridlines dialog box.

The At Interval section creates gridlines to appear at regular intervals. Only a few of the line categories can use interval lines. In the Gantt Chart and Resource Usage views, for instance, the rows and columns can have interval colors and line types. In table views, the Sheet Row and Sheet Column gridlines can also have intervals.

 tip

Any changes you make affect every line of the type chosen, unless the At Interval section has also been activated.

Five options appear in the Type drop-down list in the Normal section: no line, solid, dotted, small dashes, and large dashes. The Color drop-down list enables you to choose a color, with solid black as the default. The At Interval line type, if available, enables you to choose the type and color you want. To activate the At Interval Type fields, simply choose an interval: 2 (for every other row or column), 3 (for every third row or column), 4 (for every fourth row or column), or Other (to set your interval number).

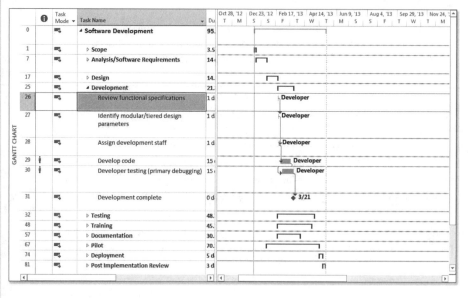

Figure 19.6
You can add clarity to a view by adding gridlines to it. Here, dashed Gantt row Gridlines were added.

Using the Outline Options

Any view that shows tasks—such as the Task Sheet and Gantt Chart views, for instance—can show information about the tasks' places in the outline structure. You can show or conceal those summary tasks, show subordinate tasks and their place in the outline through indenting, show outline numbers beside each task, and either exhibit, or not, the special symbol to show that tasks have subordinate tasks (see Figure 19.7).

...tional information about outlines, **see** *the "Defining Summary Tasks and* *...on on* **p. 154** *in Chapter 6.*

...e control in the Data group. Use this control to show subtasks, ...ific level.

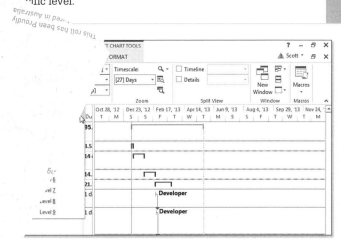

In earlier versions of Project, screen real estate was at a premium. The options Show Outline Symbol and Indent Name were key features used to compress how Project displayed views. Neither of these controls is available by default in the Ribbon; you must add them either by customizing the Ribbon or the Quick Access toolbar. They are both turned on by default.

The Show Outline check box displays either a plus (+) or a minus (−) sign preceding each summary task. A plus sign shows that this summary task has subtasks under it that are not currently shown, whereas the minus sign indicates that all tasks are being shown. The Indent Name check box indents subtasks.

The project summary task is a specific type of task; it summarizes and rolls up the entire project. Selecting the Show Project Summary Task check box (Format tab, Show/Hide) shows a project summary task at the beginning of your project's task list, with a task ID number of 0. This feature is useful to sum up projects and consolidate projects.

> ### 🌀 tip
>
> You can save space on printed reports by turning off the Indent Name option and turning on the Show Outline Number option. This way, all the tasks are aligned to the left margin, but you can still easily tell their position in the outline by using the outline number option.

The Outline Number check box (Format tab, Show/Hide) turns on and off the outline number that precedes an outline name, showing its location within the outline (see Figure 19.8). The outline number for a task includes the related summary task number. This outline number is the same for the WBS codes in the Task Information dialog box, under the Advanced tab, unless you have created a custom WBS.

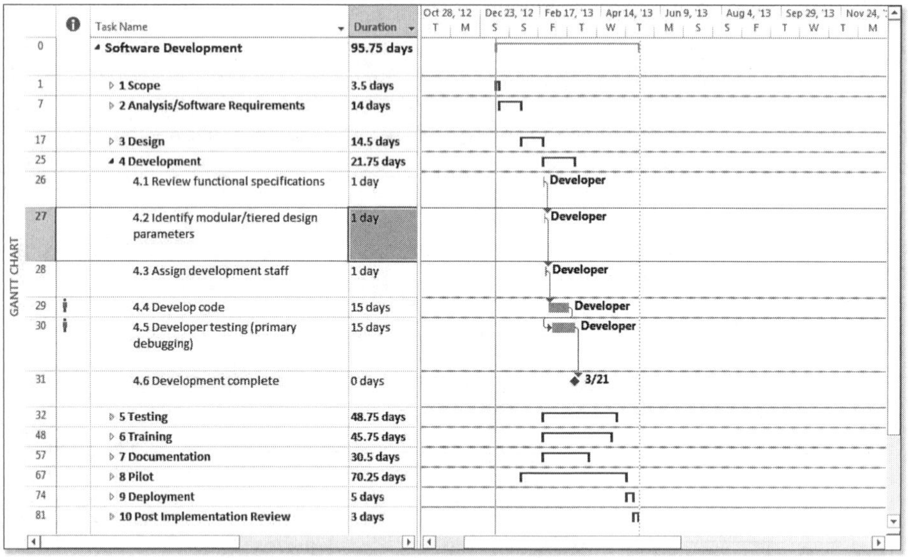

Figure 19.8 Using Outline options and summary tasks can help you organize your project. Here, the Outline number has been added in front of the task name.

The Show Summary Tasks check box (Format tab, Show/Hide) is always selected by default. If you clear the box using the Options dialog box's View tab, your summary tasks will not appear on the list. Also, if your subtasks are hidden when you turn off the summary task display, they will stay hidden. The Outline Control on the View tab is not accessible when the summary tasks are not shown. Hiding summary tasks can be useful when you are applying a filter or sorting tasks.

Formatting Timescales

A view that shows timescales, such as the Gantt Chart view, gives you the option of switching time units and date formats for each of the different levels of timescale display. Project provides you with three tiers of the timescale: Top, Middle, and Bottom.

To make changes to the timescale, open the Timescale dialog box on the View tab in the Zoom group, as shown in Figure 19.9. In the sample display area, you can preview what the timescale will look like as you switch between different options.

tip

Another way to access the Timescale dialog box is by double-clicking anywhere on the timescale itself or by right-clicking the timescale headings and choosing Timescale from the shortcut menu.

Under the shortcut menu, you will also find the Zoom option. This lets you zoom in and out of your project at several different levels, such as 1 week, 1 month, or the entire project.

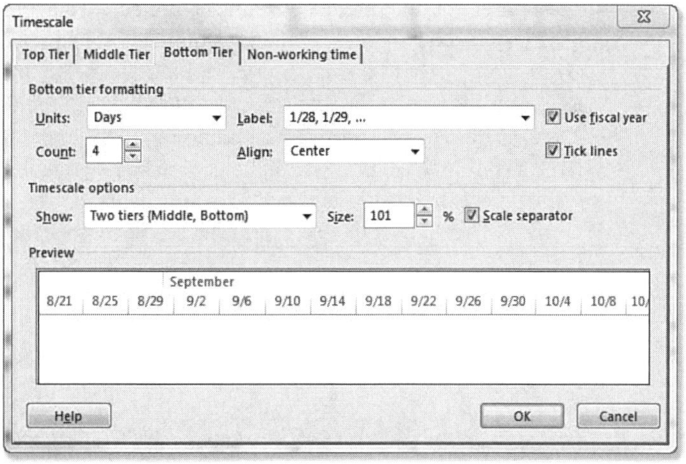

Figure 19.9
The Timescale dialog box gives you several options for displaying your timescale and lets you preview the look before deciding.

Timescale	⊠

Top Tier | Middle Tier | **Bottom Tier** | Non-working time

Bottom tier formatting

Units: Days ▼   Label: 1/28, 1/29, ... ▼   ☑ Use fiscal year

Count: 4 ⬍   Align: Center ▼   ☑ Tick lines

Timescale options

Show: Two tiers (Middle, Bottom) ▼   Size: 101 ⬍ % ☑ Scale separator

Preview

| | | | September | | | | | | | | | |
| 8/21 | 8/25 | 8/29 | 9/2 | 9/6 | 9/10 | 9/14 | 9/18 | 9/22 | 9/26 | 9/30 | 10/4 | 10/8 | 10/ |

Help   OK   Cancel

Changing Timescale Tiers

The timescale has three tiers: top, middle, and bottom. You can choose how many of them you want to use, but you must select at least one tier. You get a Timescale Error message if you try to close the Timescale dialog box with all three tiers hidden. If you select a single line on the timescale, it will be defined by the middle tier settings. Two tiers will be the middle tier and the bottom tier.

All the tiers are defined on the same dialog box, but they are defined separately. The only real rule to remember is that any units assigned to a tier must be at least as large as the units for the tier beneath it. The time span of the lower tier (including the periods specified in the Count field) cannot be longer than the timescale of the higher tier. This means that you cannot set the middle tier at days if the bottom tier is set at weeks.

Use the Units drop-down list to select which time period you want your tier to display: Years, Half Years, Quarters, Months, Thirds of Months, Weeks, Days, Hours, or Minutes. Selecting a week shows one week; if you want more than one week, you can change the Count text box appropriately. A setting of 2 in the Count text box will show two weeks. You could get the same result by selecting days and setting the Count text box at 14.

The Label option enables you to decide how you want the timescale unit displayed, as shown in Figure 19.10. Your selection depends somewhat on which units you decide to display. There are three types of labels for the time units:

tip

If the tick lines that separate the units of the scales don't change in the sample area immediately after you change the Count setting, you might need to select the Tick Lines check box twice to refresh the tick line display.

- **The specific time period named**—This would show the year, quarter number, month name or number, or day number. Many choices like this are available, some with abbreviations, full or partial specifications, numbers, or words.

- **The number of time periods within the project**—This option enables you to either start from the beginning of the project (From Start) or count down from the end of the project (From End). For instance, if the unit is Week 1 (From Start), the time periods are labeled Week 1, Week 2, and so on. You can set the same thing up using From End, only it will count backward: Week 50, Week 49, and so on. This can be especially helpful when you are first setting up a long project, before your specific start and finish dates are set. This can also be helpful if you are setting up the project to be a template, and the start and finish dates will vary depending on who is using the project.

- **None**—You can also choose to have no label, which means Project displays a timescale with tick marks only.

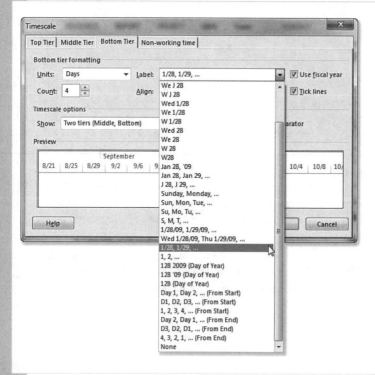

Figure 19.10
You can set the label options based on your chosen timescale units.

Using the Align drop-down list, you can align your time units labels—either left-align, right-align, or center. You can also choose whether you want separator tick lines between your larger time unit labels by selecting (or not) the Tick Lines check box.

Each tier can reflect calendar years (the default) or fiscal years. If you want to set displays and labels for periods according to fiscal years, you need to change the Fiscal Year Starts In option, as shown in Figure 19.11. You can find it on the File tab, Options, Schedule, Calendar Options for this project. Use the Fiscal Year Starts In option to set which month begins the fiscal year for your organization. The default is January, but you can use the drop-down list to change it to the month you need. If you use a month other than January, select the Use Fiscal Year check box on the Timescale dialog box to let Project know you want to use the starting month for fiscal year numbering. You can similarly change the timescale to start on a day other than Sunday (the default) by using the Week Starts On option, which is also found on the Calendar tab of the Options dialog box.

Figure 19.11 You can set the Fiscal Year definition to display on the Schedule tab of the Options dialog box.

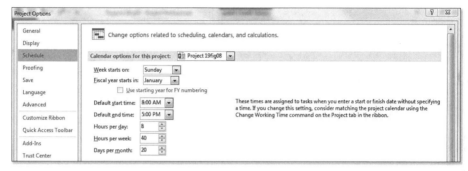

Completing the Timescale Definition

Two more options on the Timescale dialog box to discuss are the Size and the Scale Separator. These modify the overall look of the timescale. You can modify the width of the timescale units displayed with the Size box by adjusting the percentage. For instance, if you cannot fit the values for the Resource Usage view into the cells of the lowest displayed timescale units, you can enlarge the unit space by using a value greater than 100, such as 120 or 150. On the other hand, if you want a smaller view so that you can fit more of your project on paper, lower the number in the percentage box to less than 100.

Just like you can remove the ticks between the dates on your timescale, you can also remove the horizontal line between the labels. This is the Scale Separator, and you can turn it on and off using its check box.

After you are finished with your changes to the timescale, click OK to make your changes active. Your timescale changes affect only the display of the active view, just like with other formatting options. Every timescale view has its own options to format.

 caution

If you have customized your timescale settings, specifically the labels, when you use the Zoom In or Zoom Out buttons in the Standard toolbar or apply a Zoom setting from the View menu, you lose your customized settings.

Changing the Display of Non-Working Time

Project creates base calendars with working days, default and nondefault work times, and nonworking days. The Non-Working Time tab on the Timescale dialog box lets you make changes to the way your nonworking calendar time is displayed on the Gantt Chart, as shown in Figure 19.12.

> ⓦ **tip**
>
> The shortcut menu options displayed for nonworking time when you right-click the timescale bars are different from the options when you right-click the Gantt Chart. The shortcut menu from the timescale bars has the Change Working Time option. This option enables you to have access to the calendar and lets you redefine what should be considered nonworking time. The shortcut menu for the Gantt Chart view simply changes the way nonworking time is displayed. This is the same dialog box that opens when you double-click the timescale bars.

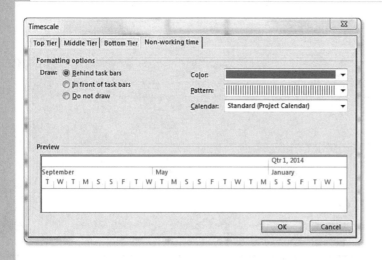

Figure 19.12
You can modify the look of the nonworking time display on the Gantt Chart view on the Non-Working Time tab in the Timescale dialog box. Here the color was changed to red and the pattern to a series of vertical lines.

You can also select which calendar you want to use when displaying nonworking time. Project defaults to the Standard calendar because it is the driving calendar unless another has been selected using the Project, Project Information command. If you have other calendars defined, select one from the Calendar drop-down list.

➤ *For additional information about calendars, **see** the "Defining Calendars" section on **p. 101** in Chapter 5.*

The three buttons in the Draw section of the Non-Working Time tab modify the way the bars that span across the nonworking time are drawn. You can change the color and pattern in which nonworking time is displayed, but remember that you cannot see the nonworking days unless at least one of your tiers in the timescale shows days or a smaller unit.

You also have options for the shading of nonworking time, which include Behind Taskbars (the default), In Front of Taskbars (which leaves a gap in the bars), and Do Not Draw. The Do Not Draw option eliminates the shading on the nonworking time. In other words, the Do Not Draw option will not change the Gantt Chart view into a five-day work week—the weekends are still shown; they just have nothing to differentiate them from the rest of the week.

> 🔍 **note**
> The choice of displaying non-working time in front of the task bars can indicate that tasks are not being worked on. This setting has no effect on the total duration of the task, just the display.

Using Page Breaks

A page break forces the beginning of a new page when you print the view, but will have no effect on the screen display, except for the optional dashed line to show where that page break is located on the list. You can change the page break line format on the Format tab, Format, Gridlines.

If you want to force a page break in the permitted views, choose any cell in the row that falls below where you want your page break. This row now becomes the first row on the new page. Now go to Insert, Page Break to add the page break. If you want to remove it later on, choose the row below the page break and go to Insert, Remove Page Break. If you want to remove all the page breaks, select all the tasks by clicking either the Task or Resource Name column heading. Alternatively, you can click the Select All square above the ID column and then go to Insert, Remove All Page Breaks.

> 〰️ **tip**
> Any of the page breaks you enter manually will only be honored by the Print command if you select the Manual Page Breaks check box in the Print dialog box. Clear it, and Project ignores your page breaks.

 For additional information about printing, **see** *the "Printing Views" section on* **p. 715** *in Chapter 22.*

Formatting the Gantt Chart Views

The Gantt Chart views are the most commonly used views for building projects and for presentations and reporting, so it makes sense that there are so many different choices available for formatting the Gantt Chart.

Formatting the Gantt Chart View Manually

There are a total of eight different groups in the Format tab for Gantt charts. We have already looked at some of the ways you can manually change the Gantt Chart view, specifically the font, timescale, gridlines, and text styles. Now we are going to look at the remaining options.

Using Gantt Chart Styles

Gantt Chart styles offer 24 different color schemes for your Gantt Chart. Whichever scheme is selected serves as a base for the more detailed options described in the following sections.

Using the Bar Styles Options

One possible way to modify the bar chart section of the Gantt Chart view is to use bar styles. Go to the Format tab, Bar Styles, Format. This brings up the Bar Styles dialog box, as shown in Figure 19.13. You can also open the Bar Styles dialog box by double-clicking on the Gantt Chart view background or by right-clicking on a blank spot on the timescale portion of the Gantt Chart to open the shortcut menu and selecting Bar Styles.

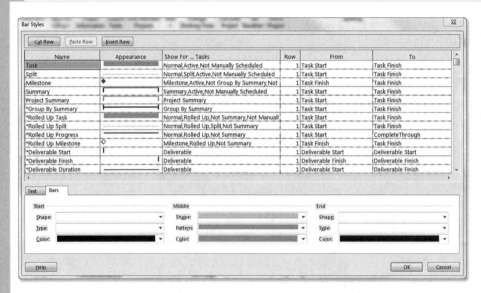

Figure 19.13
The Bar Styles dialog box enables you to make changes to the different kinds of task bars used in the Gantt Chart view.

The upper half of the Bar Styles dialog box shows the definition table, with rows for each of the bars and symbols that show up in the Gantt Chart view. The lower half has two tabs, as follows:

- The Text tab contains options for adding text to different locations around the Gantt Chart view bars.

- The Bars tab contains three different drop-down lists that set up the formatted look of the bars and symbols. You can make changes to the bar at the start, middle, and end. You can see examples of the defaults for each bar in the Gantt Chart view in the second column of the table located at the top of the dialog box.

To add a new type of bar into the table on the upper section of the Bar Styles dialog box, just choose the row you want to insert a new row above and click the Insert Row button. You can delete a bar by choosing the row it is in and using the Cut Row button. You can move your cut row to a new location by selecting the new location and clicking the Paste Row button.

Supplying the Bar Name   Enter the name of your new bar type in the first column of the definition table, located on the upper part of the Bar Styles dialog box. You can name your new bar anything you choose. This name will only be used in the legend, beside the bar symbol, when the Gantt Chart view is printed.

Defining the Bar Appearance   You can see a preview of what the bar or symbol will look like when your Bars palette definition is applied in the Appearance column in the Bar Styles dialog box. To modify the look of the sample, you will be using the Start, Middle, and End sections of the Bars tab, on the lower half of the Bar Styles dialog box.

To change the color, shape, and type of shape at the beginning of the bar or at the end of the bar, use the Start or End column, respectively. You can choose which shape you want to use from the Shape drop-down list; the Type drop-down list lets you choose whether you want a dashed, framed, or solid shape. The Color drop-down list enables you to select which color you want for your shape.

The Middle section deals with the bars themselves. You can select which shape you want the bars on your Gantt Chart view to be by using the Shape drop-down list, what pattern you want them to use with the Pattern drop-down list, and what color with the Color drop-down list. Later in the chapter, we look in more detail at the bars, in the section, "Selecting the Row for the Bar."

Selecting the Tasks That Display the Bar   The third column of the upper section of the Bar Styles dialog box, Show For Tasks, is used to define the type of tasks that use the bar. You can click this column to display a drop-down list of bar categories. To use two or more categories, use a comma to separate the names.

Here are the task types you can select in the Show For Tasks drop-down list:

- **Normal**—These tasks are neither milestone nor summary tasks. Most tasks fall into this category.

- **Milestone**—Milestone tasks are identified with Yes in the Milestone field; tasks set to zero duration are automatically defined as milestones. You can set a task as a milestone in several different ways; you can click Yes in the Milestone field, you can select the Mark Task as Milestone check box in the Advanced tab of the Task Information dialog box, or you can manually set your task to zero duration.

 note

You'll notice there are only three buttons: Insert Row, Cut Row, and Paste Row. There is no Copy Row. If you want to copy a row, you have to cut and paste it. First, select which row you want to copy, and click the Cut Row button; then immediately (without moving your selection) click the Paste Row button. That returns the original row right back to its starting place, and now you can move to where you want to insert the copy of the row and use Paste Row again. After you cut the row, you can paste it as many times as you need.

 tip

If you add an asterisk (*) to the front of the name, it will not be printed.

 tip

Because projects are often just printed in black and white, you should consider using patterns for your bars, so that they show up more easily, as opposed to just solid color bars.

- **Summary**—Summary tasks have at least one or more subtasks indented under them and are identified with a Yes entry in the Summary task field.

- **Critical**—A Critical task is any task on the critical path. They are identified by a Yes in the Critical task field, and that entry is determined by the task's slack. If slack is zero or less, normally, that task is set as critical. You can, however, change the cutoff point using the Calculation tab on the Options dialog box.

- **Noncritical**—A Noncritical task is any task not on the critical path.

- **Marked**—A Marked task is identified with a Yes entry in the Marked task field. You can set any task to Marked.

- **Finished**—A Finished task has an actual finish date (that is, Actual Finish does not contain NA).

- **In Progress**—An In Progress task has an actual start date, but no actual finish date.

- **Not Finished**—A Not Finished task has NA in its Actual Finish date field. Not Finished tasks include both In Progress and Not Started tasks.

- **Not Started**—A Not Started task has NA in its Actual Start date field.

- **Started Late**—A Started Late task has a scheduled start date later than its baseline start. These tasks might not have actually started.

- **Finished Late**—A Finished Late task has a scheduled finish date later than its baseline finish.

- **Started Early**—A Started Early task has a scheduled start date that is earlier than its baseline start.

- **Finished Early**—A Finished Early task has a scheduled finish date earlier than its baseline finish.

- **Started On Time**—A Started On Time task has a scheduled start date that is the same as its baseline start date.

- **Finished On Time**—A Finished On Time task has a scheduled finish date that is the same as its baseline finish date.

- **Rolled Up**—A Rolled Up task has its Rollup field set to Yes. Using the General tab of the Task Information dialog box, you can set the Rollup field by choosing the Roll Up Gantt Bar to Summary check box. Notice that Summary tasks do not display subtask dates unless the Show Rolled Up Gantt Bars check box is filled for the Summary task.

- **Project Summary**—A Project Summary task has a task ID number of 0, and is only displayed if you turn on the Show Project Summary Task option on the View tab of the Options dialog box.

- **Group by Summary**—A Group by Summary task is a temporary task, created by the Group By command, which has the rolled-up values for a specific set of tasks.

- **Split**—A Split task is any task that has been split into two or more sections.

- **External Tasks**—An External task is a phantom task. These represent tasks in other projects that have been linked as predecessors or successors to tasks in the current project.

- **Deliverable**—A deliverable is a tangible, measurable result, outcome, or item that must be produced to complete a project or part of a project. Bar styles for this task type, and the Dependency task type described next, can be defined as part of Project Professional and Project Server.

- **Dependency**—A dependency can be set to a deliverable that does not affect the project's schedule. Bar styles for this task type, and the Deliverable task type described previously, can be defined as part of Project Professional and Project Server.

- **Active**—New since Project 2010, tasks can be either active or inactive. Inactive tasks enable project managers to keep a record of scope cuts without impacting the current or active schedule.

- **Manually Scheduled**—Tasks can either be manually or automatically scheduled.

- **Warning**—Warnings alert project managers to potential scheduling conflicts caused by manual scheduling decisions.

- **Placeholder fields**—Placeholders are tasks that cannot be scheduled because key information is lacking. Valid Start, Finish, and Durations are required for task scheduling; otherwise, placeholders are used.

- **Late**—Late tasks are tasks that should be done as of the current status date.

- **Path Driving Predecessor**—Tasks that are driving the currently selected task if the Driving Predecessors option is chosen under Task Path (Gantt Chart Tools, Format, Bar Styles).

- **Path Predecessor**—Tasks that are predecessors to the selected task if the Predecessors option is chosen under Task Path.

- **Path Driven Successor**—Tasks that are driven by the selected task if the Driven Successors option is chosen under Task Path.

- **Path Successor**—Tasks that are successors to the selected task if the Successors option is chosen under Task Path.

- **Flag1...Flag20**—A Flag task has a custom Flag field set to Yes. You might add a Flag field to a task for data entry.

All tasks fall into one of three categories: Normal, Milestone, or Summary. You should combine the other types of tasks on the list with one of these three, to give your tasks more definition. For instance, you could create Normal, Critical and Normal, Noncritical tasks instead of just the Normal tasks, which include both Critical and Noncritical.

When a task fits into more than one category, it displays the formatting of both. If one style of formatting, however, would overwrite another, the feature lowest on the definition table is applied last and remains visible.

 tip

You can set tasks that display the bar to select all tasks *except* the one that is named by placing the word *Not* before the type name, as in Not Milestone or Not Summary.

Selecting the Row for the Bar   Every task can have up to four distinct, nonoverlapping bars drawn for it. Usually only row 1 is used, meaning there is only one row of bars for each task. If you decide to use multiple bar styles that apply to a task, then those styles will all show on the same row.

Styles at the top of the table are drawn first, followed by the styles lower on the table, which can overwrite the styles higher up on the list. If the overwriting bar is as large or larger than the one it is overwriting, it covers and hides that bar. If it is smaller, you see them both, which is why the standard progress bar appears in the middle of the standard task bar.

You can show multiple styles side-by-side, if you set them up to occupy different rows. If you wanted to see a bar set for early start and finish dates for your task, another with late start and finish dates, and a third with scheduled dates, you would define three different rows, each one corresponding to early, late, and scheduled dates.

Defining the Length of the Bar Project uses the From and To columns in the definition table, in the upper part of the Bar Styles dialog box, to determine the length and placement of all bars and symbols. You can use several different options, either the date fields or one of several measures of time (such as Percent Complete, Total Slack, or Complete Through). You can choose these from the drop-down lists. The following is a list of your options and information on how they are calculated:

- **Start and Finish**—Times and dates when your task is scheduled to start or finish.

- **Baseline Start and Baseline Finish**—Planned start and finish dates based on your task's baseline. If you have not yet saved a baseline, these fields show NA.

- **Actual Start and Actual Finish**—The recorded dates and times for the actual work start and finish on your task.

- **Start1–Start10 and Finish1–Finish10**—These are 10 custom fields you can use to store extra task start and finish date information. As you save interim schedules, they will be placed in these fields.

- **Baseline1–10 Start and Baseline1–10 Finish**—As you save your baselines, Project fills these fields with the start and finish dates, similar to the Start1–Start10 and Finish1–Finish10 mentioned earlier.

- **Deadline**—This is the date you set as a deadline for your task, instead of defining a date constraint for the task, to show when you want the task finished. Because it uses the deadline date as a single point in time, Project uses the same field as the From and To entries.

- **Preleveled Start and Preleveled Finish**—These are the scheduled start and finish dates, before the last resource leveling was completed.

- **Early Start and Early Finish**—Early Start is defined as the earliest possible start date for a task, depending on the start of the project, the schedule of the task's predecessors, the calendar, and any other constraints that might have been imposed on the task. Early Finish is the earliest possible finish date, depending on the Early Start date, the task's duration, and any linking relationships it has.

- **Late Start and Late Finish**—Late Start is the latest start date possible for a task, without delaying the finish of a project. Late Finish is the latest finish date without delaying the finish of the project. If you set a Deadline date, it will be the Late Finish date.

- **Free Slack**—Free Slack is a duration value and is defined as the amount of time a task can be delayed without it affecting the schedule of another task. If you use the Leveling Gantt view, the

Slack style is drawn from the Finish to Free Slack. This means that the bar begins at the task's finish date and is long enough to show the duration of Free Slack.

■ **Negative Slack**—Negative Slack is the amount of time needed to be saved to avoid delaying any successor task. If there is not enough time scheduled for the task, it is indicated with Negative Slack. It is usually the From column value and is paired with the Start date in the To column.

■ **Physical % Complete**—The Physical % Complete field measures the work progress against a stated goal. It does not, however, affect duration or percentage-complete calculations. You usually select this in the To value and pair it with the Actual Start in the From value.

■ **Total Slack**—When you are using fixed start date projects, Total Slack is the time a task's finish can be delayed, without delaying the finish of the project or violating a successor task's constraint. You will usually use the To value and pair it with the scheduled Finish date in the From value.

Selecting a Progress Bar Style   A progress bar shows how much of a task has been finished, and should always be drawn from the Actual Start date.

Several of the To field options for progress bars are similar to other types of bars. Some of these fields should be looked at a bit closer:

■ **% Complete**—Selecting this field draws a progress bar that corresponds to the percentage your task duration is complete. So, if your task % Complete is 65%, this progress bar will be 65% the length between the task actual start and task finish. % Complete represents the time that has passed, not the actual work completed.

■ **% Work Complete**—% Work Complete is normally calculated as Task Actual Work divided by Task Total Work, and represents the work finished, not just the time passed. This field creates a progress bar that is proportional in terms of % Work Complete to the task bar drawn from the task start to finish.

■ **Complete Through**—This is a standard field for normal tasks. Project adds the actual duration for a task to the actual start date, to determine the end of the bar. Project normally only uses this Complete Through field internally, but you can select it in the From and To columns of the Bar Styles dialog box. You cannot display this field as text in any view.

■ **Stop and Resume**—As you record actual work for a resource assignment, Project places the time and date when the actual work is finished into the Stop field, and it places that same time and date in the task Resume field. Select Resume in the To column so that a progress bar will be created to show the earliest date when work needs to resume on an assignment. This Resume bar, however, gives little information about the overall progress of the task. You can also create a progress bar from the Resume date to the scheduled finish of the task, to show the span of time during which some of the work still needs to be finished.

■ **Summary Progress**—This field applies to summary tasks. The Complete Through progress bar adds the actual duration to the actual start date, just like with normal tasks. The % Complete bar is drawn with exact proportion to the summary task duration that the % Complete field indicates. The % Work Complete bar compares the amount of completed and uncompleted work, whereas the Resume bar uses the earliest Resume date of any subtask.

Placing Text in a Bar Chart Switch to the Text tab in the middle of the Bar Styles dialog box when you are ready to enter field data to be displayed on your bar, as shown in Figure 19.14. Text can be shown to the left, right, top, and bottom of the bar, plus inside. You cannot, however, enter text into these areas yourself; you need to choose fields that contain data, such as dates, durations, percentages, and other numeric values. Any custom field you have defined and entered data into can also be displayed around the bars as well.

 tip

If you want to add text, but there isn't enough room on the row, simply add the text to a different row. A row does not require a bar; it can be used for text only. To add text to a different row, open the Bar Styles dialog box. Insert a row under the task type where you'd like to display text, such as under Normal, Noncritical. For Appearance, make the Start, Middle, and End shapes blank. In the Row column, select 2. Then, on the Text tab, set the text position as Inside and select the field to be displayed.

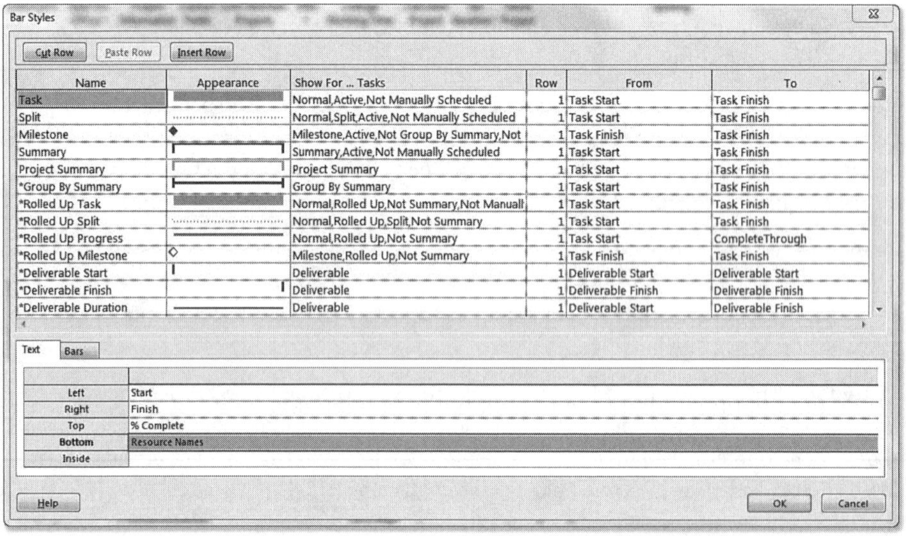

Figure 19.14 Text can be displayed by choosing one or more of the five different locations around the Gantt Chart bar in the Bar Styles Text tab.

To enter text, choose the bar you want to use from the Bar Styles dialog box; then click the Text tab, choose where you want the text to be placed from one of the five rows, and then select the field name from the drop-down list. Click OK when you are finished, or click Cancel to close the window without saving changes.

Bar Styles Definition Example

It might be helpful, when using summary tasks, to define styles that clearly indicate the overall progress for the group of summarized subtasks. You could hide all the subtasks, for instance, to help you see the bigger picture and focus on the major phases of your project. Because summary tasks look so similar, despite how many subtasks might be completed, this customization could provide more information than the standard display. With simply a glance, you can see which phases are complete, which are started but unfinished, and which have not begun yet.

Each row in the bar style box overwrites the previous row for the same type of task. Therefore, for a summary task, you would need to create rows that first check for "Not Started," then "In Progress," and then "Finished." This is a little tricky; another way to think of it is that you want the smallest subset to come last. All the tasks are summary tasks. Some of the tasks have started. Of the tasks that have started, only some have finished.

Even creating these row conditions is awkward; you need to select a task type, then enter a comma after it, and remember how to type the subsequent condition from the list or based on the default examples. There is no good way to select conditions. Project will tell you if you make a mistake, but it won't tell you how to fix it.

The good news is, it is often worth the effort. Your result is a much more readable and sophisticated Gantt chart in exchange for a bit of effort. In Table 19.1, you can see the style definitions required to draw summary bars representing changing conditions, with the results shown in Figure 19.15.

Table 19.1   Summary Task Progress Bar Styles

Row	Task Name	Bar Appearance	From	To
1	Summary Not Started	Empty	Start	Finish
4	Summary Started	Left Slant	Actual Start	Finish
1	Summary Finished	Vertical Line	Actual Start	Actual Finish

Figure 19.15
With the help of Project, you can create multiple, conditional styles for a single Gantt Chart bar, which alter format based on changing conditions.

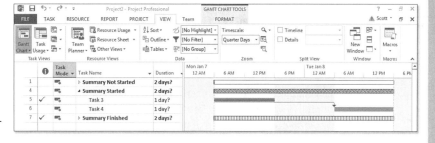

Using the Bar Options for Selected Tasks

If you want to change the appearance of the bars for only selected tasks, instead of changing a bar style, you can open the Format Bar dialog box, as shown in Figure 19.16, by selecting the Format tab, Bar Styles, Format, Bar menu. You will see that the Format Bar dialog box is similar to the lower section of the Bar Styles dialog box. Project omits the task definition portion because any changes made here would not be applied to all tasks types, but only the task(s) you select before you open this dialog box.

Any changes you make in the Format Bar dialog box are considered by Project to be manual formatting and will remain unless you reset the bar to the default. To change your task bar back to its original formatting, select it again, reopen the Format Bar dialog box, and click Reset.

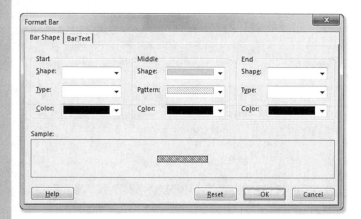

Figure 19.16
The Format Bar dialog box enables you to make quick changes to selected task bar formats.

Using the Layout Options

To modify the way bars are displayed with the Gantt Chart view, select the Format tab, Format, Layout. This opens the Layout dialog box, as shown in Figure 19.17. You can also open the Layout dialog box by right-clicking an open area on the timescale side of the Gantt Chart and selecting Layout from the shortcut menu.

If you find the task-linking lines to be distracting, you can easily turn them off. You also have the option of choosing between rectilinear line styles and straight line styles, which are the default.

You can make changes to the dates, displayed as text around the task bars, using the Date Format options. The drop-down list enables you to choose which style of date you want to use. The first option in your drop-down list is Default, which uses the format set on the General tab of the Options dialog box. Changes made here will not, however, change the default format for any date shown elsewhere in the project, such as the Start and Finish dates.

You can modify the height of your task bars using the Bar Height drop-down menu. You can set them between 6 and 24 points, with 12 points being the default.

Figure 19.17
The Layout dialog box enables you to change the appearance of task bars in the Gantt Chart view.

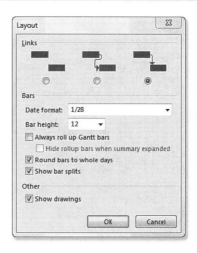

You can easily set your project up so that all tasks will be rolled up and represented on summary tasks, by selecting the Always Roll Up Gantt Bars check box. If you select this check box, all tasks behave as if the Roll Up Gantt Bar to Summary option in the Task Information dialog box has been turned on. Your milestone indicators and bars connecting subtask start and finish dates will be shown in their respective summary tasks when you choose this option.

You can also use the Hide Rollup Bars When Summary Expanded check box if you want to hide the display of the summary bar when your summary tasks are collapsed. This will also hide the usual black bar with the down-pointing end shapes that shows up under the rolled-up bars and markers. Finally, when your summary tasks are expanded and the subtasks are visible, you will not see any roll-up indicators on the summary task bars.

Figure 19.18 shows the Always Roll Up Gantt Bars and Hide Rollup Bars When Summary Expanded options turned on.

If you have a task with a duration less than the time period in the lowest displayed timescale tier, you can modify how it is displayed with the Round Bars to Whole Days check box. If you had a task with a duration of four hours, for instance, being displayed in a Gantt Chart view, where the bottom tier has been set to Days and this box is not selected, the bar shows the length for exactly four hours. If you do select the Round Bars to Whole Days check box, the bar will be extended to a full day. This affects only the display, however; the calculated start and finish dates and actual duration are still the same.

You can also select the Show Bar Splits check box if you want Project to actually show tasks being split in the Gantt Chart view. If the option is not selected, Project shows the task bar extending the entire duration of the task, including the split, from start to finish. If you select the option, however, Project shows a gap in the task bar for your split task, with the two parts connected by a dotted line.

 tip

If you want to be able to place graphics in the Gantt Chart, you need to select the Show Drawings check box.

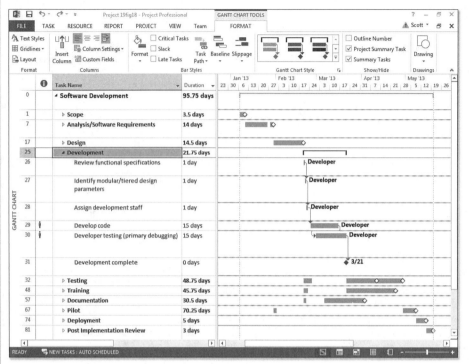

Figure 19.18
Here is an example of rolled-up markers for their sub-tasks set on summary tasks.

Using the Gantt Chart Wizard

The Gantt Chart Wizard must be added to either the Quick Access toolbar or the Ribbon. You can use the Gantt Chart Wizard to help you with formatting bars. The wizard helps you through different formatting options, as it questions you about how you want your bars to be displayed. Your options are the same as was covered in the previous section, "Formatting the Gantt Chart View Manually." However, the wizard walks you through the process, step by step.

After you open the wizard, the welcome screen appears. Click the Next button for your first screen of choices, as shown in Figure 19.19. As you make choices, you move through the appropriate steps, depending on your choices. Simply select from your options, and then click Next to move on. You can use the Back, Cancel, and Finish buttons at any time. If you have any questions, you need to get out of the Gantt Chart Wizard to use the Help button in the title bar, and then repeat your steps in the Gantt Chart Wizard to return to where you were.

 tip

If you are unfamiliar with all the formatting options available, the Gantt Chart Wizard might be a good place for you to start. You can use it to set up your task bars and then exit the wizard and use the Bar Styles and Text Styles dialog boxes to make modifications to suit you.

Your first decision concerns the basic way tasks are displayed. You begin with the choices for setting up and formatting the bars on your Gantt Chart. Your five starting options are listed here:

■ **Standard**—The default for Gantt Chart. If you have already run the wizard, you can run it again and choose Standard to undo your changes.

Figure 19.19
Setting up and formatting bars can be easy with the Gantt Chart Wizard.

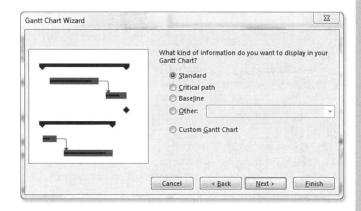

■ **Critical Path**—This is the critical path option, which concerns tasks that must be completed on time to meet the project deadline. These are displayed in red and can be helpful when you are trying to reduce the duration of your project, also known as *crashing the schedule*.

■ **Baseline**—With this option, you get two bars per task, showing the original and current schedules, such as the Tracking Gantt Chart view. This can be helpful for tracking a project already underway.

■ **Other**—There are 13 predefined formats for you to select or modify as you choose.

■ **Custom Gantt Chart**—This is your most extensive choice, and takes you through all the choices for formatting, step by step. You get to choose colors, patterns, and shapes for the Critical, Normal, Summary, and Milestone tasks. You can also add bars for baseline information and place text next to the bars.

No matter what your starting format choice is, the wizard prompts you for the type of text you want to display in and around the task bars. Not all the formats are available in the wizard's drop-down lists, but you can make custom choices to define distinct text formats for Normal, Summary, and Milestone tasks.

The last wizard question asks you how you want linking lines drawn to display dependency relationships between your task bars. After you have made all your choices, choose Finish, Format It, Exit.

 caution

Any changes that you make using the Gantt Chart Wizard will be applied to the Gantt Chart view currently being displayed. Running the wizard causes default formatting to be lost. You should instead make a copy of the standard Gantt Chart and then use the wizard on your copy. Select View, More Views, Gantt Chart, Copy. After you apply your copy, you will not have to worry about your changes; you can always go back to your original.

Formatting the Calendar View

The Gantt Chart view is not the only view to which you can easily make changes. The Calendar view can be modified in many different ways, depending on what you want to do with it. You can use the Zoom command on the View tab, or the Zoom slider on the status bar, to get in for a closer look or back off to see the big picture. This can also be helpful if you have a lot of tasks occurring all at once. The timescale can also be changed on the View tab.

With the Calendar view, you can change the height and width of the date boxes via your mouse, as shown in Figure 19.20. Move your mouse to point at any vertical line in the calendar, and the mouse pointer changes to a double-headed arrow. You can then drag this arrow left or right to widen or narrow your column. The same is true for horizontal lines, to make your date boxes taller or shorter.

 tip

If your Calendar view is set on Month, when you move lines vertically, you affect the whole week, but when you move them horizontally, you affect only that specific day of the week. For instance, if you widen Tuesday, all the Tuesdays in your month will become wider.

If you want to widen the entire calendar at once, instead of just week by week and day by day, select either the far-right vertical line, to widen the entire calendar proportionately, or the bottom horizontal line, to lengthen the calendar proportionately.

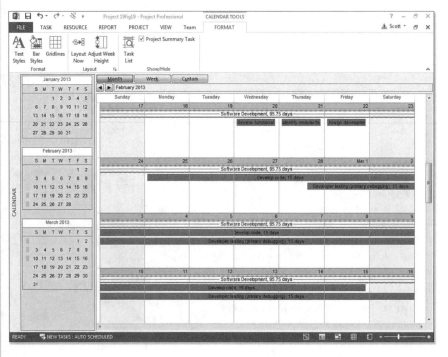

Figure 19.20
You can manipulate the size of the date boxes in the Calendar view to see more tasks per day.

The Format tab has the following options for the Calendar view: Text Styles, Bar Styles, Gridlines, Layout Now, and Adjust Week Height. The Gridlines and Text Styles options are the same as mentioned in previous sections of this chapter and are the same as the Gantt Chart view. Timescale, Bar Styles, and Layout/Layout Now for the Calendar view are unique and are covered in more detail in the following sections. Adjust Week Height simply sets the week height so that all tasks fit.

Formatting the Timescale for the Calendar

You can open the Timescale dialog box by going to the View tab, Zoom, Timescale or by right-clicking any spot in the Calendar view, other than a specific bar or heading, to open the shortcut menu. You can see in Figure 19.21 that the Timescale dialog box for the Calendar view has three tabs: one for headings and titles, one for additional data elements that can appear in the date boxes, and one for shading on certain days.

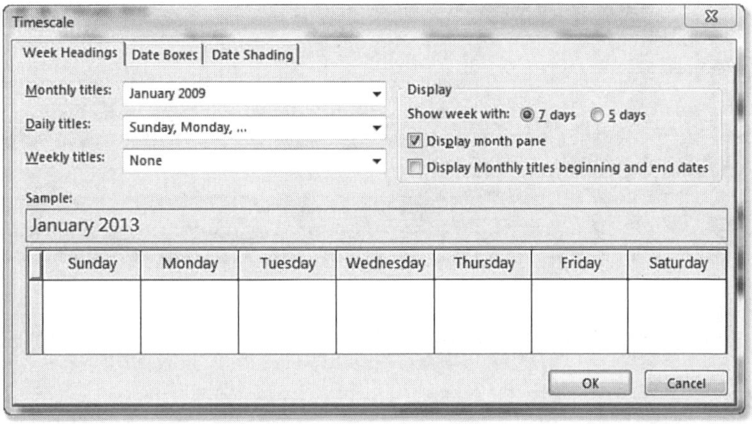

Figure 19.21
The options in the Calendar view's Timescale dialog box are different from the Gantt Chart view.

You can use the Week Headings tab to change your choices of labels for the month, days of the week, and the week itself. You can also set up either five- or seven-day weeks, plus include smaller calendars for previous and subsequent months.

With the Date Boxes tab, you can set additional data information in the top or bottom row of each of the individual date boxes. You can also use colors and patterns for more emphasis. Project's default setting for the Date Boxes tab omits the display of the bottom row, and on the top row, it includes an overflow indicator and date. The overflow indicator lets you know when all tasks scheduled for that day cannot be displayed within the date box, because of lack of space. When printing your calendar, those overflow tasks appear on a separate page.

With the Date Shading tab, you can make modifications to all the categories for working and non-working dates. With the Show Working Time For drop-down list, you can choose a base or resource calendar as your starting point. Then, select an exception type, such as nonworking days or a resource's calendar, and set the pattern and color to create the visual distinction. You can see a sample of your work to the right as you set things up.

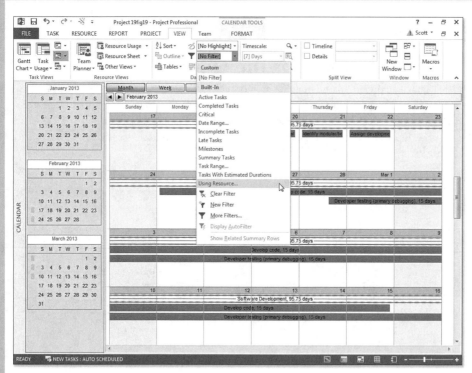

Figure 19.22
You can modify all categories for working and nonworking dates for a selected base or resource calendar.

Selecting Calendar Bar Styles Options

Just like with the Gantt Chart view, you can control how the bars in the calendar of your Calendar view appear, including text that can be added as part of the bars. To access the Bar Styles dialog box, shown in Figure 19.23, select the Format tab, Format, Bar Styles or you can right-click on the calendar to open the shortcut menu and choose the Bar Styles option.

Your first step is to choose which type of bar you want modified in the Task Type list box. Second, modify the bar type, color, pattern, and split pattern for the bar using the drop-down lists in the Bar Shape area. You can select either a bar or a line to represent the duration of a task. If you have chosen a bar, you can apply shadow for emphasis by selecting the Shadow check box. You also have a variety of patterns and colors to choose for your bars, and several different choices for different displays for split tasks.

 tip

If you select the Bar Rounding check box, any task with a duration of less than a whole day will be rounded up to a whole day. So, if you have a task that is a day and a half, it will be rounded up to show as two full days.

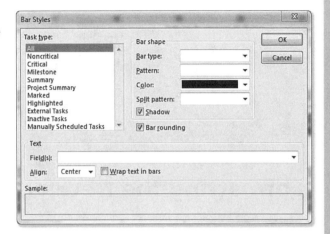

The Text area enables you to choose the fields you want shown in the bar, by either typing in their names or choosing them from the drop-down list. If you want to enter more than one field on the bar and are typing them in, separate them with commas; if you are using the drop-down list, be sure to deselect the field name and enter a comma before choosing the next one from the list. If you do not, the first field will be replaced by the second, instead of being added to it. You have the option of aligning your text either centered, left-aligned, or right-aligned. If your text is too long, you can select the Wrap Text in Bars check box. You can see results for choices made in the Sample box shown at the bottom of the dialog box, unless you have selected All in the Task Type categories list.

 caution

You might get a warning message from Project's Planning Wizard, depending on your choices in the Bar Styles dialog box, which indicates that you have calendar bars with different heights. The warning message explains how to reposition those bars.

Setting the Layout Options for the Calendar View

You can use the Layout dialog box, as shown in Figure 19.24, to display in which order your tasks appear in the date boxes. You can open the Layout dialog box by right-clicking on the calendar to open the shortcut menu and choosing Layout. Project's default method is Use Current Sort Order. You can also use Attempt to Fit as Many Tasks as Possible, which will do just what it says, without regard to the sorting. Select the Show Bar Splits check box to establish that a task that has been split displays differently from a regular task.

A split task shows a dotted outline, by default, during the portion of the task when no work is underway. Selecting the Automatic Layout check box tells Project to initiate the settings in the Layout dialog box automatically anytime tasks are edited, added, or deleted.

 tip

If the Automatic Layout check box is not selected, you need to go to Format, Layout Now or choose Layout Now from the calendar shortcut menu to apply any changes.

Figure 19.24
You can determine when and how tasks are sorted within each of the Calendar view's date boxes using the Layout dialog box.

Formatting the Network Diagram View

Getting a look at your project's logic and flow is easy with the Network Diagram view, which can be useful in the planning stages. There are several different customizations you can make to the Network Diagram view: You can change the borders, size, and shape of the nodes; you can create named data templates that specify the fields displayed in each node; and you can apply layout characteristics to task nodes.

Use of either the Zoom control on the View tab or the Zoom slider on the status bar can help to change your perspective of the project, as will applying a filter.

The Format tab provides the Network Diagram-specific options such as Box, Box Styles, and Layout. Making changes to the display of text in the Format tab for the Network Diagram view is just like the Gantt Chart view and is covered earlier in this chapter.

➡ *For additional information about the Network Diagram views, **see** the "Network Diagram View" section on **p. 375** in **Chapter 11**.*

Using the Box Styles Options

Using the Box Styles dialog box enables you to customize the boxes that surround the nodes, changing between 10 different shapes, four different border widths, and a variety of border colors. You can also make modifications to the background colors and patterns. You can open the Box Styles dialog box by going to the Format tab, Format, Box Styles or by double-clicking anywhere in the open space of the Network Diagram view (see Figure 19.25).

Default box styles have been assigned according to their types of tasks. Any critical tasks, such as summary or milestone tasks, are outlined in red with a white background; noncritical tasks are outlined in blue with an aqua background. The shape defaults are rectangles for normal tasks, four-sided parallelograms for summary tasks, and six-sided boxes for milestones.

Project sets the formatting of boxes displayed in an applied highlight filter, by default, to be the same shape as nonhighlighted nodes, but with a yellow background. Turn on the Set Highlight Filter Style option if you want to review or change the highlight settings for node types.

Figure 19.25
You have several different options you can apply to the node boxes of the Network Diagram view, using the Box Styles dialog box.

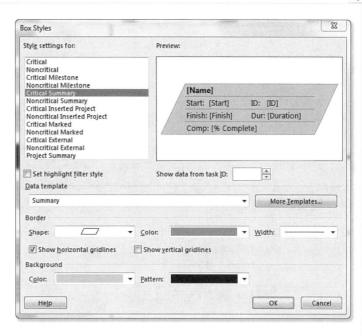

You can apply a virtually unlimited number of border colors to shapes, and they are great with a color printer to define different nodes. However, if you are not using a color printer, you should modify the border patterns to better distinguish between the types of tasks.

Turning on the Show Horizontal Gridlines and Show Vertical Gridlines options helps you view cell dividers in both the view onscreen and in print.

 tip

If you want to see how your styles will look with actual task information, instead of just the generic preview, you can enter a valid task ID number into the Show Data from Task ID entry box.

Using Data Templates for Network Diagram Nodes

Setting up a data template means that you control the contents and the row and column layouts within each node. In a template, the node definitions include the following elements:

- Box cells laid out with up to 16 cells in a 4-row-by-4-column grid

- Cell width sizing for all cells in the box

- Vertical and horizontal alignment settings for the contents of each cell

- Up to a maximum of three lines of text to be displayed in cells

- Descriptive label inserted in front of data of each cell

- Font size, style, and color options for each cell

- Fields that appear in each of up to 16 cell positions

- Date formats for the Network Diagram view displays

The contents and layout of boxes are initially defined by the supplied templates. The standard template, which is used for normal critical and noncritical tasks, displays six fields of information on a 4-row-by-2-column grid: Task Name, Start, Finish, Resource Names, ID, and Duration. The Milestone template uses a 3-row-by-1-column format and lists the Task Name, Milestone Date, and Task ID. Summary tasks use a template with a 4-row-by-2-column grid with six fields of information: Task Name, Start, Finish, % Complete, ID, and Duration.

Use the following steps to create new Network Diagram data templates:

1. Go to the Format tab, Format, Box Styles to open the Network Diagram Box Styles dialog box.

2. After the Box Styles dialog box is open, use the More Templates button. This opens the Data Templates dialog box, as shown in Figure 19.26.

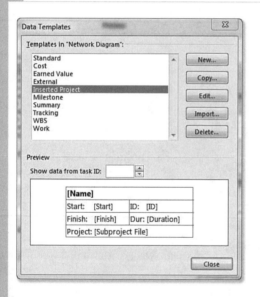

Figure 19.26
With the Data Template dialog box, you can take a look at a generic sample of a data template or choose a valid task ID to see the actual task values.

3. Use the Import button to open a box style template definition within the current file or to open one that has already been created in another file. If a second file is needed, it must already be open to allow this import.

4. Click New for a new data template. If you want to use an existing template to start with, select either Copy or Edit.

 note
The Standard data template, provided by Project, cannot be edited. You can, however, make a copy of it and then edit the copy.

5. Use the Data Template Definition dialog box, shown in Figure 19.27, for setting your options on a new template.

Figure 19.27
The Data Template Definition dialog box lets you set up the cell layout and settings for a new template.

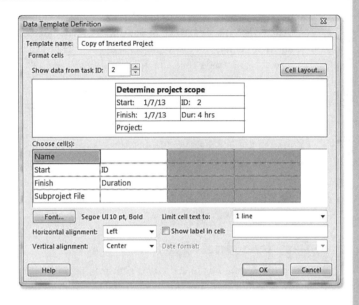

6. Name or rename the new template in the Template Name entry area.

7. Open the Cell Layout dialog box with the Cell Layout button, as shown in Figure 19.28.

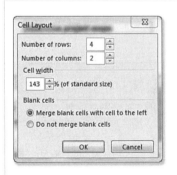

Figure 19.28
Use the Cell Layout dialog box to change the box grid and cell width.

8. Choose the number of rows and columns for the new diagram box in the Cell Layout dialog box. You can also set the cell width.

9. You should also decide handling for cells that are left blank while in the Cell Layout dialog box. The Merge Blank Cells with Cell to the Left option has been used so that the Name field appears to occupy two cells, instead of one.

10. After your layout is finished and you are ready to return to the Data Template Definition dialog box, click OK.

 note

You can choose and change more than one cell at a time by clicking and dragging, or you can use Shift+click or Ctrl+click on the multiple cells you want to change.

11. Choose your font, alignments, and number of text lines for each of the individual cells in the Data Template Definition dialog box. Select each cell in the Choose Cell(s) area and then add a prefix label to any or all cells. Finally, choose the date format for any date cells you might have.

12. After you have finished with your template definition, first click OK and then click Close in the Data Templates dialog box to return to the Box Styles dialog box.

13. Back in the Box Styles dialog box, you can apply your data template settings to nodes by selecting a task type in the Style Settings For list. Then, choose a data template from the drop-down list.

14. Click OK when you have finished. The Network Diagram view shows your change immediately.

Using the Box Options

Using the Format Box dialog box is similar to using Box Styles, but it affects only the box currently selected. A preview area is provided. You can select a data template and modify the border and background.

Controlling the Network Diagram Layout

You can control the layout of the Network Diagram by setting options in the Layout dialog box. You can also use the Layout Now command if you want to force Project to refresh the display. After the general layout is defined and applied, you can then apply task filters and group definitions to the diagram, and collapse summary tasks in the outline to hide tasks.

Selecting Layout Options

You can use the Layout command, under the Network Diagram Tools Format tab, to modify the overall look and feel of the network diagram, as opposed to just the appearance and contents of the individual network nodes. With the Layout command, you can select the options for box layout order and spacing, the style of the box connection lines, the color of the linking lines, the diagram background style and color, the drawing of task progress lines, and whether the diagram should be laid out automatically or manually.

Use these steps to set up the Network Diagram view's layout options:

1. Open the Layout dialog box, shown in Figure 19.29, by selecting the Format tab, Format, Layout, or by right-clicking on a blank spot in the Network Diagram view and choosing Layout from the shortcut menu.

Figure 19.29
You can make changes to the Network Diagram view's overall appearance using the Layout dialog box.

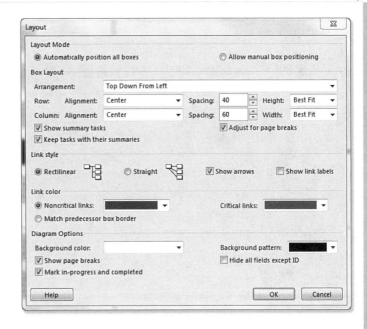

2. Select Automatically Position All Boxes in the Layout Mode area, if you want Project to maintain the onscreen layout. Alternatively, you can select Allow Manual Box Positions to allow click-and-drag movements of the boxes.

3. You can use the drop-down lists and spinners to set your row spacing, height, and alignment in the Box Layout area, as well as column spacing, width, and alignment. The settings are relative to those for other like elements; for instance, if you use a row alignment of Center to place all the boxes in a single horizontal row, all the box midlines form a straight line. If you set the column alignment to Left, all the boxes in a vertical column align with the left box edges.

4. You can use the Arrangement drop-down list in the Box Layout area to determine in what order Project draws the diagram. The default arrangement is Top Down from Left. You can see in Figure 19.30 an example of Top Down from Left. This is a common arrangement for most network diagrams.

You can see in Figure 19.31, for comparison, how a Network Diagram view might look if the arrangement were set Top Down by Month. Each column of nodes represents a month; within columns, boxes are in ID order.

 note
Your box sizes might vary, depending on the template settings applied to the box types. You can look back at the section, "Using Data Templates for Network Diagram Nodes," earlier in this chapter, for more information.

 tip
If you need to temporarily enlarge one of the Network Diagram boxes, you can move your mouse cursor over it and then pause, which enlarges the box.

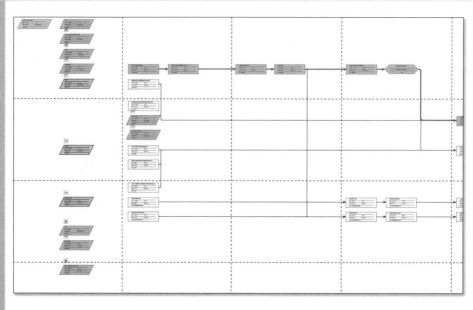

Figure 19.30
Top Down from Left, with dotted page breaks and rectilinear linking lines, is the standard diagram arrangement.

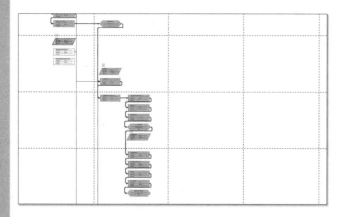

Figure 19.31
You can get a good picture of your project plan over time by using the Top Down by Month drawing of the Network Diagram view.

5. Use the Box Layout area in the Layout dialog box to make selections to keep tasks with their summaries when you are changing the layout arrangement, to show summary tasks, and to adjust for page breaks so that boxes cannot be split and printed partially on two different pages.

6. Decide which lines you want to use between diagram boxes—straight or rectilinear—and then select Show Arrows to indicate successor direction between nodes. Finally, select Show Link Labels if you want to include small dependency type labels (FS, SS, FF, SF) on each linking line.

7. Choose your pattern and color options for your linking lines and the diagram display background.

8. You can find two helpful options at the bottom of the Layout dialog box. The first is the Show Page Breaks check box, which enables you to see onscreen how the printing will be laid out without having to go to the Print Preview. The second is the Mark In-Progress and Completed check box, which draws a diagonal line (from the top left to the bottom right) across boxes for tasks with some progress, and an additional diagonal line through completed tasks.

9. If you are printing the overall structure of your plan and do not want to display any task details, you should use the Hide All Fields Except ID option, as shown in Figure 19.32.

10. After you have made all of your selections and changes, click OK.

 tip

There are two other ways to access the Hide All Fields Except ID option. You can also find it by right-clicking on the diagram background and selecting Hide Fields from the shortcut menu, or you can use the Hide Fields button on the Network Diagram toolbar.

Figure 19.32
Hiding all fields except for ID enables you to print a nice condensed schematic of your plan.

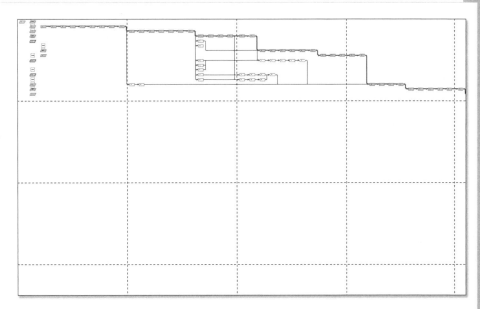

Predetermined logic exists behind each arrangement option in the Layout dialog box. If the Top Down from Left option has been chosen, Project redraws the Network Diagram view according to three standard rules of node placement, as follows:

■ Successor tasks are always located to the right of, or below, their predecessor tasks.

■ Summary tasks are always located above and to the left of their subordinate tasks.

- Linked task nodes are always connected with straight or diagonal lines, and an arrow is placed at the successor task's end of the line, to show the direction of the two tasks' relationship.

There are similar rules for other arrangement options.

Controlling Box Placement in the Network Diagram View

If you activate the Allow Manual Box Positioning radio button in the Layout dialog box, you can move around the boxes of the diagram, repositioning them for more clarity. To move a node manually, move the mouse cursor to the edge of the node, and then pause there until the cursor changes to a four-pointed arrow. You can then click and drag the border edge, moving the node to wherever you want. You can also select the node and use the Ctrl+arrow keys to move it.

Any of your predefined or custom-built task filters can be applied to the Network Diagram view. With the diagram displayed, go to the View tab, Data, Filter to apply one of the standard filters. You can also apply group definitions to the diagram. Go to the View tab, Data, Group By. There are several predefined groups: No Group, Complete and Incomplete Tasks, Constraint Type, Critical, Duration, Duration then Priority, Milestones, Priority, and Priority Keeping Outline Structure. You can see in Figure 19.33 how task nodes have been grouped into critical and noncritical task sections, which occurs when you select the Critical option. You can also select More Groups and Customize Group By to define your desired grouping.

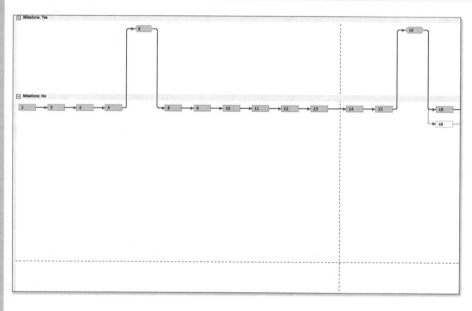

Figure 19.33 Grouping capabilities can offer you several different ways to show tasks nodes. These nodes are grouped by whether they are milestones.

You can also control the Network Diagram view display by setting up the outline detail level to be displayed. Use the Outline button on the View tab to select which level of subtasks you want to be displayed. You can also expand or collapse individual summary tasks on the screen. Just click the plus (+) or minus (−) symbol above each summary task.

Using the Zoom Command

It can be helpful to change the perspective of your view, especially using the Network Diagram view, by either zooming in to see the fine details or zooming out to see the bigger picture.

You can use the Zoom In and Zoom Out buttons to move through the various preset zoom levels, or you can use the Zoom slider on the status bar. You can select Zoom from the View tab or right-click on the Network Diagram view, and select Zoom from the shortcut menu. The Zoom dialog box is displayed, as shown in Figure 19.34. There are several preset values for zooming, or you can enter a value between 25% and 400% in the Custom text box.

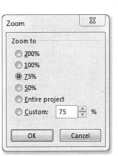

Figure 19.34
The Zoom dialog box gives you several different options on how to examine the Network Diagram view.

 tip

You can only zoom between 25% and 400% using the Zoom dialog box. If you have a large project, and use the Entire Project radio button, you will probably get an error box telling you your project cannot be displayed, because the view cannot be set below the minimum zoom of 25%.

Formatting the Task Form and Resource Form Views

Because the Task Form and Resource Form cannot be printed, the formatting options for them are limited. You can view all tasks or resources in the form when it is displayed full screen. To open these forms to full screen, select the View tab, Resource Views, Other Views, More Views, and then choose either Task Form or Resource Form from the More Views dialog box. Use the Next and Previous buttons to move through the task or resource list.

If you want to split the screen, go to either the Task or Resource tabs, Properties, Details. This creates another form in the lower pane of the split screen. The form in the lower pane of a split screen displays detailed information about the task or resource selected in the top pane.

➡ *For additional information about splitting Windows,* **see** *the "Understanding Standard Views" section on* **p. 366** *in Chapter 11.*

Sorting the Form Views

Task Form and Resource Form views can be sorted using the Sort control on the View tab.

If a form view is displayed as either full screen or the top half of a split screen, the Sort option changes the order of the tasks and resources when the Next and Previous buttons are used. If the form is in the bottom half of the split screen, applying a sort order will not have an effect; rather, the sort order applied to the top half of a split screen controls the behavior of the Next and Previous buttons on the form.

Formatting Details of Form Views

The Details option under the Format menu offers different entry field combinations that you can place at the bottom of the form. The entry fields for the Resource Form and the Task Form have similar options. Click on the entry form and then select the Format tab. When you are using the Resource Form view, various tasks assigned to the selected resource are listed. If you change the details, it alters which assigned task fields are displayed. A Task Form focuses on information about the task, including the resources assigned. So, if you change the details in the Task Form view, you are also changing what resource information or what detailed task information is shown for the selected task.

 note

You can right-click anywhere in a blank area of a form to open the shortcut menu and view a list of alternative formats for forms.

When the Task Form view is active, select the Format tab, Format, Details Schedule to see fields for when work is scheduled, plus the entry fields for imposing delay on either the task itself or on when the resource begins work on the task. You also have columns for Leveling Delay and Delay, as shown in Figure 19.35. The Leveling Delay field is a delay to the task itself, often caused when Project applies resource leveling, and is the same field that appears on the Delay table on the Detail and Leveling Gantt Charts. The Delay field, however, is a delay to the resource only. This field shows delay if the resource does not start working at the beginning of the task.

The other form details show additional entry detail fields, as shown in Table 19.2.

Table 19.2   Task and Resource Form Details

Task Form Detail	Resource Form Detail	Description
Resources & Predecessors	(Task form only)	Shows the default fields

Task Form Detail	Resource Form Detail	Description
Resources & Successors	(Task form only)	Focuses on upcoming tasks
Predecessors & Successors	(Task form only)	Shows the immediate links into and out of the task
Resource Schedule	Schedule	Shows the start, the finish, and any delays
Resource Work	Work	Shows the work fields for resources, including the Overtime field
Resource Cost	Cost	Includes Baseline, Actual, and Remaining resource costs
Notes	Notes	Shows any notes entered, usually through the Task or Resource Information dialog box
Objects	Objects	Shows any OLE objects that are attached to the task or resource

Figure 19.35
If you go to Format tab, Format, Details, Resource Schedule, when a Task Form view is active, you can display assigned resource scheduling information.

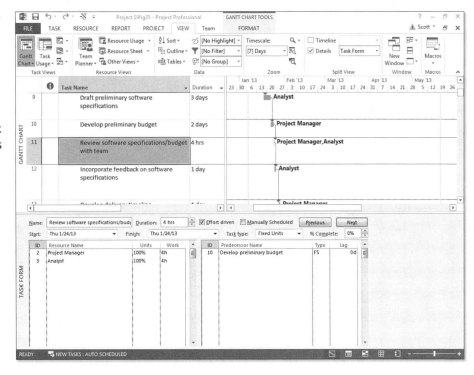

Formatting the Resource Graph View

The Resource Graph view is used when you want to look at values derived from the task assignments of one or more resources, as graphed along a timescale. You can open the Resource Graph by selecting the Resource tab, View, Team Planner, Resource Graph. In Figure 19.36, you can see a histogram or a bar chart in the lower pane of the allocated and overallocated task assignments for the resource Project Manager. The value displayed is peak units, or percentage of effort assigned during each time period.

You can graph several different measurements for a resource in a time period on each task:

- **Peak Units**—Highest assigned resource units in a time period

- **Work**—Amount of work assigned

- **Cumulative Work**—Running total of work assigned to date

- **Overallocation**—Work overallocation of the resource

- **Percentage Allocation**—Percentage of effort currently allocated

- **Remaining Availability**—Effort, in hours, still available for assignments

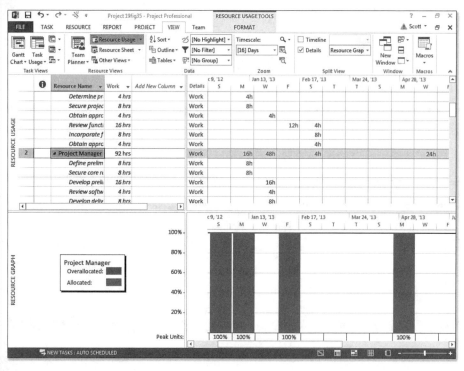

Figure 19.36
By using both the Resource Usage view and the Resource Graph view, you can see a visual representation of a resource's peak unit.

- **Cost**—Cost of assignments

- **Cumulative Cost**—Running total of cost contribution to date

- **Work Availability**—Total work availability (does not reflect assignments)

- **Unit Availability**—Total percentage availability (does not reflect assignments)

You can use the graph to show these measurements for one resource, for a group of resources, or for the resource and the group together. Values can be shown for selected tasks or for all tasks in a given time period.

When a Resource Graph view is shown in the lower pane below a task view, the display values are for one resource only. You can show the values of a given resource's assignments either by selected task or by all tasks during any period that is measured using the timescale. You can see in Figure 19.37 the assignment bars for Trainers for all tasks during each day, allowing a quick look at overassignment.

If a Resource Graph view is in the upper pane, or in the lower pane but with a resource view above it, the values are shown for all tasks, and might be for one resource, for a group of resources, or for that one resource compared to a group of resources. If you are using group data for the display, the group is defined by the current filter. For instance, if the All Resources filter, the default, is being used, the data summarizes all resources for all tasks. You can see in Figure 19.38 the total costs associated with the Testers' task assignments, relative to the total costs for all resource assignments in the period.

Figure 19.37
You can use the Resource Graph view along with the Gantt Chart view to show bars for all tasks' work in that period for a single resource.

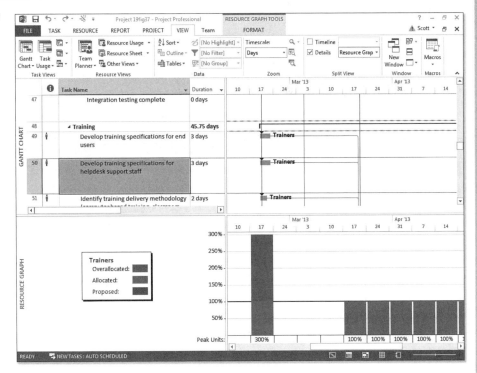

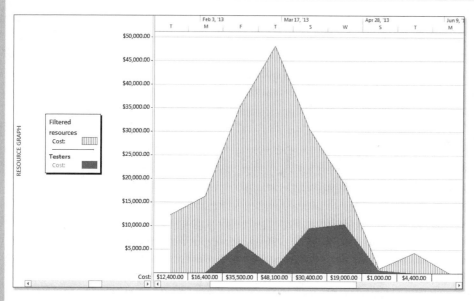

Figure 19.38
You can use the Resource Graph view to show costs associated with a single resource, as compared to the costs of all other resources.

You can see a summarization of the values displayed for different placement locations for the Resource Graph view in Table 19.3.

Table 19.3   Values Shown in the Resource Graph View

Location of Graph	Graph Value	One Resource Value
Top pane or bottom pane below a resource view	Value is for all tasks for all filtered resources.	Value is for all tasks for the selected resource.
Bottom pane below a task view	Value is for one resource but for all tasks.	Value is for one resource but for only the tasks selected in the top pane.

Reviewing the Format Options for the Resource Graph View

Zoom commands work as previously described for other views. Either the View tab, Zoom, Zoom control, or the Zoom slider on the status bar can be used.

Also, as in other views, the Format tab for the Resource Graph view contains dialog box options for formatting the gridlines and the text styles. You can change the timescale by right-clicking on it.

Because the Bar Styles dialog box has unique features concerning the resource graph, it will be discussed in the following section.

You can also change Graph options in the Data section of the Format tab. Open a Details option on the View tab, Split View. Your choices on this list of calculated values controls what information can be displayed in the timescale portion of the Resource Graph view. Because the Bar Styles dialog box options are based on these values, the Graph options are discussed before the Bar Styles dialog box is covered.

Selecting the Details to Display

Go to the Format tab, Data, Graph to open the choices you have on which values are calculated and graphed with the Resource Graph view. These choices are listed in the following sections with a brief description.

Work

The Work option is the number of units of each resource assigned to each task, measured in hours, and multiplied by the duration in hours of the task per time period display.

Project determines the amount of work to be done by the resource by looking at the number of units of the resource, the resource calendar, and the resource availability contour during the time period. If total work for the time period surpasses the available amount of resource hours, Project shows the surplus as overallocation.

 note

If Work is selected in the Details dialog box, the unit—be it hours, minutes, or days—is determined by the Work Is Entered In option on the Schedule tab of the Options dialog box. The show of costs is decided by the Currency Symbol, Currency Placement, and the Currency Decimal Digits choices on the View tab in the same dialog box.

Cost

The Cost value option displays the scheduled cost of the resource work, during a given time period. If this cost is to be prorated, as defined in the Cost Accrual field in the Costs tab of the Resource Form view, the cost appears in the time period when the work is done. If a per-use cost is associated with the prorated resource, that cost is shown at the start of the task. When the resource cost is to accrue at the beginning or end of a task, the entire cost appears in the graph at the beginning or end of the task.

Cumulative Cost

The Cumulative Cost option shows a running total of cost, based on adding each period's cost to the preceding period's cumulative cost. This measurement shows total cost over the life of the project, if you use only the group graph and include all resources in the group. See the "Using the Bar Styles Dialog Box" section, later in this chapter, for more information.

Cumulative Work

Cumulative Work measures the total work since the beginning of the project for a resource. This also includes the work during the time period shown.

Overallocation

The Overallocation value shows how much work has been overallocated for the resource for the time period. This option shows only the amount of overallocation—not any work hours occurring during the normal work day.

Peak Units

The Peak Units option measures the largest percentage of effort of a resource assigned during each time period on the graph, at any given moment.

Using the Peak Units measurement can be useful with multiple-unit resources, when the number of maximum units available is more than one. The overallocation warning is more likely to be accurate in such a case.

Percent Allocation

The Percent Allocation value shows the allocated work versus available work. Percent Allocation shows the amount of work as a percentage of the amount available.

Remaining Availability

The Remaining Availability value shows unallocated work for the resource during the time period. This option displays the unused work time still available, and is a useful option if you want to see who still has available time to work on tasks, or to see who is available when new tasks need to be assigned.

Unit

The Unit Availability option shows the same information as the Work Availability option; however, the resource availability is shown as percentages.

Displaying Work Availability

The Work Availability option is a graphical representation of the total number of hours a resource is available in a given timeframe. Based on resource minimum units and the resource calendar, this display does not reflect any work assignments that might exist in the period.

Using the Bar Styles Dialog Box

The Bar Styles dialog box helps you to set up whichever type of graph you want to display, if any, and how it will look. Your choices for graphs are Bar, Area, Step, Line, Step Line, and Don't Show. You can also use the Bar Styles dialog box to set up whether you want to see selected resource information or groups of resource information. Open the Bar Styles dialog box for the Resource Graph by making sure the Resource Graph view is active and then selecting the Format tab, Format, Bar Styles. Although a different Bar Styles dialog box appears for each of the value measurements just mentioned, they all have the same layout and are used the same way. You can see the Bar Styles dialog box for the Work value in Figure 19.39. Just like all of the Resource Graph view Bar Styles dialog boxes, this one has four main sections, plus three options at the bottom.

 note

The different areas available in the Bar Styles dialog box depend on the Details options set in the Format, Details menu.

The upper two sections of the dialog box set up the display of overallocated amounts, if relevant, whereas the lower two sections set the display of the allocated value up to the maximum amount. The sections to the left side are for specifying the display of group data. The sections to the right side are for specifying the display of one selected resource. Some of the values on the Display menu can display only two of the sections.

Figure 19.39
The Bar Styles dialog box lets you set options for displaying work on the Resource Graph view.

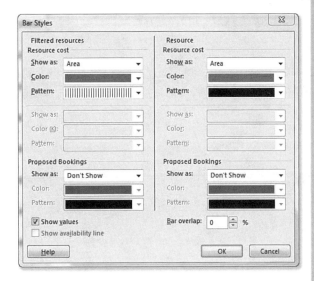

After you are finished and the dialog box is closed, you might see sets of double bars, each possibly with an upper and lower segment. The upper segment represents the overallocation measurement, whereas the lower segment is the allocation up to the overallocation level. If you see pairs of bars, the left bar is the group measurement, whereas the right is the selected resource measurement.

You will notice a similarity of the positioning of the bars to the position of options in the dialog box. Remember that the resource group is defined by the applied filter on the Resource Graph view (if the view is in the top pane or is displayed as a single pane). If no filter is applied, the group will represent all resources.

You can see in Figure 19.40 that the bar on the right is for the resource (Testers), and the bar on the left is for the group (in this case, all resources). The striped upper portion of the resource's bars represents the overallocations, and at the bottom of the graph, work values are displayed in the same time periods where the resource is allocated.

Each of these different features was defined by the dialog box. You can go back and look at Figure 19.39 to see the settings of the dialog box that affect Figure 19.40. The Show Values check box has been selected, so Project displays numeric data, along with the bars. The bars overlap by 20% to show that they are paired.

The graph shading patterns have been set by the selections in the four sections of the dialog box. For each section, you should select three features that establish how the value is displayed. You can use the Show As drop-down list to select the general format. You can choose from Bar, Area, Step, Line, Step Line, and Don't Show. Bar is the most common choice. If you select the Don't Show choice, Project suppresses all representation of the value. You can then choose the color of the image, as well as fill either the bar or area with a pattern.

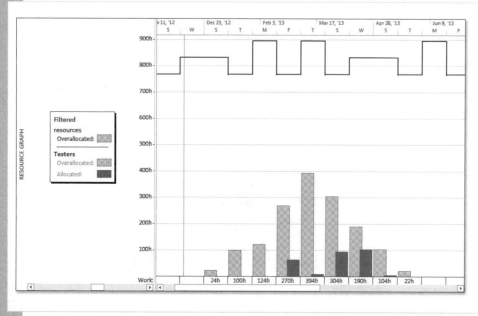

Figure 19.40
You can review over-allocation of a single resource, compared to the entire resource pool, using the Resource Graph view.

You can manage what is graphed by selecting what you want to be displayed, or not displayed, in each of the four sections of the Bar Styles dialog box. If you only want values from a selected resource, with nothing for the group values, select Don't Show from the Show As drop-down list for both left sections. If you only want the totals of all resources, select the Don't Show option for both right sections. If you select Overallocation on the Format, Details menu, the Bar Styles dialog box will have both of the bottom sections grayed out because these sections are not needed. When you are finished with your changes, click OK to execute them, or click Cancel to disregard the changes.

Formatting the Resource Usage View

If you would rather see number entries in a grid, instead of a graph, use the Resource Usage view instead of the Resource Graph view. Figure 19.41 displays the Resource Usage view in addition to Resource Graph view, so you can see the similarity and the differences between the two views. In both cases, the value being displayed is scheduled work.

You can use the Format tab to modify text styles, gridlines, and so on. You can also sort using the View tab, just like with other views. Each of these subjects, except for Detail Styles and Details, works as covered earlier in this chapter. Detail Styles and Details are covered in the following sections.

Figure 19.41
By combining the Resource Usage view and the Resource Graph view, you can see both numeric values and their graphic representations.

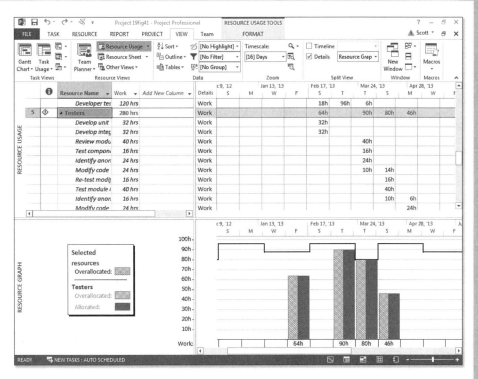

Choosing the Details for the Resource Usage View

You will find some of the same value choices in the Format tab, Details as are described in the "Formatting the Resource Graph View" section earlier in this chapter. You can choose the value you want to show in the timescale grid by picking one of these options: Work, Actual Work, Cumulative Work, Overallocation, Cost, or Remaining Availability.

If you are using the Resource Usage view in the bottom pane, under a task view, the only resources that will be displayed are resources assigned to the task that is selected in the top pane. Any work value displayed beside a resource name is the total scheduled work for that resource, across all of the tasks in the project. You will also see a breakdown of other tasks assigned to that resource shown under the resource name. In Figure 19.42, you can see a Resource Usage view below a Gantt Chart view, and how the values in the usage table show the work assigned to Movers for all the tasks during each time period.

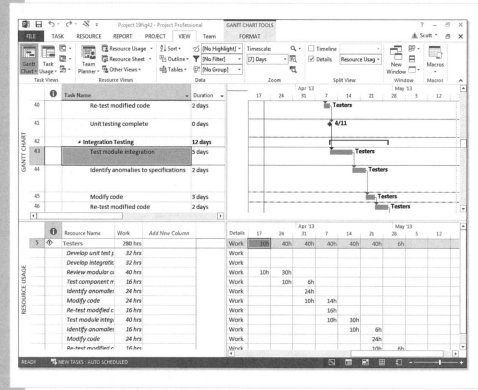

Figure 19.42
If you have a split window with the Gantt Chart view open over the Resource Usage view, you can see detailed work break-downs, by time periods and task.

Formatting the Detail Styles in the Resource Usage View

To open the Detail Styles dialog box, shown in Figure 19.43, for your Resource Usage view, first make sure that the Resource Usage view is active. Then, go to the Format tab, Add Details. With this dialog box, you can select a wide variety of fields to display for each resource assignment on the Usage Details tab. Every field shows up on its own row in the timescale grid, and you can set them up to display in a different font, background color, and pattern. Go to the Available Fields list on the left; then choose a field to be displayed and click the Show>> button.

If you do not want a field displayed, choose it from the Show These Fields list on the right, and then click the <<Hide button. If you want to change the order in which the fields will be displayed, use the Move up- and down-arrow buttons on the right side of the dialog box. The Usage Properties tab has options for aligning detail data and displaying headings for various columns and rows.

Figure 19.43
You have several different options on how to display detail in the timescale grid with the Resource Usage view's Detail Styles dialog box.

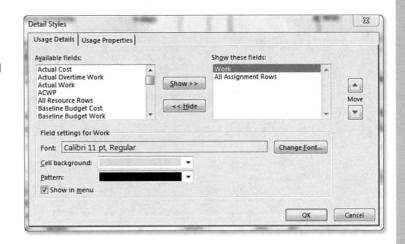

Formatting the Task Usage View

Your options for formatting the Task Usage view are the same as those for the Resource Usage view. The primary difference between the two views is the focus; whereas the Resource Usage view looks at the information from a resource's perspective, the Task Usage looks at each task, providing totals for various details and then a breakdown of each resource assigned to work on the task. In Figure 19.44, you can see that the task has three resources assigned, and each one has its own hours and costs. Also shown are the work and cost totals for the task, the related summary task, and the project.

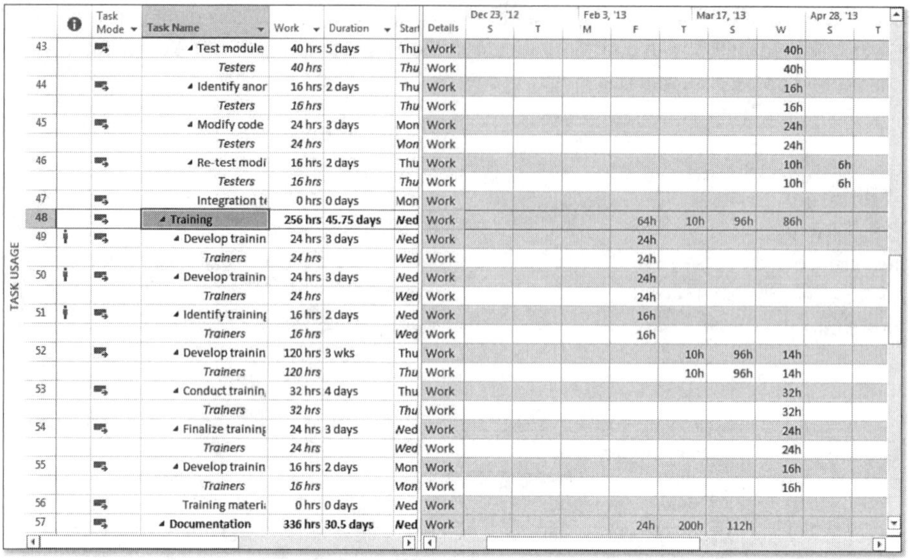

Figure 19.44
The Task Usage view can show you hours of work and costs for those work hours, which is useful information when you are making decisions about your project.

The table shown in Figure 19.44 (Task Usage view):

		Task Mode	Task Name	Work	Duration	Start	Details	Dec 23, '12 S	T	Feb 3, '13 M	F	Mar 17, '13 T	S	W	Apr 28, '13 S	T
43			▲ Test module	40 hrs	5 days	Thu	Work							40h		
			Testers	40 hrs		Thu	Work							40h		
44			▲ Identify anor	16 hrs	2 days	Thu	Work							16h		
			Testers	16 hrs		Thu	Work							16h		
45			▲ Modify code	24 hrs	3 days	Mon	Work							24h		
			Testers	24 hrs		Mon	Work							24h		
46			▲ Re-test modi	16 hrs	2 days	Thu	Work							10h	6h	
			Testers	16 hrs		Thu	Work							10h	6h	
47			Integration te	0 hrs	0 days	Mon	Work									
48			▲ Training	256 hrs	45.75 days	Wed	Work				64h	10h	96h	86h		
49	i		▲ Develop trainin	24 hrs	3 days	Wed	Work				24h					
			Trainers	24 hrs		Wed	Work				24h					
50	i		▲ Develop trainin	24 hrs	3 days	Wed	Work				24h					
			Trainers	24 hrs		Wed	Work				24h					
51	i		▲ Identify training	16 hrs	2 days	Wed	Work				16h					
			Trainers	16 hrs		Wed	Work				16h					
52			▲ Develop trainin	120 hrs	3 wks	Thu	Work						10h	96h	14h	
			Trainers	120 hrs		Thu	Work						10h	96h	14h	
53			▲ Conduct trainin	32 hrs	4 days	Thu	Work							32h		
			Trainers	32 hrs		Thu	Work							32h		
54			▲ Finalize training	24 hrs	3 days	Wed	Work							24h		
			Trainers	24 hrs		Wed	Work							24h		
55			▲ Develop trainin	16 hrs	2 days	Mon	Work							16h		
			Trainers	16 hrs		Mon	Work							16h		
56			Training materi.	0 hrs	0 days	Wed	Work									
57			▲ Documentation	336 hrs	30.5 days	Wed	Work					24h	200h	112h		

(TASK USAGE)

Formatting the Task Sheet and Resource Sheet Views

If you want to show tables of field values for the lists of tasks and resources, the Task Sheet and Resource Sheet views are your best bet. Which columns are shown on the sheet views depend on the table applied to the sheet. You can use the Format tab for both of the sheet views, but the options are limited. The View tab can be used for sorting, grouping, and filtering. All of these features are discussed earlier in this chapter.

Consultants' Tips

Use the following tips to help you in formatting views within Project.

Get Familiar with the Default Views First, Then Customize

Project offers many ways to customize views and graphs to support just about any reporting requirement. The sheer quantity of options can be overwhelming to new users. A good approach is to start off using the default views, see where they do not meet your needs, and then make copies of views to customize. For example, before changing the Gantt Chart view, make a copy of it by selecting the View tab, Task Views, Other Views, More Views. Select the view (Gantt Chart) and click the Copy button. Give it a name (such as My Gantt Chart) and click OK. This view is now displayed, ready for you to modify.

Customizing the Gantt Chart View

It is easy to get carried away with customization of Gantt views. If your organization has a Gantt standard, it can be set up as a default view in a template and saved to each user's local templates using the Organizer. Most of the Gantt views follow industry-standard symbols for tasks, milestones, and summaries. Start off with simple modifications to these styles unless you have a formal standard that you follow.

Sorting Views

When sorting your view, do not select the Permanently Renumber Tasks or Permanently Renumber Resources check box, depending on your active view. If this box is selected, the tasks or resources will be given new ID numbers. The Reset button does not return them to the original order, and filters and macros set on tasks by their ID numbers will not work. The only way to recover from this is to reopen a previously saved project file. Also, select the Keep Outline Structure check box. If this box is selected, tasks stay under their summary tasks and are sorted within their summary tasks. Clearing this box results in all tasks being sorted throughout the project.

A frequent modification made to Gantt Charts is showing resources' initials, instead of the entire resource names, beside the tasks to which they have been assigned. This can make things less cluttered.

Adding rows for Actual Work and Actual Cost to the Task Usage or Resource Usage view provides an easy place to enter actual hours and costs while you are tracking project progress.

REPORTS PART I: 2013 REPORTS

This chapter explores the new reporting features of Microsoft Project 2013 and how to customize these reports to your individual reporting needs. You also learn how to create and save new reports within your project or in your Global.mpt file for use with other projects.

Understanding the New Reports

"Basic" Project reporting was a feature set so stale it had become rare to see anyone using it. The problem was not that the feature was broken or useless; it was simply not up to modern reporting expectations. Fortunately, Project 2013 sees Microsoft introducing new and thoroughly modern reporting functionality to Project.

By default, Project 2013 contains slightly fewer reports than before, but that loss is more than made up for by the flexibility of the new reporting functionality. The default Project reports are still helpful during various stages of your project. In general, reports are an excellent way to view specific project information quickly, and are formatted in a printer-friendly fashion for easy distribution to other project stakeholders.

As highlighted elsewhere in this book, the flexibility of views and tables in Project enables you to report straight from the schedule if you want. The reality is, though, that most of your project's stakeholders will not enjoy looking at printed views, no matter how informative they are.

Reports can also be used to present great levels of detail, but as a general rule you should use them when some summarization and visualization will help you communicate better with your stakeholders.

This chapter examines how to use the new reports in Project 2013, as well as describes in detail how to customize or create new reports.

Accessing the Reports

All the reports are now available from a new tab fittingly called Report.

The Report tab is shown in Figure 20.1.

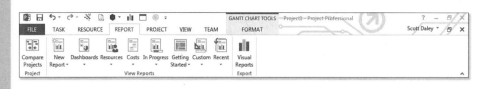

Figure 20.1
The new Report tab is one-stop for all your reporting needs.

> *For more information about comparing projects, **see** the "Comparing Project Versions" section on **p. 773** in Chapter 23.*

> *For more information about Visual Reports, **see** Chapter 21, "Reports Part II: Visual Reports, **p. 653**."*

There are three groups in the Report tab: the Project group, which includes only the Compare Projects control; the View Reports group, which is the subject of this chapter; and the Export group, which contains only the Visual Reports control. There are eight category controls. Some of these are loosely grouped report categories (Dashboards, Resources, etc.), some are more like tools (New Report), and one is a light tutorial (Getting Started). Clicking any of the controls shows a drop-down that provides you with options, including a More Reports option at the bottom that in turn opens a dialog box representing exactly the same groups, as shown in Figure 20.2. All of the reports are customizable and ready to print, and are discussed in greater detail in the upcoming sections.

The Custom category group is where reports you create appears. This process is described later in this chapter.

Single-clicking any of the report category controls displays your options under that category. From this drop-down, select the report to display by clicking it. Figure 20.3 displays the Dashboards drop-down.

Figure 20.2
More Reports leads you to an alternate representation of the View Reports group from the Report tab.

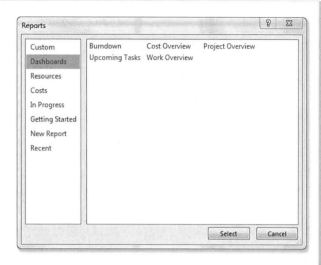

Figure 20.3
Click on Dashboards to see the Dashboards reports.

Common Report Elements

Clicking on the New Report category shows what looks like four report types: Blank, Chart, Table, and Comparison, as shown in Figure 20.4. In reality, these are simply starting points; any of these starting points cane be further modified to include any additional report elements.

The key to understanding report elements is in the Insert group under the Report Tools Design tab, as shown in Figure 20.5. You can insert images, shapes, charts, tables, and text boxes. Images, shapes, and text boxes are static design elements you can add to make your report look better or be more understandable. Charts and tables are dynamic elements that pull their contents form the project schedule itself.

The Project Overview report is a good example of multiple elements. Figure 20.6 annotates each.

> **note**
>
> While both tables and charts have pretty much the same field lists, the field list for a chart contains one additional option, the Category. This is used to specify the primary categorization for your chart.

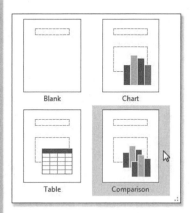

Figure 20.4
The New Report category gets you started with one of four basic templates, but you can add elements as you see fit from there.

The Insert Group

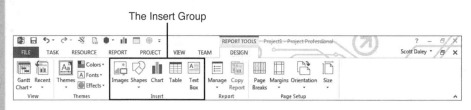

Figure 20.5
The Insert group contains all the elements you can add to your reports.

Common elements appear in most reports, as defined in the following list:

- **Text Boxes**—The heading for the Project Overview report is a text box, as are the table titles (but not the header rows). Obviously, the appearance of each individual text box is customizable as you'd expect from an Office application.

- **Tables**—Each table is driven from its own field pick list.

- **Charts**—There are a wide range of charts available for inclusion in your report.

- **Fields**—The Field List panel controls what data gets displayed on each of the dynamic elements (tables and charts). Almost all of the project fields are available, with the exception of the Project Information fields. Additionally, filters, grouping, and sort orders can be applied from the Field List panel.

Notice these common elements as you explore the reports in Project. This chapter explores how to change these elements in the upcoming section, "Customizing Reports."

▶ *For more information about customizing filters and groups, **see** Chapter 22, "Customization Almost Beyond Reason: Views, Tables, Filters, Groups, Fields, Toolbars, and Menus, **p. 699**."*

Figure 20.6
The Project Overview report contains all the common elements.

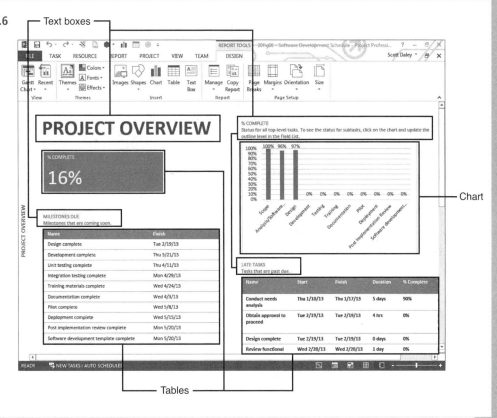

Text boxes

Chart

Tables

Dashboards Reports Category

The first reports category listed in the View Reports group is the Dashboards category. Select it, and you see five reports: Burndown, Cost Overview, Project Overview, Upcoming Tasks, and Work Overview (refer to Figure 20.3).

Table 20.1 describes these five overview reports. They all display summary information that spans the entire project and are useful as documentation of the scope of the project plan after the planning has been completed, as well as status reports throughout the work on a project.

 tip

Note that some sections of some reports require a baseline to show data.

Table 20.1 Overview Reports

Report Name	Usage	Baseline Required?
Burndown	Used to compare planned, completed, and remaining work. This kind of report is often associated with Agile projects, although considerably more work would need to go into your schedule to make this truly work for an Agile project.	Yes
Cost Overview	A cost-oriented project report that is useful for determining whether your project will stay within budget.	Yes
Project Overview	Provides a high-level view of your project's status. Useful for at-a-glance stakeholders; without modifications, it's not particularly useful for much else.	No
Upcoming Tasks	Provides a detailed view of tasks that are important this week and the next.	No
Work Overview	Used to show the summary status across major project tasks.	Yes

One of the key questions you will doubtless have when you look at reports like the Upcoming Tasks report is "What exactly is this report filtering for?" As shown in Figure 20.7, the filter is always listed on the Field List panel. Clicking on any table or chart automatically opens this panel.

But this is only half an answer. Where is the Tasks Due this Week filter described? To find that, you need to return to any of the standard views and select the View tab. In the Data group, select the Filter drop-down and click more filters, as shown in Figure 20.8.

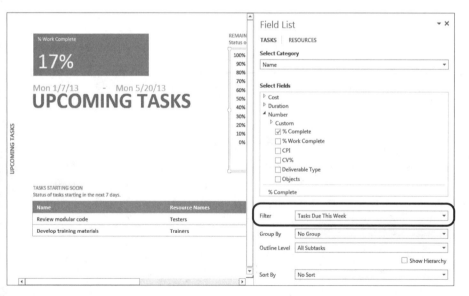

Figure 20.7
The Remaining Tasks chart on the Upcoming Tasks report uses the Tasks Due This Week filter.

Figure 20.8
There are multiple ways to reach the More Filters dialog; through the View tab is the most obvious.

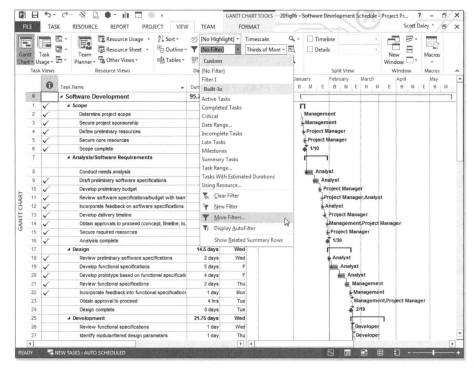

This brings up the More Filters Dialog. Scroll through it until you find the Tasks Due This Week filter, and click Edit. The full definition for the Tasks Due This Week filter is displayed, as shown in Figure 20.9.

 caution

This filter *can* be edited directly, but generally speaking that is not advisable. It is better to create a copy of the filter, then set your report reference to the new filter, thereby preserving the default. However, if you are certain that everywhere Project references this filter you want the exact same modified results, go ahead and change it.

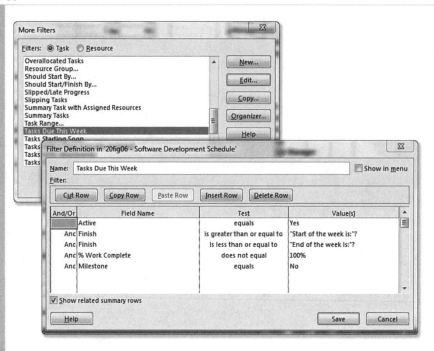

Figure 20.9
The complete defi-
nition of the Tasks
Due This Week
filter.

Resources Reports Category

The second reports category listed in the View Reports group is the Resources category.
Select it, and you see two reports: Overallocated Resources and Resource Overview, as in
Figure 20.10.

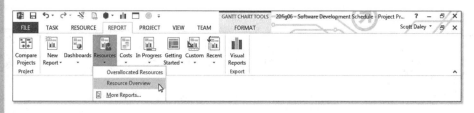

Figure 20.10
The
Resources
Category
contains
two reports.

The Resources category seems light, until you consider that reports are primarily for providing summary data to external stakeholders. Resource management can be daunting in detail, and between
the Team Planner and Resource views, Project covers it exhaustively. Table 20.2 provides a list and
description of the reports found in this category.

Table 20.2 Current Activities Reports

Report Name	Usage	Baseline Required?
Overallocated Resources	Lists all resources that are overallocated—that is, those resources that are assigned to more hours of work than the Max Units field specifies. The report can help you identify resources that are overallocated, and therefore might not finish their assignments on time. In turn, you can take an action of adding more resources to the overallocated resource's tasks to lighten the load, or to reschedule the tasks so that the work does not overlap.	No
Resource Overview	Used to show roughly how much work various resources have left on your project.	Yes

The Resource Overview report is applicable to only a small number of projects out of the box. Realistically, knowing how much work each resource on your project has remaining is only relevant if your project owns those resources for the duration. In most organizations, projects only own slices of resource time. Knowing that a certain developer only has four more hours left on your project seems like it might be useful, until you consider that this report does not show you when or for what tasks you need that resource.

Both the Resource reports run the risk of becoming very data dense in the case of a large project with significant resource pools. To overcome this, you can use the Group By drop-down in the Field List panel to group any of the individual report elements by resource group. This summarizes the report data at a higher (resource group) level. This assumes that you previously assigned your resources to a field that properly groups your resources. Figure 20.11 shows a Resource Overview report with too many resources, and Figure 20.12 shows the same report with the resources grouped by a custom field, Resource Classification.

Figure 20.11
Too many resources on the Resource Overview report...

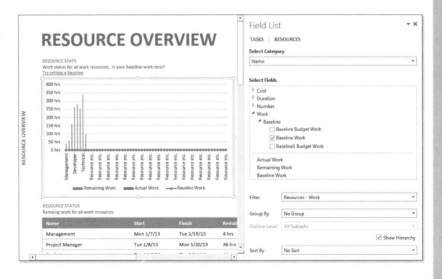

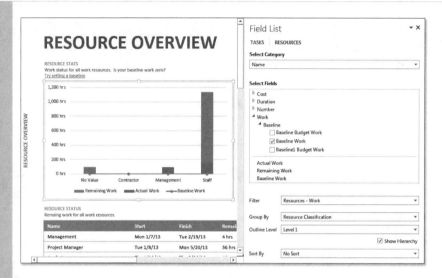

Figure 20.12
...become much
more manageable
when grouped
properly.

Cost Reports Category

The third reports category listed in the View Reports group is the Costs category. Select it, and you see five reports: Cash Flow, Cost Overruns, Earned Value Report, Resource Cost Overview, and Task Cost Overview, as shown in Figure 20.13.

Figure 20.13
The Costs
category
contains
five reports.

The Costs reports category includes five reports designed to provide an extensive assortment of cost data. Cost is one of the more significant factors in project management—that is, keeping cost under control and ensuring that the project finishes within budget. To successfully maintain and control the project's budget, you must accurately track the cost values. Table 20.3 displays all five Costs reports.

Table 20.3   Costs Reports

Report Name	Usage	Baseline Required?
Cash Flow	Shows the amount of money needed each quarter. This report can be useful for sharing with your project sponsor to ensure that the project budget is on track and executing per contract terms.	Yes
Cost Overruns	Shows a high-level summary of variances as compared with your baseline. This is primarily a backward-looking report.	Yes
Earned Value	Data is taken from the Earned Value table to compare each task's earned value (what the task has generated) to the planned value (what it was planned to generate) and actual cost. This is primarily a predictive report, if used correctly.	Yes
Resource Cost Overview	Useful for seeing which resources are costing you the most. This report, like the other resource reports, is probably best used with further modification so that resource groups and not named resources are the subject.	Yes
Task Cost Overview	This report is useful as a gut-check of your projects; considering where you are, do the costs shown look roughly correct or do they depict a growing problem?	Yes

The Cash Flow report gives you an idea of how much money you should anticipate spending each quarter, and the Cost Overruns report, well, gives you the bad news by comparing what you actually spent to what you thought you would spend. The Task Cost Overview report shows you top-level task costs, and the Resource Cost Overview shows you the cost of each of your resources. The Earned Value report is an abbreviated, easy-to-read version of the Earned Value table, displaying actual cost of tasks and the dollar value earned for the cost spent performing the work compared to what was planned. The Earned Value report is discussed in greater detail in this section.

The default Costs reports all require a baseline to be set, because cost variance is the difference between scheduled cost and baseline cost. Therefore, be sure to set the baseline. Furthermore, be sure to enter appropriate resource cost rates for these reports to be accurate. It is recommended that you synchronize the resource cost data with your financial system to ensure that the rates are correct and that the cost used for project invoicing matches that in your project schedule.

➡ *For more information about setting the baseline,* **see** *the "Working with Project Baselines" section on* **p. 432** *in Chapter 13.*

➡ *For more information about entering appropriate resource rates,* **see** *the "Defining Resource Costs" section on* **p. 252** *in Chapter 8.*

Earned Value Report

Earned value analysis is a process first developed by the U.S. Department of Defense to determine what value has been earned to date within the project life cycle as compared to what was expected to be earned to date. The earned value standard is only partially supported by Project. As shown in Figure 20.14, the Earned Value report takes its data from the Earned Value table. It compares the cost of what is being produced or generated with each task to what was planned up to the Current Date (set in the Project Information dialog box).

For the Earned Value report to be valuable, you have to ensure that the project baseline has been captured and all tracking information updated. The reason is that Earned Value data will only be calculated if a baseline has been saved on the project. If a baseline has not been saved, the Earned Value (BCWP) will be blank.

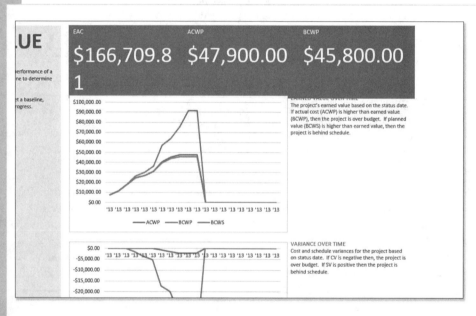

Figure 20.14
The Earned Value report conveys whether each task is earning value at the planned rate.

For more information about using earned value analysis, *see* the "Analyzing Performance with Earned Value Analysis" section on *p. 474* in Chapter 14.

In Progress Reports Category

The fourth and final reports category listed in the View Reports group is the In Progress category. Select it, and you see four reports: Critical Tasks, Late Tasks, Milestone Report, and Slipping Tasks, as shown in Figure 20.15.

Figure 20.15
The In Progress reports category contains four reports and provides assignment-related information from your project schedule.

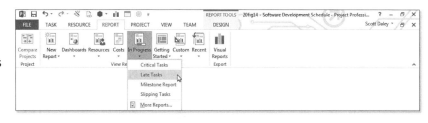

The reports in the In Progress category display various information regarding task progress. Table 20.4 lists the In Progress reports.

Table 20.4 In Progress Reports

Report Name	Usage	Baseline Required?
Critical Tasks	This report shows a list of critical tasks. These may be better seen directly on the Gantt Chart using either the Critical group or by selecting the final task and using the Driving Predecessors option in Task path.	No
Late Tasks	This report may be one of the most usable reports Project offers, if your schedule was built well. This report shows tasks that are on your critical path that are already predicted to delay your project.	No
Milestone Report	This is a useful stakeholder report if your project has a high level set of milestones to report against. For a project analyst, this report is less useful than well-constructed milestone views.	No
Slipping Tasks	Shows tasks where the predicted finish date is later than the baseline finish date. In many project schedules, this will be all the tasks.	Yes

Three of the four reports in this category do not require a baseline, yet they still seem to indicate a comparison to a target date. The question then is, to what date?

Critical Tasks relies on network analysis: What are the tasks that cannot slip without impacting the predicted project end date? The Late Tasks report relies on the Late Tasks filter, which in turn relies on the Late Finish task field. The Late Finish task field contains the latest date that a task can be predicted to finish without impacting the projects' final task delivery date. When the task finish date is later than the Late Finish date, the task is late. Consequently, there is no need for a baseline. The Late Milestones report takes advantage of the same logic. See Figure 20.16 for the exact filter definition.

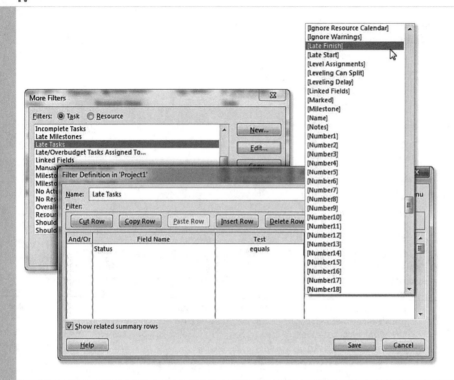

Figure 20.16
The filter defini-
tion for unbase-
lined tasks that
Project still consid-
ers late.

Miscellaneous Category Controls

There are three more category controls in the View Reports group. Getting Started includes a light
tutorial that amounts to little more than a bit of marketing material. Custom is where your custom
reports will be; more on that in the next section. Finally, Recent does just what it says—shows the
most recent six reports you have viewed, as shown in Figure 20.17.

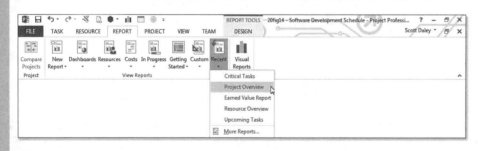

Figure 20.17
The Recent
reports cat-
egory.

Customizing Sections of Reports

Each report is made up of elements that can themselves be customized. This is what provides Project the flexibility to deliver reports to virtually any standard.

There are four primary report elements, each with its own tool tab:

- Text boxes and shapes, with the Drawing Tools tab
- Pictures, with the Picture Tools tab
- Charts, with the Chart Tools tab and two subtabs, Design and Format
- Tables, with the Table tools tab and two subtabs, Design and Layout

Additionally, clicking either a chart or a table opens the Field List panel.

Customizing a Text Box or a Shape

The text box and shape tools should be immediately familiar to any user of PowerPoint or other Office products. Enable the Drawing Tools tab as shown in Figure 20.18 by selecting a text box or shape and clicking on the tab.

Figure 20.18
The Drawing tools tab has only one subtab, Format.

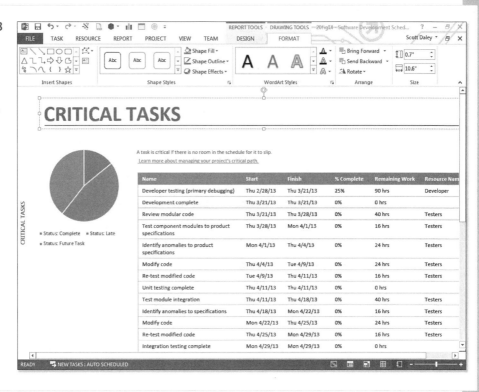

You can use the Insert Shapes group to insert new shapes. If you do add something, it becomes the focus of the Format tab.

Any selected text or Shape element is the focus of the subsequent four groups. Each control is largely a What You See Is You Get function—shape styles make your selected shape look like the selected Shape style, WordArt Styles make your font look like the selected WordArt style, and so forth.

Right-clicking a text box or shape and selecting Format Shape opens the Format Shape panel from the right, which enables still more granular customization of the shape and text box appearances, as shown in Figure 20.19.

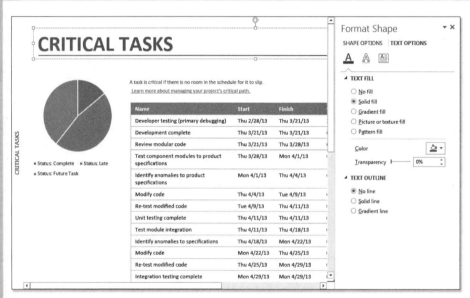

Figure 20.19
The Format Shape panel holds still more options for customization.

As you can see, the potential for customizing text and shapes is virtually unlimited.

Adding or Customizing a Picture

Clicking on the Images control in the Insert group on the Report Tools tab enables you to add any picture you want to a report. This includes logos, screen captures, or anything else, as long as it is in a standard format like JPEG or PNG. Once added, your picture becomes the focus of the toolbar and the Picture Tools tab appears, as shown in Figure 20.20.

As with the Drawing Tools tab, each control should be immediately familiar to users of other Office products. Right-clicking a picture and selecting Format Picture opens the Format Picture panel from the right, as shown in Figure 20.21.

Figure 20.20
The Picture Tools tab has only one subtab, Format.

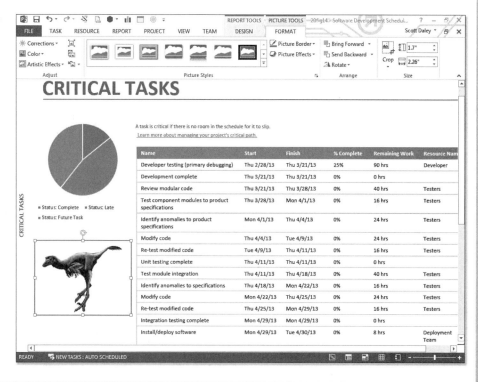

Figure 20.21
The Format Picture panel holds still more options for customization.

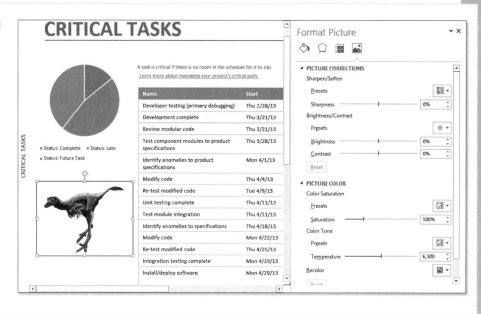

Adding or Customizing a Chart

The Chart tools should be immediately familiar to any user of other Office products. Enable the Chart Tools tab as shown in Figure 20.22 by selecting a chart on a report.

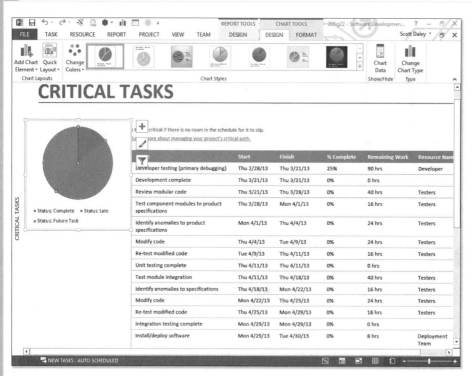

Figure 20.22
The Chart Tools tab has two subtabs, Design and Format.

Charts can also be added to any report by clicking the chart control in the Insert group on the Report Tools tab. Clicking Chart opens the Insert Chart dialog shown in Figure 20.23. Any of the charts can be added to any report, and further customized as described below. Clicking an existing chart on a report and then clicking the Chart control in the Ribbon opens the Change Chart Type dialog, which looks and works almost exactly the same as the Insert Chart dialog.

 tip

To get a better idea of how to assemble reports from scratch, use the default reports as a model.

The options for chart customization are truly intense, and alone could fill several chapters of this book. However, the What You See Is What You Get editor is helpful. Each chart element itself is composed of subelements. Right-click on any part of an inserted chart, whether inserted by you or by default. Select the Format <fill in the blank> option. A context-sensitive right panel opens, providing you options for customizing each subelement of the chart as you click on it. The Axis, Plot Area, Legend, and Chart Area all have unique formatting options, as shown in Figure 20.24.

Figure 20.23
The Insert Chart and
Change Chart dialogs differ
only in title.

Figure 20.24
Right-
clicking and
selecting
Format...
opens a
context-
sensitive
right-panel
for each
selected ele-
ment of a
chart.

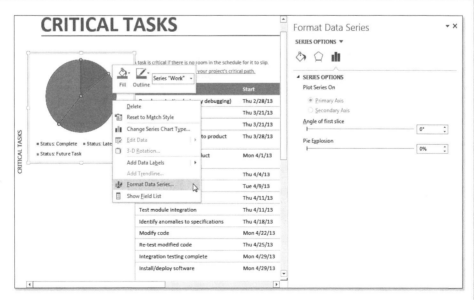

Finally, the field list for a chart can be shown either by right-clicking a chart and selecting Show Field List or by clicking Chart data in the Show/Hide group on the Design subtab of the Chart Tools tab.

Whether your chart actually makes any sense is highly dependent on selecting the right chart type to go with the right data. For example, selecting a line graph makes sense for showing a trend over time, but not for comparing one resource's work to another. That would be better depicted by a bar graph.

The Select Category drop-down determines y-axis for axis charts, and the pie slices for a pie chart. Categories available vary according to each chart type, and vary according to whether you've selected Tasks or Resources.

You have the option of applying any of the default filters, groups, or sorts, or anything you've created using the standard filter, groups, or sorts menu on the View tab. Figure 20.25 shows Field List panel for the Resource Stats chart on the Resource Overview report.

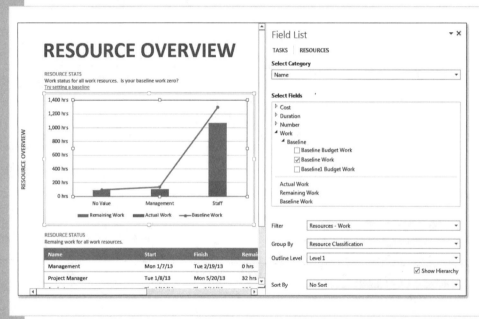

Figure 20.25
The Field List panel allows you to combine all kinds of project data with all kinds of charts—whether it makes sense or not.

The flexibility of the new reports comes with a cost—a possibly overwhelmingly high degree of complexity. However, the What You See Is What You Get environment makes it much easier to experiment and quickly learn how to make charts that look great and show exactly what you need.

Adding or Customizing a Table

The options for customizing tables are still significant but somewhat less in sheer number than the options for customizing charts. Like the other report element tabs, the Table Tools tab should be immediately familiar to any user of other Office products. Enable the Table Tools tab as shown in Figure 20.26 by selecting or inserting a table.

Figure 20.26 The Table Tools tab has two subtabs, Design and Layout.

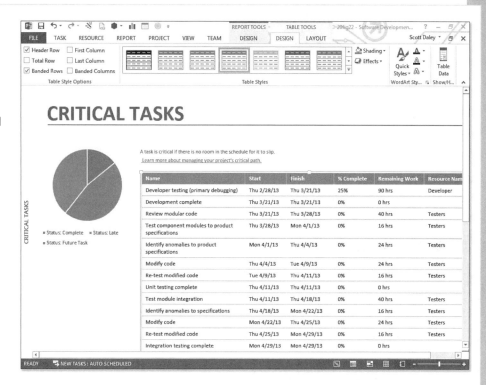

As with charts, the best way to modify table elements is to right-click on the table and select Format Shape. This opens the same Format Shape panel used with text boxes and shapes. The table, columns, rows, and individual cells can be customized by selecting them and making changes in the Format Shape panel, as shown in Figure 20.27. Whole table styles can be applied to the table by selecting them from the Table Styles group on the design subtab of the Table Tools tab.

Finally, the field list for a table can be shown either by right-clicking a table and selecting Show Field List or by clicking Table Data in the Show/Hide group on the Design subtab of the Table Tools tab.

The field list is still highly flexible, but less complicated than the Chart Field List, since it is missing the Category drop-down. Moreover, while it is possible to create a table that doesn't make sense, it's much harder to do and much easier to fix.

Figure 20.27
The Format
Shape panel
allows you
to make
big or small
changes to
your table.

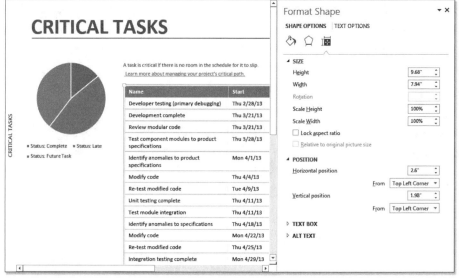

Customizing Reports

Reports are collections of the elements described in the previous section. Obviously, reports in Project 2013 are highly customizable. Similar to views and tables, reports are customized in three different ways, as follows:

- Modifying the existing report

- Creating a copy of an existing report and modifying the copy

- Creating a new report from scratch

All of these customization methods begin in the Report Tools Design tab. To access it, select any report and then click the tab. The Report Tools Design tab is shown in Figure 20.28.

Figure 20.28
The Report Tools
Design tab is your
starting point for
modifying existing
reports or creating
new ones.

The next several sections discuss the three different methods for customizing reports.

Customizing an Existing Report

As discussed in the previous section, all of the reports can be edited in a What You See Is What You Get interface, right on the report itself. Additional elements can be added from the Report Tools Design tab, and each element on the report you click on enables an additional tab. Clicking on a chart enables the Chart Tools tab. Clicking on a table enables the Table Tools tab. Clicking on either also shows the Field List panel. Finally, clicking on a text box or a shape enables the Drawing Tools tab. The Chart Tools tab is shown in Figure 20.29.

The preferred method for customizing an existing report is to copy the original report and then edit the copy. This enables you to retain the original and the modified copy together. This method is discussed in the upcoming section, "Creating a New Report Based on an Existing Report."

To modify an existing report without first making a copy, just make the changes you want. It's that simple.

 tip

There are pros and cons to modifying the existing reports. On the pro side, they continue to appear under the correct category control in the View Reports group, and you might want to make only cosmetic changes. On the con side, you will have lost your original copy of the report.

 note

You do not need to save your changes. They are saved automatically.

Figure 20.29
Any existing reports can be edited right on the spot. Clicking on any element enables the appropriate tab; the Chart Tools tab is shown here.

Creating Reports

Reports are created by copying existing ones and modifying them, or by building them from scratch. The new report appears on the list in the Custom Reports category control, and you can further customize it as you would any other report.

The next two sections describe the process of creating new reports.

Creating a New Report Based on an Existing Report

You will likely find yourself in a situation where there is a report that comes close to meeting your needs, but not completely. One option is to edit that report to your specifications, but the disadvantage to this approach is that you lose the original version when you save the changes.

As an alternative to that, Project allows you to make a copy of the existing report, enabling you to save the existing report and create a new one based on its characteristics. By making a copy of the existing report, you take advantage of its features and create an opportunity to change the aspects that do not meet your requirements.

Follow these steps to create a new report based on an existing report:

1. Open the report by selecting it from the Reports tab.

2. Select the Report Tools tab and click Manage, Rename Report.

3. Enter a new name for your report copy.

tip

If you copy an existing report that is close to what you want, most of the work in creating the report is already done. If none of the existing reports meets your needs, you have to create a new one from scratch (described in the next section).

You are done. If you check under the custom category control, you see your new report, with the name you just gave it (see Figure 20.30).

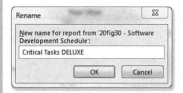

Figure 20.30
Renaming a report in the dialog box creates a copy with the new name.

The preceding procedure describes only how to create the new report from an existing one; instructions for modifying report elements were described earlier in this chapter.

Designing a New Report

Project provides you with four starting points under the New Report category on the Report tab, as shown in Figure 20.31. These are simply starting points; as described earlier, from there you can make whatever changes you want. If none of the existing reports comes close to providing the information you want, you will likely have to create one from scratch. If you want to create a Monthly Calendar report, you must use this method, because there are no existing reports of this type that are available for copying or editing.

Follow these steps to create a new report:

1. Select the Report tab, View Reports Group, New Report.

2. Select one of the four starting templates.

3. Start inserting report elements from the Report Tools Design tab.

Figure 20.31
When designing a new report, you must start from one of these templates.

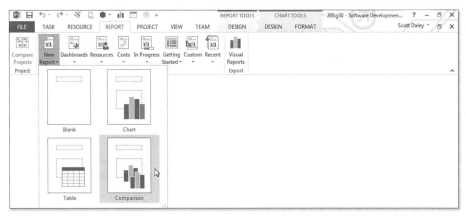

Using the Common Customization Controls

One aspect of the customization process for reports is to alter the format. Specifically, this entails modifying the theme, or the page setup options

Themes

Themes, colors, fonts, and effects are all controlled from the Themes group on the Report Tools Design tab. Themes are bundles of customizations based on colors, fonts, and effects. Once a theme is applied, the individual qualities of the theme can be modified. For example, as shown in Figure 20.32, you can select Colors, More Colors and open the Create New Theme Colors dialog.

Figure 20.32
Theme colors can be customized as you wish.

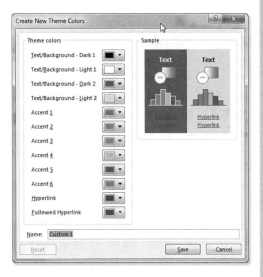

An analogous dialog exists for customizing fonts, but effects are limited to the default choices.

Choosing the Page Setup Options for a Report

The Page Setup group on the Report Tools tab dialog box is where you can change the margins of the report, page orientation, and the page size. By clicking the Page Breaks control, you can see a dynamic dotted line indicating where the page breaks will be as you change the page specifications, as shown in Figure 20.33.

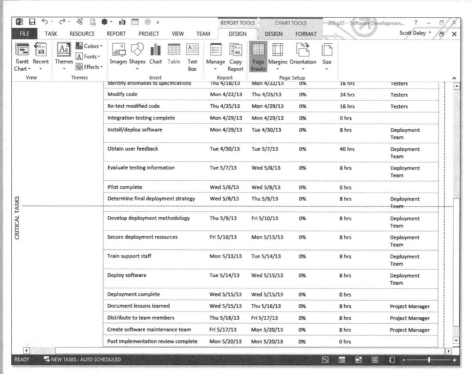

Figure 20.33 Toggle Page Breaks on to see where your printed page breaks will occur based on how you specify your margins, orientation, size, and so on.

Saving and Sharing Custom Reports

Reports you customize or create are automatically saved. However, you must also save your project file before ending your current session; otherwise, you lose the customized report (and any other work you did in that session).

There is no option to save the results of the reports, unless you create a separate file using the Create PDF/XPF under File, Export. You can also of course print reports to share them with other project stakeholders or your project team under File, Print.

It is also possible (and recommended) to make custom report definitions available to use in all your project files or share with other people working with the same project. To do so, use the Organizer to copy the reports from your project file into the Global.MPT file. You can access the Organizer from the Report Tools tab; select Report Group, Manage, and click Organizer. The Organizer appears, as shown in Figure 20.34.

Figure 20.34
Use the Organizer to copy custom reports from your project file to the Global.MPT file, or import reports from the Global.MPT file to a new project file.

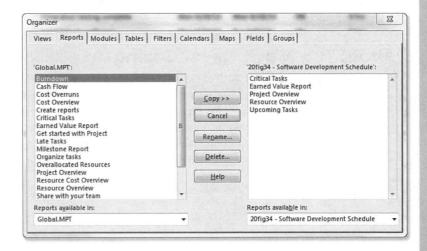

To copy reports from your project file, select them from the list on the right and then click the Copy button, as indicated in Figure 20.34. The same process works for importing reports from the Global.MPT file: Select the report from the list on the left and click the Copy button to copy it into your project file. You can also delete or rename reports in the Organizer by selecting a report and clicking the Delete button or Rename button. The various tabs on the Organizer open other areas of the project (such as Tables, Views, and so on).

➡ For additional information on Global.MPT and the Organizer, *see* Chapter 18, *"Managing Project Files Locally and in the Cloud," **p. 549**.*

Consultants' Tips

Reporting is an enormous topic. There are many good consultants that have justifiably concluded that reports are all that matters; the right report necessitates everything else. The new reports in Project enable project managers to make fewer limitation-driven compromises, and work instead toward a balance between stakeholder pandering and excessive detail.

Right Report for the Right Audience

Most of the people interested in your project are not used to looking at or interpreting Gantt Charts. Because these kinds of project artifacts are so familiar to project managers, they often forget how alien they are to people from other disciplines. Your project's stakeholders usually want to see the information summarized in a simple, visually appealing way that doesn't make them work too hard. Project's new reporting functionality enables you to present exactly what you need to in a way you can control minutely for maximum effect.

Avoid Too Much Navel Gazing

The new reports in Project 2013 are incredibly flexible, and Microsoft has done a terrific job making a complex option set accessible. However, while the new reporting tools make it much, much easier to learn how to make amazing reports, they also create the danger of spending too much time creating amazing reports. It's easy for a project manager to spend days endlessly tweaking report settings, "improving" reports, making them more attractive, more pertinent, more readable, and so on. In the end, however, reports are tools for managing stakeholders and delivering projects.

21

REPORTS PART II: VISUAL REPORTS

Visual reports are intended for export to Excel and Visio. Excel and Visio both are extremely useful tools for analysis, and of course, some project stakeholders prefer data formatted in Office applications. Visual reports are fully customizable and can be created from scratch.

This chapter discusses how to fully utilize Project's visual report templates, how to customize them to work best for you, and how to create new visual reports from scratch.

You might be wondering why you would want to use a visual report since the standard reports in Project 2013 are so versatile and attractive. As is often the case with Microsoft products, it boils down to using the right tool for the job. Visual reports provide a convenient and robust export method for project data into tools that you may be more familiar with and that are certainly more flexible.

 note

The screenshots and instructions in this chapter for Excel and Visio refer to the 2013 versions. Project 2013 is compatible with either the 2010 or the 2013 versions of Excel and Visio.

 tip

For the maximum result of clarity and professionalism in your reporting, present the source data table in your visual reports. That way, you can present your data and back it up visually with a visual report, doubling the impact of your reporting presentation.

➡ For more information about customizing and creating basic reports, as well as complete tables listing the basic reports found in each category, **see** Chapter 20, "Reports Part I: 2013 Reports," **p. 625**.

➡ *For more information about using basic and visual reports for tracking and reporting to specific audiences, see Chapter 15, "Using Reports for Tracking and Control," p. 497.*

The existing visual report templates in Project can be accessed by opening the Visual Reports – Create Report dialog box. To open the Visual Reports – Create Report dialog box, select the Report tab, Export, Visual Reports. The Visual Reports – Create Report dialog box appears, as shown in Figure 21.1.

The Visual Reports – Create Report dialog box houses 22 visual report templates, contained in seven tabs: Task Usage, Resource Usage, Assignment Usage, Task Summary, Resource Summary, Assignment Summary, and All. The 22 visual reports are divided among the first six tabs, whereas the All tab holds all 22 visual reports. Therefore, each report can be accessed from two locations: once from one of the first six tabs, and again from the All tab.

 note

You will not see Visio-based reports if you do not have Visio installed.

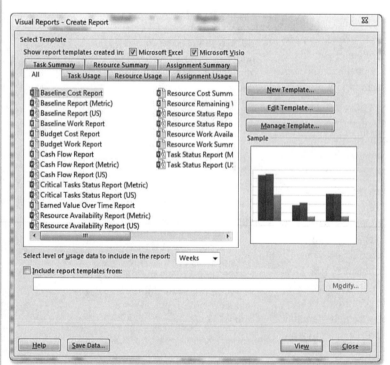

Figure 21.1
The Visual Reports – Create Report dialog box contains existing visual report templates.

You can generate visual reports in one of two formats: Excel or Visio. Notice in Figure 21.1 that some reports have the Excel icon next to them, and others have the Visio icon, representing in which tool the report is created. Each of the formats is discussed in more detail later in this chapter.

Table 21.1 lists all 22 existing visual reports, which tab they are found under, their type (Excel or Visio), and a brief description of the report data. To view a visual report, double-click on it, or select it and click View.

Table 21.1 The Existing Visual Report Templates in Project

Visual Report	Tab Location (Besides the All Tab)	Report Type Name (Excel or Visio)	Brief Description
Baseline Cost Report	Assignment Usage	Excel	A bar graph that displays baseline cost, planned cost, and actual cost for tasks (can be drilled down to project, phase, or subtask level).
Baseline Report (Metric)	Assignment Usage	Visio	A diagram that compares planned work and cost to baseline work and cost, broken down by quarter and then by task. Indicators show when planned data surpasses baseline data. Units use the metric system of measurement.
Baseline Report (US)	Assignment Usage	Visio	A diagram that compares planned work and cost to baseline work and cost, broken down by quarter and then by task. Indicators show when planned data surpasses baseline data. Units use the U.S. system of measurement.
Baseline Work Report	Assignment Usage	Excel	A bar graph that displays baseline work, planned work, and actual work for tasks (can be drilled down to project, phase, or sub-task level).
Budget Cost Report	Assignment Usage	Excel	A bar graph that displays budget cost, baseline cost, planned cost, and actual cost over time.
Budget Work Report	Assignment Usage	Excel	A bar graph that displays budget work, baseline work, planned work, and actual cost over time.

Visual Report	Tab Location (Besides the All Tab)	Report Type Name (Excel or Visio)	Brief Description
Cash Flow Report	Task Usage	Excel	A bar graph with cost and cumulative cost displayed over time.
Cash Flow Report (Metric)	Resource Usage	Visio	A diagram that shows planned and actual costs over time, broken down by resource type (work, material, or cost), with indicators if planned costs exceed baseline costs. Units use the metric system of measurement.
Cash Flow Report (US)	Resource Usage	Visio	A diagram that shows planned and actual costs over time, broken down by resource type (work, material, or cost), with indicators if planned costs exceed baseline costs. Units use the U.S. system of measurement.
Critical Tasks Status Report (Metric)	Task Summary	Visio	A diagram that shows work and remaining work for both critical and noncritical tasks. A data bar shows the work percentage complete. Critical tasks are separated from the noncritical tasks. Units use the metric system of measurement.
Critical Tasks Status Report (US)	Task Summary	Visio	A diagram that shows work and remaining work for both critical and noncritical tasks. A data bar shows the work percentage complete. Critical tasks are separated from the noncritical tasks. Units use the U.S. system of measurement.
Earned Value Over Time Report	Task Usage	Excel	Displays actual cost, planned value, and earned value over time.

Visual Report	Tab Location (Besides the All Tab)	Report Type Name (Excel or Visio)	Brief Description
Resource Availability Report (Metric)	Resource Usage	Visio	A diagram that shows work and remaining availability for each resource. Resources are separated by type (cost, work, and material). Units use the metric system of measurement.
Resource Availability Report (US)	Resource Usage	Visio	A diagram that shows work and remaining availability for each resource. Resources are separated by type (cost, work, and material). Units use the U.S. system of measurement.
Resource Cost Summary Report	Resource Usage	Excel	A pie chart that displays the division of resource cost between the three resource types (work, material, and cost).
Resource Remaining Work Report	Resource Summary	Excel	A bar graph that displays remaining work and actual work for each work resource.
Resource Status Report (Metric)	Assignment Summary	Visio	A diagram showing the work and cost values for each resource. The percentage of work complete is indicated by the shading in each box on the diagram, getting darker as the resource approaches completion of his or her assignments. Units use the metric system of measurement.
Resource Status Report (US)	Assignment Summary	Visio	A diagram showing the work and cost values for each resource. The percentage of work complete is indicated by the shading in each box on the diagram, getting darker as the resource approaches completion of his or her assignments. Units use the U.S. system of measurement.

Visual Report	Tab Location (Besides the All Tab)	Report Type Name (Excel or Visio)	Brief Description
Resource Work Availability Report	Resource Usage	Excel	A bar graph that displays total work availability, work, and remaining availability over time for work resources.
Resource Work Summary Report	Resource Usage	Excel	A bar graph that displays total work availability, work, remaining availability, and actual work for work resources.
Task Status Report (Metric)	Task Summary	Visio	A diagram showing tasks' work and percentage of work complete. Indicators show when work surpasses baseline work, when work equals baseline work, and when baseline work surpasses work. Units use the metric system of measurement.
Task Status Report (US)	Task Summary	Visio	A diagram showing tasks' work and percentage of work complete. Indicators show when work surpasses baseline work, when work equals baseline work, and when baseline work surpasses work. Units use the U.S. system of measurement.

Understanding OLAP Cubes for Visual Reports

OLAP (OnLine Analytical Processing) cubes are specially constructed databases. Normal databases are organized to reduce the space the data they contain takes up. Normal databases (or normalized databases) trade off performance for storage. OLAP databases are not so much concerned with reducing storage as they are concerned with organizing data for fast finding and fast retrieval (in support of dynamic and immediate data analysis needs). The information is organized in a single table and cross-indexed across all attributes so that a query's data results can be immediately presented rather than spending precious time searching through, organizing, and aggregating linked information. OLAP databases are referred to as *OLAP cubes* to reflect the mental picture of an analyst looking at the data first in one way, on one side of a cube, and then another—tipping the cube in various ways to examine different attributes and angles on the data. The term *cubes* also reminds you that many more dimensions are possible than the two dimensions usually considered in flat reports and spreadsheets.

Visual reports are built on a local OLAP cube (a file ending in .cub and containing the OLAP database). It is called a *local* cube because it is physically located on your local machine, rather than being served out to you from a remote database server machine. You can save this cube in your project file or export it to use elsewhere (see the section "Sharing and Saving Visual Reports" later this chapter). The data found in a visual report comes from the Project file database. From that project data, a local OLAP cube is built, which is then attached to a PivotTable and PivotChart in Excel, or a PivotDiagram in Visio (see the next section, "Understanding Excel and Visio in Relation to Project").

The 22 existing visual report templates have already been constructed. Later sections in this chapter describe how to customize these templates to better suit your needs.

 tip

You can choose not to use a template, meaning that you want to create a new visual report data query and presentation view from scratch. To create a visual report from scratch, you must first define the OLAP cube dimensions. This process is also discussed later in this chapter, in the "Reporting Capabilities" section.

Understanding Excel and Visio in Relation to Project

Because visual reports are created using either Excel or Visio, it is important to have an understanding of each of these tools, and how they are used to create and customize visual reports in Project.

Many project managers have little to no experience with Visio, and their experience in Excel is often not much more than data entry on a spreadsheet. This chapter assumes that your experience with these two tools is limited. Regardless of your skill level with Excel or Visio, this chapter provides enough detailed information that you can comfortably use them while working with visual reports. However, it is important to note that by no means does the information in this chapter give you thorough instructions on how to fully use Excel or Visio.

In other words, this chapter touches on some of the concepts that will aid you in creating successful visual reports but does not go into great detail about either Excel or Visio beyond the purposes relevant to this chapter.

 note

For a much more detailed guide to these two Microsoft Office tools, consult outside sources or other manuals written about them.

Using Excel While Working with Visual Reports

Ten of the preexisting visual report templates are Excel reports. Each Excel report includes two sheets: the PivotTable and the PivotChart. The PivotTable is essentially the data, which comes from the project file database, displayed in an Excel spreadsheet. A PivotTable has more functionality than just a sequence of rows because the data rows are listed and aggregated, enabling you to expand or collapse groups of data in the PivotTable.

The PivotChart is the visual graph or chart that illustrates the same data. A PivotChart is always associated with a PivotTable, and when you expand/collapse entries in one or the other, the action is automatically reflected in the linked partner.

 tip

Keep in mind that the PivotTable associated with a PivotChart might not be shown by default.

For example, the Baseline Cost Report is the first report listed in the All tab of the Visual Reports – Create Report dialog box. It is an Excel report. To open it, double-click on its name in the Visual Reports – Create Report dialog box, or click it once and then click View. The Baseline Cost Report is displayed, as shown in Figure 21.2.

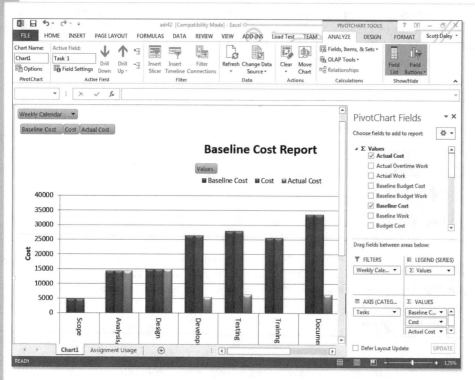

Figure 21.2
The Baseline Cost Report is an Excel report that displays Baseline Cost, Cost, and Actual Cost data.

When you open the Baseline Cost Report, the screen displays the PivotChart, or the graph, as shown in Figure 21.2. At the bottom-right corner is a scale you can use to enlarge or decrease the size of the PivotChart on your screen.

At the top of the screen, above the graph, is the familiar Office Ribbon. Click the PivotChart Tools tab.

This area provides several customization options for the PivotChart, which are discussed in greater detail later in this chapter. For now, it is important to grasp the functionality of the PivotChart

Tools section. There are three main groups in Excel 2013: Analyze, Design, and Format. If you click on any of these tabs, all your customization options for that particular tab are displayed below the toolbar. In Figure 21.2, the Design tab is selected, and all the design options are displayed underneath it.

At the bottom-left corner of the screen are three folder tabs: Chart1, Assignment Usage, and a tab to open a new sheet (refer to Figure 21.2). In Figure 21.2, the Chart1 tab is selected, meaning the screen is displaying the PivotChart. If you click on the Assignment Usage folder tab, the screen displays the PivotTable for the particular report. In this case, since the Baseline Cost Report is in the Assignment Usage category, the PivotTable is called Assignment Usage.

Figure 21.3 illustrates the PivotTable of the Baseline Cost Report, which is displayed by clicking the Assignment Usage sheet tab at the bottom-left corner of the screen.

The PivotTable screen might be more familiar to project managers with some experience in Excel. It is set up as an Excel spreadsheet, with rows and columns of information. Notice the scale at the bottom-right corner, as well as the sheet tabs in the bottom-left corner.

 note
Excel 2013 and Excel 2010 differ substantially in their presentation of PivotChart functionality, but do not differ much in the functionality itself.

 note
If you hide the PivotChart Ribbon, the tabs will still be displayed along the top of the screen. You can click on any of the tabs to display their customization options, and then repin the Ribbon if needed

Like the PivotChart, several tabs along the top of the screen hold various customization options. You can choose to display the tab details by clicking PivotTable Tools at the top, or hide them by right-clicking along the tabs and selecting Minimize the Ribbon. In Figure 21.3, the option for minimizing the Ribbon is displayed by right-clicking where the mouse is located.

PivotTables provide dynamic views that enable you to analyze project data by sorting, grouping, filtering, and pivoting. You can add or remove data fields to include in a report, and drill down into the report data. Notice in Figure 21.3 there are plus signs (+) next to the tasks in column B. In this illustration, only the phases (summary-level tasks) are listed down this column. However, you can choose to expand some or all of the summary tasks to show data at the subtask level by clicking on the plus sign and expanding the list. Because the PivotTable and PivotChart display the same data, the graph in the PivotChart also expands to show report data at the task level.

Similarly, you can collapse the data from the phase level to project level by clicking the minus sign (−) next to the project summary task in column A. The PivotTable collapses to show data at the project level, as does the graph in the PivotChart.

In Figure 21.4, the PivotTable has been collapsed to show data at the project level. The graph has been copied and pasted underneath the PivotTable to view both at the same time. You can see that the graph displays only one bar for each item in the PivotTable (Baseline Cost, Cost, and Actual Cost). Whereas in Figures 21.2 and 21.3, the data in the graph and PivotTable was drilled down to the phase level, in Figure 21.4 it is displayed at the project level.

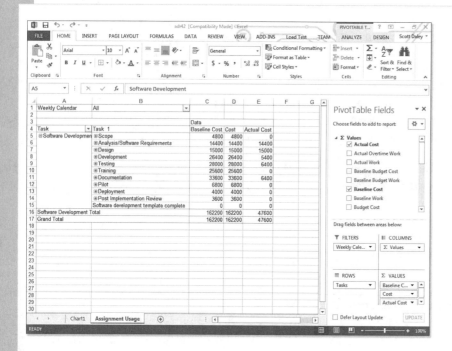

Figure 21.3
The Assignment Usage sheet displays the PivotTable for the Baseline Cost Report.

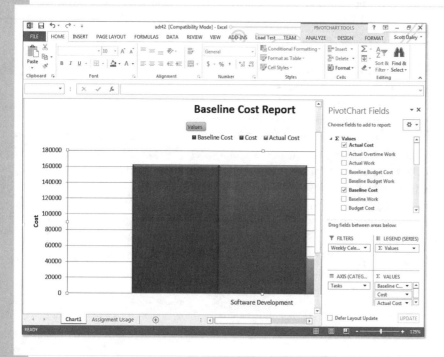

Figure 21.4
Collapse or expand the data in a PivotTable, and the graph adjusts to match your definition.

tip

It might be helpful for you to copy and paste the graph into the PivotTable screen. That way, you can view both simultaneously without having to switch back and forth on the folder tabs. To do so, select the graph in the PivotChart, copy it (Ctrl+C), switch to the PivotTable tab, and paste it (Ctrl+V) under or on top of the PivotTable.

Use Screentips to your advantage when working with PivotCharts and PivotTables. Hover your mouse pointer over a button, tab, or cell, and a Screentip appears, describing the feature, function, or cell contents. Screentips are also displayed for the chart view of the visual reports.

Adding and Removing Data Fields from PivotTables

To add or remove data fields from a report, use the PivotTable Field List. To display the PivotTable Field List, right-click on the PivotTable, and choose Show Field List. Alternatively, you can select the Options tab along the top of the screen and select Field List in the Show/Hide heading. If you are on the PivotChart screen, select the Analyze tab and click on Field List in the Show/Hide heading.

Figures 21.2, 21.3, and 21.4 all have PivotChart Fields displayed on the right side of the screen. Figure 21.5 shows how to display the PivotChart Fields using the Options tab of the PivotTable Tools menu.

The first heading in the PivotChart Fields is Choose Fields to Add to Report. To add a field, select the box next to the field name, or clear the check mark from any fields you want to remove from the report. The rest of the PivotChart Fields pane areas are discussed later in this chapter; the upcoming section "Customizing Excel Visual Reports" goes into greater detail about the specific features you can use in PivotTables and PivotCharts to customize your visual reports or create new ones.

Figure 21.5
Add or remove data fields in a visual report by using the PivotTable Field List, which you can choose to show or hide on the Options tab.

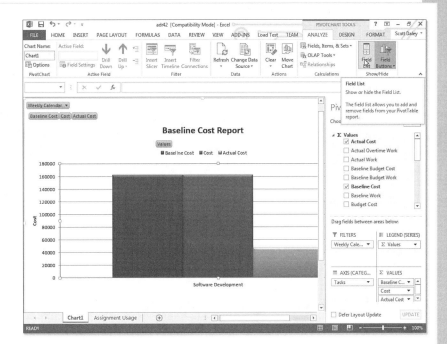

Using Visio While Working with Visual Reports

Six of the visual report templates are Visio reports, and each one has a U.S. measurement and a metric measurement system version, making for a total of 12 Visio reports.

Visio reports are composed in PivotDiagrams. A PivotDiagram is an assortment of shapes assembled in a tree structure, creating a visual format to help you summarize and analyze data. These shapes are also called *nodes*. A PivotDiagram begins with one node, called the *top node*, which is broken down into lower, subnode levels that specify aspects of the top node. For instance, a top node could be a project summary task, the next level could be the subtasks, and each subtask node can hold another level of summary tasks.

Figure 21.6 shows the Task Status Report (US), where the top node represents the entire project. The next level lists the phases, or summary tasks, of the project. The section "Customizing Visio Visual Reports" later this chapter, discusses how to drill into the data even further to display the subtask level.

Like Excel, Visio provides the capability to add or remove data fields from the report. You can also add shapes to certain nodes to represent information about the particular node's data, such as how a task is operating compared to the baseline.

A more detailed discussion on customizing Visio visual reports can be found later in this chapter; see the section "Customizing Visio Visual Reports."

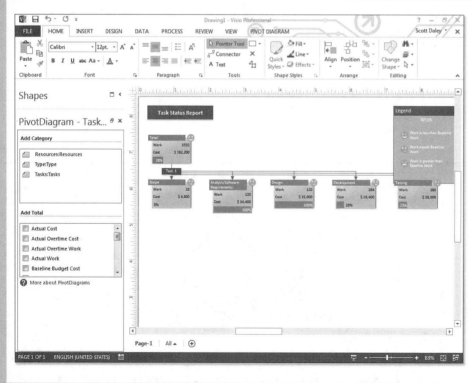

Figure 21.6
The Task Status Report (US) is a Visio report, with data displayed in a PivotDiagram.

Reporting Capabilities

Many customization options for visual reports are available that you can use to sculpt an existing template into something much more suited for your reporting purposes. In Excel, you can modify the data fields to include in a report, drill down to specific levels in the data, and completely rework the appearance of the graph in the PivotChart. In Visio, you can modify the data in the report, as well as change the look and feel of the PivotDiagram. Customizing the content and appearance of visual reports can help make them more comprehendible and visually appealing to both you and the audience you are reporting to.

Furthermore, if none of the existing visual report templates comes close to meeting your criteria for a visual report, you can create a new one from scratch.

 *For more information about customizing existing basic reports and creating new reports, **see** Chapter 20, "Reports Part I: 2013 Reports," **p. 625**.*

The following sections describe in detail the processes used to customize existing Excel and Visio visual reports, as well as create new visual reports.

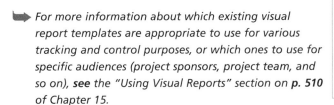 *For more information about which existing visual report templates are appropriate to use for various tracking and control purposes, or which ones to use for specific audiences (project sponsors, project team, and so on), **see** the "Using Visual Reports" section on **p. 510** of Chapter 15.*

> **note**
>
> The upcoming sections describe the theory and processes associated with customizing and creating visual reports in general. Data content in the forthcoming examples is irrelevant.

Customizing Excel Visual Reports

Excel visual reports are extremely versatile in their customization options. This section first discusses how to edit or customize the data within a report, and then how to customize the appearance of the report.

Customizing Data in an Excel Visual Report

Three major steps are involved in editing the data found in an Excel visual report. The first two are done before you actually open the report, and the third is done within the PivotTable screen. You might find that you need to use all three methods to fully achieve what you are after.

Inserting and Removing Fields   The first step is to use the Visual Reports – Field Picker dialog box to insert or remove fields to include in your report. To open it, first open the Visual Reports – Create Report dialog box (Report tab, Visual Reports). Refer to Figure 21.1. Then, click the report you want to customize and click the Edit Template button. The Visual Reports – Field Picker dialog box appears, as shown in Figure 21.7.

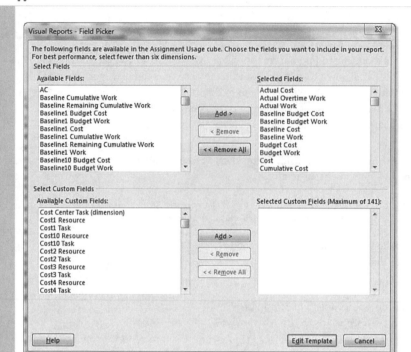

Figure 21.7
Edit the contents of a visual report in the Visual Reports – Field Picker dialog box.

As illustrated in Figure 21.7, the Visual Reports – Field Picker dialog box has two areas: Select Fields and Select Custom Fields. In the Select Fields section, at the top, are two headings. The first heading is Available Fields, which lists all the available Project predefined fields you can insert for use in your report. To select a field for your report, click on it in the Available Fields list and then click the Add button. The field disappears from the Available Fields list and appears in the Selected Fields list on the right.

Working with Selected Fields The Selected Fields column lists all fields selected to be included on the PivotChart Fields. Fields found in the Selected Fields list are not automatically included in the report; you must select them again from the PivotChart Fields to actually include their data in your report.

 tip

In the Visual Reports – Create Report dialog box, you can choose to display only Excel reports or only Visio reports by selecting the boxes underneath the Show Report Templates Created In heading at the top of the dialog box. This might make it easier to decide which report you want to edit.

This mechanism is intended to enable you to preselect a set of fields that could be valid for inclusion in the report. You can opt to remove a field from the PivotChart Fields List if you know that you will not use it. To do so, select it from the Selected Fields list and click the Remove button. The removed field now appears highlighted on the Available fields list. Because it is highlighted, it is still selected, so if you removed it from the Selected Fields list by mistake, just click Add and the field will be returned to the Selected Fields list.

You can also remove all the fields from the Selected Fields list by clicking the Remove All button. This clears the Selected Fields list, so you can start over with exactly the fields you want to be able to include in your report. However, if you click the Remove All button by mistake, all the removed fields remain highlighted in the Available Fields list, and you can undo the action by clicking the Add button immediately after, returning them to the Selected Fields list.

 note

Select only the fields you will need. It will be easier to work with a small set when you build your report.

Notice that some of the fields listed in the Visual Reports – Field Picker dialog box have the word *dimension* next to them in parentheses (see Figure 21.7). This indicates that the particular field represents a major category in the OLAP cube; it is a significant field in report data and analysis.

The bottom half of the Visual Reports – Field Picker dialog box functions the same as the top half but is dedicated to custom fields only.

 caution

It is important to select no more than six dimension fields for your report. Selecting more than six dimensions significantly increases the amount of data and complexity of the PivotTable and therefore decreases the performance and usability of your report.

> *For more information about creating and modifying custom fields,* **see** *the "Creating and Customizing Fields" section on* **p. 745** *of Chapter 22.*

When you are finished selecting or removing fields from the Visual Reports – Field Picker dialog box, click Edit Template to close the box and apply your changes. To close the box without changing anything, click Cancel.

Define the Time Period   After you have selected the fields to include in your report's PivotTable Field List, it is time to define the time period of the report. This is the second of the three major steps of editing the data in a visual report.

 note

The Selected Custom Fields list has a maximum limit of 141 custom fields.

In the Visual Reports – Create Report dialog box, underneath the list of existing report templates, you see the heading Select Level of Usage Data to Include in the Report, followed by a drop-down list. The drop-down list contains the following options: Years, Quarters, Months, Weeks, and Days. Select from one of these five options to define the level of information to drill down into your report. By default, Project selects the level most appropriate for that particular report. If Weeks is selected, you can drill into the report to view weekly data.

 note

Defining the time period of the report is the second of the three major steps of editing the visual report.

 note

Not all fields are available in both Excel and Visio reports. Some fields are only available in one or the other. Furthermore, if you are unable to locate a field you want to include in your report, it might be stored in a different data category.

For example, some fields you might think of as Task Summary fields are actually Assignment Summary fields. If you cannot find a particular field from a report under the Task Summary tab of the Visual Reports – Create Report dialog box, try to look at reports under the Assignment Summary tab.

For instance, the Earned Value Over Time Report shows Earned Value, Planned Value, and Actual Cost data over time. If you select Weeks from the level of usage data drop-down, you can drill into the data to weekly information. However, if you select Days, you can drill even further, into daily information. This does not mean that you *have* to display daily information; you can still show Earned Value data for the quarter or year. But, if you select Days, you have the capability of drilling down to daily information. Therefore, it is recommended that you select a smaller time unit, such as Weeks or Days, if you plan on drilling into that data. If not, it is recommended that you select a larger time unit, such as Quarters or Years.

To define the time unit for your report, first click on the report in the Visual Reports – Create Report dialog box and then make your selection from the drop-down list.

Customizing the PivotTable   The third step in editing the data in your report is performed in the PivotTable. To access it, open the report by double-clicking on it or clicking it once and then clicking View in the Visual Reports – Create Report dialog box. The report will then be displayed.

For this discussion, the Baseline Cost Report is used. Figure 21.8 shows the PivotTable for the Baseline Cost Report, with the graph copied and pasted underneath.

A previous section in this chapter, "Using Excel While Working with Visual Reports," briefly described how you can drill into data by collapsing or expanding the information on the PivotTable. Click the plus sign (+) to expand the data, and the minus sign (−) to collapse it. The graph adjusts itself to match your choices. For example, notice in Figure 21.8 that the second quarter for 2013 (Q2) has been expanded to show weekly data. The PivotTable shows the weekly data for Q2, as does the graph.

The PivotChart Fields was also mentioned previously. Items selected in the PivotTable Field List appear as field data in the PivotTable and on the graph. In Figure 21.8, Actual Cost, Baseline Cost, and Cost are selected, and thus appear as field data in the report. Budget Cost is by default selected for this particular report, but has been cleared and thus removed from the report.

All the data field options listed in the PivotTable Field List are taken directly from the Selected Fields and Selected Custom Fields lists in the Visual Reports – Field Picker dialog box, discussed earlier in this section.

In the bottom half of the PivotTable, underneath the Choose Fields to Add to Report area, are four other areas: Report Filter, Legend (Series), Axis (Categories), and Values. Drag fields into the Report Filter section to filter for any attributes before inserting the data into the PivotTable. You can add fields as column information by dragging and dropping them

note

The level you choose impacts the performance and complexity of the report. Lower levels increase the amount of data presented by the report (reducing performance). Lower levels might also present too much detail, confusing your audience or focusing their attention on a level of detail that detracts from the main point of the report.

note

Organizing the filtering, layout, and presentation of the report is the last of the three major steps of editing the visual report.

note

You must define the Selected Fields list and the time unit level (as discussed earlier in this section) before opening the visual report to edit. Otherwise, those definitions will not be included in the visual report.

Figure 21.8
Make data modifications to an Excel visual report in the PivotTable. In this case, the Baseline Cost Report is being edited.

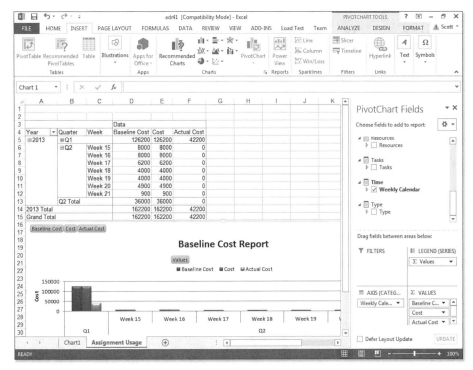

into the Column Labels box (sometimes called the Legend Fields box on the PivotChart screen), or as row information in the Row Labels box (or the Axis Fields box on the PivotChart screen). The Values box can hold any of the value fields from the PivotTable Field List; drag and drop them into this box or place check marks in their corresponding boxes.

You can make changes to the PivotTable by dragging and dropping fields from the Field List into or between these areas or to location-sensitive areas in the PivotTable itself.

Underneath these four areas is the option Defer Layout Update. Select this box if you want to make changes to the PivotTable but do not want the changes to happen immediately. To defer the update of the PivotTable, select this box, make your changes, and when you are ready to update the PivotTable, click Update.

At the top of the PivotTable Field List is a button with a drop-down list that enables you to choose the layout of the PivotTable Field List. Click the button, and your layout options appear, as shown in Figure 21.9.

 note

You can get comfortable with the location-sensitive areas in the PivotTable by dragging fields from the Field List directly to a location-sensitive area in the PivotTable and seeing where the field shows up in the four quadrants at the bottom of the Pivot Table Field List pane.

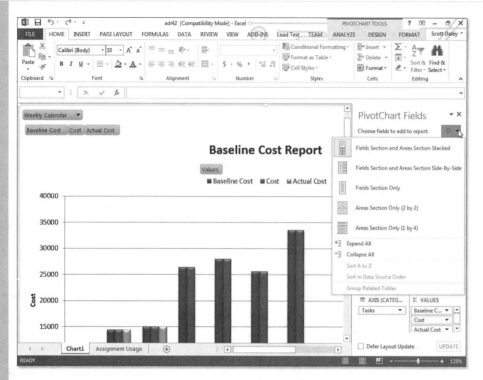

Figure 21.9
Choose
the layout
of the
PivotChart
Fields from
the drop-
down list
at the top
of the Field
List box.

In the PivotTable itself, you can also make adjustments using the drop-down arrows that appear in some of the cells. For example, in Figure 21.8, next to the Word Year is a drop-down that will open a filter, allowing you to select the time frame for your report. In other words, in this example, the data is filtered to include only 2013. If you click that drop-down arrow, you can expand or narrow the filter.

For example, in Figure 21.10, the PivotTable has been selected to filter for only tasks in the Scope phase of the project. You can select the box next to Select Multiple Items to filter for more than one phase or task. When you have made your selection, click OK, and the PivotTable only displays data for what you selected.

The same concept applies to the drop-down list in the Year cell. Select it and choose which year to display data for, or drill into each year and choose the quarter or week.

If you are viewing the PivotChart screen, you can display the PivotTable Field List, and drag and drop data fields directly from the PivotTable Field List into the PivotChart. They will then be included in the chart, and thus the report.

**Figure
21.10**
Choose
specific task
levels to
filter for by
clicking the
drop-down
arrow at
the top
of the
PivotTable.
In this
case, only
Baseline
Cost data
for the
Scope
phase level
has been
displayed.

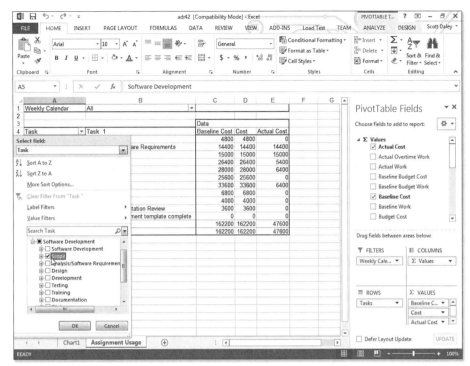

Customizing the Appearance of an Excel Visual Report

Like modifying the data of a visual report, the appearance of an Excel visual report can be altered significantly. There are many reasons why you might want to spend time modifying your visual report. The graphs in the PivotChart screen at first appear simple when compared to a graph with a few basic modifications. Therefore, improving the appearance of your visual report makes it more professional looking and impressive.

 tip

Incorporate organizational presentation standards when generating your reports. Many clients, team members, or other project stakeholders will react more positively to a report that appears in a standard corporate format or that just appears more polished than what they are accustomed to. On the other hand, spending too much time on the appearance of a report can overshadow the data it holds. Find a comfortable compromise between style and necessity. With a few simple touches, you can make your report stand out much better than originally designed.

Another reason to modify the appearance of an Excel visual report is to clarify or better emphasize the data. Perhaps you feel a column will make the report easier to understand than a line graph or pie chart. Excel reports enable you to choose different visual representations of the data in the report. Experiment to find what works best for you and be consistent in your reporting techniques for best results.

Customizing the Appearance of Chart Types   The Cash Flow Report is an Excel visual report that displays Cost as columns and Cumulative Cost as a line over time. You can change not only the appearance of this data (from a line to a column, and so on), but you can also change the appearance of the chart types (columns or lines) themselves.

For instance, perhaps you do not like having columns and lines on the same graph. You could opt to display Cumulative Cost as a column rather than a line. To do so, right-click on Cumulative Cost in the legend, or on the line itself, and choose Change Chart Type from the list options. This opens the Change Chart Type dialog box, as shown in Figure 21.11.

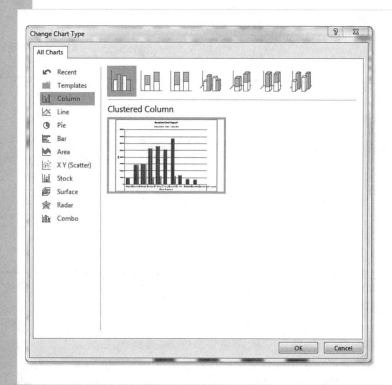

Figure 21.11
Select the type of line, bar, column, or other chart type for your data in the Change Chart Type dialog box.

In the Change Chart Type dialog box, you can choose from Column, Line, Pie, Bar, Area, X Y (Scatter), Stock, Surface, Radar, and Combo chart types, as well as from a template, for your chart data. In this case, because the Cost data is displayed as a column, you might also want to choose one of the Column options for the Cumulative Cost data as well.

Figure 21.12 shows what the Cash Flow report looks like if you change the original line chart type for Cumulative Cost to the first Column option in the Change Chart Type dialog box.

You can change the chart type in any of the Excel PivotChart visual reports by following the same process:

1. Right-click on the chart type you want to change and choose Change Chart Type. This opens the Change Chart Type dialog box.

2. In the Change Chart Type dialog box, choose from the many different options for each chart type.

3. When you have made your selection, click OK to apply the change and close the dialog box.

Figure 21.12 Changing the Cumulative Cost data from a line to a column might improve the clarity of the data in your report.

After you have chosen the chart types to visually represent your data, you can make further modifications to the chart types themselves. In Figure 21.11, you probably noticed that there are many options for each chart type. For example, there are seven different Column options.

Some of the chart types, such as the XY (Scatter) chart and the Stock chart, are not compatible with PivotTable based data. If you choose one of these, you see the message in Figure 21.13.

Figure 21.14 shows how easily charts can be represented in three dimensions.

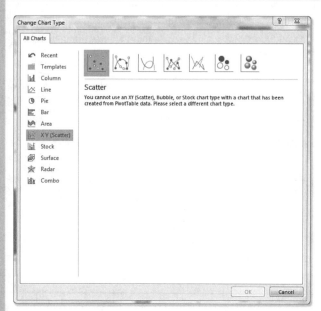

Figure 21.13
If you mistakenly choose an incompatible chart type, Excel lets you know.

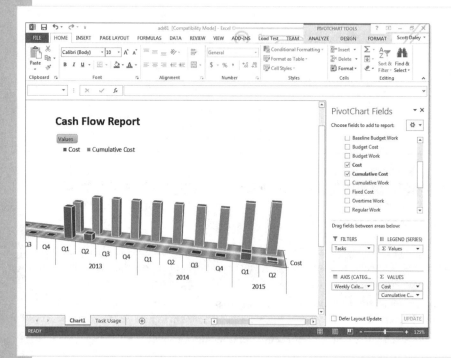

Figure 21.14
Data can easily be represented in three dimensions.

The Design tab of the PivotChart Tools option tabs also provides options to change the chart type in your graph. Click on the Design tab to list the options available to you in the Ribbon underneath the tabs, as shown in Figure 21.12. The Design tab lists alternative ways to customize the look of your data chart types.

You can open the Change Chart Type dialog box by clicking on the Change Chart Type option on the Design tab.

Customizing the Walls, Borders, Axes, and Text of an Excel Chart   Although the data chart types generally are placed in the foreground of a PivotChart, you also have the ability to customize the background and sides of the graph. Adding a few minor changes to the background and side walls of a visual report can give it a bit of an artistic flare while helping the data in the foreground stand out.

To modify the background and side walls of a graph, you must open the Format Walls panel. To do so, double-click on one of the walls in the graph. Alternatively, you can click on the Format tab, and on the Current Selection heading on the left side of the Format Ribbon, choose Walls from the drop-down list, and click Format Selection. Both methods open the Format Wall panel, as shown in Figure 21.15.

The Format Wall panel has several formatting options, listed on the left. The Fill option enables you to customize the appearance of the walls themselves. Choose from No Fill for empty white space, Solid Fill for a solid color, Gradient Fill for a gradient color scheme, Picture or Texture Fill to insert a picture or preset texture, or Automatic to use the default Excel choice.

Figure 21.15
Change the background and walls for your graph in the Format Walls panel.

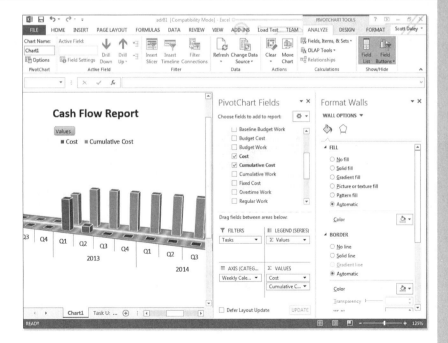

The Border section enables you to format the border lines of the graph. The Shadow option provides customization capabilities for the graph's shadow, and the 3-D Format and 3-D Rotation selections enable you to customize the three-dimensional options for the graph.

The floor of the graph can also be formatted. To do so, select the Format tab, and on the Current Selection heading on the left side of the Format Ribbon, choose Floor from the drop-down list and then click Format Selection. The Format Floor dialog box appears, which operates in the same fashion as the Format Walls panel.

Figure 21.16 shows an example of a graph after making modifications in the Format Walls panel and the Format Floor dialog box. A gradient fill has been selected with some slight shadowing effects. It is best to take a little time to experiment with all of these options and determine what works best in your reports.

note

The illustrations in this book appear in black and white. However, many of the customization options for Excel PivotCharts include color. If you are printing a report on a color printer, be sure to take advantage of the color customization options.

For more information about printing a visual report, see the section "Sharing and Saving Visual Reports" later in this chapter.

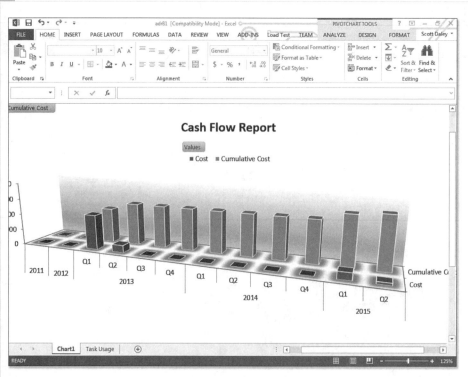

Figure 21.16
The walls and floor have been given a gradient fill and a light shadowing effect, which helps to make the data stand out more and improve the overall appearance of the graph.

Besides the walls and floor, you can customize every aspect of the graph by selecting a particular option from the drop-down list on the Current Selection heading of the Format tab. After you choose which aspect you want to modify, click the Format Selection button, and a dialog box appears in which you can make the changes. You can also open an item-specific dialog box by right-clicking directly on the item you want to modify, such as the legend or axis lines, and choosing the Format (item) option at the bottom of the list. This opens the appropriate dialog box for that particular item.

Here are the items you can customize on your PivotChart:

- Back Wall
- Chart Area
- Chart Title
- Floor
- Horizontal (Category) Axis
- Legend
- Plot Area
- Side Wall
- Vertical (Value) Axis
- Vertical (Value) Axis Major Gridlines
- Vertical (Value) Axis Title
- Walls
- Series (there might be several of these, depending on the chart data in your graph)

note

You do not need to modify all walls in the same fashion. That is why you have the option to customize the back wall and the side wall. Choosing the Walls option customizes both.

Customizing Labels on an Excel PivotChart The Add Chart Element control in the Chart Layouts group on the Design tab provides several customization options for specific areas of your PivotChart. The Axes and Background headings enable you to customize these items similarly to the methods described in the previous section.

The Add Chart Element can be useful to customize the Chart Title, Axis Titles, and Legend information. Also, you can change the display of the Data Labels, and choose to display the Data Table, which is similar to the PivotTable, only it is not interactive.

Figure 21.17 displays the Add Chart Element button clicked and the various options found under the Data Table selection.

Resolving Text Overlapping in an Excel PivotChart Sometimes, when you drill into your data, the text along the horizontal axis overlaps, simply because there is not enough room to display it (see Figure 21.18). All the text data along the horizontal axis is overlapping.

You can fix this problem by right-clicking on the text and choosing Format Axis. This opens the Format Axis panel. In the Format Axis panel, choose Alignment, and then rotate the text either 90 or 270 degrees, as shown in Figure 21.19. The text will then be displayed vertically, so it does not overlap, as shown in Figure 21.20.

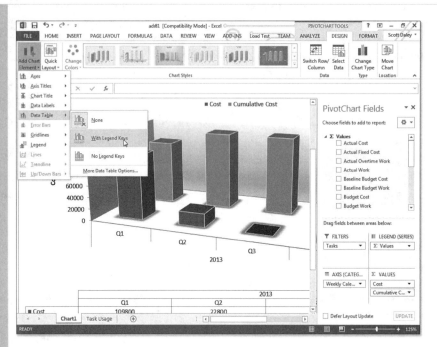

Figure 21.17
Customize the layout and appearance of the various labels found in your graph by using Add Chart Element.

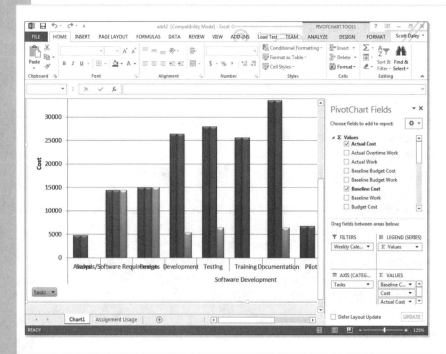

Figure 21.18
Drilling into the data can cause the text data to overlap, making it nearly impossible to read.

Figure 21.19
Rotate the text data in the Format Axis panel to fix the overlapping problem.

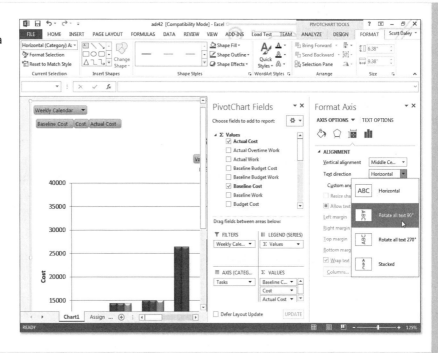

Figure 21.20
The text data has been rotated 90 degrees, making it much easier to read.

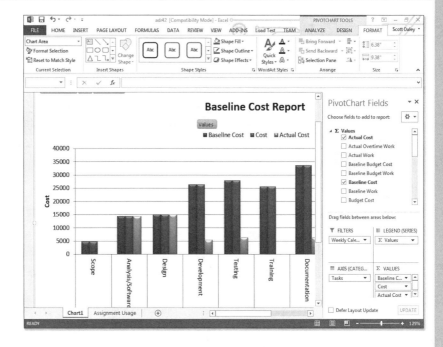

Customizing Visio Visual Reports

As mentioned previously, Visio reports are built using a PivotDiagram. Therefore, to customize a Visio visual report, you must understand the essentials of customizing a PivotDiagram.

 note

Visio does not come standard with Microsoft Office. To use the Visio visual reports in Project, you need to install Visio as well.

Formatting a PivotDiagram

Visio shares the Ribbon with Word or other Office tools. You can hover your mouse pointer over any button or feature in Visio, and a Screentip appears that describes that particular item.

Generally, when you open a Visio visual report, it chooses a zoom factor that shows the entire diagram. Usually it is too small to read, so you need to zoom in to work with it. To do so, click the View tab, Zoom and choose how much you want to zoom in, or just type in the percentage. The PivotDiagram then zooms in accordingly.

The PivotDiagram tab is unique to Visio visual reports, and it contains options specific to this type of diagram. Figure 21.21 shows the PivotDiagram tab.

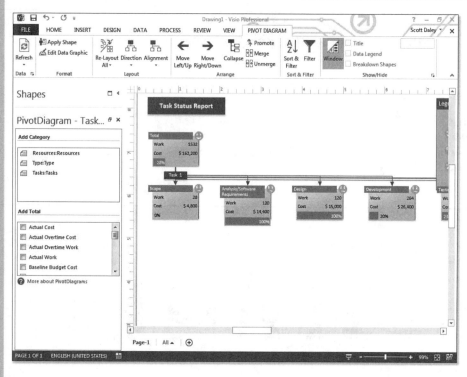

Figure 21.21
The PivotDiagram tab provides several formatting options for the Visio PivotDiagram.

Table 21.2 shows the icon, name, and a brief description of the nine command buttons found on the PivotDiagram tab.

Table 21.2   Key PivotDiagram Tab Functions

Toolbar Icon	Name	Brief Description
Refresh Data	Refresh Data	Refreshes the data in a PivotDiagram.
Apply Shape	Apply Shape	Inserts a shape into the PivotDiagram. Select the node(s), click Apply Shape, and in the Apply Shape dialog box, choose the shape you want to apply and click OK.
Edit Data Graphic	Edit Data Graphic	Select a single item and make detailed and/or conditional changes in appearance.
Re-Layout All	Re-Layout All	When you manually move nodes by dragging them to other areas on the PivotDiagram, this button resets them to their last predefined location. This action applies only to the manually moved nodes.
Direction	Layout Direction	Changes the node layout direction: Top-to-Bottom, Bottom-to-Top, Right-to-Left, or Left-to-Right.
Alignment	Layout Alignment	Changes the node layout alignment: Left, Center, Right, Top, Middle, or Bottom.
Merge	Merge	Merges two or more nodes.
Unmerge	Unmerge	Unmerges merged nodes.
Move Left/Up	Move Left/Up	Moves selected item(s) left or up.
Move Right/Down	Move Right/Down	Moves selected item(s) right or down.

Click the expand control in the Show/Hide group and the PivotDiagram Options dialog box opens, as shown in Figure 21.22. In the PivotDiagram Options dialog box, you can choose from many different formatting options for both the diagram and the data, including showing the title, legend, connections, and breakdown shapes.

Many formatting options are also available when you right-click any node or shape in the PivotDiagram. You can list tasks or resources associated with a particular node, apply a shape, or apply other Format, Data, and Shape formatting options listed when you right-click. For the Format option, you can edit the node's text, connecting line, or fill (the fill is the appearance of the node box). For the Data option, you can edit or remove a data graphic, which is used as an indicator to the status of the data. The Shape option lets you format any shapes in the PivotDiagram.

caution

Not all nodes can be customized with all options. For example, you cannot collapse a node that does not have "children" (other nodes attached to it at lower levels).

Figure 21.22
The PivotDiagram Options dialog box provides several basic formatting options for the PivotDiagram.

Changing the Look and Feel of a PivotDiagram As with the Excel PivotCharts, you can change the background appearance of a PivotDiagram. When you first open a Visio visual report, a pane appears on the left side of the screen (refer to Figure 21.21). If you maximize the Shapes group, collapse the PivotDiagram heading, it reveals More Shapes, Quick Shapes, PivotDiagramShapes, Workflow Objects – 3D, and Department – 3D. Each of these tabs holds several items you can insert into the PivotDiagram by dragging them from the pane and dropping them into the PivotDiagram.

note

Data graphics can be used to indicate the status of the data represented by a Visio shape.

Select the Design tab on the Ribbon. In the backgrounds group, you can change the Background or the Borders and Titles. Click Backgrounds and select a background.

Figure 21.23 shows a PivotDiagram with the Background World inserted. The Backgrounds menu is expanded for illustration purposes.

To remove a background, you can use the Multiple Undo feature on the Standard toolbar. Or, you can select No Background from the Backgrounds menu. The background will be removed.

Another way to change the look and feel of a PivotDiagram is to apply a theme to it. To do so, click the Theme button, also located on the Design tab (see Figure 21.24).

> **note**
>
> By default, the report's title is displayed in the upper-left corner of the PivotDiagram. You can select it and move it, as well as format the title's text like you would in Microsoft Word.

Figure 21.23
Choose from any of background options.

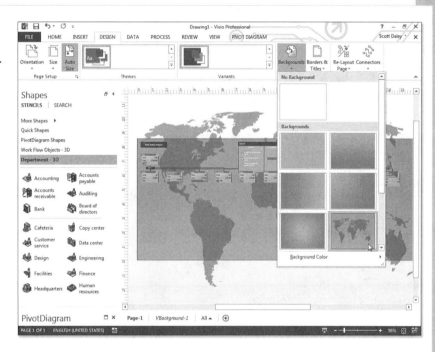

Figure 21.24
Apply a theme to the PivotDiagram to change the colors of the nodes, using a predefined color scheme.

The Themes group provides a number of different color schemes for the nodes themselves. The Variants group provides different selections for the shapes and styles of the nodes.

Customizing the Data in a PivotDiagram

Like the Excel reports, you can insert data fields to be included in your PivotDiagram using the Visual Reports – Field Picker dialog box. To access it, open the Visual Reports – Create Report dialog box (Report tab, Visual Reports), select the Visio report you want to customize, and click the Edit Template button. This opens the Visual Reports – Field Picker dialog box, in which you can add fields to or remove fields from the list in the same way as discussed in the previous section, "Customizing Data in an Excel Visual Report." Click OK when you are finished, and open the Visio report.

There are two main areas to add data to a Visio PivotDiagram: Add Category and Add Total. Both are located on the pane on the left side of the screen, as illustrated in Figure 21.25.

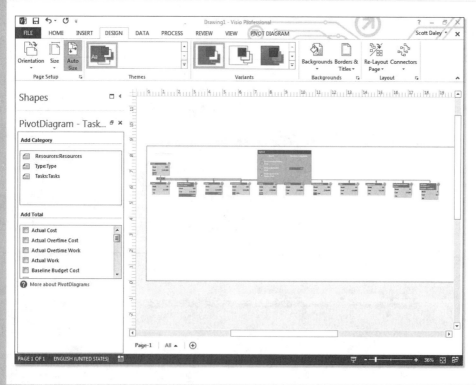

Figure 21.25
You can use the Add Category and Add Total panes to add additional fields and categories of fields to your Visio report.

In the Add Category area, you can choose the level of tasks or resources to display in the diagram. For example, if you are working with the Task Status Report, the diagram lists the Work and Cost values for each summary task, along with indicators of how the data compares to the baseline data. You might want to drill further into the subtask level, or display resource information for each summary task. Furthermore, you can select specific nodes to add categories to, or add them to the entire diagram.

Figure 21.26 shows the Task Status Report (US), with the resources displayed for the Scope summary task and the subtasks displayed for the Design summary task. To display resources for a node, select it, and in the Add Category box, choose Resources. Similarly, to display another level of tasks, choose the node(s) you want to expand, and select Tasks from the Add Category box. A drop-down list displays the levels of tasks you are able to drill into (Task 1, Task 2, Task 3, and so on). Select the level you want to display, and those subtasks will be displayed underneath the node(s) you selected.

Figure 21.26
Use the Add Category box to display additional category information, such as resources and other task levels.

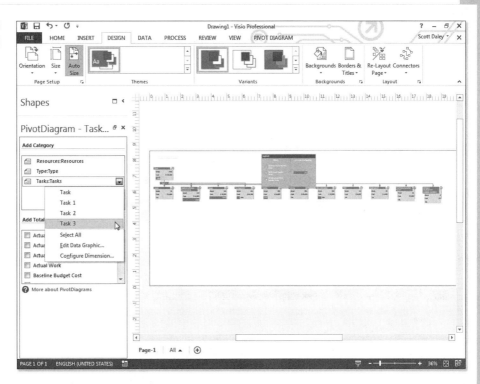

 note
By default, lower levels of tasks or resources are displayed underneath the node you selected. However, you can change the layout and alignment of the tree structure in a PivotDiagram using the PivotDiagram tab.

To remove the newly inserted category, select the node(s) that the tree is attached to, and in the PivotDiagram tab, select Collapse from the drop-down list.

The Add Total box functions similarly to the PivotTable Field List of an Excel PivotChart. Select the boxes next to the data fields you want to include in the PivotDiagram, or clear the selections you want to remove. For example, in the Task Status Report, you might want to include Actual Cost and Actual Work into the diagram to compare with the Cost and Work values. Select the Actual Cost and Actual Work check boxes, and they appear in each node, as illustrated in Figure 21.27.

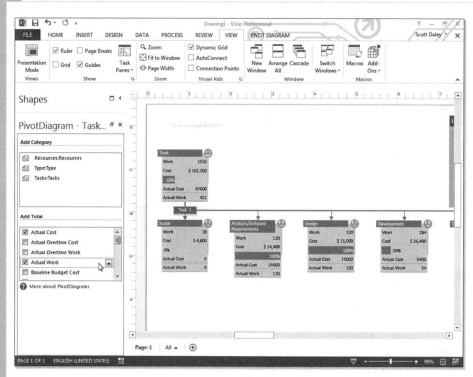

Figure 21.27
Use the Add Total box to display additional data fields or remove fields from the PivotDiagram.

On the Pivot Diagram tab, there is an Apply Shape button. To add a shape to a node, select it and click the Apply Shape button The Apply Shape dialog box appears, as shown in Figure 21.28. Choose the shape you want to apply and click OK. The shape is then attached to the node.

The Refresh Data button to the left of the Apply Shape button is also found on the PivotDiagram tab. It refreshes the data in the PivotDiagram to apply any changes made to the project file.

The Shape Data Box If you want to examine all the information related to a node, you can do so in the Shape Data box. To display it, right-click on a node and choose Data, Shape Data. The Shape Data box appears, as shown in Figure 21.29.

 tip

Shapes can be very helpful graphical indicators of the data or category of a particular node or group of nodes.

Figure 21.28
In the Apply Shape dialog box, choose the shape you want to apply to the node you selected.

Figure 21.29
The Shape Data dialog box enables you to view specific data information for any particular node. This one has been manually expanded.

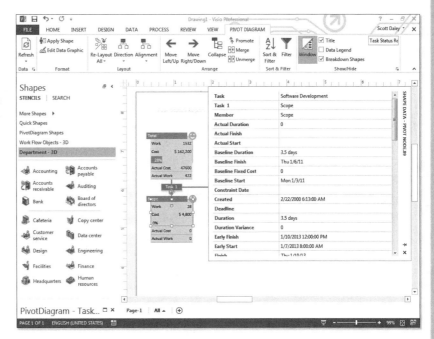

The Shape Data box is an excellent way to view all the information associated with a node, as it is sometimes difficult to see everything in the node itself.

Although the Shape Data box is primarily intended for viewing detailed information, you can change some of the data by typing directly into a particular field. Also, if you right-click the node and click Data, Define Shape Data, the Define Shape Data dialog box appears, as shown in Figure 21.30. Use the Define Shape Data dialog box to define further information about the node you selected.

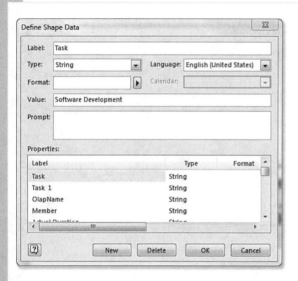

Figure 21.30
In the Define Shape Data dialog box, you can define additional information regarding the node you selected.

Helpful Tips for Customizing Visio Visual Reports   Visio provides the capability to create a report within a report. That is, you can create another type of report that includes data fields from your original report, outside the Visio PivotDiagram format. To do so, select Review, Reports on the Ribbon. This opens the Report Definition Wizard, which walks you through the process of creating an alternate report via Visio. These reports can be generated using Excel, HTML, Visio Shape, or XML format.

Creating Visual Reports Using Excel

If none of the existing visual reports completely meets your needs, you can create a new report from scratch. To create a new Excel visual report, you must first open the Visual Reports – Create Report dialog box by selecting the Report tab, Visual Reports from the main menu.

In the Visual Reports – Create Report dialog box, click the New Template button. This opens the Visual Reports – New Template dialog box, as shown in Figure 21.31.

To create a new Excel visual report, follow these steps:

1. In the Visual Reports – New Template dialog box, select Excel from the Select Application area.

2. In the Select Data Type area, choose from Task Usage, Resource Usage, Assignment Usage, Task Status, Resource Status, and Assignment Status. To help make the right decision, ask yourself whether the report will primarily focus on task, resource, or assignment data, and make your selection based on that decision.

Figure 21.31
Create a new Excel visual report by selecting Excel in the Visual Reports – New Template dialog box.

3. After you choose your data type, select the fields to include in your report by clicking the Field Picker button, which displays the Visual Reports – Field Picker dialog box (refer to Figure 21.7).

4. In the Visual Reports – Field Picker dialog box, choose which fields you want to include from the Available Fields or Available Custom Fields boxes, and click Add to insert them into the Selected Fields or Selected Custom Fields boxes. These fields are then available for you to include in your report data by selecting them from the PivotTable Field List. You can also remove fields that you do not want to use in your report. When you have finished choosing your data fields, click OK to close the Visual Reports – Field Picker dialog box and return to the Visual Reports – New Template dialog box. Refer to the section, "Customizing Data in an Excel Visual Report" earlier in this chapter for more information about the Visual Reports – Field Picker dialog box.

5. To complete the creation of your new visual report template, click OK in the Visual Reports – New Template dialog box. This opens a blank Excel PivotTable, as shown in Figure 21.32.

 tip

If you want to include time-phased data in your report, choose Task Usage, Resource Usage, or Assignment Usage as your data type. These three data types enable you to display time-phased data.

To insert data fields into the blank PivotTable, you can drag and drop them onto the table itself, select them in the PivotTable Field List, or drag and drop them into the Values box at the bottom of the PivotTable Field List. Scroll down past the data fields in the PivotTable Field List to find Tasks, Resources, or Time options, depending on the data type you chose when creating the report. You can drag these category fields into the Filters, Columns, or Rows boxes at the bottom of the PivotTable Field List, or select them in the list. If the Defer Layout Update option is cleared, the PivotTable changes based on the modifications you make as you make them.

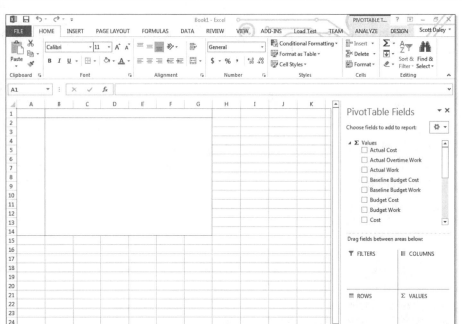

Figure 21.32
When you create a new Excel visual report, a blank PivotTable appears, in which you can place your data fields to construct the report.

Perhaps you want to create an Excel report that shows your Actual Work and Actual Cost over time thus far in your project. You would select the boxes next to these fields in your PivotTable Field List. Also, you can insert Tasks and Time by selecting those boxes and dragging them into the areas where you want them to be displayed.

If you click the File tab, the familiar Office page in Figure 21.33 appears. Saving and printing your report are discussed in greater detail in the section "Sharing and Saving Visual Reports" later in this chapter.

As you are constructing your PivotTable, you can also create the PivotChart for your report. To do so, select the Insert tab from the main menu and choose what kind of PivotChart you want to create from the Charts section of the Insert Ribbon. You can choose from Column, Line, Pie, Bar, Area, Scatter, and Other Charts Each chart type has several two- and three-dimensional options.

In Figure 21.34, a PivotTable has been created to display Actual Work and Actual Cost for all tasks in the project over time. The Tasks category is collapsed to show total project data (but can be expanded to show lower task levels). Also, the Time category has been expanded to show the first

 tip

It is best to have a general idea of how you want to organize your report and what data and categories you want to include. Then, as you are building your report in the PivotTable Field List, experiment with the formatting of the data by dragging and dropping the data fields and categories into different rows or columns until you are happy with the results.

quarter data for 2013. A PivotChart has also been defined to show the data in a three-dimensional column format.

Figure 21.33
Clicking the File tab opens the familiar Office gallery page, in which you can save, open, print, or perform other Office commands.

Figure 21.34
Insert a PivotChart to your PivotTable using the Chart area on the Insert tab.

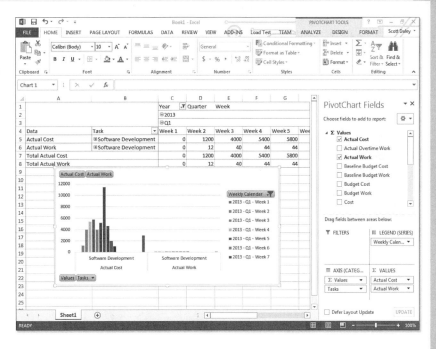

If you want to place your PivotChart on a separate sheet from your PivotTable, select the PivotChart, and on the main menu, select the Design tab. At the right side of the Design Ribbon is the Move Chart option. Click on this option, and a Move Chart dialog box appears, in which you can opt to move the chart to a different sheet.

You can continue to modify your PivotTable and PivotChart using the methods discussed previously in the section "Customizing Excel Visual Reports."

Creating Visual Reports Using Visio

Creating a new Visio visual report is similar to creating a new Excel report. To create a new Visio visual report, follow these steps:

1. Open the Visual Reports – Create Report dialog box by selecting the Report tab, Visual Reports from the main menu.

2. Click the New Template button to open the Visual Reports – New Template dialog box.

3. In the Visual Reports – New Template dialog box, select either Visio (Metric) or Visio (US Units), depending on which measurement system you want to use in your report.

4. Select your data type from the six options in the Data Type drop-down list, and use the Field Picker to add data field options to or remove them from your report.

5. When you have finished selecting the fields to be included in the report, click OK to create the report. A new PivotDiagram opens.

Figure 21.35 shows a new PivotDiagram that has been created to display Actual Work and Actual Cost for each quarter in the project. Themes and Variants have been applied using the Design tab.

You can define which categories to include as nodes (tasks, resources, and so on) using the Add Category box, and define the data each node holds in the Add Total box. You can also format the nodes themselves by right-clicking on them and choosing from the available formatting options, or by using the PivotDiagram tab or Theme options.

If you want to change the title, right-click on it to format the text. You can also move it by dragging it.

Continue to modify your PivotDiagram using the methods discussed previously in the section "Customizing Visio Visual Reports."

Figure 21.35
Use the Add
Category
and Add
Total boxes
to insert
data into
your new
Visio report.

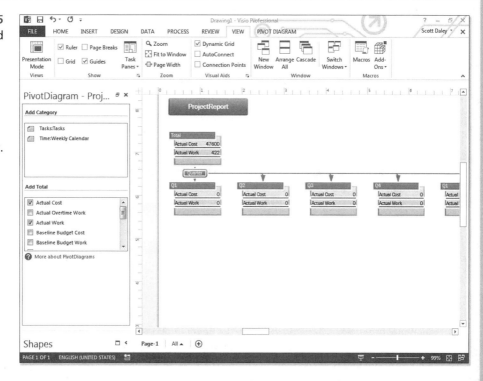

Sharing and Saving Visual Reports

The 22 existing visual report templates are designed to contain specific project data, and are excellent starting points for customizing your own visual reports using the methods discussed throughout this chapter. When you make changes to a report template, or when you create your own, you have the ability to share not only the data but the format of the report you have modified. That way, if you or other project managers want to use the same report format for future project files, it is saved and stored properly and does not have to be re-created.

You can save the modified or new report as a template using both Excel and Visio. Also, you can save it as a cube (to open in Excel) or a database (to open in Excel or Visio). Whereas a template saves the report's format definition with no actual data, a cube includes the specific project reporting data. That way, you can access the report, including the project information, from Excel or Visio without having to open Project. A database also includes specific project data but is smaller and more specific than a cube.

Saving a Visual Report Template Using Excel

If you have customized or created a new Excel visual report, and you find that the report format works very well, you might want to save the format for use in future projects. To do so, follow these steps:

1. In Excel or Visio, from the File tab select Save, which opens the Save As dialog box. Give your new report template a specific name that describes the functionality of the report and is unique from the other existing Excel report templates. When you have entered the template's name, click Save.

2. A box appears asking you if you want to clear the data before saving the template. Click Yes, and the template is saved as specified in the Save As dialog box.

By default, when you click Save and close the Save As dialog box, the report template is saved along with the other existing visual report templates. It appears on the list in the Visual Reports – Create Report dialog box, not only for your current project file, but for all project files you open or create.

However, you might choose to save it in another location on your computer or network. If that is the case, the new template might not appear in the Visual Reports – Create Report dialog box automatically; you might have to browse for it. To do so, select the Include Report Templates From check box in the Visual Reports – Create Report dialog box and click the Modify button to browse for the template.

 note

The new report template does not appear in the Visual Reports – Create Report dialog box until you close the box and reopen it after the template has been saved. Once you reopen the dialog box, the report appears in the list.

 note

Sometimes, selecting the Include Report Templates From box is enough to display the new report template; you might not have to browse for it when you check this box.

Saving a Visual Report Template Using Visio

To save a customized or new Visio report as a template, repeat the process described in the previous section. Click the File tab, Save button, which opens the Save As dialog box. Name your report, and click Save. By default, it is saved in the same folder as the other existing visual reports, and appears every time you open the Visual Reports – Create Report dialog box (if the box is currently open, you have to close it and reopen it to see the new template).

If you choose to save it elsewhere, you have to select the Include Report Templates From check box in the Visual Reports – Create Report dialog box and browse for it using the Modify button if it did not automatically appear when you checked the box.

Saving a Reporting Cube

There will be times when you want to save the reporting data in your project file outside your project. You can save the data as a cube, which is larger than a regular database, to be opened later in Excel. To do so, follow these steps:

1. Click the Save Data button on the Visual Reports – Create Report dialog box. This opens the Visual Report – Save Reporting Data dialog box, as shown in Figure 21.36.

   In the Visual Reports – Save Reporting Data dialog box, you can choose to save reporting data as either a cube or as a database. As previously mentioned, a cube is larger than a regular database.

2. To save your reporting data as a cube, use the drop-down menu to choose from Task Usage, Resource Usage, Assignment Usage, Task Summary, Resource Summary, and Assignment Summary.

Figure 21.36
Save reporting data as a cube or as a database using the Visual Reports – Save Reporting Data dialog box.

3. Click the Field Picker button to open the Visual Reports – Field Picker dialog box and select your fields as described previously in this chapter.

4. When you have chosen the cube and its accompanying fields, click Save Cube. The Save As dialog box appears, and you can designate the location where you want to save your cube.

To access the saved reporting data, follow these steps:

1. Open Excel. On the Insert tab, select either PivotTable or PivotChart from the Tables heading. This opens the Create PivotTable or Create PivotChart dialog box, depending on what you selected on the Insert Ribbon (see Figure 21.37).

2. Select Use an External Data Source, and click Choose Connection. This opens the Existing Connections dialog box.

3. Click the Browse for More button, and browse for the location where you saved the cube. When you find it, select it and click Open; then click OK on the Create PivotTable (or Create PivotChart) dialog box.

4. A blank PivotTable or PivotChart appears, and when you select data fields from the PivotTable Field List, the reporting data from the project file is displayed as the data values in the chart.

Figure 21.37 shows the Create PivotTable dialog box.

Figure 21.37
To import data from a saved cube, select Use an External Data Source. Then browse for your saved cube by clicking the Choose Connection button on the Create PivotTable (or Create PivotChart) dialog box.

Saving a Reporting Database

To save the reporting data as a database, open the Visual Reports – Save Reporting Data dialog box as instructed in the previous section and click Save Database. This opens the Save As dialog box, which you can use to define the name and location where you want to save the reporting database.

After you have saved the database, you can open it in either Excel or Visio.

To open it in Excel, follow these steps:

1. Open Excel, and on the Insert tab, choose PivotTable or PivotChart on the Tables heading. This opens the Create PivotTable or Create PivotChart dialog box (refer to Figure 21.37).

2. In the Create PivotTable (or PivotChart) dialog box, select Use an External Data Source and then click Choose Connection.

3. In the Existing Connections dialog box, select Browse for More, find your saved database, and click Open. This opens the Select Table dialog box.

4. In the Select Table dialog box, choose the database table to insert into the PivotTable or PivotChart and then click OK. Click OK on the Create PivotTable or Create PivotChart dialog box, and the blank PivotTable or PivotChart is inserted.

5. Select the data fields from the PivotTable Field List, and the reporting data from your original project appears as data values in those fields.

To open the reporting database in Visio, follow these steps:

1. Open Visio, and choose Data, Link Data to Shapes. This opens the Data Selector dialog box.

2. On the Data Selector dialog box, choose Microsoft Office Access Database and click Next.

3. Browse for your existing database by clicking Browse on the next screen. Select it and click Open.

4. Click Next to advance to the next screen, and choose your rows and columns to include. By default, All Columns and All Data are selected. Click Next and then click Finish.

5. Select the data fields from the Add Total and Add Category boxes to include on the PivotDiagram. The reporting data from your project is displayed as data values.

Printing a Visual Report

When you have finished customizing or creating your report and saved it appropriately, you might also want to print a copy of your report to share with your project team or other project stakeholders.

In Excel and Visio, as in any Office product, click the File tab and Print. You see the standard print options, as well as a print preview. Verify your report, and then click Print.

 caution

Not all printers are capable of printing color documents. If you must have a printed report in color, be sure to verify on the Print Preview screen that it will in fact be printing in color. If it shows up black and white on the Print Preview screen, you need to change the printer to use in the Print dialog box to a printer that can print in color.

Consultants' Tips

Visual reports are a powerful feature for communicating with project stakeholders if used well.

80/20: Choose the Right Data Resolution for Your Reporting Goals

Successful reports communicate information within the correct context. The wrong context can cause confusion, which in turn can sometimes be cleared only through an amazing amount of effort that could have been avoided if the context had been provided. Data resolution is often a critical part of providing the right context. For example, tracking project status daily is a waste of effort if the team is only updating the status weekly. Worse, reporting that daily status and drawing conclusions from are even bigger wastes of time. When you present information, presenting more than is needed causes miscommunication. People naturally look for patterns from which to draw conclusions. Presenting too much information provides the opportunity to look for patterns that are irrelevant. But the assumption by your audience is always going to be that if you provide the information, it must be relevant.

Save Customized Reports as Templates for Later Use

Project visual reports provide a variety of customization options; therefore, when you identify report definitions that work best for you, it is important that you save them as templates for future use. Using visual reports' templates can be a great way to save time in your future projects. In addition, templates can be used to standardize the format and data across your organization as your project managers can share the templates they create. Having consistent, informative reports can help you effectively communicate your project information to your project team and project sponsors, as well as help you better understand problems occurring in your project.

22

CUSTOMIZATION ALMOST BEYOND REASON: VIEWS, TABLES, FILTERS, GROUPS, FIELDS, TOOLBARS, AND MENUS

Project managers are busy people who must plan, adjust, and communicate change quickly and efficiently. This chapter shows you how customization can save time and improve your ability to find the schedule information you need, when you need it. This is a long chapter, but it can be consumed as-needed, in parts.

Views, tables, filters, groups, and fields are all helpful ways of organizing specific aspects of your project. They are useful for displaying or reporting various characteristics or phases within your project. Furthermore, they are all related. Views are composed of different kinds of tables. Tables can be filtered or grouped to display common traits within the table entries. Tables can also include custom fields, which contain specific project information, such as customized schedule "stop light" indicators driven by formulas. Each of these elements can help you to more effectively manage your project based on the specific information each provides and how they are formatted or configured. All these concepts are discussed in greater detail throughout this chapter.

Additionally, this chapter helps you learn how to better manage the Ribbon, the Quick Access toolbar, and the status bar. Because you use some commands regularly, some on occasion, and the rest not at all, personalizing the Ribbon and toolbars helps you increase your efficiency.

> **note**
>
> Something to keep in mind while reading this chapter is the difference between tasks (work that needs to be done) and resources (the people, tools, and equipment necessary to get the work done) and how they apply to views, tables, filters, groups, and fields. For instance, different tables are available to view tasks rather than resources, and vice versa. This is important to remember because although the methods for customizing and creating views, tables, filters, groups, and fields for tasks and resources are the same, the end result often is not, simply because tasks and resources are two different entities within Project. For example, Resource Names is a field in the default Task Entry table, but several resource tables have fields in which you define the resource name.

➡ *For additional details on what you can view in Project, **see** the "What Can I View Using Microsoft Project?" section on **p. 357** in Chapter 11 and the "Viewing Strategies" section on **p. 359** in Chapter 11.*

In short, all the methods and concepts discussed in this chapter are related; some processes might require an understanding of other processes, such as creating a custom table to insert into a custom view. Also, bear in mind that different views, tables, filters, groups, and fields appear or function differently for a task than a resource.

> **tip**
>
> Most of the dialog boxes discussed in this chapter have a Help button. The Help button can be a great resource for answering questions or guiding you through a process you might be confused about.

Creating and Customizing Tables

As previously mentioned, Project contains tables that hold and define a wide variety of information within a project. Tables are composed of rows and columns that are customizable in many aspects, and are the foundation for sheet views within Project. In any table row, column, or field, you can define not only the information it houses, but also its appearance within the table. You can adjust the width, height, and text alignment of a table's columns. Furthermore, you can add, delete, and move columns to better suit your needs.

With Project, by far the easiest way to create a new table is to customize whatever view you are looking at by adding new columns, and then selecting the View tab, Data, Tables, Save Fields as New Table. Name the table. Your new table is automatically available under the Custom section of the Tables menu.

> **note**
>
> Be aware that if you use this method to modify a table, you are also modifying the original.

➡ *For more information about formatting screens and views, **see** Chapter 19, "Formatting Views," **p. 569**.*

To create and customize a table from scratch, select the View Tab, Data, Tables, More Tables. This opens up the More Tables dialog box, with the currently displayed table highlighted, as shown in Figure 22.1.

Figure 22.1
The More Tables dialog box is the starting point for creating and customizing a table.

The More Tables dialog box is similar to the More Views dialog box discussed later in this chapter. The major difference is the choice of displaying Task and Resource tables, which is found at the top of the dialog box. Selecting Task displays all the task tables, and selecting Resource displays all the resource tables. One or the other is selected automatically, depending on the view you were displaying when you opened the More Tables dialog box. If it was a Task view, the Task tables are listed, and vice versa if it was a Resource view.

To change a table on your current view, highlight the table you want to display and click Apply. Project lets you display only applicable tables for the current view; you cannot display a Task table on a Resource view, and vice versa.

The rest of the More Tables dialog box works like the More Views dialog box. If you want to edit a table, saving the changes and replacing the original table, highlight the table and choose Edit. If you want to edit a table but do not want to replace the original, choose Copy. To copy a table to or from the Global.MPT file, choose Organizer (this feature is discussed at the end of this chapter in the section "Organizing Views and Other Custom Elements in Project Files").

To create a new table, follow these steps:

1. Open the More Tables dialog box by selecting the View Tab, Data, Tables, More Tables.

2. In the More Tables dialog box, select New. This opens the Table Definition dialog box, as does choosing Edit or Copy. Notice how all the fields are blank; you create the new table by entering values in these fields. If you chose Edit or Copy, these fields would already be defined based on the original table you were editing, and you would edit the original table by changing the entries in these fields (see Figure 22.2).

The following sections discuss the various fields in the Table Definition dialog box and the process for creating and customizing tables.

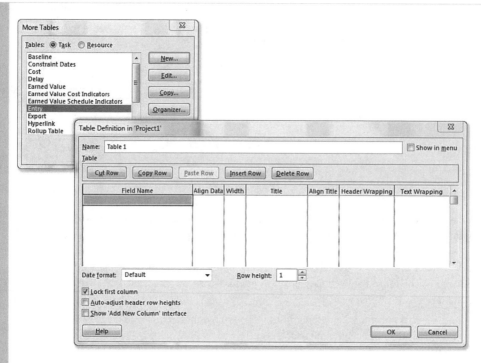

Figure 22.2
Create a new table or edit an existing one in the Table Definition dialog box.

Entering a Table Name

As with any name in Project, your table name should be unique and specific to what is defined in the table. This applies to new tables and edited ones. Even if you are making minor adjustments, you want the name to reflect those modifications. If you are copying an existing table, you need to make sure you give it a new name; otherwise, you end up with two different tables that have identical names.

As with views, you can include an ampersand symbol (&) directly before any letter you want to designate as the hotkey. This way, if you save the table to the main Table menu (View tab, Data, Tables), you can type the hotkey letter as a shortcut to the table. To save the table to the main Table menu, select the Show in Menu check box before you click OK. The new table appears in the Custom grouping.

For more information about hotkeys, see "Entering the Name of the View" later in this chapter.

Adding and Changing the Columns in the Table

To add a new column in your table, there are several fields in the Table Definition dialog box to define information about the column. The following list describes each of these fields:

- **Field Name**—Choose the field name by clicking in the Field Name field and selecting from the drop-down list (see Figure 22.3). You cannot create your own; you must use one from the drop-down list. You can, however, rename it so the name is displayed the way you want it to read. (See the "Title" section of this list.) After you choose a field name and click in another area of the Table Definition dialog box, three other fields are automatically filled in with default values: Align Data, Width, and Align Title.

- **Align Data**—In this field, you have three choices available in the drop-down list: Left, Center, and Right. The one you choose is how the data in each cell will be displayed. If you choose Right, it will be as far to the right in the cell as possible. Choosing Center centers the data in the cell, and Left lines it up all the way to the left. The default choice is Right.

- **Width**—In the Width field, you simply define the width of the column. The default is 10 characters, and you can increase or decrease that value by using the up and down arrows on the right side of the field or by typing in the number of characters you want the width to be.

- **Title**—The Title field is where you define the text you want displayed as the header of the column. For example, in the Task Entry Table Definition dialog box, the third entry under Field Name is Name, but its Title entry is Task Name. You can see that Task Name appears at the top of the column in that particular table. Thus, the Title field is where you change the display name that you selected as your field name. You can leave the Title field blank, and the column header will be displayed as its field name.

- **Align Title**—This field is similar to the Align Data field. Again, you have a drop-down list with three options: Left, Center, and Right. Your choice determines how the text in the column header (the top of the column in the table) is displayed. This alignment does not have to match the alignment you chose for the data. You could have the title aligned to the right and the data in its subordinate cells aligned in the center. It might be helpful to visually align the title and the cell data differently to emphasize the column header.

- **Header Wrapping**—In this field, you have two choices in the drop-down list: Yes and No. This applies only if you have a long column header title that does not fit in the cell. If you select Yes, Project automatically wraps the title to fit in the cell.

- **Text Wrapping**—In this field, you have two choices in the drop-down list: Yes and No. This applies only if you have long text that does not fit in the cell. If you select Yes, Project automatically wraps the text to fit in the cell.

 tip

If you have never created a new table before, it might be a good idea to open a familiar table's Table Definition dialog box to see how it is defined. For example, you are probably familiar with the Task Entry table (the left side of the Gantt Chart view).

To view its Table Definition dialog box, switch to the Gantt Chart view and choose View, Table, More Tables. Then, select Task at the top of the More Tables dialog box, select Entry, and click Copy. The Table Definition dialog box appears, with all the Task Entry table's characteristics defined. You can play around with it and see the effects of your modifications without losing the original Task Entry table.

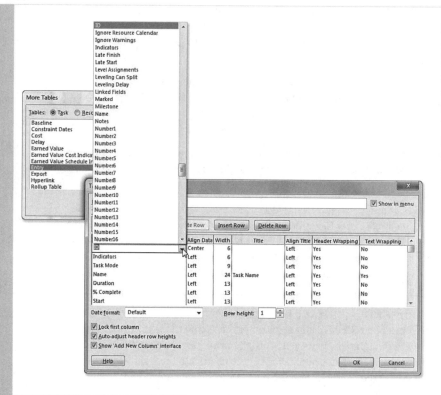

Figure 22.3
Click in the Field Name field to choose from the drop-down list. Other fields in the Table Definition dialog box also have drop-down lists to select from.

Any time you make an entry in the Field Name field, you create a new column. Furthermore, the columns are displayed in order. Reading them from top to bottom is the same order they will be in from left to right on the table. Therefore, you want to keep the order in mind as you are creating or customizing your table. If you want to insert a column somewhere in the middle of the table, select any field where you want to put it, and click the Insert Row button. A blank row is created for you to enter the column information, and all other rows, including the one you selected, move down to make room for it.

To delete a column from the table, select a field in its row and click the Delete Row button. Or, if you want to replace the deleted column, you do not have to delete it. Simply click in the Field Name field for the column you want to delete, and select the field name you want to replace it with. Then fill in all the information for the new column.

You can also cut and paste the rows to rearrange columns in the table. Select any field in the row for the column you want to move, and click the Cut Row button. Then, select any field in the row you want to move it to, and click the Paste Row button. The new column information is pasted in the row you selected, and all other rows beneath it, including the one you selected, move down to make room for the pasted row.

Completing the Definition of the Table

You can select the date format to use in the table if you want to change it from the default. The default date format is defined on the View tab of the Options dialog box (Tools, Options). Changing the date format applies only to the table and not to other tables or views within the project.

Next to the Date Format field is the Row Height field. By default, it is set at 1, which means one row of text is displayed for each task or resource row in the table. You can change this by entering a number or using the up and down arrows, which makes all rows on the table that height. Alternatively, you can change the height of individual rows without changing all the rows on the table. This is done outside the Table Definition dialog box by clicking and dragging on the individual row dividers.

 For more information about changing individual row height in a table, **see** *the "Adjusting the Height of Task Rows" section on* **p. 149** *in Chapter 6.*

Selecting the Lock First Column check box is useful when working with a table that has columns displayed to the right that you have to scroll to see. If selected, this feature displays the first column as a means for you to keep track of the row information. For instance, if your first column (the top column entry row in the Table Definition dialog box) is Task Name, and you have the Lock First Column box checked, you can scroll all the way to the right and your task names will always be displayed.

By default, this box is checked. The disadvantage, however, is that this column cannot be edited in the table itself, because it is locked. Also, the column header (the Title) is not displayed in the table when this box is checked.

By default, the check box is selected for Auto-Adjust Header Row Heights. This feature is applied when you change the width of a row. If you decide to make a row narrower, the column header (the Title) might not be able to fit with the smaller width. If this box is selected, Project wraps the header to fit by using more rows. If it is not selected, the header will only be partially displayed (as much as will fit with the new, narrower width).

Figure 22.4 shows a Table Definition dialog box. A table has been customized from the standard Task Entry table. To re-create this, follow these steps:

1. Set the Task Sheet as your view by selecting the View tab, Task Views, Other Views, Task Sheet.

2. Stay on the View tab, Data, Tables, More Tables. Entry is selected in the More Tables dialog box.

3. Choose Copy to customize the Task Entry table without losing the original.

4. The Table Definition dialog box appears, and you can define the table based on the information in the previous sections. In the example in Figure 22.4, the % Complete and % Work Complete fields have been added to view the task's progress.

> **note**
>
> The example in Figure 22.4 is meant to convey the theory behind customizing a table; it is not necessarily the best way to view task progress. The newly customized table in this example is called "Task Progress," but other tables already built into Project are better for tracking a task's progress.

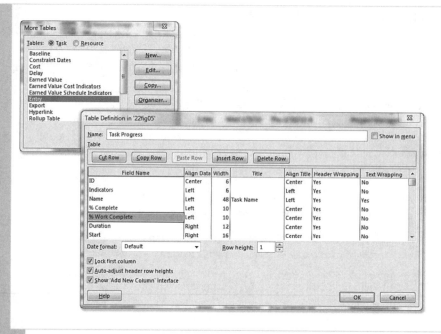

Figure 22.4
The Task Entry table has been customized into a new table, called Task Progress, by inserting the % Complete and % Work Complete fields.

Figure 22.5 shows the newly customized Task Progress table itself as applied to the Task Sheet view.

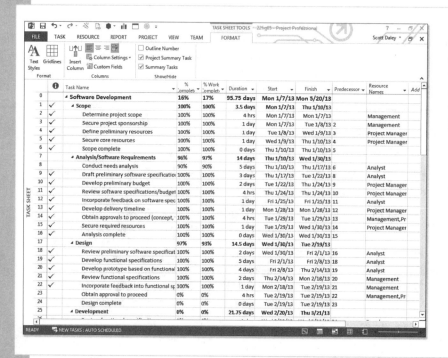

Figure 22.5
The Task Progress table is displayed in the Task Sheet view. This is the table defined in Figure 22.4.

Changing Table Features from the View Screen

You can make many of the table customization or creation modifications without using the Table Definition dialog box. You can access the Field Settings dialog box to make changes to particular columns in the table.

To open the Field Settings dialog box, right-click the column header and select Field Settings. The Field Settings dialog box appears, as shown in Figure 22.6. Notice that the entry fields in the Field Settings dialog box are similar to those found in the Table Definition dialog box.

Figure 22.6
Modify column information in the Field Settings dialog box.

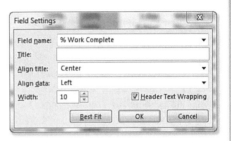

You can change column information in the following fields: Field Name, Title, Align Title, Align Data, and Width. Although in a slightly different order, these are the same fields in the Table Definition dialog box. Header Text Wrapping is also an option, only here it is a check box instead of a Yes/No field.

The major difference between defining this information in the Field Settings dialog box versus the Table Definition dialog box is the Best Fit button in the Field Settings dialog box. When you have entered all the information you want, you can click OK to apply the changes and close the box. Alternatively, you can click the Best Fit button, which applies all the information and closes the box, but the column width is automatically calculated by Project. The width is defined to fit the longest entry in the column.

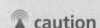 **caution**

Choosing the Best Fit button fits the longest entry onto one long line of text. This can make for very wide columns if you have long entries such as the task name.

You can also insert a new column in the table without using the Table Definition dialog box. To do so, highlight the column where you want to insert the new one by clicking its header. Then, insert it in one of two ways:

- Right-click the column title and choose Insert Column.

- Press the Insert (Ins) key.

A list of field names appears. Select a field. The new column is inserted in place of the one you highlighted, and all columns to the right shift over to make room for the new one.

To hide or delete a column without accessing the Table Definition dialog box, do one of the following:

- Highlight the column by clicking its header and then press the Delete (Del) key. This removes the column from the table entirely.

- Right-click the column header and choose Hide Column. This also removes it from the table entirely.

- Drag the right divider line for the column from right to left until the column is hidden. This does not remove the column from the table, but sets its width to zero.

If a column was hidden or deleted, you must reinsert it to get it back using any of the methods described in this section or using the Table Definition dialog box. If you used the mouse to drag the width to zero, you can use the mouse to reopen it. This might be tricky because the column is not displayed; slowly drag the mouse over the area where it was hidden in until the pointer becomes a vertical line with horizontal arrows and then drag it open.

Row heights can be changed as well by dragging the border of a row with the mouse.

Creating and Customizing Views

Project is equipped with dozens of views, all of which are beneficial depending on specifically what you want to display on the screen. Moreover, these views are divided into single-pane views, in which the view is displayed on the entire screen, and combination views, which are composed of two different views combined onto one screen separated by a divider bar. The Team Planner view is still a third kind, with special characteristics not shared by either of the other types of views.

In addition to these views, you have the ability to copy or edit the existing views to create new ones, or create new views entirely from scratch. Editing existing views and creating new ones is done in the More Views dialog box, shown in Figure 22.7. To open it, select the View tab, Task or Resource Views, Other Views, More Views.

Four buttons appear along the right side of the More Views dialog box:

- **New**—Use the New button to create a new view from scratch.

- **Edit**—Use the Edit button to edit an existing view, replacing the original view with the newly edited version.

 caution

You must remember if you hide a column using your mouse because Project gives no indication of a hidden column.

 note

There are advantages to changing table features from the View screen as opposed to the Table Definition dialog box. The Table Definition dialog box is beneficial to making changes to multiple rows at once, and other methods such as accessing the Field Settings dialog box aid in modifying columns one at a time.

 note

A view is composed of a table, a filter, a group, and a screen. It is not necessary to create a new filter and table for a new view; you can use existing ones, but they must be defined in the New View dialog box. Not all views allow the selection of alternate tables, groups, and so on.

■ **Copy**—Use the Copy button to edit an existing view without replacing the original, so you are left with both the original and your edited version.

Figure 22.7
Edit and create views using the buttons along the right side of the More Views dialog box.

■ **Organizer**—Use the Organizer button to open the View tab Organizer dialog box, where you can rename or delete views, and copy them to or from the Global.MPT file or any other Project file that is open in your current session. This is helpful if you create or customize a view and want to use it in other projects, or to use a view you have created or customized in a previous project that was copied to the Global.MPT file. This is discussed more at the end of this chapter in the section, "Organizing Views and Other Custom Elements in Project Files."

 For additional information about Global.MPT and the Organizer, **see** *Chapter 18, "Managing Project Files Locally and in the Cloud,"* **p. 549**.

Regardless of which option you choose to customize or create your view (New, Edit, or Copy), the process is similar. If a view is almost, but not completely, what you are looking for, choose the Edit or Copy button to customize that view to your specific needs.

> **tip**
> It is wise to use the Copy button to create a copy of a view for further edits instead of customizing one of the out-of-the-box views. That way, you do not replace the original view after you edit it. Unless you are positive you will never need the original view, use the Copy button. After you select the Copy button, the first thing you should do is change the view name so no one confuses it with the original.

If none of the views in Project meets your needs, create a new view by clicking the New button. The Define New View dialog box appears, as shown in Figure 22.8.

Depending on which option you choose (Single view or Combination view), another dialog box appears. If you are creating a Combination view, you must define the new view's name and choose the two views to be displayed in the top pane and the bottom pane, as shown in Figure 22.9.

This is a brief summary of creating a Combination view; the process is discussed further in the upcoming section "Creating a Combination View" later in this chapter.

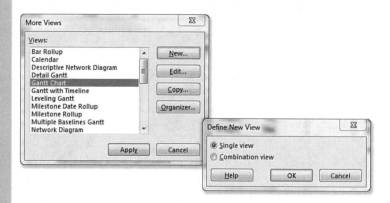

Figure 22.8
In the Define New View dialog box, you can create a new Single view or Combination view.

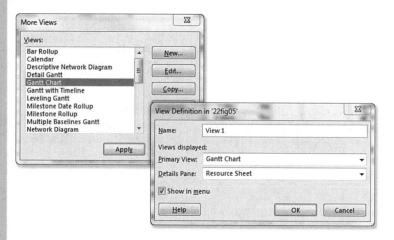

Figure 22.9
To create a new combination view, enter the name and choose which existing views to display in the top and bottom panes.

If you are creating a new Single view, a different version of the View Definition dialog box appears (see Figure 22.10). This is the same dialog box you use if you select Edit or Copy. You would, of course, define the name in the Name field; then choose the screen, table, group, and filter from their respective drop-down lists. These are discussed in greater detail in the following sections.

 note

If one or more panes in your new Combination view are to include another customized or created view, you must customize or create that view first; then select it from the drop-down list when selecting the top and bottom panes in the View Definition dialog box.

Figure 22.10
Create a new Single view in this version of the View Definition dialog box.

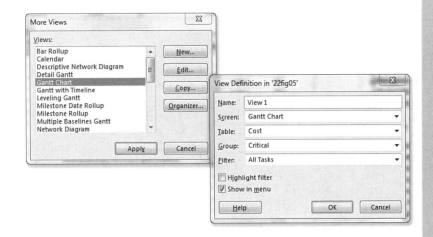

Entering the Name of the View

Similar to naming tasks or resources, it is important to choose a name for a view that is unique and clearly identifies the features the view incorporates. Otherwise, a few months down the road, you might find yourself wasting time searching through ambiguous view names for the one you want.

If you want to include your view in the main drop-down list that appears when you select View, select the Show in Menu check box. If not, leave it unchecked. The view still appears in the More Views list (View tab, Other Views, More Views).

Also, just like with tables, you can designate a hotkey letter to use when selecting the view as a shortcut if you select Show in Menu. Simply put an ampersand symbol (&) before the letter you want to designate as the hotkey. Then, in the main View drop-down list, the hotkey will be underlined, and you can type that letter to select the view.

 note

The hotkey can be any letter in the view's name, not just the first letter. Be sure that this letter is unique; otherwise, you still have to select from all the views that have identical hotkeys. This hotkey shortcut applies only in the main View list; in the More Views list, you can press the first letter of the view name you are looking for, and select from all views that begin with that letter.

Selecting the Starting Format

When customizing or creating views, you must start with an existing screen and make your changes from there. All views must use one of the basic screens as its foundation, and all basic screens are already defined in Project. Choose this "starting point" screen from the drop-down list in the Screen field of the View Definition dialog box (refer to Figure 22.10).

Sixteen basic screens are found in the drop-down list, as shown in Figure 22.11. Notice that some of them are resource screens, and some are task screens. Be sure to have a clear idea of whether the view you are creating is a resource or a task view.

Some views can be modified more than others; you just have to experiment to see which one is most suitable for your needs. You can also change the formatting on most of the screens. Over time, you will become more familiar with the basic screens and will know which one to select to meet your specific view requirements.

 tip

You are only able to define the starting view in the Screen field if you are creating a new view. If you are editing or copying an existing view, the Screen field is automatically filled in because you cannot change the view you are editing or copying.

➡️ *For more information about formatting screens and views,* **see** *Chapter 19, "Formatting Views," **p. 549**.*

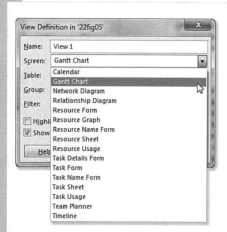

Figure 22.11
Choose from the 16 different default views, which are the foundation of any new view you create in Project.

Selecting the Table for the View

Depending on the view you have selected, you might have to select a table. Not all views display tables, but many do. If the view you have selected does not display a table, the Table field in the View Definition dialog box is grayed out so you cannot make a selection. The following screens require a Table field entry:

- Gantt Chart

- Resource Sheet

- Resource Usage

- Task Sheet

- Task Usage

If you are using one of these screens, select the table you want from the drop-down list in the Table field in the View Definition dialog box (refer to Figure 22.10). The list displays all the tables that can be used with the screen type you have selected. For instance, if you chose a resource screen type, such as Resource Usage, the Table drop-down list displays all the possible tables to use for that particular screen and does not include task tables.

Also, if you have any customized tables that would apply to the screen type, they will be in the drop-down list. If you want to select a customized table, you must create it before you create your view. This process is described in the section "Creating and Customizing Tables" earlier in this chapter. The same applies to custom groups and filters.

Selecting the Group for the View

After defining a table for your view, the next option is the Group field. Your selection in the Group field determines how Project arranges the table entries in your view. You can choose No Group, and the tasks or resources are sorted according to their ID number. If you choose a custom group, it must exist prior to selection, as discussed in the section "Creating Custom Groups" later in this chapter.

Selecting the Filter for the View

The last step in creating or customizing your view is defining the filter to apply to it. The options in the Filter drop-down list are all of the possible filters you can use based on your other entries in the View Definition dialog box. Depending on your screen type, the top choice in the Filter drop-down list is All Tasks or All Resources. Select this option if you do not want Project to filter the task or resource list for anything more specific.

After you have chosen your filter, you can also select the check box next to Highlight Filter. If this option is selected, Project displays all the tasks or resources, and the ones that the filter applies to will be highlighted. For instance, if you chose the Completed Tasks filter and select the Highlight Filter check box, all the completed tasks will be highlighted in the list. The method of highlighting (bold, underline, italic, and so on) can be defined on the View tab, Data, Highlight, New Highlight.

As with tables and groups, you can create a custom filter and apply it to your custom view, but you must create the custom filter before you create the custom view. This process is described in the section "Creating and Customizing Filters" later in this chapter.

 note

You must define all fields in the View Definition dialog box except for when a field is grayed out. However, after you create your view, the entries in these fields are really just starting points when you first launch the view. You can apply different tables, groups, or filters, just like any other view in Project, after you have created and applied the custom view.

Displaying the View Name in the Menu

After you have created a view, it appears in the More Views dialog box (View tab, Other Views, More Views). If you want it to appear in the main View menu, select the Show in Menu check box (refer to Figure 22.10).

You probably want to include the new view in the main View menu if you will be consistently using it. If not, you might not want to clear the Show in Menu check box, just to keep it out of the way until you need it.

Saving the View Definition

After you have entered all applicable information in the View Definition dialog box, click OK (or Cancel to exit without making any changes). The More Views dialog box is still displayed, and the view you just created or edited is highlighted in the list. To display the view immediately, click Apply. To exit the More Views dialog box without displaying the new view, click Close. The new view is saved and ready to be applied.

You can also continue working with any of the views by clicking the New, Edit, or Copy button.

Alternatively, click the Organizer button to open the Organizer dialog box to save the new view to the Global.MPT file for use in other projects. As previously mentioned, this is discussed further at the end of this chapter in the section "Organizing Views and Other Custom Elements in Project Files."

Creating a Combination View

The previous sections described copying views, editing views, and creating new Single views. This section focuses on creating new Combination views.

As mentioned previously, a Combination view displays two Single views on the screen simultaneously. Creating Combination views is similar to creating Single views. To create a Combination view, follow these steps:

1. Open the More Views dialog box by selecting the View tab, Other Views, More Views.

2. Open the Define New View dialog box by clicking the New button (refer to Figure 22.8).

3. In the Define New View dialog box, select Combination view and click OK. A version of the View Definition dialog box appears, and this time it is designed to create a Combination view rather than a Single view, as discussed in the previous sections (refer to Figure 22.9).

4. Name the new Combination view as you would a Single view. Choose a name that is descriptive and unique, and place an ampersand symbol (&) directly in front of the letter you choose to be the hotkey. If the view appears in the main View menu, you only have to type that hotkey to select the view from the list.

5. The next step is to select the top and bottom panes for the Combination view. Use the drop-down lists in the Top and Bottom fields to do this. All Single views are displayed in these two lists, including any recently created or customized views. You cannot display the same view in both panes; you must select different views for the Top and Bottom settings.

6. When you have made your selections, decide whether you want to display the new Combination view in the main View menu by selecting Show in Menu. Leaving it blank still saves the new Combination view in the More Views dialog box.

7. Click OK to save the view and exit back to the More Views dialog box, where you can immediately apply the new Combination view, or any of the other options described in the previous section "Saving the View Definition."

This process can become slightly more complicated if you want to create a new Combination view but the Single views you want to use are not yet defined. Essentially, you have to start at the bottom and work your way up.

You must first create the Single views you want to use. But before you can do that, you must create any custom tables, groups, and filters (remember, a Single view requires you to define all these fields unless they do not apply to the screen type). Creating custom tables, groups, and filters is covered in the following sections. If the tables, groups, and filters you plan to use for the Single views already exist, you do not have to create new ones.

After you have an idea of the tables, groups, and filters you plan to apply to your Single views, you can create your Single views. Select the View tab, Other Views, More Views, and click the New button. Choose Single View, click OK, and follow the process described in the previous sections.

If you want to format either of the Single views, do that as well before creating the Combination view.

 For more information about formatting views, **see** *Chapter 19, "Formatting Views," p. 569.*

When all that is finished to your satisfaction, create the Combination view using the process described earlier in this section. The newly created Single views appear in the Top and Bottom drop-down lists in the combination View Definition dialog box.

🔵 tip

If you have edited a standard view and saved it, thus replacing the original standard view with the edited view, and you want to get the original view back, you can do that in the Organizer dialog box. Click the Organizer button on the More Views dialog box, select the original view from the Global.MPT file, and click Copy. This brings the original view back into your project and overwrites your new view unless you have changed its name. It is assumed that the original view in the Global.MPT file has not been overwritten.

Printing Views

Sometimes you might want to print a hard copy of the data within a view. Hard copies can be helpful for preparing reports or presentations, showing other people who do not have immediate computer access, and analyzing while traveling—or you might just be the type of person who prefers paper to computer screens. Whatever the case is, the following sections discuss how to print views in Project.

Preparing Your Screen and Choosing Fundamentals for Your Printed View

When you print a view, the printed paper displays the exact data that is on your screen when you print it. Therefore, before printing your view, be sure that all tables, fields, filters, and groups are applied or displayed exactly as you want them to be. You learn how to customize and display all these items throughout this chapter.

The first step is to choose the appropriate view to print. If you are printing a view with a timescale, such as the Gantt Chart, the timescale that is displayed is what will be printed. You can zoom in or out using the Zoom slider on the status bar. Zooming changes the time units; zooming in displays smaller units, such as hours and minutes, and zooming out displays larger units, such as days, weeks, thirds of months, months, quarters, half-years, and years.

Alternatively, you can change the time units by choosing Format, Timescale, and selecting the time unit you want from the drop-down list in the Unit field. When you click OK, Project adjusts the timescale accordingly, based on your selection. When viewing the entire project timescale, select the View tab, Zoom, Entire Project.

If your screen is split into two panes, you must choose which pane to print. If you choose the top pane, all data is printed (unless it is filtered, in which case only the filtered data is printed). Because the bottom pane shows data based on the selection in the top pane, only data related to that selection is printed if you choose the bottom pane.

 tip

As mentioned before, a column must be completely visible on the screen to be printed. If a column is hidden and you want the data to print when you print the view, move it so it is displayed on the screen by inserting it somewhere else or dragging a divider bar that might be hiding it. Alternatively, on the View tab in the Page Setup dialog box (which is discussed in the upcoming sections), you can choose to print all columns, whether or not they are displayed. Select File, Print, Page Setup, and on the View tab, select the Print All Sheet Columns check box.

Filtering, Sorting, Grouping, and Enhancing the Display

You might want the printed view to focus on a more specific aspect of the project and not all the tasks or resources. In this case, apply a filter to the display before you print it. Applying and customizing filters are covered later in this chapter.

Similarly, you might want your printed view to display task or resource data in a different order than what is on your screen. You can apply a custom group, which is discussed later in this chapter, or use the Sort or Group By command.

➡ *For more information about using the Sort and Group By commands,* **see** *Chapter 11, "Using Standard Views, Tables, Filters, and Groups to Review Your Schedule," p. 357.*

Formatting the text data can enhance your printed view and make it easier to examine. You can highlight selected tasks or resources, display items in bold, italic, or underline, or change the font and size. Also, you can customize gridlines, as well as column and row separator lines. All of these formatting options, as well as additional ones, must be performed before you print your view.

➥ *For more information about formatting views, **see** Chapter 19, "Formatting Views,"*
p. 569.

Using Page Breaks

Like other Microsoft tools, page breaks are inserted automatically for multiple-page printed views. You can, however, insert them yourself in specific areas. For instance, if you are printing a task or resource list, you might want a certain task or resource to be at the top of a page. When you insert a page break at a specific task or resource, that page break is tied to that item, and not the location in the list. In other words, if you move the task or resource, or filter, group, or sort the list, the page break stays with the task or resource, wherever it moves to within the list.

Furthermore, you can insert page breaks, but still opt to ignore some or all of them in the final dialog box before you print. This feature is handy in case you want to print a special version of the view without having to insert the page breaks again later.

With Project, inserting a page break requires you to first add the Insert Page Break to either the Ribbon or the Quick Access toolbar (right-click on either, select Customize, and from the Commands not on the Ribbon group, select Insert Page Break). To insert a page break, select the row directly underneath the intended page break and then click Insert Page Break. The manually inserted page break appears as a solid line.

To remove a page break, the Remove page break control must be added to either the Ribbon or the Quick Access toolbar. Select the row just below the existing page break and then select click Remove Page Break. The line disappears. You can also remove all page breaks by selecting all rows (click the upper-left column heading) and clicking Remove All Page Breaks—which also must be added to either the Quick Access toolbar or the Ribbon.

 tip

By properly inserting page breaks, you can print different aspects of the same project to give to different people. For instance, you could print different parts of the overall task list for different resources that are responsible for those specific tasks, without having to print the entire list for them and without having to create separate project files.

Using the Page Setup Dialog Box

The Page Setup dialog box is where you can change the appearance of printed view pages. You can modify margins, orientation (landscape vs. portrait), headers and footers, and so on. Changing a view's page setup applies to that view only, not to any other views within the project.

To open the Page Setup dialog box, choose File, Print, Page Setup. Figure 22.12 displays the Page Setup dialog box.

There are multiple tabs in the Page Setup dialog box. Choose one to display and edit the specific settings for that particular tab. The usage of these tabs is covered in the following sections. Although the functionality of the tabs goes in order (beginning with Page and moving left to right), the section headings refer to the action and not necessarily the Tab title.

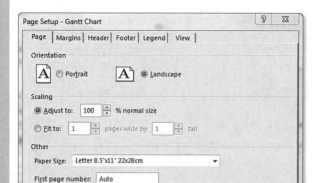

Figure 22.12
Change the appearance of printed pages in the Page Setup dialog box. This dialog box has the Page tab active.

 tip

If you've added the Page Setup control to the Quick Access toolbar, the Print Preview button will be available. At any time when working in the Page Setup dialog box, you can preview what the printed pages will look like by clicking the Print Preview button, located at the bottom of every tab. Or, while working in the Page Setup dialog box, changes will be reflected in the Print Preview pane on the File tab right after you click OK.

Selecting the Orientation

Under the Page tab, the first choice you can make is the Orientation field. The orientation refers to the layout of the printed page. You have two choices: Portrait (taller and narrower) and Landscape (shorter and wider). If you are printing a long list, or if you are adding the printed view to another document, you might want to choose Portrait because that is the normal orientation for most other text documents and because you can fit more rows in your list onto one page. On the other hand, if you have a large timescale, you would probably want to use the Landscape orientation because it can accommodate more of the timescale.

Scaling the Printout

Also under the Page tab is the Scaling field. Scaling is used to enlarge or reduce the size of your printouts. You can use a percentage in the Adjust To box, or specify a number of pages in the Fit To boxes.

For instance, if you look at the Print Preview pane, and see that your list runs just over one page, you might want to reduce the size so that it fits onto one page rather than print the extra page just for a few items.

Also, you can print multiple pages onto one sheet of paper. To do so, click the Options button and change the Pages Per Sheet field to however many pages you want on each printed sheet of paper. For example, if you entered 2 pages wide by 1 page tall, and change Pages Per Sheet to 2, your printed sheet would have two pages—one on the left half of the page and one on the right (see Figure 22.13). If you entered 1 page wide by 2 pages tall, it would still print two pages onto one printed page (if your Pages Per Sheet was set to 2), only this time they would be on the top and bottom rather than the left and right.

 tip

Use the Print Preview pane relentlessly until you have scaled the printout exactly how you want it. This saves time and paper! If you are enlarging or reducing the scale to fit on one or more pages, try the Adjust To % field. If you are trying to fit multiple pages onto one sheet, try the Fit To fields with the Pages Per Sheet field defined correctly. After you are comfortable using these features, you can experiment more to find the method you prefer.

Figure 22.13
If you defined the Scaling field of the Page tab in the Page Setup dialog box as 2 pages wide by 1 page tall, and the Pages Per Sheet field was set to 2 (found by clicking the Options button), each printed page would have two pages on it—one on the left and one on the right.

Designating Paper Size and Page Numbering

At the bottom of the Page tab in the Page Setup dialog box, you can set the paper size as well as the first page number. To set the paper size, choose from the drop-down list in the Paper Size field. You can also use the printer Properties dialog box to set the paper size (choose File, Print, Properties).

Set the page numbering by entering the first page to print in the First Page Number field. By default, Auto is selected. Do not change this field unless you want Project to begin printing on another page besides the first one. For example, if you have a multipage view to print but do not need the first two pages, enter **3** in the First Page Number field, and the first page to print will be the third page.

Specifying Margins and Borders

The second tab in the Page Setup dialog box is the Margins tab. Like its name suggests, you set the margins using this tab. The default margin for all four borders is one-half inch (0.5"), meaning that there will be at least one-half inch of space between the edge of the printed page and the data it contains (see Figure 22.14).

Borders surround the page with a box. You can opt to display borders, which places a box around the data at the specified margin measurement (in this case, one-half inch from the edges of the paper), or not to display borders, leaving the area outside the margin blank. You can also opt to display borders around the outer pages only, which makes it easier to find the beginning and end of a multipage list or other view. This is done on the bottom of the Margins tab under the Borders Around field. By default, borders are selected to be displayed.

 note

Project always places a margin of one-quarter inch (0.25") on all printed views, even if you set the margins to zero.

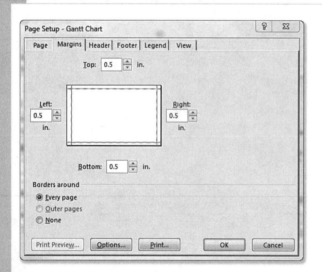

Figure 22.14
Set margins for the printed view under the Margins tab of the Page Setup dialog box.

Using the Header and Footer Tabs

The Header and Footer tabs look almost identical, except for the fact that the Header tab is for headers (that is, summary displays at the top of the page), and the Footer tab is for footers (that is, summary displays at the bottom of the page). Both tabs have a Preview box at the top that displays in real time the header or footer you are creating. You cannot make entries in this box, but you can make entries in the box below it (see Figure 22.15).

Figure 22.15
Define header and footer information for your printed view in the Header and Footer tabs. This example shows the Header tab.

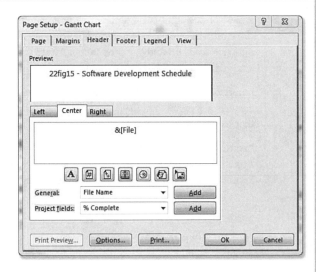

You can enter a maximum of five lines of header text and three lines of footer text on each page of a printed document.

The Alignment tabs give you three options: the left side of the page, the center, or the right side. You can enter different data in all three alignment tabs, and the header or footer displays it all.

Below the Alignment tabs is the header or footer entry box. Use this box to enter any text you want to define as the header or footer for the Alignment tab you selected above the box.

Directly below the entry box is a row of seven buttons that you use to format, insert system codes, or insert pictures into the header or footer (refer to Figure 22.15). Hover over any of these buttons for a Screentip to help you identify the button's purpose. The seven buttons are described in the following list, moving from left to right:

- **Format Text Font**—When you click this button, the Font dialog box appears, enabling you to format the font, font style, size, color, and script for the text in the header or footer. If you want to format only part of the header or footer, highlight it using the mouse, and click the Format Text Font button. Your definitions in the Font dialog box apply only to the highlighted items. You can format different text in different ways on each of the Alignment tabs.

- **Insert Page Number**—When you click the Insert Page Number button, Project inserts the following code: **&[Page]**. While this is displayed, only the page number is actually printed. Therefore, if you want the word *Page* to be displayed, you must type it before the page number code. For example, for the printed view to display "Page 5" on the fifth page of the document, you would enter **Page** (including a space after the word *Page*) and then click the Insert Page Number button, so it would look like this in the Preview box: **Page&[Page]**. The result would be "Page 5" on either the header or the footer (depending on which tab you were working in).

- **Insert Total Page Count**—This button is similar to the Insert Page Number button in that it displays a code when you click it: **&[Pages]**. This code represents the total number of pages *only*, and not the current page number. Therefore, if you wanted the header or footer to display "Page 3 of 5" on the third page of a five-page document, you would enter **Page** (including a space after the word *Page*), click the Insert Page Number button, and then enter **of** (with a space before and after the word *of*) and click the Insert Total Page Count button, so the Preview field would look like this: **Page&[Page] of&[Pages]**.

- **Insert Current Date**—This button also displays a code: **&[Date]**. When printed, the current date, according to your computer, is displayed in your header or footer. The date displayed is the date that the document is printed.

- **Insert Current Time**—This button displays the code **&[Time]**. Again, this is only a code; the time (based on your computer) is printed in its place. The time displayed is the time the document is printed.

- **Insert File Name**—This button inserts the code **&[File]**. As with the other codes, this will not actually be printed, but the project file name will be, as displayed in the Preview box. Unless you have Windows set to display file extensions (such as .mpp), the extension is not displayed with the filename.

- **Insert Picture**—When you click this button, the Insert Picture dialog box opens, from which you can browse your files for the picture or image you are looking to insert. This can be any type of picture file, such as WMF, PCS, CGM, TIF, BMP, or GIF. This button is especially useful when inserting a company logo into a header or footer.

 tip

Printing the date and time as a header or footer can be useful, especially when you produce several revisions of the document.

 tip

A good way to please your clients is to insert their company logo as a header or footer on your printed documents for the project they have hired you to manage.

Using the Drop-Down Lists in the Header and Footer Tabs

Below the seven buttons in the Header and Footer columns are drop-down lists for the General and Project Fields boxes. These can be used in addition to the seven buttons for entering project data into a header or footer.

The first drop-down list, General, contains the same data provided by the seven insert buttons (such as Total Page Count), as well as information from the Project Properties dialog box (such as Project Title), which can be defined by selecting File, Properties.

➡ *For more information about the Project Properties dialog box,* **see** *the "Set Project Attributes" section on* **p. 32** *in Chapter 2.*

The Project Fields drop-down list can be used to insert many fields found within the project. This list includes any fields regarding cost, duration, work, and dates, as well as custom text and custom number fields.

To insert project data into a header or footer using these two drop-down lists, make the selection and click the Add button next to the appropriate box.

Using Legends

Besides headers and footers, you can insert legends into your printed views or reports to further describe the contents of the document. A legend can be especially helpful in explaining graphic elements in your document, such as the timescale on the Gantt Chart view.

Figure 22.16 shows the Page Setup dialog box open to the Legend tab. This is the area where you define the settings for the legend. Notice the similarities to the Header and Footer tabs.

Figure 22.16
Define legend information for your printed document in the Legend tab.

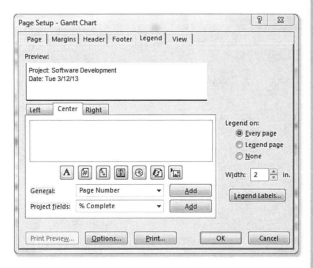

The Legend tab has Alignment tabs in which you can enter up to three lines of text in each area (Left, Center, and Right). These three lines of text can be different for each of the three Alignment options. By default, the project name and date are entered on the left side of every page, as defined in Figure 22.16.

Below the Alignment tabs is the text box in which you can type in text, or use the same seven buttons as the Header and Footer tabs. The buttons are used exactly as described in the bulleted list in the previous section "Using the Header and Footer Tabs" to format, insert system codes, or insert pictures into the legend. Also, the two drop-down lists, General and Project fields, below the seven insert buttons function the same as described in the previous section to insert specific project information into the legend.

Under the Legend On field, you can choose where to display the legend. Choosing Every Page displays the legend at the bottom of every page in the document. Choosing Legend Page prints the legend once on a separate page at the end of the document. Choosing None displays no legend anywhere.

As much as half of the legend area can be occupied by text. The width of the legend text area is defined in the Width box by choosing a number between 0 and 5 inches. This number represents the amount of space devoted in the legend area to text. Therefore, if you enter **0**, the entire legend area is devoted to graphics and no text. If you type **5**, the entire legend area is devoted to text. By default, the entry is 2 inches.

Selecting Special Options for Views

The View tab is the final tab on the Page Setup dialog box (see Figure 22.17). In the View tab, you set specific options for printing different views. Not all of these options are available for all views; some options might be dimmed out if they are unavailable.

Figure 22.17
Set special view options in the View tab.

 note

When you're printing the Calendar view and you open the Page Setup dialog box from the Page Setup control you added to the Quick Access toolbar or the Ribbon, the View tab in the Page Setup dialog box appears different from the one shown in Figure 22.17. The Calendar view version of the View tab is covered later in this section.

The following list describes the options in the View tab. Place a check in the box next to each option to activate it:

- **Print All Sheet Columns**—Select this check box when printing a sheet view (such as Gantt Chart, Task Sheet, Resource Sheet) to print all columns in the view, regardless of whether they are displayed on the screen when you are ready to print.

- **Print First *X* Columns on All Pages**—This option enables you to print the first three (or any number you specify) columns on all pages. This overrides the default of printing the first three columns (ID number, Indicators, and Task Name columns) on the first page only. This is a great feature to enable if you have a table in your printed view that extends multiple pages, and you are not going to fasten it together. When you get to page 5, for example, you will not have to go back and look at page 1 to see which task is in a certain row because the first few columns will be printed on all the pages.

- **Print Notes**—This option prints the notes you have attached to tasks or resources. The notes are printed on a separate page.

- **Print Blank Pages**—By default, all pages are set to print. You can clear this box if you do not want any blank pages that might exist within your document to print.

- **Fit Timescale to End of Page**—Select this box to ensure that a timescale unit does not break across two pages. For example, on the timescale, if a week begins on one page and ends on another, you can select this box to make sure that the entire week is printed on the same page rather than being broken up over two pages.

- **Print Column Totals**—This feature adds a new row at the bottom of the printout, which houses the totals for each column.

- **Print Row Totals for Values Within Print Date Range**—This feature adds a column at the end of the printout that houses data totals for each row within the date range you specify in the Print dialog box (which is discussed in a few sections). The row totals column always prints on a separate page, after the timescale and before the notes.

> **note**
>
> It is always good practice to attach notes to tasks or resources, especially to communicate scope, constraints, assumptions, and limitations.

As mentioned before, when you're printing a Calendar view, the View tab in the Page Setup dialog box contains different options, as displayed in Figure 22.18.

Figure 22.18
The View tab in the Page Setup dialog box for the Calendar view contains different options.

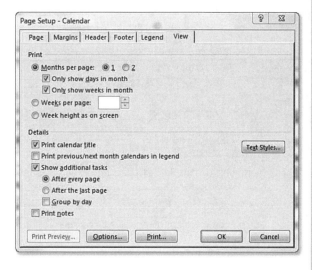

The following list describes the options for the View tab when printing the Calendar view:

- **Months Per Page**—Choose to print either one or two months on each page. Selecting Only Show Days in Month means that if the month starts in the middle of a week, the days before it in the same week (the last days of the previous month) will be displayed as blank boxes. Selecting Only Show Weeks in Month means that weeks from other months will not be printed.

- **Weeks Per Page**—If you have many tasks and want to print only one or a few weeks on each page, choose this option and specify the number of weeks per page to print. However, if you select eight weeks or more, it becomes unreadable (the same reason you can only select up to two months per page in the previous option).

- **Week Height as on Screen**—This option matches the printed calendar with the week height on the screen display.

- **Print Calendar Title**—This feature prints the calendar title at the top of each page.

- **Print Previous/Next Month Calendars in Legend**—This feature prints a miniature version of the previous and next months' calendars to appear in the legend. Only the dates are displayed and not any project information. Be sure the legend is set to something other than None in the Legend On field on the Legend tab.

> **note**
>
> You can only select one of these three options: Months Per Page, Weeks Per Page, or Week Height as on Screen.

- **Show Additional Tasks**—Sometimes you might have more tasks than can fit on the calendar. Select this box, and Project prints an overflow page containing these extra tasks. Choose to print an overflow page after every page (After Every Page check box), or at the end of the printout (After the Last Page check box). Also, you can select Group by Day, which lists the extra tasks for each day on the overflow page. If a task is worked on over several days, it is listed every day if the Group by Day box is selected.

- **Print Notes**—This option prints the notes for tasks on a separate page after the calendar or overflow page (if it exists). The Task ID and name appear with the note.

- **Text Styles button**—This button opens the Text Styles dialog box, which enables you to format the font type for any text within the printout.

Previewing the Printed View

As previously mentioned, a print preview is provided automatically when you select the File tab, Print (see Figure 22.19).

Use the arrows at the bottom right of the screen to scroll through various pages in the print preview. Next to the arrow buttons is the actual size button. Alternatively, you can click on the screen to switch back and forth between actual and preview size.

The buttons next to the actual size button are for displaying one or multiple pages on the same screen.

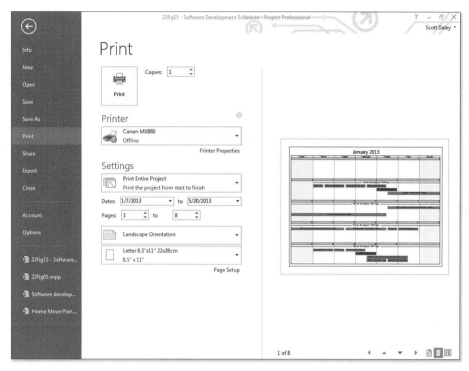

Figure 22.19
Simply selected print from the File tab to preview what the actual printout will look like.

Printing

Selecting the Number of Copies to Print

Enter the number of copies you want to print in the Copies field next to the Print button, or select the number of copies to print from the drop-down.

Selecting the Printer

You can choose the printer to send your document to. Be sure you are using the correct printer. If the printer you want is not an option from the Printer drop-down list, you might have to add it by using Start, Printers and Faxes, and selecting Add a Printer in the Printer Tasks panel. If you are unsure of a network printer setup, it might be beneficial to contact the person in your organization who is responsible for such issues, or consult the printer manual.

Selecting the Pages to Print

In the Settings area, select the pages you want to print. Generally, you want to print them all, so Print Entire Project is selected as the default. But you might want to print only some pages within the document. You can print specific dates, specific pages, or a combination of the two.

By default, All is selected, meaning Project prints the entire timescale from the project's start date to its finish date. However, you can define a more specific date range in the Dates From and To fields.

Choose the Print Left Column of Pages Only option to print only the pages in the left column of a multiple-page layout in the Print Preview screen.

Selecting the Orientation and Paper Size

Also in the Settings area, select the paper orientation (Landscape or Portrait), and select the paper size. As described previously, you can click on Page Setup for still more options.

After you have selected all your print options, it is finally time to print your document. To do so, click the Print button (see Figure 22.20).

> **tip**
>
> As discussed in the previous section "Preparing Your Screen and Choosing Fundamentals for Your Printed View" be sure that the correct time units are displayed on your timescale screen before you print.

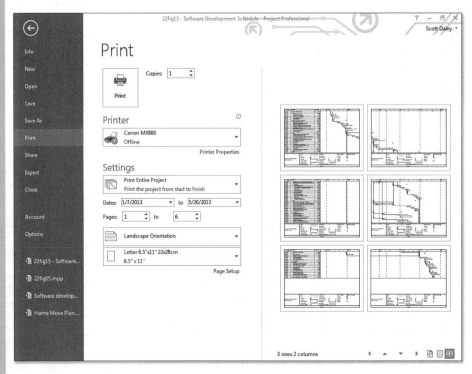

Figure 22.20
Choose where to print, how to print, how much to print, and how many to print in the Print dialog box.

Creating and Customizing Filters

Just as tables define which columns and rows are displayed for tasks or resources, filters define which tasks and resources are shown in a table or view. A filter is always applied to any view. By default, the initial filter is All Tasks or All Resources (depending on whether you are displaying a task or resource view), which shows all the tasks or resources in a project (as their titles suggest). If you apply a highlighted filter, all tasks or resources are displayed, and those selected by the filter are highlighted.

 note

Filters defined here can also be used in Reports.

As with views and tables, there is a More Filters dialog box you use to edit, copy, or create a new filter (see Figure 22.21). To open the More Filters dialog box, select the View tab, Data, Filter, More Filters.

Figure 22.21
You can edit, copy, or create a new filter in the More Filters dialog box.

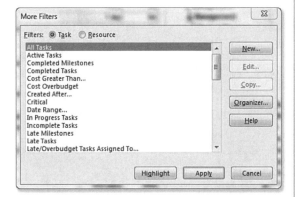

As with the More Tables dialog box, you can choose to display either the Task or Resource filters at the top of the box. The same buttons appear on the right: New, Edit, Copy, Organizer, and Help. Choosing New creates a new filter, Edit modifies an existing filter and replaces the original, Copy modifies an existing filter (saving both the original and the modified version), and Organizer aids in saving filters to the Global.MPT file (as well as other features described at the end of this chapter).

The Help button is a good resource if you are confused about any part of creating or customizing filters.

Before you begin to customize or create a filter, you want to have a good idea of exactly what you want the filter to do. It might be helpful to view the functionality of the existing filters to give you a better idea of what you already have available. If you find a filter that comes close to meeting your needs, you should use the Copy command to modify the filter appropriately without losing the original. If none of the filters are close to what you are looking for,

 note

In a Combination view, no filter can be applied to the bottom pane because the bottom pane is already filtered and controlled by what is selected in the top pane.

create a new one with the New button on the More Filters dialog box.

To view the functionality of an existing filter, choose it from the list, and click the Copy button (or the Edit button if you want to replace the original). This opens up the Filter Definition dialog box, and the definitions for the filter are displayed. If you click the New button, the Filter Definition dialog box appears with no information defined. Figure 22.22 displays the Filter Definition dialog box opened as if you were going to modify a copy of the Date Range filter.

The upcoming sections refer to Figure 22.22 while discussing the different fields used to create or customize a filter.

 note

If you select All Tasks or All Resources, you cannot choose Edit or Copy. These filters are permanent, because they really do not filter for anything. Instead, they display all the tasks or resources in your project.

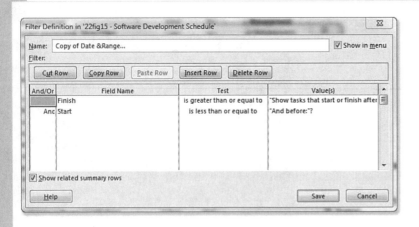

Figure 22.22
You can make changes to the Date Range filter or most of the other filters, or create a new filter, in the Filter Definition dialog box.

Naming a Filter

As with naming views and tables, choose a name for your filter that is definitive and unique. Select the Show in Menu box if you want the filter to be in the main filter list (Project, Filtered For) as well as the filter drop-down list on the Formatting toolbar. Place an ampersand symbol (&) directly in front of any letter in the name you want as the hotkey (see the Name field in Figure 22.22; the ampersand symbol is in front of the letter *R*). That way, in the main filter list, you can press the hotkey as a shortcut to select that particular filter and then press Enter to apply it.

Defining Filter Criteria

For each test Project is to conduct within the filter, you must create a row in the Filter Definition dialog box. For example, the Date Range filter performs two tests, and each test is defined on its own row in Figure 22.22. Project internally tests all tasks to the criteria, and if they meet the criteria, they are displayed when the filter is applied.

Four columns are used to define the criteria for a filter:

- **And/Or**—This column is used if multiple tests are performed in the filter. The top row is blank because it is the first test. Beginning in the second row, you would define this column by choosing And or Or from the drop-down list. If you choose And, the test criterion must be met for the task or resource to be included in the filtered list. If you choose Or, this indicates that only some of the tests must be met. In Figure 22.22, And is chosen, meaning that the task must meet criterion for both tests to be included in the filtered list. If Or was chosen, the task would only have to meet the criteria for one of the tests.

- **Field Name**—In this column, select the name of the field you are testing. The field relates to the task or resource table you will apply the filter to. For example, in Figure 22.22, in the first row, Finish is selected because the first test will be performed on the Finish field for all tasks. You can type in the field name or choose from the drop-down list.

- **Test**—This column defines the actual test that is to take place. Make your Test selection from the drop-down list. In Figure 22.22, the filter is defined to test whether the Finish field is greater than or equal to the entry in the Value column, and whether the Start field is less than or equal to the entry in the Value column in the second row. If a task's Start and Finish fields contain an entry that is within these defined boundaries, that task is displayed when the filter is applied.

  The table at the end of this list (see Table 22.1) describes all the test options and their meanings. The various Within and Contains tests are described in the upcoming section "Using More Filter Criterion Tests."

- **Value(s)**—This is the final column used in defining the criteria for the test. In this column, you enter a value for what the test is actually testing for. To make an entry in the Value(s) field, you can type it in, choose from the drop-down list, or create a prompt for interactive filters. Interactive filters open a dialog box asking for input when the filter is executed. This is discussed in greater detail in the upcoming section "Using Interactive Filters."

In Figure 22.22, in the first row, the test is whether the Finish field of a task is greater than or equal to a value. In this case, you would enter a date in the Value(s) field, thus completing the criteria for that particular test. Therefore, the complete test would be whether the Finish field is greater than or equal to the date you entered in the Value(s) column. In other words, if the task's finish date is the same date or later than the date you specify in the Value field, it has met the criteria for that particular test. If it meets the criteria for all other tests as defined in the Filter Definition dialog box, it will be displayed when the filter is applied.

You have to enter two values in this column if you are defining the Test column as Is Within or Is Not Within. In this case, separate the two value entries with a comma and include them on the same row.

Table 22.1   Filter Test Option Names and Their Meanings

Test Name	Meaning
Equals	The entry in the Field Name column must match the entry in the Value(s) column exactly.
Does Not Equal	The entry in the Field Name column must differ from the entry in the Value(s) column.
Is Greater Than	The entry in the Field Name column must be more than the entry in the Value(s) column. If the entries are dates, the date in the Field Name column must be later than the date in the Value(s) column.
Is Greater Than or Equal To	The entry in the Field Name column must be equal to or more than the entry in the Value(s) column. If the entries are dates, the date in the Field Name column must be the same date or later than the date in the Value(s) column.
Is Less Than	The entry in the Field Name column must be less than the entry in the Value(s) column. If the entries are dates, the date in the Field Name column must be earlier than the date in the Value(s) column.
Is Less Than or Equal To	The entry in the Field Name column must be equal to or less than the entry in the Value(s) column. If the entries are dates, the date in the Field Name column must be the same date or earlier than the date in the Value(s) column.
Is Within	The entry in the Field Name column must be on or between the range of the two entries in the Value(s) column.
Is Not Within	The entry in the Field Name column must be outside the range of the two entries in the Value(s) column.
Contains	The entry in the Field Name column must contain the string of characters in the Value(s) column.
Does Not Contain	The entry in the Field Name column must not contain the string of characters in the Value(s) column.
Contains Exactly	The entry in the Field Name column must contain the exact string of characters in the Value(s) column. There might be more than one string of characters in the Value(s) column; if this is the case, the entry in the Field Name column must contain exactly one of the strings of characters in the Value(s) column. The strings of characters in the Value(s) column are separated by commas.

To insert a test row before one that already exists, select the existing row and click Insert Row. A new blank test row appears above the existing one.

When you apply the filter, you can also opt to display the summary data for the filtered tasks by checking the box next to Show Related Summary Rows. This can apply to a resource filter as well; if you are filtering for tasks assigned to a resource, selecting this box displays the summary data for the resource's assigned tasks.

After you are satisfied with your entries in the Filter Definition dialog box, click the Save button to return to the More Filters dialog box. Select the filter and click Apply to apply the filter immediately, or click Close to save the filter for later use. You can also click Highlight to apply the filter immediately, displaying all the tasks or resources and highlighting the filtered ones.

 tip

You might want to practice creating a new filter that displays all the subtasks of a project. This helps you get familiar with the process of creating and customizing filters, and leaves you with a useful custom filter. To do so, remove all summary tasks and milestones (see Figure 22.23).

Figure 22.23
In this newly created filter called Subtasks, the summary and milestone tasks are defined as "No," meaning they are not displayed when the filter is applied.

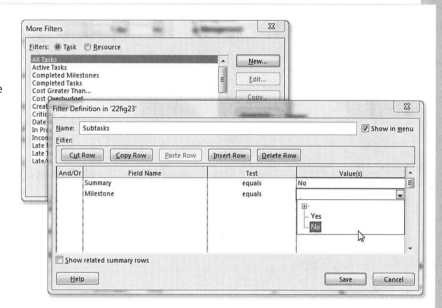

Using More Filter Criterion Tests

As you are creating or customizing a filter, you have limitations in your definitions, depending on the tests you are creating. For example, many entries in the Value(s) column are a choice between Yes and No only. If you have entered invalid information into any of the columns when defining tests in the Filter Definition dialog box, Project warns you and instructs you to go back and fix the problem (see Figure 22.24).

Figure 22.24
This warning box appears when you have created an invalid test in the Filter Definition dialog box.

Table 22.1 displays all the test options available when defining filters. The first few are easy to understand, but the last five (Is Within, Is Not Within, Contains, Does Not Contain, and Contains Exactly) are slightly more complex.

Is Within and Is Not Within Tests

When using the Is Within or the Is Not Within tests, you are defining the filter to test according to a range of values. You define this range in the Value(s) column, entering the endpoints for the value range together in the same row, separated by a comma. The endpoints you enter are included as part of the value range. Thus, if you use the Is Within test, you are filtering for a value within the value range you define, including the endpoints. If you are using the Is Not Within test, you are filtering for a value that is outside the endpoints for the value range you define.

Perhaps you want to filter for tasks that are resourced by either management or a project manager. You would enter those values in the Value(s) column, surrounded by tick marks, separated by a comma. Project would then filter for all tasks whose resource names are management or project manager when the filter is applied, as shown in Figure 22.25.

The same methodology applies to the Is Not Within test; if you want to filter for tasks with resources that aren't management or project manager, use the Is Not Within test.

Contains, Does Not Contain, and Contains Exactly Tests

The Contains test filters for a specific string of characters you enter in the Value(s) column. This test is especially helpful when you want to filter for words in a task or resource name, or in any text field.

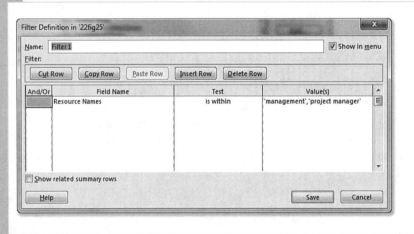

Figure 22.25
To filter for tasks within certain values, use the Is Within test.

Type the word or string of characters in the Value(s) column when using a Contains test. When you apply this filter, Project displays all tasks or resources whose name contains the word or string of characters you entered. For example, if you wanted to display all tasks that have the word *expense* in their name, you would type **expense** in the Value(s) column, as shown in Figure 22.26. You could define this test in a new filter or as an additional test to an existing one.

Figure 22.26
To filter all task names for the word expense, type it in the test's Value(s) column.

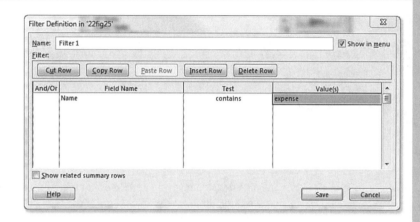

note

Project filters for plural versions of words when using the Contains test, as long as the plural version contains the string of characters you define in the Value(s) column. In the preceding example, if you had tasks that contain the word *expenses* in their names, Project would select those when the filter is applied, as well as tasks with the word *expense*, because both actually contain the string of characters that spell out "expense." The Contains Exactly test, however, would not select both; it would select only the exact string of characters in the tasks' names.

If you were to perform the preceding test using Does Not Contain, Project would list all tasks whose names do not have the word *expense* anywhere in them.

The Contains Exactly test performs much like its title suggests. If you enter a string of characters in the Value(s) column for a Contains Exactly test of the task names and then apply the filter, Project displays all tasks whose names contain *exactly* the string of characters you defined. Therefore, if you enter **expense**, Project will not display tasks whose names have the word *expenses*, because the string of characters is not exact.

Similarly, if you have two or more words in the task name, and only enter one word in the Value(s) column, the words in the task name will have to be separated by a comma (see Table 22.2).

Table 22.2   Examples of Task Names That Would Be Selected with the Different Contains Filters Using "Expense" in the Value(s) Column

Task Name	Contains	Does Not Contain	Contains Exactly
Calculate May Expenses	X		
Calculate May Expense	X		
Expenses, May 2010	X		
Expense, May	X		X
Calculate May Expenditures		X	

In Table 22.2, the five listed task names are all filtered for the word *expense* using the three different Contains tests. If the test displays the task when the filter is applied, it has an X in that column.

In short, the Contains Exactly test is useful for fields that have comma-separated entries and for finding fields that have the string of characters exactly. The Contains test is useful for searching for fields that contain the string of characters somewhere, regardless of what else is in the field.

note

The string of characters is not case sensitive. In Table 22.2, you could filter for "Expense" or "expense," and the results would be the same.

Using Wildcards in the Value(s) Column

You might encounter a situation where you want to filter for a string of characters, but the string of characters might have slight variations within your project. To solve this problem, you can use wildcards in your definition. However, to use wildcards, you must use the Equals or Not Equals tests only.

A wildcard in Project is similar to a wildcard in a game of poker; it can represent any character in the string. During an intense game of poker, the dealer might call "deuces wild," meaning that all the "two" cards in the deck are wild and you can play them as any card you want (such as an Ace, King, and so on). In Project, the same theory applies. You can use the wildcard characters to represent any other character.

The wildcard characters you use are the asterisk (*) and the question mark (?). The asterisk represents any number of missing characters, including no characters, and the question mark represents a single missing character.

When you define a string of characters, the characters that are not wildcards must be in the places you defined them to be selected in the filtering process. The wildcards can be any character, or number of characters, as long as the non-wildcard characters are in place.

For example, if you enter **t?p** in the Value(s) column using an Equals or Not Equals test, Project would filter for fields that have such entries as top, tip, t4p, t0p, and so on. Similarly, if you enter **t*p**, Project filters for t55p, tp, temp, t739stp, and so on.

Furthermore, you can search using a wildcard character. To do so, place a caret symbol (^) directly before the wildcard character. You must begin and end the string with an asterisk. For example, to search for fields that have a question mark (?), you would type ***^?***.

Using Interactive Filters

As previously mentioned, you can create a prompt for an interactive filter in the Value(s) column of the Filter Definition dialog box. An interactive filter is a flexible filter that does not always search for the same value when the filter is applied. Instead, you are prompted for input, and your response provides the value(s) to test for. You can distinguish interactive filters from regular filters because they have an ellipsis (...) after their name.

To create an interactive filter, type a message in the Value(s) column when creating a filter test in the Filter Definition dialog box. Surround your prompt with double quotes (" ") and end it with a question mark (?). Then, when the filter is applied, the prompt is displayed in a dialog box, and Project waits for you to answer the prompt. You receive a separate dialog box prompt for each test you create in the Filter Definition dialog box.

In addition, you can enter more than one prompt on the same row if you are using an Is Within test or another test that requires two values. Enter each prompt surrounded in double quotes and ending with a question mark, and place a comma in between prompts, so it looks like this: **"Prompt 1"?, "Prompt 2"?**. Both prompts will be included in the same dialog box when the filter is applied.

Project already contains several interactive filters. You can view any of them. For example, open the More Filters dialog box (View tab, Data, Filter, More Filters) and choose any of the filters that have an ellipsis at the end of the name, such as Created After.... Click the Copy button to display the Filter Definition dialog box, as shown in Figure 22.27.

Notice the Value(s) column in this example. This is how a value prompt for an interactive filter should be displayed.

If you were to apply this filter, a small dialog box would appear, prompting you to choose a date as the value. Project would then filter for all tasks created after the date you specified (see Figure 22.28).

Perhaps you want to change a filter to an interactive filter. To do so, simply change the Value(s) column entry or entries to the appropriate interactive filter format. For example, open the Filter Definition dialog box for In Progress Tasks and follow these steps:

1. If you are copying the filter, give it a unique name.

2. In the Value(s) column for the first test row, replace NA with the interactive prompt. Whatever you put inside the double quotes will be prompted in the dialog box. Type something like this: **"Define the start date:"?**.

3. Define the interactive prompt for the second test row in the Value(s) column. Type something like this: **"And the finish date:"?**.

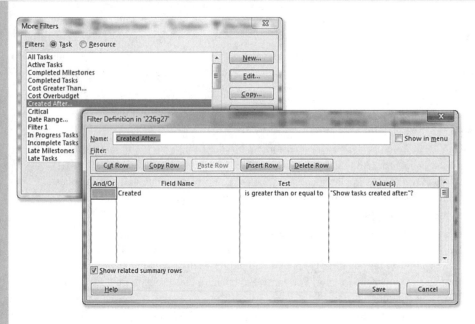

Figure 22.27
Define value prompts for interactive filters in the Filter Definition dialog box.

Figure 22.28
When you apply an interactive filter, Project prompts you with dialog boxes like this one to define value information for the filter.

4. Select the Show in Menu box if you want the interactive filter to be displayed in the main Filtered For menu. It automatically is displayed in the More Filters list. Click Save, and then click Apply. The first dialog box appears, prompting you to define the start date for the filter. Then, the second dialog box appears, prompting you to define the finish date.

Creating Calculated Filters

A calculated filter compares the values of two different fields of a task or resource. Cost Overbudget and Work Overbudget are both examples of a calculated filter. Figure 22.29 shows the Filter Definition dialog box for Work Overbudget. Notice that the Value(s) column in the first test row is Baseline Work surrounded in brackets ([]). The brackets indicate that this is a calculated filter, because the test value is also a field name, as indicated on the second test row.

When creating a calculated field, you enter a task or resource field in the Value(s) column surrounded by brackets ([and]), and then you must define the value for that field. In other words, the example in Figure 22.29 defines Actual Work as being greater than Baseline Work for the task to be selected when the filter is applied. However, you must also give Baseline Work a value, which takes place on the second line. You cannot compare two fields unless they both have a value.

Figure 22.29
The Baseline Work is a test value as well as a test field in this calculated filter.

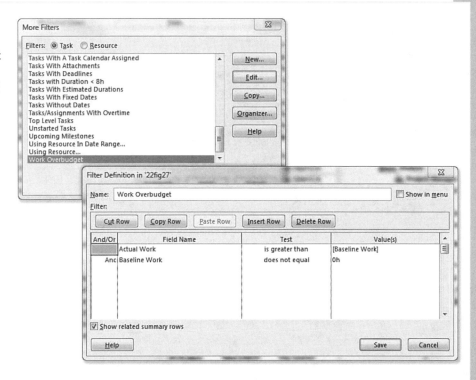

Creating Multiple Criteria Filters

As previously mentioned, if you have more than one test in a filter, each test is defined on its own row in the Filter Definition dialog box. The And/Or column is used to define the relationship of the tests. The order of the tests is important; if you have two or more tests, the And/Or column of the second row determines its relationship to the test above it, and so on. If you enter **And**, both tests must be met. If you enter **Or**, either test must be met to be selected when the filter is applied.

Furthermore, you can group multiple criteria together when defining a filter. Look at the Incomplete Tasks Filter Definition dialog box in Figure 22.30.

The first test states that for a task to be incomplete, its % Complete must not equal 100%. But, there is another way to define a task as incomplete, as the second test criterion indicates. Following the first test criteria, there is a row that reads only "Or," and is shaded in gray. This row indicates that multiple criteria are used to define this filter, and because it reads "Or," only one of them must be met.

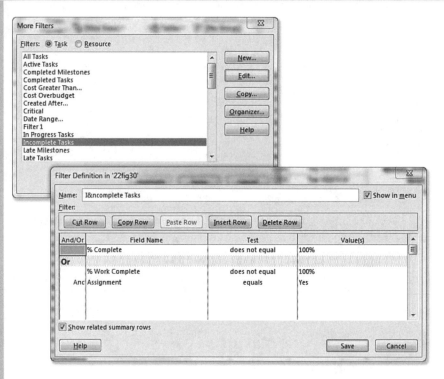

Figure 22.30
Define multiple criteria for filter tests by inserting a blank row with only the And/Or column defined.

The second set of criteria, on the third and fourth rows, has two tests that must be met, indicated by the And in the fourth row. They state that % Work Complete must not equal 100%, and that the task is assigned to at least one resource. If a task meets both of these criteria, it will be selected when the filter is applied, just as it will be selected if it meets the criteria defined on the first line.

To insert a row similar to either of the additional rows in Figure 22.30, simply select a blank row, and either choose And or Or. Define nothing else in the row. When you click out of that row, it will be shaded in gray, and the And or Or entry will be in bold and placed all the way to the left of the row, indicating that there are multiple criteria tests for that particular filter.

 tip

Remember, the order in which you define the tests is the order in which the tests will be performed in Project. The And/Or column relates directly to the row above it.

Creating Custom Filters with AutoFilter

Another option for creating custom filters is the AutoFilter. To use this feature, select the View tab, Data, Filter, Display AutoFilter. No dialog box appears just yet, but you can tell you have turned on the AutoFilter feature if the column headings on the table you are displaying now all have drop-down arrows in them (see Figure 22.31). If you click on one of those drop-down lists and select Filters, Custom, the Custom AutoFilter dialog box appears (see Figure 22.31).

Figure 22.31
The Custom AutoFilter dialog box is another option for defining test criteria for a filter. Notice behind the dialog box the drop-down arrows in all the table column headings.

The first field in the dialog box is already defined as a filter test, depending on which column's drop-down list you opened. If the field you chose was a task name, Contains is the test used, because you are filtering the task names for a string of characters. If you chose a field such as Duration or Start, Equals is entered as the test in the first field.

Next to that field is the Value(s) field, although it is not labeled as such. In Figure 22.31, the Custom AutoFilter dialog box was selected from the Task Name column, so you would define the string of characters in the second box. Then, you have the option to define another test in the filter. Choose And or Or, and repeat the process on the second row in the dialog box.

When you have defined your tests in the Custom AutoFilter dialog box, click OK to apply the filter. The next time you access the dialog box from the Task Name AutoFilter drop-down list, the criteria you defined will be in place, and you can edit it if you want.

If the custom AutoFilter is one you find particularly useful, you might want to save it for later use. Click the Save button, which opens the Filter Definition dialog box with the tests already defined. Enter the remaining information in the Filter Definition dialog box, and select the Show in Menu check box if you want the filter to show in the Filtered For menu found by going to the View tab, Data, Filter.

Creating Custom Groups

Grouping is a great way to organize your task or resource list to better assess your project. When you organize the task or resource list into groups, the individual data for each item is rolled up to display the information for the group instead, temporarily hiding some of the clutter on your screen and generating useful summary information.

Creating a custom group is similar to creating a custom filter. The following sections describe the process of creating custom groups.

Accessing Custom Groups

Like other topics in this chapter, you start creating a custom group by opening the Group Definition dialog box. To do so, open the More Groups dialog box by selecting the View tab, Data, Group By, More Groups. In the More Groups dialog box, you are presented with familiar options. Select from a Task or Resource list, and click one of the buttons to the right.

As usual, New opens the Group Definition dialog box to create a new group, Edit lets you edit an existing group (replacing the original), and Copy lets you edit an existing group without replacing the original. Click one of those buttons, and the Group Definition dialog box appears (see Figure 22.32). You can also go directly to the Group Definition dialog box by selecting the View tab, Data, Group By New Group By.

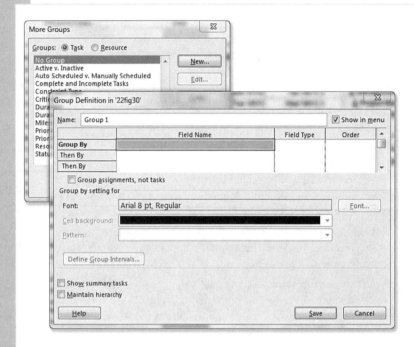

Figure 22.32
Create and customize groups in the Group Definition dialog box. In this example, the New button was clicked to create a new group.

As with views, tables, and filters, choose a unique and descriptive name for the group you are customizing, and enter it in the Name field. Select the Show in Menu box to display the group under the Custom group heading in the main Group By menu. It automatically appears in the More Groups dialog box list whether you check the box or not.

Selecting Grouping Fields

Select the grouping fields from the drop-down lists in the Field Name column of the Group Definition dialog box (refer to Figure 22.32). You can select up to 10 grouping levels, with each selection defining a more detailed grouping criteria. Therefore, the top selection is the broadest group, and the more fields you select, the more refined the group definition becomes.

After you have selected the field name in the Group By row, there are two more columns to define. The Field Type is filled in automatically based on the Field Name, and usually cannot be modified. By default, Ascending is entered in the Order column. You can change it to Descending from the drop-down list, depending on the order you want the group to be displayed when it is applied to the screen. Continue these selections on the following Then By rows up to 10 times. There is no pre-view; you must click OK to view the result.

 note

It is important to point out that the Group field for a resource is different from the concept of grouping. When you create a resource list, you have the option to define a group the resource falls into using the Group field. This is not the same as the grouping feature described in this chapter.

Underneath the Group By and Then By rows is the check box Group Assignments, Not Tasks/Resources (depending on whether you are working with a task or resource list). This box is cleared by default, so each assignment for each task or resource is displayed in the group. Decide which is best for you, and then format the grouping with the Font, Cell Background, and Pattern fields.

Defining Group Intervals

In the Group Definition dialog box, you have the option to define the group intervals. To do so, select a field name from the Group By or Then By rows, and click the Define Group Intervals button. The Define Group Interval dialog box appears, as shown in Figure 22.33.

Figure 22.33
Define group intervals in the Define Group Interval dialog box.

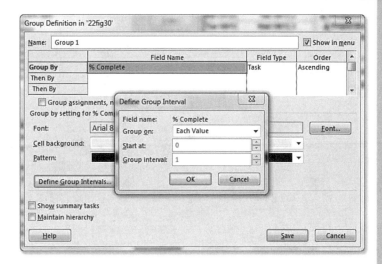

Field Name is automatically entered using the field name selected when you open the Define Group Interval dialog box. In the Group On field, Each Value is selected by default. You can change this entry using the drop-down list, which gives you different options based on the Field Name setting. Depending on your Group On selection, you can define the Start At and Group Interval fields. For instance, you can group date values by intervals of minutes, hours, all the way up to years. You can group numeric values in any interval, and the grouping can start on a number other than 1 (sometimes including negative numbers). You can group text values by the first few characters, and so on.

You can use Group Interval to define intervals for the groups and the starting value for the selected field. For example, if you are grouping on the amount of work instead of a different grouping for each different work value (1 hour, 2 hours, 3 hours, and so on), you can specify groupings in four-hour intervals. The first grouping, defined in the Group By field, would be 0–4 hours, the second grouping (defined in the first Then By field) would be 5–8 hours, the third grouping (defined in the second Then By field) would be 9–12 hours, and so on.

When you have completed your entries in the Define Group Interval dialog box, click OK. After you are finished with the Group Definition dialog box, click OK, and you are back to the More Groups dialog box. Click Apply to apply the group immediately, or click Close to save it for later use. It will always be displayed in the More Groups dialog box and possibly in the main Group By list if you checked the box next to Show in menu.

Formatting Group Displays

As previously mentioned, you can format the group display in the Group Definition dialog box. Each group level has its own setting for font size, background color, and pattern.

Groups look and behave like outlines. As with an outline, you can show or hide levels of the group using the Show button on the Formatting toolbar. Also, you can use the Show and Hide buttons on the screen, which look like either a small right-pointing triangle or a small down-pointing triangle, as shown in Figure 22.34.

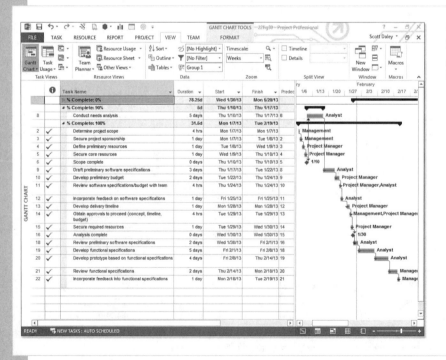

Figure 22.34
Show and Hide triangles using Group By on % Complete.

note

It is important to use cell background colors sparingly to ensure that your Group By screen does not become unreadable and overwhelmed with color. This is especially important when you are grouping on multiple fields.

Saving Custom Groups

The group is always saved to the More Groups list, and it's saved to the main Group By list under the Custom heading if you selected Show in Menu. You can also save it so it is available in other project files using the Organizer. This is discussed in greater detail in the section "Organizing Views and Other Custom Elements in Project Files" at the end of this chapter.

Creating and Customizing Fields

As you must be aware of by now, Project is equipped with dozens of different task and resource fields in which you store all your various project data. In addition to those existing fields, you can create and customize fields to better suit your project and make your life as a project manager less hectic.

For example, you might want to have a field to define the status of a task besides % Complete, such as whether or not the resource has approved the assignment. Or, perhaps your organization has a unique system of classifying resources, and you want to implement that system into your tables. A variety of custom fields and field types within Project is available for you to customize.

There are separate sets of custom fields for task and resource information. The default names are identical, and you can give them different aliases as you are customizing them. The numbers in the following list represent the number of available custom fields for that particular type:

- **Text1–Text30**—Alphanumeric text up to 255 characters

- **Number1–Number 20**—Any positive or negative number

- **Cost1–Cost10**—Number values (formatted)

- **Date1–Date10**—Any valid date value

- **Duration1–Duration10**—Any duration value, such as 4w (four weeks)

- **Start1–Start10**—Any valid start date value

- **Finish1–Finish10**—Any valid finish date value

- **Flag1–Flag20**—Yes/No values

- **Outline Code1–Outline Code10**—User-defined alphanumeric outline structures

For details about custom fields, **see** *the "Defining Custom Fields" section on* **p. 112** *in Chapter 5.*

The following sections discuss defining custom fields.

Accessing the Custom Fields

Technically, custom fields already exist. They are present in every drop-down list that contains predefined fields, such as in the Field Name column of the Group Definition dialog box, even if you have not given them a specific value.

Therefore, you cannot actually create custom fields; rather, you modify—or *customize*—the ones that already exist. Each type has at least 10 different fields, so there should be an ample amount of fields to customize within your project.

Define values for custom fields in the Custom Fields dialog box. To access it, select the Project tab, Properties, Custom fields (see Figure 22.35).

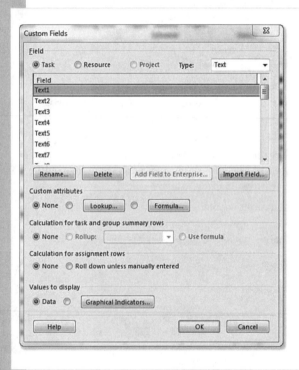

Figure 22.35
Define values for custom fields in the Custom Fields dialog box.

When you open the Custom Fields dialog box, select the custom field general type by choosing Task or Resource and selecting one of the category types from the drop-down list in the Type field. The drop-down list contains all nine field types from the list in the previous section. After you have selected the type, the names of all the available custom fields are displayed in the Field box. Select the one you want to customize.

Naming Custom Fields

The custom field names, such as Cost1, Cost2, and so on, are permanent. However, you can give them an alias; that way, each custom field has a much more descriptive name associated with it.

To do so, click the Rename button, and enter the name you want as the alias. After you click OK, the new name is displayed with the old one in parentheses next to it.

The new name/old name pair now appears in all drop-down lists. However, only the new name is displayed anywhere the custom field is used—even if the field was used before it was renamed.

Creating Calculated Custom Fields

A custom field's data can be derived from values in other fields in your project. Also, you can apply calculations or custom formulas to a custom field to determine its value. This is done on the bottom half of the Custom Fields dialog box.

Specify value behaviors in custom fields in the Custom Attributes section of the Custom Fields dialog box. By default, None is selected. You can opt to create and assign a lookup table or formula to obtain the value of the custom field.

To apply a lookup table to the custom field, click the Lookup button. A lookup table is a value list that the user can select from to enter a value in the custom field. The options you define appear in a drop-down list in the field. Figure 22.36 displays the resulting Edit Lookup Table dialog box.

Figure 22.36
Create and edit a lookup table for a custom field in the Edit Lookup Table dialog box.

In the Edit Lookup Table dialog box, you can define default values, define and restrict available entries for the custom field, or import a lookup table. Enter acceptable values on as many rows as necessary. You can also add optional descriptions of the values to the right in the Description column.

Select the check box next to Use a Value From the Table as the Default Entry for the Field if you always want the selected value to appear in the field as the default entry. Then, select the Display Order for Lookup Table: By Row Number (the order in which you entered the rows), Sort Ascending, or Sort Descending. Click the plus sign (+) button if these options are not already displayed. When you choose, click Sort. Below that, set the data entry options. If you want to allow users to enter values that are not on the value list, check the box next to Allow Additional Items to be Entered into the Fields. The value they enter is then added to the list.

You can also import a lookup table by clicking the Import Lookup Table button and following the instructions in the Import Lookup Table dialog box.

When you are finished, click Close.

Alternatively, you can apply a formula to the custom field to compute and enter their values. A formula is especially useful to calculate values that you might use to determine variance from the plan. For example, you might want to have graphical indicators calculated based on the task progress compared to the baseline.

To apply a formula, click the Formula button, which is next to the Lookup button in the Custom Fields dialog box. The Formula dialog box appears, as shown in Figure 22.37.

tip

You could create a custom field to track the task baseline finish and actual finish dates, and display the status of the task accordingly. That way, you can easily view which tasks have no baseline, are on schedule, or are late by more than five days.

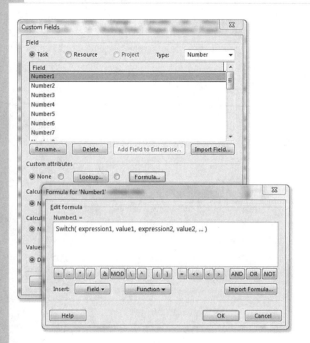

Figure 22.37
Define formulas for custom fields in the Formula dialog box.

Type in the formula you want to use, or import it from another source on your computer as you would import a custom field or lookup table. If you are building a formula, type it directly into the Edit Formula area. You can use the Insert Field drop-down menu, which lists all allowable Project fields, or the Insert Function drop-down menu, which lists all possible predefined functions that can be used in custom field calculations, to assist you. You can also use the operator buttons.

When you are finished, click OK. A warning box appears. You always get this warning when you complete a formula: "Existing data in the custom field will be deleted, because all values will now be calculated by the formula." If that is okay with you, click OK; if not, click Cancel.

note

You do not have to type in the equal sign (=) in the Edit Formula area; Project automatically adds it.

Controlling Custom Field Behaviors

The Calculation for Task and Group Summary Rows section in the Custom Fields dialog box enables you to control custom field calculations for summary rows and for use in custom groups. By default, no value is entered on summary or group rows for custom fields.

You can set the summary and group-level fields to use the formula set for the custom field if you have defined one. Or, at the rollup level, you can set them to perform single mathematical operations. The choices for math operations are Average, Average First Sublevel, Maximum, Minimum, and Sum. The Average First Sublevel option, which is applicable to grouping, prevents a field value from being carried up in the calculations from very detailed groups into less-detailed groups.

The Calculation for Assignment Rows section of the Custom Fields dialog box has only two options. Select the None radio button if the assignment row has no rolled-up values or formulas associated with it. The other option is Roll Down Unless Manually Entered.

note

You can only select Use Formula if the custom field uses a formula, defined in the Custom Attributes section of the Custom Fields dialog box.

Creating Custom Indicator Fields

Rather than display the actual values, Project enables you to display graphical indicators instead, which you customize to represent a range of values. This is useful to save space on your screen by avoiding clutter, as well as to preserve confidentiality; you might not want people to view the exact values, but just an overview represented by an indicator. For example, if you created a formula to calculate the schedule status of a task compared to baseline, you can then create indicators to display the status in a graphical format.

In the Values to Display section of the Custom Fields dialog box, select the Data radio button to display actual data in the field contents in all views in which the field appears. Alternatively, select the radio button next to the Graphical Indicators button and click the Graphical Indicators button to specify the criteria and associated indicator images to be displayed in the field in place of data. The Graphical Indicators dialog box appears, as shown in Figure 22.38.

In the Graphical Indicators dialog box, you can define the indicators to use for certain values of the custom field. Use the drop-down lists to guide you through the process.

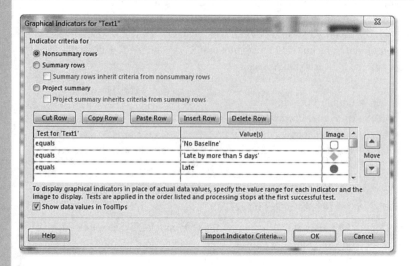

Figure 22.38
Graphical indicators, defined in the Graphical Indicators dialog box, are useful when you do not want to display actual values in custom fields.

You can also import the graphical indicator criteria by clicking the Import Indicator Criteria button and choosing the criteria to import from another project or the Global.MPT.

Click OK when you are finished to apply the graphical indicator, or click Cancel to exit the dialog box without making the changes.

It is a recurring theme for many companies to want to capture specific job codes or cost accounting codes associated with their organization. To accomplish this, an Outline Code should be used, especially if you need to control input so that the codes conform to a predefined hierarchical structure. Similar to many of the custom field types listed in the beginning of this section, a specified lookup table can be created for the Outline Code. In fact, all the other options on the Custom Fields dialog box, when creating the other types of custom fields, are not available, such as the Calculation for Task and Group Summary Rows, Calculation for Assignment Rows, and Values to Display options, as shown grayed out in Figure 22.39.

Unlike the other field types, each Outline Code must have a predefined code mask, as shown in Figure 22.40. The code mask is used to define the format, sequence, length, and separator of each level and value in the lookup table. When entering the structure and values in the lookup table, each value is matched up against the defined code mask to ensure that there is not a mismatch.

Another option exclusive to Outline Codes is the ability to Allow Only Codes That Have No Subordinate Values. If this option is chosen, you will only be able to enter additional values into the Outline Code custom field if it is at the lowest level. If you do not want any additional values entered into the Outline Code lookup table, both of the options underneath Data Entry Options must be cleared.

 tip

A common practice in Project is to use graphical indicators for schedule status or budget status. Use the colors of a traffic light: A green indicator means your schedule or budget status is on schedule, yellow means it is late, and red means it is significantly late.

Figure 22.39
Outline Code field type with only the Lookup table option available.

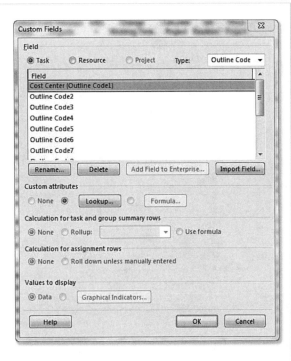

 tip

Ideally, you want to define the code mask for the lookup table first and then begin to enter the values into the lookup table as needed. If any of the values you have entered do not match the code mask, the item will be displayed in red in the lookup table. In addition, if you try to save the lookup table and at least one of the values does not match the code mask, you receive the following message, "One or more code values in the lookup table is invalid. A value is invalid when it does not match the mask defined for the code, includes the separator character, is a duplicate of another value, or exceeds 255 characters in length."

Five action buttons are specific to the Outline Code custom field. They make up the last five buttons under the Lookup Table section in Figure 22.40. Each of these buttons can be used to manipulate the lookup table during the active working session:

- **Outdent**—Decreases value or parent code of the selected item by moving it to the left.

- **Indent**—Increases value or parent code of the selected item by moving it to the right.

- **Show Subcodes**—Displays all the subcodes underneath a selected parent code.

- **Hide Subcodes**—Hides all the subcodes underneath a selected parent code.

- **Show All Subcodes**—Displays all the subcodes in the lookup table regardless of the item selected.

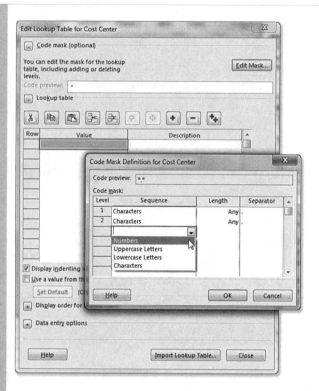

Figure 22.40
Outline codes can be "masked" so that only certain types of values can be entered.

An example of a Cost Center lookup table can be found in Figure 22.41. The code mask consists of two levels, different characters (letters and numbers), and a period (.) as the value separator.

To put the code to use, it needs to be inserted into an existing view by one of the methods described in this chapter. For simplicity, just right-click a column in your existing view and select Insert Column. Choose the new field you want to include in the view (in this case, it is Cost Center Outline Code1).

After the field is included in your active view, a selection can be made from the Cost Center field. Figure 22.42 shows this process. You can see that all the values in the drop-down appear as they did in the lookup table with one exception; the description is attached to the code value. After a value is selected, the parent level value is concatenated with the separator and selected value. This concatenation holds true regardless of the number of levels you have designated.

 tip

Be sure to give outline code values appropriate descriptions. This ensures that whenever you or someone makes a selection from the outline code field, there will not be any confusion as to what the value means. This is especially important when the defined values contain only numbers.

Figure 22.41
This Cost Center lookup table is an example of a fully defined Outline Code.

Figure 22.42
The Cost Center code column is added to the Gantt Chart view and enables you to select a value for each task in the view.

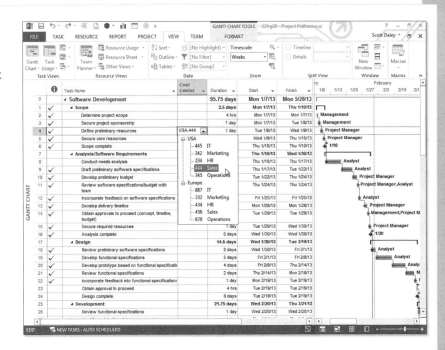

Managing Custom Fields

After you are done with the Custom Fields dialog box, click OK. Your custom field will be stored in the project, and you can insert it anywhere you can insert fields. You can also save it to your Global.MPT file for use in other projects. The next section describes that process.

Organizing Views and Other Custom Elements in Project Files

Throughout this chapter, you have read about saving your views, tables, filters, groups, and custom fields not only to the project you are working on, but to your Global.MPT file, for use in other project files. Finally, the moment has arrived when you will better understand what that means.

Every time you open Project, the Global.MPT file loads with the project file. After you have worked on your project file, everything you saved or created is saved to the project file, but not the Global. MPT file. However, you can save items to the Global.MPT file, thus allowing them to be used in other project files. To do so, follow these steps:

1. Click the Organizer button, which is found on the File tab, Info. This in turn opens the Organizer dialog box, as shown in Figure 22.43.

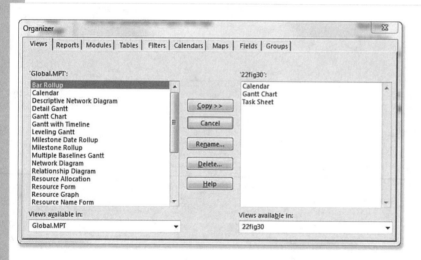

Figure 22.43
The Organizer aids in saving customized items such as views, tables, filters, groups, and fields.

2. The Organizer dialog box has several tabs for custom items. Click on the appropriate tab (if you want to save a custom filter, click the Filters tab). If you opened the Organizer dialog box from the More Filters dialog box, you will already be on the Filters tab. You must select the Fields tab to save custom fields because there is no corresponding More Fields dialog box. The left side of the box shows all items applicable to that particular tab that are saved in the Global.MPT file. The right side shows all custom items for that tab that you have created in the current project

file, plus all the standard items you have used during the current session (in other words, if you were in the Filters tab, it would show all the custom filters you have created as well as all the filters you have used in the current session).

3. Select all the items from your project (on the right side) that you want to save in the Global.MPT file, and click the Copy button. The items are then copied to the Global.MPT file. You can copy multiple items at once by holding down the Ctrl key as you select the items.

4. The Cancel button changes to Close once the items are copied. You can copy additional items, choose a different tab, or click Close to complete the copy process.

Now, any time you create a new project file, these items will be available.

In addition, you can use the Organizer dialog box to rename or delete items from the Global.MPT file or other current project files. To delete an item, simply select it from the appropriate list, and click the Delete button. Project asks you to confirm the deletion; select Yes to delete the item and No to cancel the deletion. If you want the item deleted from both lists, you must delete it from both lists (Project does not do it automatically).

To rename an item, simply select it and click the Rename button. Type the new name in the Rename dialog box that appears, and click OK.

You can also use the Organizer dialog box to copy items from one project file to another without using the Global.MPT file. Be sure both files are open, and at the bottom of the Organizer dialog box, select them from the drop-down lists on the left and on the right. Then, follow the same procedure described previously.

The Organizer is updated if you upgrade to Project from an earlier version. Your old Organizer still exists, combined with the new one.

 For additional information about the Organizer, **see** *the "Manipulating Objects Using the Organizer" section on* **p. 565** *in Chapter 18.*

 tip

As mentioned before, all customized items are displayed in the Organizer dialog box, as well as items that have been used during your current session. It might be helpful to keep track of the items you have customized; that way, they will not be confused with the standard items that appear with them. This is in case you want to copy custom items only.

 caution

Be sure to copy custom items that relate to each other. For example, if you copy a custom view, be sure to also copy any tables, filters, groups, and so on, customized for that particular view.

 note

You cannot rename a custom field in the Organizer dialog box. To rename a custom field, open the Custom Fields dialog box (Tools, Customize, Fields).

 tip

If you are working with several project files, it might be beneficial to designate a project file as a holding vessel for storing and retrieving your customized items. This is especially practical if you run a shared copy of Project on a network and you cannot save items to the Global.MPT file that is used by everyone else on the network.

Customizing the Ribbon

The Project Ribbon (see Figure 22.44) is roughly organized by the most immediate goals of a Project user: Create a task, manage a resource, manage your project, report on your project, alter your view of your project, or customize a particular view. The File tab is where you find common Office functions, as well as options specific to Project.

Figure 22.44
The Ribbon is broken down into tabs and groups.

Each tab is broken down into groups. These groups are mostly sensible collections of operations and controls, with occasional exceptions.

To begin customizing the Ribbon, right-click anywhere on the Ribbon and select Customize the Ribbon.

The Project Options (see Figure 22.45) window opens. You can reach this same window by selecting the File tab, Options, Customize Ribbon. Note that the Customize the Ribbon pane is broken into two columns: the Choose Commands From column and the Customize the Ribbon column.

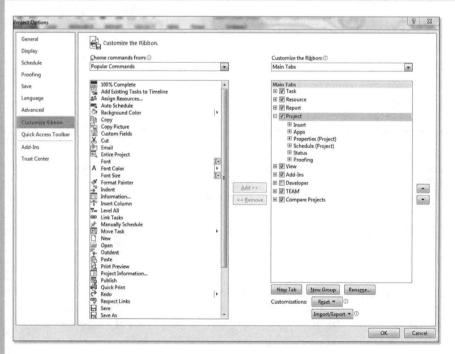

Figure 22.45
You customize the Ribbon through a simple graphical interface.

Before you make any customizations to the Ribbon, use the Choose Commands From column to explore the default configuration of the Ribbon. Hovering over a particular command in the command list shows the location in the Ribbon for that command, if it is in the Ribbon by default (see Figure 22.46). This is a useful feature that prevents you from duplicating commands in multiple locations on the Ribbon.

> ## tip
>
> The Quick Access Toolbar can be used for high-frequency commands. It is addressed later in this chapter.

Figure 22.46
Use tooltips by hovering over commands in the Customize the Ribbon column to find default locations for commands on the Ribbon.

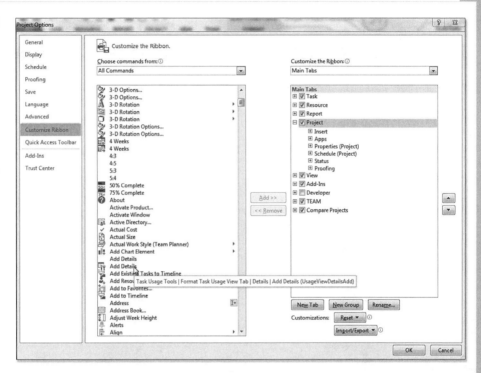

The Choose Commands From drop-down has nine separate filters, most of which are self-explanatory (see Figure 22.47). Three key filters help you make customizations that you won't regret later: Popular Commands, Commands Not in the Ribbon, and All Commands. Longtime users of Project find that most of the commands they are familiar with and need are already somewhere in the Ribbon. If you can't find a command in Popular Commands, look in Commands Not in the Ribbon. If you can't find a command there, look in All Commands.

The Customize the Ribbon drop-down contains three choices, as shown in Figure 22.48: All Tabs, Main Tabs, and Tool Tabs. Main tabs are the tabs visible by default. Tool tabs are the context-sensitive tabs that appear above the Format tab. For example, when the Gantt view is selected, the Format tab is the Gantt Chart Tools tab. When the timeline is selected, the Format tab is the Timeline tools tab.

tip

Unless you know exactly what the command name is, there's a good chance you still won't find it. Do not despair. Most likely you expected to find the command you are looking for alphabetized by the command name. Unfortunately, many commands are prefaced with words you might not expect, such as Display, Hide, or Show. Use the All Commands list and search command by command. If you find yourself customizing the Ribbon frequently, you'll notice a rough naming logic that makes finding commands more predictable.

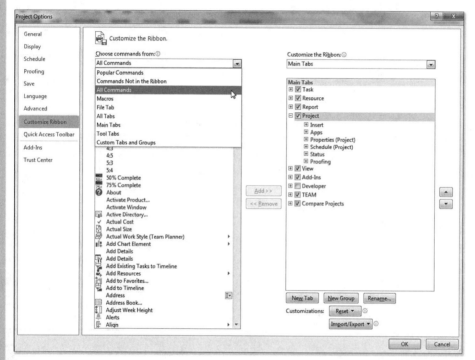

Figure 22.47
The Choose Commands From dropdown menu helps you find the command you are looking for.

Figure 22.48
The tabs are broken down into two types: Main and Tool. All Tabs can also be selected to display all tabs at once.

You can control the visibility of the tabs by checking and unchecking the boxes to the left of the tab name (see Figure 22.49). You cannot delete default groups. To rename a tab or group, select the target item and click the Rename button.

Figure 22.49
You can hide tabs to simplify the Ribbon, if needed. In this example, the Developer tab is not shown.

Although you can rename default Ribbon tabs and groups, you cannot add commands to default Ribbon groups. To add commands to the Ribbon, you must create a custom group. The custom group can be on either a default tab or a custom tab.

To create a custom tab, select a default tab and click the New Tab button. A custom tab with the default name New Tab (Custom) appears directly below your selection. Select the new tab and click Rename to provide a new name.

To create a custom group, select a tab or group and click New Group (see Figure 22.50).

Adding new commands is simply a matter of selecting a command from the Choose Commands From column and clicking Add. Remove commands by selecting a command from the Customize the Ribbon column and clicking Remove (see Figure 22.51).

As with all modern Office products, you can export or import your customizations to an Exported Office UI file by clicking Import/Export (see Figure 22.52). This can be particularly useful for project managers working in a group with a well-structured methodology that can be reflected in the Ribbon. For instance, new or junior project managers might benefit from a simpler, more focused features set. Or entirely new groups can be created to reflect unique stages or functions in a team's project management life cycle.

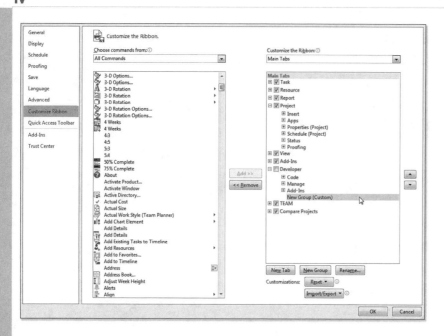

Figure 22.50
You can position new custom groups or entire tabs by selecting an existing group or tab, as needed.

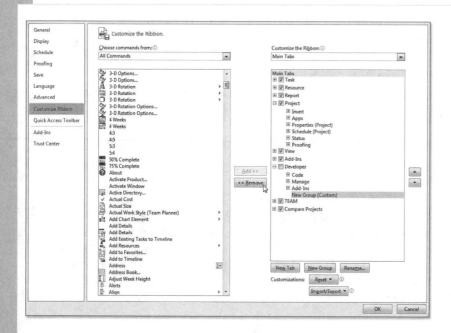

Figure 22.51
Add and remove commands with a button click.

Figure 22.52
Exporting your customizations is easy, enabling a standard Project Ribbon look and feel across a small team of users.

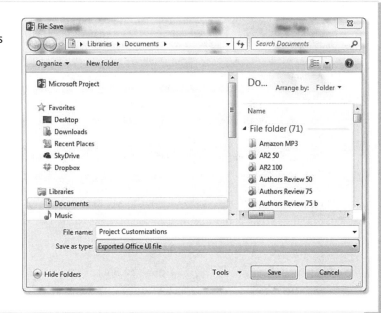

Finally, all customizations can be reset by clicking Reset. You are offered the option of resetting the entire Ribbon or just the selected tab (see Figure 22.53).

Figure 22.53
You can always undo all your customizations by using the Reset button.

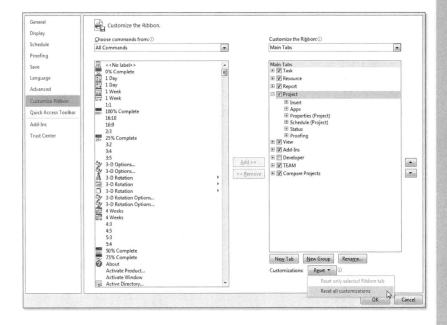

Customizing the Quick Access Toolbar

Customizing the Quick Access Toolbar is almost exactly the same as customizing the Ribbon. The key difference is that the Quick Access Toolbar starts out with only three buttons: Save, Undo, and Redo. Even these can be removed, however. When you customize the Ribbon, you should usually try to find out whether the command you want to add is on the Ribbon already and where it is.

To begin customizing the Quick Access Toolbar, right-click anywhere on the Quick Access toolbar and select Customize the Quick Access Toolbar. As shown in Figure 22.54, you can select the Quick Access Toolbar position the same way, or with a check box at the bottom of the Choose Commands From column.

tip

When you customize the Quick Access Toolbar, you want to include common commands you use frequently. Whether they are already on the Ribbon is less relevant.

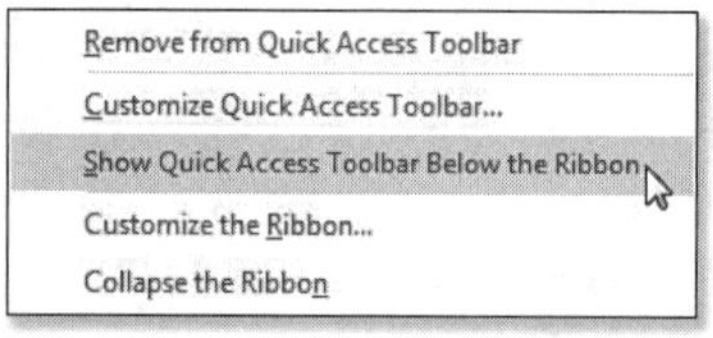

Remove from Quick Access Toolbar

Customize Quick Access Toolbar...

Show Quick Access Toolbar Below the Ribbon

Customize the Ribbon...

Collapse the Ribbon

Figure 22.54
You can show the Quick Access toolbar above or below the Ribbon.

The Project Options window opens (see Figure 22.55). You can also get to this window by selecting the File tab, Options, Customize the Quick Access Toolbar. Note that the Customize the Quick Access Toolbar pane is broken into two columns: the Choose Commands From column and the Customize Quick Access Toolbar column.

The Choose Commands From menu contains 25 filtering options (see Figure 22.56). Most are Ribbon locations. The top four, however, are different: Popular Commands, Commands Not in the Ribbon, All Commands, and Macros. Unlike the Ribbon, the Quick Access toolbar is basically empty.

In most cases, you will be looking for a command you use all the time or a command that is not in the Ribbon by default. Because duplication is not an issue, you will be as likely to use the Popular Commands filter and the Commands Not on the Ribbon filter.

tip

As with customizing the Ribbon, expect many command names to be alphabetized oddly, sometimes prefixed by a verb, sometimes not, and other times named entirely unpredictably. You will occasionally need to sift through every command line by line to find what you are looking for.

Figure 22.55
Customize the
Quick Access
toolbar through
a simple graphi-
cal interface.
The Quick Access
toolbar is basically
blank before you
customize it.

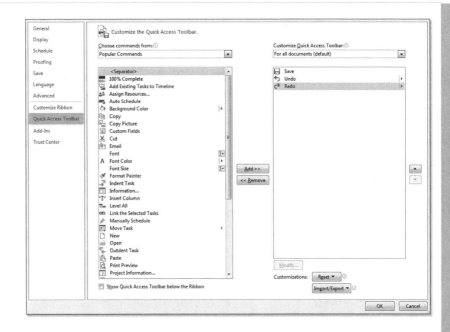

Figure 22.56
The Choose
Commands From
menu helps you
find the command
you are looking
for.

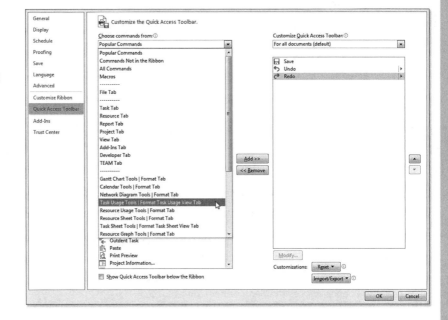

There are two options for using the Customize Quick Access Toolbar menu: for all documents or for the specific project you are working on. In general, project managers managing multiple projects use the same commands and want the same quick access regardless of specific project. Use your best judgment.

Adding and removing commands from the Quick Access toolbar is even simpler than customizing the Ribbon because there are no tabs and groups to be concerned with. Simply select the command from the Choose Commands From column and click Add to put the command on the Quick Access toolbar (see Figure 22.57). Remove commands by selecting them in the Customize Quick Access Toolbar column and clicking Remove.

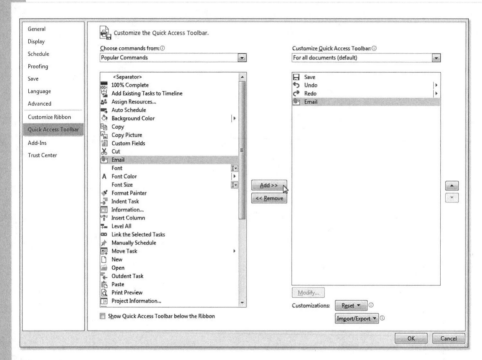

Figure 22.57
Add and remove commands with a button click.

As with all modern Office products, you can export or import your customizations to an Exported Office UI file by clicking Import/Export (see Figure 22.58). As with the Ribbon, this might be useful in a highly structured group of project managers in which individuals can benefit from a unified Quick Access toolbar. Of course, this can also be used to maintain the consistency of one power user's Project experience across multiple copies of Project.

Finally, you can undo all customizations by clicking the Reset button. You have the option of resetting the Quick Access toolbar or all customizations.

Figure 22.58
Exporting your customizations is easy, enabling a standard look and feel across a small team of users.

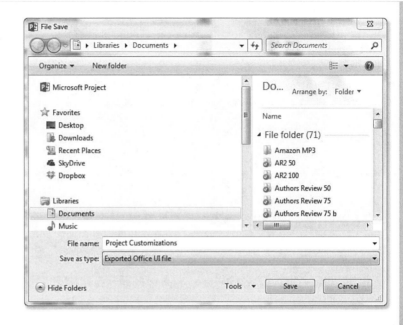

Customizing the Status Bar

The status bar is at the bottom of your Project screen by default. It includes three obvious elements: the New Tasks mode, the view shortcuts, and the Zoom slider. Right-clicking on the status bar reveals 11 options, all of which except Macro Recording are turned on by default (see Figure 22.59).

Figure 22.59
The status bar has 11 options.

The Cell Mode is an indicator that toggles depending on whether you are entering something in a cell. This is occasionally useful when, for some reason, commands are grayed out. For example. Cell Mode indicates *Enter*, indicating that you need to press Enter or otherwise leave Enter mode for the grayed-out command to return to an active state.

Calculation is a little bizarre. When the File tab, Options, Schedule, Calculation, Calculate Project After Each Edit is Off, Calculation in the status bar customization window says On—but the indicator that appears in the status bar says Calculation: Off. See Figure 22.60 for clarification.

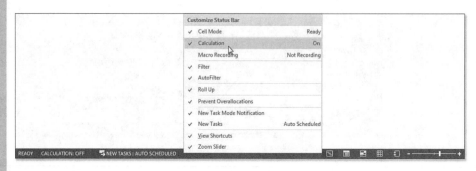

Figure 22.60
The Calculation option might be confusing—the notification area correctly shows that Calculation is off.

Including Macro Recording on the status bar provides a control for starting and stopping macro recordings. You can reach this same macro recording control from the Developer tab, Code, Record Macro command (the Developer tab is made visible by customizing the Ribbon).

Filter, AutoFilter, Rollup, Prevent Overallocations, and New Task Mode Notification (see Figure 22.61, not all are shown) are all notifications that appear when their various trigger conditions are met. Otherwise, they are invisible.

Figure 22.61
The status bar indicates when certain conditions are met. In this case, the view has a filter applied, so that is indicated in the status bar.

Finally, the View Shortcuts and Zoom slider controls can be turned on or off, as needed. You cannot add views to the View Shortcuts control.

Consultants' Tips

Create Views the Right Way

Project comes with a number of helpful views, but of course, no one can anticipate everyone's needs. Creating new views might seem to be a complex task at first, but if you map out what you want to see and how you want to see it, it is not that difficult.

Just remember that a view is composed of a table, filter, group, and screen. A good approach is to find a "like" view whenever possible, and then copy and modify the view to meet your needs. This ensures that the default view is never overwritten. If you cannot find a "like" view, create a new one. Similarly, if you cannot find a "like" table to build your view off of, create a new table. Next, go back to the view definition to add the filter and group information.

Test it to make sure it works correctly and, assuming it does, use the Organizer to put the view into the Global.MPT file, so it will always be available in future projects.

Name Organizer Objects Appropriately

It is critical to ensure that all views, tables, fields, filters, and groups are named appropriately with easily recognizable and descriptive names. This ensures that whenever you or someone else accesses these items, there will not be any confusion as to what the object's true intention is.

Resolve Unexpected View Results

While analyzing a project view, you might not see the expected results or it might appear that information that should be present has disappeared. When this occurs, first check to make sure that there is not an active filter applied to the view. Most likely, changing the Filtered For option to All Tasks resolves the issue.

Know Your Audience When Using Graphical Indicators

When selecting graphical indicators associated with a custom field, be cognizant of the fact that there might be users who are color blind and will not benefit from certain indicators such as "stop light" schedule indicators with red, yellow, and green circles. If this is the case, consider using another set of indicators, such as schedule indicators with faces (a smiley face for on schedule, a straight face for late, and a sad face for substantially late).

In addition, when setting up your custom fields for cost or schedule status, be sure to include a No Baseline value to identify those projects or tasks that do not have a baseline. Otherwise, the values that do not have a baseline show an error. In addition, this enables you to identify those tasks that do not have a baseline and take the appropriate actions to baseline them.

Keep an Excel Configuration Workbook

You should keep a personal list of all the customized objects you have created so that you know what is available to you and other users. You might consider creating an Excel configuration workbook with a worksheet for each type of object (tables, views, groups, filters, and fields). This saves you time in the long run in that you will not have to jump directly into a particular project schedule and navigate around until you find the object you are looking for. With a central configuration table, you can open the Excel spreadsheet and immediately locate the customized item you are looking for. In addition, you want to make sure you keep the configuration table constantly updated.

Making the Most of the "Ribbon"

If you need to add items to the Ribbon, first use the customization interface for finding "missing" commands. Most often, they are hidden in plain sight, already on the Ribbon by default.

Second, use the Quick Access Toolbar rather than modifying the Ribbon. Using the Quick Access Toolbar makes it easier to move from one user's version of Project to another, and usually there are a surprisingly small number of high-frequency commands.

Finally, save significant customizations of the Ribbon itself for true workflow-type enhancements in situations where it makes sense to "guide" managers and planners through a process.

23

WORKING WITH MULTIPLE PROJECTS

Project managers work with multiple projects for a variety of reasons. Sometimes projects that are *logically* unified are broken up according to performing organization. Complex programs are frequently managed by a program manager and multiple project managers, with each Project file corresponding to a component of the program. Finally, project managers are often asked to manage multiple independent efforts that all share the same resource team.

This chapter deals in particular with projects that are either closely interrelated or components of a larger program. Project provides tools for sharing resources and tracking tasks across projects that can be particularly helpful for complex efforts that require multiple Project files.

Using Windows Commands

There might be occasions when you need to work with more than one project at a time. Here are some examples:

- You have two tasks in different projects that are dependent on each other—for instance, if the start date for a task in one project is dependent on the finish date of a task in another project.

- You have several projects placed under your supervision. For example, if you are a program manager and need to see the status of projects within the program, you can create a program-level master project. Even if the projects within the program are managed by different project managers, the master project enables you to get an overall status and insight into how the entire program is executing.

- You have a project that is too large and has become difficult to manage. You can break down this project into smaller, more controllable projects and then link them back together into one master project to see the high-level status. This has a similar benefit to outlining a project, but on a larger scale.

- You find yourself with several projects using the same set of resources, which need to be coordinated to prevent overallocations.

- Although this is now a very rare scenario, you have a project that is too large to fit your organization's computer memory capacity. You can break it down into smaller projects to bypass these confines.

Project can support a practically unlimited number of simultaneously open projects. You will want to use the least amount of fies required to manage your master project. If multiple projects are open simultaneously, you can use the View tab, Window, Switch Windows control to move between your open files. The list of open project files appears in the Switch Windows menu, as shown in Figure 23.1. The active window is designated by a check mark, and if you have more than nine files open at a time, a More Windows option appears at the bottom of the Switch Windows menu; selecting More Windows shows all the open project files. You can then select the project file you want to activate, and all other files will be moved to the background.

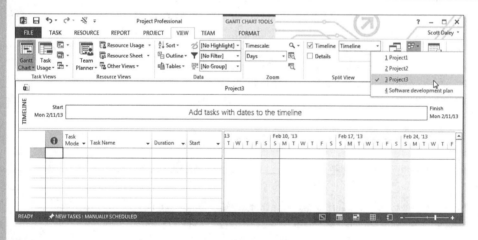

Figure 23.1
You can switch between all open project files by using the Switch Windows menu.

 note

You can also access a list of files on the File tab, Recent Projects. This list shows the most recently accessed files, but this does not mean that these files are currently open. You can control the number of files in this list by selecting the File tab, Options, Advanced, Display, Show This Number of Recent Projects.

Besides switching between screens, you can also use the View tab, Split View, Details command to divide the screen for combination views of a single project. These can be useful when dealing with different areas of a large project file. For instance, you can open the Resource Usage view in the upper section of the screen, and the Gantt Chart in the lower. You can then view and change specific resource assignments in the upper view while reviewing the effects in the Gantt Chart view in the lower part of the screen.

➡ *For additional information on working with views, **see** Chapter 11, "Using Standard Views, Tables, Filters, and Groups to Review Your Schedule," **p. 357**.*

Viewing All the File Windows at the Same Time

If you want to view multiple files at the same time, you can open them all onscreen, in their own distinct windows, by using the View tab, Window, Arrange All command. The Arrange All command creates windows for every project you have open, so remember to only open the projects you want to view in this arrangement. When you use the Window, Arrange All command, the last project opened appears in the top-left corner of your screen. The number of windows opened depends on your processor, memory, and screen size, but managing more than five or six projects in one multitiled screen is usually impractical.

Each window is sized and moved so each can be seen onscreen at the same time. This process tiles your windows, depending on how many projects are open at the same time. Each filename is shown in its title bar, and the active window is identified by the active pane indicator and active window color scheme, as shown in Figure 23.2.

Figure 23.2
The View tab, Window, Arrange All command makes it easy to open several windows with different projects at the same time.

tip

The Window, Arrange All command can be useful when you want to compare a saved version of a project with a current project, side by side. For example, if you wanted to compare last month's status with the current status of the project, you can open both files with the Window, Arrange All command, and compare specific tasks using the AutoFilter function. This provides a side-by-side comparison of the changes made over time. Although you can save up to 11 full baselines at a time, some project managers prefer saving versions of the same file, perhaps at the end of the month, to allow for review, comparison, contrast, and analysis of project data.

You can also use the Compare Project analysis tool. Select the Project tab, Reports, Compare Projects. This enables you to open two files and then build a comparison file by merging your two selected files, displaying their differences, discussed later in this chapter.

When viewing multiple project windows in one screen using the Window, Arrange All command, the Ribbon and the Quick Launch bar control the active project.

If you maximize one of the open windows, all other windows become maximized as well. You cannot, however, see the other files, because the active window covers the whole screen. To switch between project files when the window is maximized, use the Switch Windows menu.

Hiding and Unhiding Open Windows

You might come across a situation where you have open project files, but do not want to include them in the Arrange All display. Rather than closing them, you can use the Hide command to hide them. To hide a file, it must first be the selected, active file. Then select the View tab, Window, Hide. That file will be hidden and the next file becomes the active project in the window. To unhide a file, choose the Window, Unhide command, and the Unhide dialog box opens, showing you the list of any and all files you have hidden. Select the file you want to unhide and click OK; it becomes the active file. If you have any hidden files when you exit Project, you are prompted to save them, if necessary.

Using the Save Workspace Command

When you are working on several files at once and want to be able to go back to what you are working on later, you can save the workspace. The workspace includes all the files you have open and saves your current setup in addition to saving the individual files. The workspace does not save a second copy of the files, but rather creates a pointer to the originals. Follow these steps to save a workspace:

1. Add the Save Workspace command to the Quick Launch bar.

2. If you have any unsaved changes to the individual files, the File Save dialog box opens, prompting you to save those individual files. Click Yes to close the File Save dialog box.

3. In the Save Workspace As dialog box, browse to the directory to which you want to save your files on the right, if you do not want to use the default directory. Project automatically provides a default Resume.mpw name. You can change it by entering a new name in the File Name box.

4. Click the Save button when you are finished.

5. Reopening these files is as easy as going to File, Open and selecting the workspace file.

 *For additional information about workspaces, **see** Chapter 18, "Managing Project Files Locally and in the Cloud," **p. 549**.*

> **note**
> Project automatically saves all workspace files with the .mpw extension.

Comparing Project Versions

Project makes it easy to compare the first draft of your project with a revised version, letting you analyze the differences between cost, duration, resources, work, and other data. This helps you to look at and report the net effect of your changes. After you have made your revisions, you can use the File tab, Save As to save your new version.

> **caution**
> If you are using Project Professional in conjunction with Project Server, you can run into a special situation with the resource pool. Keep in mind that if you are using a resource pool, when you create two versions of a project, they are both drawing from that common pool, which causes duplication of your assignment information, and invalidates your available information. After you are done comparing your versions, make sure you select the version you do not plan to use and break the link to your resource pool.

To compare the new project schedule to your original, follow these steps:

1. Open the newest version (Version 2) first; then open the original (Version 1) and reactivate Version 2. This positions Version 2 as the later version when you use the Compare Project Versions dialog box.

2. Select the Report tab, Compare Projects (see Figure 23.3).

Figure 23.3
Use the Compare Project Versions dialog box to select options for comparing two versions of a project.

3. Choose the correct task and resource tables in the section; then click OK. A third project sched-ule is created that contains the data from both Version 1 and Version 2 files. This is not a full-fledged project schedule and is used as a placeholder for the comparison information.

4. The comparison report includes three windows showing a comparison report and the two com-pared projects, as well as a new Compare Projects tab in the Ribbon (see Figure 23.4). The View tab toggles between a resource and a task comparison. The Show tab enables filtering and hid-ing/showing the Legend. Use the Close Comparison command when you are finished. This closes the Comparison window but does not close any of the projects, including the comparison report (see Figure 23.5).

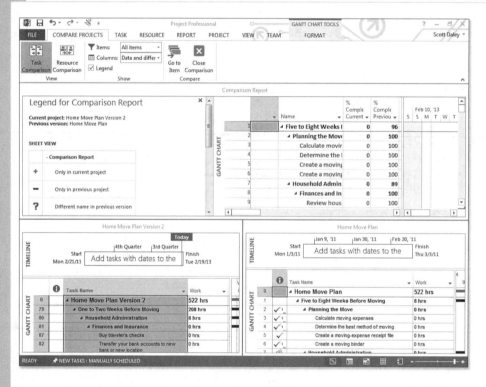

Figure 23.4
The Project Versions legend helps you to com-pare and contrast your two different projects.

When you are using the Comparison Report project, a custom table is applied to the task sheet. For every table selected from Version 2, it displays three custom fields. For instance, if you had selected the Entry table in Version 2, the Comparison Report shows three Entry tables: Version 1, Version 2, and the difference version.

Table 23.1 breaks down how this works.

Figure 23.5
The Comparison Report table uses Gantt bars and a custom table to compare the two versions of a project.

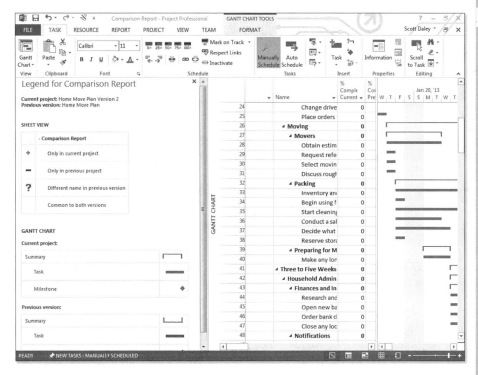

Table 23.1 The Comparison Report: Task All Columns Table Utilizes Several User-Defined Fields

Field Label	(Actual Field Name)	Version: Data Type
Duration: V1	(Duration 1)	Version 1: Duration
Duration: V2	(Duration 2)	Version 2: Duration
Duration: Diff	(Duration 3)	Comparison version: Duration
Start: V1	(Start1)	Version 1: Date
Start: V2	(Start2)	Version 2: Date
Start: Diff	(Duration 4)	Comparison version: Duration
Finish: V1	(Finish1)	Version 1: Date
Finish: V2	(Finish2)	Version 2: Date
Finish: Diff	(Duration 5)	Comparison version: Duration
Predecessors: V1	(Text1)	Version 1: Text
Predecessors: V2	(Text2)	Version 2: Text
Predecessors: Diff	(Text3)	Comparison version: Text

Field Label	(Actual Field Name)	Version: Data Type
Resource Name: V1	(Text4)	Version 1: Text
Resource Name: V2	(Text5)	Version 2: Text
Resource Name: Diff	(Text6)	Comparison version: Text

If you try to have too many user-defined fields when you use Compare Project, you might receive a warning because Compare Project has a limited number of custom fields available to show all the data.

Because the Comparison Report project uses its own set of custom fields, it does not change any of the custom fields in your project files. Custom fields are listed the same as all of the other fields when run through the Comparison Report, showing Version 1, Version 2, and the difference version.

Displaying Tasks from Different Projects in the Same Window

Project supports two viewing techniques for displaying tasks from different projects in the same window. First, you can use the Project tab, Insert, Subproject command to combine multiple project files. This enables you to edit, view, print, and even link multiple projects' tasks in one view. You can change the view to add a column to identify the project file each task came from, such as a column with Project field selected, which enables you to see the origin project of each task. You can sort and filter the task list the same way you would a regular project file. You can apply any table or view to the combined file, including the Network Diagram view, and insert and delete tasks. In addition, you can print views or reports from the merged project.

Second, you can use the View tab, Window, New Window command. This assumes that all the files being combined are already open.

You can read more about the first approach in the "Combining Projects into One File Using the Insert Project Menu" section later in the chapter.

Using the New Window Command

The New Window menu has two major functions. First, you can use it to open a new window for the same file. This new window is designated with a colon and number; for instance, if you had a file titled New Project, and opened a copy with the New Window menu, you would now have a window for the file named NewProject:2.

The other major function of the New Window menu is for creating master and sub relationships between two or more files. A master file is one or more files combined together from several sub files.

Follow these steps to combine tasks from multiple subprojects into one master file:

 tip

The New Window menu can also be helpful for editing the same file in two different windows. For instance, you can show a summary task in one window and make edits to tasks in another.

1. Open the New Window dialog box by selecting the View tab, Window, New Window, as shown in Figure 23.6.

Figure 23.6
Use the New Window dialog box to combine multiple projects into a one-window view.

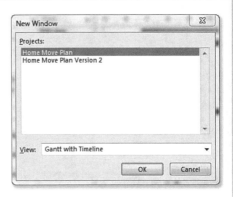

2. Select all the files you want included from the Projects list, holding down the Shift key to highlight them. You can use the Ctrl key if you need to add nonadjacent filenames to your selection.

3. You can select which view you want your new window to open by using the View list box at the bottom of the dialog box. The Gantt Chart is the default, but you can always go back and change the view later, after the new window has opened.

4. Click OK when you are finished and ready to display your new window.

Your new window is named Project(*number*), where (*number*) is the consecutively assigned number given each time you create a new project. You can save your new file by using the File, Save command. A separate entry for Project(*number*) is also added under the Window menu in addition to the project files you already have open.

When any of the task sheet views are active, including any of the Gantt Chart views, the Indicators column displays an icon for an inserted project, as shown in Figure 23.7. If you hover your mouse cursor over the icon, the name of the source file and its location are displayed. The icon simply tells you that the inserted project is pointing to the source file that contains the tasks. If you use the Gantt Chart view for each inserted file, the corresponding project summary task name will be shown and the task ID for this project summary task will indicate the order in which the selected files were merged. Use the outline symbol in front of the project summary task name if you want to hide the details of the task, just as though you were working with the tasks in an outline. You also see a gray taskbar in the timescale side of the Gantt Chart view, which represents the Project Summary task and looks just like the regular summary taskbar.

 note
You can select the View tab, Data, Outline to choose the level of outline detail you want displayed.

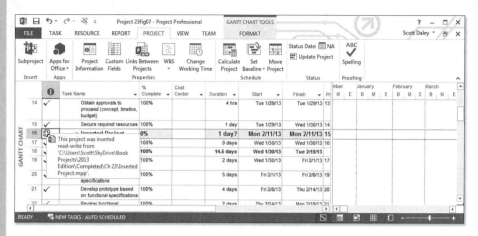

Figure 23.7
Holding your cursor over the icon in the indicator column shows information about the inserted projects.

 tip

If you want like to see a different view of a project quickly, without losing all of your layout information in the current view, you can create a new window with the new view. This way, you could have the Gantt Chart view open with a split screen showing the Task Usage view in the lower half, and then open a new window with the Resource Sheet view, enabling you to use filters on the Resource Sheet view without changing the layout information you have set up for your Gantt Chart view.

To do so, select the View tab, Window, New Window and highlight your current project. That opens another window with your current project as the active one. It is, essentially, creating more than a standard combination view—you can now see two separate combination views, two full-screen views, or one combination view and one full-screen view, all from the same project. When you do this, you will be opening another copy of the same file with the same name, with an addition of :2, such as Home Move Project and Home Move Project:2. You can then use either the Window menu or Ctrl+F6 to move between them. Any changes you make and save are saved to both versions of the file. You have, in essence, only one file open; it is just displayed in two separate windows.

Filtering and Sorting Consolidated Projects

When you first create a consolidated project, the tasks are grouped by the file they originally came from. You can sort the list using the Sort command, or filter tasks with the Filter drop-down list or AutoFilter method. If you want to sort the list, go to the View tab, Data, Sort, Sort By. This opens the Sort dialog box. At the bottom of the Sort dialog box is the Keep Outline Structure check box. If you want to change the order of tasks from their original grouping of which project they came from, you need to clear this box. You can now, for instance, sort your list by start date, and the tasks from all the consolidated project files will move out of their original start date. Remember that your predefined sort options on the Sort menu are set to sustain the outline structure, and if you turn off the outline structure, the subtask level expanding and collapsing will not work.

Figure 23.8 shows that the task list for the two inserted projects has been sorted by start date. The Project field column has been added to the table, so you can see the name of the source project for each task. The outline indenting option has been turned off, and the summary tasks and project summary tasks have been hidden. You can make the same changes using the show/hide group on the Format Gantt Chart tab.

Many of the task names in Figure 23.8 are duplications of one another. Many managers find that common tasks occur in almost all similar-type projects. Following good project management practices and creating project files from existing files or templates causes some repetition of task names when you combine projects into a master file. Adding the Project column is an easy way to identify the source of each task.

Figure 23.8
You can sort a file with inserted projects to make it easier to find when tasks from different projects are scheduled.

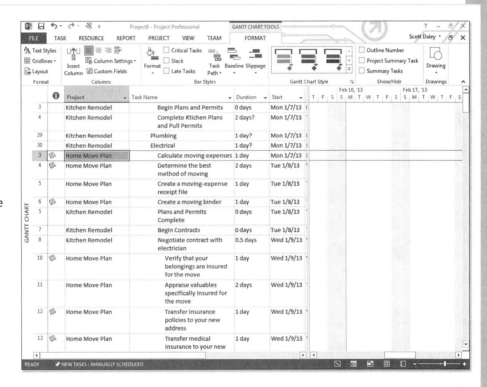

Besides filtering and sorting, there are other formatting options you can use with your consolidated file, such as Bar Style formatting and layout commands.

Project treats individually inserted files as summary tasks with subtasks in new consolidated files. Each has its own critical path.

If you want to set up a critical path across all the projects and tasks within a combined file, follow these steps:

1. Open the Options dialog box by selecting the File tab, Options.

2. Select the Schedule tab.

3. For inserted projects to be calculated like summary tasks, turn on this feature by selecting the Inserted Projects Are Calculated Like Summary Tasks check box, shown in Figure 23.9. Your files do not have to be linked to use this feature.

> *For additional information about task dependencies, **see** the "Linking Tasks" section on **p. 186** in Chapter 7.*

 tip

The cross-project task dependencies are important if you really want to manage the critical path. If you do not establish the task dependencies, your critical path simply becomes the point where the two projects happen to converge. To use the critical path properly, you must establish your task dependencies.

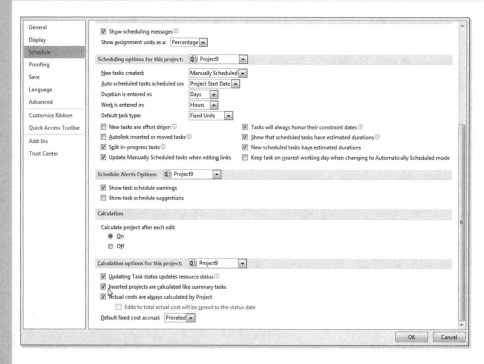

Figure 23.9
If you treat your inserted files as summary tasks, you can show the critical path across your combined files.

Creating Master Projects

You will find several advantages to managing large and complex projects in smaller, separate files. You can more easily share files among coworkers, and you can print and transmit several small files faster than one large file.

When you need to analyze, review, and report on your project, you can take each of the individual files and create a master/sub-project structure, combining the files into one. You can save this consolidated file and use it later, so you do not have to re-create it each time. An advantage of this approach is that these master/sub-projects can be multilevel: You can show consolidated projects at different levels, such as the departmental, functional, regional, and perhaps even the national or international level.

You can use two methods to combine files into a master/subproject structure. The first method, using the New Window command, was discussed earlier in the chapter. For more information, see the "Displaying Tasks from Different Projects in the Same Window" section. The following sections discuss the second method for combining files: inserting files into a new master project schedule. Important master file issues, such as maintaining the combined file, removing the subproject, and linking between combined files are also discussed in the following sections.

> **⚠ caution**
>
> One issue with using master and sub files is the potential of having broken connection links. For example, if you have the sub files stored in a shared location on the network and the project manager moves a linked project to a different location, the link within your master will be incorrect and Project will not be able to open that project.

Combining Projects into One File Using the Insert Project Menu

To insert one project into another, or to create a combined project from two original projects, select the Project tab, Insert, Subproject. Follow these steps to insert an entire project into another:

1. Choose the task row where you want to insert the new project. When the new tasks are inserted, the existing task moves down one row.

2. Open the Insert Project dialog box by selecting Insert, Project, as shown in Figure 23.10.

Figure 23.10
The Insert Project dialog box assists you in opening and inserting one project file into another.

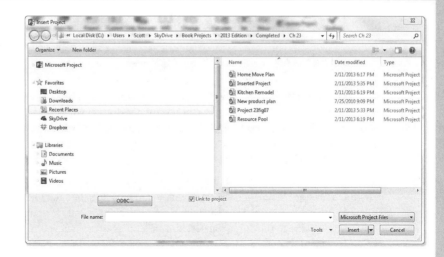

3. Choose which of the files you want to insert.

4. If you want to insert a read-only copy of the project into the file, use the Insert drop-down list at the lower-right corner of the Insert, Project dialog box to select that option. This enables you to make changes to the source project in the master project, but you will not be able to save those changes back to the source copy. This option could be helpful, for instance, if you want to allow someone to see the effect of the changes he or she wants to implement. That person cannot actually make the changes; rather, he or she needs to discuss them with the individual project managers in charge of the source project. This prevents project managers from inadvertently making changes to another project manager's project. If you do not use the read-only option, it always defaults to the regular Insert with Full Read and Write Permissions.

5. You create a link to the inserted project unless you clear the Link to Project option. If you clear the Link to Project option, you will, in effect, be copying tasks from the source project. If you don't clear the Link to Project option, any changes made to the master files will also be made to the inserted file, on a bidirectional basis. If the file was inserted as read-only, any updates from the source to the master project files work, but updates from the master file back to the source files will not work. If the files are inserted in a full read-write capability, you still have the option of not saving changes to individual files.

6. Click OK when finished. This newly created file is now a master file and is separate from your original sub file.

 note

The ODBC button on the Insert Project dialog box is for inserting data stored in a database.

 tip

When inserting multiple files into the same location of a master project file, click them in the order you want them displayed. Select the first one and then press and hold the Ctrl key while you pick your other projects in the order in which you want them to appear. If you simply want to select an adjacent block of files, and do not care about their order, choose your first file, hold down the Shift key when selecting your last file, and all files between the two will be automatically chosen to be placed in the master project file.

Working with Inserted Projects

For information about your inserted project, you can use the Advanced tab on the Task Information dialog box. You can open the dialog box by selecting the Task tab, Properties, Information. After you have accessed the Task Information dialog box for a task from your inserted project, the title of the dialog box changes to Inserted Project Information, and the Advanced tab displays the details of the source project file. The title bar indicates that you have selected the task from an inserted project, as shown in Figure 23.11.

You have the option to maintain a link with the individual files. You can choose whether changes made to the master file link back to your original file by using the Link to Project check box. When the Link to Project check box is selected, any content-related changes you make to the new master file are also be made to the original inserted files. The link between your original source file and the new file is created by default. However, any changes made to the formatting in the new window are not reflected in the source files. This enables you to make formatting changes in the new window, to assist in telling the two combined projects apart, or printing reports for different audiences, without your changes being saved back to the original working file.

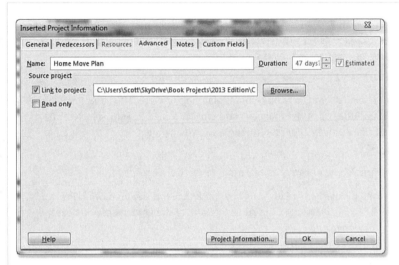

Figure 23.11
You can see the link to the source file and gain access to project information using the Task Information dialog box for an inserted project.

As mentioned previously, the read-write option is the default, but you can change that to read-only, if you prefer. To do so, select the Read Only check box to protect your original source files from changes. If you use the Read Only check box, your inserted files show an icon in the Indicators column of the Gantt Chart view. This icon is an exclamation point and indicates that the file is read-only. Hovering your mouse cursor over the icon brings up information about this condition.

If you need to change the link to another file, or fix a link for a file that has been moved or renamed, the Browse button enables you to select a new, moved, or renamed file. Later sections in the chapter cover moving, deleting, and renaming of the inserted projects.

You can also click the Project Info button to open the Project Information dialog box for your source file. You can find the Project Info button in the lower section of the Inserted Project Information dialog box. If the Project Information button is grayed out, expand the inserted project summary task and then try again.

 note

The original source file location reference is stored in the Subproject field for inserted project tasks. If the Read Only check box has been selected, a Yes is stored in the Subproject Read Only field. These fields can be seen only if you add them to a table. If you clear the Link to Project check box, the inserted source project becomes a normal summary task and file location references are not shown.

Not only can you create inserted projects at any level of an outline, you can then insert that consolidated project into another project. Project makes sure that no circular references exist within the levels.

Breaking Apart a Large Project Using Inserted Projects

Now that you know how to insert projects, you can also create inserted projects by moving tasks from a large project into new project files, and then designating these new files as inserted projects. When you move one or more tasks that are linked to tasks that remain behind, you lose those links and have to reestablish them later. It is easier, therefore, to copy the tasks that are going to become new project files and paste the copied tasks to a new file. Then you insert the project file, change the links, and finally delete the original copied tasks.

Follow these steps to move tasks to a new project file:

1. Highlight the entire row of task IDs for the tasks you are planning to move. This guarantees that all fields are selected and that all of the relevant data will be copied. If your selected tasks include a summary and all the subtasks indented underneath, you can just select the summary task instead.

2. Go to the Task tab, Clipboard, Copy, to copy the task data to the Clipboard.

3. Select the File tab, New, Blank Project to create your new project file. If the Prompt for Project Info for New Projects check box is selected on the Advanced tab of the Options dialog box, the Project Information dialog box opens.

4. Select the Name field of the first task in the new file; then go to Edit, Paste, or use Ctrl+V, to paste the new task data into the new project.

5. Save your new file by selecting the File tab, Save. Fill in the name in the resulting dialog box and click Save.

6. Open the Switch Windows menu and select the filename in the list at the bottom to return to your original file.

7. Choose where you want your inserted project to appear, and insert the project as described earlier in the chapter in the "Working with Inserted Projects" section.

Master Projects Using Hammock Tasks

A *hammock task* is a task dependent on external dates for the start date, finish date, and duration. These tasks are called hammock tasks because of the hammock shape created, as shown in Figure 23.12, which determines the distance between the points to which the task needs to be attached.

As scheduled dates in other tasks change, the duration and start and/or finish dates of the hammock task change as well. If you have three tasks (Tasks A, B, and C), as shown in Figure 23.12, Task C must start on the finish date of Task A, and must finish by the finish date of Task B.

The span of time between the dates of Tasks A and B dictates the available time to accomplish Task C. For example, if the date for Task A changes, the start date for Task C changes as well. If the date for Task B moves, Task C must finish appropriately. The difference between the dates on Tasks A and B determines the duration for Task C.

Figure 23.12
Hammock tasks are
so named because of
the way one task is
slung between two
other tasks.

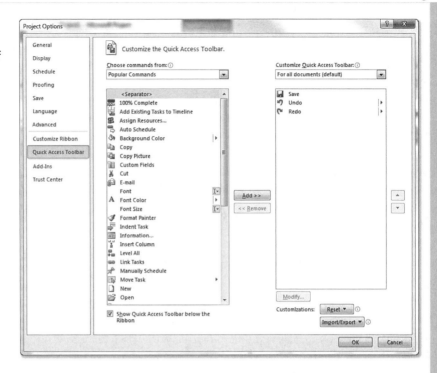

If you have Tasks A, B, and C linked together in a predecessor
relationship, and you create a new task, Task D, with the start date
coming from Task A's start and the finish date coming from Task
B's finish, Task D acquires the start date of Task A and the finish
date of Task B. If Task C is delayed (the duration changes), the
duration of Task D also changes.

Use the following steps to establish a hammock task:

1. Right-click the cell that contains the date that determines when
   the hammock task starts and select Copy Cell.

2. Right-click the hammock task start date cell and select Paste
   Special.

3. In the Paste Special dialog box, select Paste Link and then click
   OK.

4. Right-click on the cell containing the date that determines when the hammock task finishes and
   then select Copy Cell.

5. Right-click the hammock task finish date cell and select Paste Special.

6. In the Paste Special dialog box, select Paste Link and then click OK.

> **tip**
>
> Hammock tasks can be useful
> at the top of a project sched-
> ule to reflect key milestones
> within your schedule. Use the
> hammock method to dupli-
> cate task names and start and
> finish dates. Then, when the
> parent milestone changes,
> the hammock task shows the
> updates.

To use hammock tasks in a master project, use the following steps:

1. Using the procedures previously described, create a master project containing one or more subprojects so that each subproject is a Summary task.

2. Add a new Summary task called *Dynamic Links* (the name is not important, but it makes it easier to find) in the workspace and create several blank rows beneath the summary.

3. Create the hammock tasks as described previously.

4. After all the hammock tasks are created, continue to expand the master project and copy (from the Dynamic Links section) the linked tasks and paste them into the master. This creates "double-hammock tasks" or "duplicated existing links."

After all the desired links have been created in the master project, save the Dynamic Master Schedule file. Click Yes to All to save the master, with the newly added links. Once the dynamic links file and linked hammock tasks are created, opening the master project causes the dynamic links file to be opened in the background. Subsequently, all of the linked enterprise projects that feed the updates to the master project are opened. The master project now includes duration-based schedule data from the subprojects, rather than using links between tasks or milestones.

You should not specify a predecessor for a hammock task. Only Paste Linked dates determine start and finish. You may, of course, specify predecessors for the tasks from which dates are paste-linked into the hammock task.

 tip

To test your hammock task, change the duration of the task that provides the start or finish date of the hammock task, to see if the hammock task reflects the changes.

You can also double-click on the small triangle in the lower-right corner of hammock task. This opens the parent cell.

 caution

The hammock tasks necessarily contain a date constraint. You cannot clear this type of constraint.

Also, if you later go back and directly edit any one of the hammock task's Pasted Link fields, the hammock relationship is removed for that field.

Maintaining Inserted Projects

To replace an inserted project, you can change the name in the source project by selecting the Advanced tab of the Task Information dialog box. Use the Browse button to find the file instead of typing it in. If you just delete the filename, you will sever the link between the two projects, and your inserted project task will become a single task with a 1-day duration by default. If you change the filename to an already existing file, that file will be used as the source project file, instead of the previous file. If you enter a filename Project cannot find, Project automatically opens the Browse dialog box, shown in Figure 23.13.

Be careful when moving or renaming projects used as inserted projects. If you want to try to open a project that contains an inserted project and Project cannot find the file, the Browse dialog box from Figure 23.13 opens. Locate the file before proceeding to maintain your links.

Figure 23.13
The Browse
dialog box
opens if
you need to
re-identify
an inserted
project
when the
original
is moved,
deleted,
renamed, or
cannot be
found.

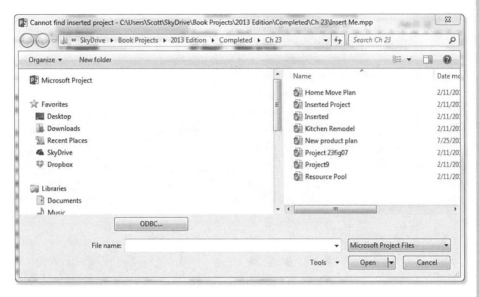

---

 note

Project will not alert you of a lost link on inserted project files until the outline for the file is expanded in the combined file. A combined file always opens collapsed down to a single summary line for every inserted project, regardless of whether the outline was expanded when the combined file was saved and closed.

If you plan to maintain several subprojects rolled up into a master file, it would be useful to investigate how best to organize and catalog the repository of files. Just as with a filing cabinet or a computer hard drive, you can save a lot of time by setting up an appropriate filing system to organize your files, as well as maintaining the linkages built into the master project.

Identifying Tasks That Are Inserted Projects

Besides the inserted projects indicator in the Indicators column, you can also use the Subproject File field, which stores the name of the inserted project. You can set up a table displaying that field to help you identify the tasks.

Every Subproject File field entry has to contain a filename and extension, which are separated by a period. Figure 23.14 demonstrates a filter definition for displaying inserted projects, which filters the Subproject File field for any entry containing a period. Enter a period into the *contains* test to find the value you are looking for.

➡ *For additional information about filter definitions,* **see** *the "Creating and Customizing Filters" section on* **p. 729** *in Chapter 22.*

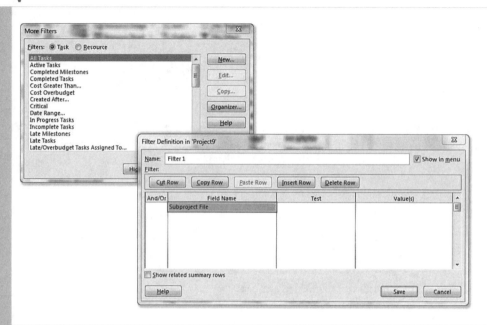

Figure 23.14
You can create a filter to find inserted projects by searching for the period in the Subproject File field.

Removing Inserted Projects

Removing an inserted project is identical to the way you remove a summary task. Select the inserted project and either press the Delete key on the keyboard or right-click the task ID and select Delete Task from the shortcut menu. A warning message is displayed to let you know you are deleting more than one task, as shown in Figure 23.15.

Figure 23.15
This warning dialog box appears when you attempt to delete inserted projects.

Creating Links Between Tasks in Separate Projects

You can easily create links between projects. One method is to link tasks of one project together as the predecessor or successor to a group of tasks in another project. For example, a detailed landscape project cannot begin until the home construction project is completed and the lot is cleaned of construction debris. If you need to monitor the construction project's progress to efficiently schedule your workforce, you might want to link a group of tasks. Another way to accomplish this is to link a single task from one project to a single task in another.

If you have already inserted one project inside another, you can simply expand the inserted project task list, and then choose the tasks to be linked. To do so, select the Task tab, Schedule, and use the Link Tasks tool. Use the View tab, Window, Arrange All if you want to display both projects at the same time, and then select the tasks you want linked. You can also enter the full path of the project file and task ID into the Predecessors or Successors task fields, as follows:

Drive:\directory\subdirectory\filename.ext\taskIDnumber

If, for instance, your predecessor is Task 13 in the project file new-product.mpp, stored in the directory C:\Projects\Development, you would enter the following into the Predecessors field:

C:\Projects\Development\newproduct.mpp\13

Although this functionality can be used, it is rare to see it used in practice due to the possibility of making entry errors.

A cross-link between files can use any of the standard relationships (Finish-to-Finish, Finish-to-Start, Start-to-Finish, or Start-to-Start), plus lag and lead times are supported.

 For additional information about creating links between tasks, see the "Linking Tasks" section on *p. 186 in Chapter 7.*

After the link is established, the name of the task being linked to, along with the duration, start, and finish, appear in gray text. If the linked task has a duration, a taskbar also appears in gray. If the linked task is a milestone, the milestone marker will be gray. Double-clicking on the linked task opens the original project plan that contains that task. If the source project for the linked task is open, the linked task from the destination project plan also appears in gray, and you can double-click it to return to the original project file. When you open the Task Information dialog box for either of the two grayed-out tasks, information about those tasks is displayed, but you can change only the note entries.

For instance, suppose you are using separate files for two new projects in development. The design work for the second product prototype begins after the prototype for the first product is finished. If the two tasks from separate files have been linked together, Project includes placeholder tasks for both files. An external successor task in the First New Product file would look as shown in Figure 23.16.

 note

With networked computers, it is not necessary to use a drive name; you can use a network share instead. The format for this could be the following:

*sharename**directory*\ *subdirectory**filename.ext*\ *taskIDnumber*

You can even keep files on an FTP site, and then insert them into a project using the Insert Project dialog box, by pulling up the predefined FTP site in your drop-down list box for the Look In field.

 caution

Any notes or other data column changes entered for a grayed-out task will not be saved back to the original task.

note

If you create a link to a task in another project file, the External Task field is set to Yes. This enables you to create a filter for all tasks with external links. A filter like this, plus a table including the Predecessors and Successors column, provides a view of all the external links and their sources.

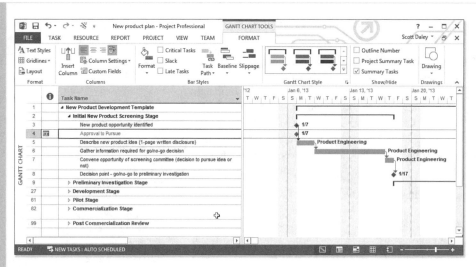

Figure 23.16
You can set up predecessor or successor tasks that are linked back to another project. These tasks will be shown in gray.

Notice the gray text of the task named Approval to Pursue. The Approval to Pursue is part of the New Product file only to the extent that it is a predecessor to the Describe New Product Idea task. You can double-click these tasks, and the Approval Process file opens, as shown in Figure 23.17. In the Approval Process file, you see the gray text from the first Describe New Product Idea task. Once again, this task is part of the Approval Process plan only to the extent that it is a successor to the Approval to Pursue task. Double-clicking the gray Describe New Product Idea task returns you to the New Product file.

> **caution**
> Make sure you do not delete the gray task, because this will break the bidirectional links between the files the next time they are opened.

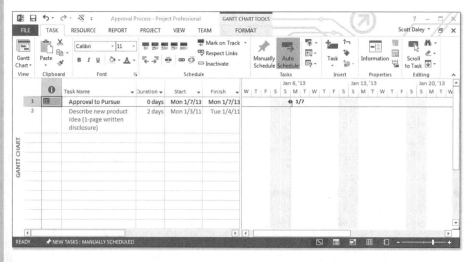

Figure 23.17
You can easily jump back and forth between projects by double-clicking on the grayed-out cross-linked tasks.

Now that the two projects are linked together, any changes to the New Product file that affect the Prototype Complete task also affect the Second New Product file.

If you open a file that has cross-linked predecessors, the Links Between Projects dialog box opens if any changes have taken place to the external tasks. You can also open this dialog box by selecting the Project tab, Properties, Links Between Projects. This dialog box not only refreshes any changes made to the external files, but also reestablishes file locations or deletes links. You can see which changes have occurred in the Differences column, and in Figure 23.18, you can see that the full path is shown for the selected tab in the title bar.

Figure 23.18
You can see if any changes have been made in cross-linked tasks with the Links Between Projects dialog box.

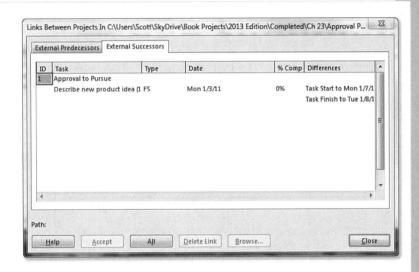

If you accidentally create any links that might cause a circular relationship between tasks, such as one task acting as the predecessor and successor for another, a warning dialog box appears, as shown in Figure 23.19. You need to remove the conflicting link to prevent this from reappearing.

Figure 23.19
If you accidentally create a circular relationship, a warning appears, and you need to remove the conflicting link.

Sharing Resources Among Projects

Project managers who have several projects executing at the same time often use the same set of resources. It can, however, be difficult to manage the same resources in several different projects.

You cannot always see which resources have been assigned and what they are doing for all projects. You can have Project store that resource information in one file, and only the assignment information in the project files. You can enter all of the resources into one project file and instruct other project files to use resources defined in this file, your shared resource pool file. The project file that contains your shared resource pool does not require and should not contain any tasks.

If several projects share the same resource pool, you can open all of your projects at the same time to display the allocation of resources across your projects. Project warns you when a resource is being overallocated because of conflicting assignments in different projects. You can then use the leveling feature to resolve resource overallocation by delaying tasks in different projects.

➡️ *For additional information on resolving resource overallocations,* **see** *Chapter 24, "Resolving Resource Allocation Problems,"* **p. 801.**

The steps shown in this section for sharing resources work only with Project Standard or Project Professional if it has not been linked with Microsoft Office Project Server.

Creating the Shared Resource Project

The easiest way to create a resource pool is to create a project file with no tasks, simply containing a list of all your resources. To create the resource pool, follow these steps:

1. Open a blank project schedule by selecting the File tab, New, Blank Project.

2. Switch to the Resource Sheet view by selecting the Resource tab, View, Resource Sheet.

3. Enter your resource data, including resource names, types, rates, and so on.

4. Save this file with a recognizable name that indicates the file is the resource pool, such as Shared Resource Pool.

Using the Resource Pool

Use the Resource tab, Assignments, Resource Pool, Share Resources command to associate the resource pool file to your project schedule file. When both files have resources defined in them at the time the link is established, the resource pool will be enlarged to include all the resources in both files. If both projects use the same resources (although this is not recommended) but have different definitions, you must select which file takes precedence. You can set this up using the Share Resource dialog box, which provides a check box to set precedence.

After your resource pool sharing link is established, look at the Resource Sheet view of either file to see the complete list of resources. You can change the resource definitions in either file if needed. When you close the files, make sure each one includes a copy of the entire resource pool. This enables you to open the project file that uses the resource pool independently of the file that actually contains the resources, if needed, to change and manage that project file.

Follow these steps to allow a project file to use resources from another file:

1. Open both of the project files: the file containing the resource pool and the file that will be sharing the pool. Confirm that the active project is the file sharing the pool, not the pool itself.

2. Open the Share Resources dialog box by selecting the Resource tab, Assignments, Resource Pool, Share Resources command (see Figure 23.20). Select the Use Resources option button, and then select your resource pool from your currently open files using the From drop-down box.

Figure 23.20
The Share Resources dialog box helps you to link your resource pool to other project files.

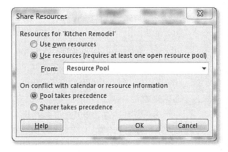

3. Choose the Pool Takes Precedence option button to avoid conflicting definitions between your two pools (the resource pool and the file sharing the pool). If you want your sharing pool to control resources, select the Sharer Takes Precedence button.

4. Click OK to finish.

If your resource pool file is not open when a connected file opens, the Open Resource Pool Information dialog box is displayed, as shown in Figure 23.21. Here, you can choose to have Project open the resource pool, plus all other project files that use those resources.

 tip
You can select the shared resource pool and display the Resource Usage view to see all the resources shared with other schedule files. Insert the Project column to see associated schedules. Split the screen with Resource Usage on the top and Resource Graph on the bottom to see assignment workload profiles for selected resources.

Figure 23.21
You can open your resources with the Open Resource Pool Information dialog box.

You have a few different options with the Open Resource Pool Information dialog box, as shown in Figure 23.21. The Open Resource Pool Information dialog box appears after you open the Project file containing your shared resource pool. Using the first option, you can open the resource pool and see assignments across all shared files. Any changes made to the shared file are immediately reproduced in the resource pool file. Project might claim that the pool file will be opened as read-only, but this is a bit misleading. The truth is the resource pool accepts changes to resource assignment information, so it is not entirely read-only. The pool is temporarily locked, however, to prevent other shared files from making changes to the pool. The shared resource pool is changed to read-write, saved, and then returned to read-only status when you save your project file and click OK to the Save Pool challenge dialog box.

The other option in the Open Resource Pool Information dialog box lets you open and work on a project file without having to also open the resource pool. With only one file open at a time, this should increase your computing performance.

caution

When you open a file that shares resources with the resource pool, but do not open the resource pool, any changes you make will be saved to the file, but the resource pool will not be immediately updated. Any changes made are not included until the resource pool and all sharing files have been opened at the same time, or you have saved all the projects. Your options for opening the resource pool are shown in Figure 23.22.

Figure 23.22
How you open your resource pool file determines the access to and behavior of that file.

If you open the resource pool file without opening another linked file first, the option you select on the Open Resource Pool dialog box establishes your accessibility and how the pool will be updated. If you use the read-only option, you can make changes and see the results instantly in a copy of the last-saved version of the pool file, but any changes made in real time by another user will not be reflected until the pool has been closed and reopened. You can refresh the pool with current information, however, when you have multiple users working on it. Select the Resource tab, Assignments, Resource Pool and select the Update Resource Pool option. This saves changes to the stored resource pool, and then you can go to the Resource tab, Assignments, Resource Pool, Refresh Resource Pool to load a fresh copy of the pool into your open resource pool window. When these two options are grayed out and unavailable, this means that the file-sharing environment is updated, and refreshing is unnecessary.

The second option when you open your resource pool file is to open the file with read-write capabilities. The read-write option itself has two choices—you can have complete editing control over the pool file, but lock out other users while you have the file open. Alternatively, you can open the resource pool as read-write, along with all the shared files. This forces Project to retrieve the last saved versions of all the attached files and rebuild the pool.

After you have set up a project to share another project's resource file, if the resource pool is open in read-write mode, any changes made to the resource pool while both files are open will be saved back into the shared pool, and both files are updated immediately.

However, when you are working with a dependent project file alone, and changes are made in the resource sheet of that project, the changes will not be saved back to the resource pool until you try to either close or save the file. If you add only new resources with different names, these resources are added to the resource pool when it is next opened in read-write mode.

If you make changes to the definition of the resource, such as the pay rate, maximum units, or working days on the resource calendar, it is possible those changes might be lost if both files are loaded in memory together the next time. If you selected the Pool Takes Precedence option button in the Share Resources dialog box, changes will be lost if you make them in the sub file. If, however, you selected the Sharer Takes Precedence option button in the Share Resources dialog box, your changes will be updated within the resource pool. The Pool Takes Precedence option is the default button, so changes to the definitions of your resources should always be made to the resource pool, if possible.

 tip

It is a good idea to occasionally open your resource pool file and all the shared files along with it, to force the most up-to-date information into all the files. This can also alert you if any files have lost or corrupted links.

Open only the shared resource pool and then use the Resource Sharing menu. A dialog box is present to enable you to select any or all associated project schedules. You can also use the Break Links option to remove resource sharing. A copy of the shared resources is saved within the selected schedule(s) if you break the sharing link.

 tip

For best practices, the resource pool is the only file where the underlying resource details are changed. In most cases, organizations only have one or two people to serve as resource managers, custodians of the resource pool, and they should be the ones entering and making changes to resource details, such as maximum units, pay rates, calendars, and so forth. Sharing files should be connected to the pool, and the Pool Takes Precedence option should be selected in the Share Resources dialog box.

Discontinuing Resource Sharing

You can quit sharing resources whenever you choose. To do so, open the file using another file's resources, and then go to the Share Resources dialog box by selecting the Resource tab, Assignments, Resource Pool, Share Resources. In the Share Resources dialog box, select the Use Own Resources option button. The resource pool will be no longer available to this file. However, if any resources that were assigned to tasks in the file have been copied into the file's resource list, they are now saved with that file. Also, any resource in the file being shared from the resource pool of another project will be copied into the local resource sheet and will remain there after sharing has been disconnected.

Follow these steps to discontinue a project file's dependence on another file's resource pool:

1. Open the file you want to make independent and use its own resources.

2. Set up this file as the active file window.

3. Open the Share Resources dialog box by selecting the Resource tab, Assignments, Resource Pool, Share.

4. Select the Use Own Resources option button.

5. Click OK to finish. A confirmation of resource connection removal between your sharing file and the resource pool file is displayed.

 note

It is also possible to break a sharing link in the other direction by opening the resource pool file, bringing up the Share Resources dialog box, and clicking on the Break Link button.

Identifying Resource Pool Links

Resource sharing connections are recorded both in the resource pool file and the file that uses the resource pool. You can open the Share Resources dialog box (Resource tab, Assignments, Resource Pool, Share) to show the linking information in both file types. The layout of the dialog box also shows you which of the two file types is active.

Project knows which file is the resource pool file and changes the Share Resources dialog box when you need link-management options.

 tip

As you experiment with inserted projects, cross-project links, and shared resource pools, it might be helpful to include columns for External, Linked Fields, Predecessors, Successors, Subproject File, Subproject File Read-Only, and Notes. This way, as you are trying different options, you can see what is happening and where Project is storing the information.

Viewing Resource Loads Without Sharing a Pool

Having many project managers attaching their files to a single resource pool can cause problems. Too many attached projects will degrade performance, and other managers might have problems making and saving changes to their files, especially if someone has opened all the shared files by mistake. If your primary reason for pooling is to summarize and report on the resource assignments for several different files, Project gives you another option that does not require links to the resource pool.

If two or more projects have been linked together, as mentioned earlier in the chapter, Project creates a combined list of resources assigned to each of those files. If you break those links, Project re-creates a list of resources from all the linked files. Resource names from each of the files are matched up, and the assignments totaled. You can then use the Resource Usage view to show the sharing of work by resource between all the linked projects in a particular file.

If you want to build this combined resource list, select the Project Summary task (if this isn't visible, use the Format tab, Show/Hide, Project Summary task to make it visible). Open the Inserted Project Information dialog box, go to the Advanced tab, and in the Source Project area, clear the Link to Project option, as shown in Figure 23.23. Your Gantt Chart view now shows tasks renumbered consecutively, and duplicate task IDs no longer exist. You can now create a separate consolidated file, with file links included, to edit projects from this level.

Figure 23.23
You can use the Inserted Project Information dialog box to create a combined resource list across projects by unlinking your consolidated files.

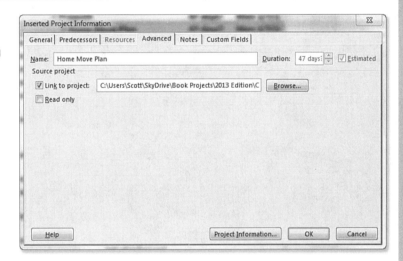

 tip

If you decide to use the aforementioned method to create a consolidated resource list, make sure that you have a separate file acting as your resource information pool. You should have someone in your organization keep the resource detail information (pay rate, nonworking time, and so on) in a separate and up-to-date file. When updates are then made to that file, all project managers should open their Project files, link them to this resource file to upload the most recent resource information, and then break the resource-sharing link and save their files.

Saving Multiple Files in a Workspace

Project supports a concept of workspaces. A workspace represents all the files you have currently open in Project and enables you to capture a work setup that you can easily access by opening a previously saved workspace. Workspaces do not create copies of the project files, but rather provide pointers to the file locations that are opened once you open the workspace.

If you are using a shared resource pool, you can save the pool and resource-sharing files into a workspace file simultaneously. To do so, add the Save Workspace command to the Quick Launch bar; then select Save Workspace. This saves all open pool and shared files together; this workspace file is assigned the name resume.mpw by default.

You can open files attached to the resource pool easily by opening the resource pool first, and then using the Share Resource dialog box by selecting the Resource tab, Assignments, Resource Pool, Share Resources. This displays a list of all the sharing files attached to your resource pool in the Share Resources dialog box, and you can open all of them at the same time, using the Open All button, as shown in Figure 23.24. To open individual sharing files, simply choose the filename in the Sharing links area and then select Open.

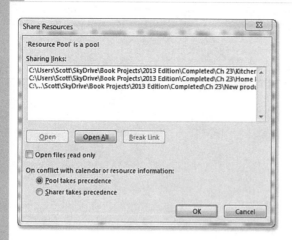

Figure 23.24
The Share Resources dialog box lets you open one or all of your resource pools' sharing files.

Consultants' Tips

Using Master Files

Using master project files can be a useful technique when you need to view the high-level status of multiple projects. Master files are often used for program-level information. Although this feature can be helpful, you should use it with caution. To avoid broken links, ensure that the location of the source (sub) files inserted into the master is well maintained. In addition, if you have multiple people working on the project files, including the master, establish file-sharing policies so that the changes made to files are not overwritten.

How Do I Tell Which Task Is from Which Project When They Have the Same Names?

Make sure that you only have the files that you need open; it will simplify the look of your workspace. You can also insert the Project field into your view, which helps you distinguish the source of each task.

Sharing Resources Between Projects

If you are not using Project Professional in conjunction with Project Server, and you work in an environment with multiple project managers, it can be useful to set up a shared resource pool. Resource overallocation problems silently sap the effectiveness of an organization without ever appearing on an individual project manager's schedule. The shared resource pool enables you and other project managers in your organization to view where and which resources have already been allocated, contributing to more accurate and realistic planning, tracking, and reporting.

Even if you are not sharing your resource pool with other project managers, it can be beneficial to set up one. It can save you time from reentering the resources you use often and also predict resource availability more accurately.

24

RESOLVING RESOURCE ALLOCATION PROBLEMS

One of the most difficult conditions facing project managers is how to identify and correct resource workload bottlenecks. This chapter helps you with the following:

- Understanding how resource allocation problems can occur

- Determining how to visualize resource workload problems

- Using techniques to correct overallocation conditions

Understanding How Resource Allocation Problems Occur

You should have a firm understanding of how resource allocation problems can occur. Some problems are very real and stem from your project's business context (like unreasonable deadlines). Others boil down to misuses of Project. This chapter introduces you to a wide range of corrective techniques and cross-references to other chapters in this book.

➡ For additional information on simplified project management and tracking, **see** Chapter 2, "Microsoft Project Quick Start," **p. 15.**

➡ For a discussion about detailed progress tracking, **see** Chapter 13, "Tracking Your Project Progress," **p. 431.**

Why Should I Care About Resource Workload Conditions?

Overloaded resources threaten the outcome of the task deliverables and consequently your entire project. In these circumstances, the end date Project calculates for your project is fictitious.

The performance of each resource on tasks determines the overall success or failure of the project. You dramatically increase the risks to your project if you choose to ignore resource allocation issues.

Your schedule probably has named resources you plan to use throughout the project life cycle. Some resources might report directly to you during the normal course of business, so you have direct responsibility to apply those resources in ways that satisfy overall project and staff management goals.

Some resources might report to other staff managers, so those resources are shared by multiple projects throughout the organization. Chances are you must negotiate to use shared resources, so as the project manager, you are responsible for building the argument for your project's resources (even if your argument is ultimately presented by someone else).

Organizations often need to provide project life cycle budget forecasts. Typical financial forecasting models are done using Microsoft Excel to show expected spending levels in the future. You can also use Project with a resource cost structure to make these forecasts, but if Excel is currently in use, shifting to Project is a significant step.

You can use the robust features of Project to forecast resource workloads and costs for overall task delivery. These resource forecasts help you build a strong business case while also strengthening your argument to use certain shared resources that perform project task activities.

What Is the Problem?

The key challenge for the project manager is to identify actual resource workload conditions and then resolve the inevitably conflicted demands.

Exaggerated actual work and cost are common problems that create the appearance of overload. These false data can also cause unexpected errors in overall budget forecasts.

During early planning stages, you might choose to use a combination of Manually Scheduled mode and the Team Planner. Or, you might be focused on managing a defined team's availability and utilization. Figure 24.1 shows a simple resource overload condition using the Overallocated Resources report.

> **caution**
> Note that using the Team Planner to move assignments creates constraints on auto-scheduled tasks. These constraints compromise Project's capability to predict completion dates for your project.

Figure 24.2 shows a simple example of an overload resource condition using auto-scheduled tasks. Notice how the resource graph shows that the Russ resource is clearly overloaded for a period of time. If the project manager changes the %Complete on the summary task, Actual Work and Actual Cost data are exaggerated.

Figure 24.1
The Overallocated
Resources report
indicates that Russ
and Becky are not
likely to make
everyone happy.

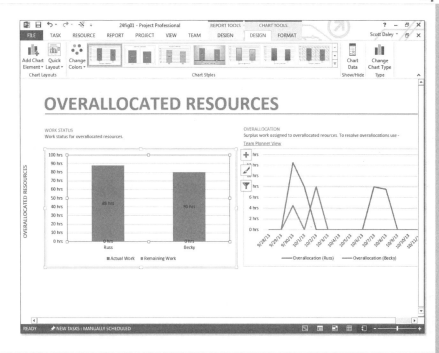

Figure 24.2
A combination view
of Gantt Chart and
Resource Graph is
a simple way to see
how resources are
allocated for each
task within your
schedule.

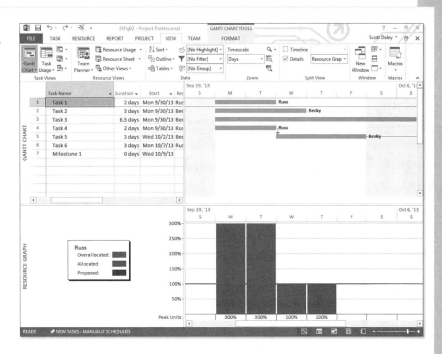

Another common but less obvious condition is the effect on your project when other project managers overload the same resources you expect to use in your project.

 note

Where possible, you should model external demand in your schedule, typically by reducing resource availability. However, sometimes it makes sense to model external demand with "dummy" tasks, depending on whether this makes it easier to visually identify problems.

What Causes Resource Overallocation?

Many common problems can cause resource overallocation issues. Arbitrary delivery dates are the primary cause. Additional causes include competing projects, unexpected discoveries, emergency conditions, and so forth. Project managers instinctively understand these conditions, so the trick is expressing those conditions within Project.

Many common problems stem from the use of Project features, such as the following:

- Using Task Type settings that affect the way resource workload is calculated

- Not understanding the relationship between a task's duration, work, and resource units

- Creating a task assignment on more than one task during a specific overlapping time period (for example, tasks running in parallel)

- Assuming that resources are 100% dedicated to each task

- Not using Project views, groups, and filters to isolate overloaded resources

- Ignoring task links and overlapping tasks

 caution

Using Manually Scheduled task mode does not lead to resource allocation problems in and of itself. In fact, in situations where resource utilization is more important than completing projects, it actually makes resolving resource allocation issues easier.

When Should I Ignore Resource Allocation Problems?

Well, never. However, there are times when you can pay less attention to them:

- If you have dedicated teams under your complete control.

- If you are not in fact responsible for the project outcome, and instead you are simply tracking time spent against tasks.

- If you have unlimited budget and no specific delivery timelines.

- If you have excess resources.

All other project conditions demand your attention to resource workload conditions.

The bottom line is simple and straightforward: Ignore resource workloads, and you increase the risk of facing embarrassing project and budget failures.

Visualizing Resource Allocation Conditions

Project provides several mechanisms to view and manipulate resource allocation data. This section shows features commonly used to examine resource workload conditions, including the following:

- Resource Max Units and calendars

- Team Planner

- Resource graph

- Resource sheet

- Split views

- Resource usage time-phased data

- Grouping, filtering, and sorting tasks and resources

- Review task relationships

The simple example shown in Figure 24.2 is used for the remainder of this chapter to demonstrate these concepts. You might want to create your own version of this example to follow along in the upcoming sections.

Resource Max Units, Calendars, and Other Settings

Each resource in your project schedule has certain settings that enable you to specify the general properties for those resources. Each one of the properties is an attribute about the resource—for example, calendar, availability dates, cost, email address, and so forth.

> ➡ *For additional information about calendars,* **see** *the "Defining Calendars" section on* **p. 101** *of Chapter 5.*

One of those properties is called Max Units, which enables you to set a maximum capacity for resource availability. The default setting for the Max Units field is 100%. The Max Units setting does not prevent you from overloading a resource, but rather gives you a visual queue when overload conditions are present.

Figure 24.3 shows a Resource Sheet view with a list of individual named resources with a variety of settings. Max Units for Russ and Becky are set to 100%, indicating that they are generally available full-time. G_Implementer is a generic resource set to 500%, indicating that five full-time workers are available from a general pool of system implementers.

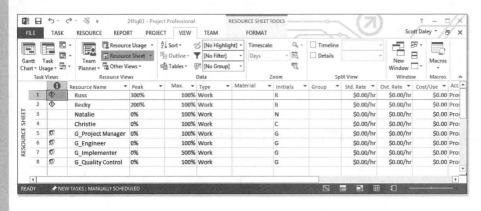

Figure 24.3
The resource row color and font change when the resource workloads exceed the Max Units threshold value.

Resource calendars in combination with the Max Units also affect the amount of work a resource can be scheduled to perform during a given point in time. The individual resource calendars enable you to specify the expected working schedule for the resource. The calendar settings also enable you to specify exceptions to working periods.

The resource calendar has a direct impact on work when you assign a resource to a task. By default, the resource calendar drives the task duration, work, or resource units. If, however, you change the task attributes to Ignore Resource Calendars, you can create a resource overload condition that will not be reflected by Project. Figures 24.4 and 24.5 illustrate before and after conditions when you use this setting.

 tip

Use shared resource pools to establish Max Units, working calendars, exceptions, and so forth. Then you do not have to alter every resource calendar in every schedule when resource vacations are planned. Just remember to open and resave each affected schedule to update the affected tasks. Another way to handle this shared resource condition is to use the Project Server Enterprise Global Resource Pool features.

Another shared resource tip: Open one project schedule and use the Resource Usage view to see all the projects related to the selected resources. You see which project schedules should be updated when a resource calendar changes.

Each of the tasks is Fixed Work, and each resource uses a standard calendar. You can overload Natalie if you force a 12-hour-per-day calendar on her task and also set the flag for the task to ignore the resource calendars. Now Natalie is forced to work longer hours per day to get the job done, thus overloading the resource allocation. Project, however, does not highlight this as an overload because the resource calendar is ignored.

 caution

Notice how the resources on the task in Figure 24.5 do not appear overloaded. You need to be careful about using the task feature that ignores resource calendars.

Figure 24.4
Before the task ignores resource calendars.

Figure 24.5
After the task ignores resource calendars—Natalie suddenly appears to be much more productive.

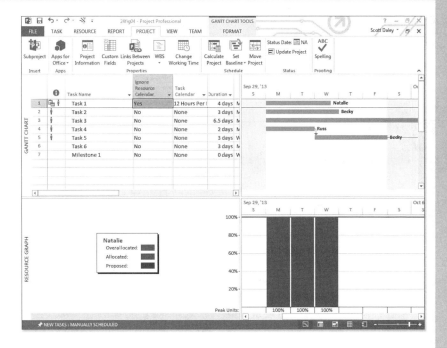

Team Planner

The Team Planner is a graphical tool for both identifying resource overallocations and changing them, right on the spot. By combining a project timeline with a list of resources, unscheduled tasks, unassigned tasks, and a Gantt Chart, it is possible to smooth resource demand by simply dragging screen elements from one section to another, or by dragging Gantt bars (see Figure 24.6).

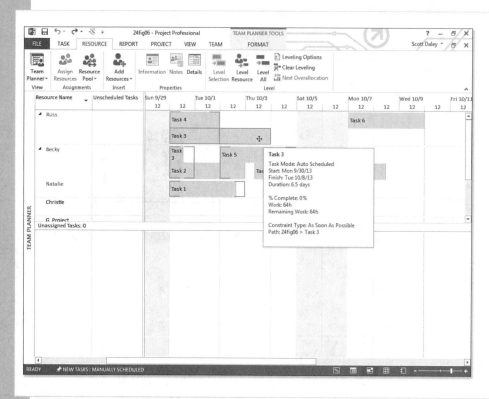

Figure 24.6
You can easily identify and resolve resource overallocations by simply dragging Gantt bars in the Team Planner.

Resource Graphs

Resource Graph views are helpful to get a quick overview of resource workload conditions. This type of view is especially helpful when you split the window, showing the Gantt Chart view at the top and the resource graph in the bottom half. Figure 24.7 shows an example of a split window with the resource graph. The resource list in the resource graph changes as you select a single task or multiple tasks from the Gantt Chart view. You can easily see the overall workload conditions for each resource across a given timescale.

 tip
Remember to pan right and left in the resource graph's Names section to see each resource condition for the selected tasks.

Figure 24.7
Split window with resource graph, where you can use the horizontal scrollbar on the left side of the resource graph to switch between resources.

 caution

Be aware that the resource graph color might indicate overloading conditions, based on the current zoom factor for the time display. Project stores data at a minute-by-minute resolution, so you might see overallocation conditions when work overlaps anywhere within the time period, such as month, week, day, and so forth.

 tip

Did you know that you can change the resource graph format and details if you right-click in the resource graph area? You can select from a variety of graph styles and color formats. Try using the Percent Allocation display.

Resource Sheet

The Resource Sheet view provides a quick way to find overallocated resources, which display in red. You can inspect various resource settings such as Max Units, Standard and Overtime Rates, and Base Calendars.

You can quickly see overallocation conditions by looking for the following:

- Red-colored rows indicate that the cumulative resource workload exceeds the Max Units value in a time period.

- The Information Indicators column shows a graphic icon under which you see a warning message about leveling.

- If you display the Overallocated column and see the Yes condition, the resource is overallocated.

Figure 24.8 shows an example of useful display features for overallocated resources.

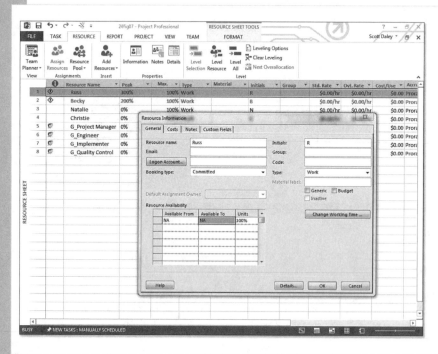

Figure 24.8
You can drill into additional details when you double-click a resource to inspect conditions such as Availability From Units for specific date ranges, Working Time (reached from the General tab), Effective Dates for Costs (not shown, on the Costs tab), and so forth.

➡ For additional information about resources, **see** Chapter 8, "Defining Project Resources," **p. 235**.

 tip

Use the Format tab, Format, Text Styles to alter the display colors for overallocated resources. Try using background cell colors and font settings to highlight important resource conditions.

Split Views and Windows

The preceding sections show simple examples of using split views to see a combination of task and resource information. This section explores this powerful feature in greater detail.

➥ *For additional information about resource views,* **see** *the "Working with Resources" section on* **p. 258** *in Chapter 8.*

You should already be familiar with the various ways to split the screen into two sections. But did you know there are several combinations of split views that are helpful for determining resource workload conditions?

Figure 24.9 shows an example of a Resource Sheet view in the top half of the screen and with projects and tasks listed in the bottom half of the screen. You can see a lot of helpful information in the lower half of the screen as you navigate to each resource in the resource sheet. You can also see cross-references to other projects and tasks if you are using a shared resource pool.

Figure 24.9
The Resource Sheet view with Task Details is a great way to navigate each resource in the resource sheet.

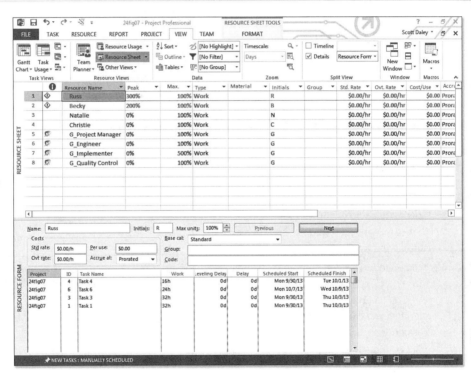

Figure 24.10 illustrates a good use of both the resource sheet and resource graph. You can select one or more resources in the top half of the screen and then see the graph in the lower half.

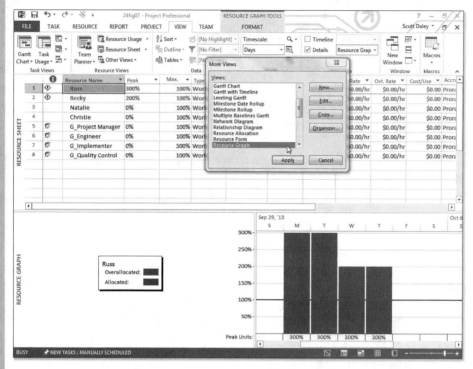

Figure 24.10
You can also combine Resource Sheet and Resource Graph views in a split window, which enables you to select and view over-allocation conditions for more than one resource.

If you have a higher-resolution monitor, you can also use another helpful viewing method whereby you divide the Project session screen into multiple individual windows. Figure 24.11 shows an example where the single Project session has two windows referencing the same schedule. Notice that each window's title bar has the name of the project with a suffix window number.

This window arrangement is easily created by selecting the View tab, Window, New Window to display another view for this project. You can then use the View tab, Window, Arrange All command so you can see each active window within the same Project session.

This multiwindow option gives you a lot of flexibility in viewing resource allocation issues.

 tip

When you make a change within any project window, those edit changes are applied to the project in all windows.

 caution

Be aware that the timescales are controlled independently in each window and are not synchronized.

Figure
24.11
If you have
a higher-
resolution
monitor
than shown
here, the
multiple-
windows
feature in
Project is
useful for
adjusting
allocation
within your
project
schedule.

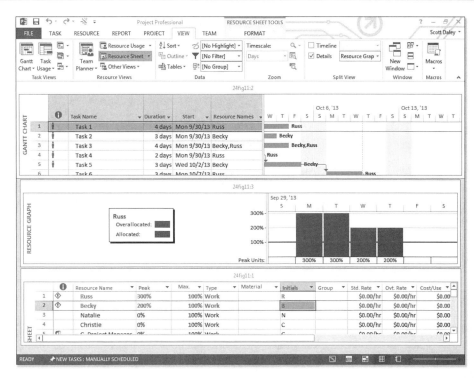

Resource Usage Time-Phased Data

You might be familiar with the basic Project usage data, whereby you can drill into greater detail for resource assignments on tasks. Usage data is central to the core data about all assignments. This core data is typically called *time-phased* or *timescaled* data and is stored within Project at the minute-by-minute level of detail.

> For additional information about assigning resources to tasks, **see** the "How-To's: Modifying Resource Assignments" section on **p. 336** in **Chapter 10**.

The Resource Usage view is helpful if you need to see the details about resource allocation. You can use this view to isolate overallocation issues.

Figure 24.12 illustrates a typical Resource Usage view showing several helpful data fields. You can add data columns on the left side of the screen or add data rows to the right side. You can also split the screen to show a combination of Resource Usage and Resource Graph information. The combination of these data fields and viewing layouts gives you a lot of resource allocation information.

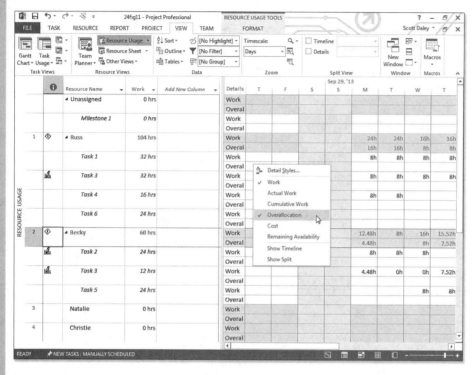

Figure 24.12 Adding more field columns to the Resource Usage view is a great way to combine information and analyze the resource allocation conditions.

 tip

Right-click in the Resource Usage detailed data to add more data fields, change the color display, and so forth. Use the menu command Format, Text Style to show overallocated resources using special colors and font characteristics.

You can copy/paste data in the detailed data display within a usage view. Try copying data rows and then pasting that data into Microsoft Excel for additional analysis. You can also use Visual Report to export data to Excel.

Groups, Filters, and Sorting Tasks with Resources

Project provides several helpful features to rearrange the resource data. You can use combinations of these features to view resource overallocation conditions:

- Grouping

- Filtering

- Setting colors

- Sorting

- Resource allocation fields

Figure 24.13 shows an example of a customized group for a resource sheet. The group has some simple criteria used to rearrange resource information display with key structures at the top of the list. This group uses the data fields Overallocated, Peak (units), and sort criteria to arrange the resources in a simple view. The Format tab, Format Text Styles was also used to create a color schema showing overallocated resources in bold text.

Figure 24.13
You can group the list of current resources based on overallocation and peak units to
highlight problems.

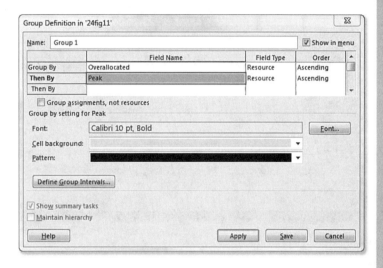

 For additional information about using groups in views, **see** *Chapter 11, "Using Standard Views, Tables, Filters, and Groups to Review Your Schedule,"* **p. 357.**

You should consider using creative combinations of features to group, filter, and color resource information to make flexible views for analyzing resource allocation conditions.

Review Task Relationships

The structure you select for your activity breakdown list also has a direct impact on resource allocation. You can overload resources if you assign those resources to multiple parallel activities. You can also create resource overallocation conditions if you are using features to create task-level overlap conditions. Therefore, you should examine the task's relationships to resource assignment information.

Consider combining a task Gantt Chart view with a Resource Usage view if you want to examine overallocation issues. Figure 24.14 provides an example of viewing task relationships and resource allocation. This view uses another simple tactic—selecting multiple tasks within the top view and then scrolling through the resources in the bottom view.

Figure 24.14
Analyzing the task relationships in the top part of the split Gantt Chart view and the resource allocations in the bottom can help you determine the source of resource allocation problems.

Strategies for Correcting Resource Allocation Problems

Project provides several techniques you can consider for correcting certain resource overallocation conditions. You might decide to use one or more of these techniques to address the issues you observe within your project schedule. You should also know that a single feature might not provide the total solution you seek, so you might need to explore multiple strategies, such as the following:

- Review the business goals

- Replace resources

- Split tasks

- Link tasks

- Adjust resource units

- Use automated resource leveling

- Use manual task mode or assignment contouring

Process Check: Review Project Scope and Other Business Issues

A review of the business goals is always the first thing you should consider when you have project scheduling or resource allocation issues. Consider business conditions, such as overall project scope, budget, timeline, and so forth.

You might decide that resource overallocation is caused by intermediate or final milestone timelines, but the budget cannot withstand additional overtime costs for workers to meet those dates. This condition might cause you to simply extend the project timeline. You should use a formal change-management process to record this information as important artifacts of the project history.

The overall business issues might require that you take steps within tools such as Project to correct these conditions. The remainder of this chapter provides guidance on strategies to address resource overallocation conditions.

Replacing or Adding Resources

One obvious strategy to relieve overbooked resources is to add resources or use resource-substitution techniques. You might decide to replace overloaded resources with those that have greater availability to work on specific tasks.

The first action you take is to understand which resources could be used for substitution. You can use various viewing techniques shown in the beginning of this chapter to find the resources that are overallocated. You can then use the Project Assign Resources feature to replace overloaded resources.

Figure 24.15 shows a simple example using the Assign Resources feature to replace one resource with another. The technique is straightforward:

1. Select the task containing the overloaded resources.

2. Select the Resource tab, Assignments, Assign Resources to open the Assign Resources dialog box.

3. Select the target resources for replacement and click the Replace button.

4. Select the substitution resource, optionally set the resource units, and then click OK.

Also consider the impact to resource workloading when you replace a resource on tasks. You might accidentally overload the newly assigned resource on other tasks within your project or other projects using that same resource.

 *For additional information about manipulating resource assignments, **see** Chapter 10, "Scheduling Single and Multiple Resource Assignments," **p. 301**.*

 tip

Click the Graph button (not shown in Figure 24.15) in the Assign Resources dialog box to see Assignment Work graphs with Availability information.

tip

Select the View tab, Data, Filter, Using Resource to rearrange the task list to show those tasks with the overallocated resources. You can select some or all of these tasks and use the Assign Resources function to do a mass substitution.

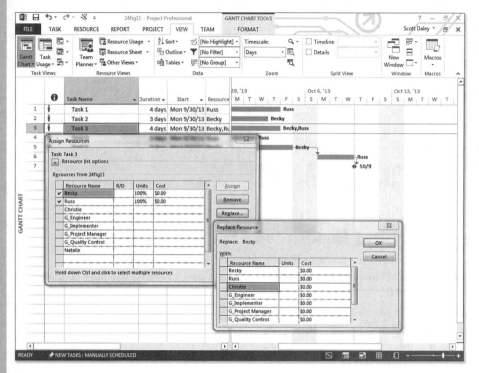

Figure 24.15
You can use the Assign Resources feature to replace resources if resources are over-allocated.

Splitting Tasks

You might find opportunities to use task slack when you examine the overall schedule critical path. One of the ways you can use task slack is to split task work into multiple segments. You should use this technique only on those tasks that do not require continuity of work and can be stopped and started easily. Figure 24.16 shows a simple example where task work activity has been split into multiple segments to correct overallocation for a specific resource. This simple example also illustrates how the critical path and related milestone can still be achieved by using this split task technique. This example shows how Becky could have started working on a task, paused on that task to do the original critical path work, and then resumed work on the original task.

 tip

Notice that a split task condition retains the original Duration value, but the finish date moves.

Figure 24.16
You can split tasks into smaller segments to lighten the workload and correct resource overallocation issues.

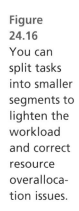

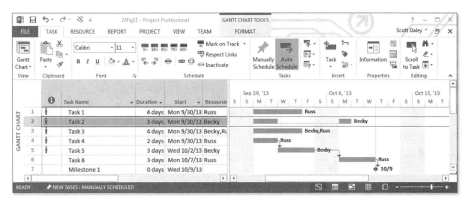

Linking Tasks

A simple way to clear some resource overallocation issues is to manually change the task linkage sequence. Figure 24.17 shows a simple overallocation condition where tasks are scheduled in a parallel sequence; this parallel activity condition overloads resources.

Figure 24.17
Parallel scheduled tasks can often cause resource overallocation.

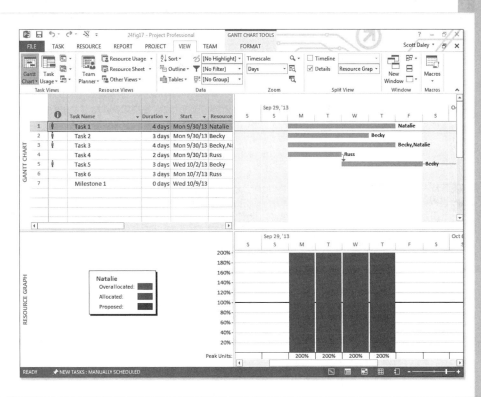

You should review the critical path of tasks to see whether you have activity slack that can be used to shift dates by linking tasks. Figure 24.18 shows the effect of linking tasks. This relieves some overallocation conditions but might have a direct impact on final milestone delivery dates.

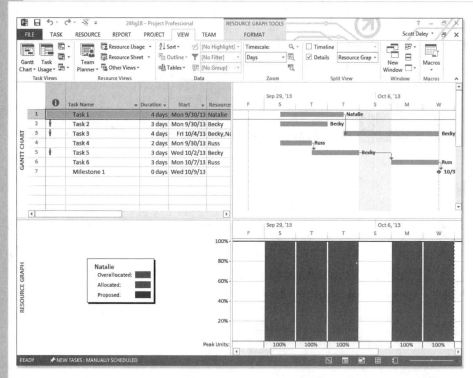

Figure 24.18
You can also use a technique of linking tasks to solve resource overallocation issues.

Adjusting Resource Units

You might decide to assign a single resource to multiple task-parallel activities. You must be careful to examine the resource Units factor for each of these work assignments so that you can understand resource overallocation issues.

You can use a few manual techniques to adjust the resource Units factors for resource assignments. Examples of these techniques include the following:

- Change the resource Units within the Resource Names column in a Gantt Chart, as shown in Figure 24.19.

- Split the screen and adjust the resource Units for selected tasks.

- Use the Assign Resources window to change Units.

- Use a Task Usage view to alter the resource assignment Units.

- Use a Resource Usage view to alter the resource assignment Units.

**Figure
24.19**
Resource
Units can
be adjusted
to reduce
overalloca-
tion condi-
tions for
specified
resources.

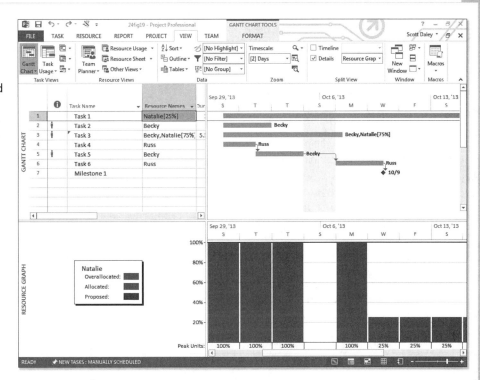

Using the Level Resources Tools

Project has a specific feature called *leveling* that enables you to automatically alter resource assignment timelines, thus adjusting overall resource overallocation conditions.

 caution

The Level Resources tool does *not* optimize resource utilization. It only *levels* resource demand, and in the process it often creates huge areas of resource underutilization. With lot of futzing, these underutilizations can be made less bad, but you *will* need to use manual editing techniques to tune resource assignment details beyond the automated leveling results.

The leveling feature adjusts the tasks/assignments within your schedule with two basic actions:

- Setting a delay on the task/assignment

- Splitting a task

This feature is found on the Resource tab in the Level section. You need to understand the basic features of the Level Resources tool before you use those features to alter your schedule.

You should become familiar with every feature of the Level Resources dialog box to gain confidence before applying this tool to your project schedules. You will then recognize typical scenarios where this tool can be helpful in solving resource overallocation conditions. Consider using the leveling features for conditions such as these:

- The schedule might have several parallel tasks, with slack, assigned to a given resource.

- You might choose to level the schedule and then later clear the leveling on selected tasks for subsequent manual intervention.

- You might choose to level task assignments within a specific date range.

You should now ask the question: "What does the leveling tool do with my schedule?" The resource leveling tool uses a simple strategy to reduce workload conditions for resource assignments by altering the start and finish dates. The following general actions are taken to resolve resource assignments considered overallocated compared to the Max Units setting for the resources:

- Apply a task's or resource assignment leveling delay factor, thus adjusting the start and finish dates for a given resource on a task.

- Split a task's work activities into multiple segments, effectively moving some assigned work to the future. This action alters the finish date for the task.

You also need to understand that the Level Resources tool has certain limitations (that is, actions it will not perform). These are summarized as follows:

- Resource assignment work is not altered.

- Resource assignment units are not adjusted.

- It will not make assignment changes to fully utilize resources.

- Resource calendars and Max Units settings are not modified.

- One resource is not substituted for another.

- Task Duration data fields are not directly modified.

- Task Type settings are not changed.

- Generic, budget, cost, and material resources are not leveled.

- Some combinations of resource assignments, actual work, date constraints, and so forth can create conditions that cannot be resolved by the leveling algorithm. These conditions can cause error or warning messages that you must acknowledge.

- It will not move a task/assignment to start earlier to resolve an overallocation.

The Level Resources tool has internal limitations that cannot solve certain overallocation conditions. Figure 24.20 illustrates an example of unresolved resource allocation conditions. You need to examine these conditions and take manual action.

The next section enables you to practice with some simple leveling examples so that you can learn more about this tool. You should build some simple schedule examples to practice with the tool and learn about the features.

tip

Use the embedded Help button to understand details about each feature within the Level Resources dialog box. Look for the key phrase "about resource leveling."

Figure 24.20
Unresolved resource allocation conditions.

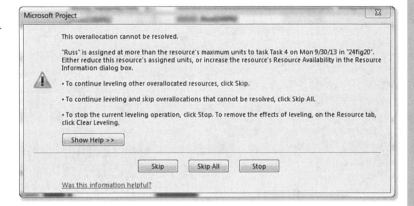

tip

Make a copy of your schedule and experiment with different resource leveling settings to see the effects on your schedule timeline. Try variations of the leveling settings to understand what this tool will do to the task and resource conditions. Save intermediate copies and then use the Compare Schedules Wizard to see the differences among the schedules.

Scenario 1: Simple Level Example

Let's say you want to use the leveling tool to redistribute the workload for the Russ resource. Select the Resource tab, Level, Level Resource to review the defaults before clicking on the Level Now button. You might see scheduling warnings, in which case you should see a result similar to the one shown in Figure 24.21. The unresolved scheduling issues are discussed later.

Notice how the Gantt Chart has been changed to show conditions, such as the task date shift due to leveling delays, the change to the overall critical path, possible task-split conditions, and so forth.

Also notice how the lower half of the screen shows a resource assignment delay factor that adjusted the finish date for a specific resource on a specific task. These are examples of how the leveling tool might alter the resource assignments to reduce overallocation conditions.

Select the Resource tab, Level, Level Resource, Clear Leveling to undo the leveling delays.

 tip

Show the Leveling Delay column to see any delay factors applied to tasks.

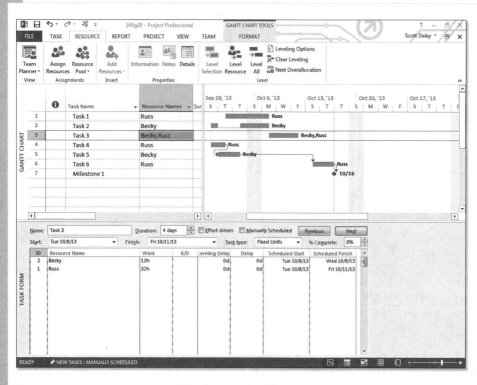

Figure 24.21
Simple leveling example with default settings.

Scenario 2: Level Example Within Slack

This example illustrates how the leveling tool produces different results, with possible warning messages, when you restrain the solution to within the available critical path slack. Select the Resource tab, Level, Level Resource and then check the Level Only Within Available Slack box in the resulting dialog box. The purpose of this setting is to attempt to level the resources without pushing out project or intermediate milestone dates. Click Level Now to see the results.

You might have to acknowledge warning messages indicating that a unique solution cannot be found. Click the Skip button to watch a series of messages appear. Figure 24.22 shows an end-result example of this solution. Take some time to carefully examine task and resource assignment leveling delays. Use combination view layouts to visualize the results.

Figure 24.22
Leveling example constrained within available slack.

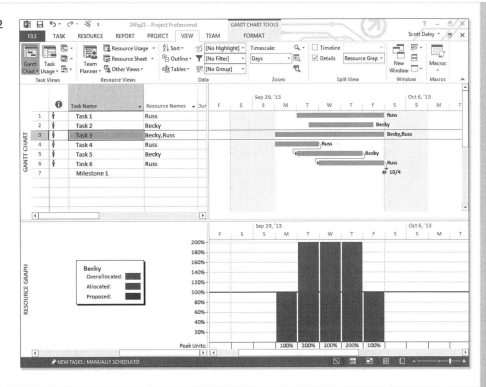

Scenario 3: Clear Leveling on Selected Tasks

Let's say you like some of the leveling results, but you want to override certain task results. Run the leveling tool again, but this time click Clear Leveling and then select Selected Tasks. The tool removes the leveling delay conditions from the selected tasks, so you can perform other manual operations for those resource assignments, as shown in Figure 24.23. You might then fine-tune some of the tasks by using other techniques.

Figure 24.23
Clear Leveling for selected tasks to manually change the leveling conditions.

Scenario 4: Leveling After Rescheduling Uncompleted Work

Let's say your schedule is in progress and some tasks have started but are behind schedule. Furthermore, you have a business process that requires rescheduling uncompleted work into the future weeks. You might want to use the Level Resources tool after that action.

This example shows the following:

- Some actual work has been posted on certain tasks.

- Incomplete work has been rescheduled using the menu command Tools, Tracking, Update Project, Reschedule Uncompleted Work After Date: (status date).

- You might have set task-level priorities and then used the leveling feature Priority, Standard.

You might want to reexamine the resource-loading issues that could have occurred as a result of these actions. You might want to use the Level Resources functions to mitigate overallocation conditions, as shown in Figure 24.24. This example focuses on the tasks assigned to Russ, so the task priority has been adjusted so that those tasks are considered before other tasks.

 caution

The leveling tool produces different results for tasks with posted actual work. Sometimes the Clear Leveling function might not remove all leveling conditions previously established. This might cause the leveling tool to create conditions that you do not expect. You should practice leveling schedules that contain actual work.

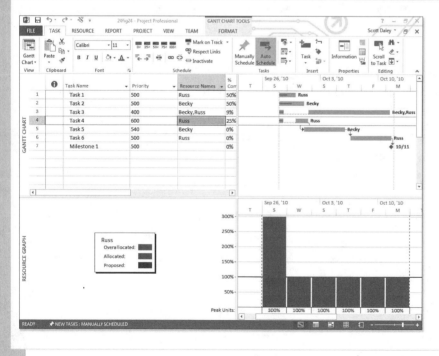

Figure 24.24
Releveling after posting actual work.

You should now have a better overall understanding of how the Level Resources tool works. Use the tips in this section and refer to the "Consultants' Tips" section at the end of this chapter for more discussion of this topic.

Manual Strategies to Correct Resource Allocation Problems

There are four additional manual edit strategies you can explore within Project. Each of these strategies requires a lot of detailed investigation and editing, so you should consider them as a last resort to reduce resource overallocation conditions. These strategies involve the following general features:

- Using Manually Scheduled task mode and the Team Planner

- Using resource assignment contour patterns to structure work

- Editing resource work details in the Usage views

- Inserting manual delays or dates for resource assignments

The following sections summarize each of these strategies.

Strategy 1: Use Manually Scheduled Task Mode and Team Planner

The Team Planner is built for manual resolution of resource allocation issues. It works with either auto-scheduled tasks or manually scheduled tasks, but it works best with manually scheduled tasks.

Auto-scheduled tasks ideally rely primarily on network logic to determine when tasks are scheduled for start and finish dates. The Team Planner enables planners to completely ignore task network logic in favor of allocating resource capacity. Consequently, it makes sense to use the Team Planner primarily to manage manually scheduled tasks, or to manage very near-term tasks only (see Figure 24.25).

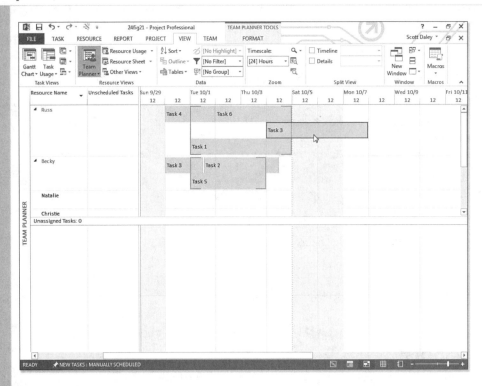

Figure 24.25
The Team Planner and manually scheduled tasks enable the planner to do as he or she pleases.

Strategy 2: Use Resource Assignment Contours

Project provides a specialized set of detailed work contour patterns for each resource assignment. You can see only the contour options if you are using a Resource or Task Usage view. Figure 24.26 shows the list of predefined Work Contour settings. The standard default is Flat, but you can alter the work distribution profile by selecting one of the alternative structures.

You can use this feature if you want to set one task assignment to front loaded and another assignment to back loaded. This would enable you to redistribute the work on tasks. The Usage Work data is redistributed for the affected task, so you should carefully inspect the impact on task duration dates.

Figure 24.27 shows an example of how a single resource is initially overloaded for two tasks, shown at the top of the screen. The overallocation condition is reduced after front-loaded and back-loaded contours are applied. Also notice that the dates for the tasks have been shifted as a result of recontouring the assigned work.

 caution

The predefined work contours redistribute all the task work for the selected resource. This might result in a task duration change. You might also see unexpected results if you alter individual resource assignment contours on tasks that have actual work.

Figure 24.26
You can use the resource assignment contour profiles to help you manually level the distribution of work.

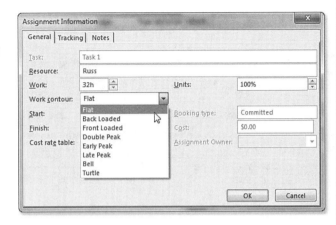

Figure 24.27
Resource assignments using front and back loading.

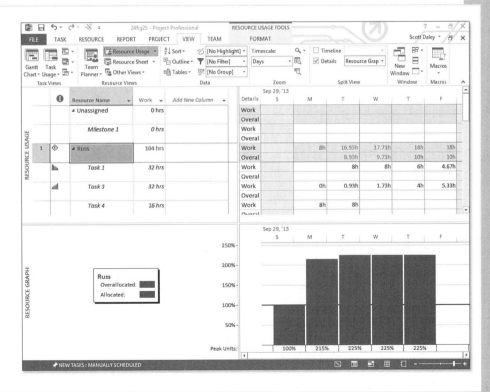

Strategy 3: Manually Edit Resource Assignment Work in Usage Views

On a project of any size, manually editing the specific work details within a Usage view to distribute the workload on task assignments will quickly consume your entire day, but you can do it. If you find yourself too involved in this, though—change the task mode to Manually Scheduled.

The Indicators messages for assignments show that data has been edited, and the Work Contour profile shows Contoured when you perform a manual edit on the Usage data.

Figure 24.28 shows an example of manual edits to an overloaded resource condition. This method enables you to explicitly modify the work profile details to create any overall workloading condition you want to schedule.

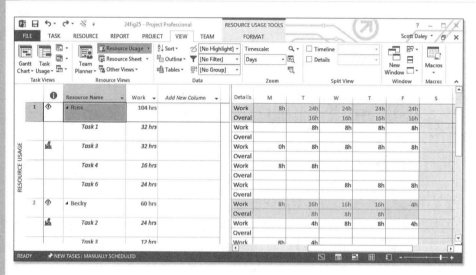

Figure 24.28
Manually edited resource assignment work contours.

> ⚡ **caution**
> Manually contoured assignment work details will be erased if you use one of the predefined contour types.

Strategy 4: Use Manually Edited Assignment Delays and Dates

Frankly, just because you can manually edit delays and dates doesn't mean you should. Again, if you find yourself doing this routinely, consider changing the task mode.

If it makes sense, you can split the screen, showing the Resource Schedule in the lower half of the screen. This view arrangement enables you to set conditions individually, such as the following:

- Resource work and units

- Assignment start and finish dates

- Assignment delay factors

Figure 24.29 illustrates this kind of view and controls, but it might take you a long time to fine-tune a view that is optimal for your situation. You see task-split conditions if you establish delay factors or fix individual resource start dates.

Figure 24.29
Split-screen
assignment
edits.

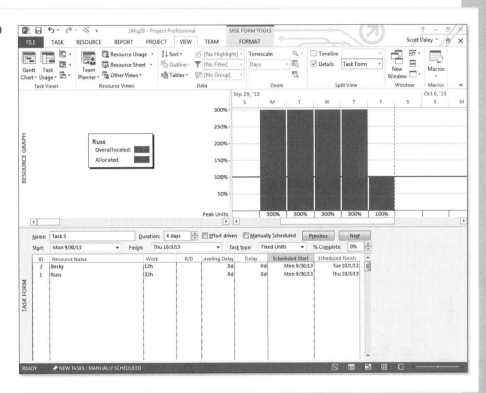

Consultants' Tips

This section provides some suggestions that you should consider.

Use Team Planner and Manually Scheduled Tasks Where Appropriate

The Team Planner is an amazing tool for resolving resource allocation issues, but it puts constraints on auto-scheduled tasks that limit Project's capability to predict start and finish dates. Conversely, manually scheduled tasks do not take advantage of Project's predictive capacity at all, making them easier to understand but more labor-intensive to work with.

During project execution, consider using Manually Scheduled mode for LOE (Level of Effort)-type tasks, and Auto Scheduled mode for the rest. Use the Team Planner to identify and resolve short-term resource issues, but use the other techniques discussed in this chapter for long-term resource issues.

That said, if you find yourself constantly working in the Usage views adjusting resource hours and start times, switch to Manually Scheduled mode and don't look back.

Establish Guidelines for Resolving Resource Allocation Issues

Consider establishing some general-process guidelines for project managers to resolve resource allocation conditions. The following items are recommended:

- Examine task sequence links starting from or leading to intermediate or terminating milestones. Use these milestones to establish deadlines or constraints.

- Use a standard set of multiple views and windows to review resource allocation issues. Consider using a common Global.mpt file shared among Project users in your organization.

- Determine which edit and update strategies are most likely to produce the desired results for tracking project progress and managing resource allocation.

- Use temporary copies of schedules to practice solving resource allocation problems. Use the Compare Schedules Wizard to see the before and after details in an overlaid view.

Examples of Resource-Leveling Scenarios

You might discover or want to test many different resource-leveling scenarios. The following list should give you some ideas:

- **Scenario 1**—Use basic leveling on schedules that do not use task links of constraints.

- **Scenario 2**—Level with resources that have calendar exceptions for working periods.

- **Scenario 3**—Level tasks containing Actual Work or nonzero %Complete.

- **Scenario 4**—Level tasks with fixed-start-date or start-no-later-than-date constraints.

- **Scenario 5**—Level tasks with various Task Priority settings from 1 to 999. A variant scenario includes tasks with Priority set to 1000, meaning the leveling tool ignores these tasks.

- **Scenario 6**—Level tasks with several resource assignments that include full-time and part-time units.

- **Scenario 7**—Level tasks that ignore resource calendars.

- **Scenario 8**—Level schedules with a mix of task types, such as fixed duration, fixed work, and fixed units.

Receiving an "Overallocation Cannot Be Resolved" Warning

If you are receiving an "overallocation cannot be resolved" warning, perform the following:

- Check for resources that are assigned over their set Max Units.

- Check for constraints that prevent a task or assignment being delayed.

- Remove the option Level Only Within Available Slack on the Leveling dialog box.

Resource(s) Indicate Overallocation Condition After Leveling

If your resources indicate an overallocation condition after leveling, change the leveling calculation option to a smaller time interval (hour by hour).

25

EXPORTING AND IMPORTING PROJECT DATA

You might occasionally have the need to exchange project data with other applications or file formats. For instance, you might have a resource list in an Excel spreadsheet you want to import into the Resource Sheet of Project to build your project team. Or, you might need to send a simple project task list to others, but you cannot use an .mpp file because the people who need the file do not have Project. In another case, you might need to export particular project data such as actual resource hours or costs, so that other systems can use the data for reporting purposes.

This chapter covers the various forms of importing and exporting data to other applications or file formats to help you with similar situations. In some cases, you might want to consider a simple cut and paste for data exchange. Weigh the time and cost benefits of performing an elaborate import/export process, something that might be occasional or difficult. This chapter focuses on a built-in feature of Project that uses maps to translate data from one file or application format to another.

In many cases, creating a map to export data is simple for some applications, whereas creating a map to import data might be a bit more difficult. In addition, maps can be saved and reused, so the data maps might be well worth your time if you have a consistent data import or export requirement. Project has a handy wizard to guide you through your data-mapping decisions for the various file formats or applications you might use.

In previous versions of Project, exporting data was frequently used to create reports. The new 2013 reports and visual reports are often a better choice now.

➡ *For additional information about visual reports, **see** Chapter 21, "Reports Part II: Visual Reports, **p. 653**."*

Exchanging Project Files Across Microsoft Project Versions

First, you might wonder about sharing project files (.mpp file format) with other versions of Project. Project 2013 is backward compatible with many older versions of Project (2000-2010), enabling you to open and use older versions of Project files. When you open an older version of a project file in Project, there might be some changes to the layout, and the Gantt Chart now appears as the new version, but all the schedule's data from the previous version is included.

If you created a file in Project 2013, you have two options to open it later with an older version of Project. First, you can simply save your project as a 2013 version, and then open it with an older version of Project.

Your other option when you need to open a Project file in an older version of Project is to save your project file into the 2000–2003 or 2007 format while you are in Project 2013. When you select this option, Project warns you that this format might leave out data due to incompatible features, as shown in Figure 25.1. You have the choice of continuing with saving your file or canceling the save operation.

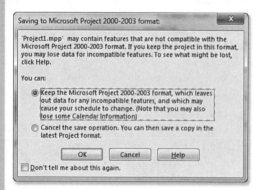

Figure 25.1
Project 2013 warns you about the changes that will be made to your version file when you try to save it to an earlier format.

 caution

When you save a 2013 version file to an earlier format, you lose any data in Project fields that are not available in the older versions. This might include anything entered as a Cost or Budget Resource and manually scheduled tasks. The Cost or Budget Resources will be changed to either work or material resources, depending on how you set them up in your 2013 version. In addition, fields in the 2013 version, but not in the earlier version, will be included as "unavailable" with the values listed as "NA" when viewing them with earlier versions of Project.

➡ *For additional information about compatibility of other versions of Project,* **see** *the "Version Compatibility" section on* **p. 552** *of Chapter 18.*

Exchanging Project Data with Other Applications

Sharing information with other Microsoft Office applications, such as Excel, Word, Access, and Visio, is easy in Project. There are several alternatives for sharing project data between the different applications.

First, you can use the Copy and Paste commands to transfer project data into any of the Microsoft Office programs and many other applications as well. You should use this method for simple and occasional data transfer. However, remember that when you paste an entire task row of data from Project, you retain the data in the fields, but lose some of the calculation capabilities that exist in Project (such as Duration * Resource Units = Work). And if you copy and paste task data from another application (such as Excel), Project calculates key fields.

➡ *For additional information about using Copy and Paste in Project,* **see** *Chapter 26, "Manipulating Data Using Other Applications,"* **p. 873**.

You might be using a particular file format or a particular application to exchange data. In most cases (importing tasks from Outlook uses its own method), when you start the import or export process, Project provides an Import/Export Wizard that can help you map fields between Project and other applications, such as Excel, or other file formats, such as text- or comma-delimited.

Later sections in this chapter discuss the wizard and other methods for exchanging data with applications, such as Excel and Outlook, and other file formats, such as Text and XML.

File Formats Supported by Project

Although you will almost always save your files as Project files (.mpp files) for your usual project operations, occasionally you might want to use a different file format for opening and saving project data using the File, Open and File, Save As commands. When you select one of these other file formats presented when using one of the commands, you can open, read, write, and save project data into formats other than the .mpp Project format.

All Project nonnative file formats can support only a portion of the Project data. You will use the Import/Export Wizard as described in the section "Working with Import/Export Maps to Select Your Project Data" to guide you through the process. You might also use the same process for just selecting particular fields in Project to export. Some file formats, such as Excel Workbook, enable you to transfer an Excel template of basic project data or all project data (by selecting the Add All button during the mapping process).

The process of selecting how you want to exchange project data is described in the section, "Working with Import/Export Maps to Select Your Project Data."

tip

If you plan to use a nonnative file format for exporting project data, you should experiment with it to understand its capabilities and limitations.

➡ *For additional information about the different file formats supported in Project,* **see** *Chapter 18, "Managing Project Files Locally and In the Cloud,"* **p. 549**.

As of version 2007, Project no longer supports using import/export maps with Microsoft Access. Data transfer between Project and Access now occurs though simple cut-and-paste operations or through the use of visual reports. Also, Project does not support exporting to HTML.

 *For additional information about visual reports, **see** Chapter 21, "Reports Part II: Visual Reports, p. 653."*

Working with Import/Export Maps

Import/export maps specify which tables and fields from a foreign data format correspond to the correct tables and fields in Project's native format. Importing and Exporting in Project relies on maps, but in the end you are simply "saving as" a different file type and exporting, or opening a different file type and importing.

You can use the predefined maps, but you can also set up your own map, defining tables to match Project. In some file formats, you can export only selected fields from the project file, such as with text formats. Although in other cases, such as with the Excel file format, you can save almost the entire project. It might be impractical to do this, so you might choose instead to save selected information. For instance, if a fellow project manager asked for only a few fields such as a simple list of task names, scheduled work, and actual work from your project, you could save just the requested data from your project into an Excel format using the Export Wizard and an export map.

When selecting fields of project data using one of the export formats, you use an export map to define which of the fields you want to export from Project. An example of this process is shown later in Figure 25.11. You also need to name the table or tables where the fields will be stored.

If you make changes to the values in another format when exporting it, and then import the data back into Project, you need to make sure you use the same map, or set up a new one with the same changes you made when exporting. This import map helps Project know where the data being imported needs to be inserted within the Project data structure.

 note

This and the following sections describe what maps are and how they work. You could also skip ahead to the "Creating and Using an Export Map" section for the practical steps involved.

 note

When exporting all project data to a Microsoft Excel format by selecting the Add All button, you might receive a warning that the project contains too many fields. The maximum number of fields to be imported is 255.

note

Time-phased data cannot be imported from or exported to Project using the import/export maps. If you need to export time-phased data, use visual reports.

Understanding Import/Export Maps

You can define three tables when building your own import/export map, as follows:

- An assignment table for values matching Project assignment fields
- A resource table for values matching Project resource fields

■ A task table for values matching Project task fields

For each table in a map, you must specify the field name in Project and the equivalent data location in the foreign format. You can add all the Project fields to a table or add the same set of fields from an already defined table in Project using the Option button.

When exporting maps, you can select a subset of tasks or resources in the project using the pre-defined filters.

 *For additional information about predefined filters, **see** the "Understanding Filtering and Grouping" section on **p. 393** of Chapter 11.*

When building import maps, you must decide how the imported data fits into an open Project file. You have three options, as follows:

■ You can insert your imported records into a new Project document. A new .mpp file is created with the field values you have chosen. This is a standard .mpp file with no links to the source of the imported data. When you save it, the source data is not updated.

■ Your imported records can be appended to the tasks, resources, and assignments that already exist in the open project file. These new tasks, resources, and assignments are added below the existing corresponding fields.

■ You can have your imported values merged into the existing project to update the existing tasks, resources, or assignments. If you use this option, Project attempts to match the records being imported with those in the current file. You have to define one field as the key field when matching the records. For instance, you could be importing resource names and standard rates to update the pay rates for resources on the project team. In such a situation, you would most likely use the resource name as the key field.

> ### ⚠ caution
> The default installation of Project will not allow you to save a project file in xls format. Unless you change the Legacy Formats option to Allow Loading Files with Legacy or Non Default File Formats under the File tab, Options, Trust Center, Trust Center Settings, Legacy Formats, you get an error message stating "You are trying to save a file in an older file format. Your settings do not allow you to save the file in older file formats. To change your setting, navigate to the 'Security' tab in the Options dialog box."

Import/export maps can be used for different file formats. If you create a map for importing data from Excel, you can use the same map to import data from a text file. Keep in mind that different file formats can often convert nontext fields into different field types and values.

 ### note
If you decide to save Project data into a non–Project format, Project changes the options shown on the import/export map to match the format you have selected. If, for instance, you choose Save As for a text format and then use an import/export map designed for working with an Excel workbook, the workbook options will be replaced with text options.

caution

caution is advised when importing data into Project using a map. Maps are designed for one particular database or worksheet, with specific tables or fields that might not work in another data source. Be sure to check the structure of the map before using it to import data.

When you create import/export maps, they are saved in the Global.mpt file instead of the active project file. To change the name of a map, you do not need to use the Organizer; you can change the map name when you are editing it. You do, however, have to use the Organizer if you want to delete a map.

 tip

If you want to share a map with other users, use the Organizer to copy your map into an open project file and then save the project. Other users who can open your project file can copy the map to their Global.mpt files using the Organizer.

➡ *For additional information about the Organizer and the Global.mpt file, **see** Chapter 18, "Managing Project Files Locally and in the Cloud," **p. 549**.*

Reviewing the Predefined Import/Export Maps

Project contains 10 predefined import/export maps. They are listed and described in Table 25.1.

Table 25.1   Predefined Import/Export Maps

Map	Description
"Who Does What" report	Exports a table that lists resources and their task assignments
Compare to Baseline	Exports a table that lists all tasks with scheduled and baseline values
Cost Data by Task	Exports a table that lists task costs
Default Task Information	Exports or imports the basic task fields included in the Task Entry table
Earned Value Information	Exports the task's earned value fields
Resource "Export Table" map	Exports all the fields in the predefined resource's Export table
Task "Export Table" map	Exports all the fields in the predefined task's Export table
Task and Resource PivotTable report	Creates Excel PivotTables for tasks and resources

Map	Description
Task List with Embedded Assignment Rows	Exports a table of tasks and their assigned resources
Top Level Tasks list	Exports tables with data for tasks at the top outline level

The next sections of this chapter discuss each map in more detail, covering how they were created and how to get the most efficient use out of them. Each of these maps was designed to export data from Project into another format. Although some were designed for specific file formats, any map can be used to export any format. Of course, they work best when used with the format for which they were created. Some of the maps were also designed for importing, but can be used to export. Take caution when using any map to import data because you might receive an unexpected result.

 note

Project exports values for duration and work fields as text and not as numeric data. Project attaches a time unit as part of the text value, such as "5d" representing five days.

Imported data placed in a new Project document does little harm because it is a new document and you can simply close it. Import maps can also be set up to append imported data into an active file, or merge the imported information to an existing task or resource record, and that can cause issues if your import data and your project both are not structured correctly for the map you chose. Project updates existing field values with data from external documents. When the map in the Map Selection dialog is set to append or merge, activating the file listing alters the data in your open Project file.

Using the "Who Does What" Report Map

A good use of the "Who Does What" report is to export Project data to an Excel format using the map. The Excel spreadsheet, similar to the Resource Usage view in Project, shows the list of resource names and task assignment names, in the same column, but does not indent the assignment names under their resource names. Included under each assignment are columns for Start, Finish, and Scheduled_Work field values. The exported data for the Scheduled_Work field is text data, instead of numerical, and the unit "hrs" is added as part of the text value.

Although this map works well when saving to an Excel spreadsheet format, you can also save to a text or comma-separated values (CSV) file. If you save it to one of these formats, your resource rows will be identical to the assignment rows and the data is separated by a tab (default selection) or another separator that you specified, such as a space or a comma. These two formats are useful when you plan on importing the data into another system or a database.

 tip

When saving your data to an Excel, text, or CSV format, you should change the "Who Does What" report map, adding the field named Assignment to the table, to help distinguish resource names from task assignment names. The resource rows in the list have No in the Assignment field, whereas the assignment rows have Yes. By applying Excel's conditional formatting, you can bold the resource rows, because of the No value found in the Assignment column. For more information, see the section, "Exporting Project Data to an Excel Worksheet," later in this chapter.

Using the Compare to Baseline Map

The Compare to Baseline map exports a table titled Baseline Comparison, which lists all tasks, including their start and finish dates, plus their scheduled, baseline, and variance values for duration, work, and cost. This map works the same for spreadsheet and text formats.

Using the Cost Data by Task Map

The Cost Data by Task map exports a table titled Task Costs, which lists all the tasks (fixed cost, cost, baseline cost, cost variance, actual cost, and remaining costs), plus their cost values.

Using the Default Task Information Map

The Default Task Information map exports or imports basic task fields included in the Task Entry table: ID, Name, Duration, Start Date, Finish Date, Predecessors, and Resource Names. This map works the same for all file formats.

Using the Earned Value Information Map

The Earned Value Information map exports the earned value fields for tasks into any file format. This includes Task ID, Task Name, BCWS, BCWP, ACWP, SV, CV, Cost (EAC), Baseline Cost (BAC), and VAC.

Using the Resource "Export Table" Map

The Resource Export Table map exports the fields included in the predefined resource's Export table. This Export table is an inclusive list of 24 resource fields, covering the definition of the resources, as well as scheduled, baseline, and tracking sums for work and cost for each resource.

Using the Task "Export Table" Map

The Task Export Table map exports almost all the fields included in the predefined task's Export table. This Export table contains more than 70 fields, including the task definition fields: Values for Scheduled, Baseline, Actual Work, Cost, Duration, Start, and Finish, as well as several user-defined fields, such as Cost, Duration, Number, and Flag.

Using the Task and Resource PivotTable Report

The Task and Resource PivotTable map creates an Excel document with two PivotTables summarizing the total costs of the resource assignments. Each PivotTable is organized by resource groups, and in each group by resource name. Four sheets are included in each Excel file, as follows:

- The Tasks sheet provides all the data for the Task PivotTable and includes the following columns: Resource Group, Resource Name, Task Name(s), Duration, Start, Finish, and Cost. If you outlined your project, a Task Name column for each outline level is included, plus all summary task names for a subtask appear on the row for the subtask. Outline level 1 summary tasks are placed in a column named Task Name1, outline level 2 summary tasks are placed in a column named Task Name2, and so on.

- The Task PivotTable sheet displays, for each resource group, the tasks that each resource in the group is assigned, plus the task duration, start, and finish. Cost for each assignment is the PivotTable's Data field and includes summary costs for each task and summary task, for each resource, and for each resource group.

- The Resources sheet lists data for the Resource PivotTable and includes the Resource Group, Resource Name, Work, and Cost fields.

- The Resource PivotTable displays the work and cost totals for each resource group and each resource within the group. Totals are not broken down by task.

---

 note

When a project has more than two outline levels, Project creates data sheets and PivotTables, but cannot lay out the fields for the Task PivotTable, which causes that sheet to appear empty. To fix this, you have to manually lay them out in Excel. To do this, select all the information in the Tasks data sheet you want to include as part of the PivotTable and click Insert. Next, click the PivotTable button. From here, you can select where you want the PivotTable to be created. You most likely want to create a new worksheet and click OK. A new blank PivotTable appears where you can drag and drop the fields you want included into the PivotTable.

You can read more about working with PivotTables later in this chapter, in the section, "Exporting Project Data to an Excel PivotTable."

Using the Task List with Embedded Assignment Rows Map

The Task List with Embedded Assignment Rows map exports a table of tasks and their assigned resources. The best use of this map is for exporting a table that includes all the resource assignments for each task, along with the Work, Duration, Start, Finish, and % Work Complete fields for each assignment. In addition to using this map to export to Excel, you can also use it for the text and CSV formats.

Using the Top Level Tasks List Map

The Top Level Tasks map exports a table showing only the outline level 1 tasks. This includes the following fields: Task ID, Name, Duration, Start, Finish, % Complete, Cost, and Work. This map works with all file formats.

Creating and Using an Export Map

An export map is easier to create than an import map, because Project field names are the source of the data, and it is easy to create field names in the target format similar to Project field names. It can be much harder to relate imported field names in the source format with the field names in Project.

The following steps take you through creating an export map by using an example of exporting Project cost data to an Excel worksheet:

1. Open the Project file containing the data you want to be exported.

2. On the File tab, select Save As (alternately, use File tab, Export, Save Project as File).

3. Choose the directory location from the Save In list box.

4. In the Save as Type list box, select Microsoft Excel Workbook (*.xls).

5. Click the Save button to open the Export Wizard dialog box.

6. Click the Next button to open the Data dialog box.

7. Choose the Selected Data option and click the Next button. This opens the Map dialog box.

8. Choose the New Map option and click the Next button. This opens the Map Options dialog box.

9. Choose one or more data types to be exported: tasks, resources, or assignments. Because this is being exported to an Excel file, you also have the options of exporting the headers and including assignment rows. In Figure 25.2, all three have been selected, and the Export Includes Headers option has been selected as well.

10. Click the Next button to open the Task Mapping dialog box.

11. Enter a name for your table into the Destination Worksheet Name field. The more descriptive the name for your table, the easier it is to remember why you built it.

12. You can limit any of the tasks being exported by selecting one of the filters in the Export Filter field, as shown in Figure 25.3. You can choose any of Project's predefined filters, or any you might have defined ahead of time, but you cannot design a new filter at this point.

 tip

If you plan to add data to overwrite an existing document, you should create a copy of your document for testing as you create your new map. If there are problems, you will not lose your previously saved document, and if your map works as planned, you can keep the newly created document and delete the previously saved version.

 tip

If you find you need a filter that is not included in the list, you have to cancel out of the Export Wizard, create your new filter, and then start again at the beginning of the Export Wizard in step 1.

➡ *For additional information about creating filters,* **see** *the "Creating and Customizing Filters" section on* **p. 729** *of Chapter 22.*

Figure 25.2
You can select which type of data table you want to create with the Map Options dialog box in the Export Wizard.

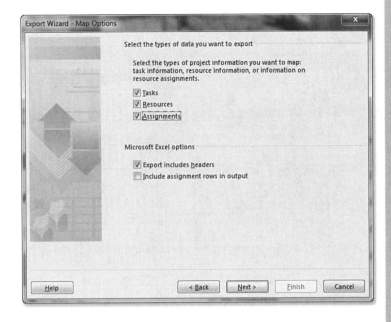

13. You now need to define which task fields you want to export in the mapping table. List each of the fields you want to be exported in the From: Microsoft Office Project Field column.

    You can use the drop-down menus listing Project's predefined fields by clicking on the cell that displays the Click Here to Map a Field prompt. After you have selected a data field, you can click on the corresponding cell under To: Excel Field, and Project automatically creates a name for your worksheet field, as shown in Figure 25.4.

14. After you have chosen the fields you will be exporting from the list of Project fields, you can either press the Enter key after selecting each field, press the Tab key on your keyboard, or click on the corresponding To: Excel Field cell. Any of these actions insert a default field name into the cell. You can see a sample of the fields you have added and their data in the Preview box below the mapping table.

    You can change your export field name if you want, instead of using the name supplied by the Project.

 caution
If you change the export field name, make sure that you do not violate any of the field-naming rules for the format you are creating, such as using periods, exclamation points, or square brackets.

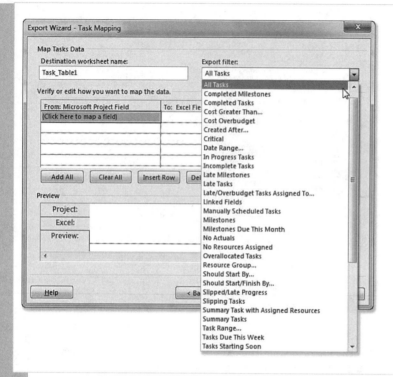

Figure 25.3
Name your destination document and choose an Export filter in the Task Mapping page of the Export Wizard.

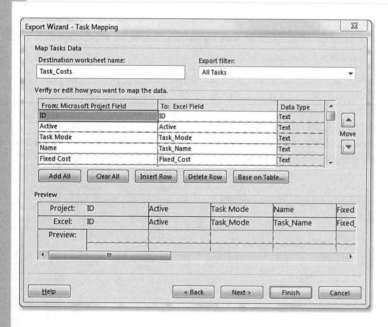

Figure 25.4
Choose which fields you will be exporting with the Task Mapping page of the Export Wizard.

15. Several buttons can help you manage the field mapping table, as shown in Figure 25.4:

  ■ If you need to move a field row in the list, highlight the row you want to move and use the Move arrows to the right of the mapping table. They move the row up or down the list.

  ■ Use the Add All button to insert all the Project task fields. Project has a limitation of 255 fields for exporting. If you are selecting several tables, you want to use this selection with caution. If your selection exceeds 255 fields, the Export Wizard displays an error message and you are required to decrease the number of fields in the map.

  ■ Use the Clear All button to clear the mapping table.

  ■ Use the Insert Row button if you need to place a blank row into the middle of the list. Select a row, click the Insert Row button, and all the rows move down to create an empty row above the one you selected.

  ■ Use the Delete Row button to remove a field row.

  ■ You can add a predefined map to your mapping table by using the Base on Table button. Clicking this button pulls up a list of the Project-defined task tables in the Select Base for Field Mapping dialog box, as shown in Figure 25.5. Choose which table you want to use and click OK. Any entries previously made in the mapping table are cleared, and the fields defined in the table you choose are placed in the mapping table instead.

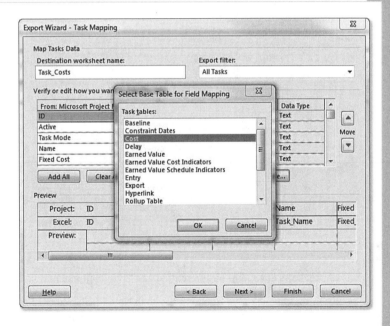

Figure 25.5
The Select Base Table for Field Mapping dialog box lets you fill in your mapping table with one of the Project predefined tables.

16. After you have finished with the task mapping table, click the Next button to move on to the next table to include in the export. Because all three data types were chosen for this example

(refer back to Figure 25.3), your next window is the Resource Mapping page, shown in Figure 25.6. You need to fill out this mapping table by repeating steps 11 through 15. Click the Next button to continue through the wizard.

17. Your next page is the Assignment Mapping page, because this example uses all three types of data. When building your own export map, you may or may not use this many steps. Filling out the assignment mapping field is like using the first two mapping fields. Assignment records are created from combined task and resource cost summaries.

18. After you have finished with the Assignment Mapping page, click the Next button. You now see the End of Map Definition page.

 note

Because there is no table in Project for assignments (they appear in the Task Usage and Resource Usage views, and some other forms), you will not be able to select a table as a template for the fields to be included. There are also no filters defined for assignments. You will notice that both of these options are grayed out.

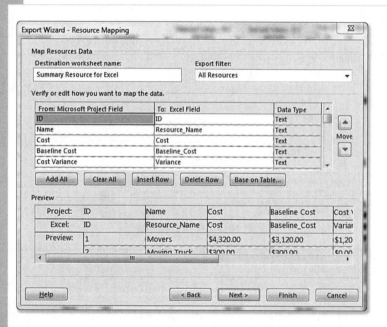

Figure 25.6
You can define the resource mapping table the same way you defined the task mapping table.

19. Click the Save Map button to open the Save Map dialog box, as shown in Figure 25.7.

20. Enter a name for your map in the Map Name field and click the Save button. This returns you to the End of Map Definition dialog box. You should use a descriptive name to help you remember why you created this map.

21. Click the Finish button to export your chosen data to a new Excel document.

Figure 25.7
It is always a good idea to save your map, even if you do not plan to use it again. This saves you from having to create it again.

 tip

When you are building a map for one file format, such as Excel in the previous example, and then use the same map to exchange data with another application in a different format, such as text, you will get varying results. For example, the formatting in the Excel format will be lost and, depending on the separator chosen, each data field will be separated by the designated delimiter (tab, space, or comma). For specialized maps such as the one you just created, it is a good idea to include the application type in the map name.

If you are planning on using your export map later to import data into Project, as described in the next section, you should include the Unique ID field in your export. Because the Unique ID number will not change after a task has been created, this makes it a reliable key field when importing data at a later time.

Creating and Using an Import Map

If you want to import data into Project from another source application, you need to either find a workable import map or create your own. If the data was exported from Project originally, you can import your data with the same map you used to export it. You can also edit your export map if you want to make some changes and then save it as a new import map.

Your options for an import map are a little different from those used when building an export map:

- Your source tables are already defined, unlike in the export map, where you had to define your target tables. There might be, for instance, several tables in the source document with task information included in them. You have to select which table contains the task data you need. You also have to identify the source tables appropriate for supplying your resource or assignment fields.

   If your source was created with an export map, it will be easier to import it back into Project because the field names will be recognizable. If your source table was created by some application other than Project, you have to match your field names with Project internal fields.

- Project filters data during an import. If you want to include only some of the records from your source, you have to filter the source first to create a new data source document and then import it into Project. Otherwise, you have to import all the data into Project and then delete the necessary data.

- When you are using an import map, you can select whether you want the imported data to be stored in a new project file or inserted into an existing one. You can add the imported records to information that already exists in Project, or you can merge the imported data, using it to update selected fields for already existing tasks or resources.

Import steps are very similar to export steps. As an example of importing from another file format, see how to import the cost Excel spreadsheet created earlier in the section "Creating and Using an Export Map."

If you want to add your imported data to an existing project, you need to open that project before beginning the import process. If you do not want to add your imported data to an existing project, it does not matter which project documents are open, because Project creates a new document. Follow these steps to import data using an import map:

> **tip**
>
> The Save As and Export options under the File tab both serve largely the same purpose.

1. In Project, select the File tab, Open, as shown in Figure 25.8.

2. Choose your location. For example, click Computer, Browse to open a file on your local machine.

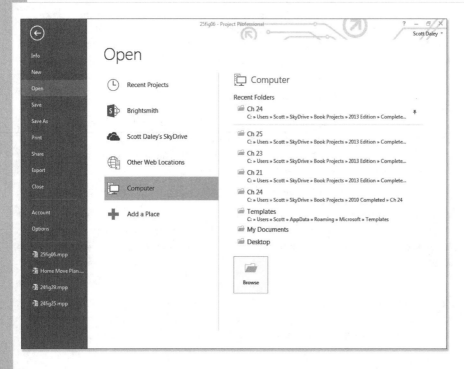

Figure 25.8
The Open page enables you to select other file types to open.

3. In the Files of Type list box, choose the format of your data source.

4. Select the data source file from the file list and click the Open box. This opens the Import Wizard dialog box.

5. Click the Next button to move to the Map dialog box.

6. Choose the Use Existing Map option, as shown in Figure 25.9. To create a new import map, choose the New Map option; then follow the techniques shown for creating an export map in the previous section "Creating and Using an Export Map." Click the Next button to move to the Map Selection dialog box.

7. Choose the map you want to use to import your data. Be careful when choosing a map; it defines the way you import your data. In this example, the export map created in the previous section "Creating and Using an Export Map" is used to import the data. Click Next to move to the Import Mode dialog box.

Figure 25.9
You can either create a new map from scratch and select the tables and fields to include in the import or use an existing map in Project.

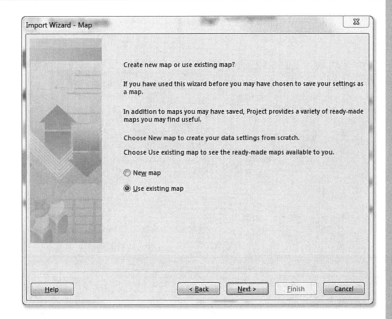

8. You have three options in the Import Mode dialog box: Import Your File as a New Project, Append the Data to the Active Project, and Merge the Data into the Active Project. After you have decided which of these options works best for you, click the Next button to move to the Map Options dialog box.

9. Select the types of data you want to import: Tasks, Resources, or Assignments. If you are using an export map you have already set up to import your data, Project enters this data for you, although you can amend it if you choose. After you are finished, click the Next button.

tip

If you are importing an existing text delimited document, you can only choose a single type of data to import (Task, Resources, or Assignments). You are prompted with radio buttons instead of check boxes when importing other formats. You can read more about importing text delimited documents later in this chapter, in the section "Working with Text File Formats."

10. Project now opens the Mapping dialog box for the first type of data you chose in step 9. So, if you selected to import task data, Project opens the Task Mapping dialog box.

11. Look through the Mapping dialog box for each type of data that is being imported to make sure your settings are exact. You can check the list of names in the Source worksheet name field to confirm that the right table has been chosen for the type of data in each Mapping dialog box.

As you can see in Figure 25.10, the Task Mapping dialog box for the importing map is the same as the export map created in the previous section. The Source Worksheet Name list has been highlighted to show the tables available.

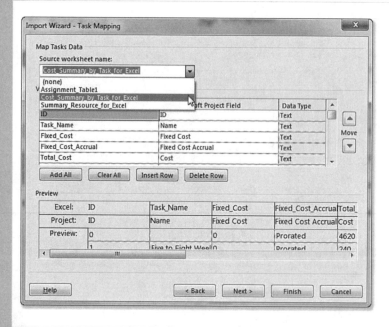

Figure 25.10
The mapping fields box that you set up as an export map has a few different options when it is used as an import map.

12. Click the Next button to move to the Resource Mapping or Assignment Mapping dialog boxes. Confirm your settings in each of these.

13. If you decided to merge your imported data, the Set Merge Key button appears on each of the Task, Resource, and Assignment Mapping dialog boxes. You must use this merge key button

in each of the Mapping dialog boxes you have active. Merge Key is a field with identical values in both the existing Project file and the imported tables. The task ID field, for instance, matches tasks as long as the task list has not been changed since the data was exported. This is why you should use the Unique ID field, as mentioned in the Tip at the end of the section "Creating and Using an Export Map."

After you have chosen your key field, click the Set Merge Key button. The field name changes to MERGE KEY:*field name*. The ID field has been chosen as the merge key in the Task Mapping dialog box, as shown in Figure 25.11. If you later find that you need to change the Merge Key field, choose a new key field and click the Set Merge Key button again.

 note

You must use the Unique ID field if you want to merge assignment data.

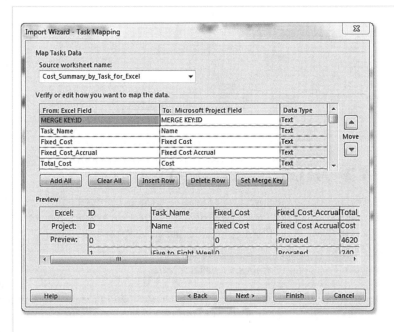

Figure 25.11
You need to choose a field to serve as the merge key field to help identify matching records when you are importing data to be merged with the existing data.

14. Click the Next button to move to the End of Map Definition dialog box. If changes have been made to the map, and you want to save it by a new name, click the Save Map button.

15. Click Finish to import your data into your project.

Some errors might appear in the mapping tables if you select the wrong map, as shown in Figure 25.12. If your map source field names do not exist in the file you have opened, the field name entries appear in red and have an "OUT OF CONTEXT:" prefix in the From: Excel Field column.

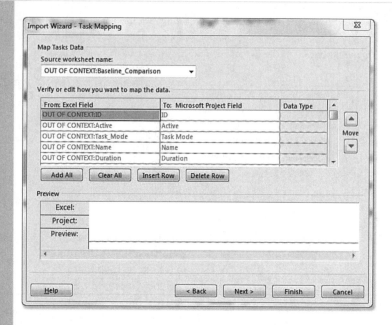

Figure 25.12
If the wrong map has been chosen to import data, you see several OUT OF CONTEXT errors in your mapping fields.

Exchanging Data with Microsoft Excel

You have two options when exporting field data into Microsoft Excel—you can export it either as worksheet data or as PivotTable data. You can also import table data from Excel worksheets, but not from PivotTables. When you export to Excel, Project creates an Excel file in the Excel (.xlsx) format. You can import Excel 4.0 format documents or later, including Excel 97–2003.

You can also exchange data between Project and Excel using visual reports.

➡ *For additional information about visual reports in Project,* ***see*** *the "Using Excel While Working with Visual Reports" section on* ***p. 659*** *of Chapter 21.*

If you create an import/export map for the Excel format, there are a few differences you should keep in mind:

- You can export using either an export map or an Excel template. The Excel template exports a predefined set of Task, Resource, and Assignment fields, and creates a separate worksheet for each of the data types.

- You have the option of exporting field names as the first row of each worksheet. If you choose not to export field names, the field data will be entered in row 2 of the worksheet, and if you want column titles, you have to add them in separately later.

- You can include assignment rows, like those shown in the tables of the Task Usage and Resource Usage views. These worksheet rows are not outlined and indented automatically in the Excel workbook as they are in Project.

Excel's Group and Outline commands can be used to group assignments under the task or resource, making it possible to display or hide the assignment rows, as in Project. However, you have to group each set of assignments by hand, and they are not indented when the assignment rows are shown.

 tip

You should change Excel's grouping direction before using Excel's Group and Outline command. In Excel, open the Data tab and then click on the small box in the lower-right corner of the Outline box. This opens the Settings dialog box, and you need to clear the Summary Rows Below Detail check box. This places the outline symbols for grouping, the plus and minus indicators, to the left of the task or resource name, as in an Assignment view, instead of at the bottom of the list of assignments in each group.

 caution

Sort in Excel with caution. If you sort the rows in a worksheet, you might not be able to tell which assignments go with which tasks or resources.

Exporting Project Data to an Excel Worksheet

Import/export maps that have been created for another format, including any of the predefined maps, can be used to export the Project data into Excel. If you use an existing map, you might then want to save it with a different name, so you know it was used for exporting data to Excel.

Follow these steps to export Project data to an Excel workbook:

1. Open the Project file containing the data you want exported.

2. Open the Save As dialog box by selecting the File tab, Save As. Choose the location of your new file in the Save In list box; then change the Save as Type to Microsoft Excel Workbook 2007 (*.xlsx), enter a name in the File Name text box, and click the Save button (or, as indicated earlier, use File tab, Export to accomplish the same).

3. Project opens the Export Wizard dialog box. Click the Next button to open the Data dialog box.

4. Choose the Selected Data button, and then click the Next button to go to the Map dialog box. The Project Excel Template button is discussed later in this chapter.

5. Choose the Use Existing Map button. To create a new import map, choose the New Map option and then use the same steps for creating an export map as outlined in the section "Creating and Using an Export Map" earlier in the chapter. Click the Next button to open the Map Selection dialog box.

6. Select an export map, and click the Next button to open the Map Options dialog box.

7. Three types of data can be exported to Excel—tasks, resources, and assignments. Not all options are active, depending on the type of export map you selected. The options for the Default Task Information export map in the Map Options dialog box are shown in Figure 25.13.

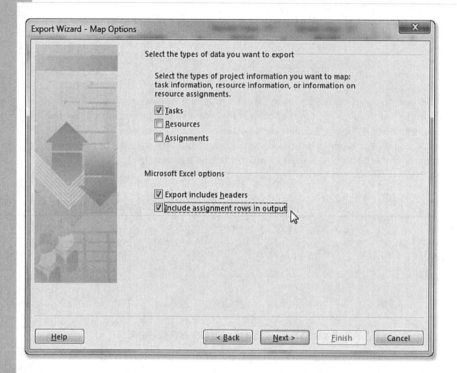

Figure 25.13
For help in identifying which records are tasks or resources and which are assignments, use the Include Assignment Rows in Output check box.

8. Select the Export Includes Headers check box. With this option selected, the first row of data on each sheet in the workbook now displays field names as column headers. If it is not active, no label appears at the top of each column.

9. Select the Include Assignment Rows in Output check box if you want your tasks and resources to show details by assignment, as in the Task Usage and Resource Usage views. Remember to include the field named Assignment in the Task Mapping dialog box, so you can distinguish assignments from tasks or resources. Click the Next button to move to the Task Mapping dialog box.

10. Select your task fields that are being exported to Excel to confirm that the settings are correct. You see a destination worksheet name for the worksheet that receives the task data, as shown in Figure 25.14.

> ## 🔆 caution
> When you are exporting the rows for the assignment details in a task mapping, the assignment rows appear to be extra tasks in the workbook that is created. If you later import the data back into Project, your resource assignments will now be listed as tasks, even if you include the Task Assignment field in the exported data. Also, any exported assignment details in a resource mapping result in the assignments being treated as additional resources, and you will not be able to import them back into Project.

Figure 25.14
The Task Mapping dialog box lets you confirm that your exported data is going into the correct worksheet and that you are exporting all the fields you want to use, plus you can add any extras to a predetermined export map.

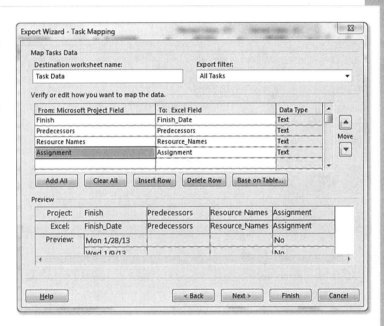

11. If you selected to include resource and assignment data in the Map Options dialog box, in step 7, you need to continue through the Resource Mapping and Assignment Mapping dialog boxes. After you are finished with your data mapping dialog boxes, you reach the End of Map Definition dialog box.

12. Click the Save Map button and give your export map a unique name when the Save Map dialog box appears, so if you ever want to import the data back into Project, you already have the exact Import/Export map set up. Click Finish when you are done to export your data to an Excel workbook.

When you export data into Excel, the application creates a worksheet for each of the tables defined in the export map in Project, as shown in Figure 25.15. Because the option Export Includes Header was selected, the field names appear in the first row of the worksheet, and the assignments for each resource are listed under the row for that resource.

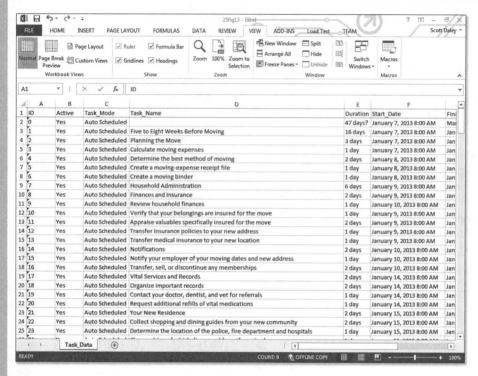

Figure 25.15
Project exports data into an Excel workbook, listing the assignments for each task below the task name.

When you open the Import/Export Wizard, the option for Project Excel Template appears in the Data dialog box and is used for exporting data into Excel. The option exports data to Excel easily, using a standard list of fields for task, resource, and assignment information. These fields are listed here:

- **Task fields**—ID, Name, Duration, Start, Finish, Predecessors, Outline Level, and notes.

- **Resource fields**—ID, Name, Initials, Type, Material Label, Group, Email Address, Windows User Account, Max Unites, Standard Rate, Cost Per Use, and notes.

- **Assignment fields**—Task Name, Resource Name, % Work Complete, Work, and Units.

The Project Excel Template option exports data to three Excel worksheets—Task_Table, Resource_Table, and Assignment_Table. These show data described by the worksheet name. You can see in Figure 25.16 an Excel workbook created with the Project Excel Template option and then formatted by the user.

Figure 25.16
Using the Project Excel Template option is a quick and easy way to export data from Project into Excel.

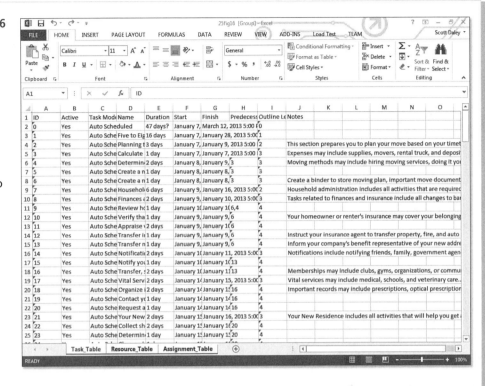

Exporting Project Data to an Excel PivotTable

An Excel PivotTable summarizes data in cross-table calculations, offering flexibility to change the layout of the PivotTable quickly. Project exchanges data with Excel PivotTables using visual reports.

➡ *For additional information about using visual reports in Project, **see** the "Using Excel While Working with Visual Reports" section on **p. 659** of Chapter 21.*

Importing Project Data from the Excel Format

Use caution when importing data from Excel into Project. Your data must be mapped correctly to the Project fields, and the data types must be correct for each field; otherwise, you will run into problems.

 caution

As mentioned previously in this chapter, if the Excel workbook was created by exporting tasks or resources from Project, and if the option to include rows for resource assignments was used, some of the rows in the workbook will be tasks or resources, whereas others will be assignment details. Do not import data from a workbook with assignment details included. Find and delete the assignment details before you import the data back into Project.

The following example shows you how to add a list of new employees to the resource sheet in a Project file. The list has been created and stored in Sheet 1 of an Excel workbook. The names are imported to the Resource data in the New Product Project file. The column headings are not perfect matches for the Project field names, and the Overtime Rate field uses text entries, whereas Project expects numbers. You can see an example of the worksheet in Figure 25.17.

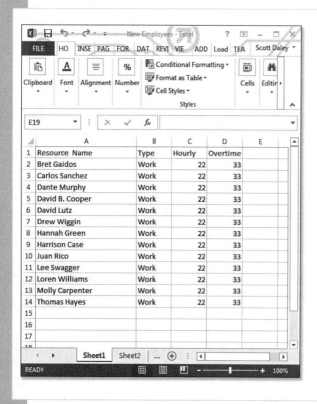

Figure 25.17
Information such as new resources and their pay rates can be imported into Project from Excel, using an import map.

Follow these steps to import data from Excel into a Project file:

1. Open the Project file into which you want to import your data. If you do not have a file open, Project creates a new document for your imported data.

2. It is a good idea, but not required, that you change your project to a view that shows the data you are importing. Having the view open can be useful if you are unsure of which Project field names are needed for your imported data. In the example set up earlier, opening the Resource Sheet view shows you that the employee's name should go into the Resource Name column, but the name of that field is simply Name. You can find the real field name for a column by right-clicking the column heading and selecting Field Settings, shown in Figure 25.18, to open the Column Definition dialog box.

Figure 25.18
You can learn information about Project's columns, such as their field names versus their titles, in the Field Settings dialog box.

3. Select the File tab, Open to show the Open dialog box; then change to file type in the Files of Type selection box. In this case, you change it to Microsoft Excel Workbook.

4. Select the location where your Excel workbook has been saved in the Look In list box and then find your file and click the Open button. This opens the Import Wizard dialog box.

5. Click the Next button to move on to the Map dialog box. Select the New Map option and click the Next button to open the Import Mode dialog box.

   The Import Mode dialog box is where you have the option of how you want to import your data into Project: As a New Project, Append the Data to the Active Project, or Merge the Data into an Active Project.

6. Select how you want to place your import data into Project. For this example, click the Append the Data to an Existing Project option. Click the Next button to move on to the Map Options dialog box.

   The Map Options dialog box contains options for what kind of data you want to import: Tasks, Resources, or Assignments.

7. Click the Resources box as the type of data to import. Although this example shows how to import data containing new employees and their pay rates, you could just as easily create task data listing the tasks in your project.

   Confirm that the Import Includes Headers box is selected. If this box is cleared, the map's field list does not show the Excel column headers; it simply numbers the columns. This creates difficulties, so you need to find out which Excel column maps to which Project field, as shown in Figure 25.19.

8. Click the Next button to move to the Resource Mapping dialog box.

9. Choose the source worksheet name in the Source Worksheet Name list. This is the worksheet to which you have saved your information, most often Sheet 1, which is what is used for this example also.

   After you choose the worksheet, Project fills in the From: Excel Field columns on the left side of the mapping field with the column headings you set up in your worksheet. Project also tries to find matching field names from the project to enter into the To: Project Field column on the right side of the mapping field. Not all of the Excel field names used were matched in the Project Resource Field column, as shown in Figure 25.20.

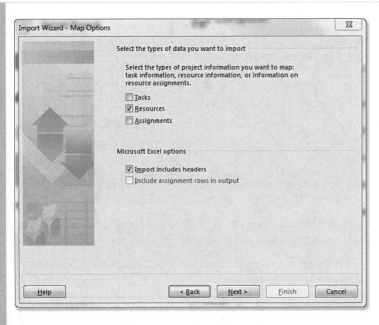

Figure 25.19
Importing the headers from your Excel worksheet helps you match your imported data with the correct Project fields.

Figure 25.20
Project matches the column headings from your Excel document when possible, but it might not always find the right match, and you have to enter them yourself.

10. Enter the correct field names in the To: Microsoft Project Field column of the mapping table for each of the fields in the From: Excel Field column, as shown in Figure 25.21.

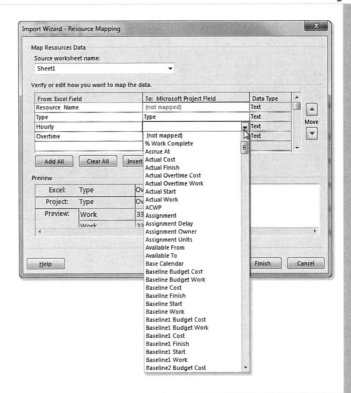

Figure 25.21
Use the Project drop-down list of field names to find the correct field for your imported data.

11. After you have finished filling in the field names, click the Next button to move to the End of Map Definition dialog box. Click the Save Map button if you want to save your import map. Do not forget to give it a unique name. If you do not want to save it, click the Finish button to import your data. In this example, it is added to the end of the Resource sheet list, as shown in Figure 25.22.

When Project has a problem importing data, you might receive a warning message, as shown in Figure 25.23. Or you might simply crash Project. Project is very rigid when importing task data, as you can see from this warning, where Project found a mismatched Duration value in the imported data. If you happen to see one of these error messages while importing data, you have three different options:

- Click Yes to keep importing data, and to continue receiving error messages if more exist. This is your best option, unless you know specifically what the problem is and how to correct it in Excel. This option continues importing the data, and you can find and fix the problem in Project after the import is complete.

- Click No if you want to continue importing data, but do not want to receive any more error messages. This option can create problems, because you will not know if there are any more errors in your imported data.

- Click Cancel to quit importing your data.

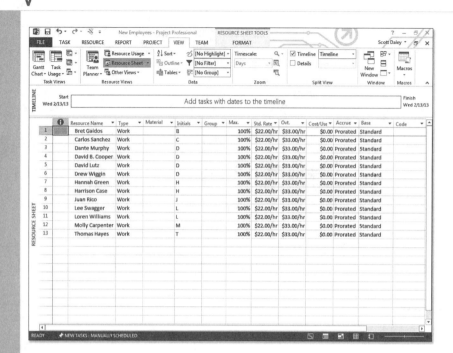

Figure 25.22
Project adds new resources to the project resource list, with the use of an Excel import map.

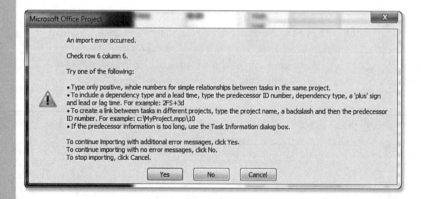

Figure 25.23
If Project encounters a problem with mismatched data during an import, it might warn you with this window, or it might simply stop working.

> **⚠ caution**
>
> If your imported data does contain mismatches, it will not be imported into Project even if you select Yes from the warning dialog box (see Figure 25.23). Project instead shows a default value, and you need to find the holes left by this mismatched data and enter the correct information.
>
> If you do encounter the warning dialog box, you should save the source references listed. These references can assist you when you go back to find and fill in the holes left by the missing data.

Working with Web-Enabled Project Data

Beginning with Microsoft Project version 2007, you can export project data in the XML format, but you can no longer export into HTML. Exporting into XML enables you to publish Project data onto web pages, which can be used for reviewing most all of the project information on either the Internet or a corporate intranet. Unlike with HTML, you can import XML data into Project as well. XML is a versatile format because of its structured form and can be easily imported into many other applications and formats.

Follow these steps to save a project to an XML file:

1. Open the Project file containing the data you want to export.

2. Go to the File tab, Save As (or Export) to open the Save As dialog box. Then select the directory for your new XML file in the Save In list box, and name your file.

3. Choose the XML Format (.xml) file format; then click the Save button. Your project has now been saved as an XML file.

> ## note
>
> When you are saving a project into the XML format, you cannot export selected data only; you must export the entire file. The Project data within the file is structured by nodes. You can expand each node to view the groupings of data, such as Task, Resource, and Assignment.

Working with Text File Formats

Project supports two ASCII text formats: the tab-delimited format and the comma-separated values (CSV) format. Import/export maps for these formats are nearly identical to the import/export maps of Excel, with one important difference. In Excel, you can import or export all three data table types at the same time: tasks, resources, and assignments. When you import/export text formats, you can select only one of these three data tables at a time.

Exporting Project Data in the Text Formats

Follow these steps to export a list of summary tasks with their start and finish dates to a text file:

1. Open the project from which you want to export your summary tasks.

2. Go to the File tab, Save As, and browse to the directory for your new text file in the Save In list box.

3. Choose the file format you want to use in the Save as Type list box. If you want a tab-delimited file, select Text (Tab Delimited) (*.txt). This format places tab characters between each of the data fields in the record, with paragraph marks to separate the records (a carriage return and line feed).

   If you want a comma-delimited file, select CSV (Comma Delimited) (*.csv). This format places commas between each of the data fields in the record (with quote marks surrounding field values that contain commas themselves) and separates the records with paragraph marks.

4. Click the Save button (if you see a warning when you click Save, see the Caution in the section "Understanding Import/Export Maps" of this chapter). This opens the Export Wizard dialog box. Click the Next button to go to the Map dialog box.

5. In the Map dialog box, choose whether you want to use an existing export map or create a new one. This example creates a new map. Click Next to move to the Map Options dialog box.

6. Choose which type of data you want to import from the Map Options dialog box: tasks, resources, or assignments. You can choose only one of the three, unlike in an Excel export map. See Figure 25.24 for more details.

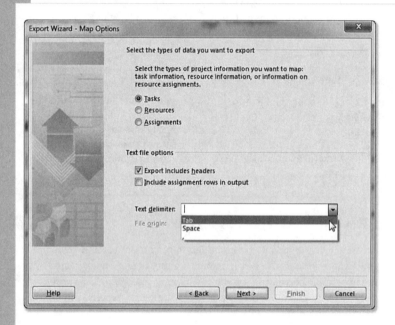

Figure 25.24
You can choose only one data table at a time in the Map Options box when you are saving your data to a text file.

7. If you want your exported data labeled, leave the Export Includes Headers box selected.

8. If you want your assignments included, select the Include Assignment Rows in Output box. Keep in mind that your assignments will be indistinguishable from your tasks or resources, unless you include the Assignment field in the field mapping box to identify them.

9. Choose your text delimiter from the drop-down list if you want to use either a comma or a space as the delimiter, instead of the tab character, which is the default.

10. Click the Next button to open the Mapping dialog box. You can now select the data type you want to include in your text file. This example includes the Name field, the Start_Date field, and the Finish_Date field, while using the Summary Task export filter, as shown in Figure 25.25. Also notice that the Destination Table Name text box is unavailable when importing or exporting text-formatted data.

11. Click the Next button to proceed on to the End of Map Definition dialog box.

12. If you made a new export map and want to save it, click the Save button, and then give the map a unique name, such as Export Summary Tasks to Text, so you can identify it more easily the next time you choose to use it.

13. Click the Finish button to create the file.

Figure 25.25
The Summary Task filter limits the tasks exported, thus making data management easier.

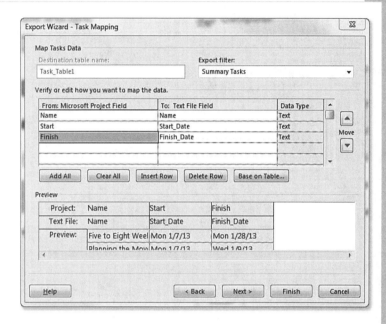

You can open the text file in Notepad or any other text editor. You can also import it into any application that can import tab-delimited text files. You can see how the example, with some minor formatting, creates a nice list of your summary tasks and their start and finish dates, as shown in Figure 25.26.

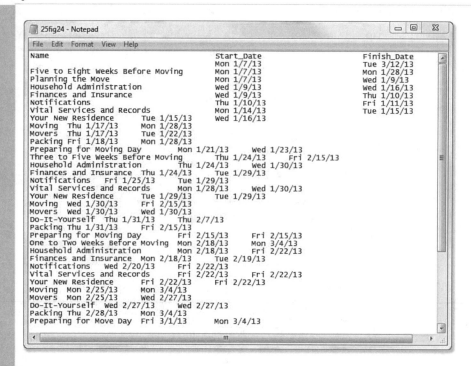

Figure 25.26
With a little bit of formatting to create better spacing between the summary task names and the start and finish dates, you can create an easy-to-read text file in Notepad.

Importing Project Data from Text Formats

You can import a text file in a similar manner as importing an Excel file. However, as when you are exporting, you can import only one type of data at a time. This means you have to import your tasks, resources, and assignments separately. Also, as with Excel formats, you will probably encounter problems matching field names if your import source file was not exported originally from Project. Refer to the earlier section "Importing Project Data from the Excel Format" for more information on this topic.

When you are importing a text file, you have one additional option that was grayed out for exporting (refer to Figure 25.24). The File Origin text box lets you specify whether a different character set has been used as the source data. The default is Windows (ANSI), but you can also choose DOS, OS/2 (PC-8), or Unicode. This assists you in importing your data more correctly, if for example the text files originated from an international environment using Unicode.

Importing a Task List from Outlook

Because many organizations use Outlook to track their calendars and to-do lists, you can import your tasks straight from Outlook. In Figure 25.27, you can see a list of tasks that have been entered into Outlook.

Figures 25.28 and 25.29 show additional information you can enter into an Outlook task, such as notes and the duration for tasks. Double-click on the task when you want to add more information.

Figure 25.27
With the help of Project, you can enter a task list in Outlook and then import it into a project file.

Figure 25.28
You can add notes in Outlook through the Task tab.

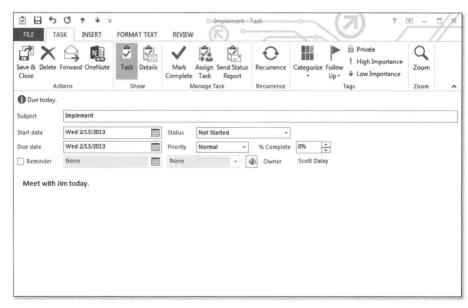

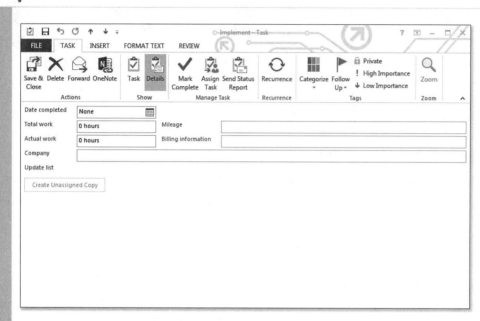

Figure 25.29
You can specify details about the task(s) by clicking the Details button in Outlook.

Follow these steps to import a task into Project from Outlook:

1. Enter your task information in the Tasks section of Outlook. You can add the start date, duration, due date, and even notes if necessary.

2. Open the project into which you want to import the Outlook tasks, or a blank project file to start a new project.

3. Go to the Task tab, Insert, Task, Import Outlook Tasks to open the Import Outlook Tasks dialog box, as shown in Figure 25.30.

4. Choose which tasks you want to import by filling the check box in the first column for each task. Use the Select All button to choose every task on the list.

5. Click OK to import the Outlook tasks.

Project imports your Outlook tasks in alphabetical order, as shown in Figure 25.31. After you have imported the tasks into Project, you can drag them into the preferred order, plus set their dependencies and constraints, and so on. You also see that the start date for each imported task has been set to the start date of the project. The dates associated with the tasks, when created in Outlook, are not imported.

Figure 25.30
Use the Import Outlook Tasks dialog box to select and import tasks to be imported into Project.

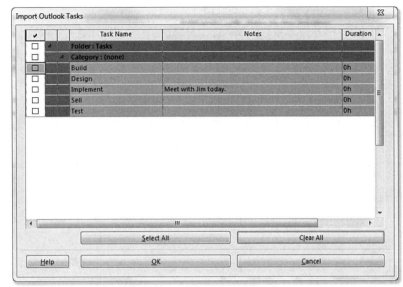

Figure 25.31
You can see how Project imports tasks from Outlook in alphabetical order, including the duration and any notes added in Outlook.

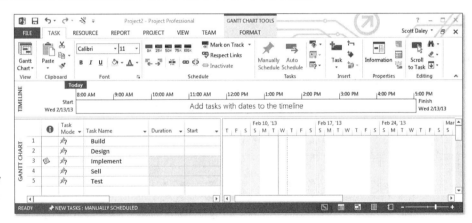

Consultants' Tips

Import/Export as a Legacy Feature Set

Import/export functionality is still useful in some cases. At this point, however, it is more of a legacy feature set superseded by the new reports and visual reporting. In general, start with either reports or visual reports to export data and use import/export functionality as a last resort.

Design the Data Layout Prior to Import/Export

Even if on paper only, you should design the data layout for the information you want to import or export before trying to import/export it. The mapping process can be frustrating without some preliminary thinking. You might use the data exchange process to create some reports for yourself in other applications, such as in Excel, to help you analyze issues with your projects offline. For instance, you could use the Compare to Baseline map to print an Excel report and then review it later for analysis.

Using Export/Import Versus Copy/Paste

Although this is a rare situation, if you have ever seen Project data crash in a previous version for a given file, consider cutting and pasting the data you need rather importing the data. The original data setup might be corrupt, and by importing the data, you might be taking some of the issues with you.

Copying and Pasting Using Excel

If you decide to copy and paste using Excel as the transfer agent, think ahead to get the intended summary/task/assignment structure set up. Map the exact columns to use for the copy-and-paste operation.

Be Aware of Additional Data When Importing/ Exporting

A project file has hundreds of fields, and sometimes you will be unaware of certain data in the project file by viewing only a few columns. For instance, you will often miss transferring data in the actual work and cost or baseline fields to other file formats if you do not know it is there. Prior to data transfer, consider displaying extra columns to determine whether "hidden" data exists.

Using the XML Export Will Not Keep Some of the Usage Data

If you are using XML output, you might *not* get all the detailed data in the Usage views. For example, when viewing the Resource Usage view, you can see time-phased data for each resource assignment, but when the project is exported into XML format, it will not contain this time-phased data. Specifically, a resource might have worked eight hours a day for the past three weeks, but you will not be able to see this when the project data is exported to XML format.

MANIPULATING DATA USING OTHER APPLICATIONS

A solid project plan is more than just a schedule. There are project charters, requirements, and design specifications. There are contracts and permits. Often there are custom cost models that are simply easier to implement in a spreadsheet than in Project. Finally, there are obviously times when Project data needs to be inserted into another document, such as a monthly report.

Project makes it possible to link these kinds of project artifacts with tasks in Project, and to put Project data into other applications. This enables the project manager to use her primary tool as the single control point for everything related to her project. This chapter explains the various mechanisms used to tie documents and other objects back to related tasks in the Project schedule.

 note

Many of the features discussed in this chapter have not changed for years, and clearly echo a time before Office 365, SharePoint, and "The Cloud." Nonetheless, these features highlight the enduring flexibility Project provides for many different kinds of work environments and requirements.

Copying Data Between Applications

In this chapter, you learn how to exchange individual field values and objects between files, and use the Copy and Paste and Insert Object commands. You discover that data you paste into Project, plus any objects you might insert, can be linked back to their original source. This enables you to update the Project document to show the most current values in a source file. Although in some cases you might need the rigor and preciseness of using an import/export map to exchange data between fields, as described in Chapter 25, "Exporting and Importing Project Data," the cutting and pasting or linking of objects often suffices for most of your project needs. For instance, you might need to just link a Word document that contains the specifications associated with a task in your project that indicates the Create Specifications Document task is complete. Or you might need to copy and paste the same set of tasks for a phase that a colleague created in an Excel spreadsheet, and it simply is not worth the time and trouble to perform the data mapping.

 note

Time-phased data is not handled by import/export maps, but it can be exported using visual reports.

Use the Clipboard to copy and paste data from one application's document (the source) into another application's document (the destination) if you do not need to transfer all of the information in a file (for instance, you only need one or a few values from your source document). In such a case, Project can be either the source or the destination document when exchanging data. Simply paste a copy of your values. Alternatively, you can paste a permanent link that shows the current value from the source document that can also be updated as needed to show changes in the source document.

If you are using the Clipboard to paste data into a table (a series of cells, such as the list of resources in the Gantt Chart view) in Project, it is important to choose the correct field receiving the data. When importing files with the import/export map, you can define which field the data will be placed in, but when you are using Copy and Paste, the location depends on which field you select.

When pasting a single value, it is easy to pick the right recipient field, but if you are copying a block of two or more columns of values, you need to be in a table view in Project that has the appropriate columns alongside one another in the same order as your copied block of values. This often requires you to define a custom table in Project to show the data field columns in the same order as the data being copied. When pasting data into Project, you might also have to have a custom table with like columns of data from the source open in the current view.

➡ *For additional information about custom tables, **see** the "Creating and Customizing Tables" section on **p. 700** of Chapter 22.*

In Figure 26.1, the Excel worksheet layout contains fields for resource names as well as the cost rates for each resource. If you open the Entry table in the Resource Sheet view, you see that it does not match this layout. There are five other columns between the Resource Name and the Standard Rate columns. Therefore, if you want to cut and paste your information from your Excel worksheet into a Resource Sheet view, you need to create a custom Entry table in Project that looks like your Excel sheet and hides the five columns, so your information can be pasted correctly, as shown in Figure 26.2.

Be sure to select the cell that should receive the upper-left cell of your block of pasted cells before you execute the Paste command. The cell containing Thomas Hayes was chosen before pasting, as shown in Figure 26.2.

Figure 26.1
If you want to correctly paste your spreadsheet data into Project, you must create a custom table with the columns laid out identical to your spreadsheet.

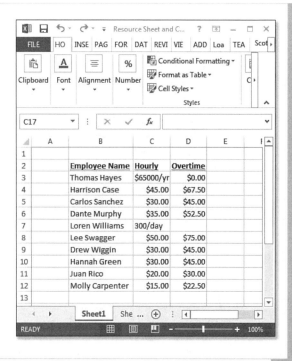

Figure 26.2
You can create a custom resource table to accept the data pasted from the spreadsheet shown in Figure 26.1.

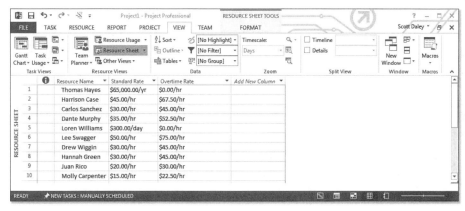

Copying Data from Other Applications into Project

Follow these steps when copying data into Project from another application:

1. Choose your source data. You can choose a single value, or several values, as shown in Figure 26.1. When choosing several values, be sure the layout of your values matches the order of the values in the Project table serving as the destination.

2. Move the data to the Clipboard using Edit, Copy; Ctrl+C; or the Task tab, Clipboard, Copy command on the Ribbon.

3. Open Project and choose which view contains the table with the columns in the same order as the data you are copying, as shown in Figure 26.2.

4. Choose the resource or task row and field in the table that is receiving the data. If you choose blank rows, Project creates new resources or tasks with the copied data. If you select rows that already contain data, Project replaces the existing data with the newly copied data.

5. Paste your data to Project by selecting Edit, Paste; Ctrl+V; or the Task tab, Clipboard, Paste command on the Ribbon.

> **caution**
>
> If, while copying and pasting, you overwrite an existing resource, you are simply changing field values for that resource. Any tasks assigned to that resource are still assigned to it, even if the resource name might have changed.

Using the Paste command places a static copy of the current value from the source document into your selected field. Project does not automatically update this value if the source document is changed.

If you paste into a field that does not support the data type you are importing, you see a pasting error, such as the one shown in Figure 26.3. For instance, the data from Figure 26.1 contained the text value N/A in cell D7, and in Figure 26.3, Project tells you that it is unclear what to do with that value in the Overtime Rate field. The error message shows you that the error was detected in ID 5 in the Overtime Rate column. Error dialog boxes give you three option buttons, as follows:

- **Yes**—Choose Yes to continue pasting and receiving error messages. Your mismatched value are pasted into the cell, and Project tries to make sense of it.

- **No**—Choose No to continue pasting, but without receiving any more error messages. Project pastes the mismatched value into the cell and ignores any more mismatched values it encounters.

- **Cancel**—Choose Cancel to terminate your pasting operation. If you are pasting a block of values and some have already been pasted, using the Cancel button causes the already pasted values to remain in the Project document, but no more of your values will be added.

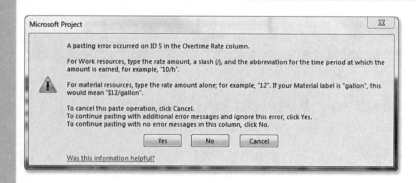

Figure 26.3
Project opens an error message dialog box to tell you where the error occurred and what kind of data is expected.

note

When you are pasting data from another application into Project, Project gives you an error if you use a slash (/), such as in Figure 26.3. The only exception to this would be if you used it as an abbreviation for a time period at which an amount is earned. For instance, $10 per hour would be represented as 10/h.

 caution

When you are pasting dates into the Start or Finish fields for a task, the default Task Mode matters. If your task mode is Manually Scheduled, you simply paste the dates. If your task mode is Auto Scheduled, you create soft constraints for those tasks (Start No Earlier Than constraints in projects scheduled using a start date, and Finish No Later Than constraints in projects scheduled using a finish date). To change those constraints, go to the Task Information dialog box and select the Advanced tab. If you select As Soon As Possible, you can reset the constraint type to the least constrained.

➡ *For additional information about types of constraints and their removal, **see** the "Defining Constraints" section on **p. 211** of Chapter 7.*

Copying Project Data into Other Applications

Follow these steps when you want to copy data from Project into another application:

1. Choose a view and apply a table displaying the data you want to copy to another application.

2. Choose your source data; you can select a single value, several adjacent values, whole rows or columns, or all the cells in the table:

   ■ If you want to select an entire row, click the ID number for the row or rows.

   ■ If you want to select entire columns, click the column headers.

   ■ If you want to select all the cells in the table, click the Select All button above the ID numbers and to the left of the other column headers.

3. Copy the data to the Clipboard by either selecting the Task tab, Clipboard, Copy or pressing Ctrl+C.

4. Open the other application and choose the location to which you want to paste your data, and paste it from the Clipboard. Word and Excel both have the Paste command on the Home tab of the Ribbon.

In Figure 26.4, a block of data is copied from the Resource Usage view into an Excel worksheet. Before the data to copy was selected, the Cost table in Project was changed to include the Assignment field. After the data was pasted into Excel, the user added the heading at the top of each column in the worksheet (Resource Name, Cost, and Assignment). Final formatting on this worksheet might include using the Assignment column to separate the rows containing resource data from those containing assignment data.

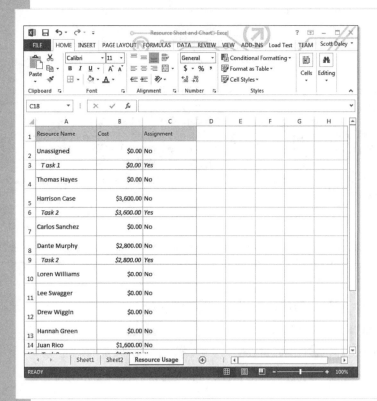

Figure 26.4
Data copied from Project's Resource Usage view has been pasted into Excel and is now ready for final formatting.

 tip

There are three steps you must follow if you want to copy and paste information contained in the time-phased grid of either the Resource Usage view or Task Usage view:

1. Choose the desired information in the table; then copy and paste it to the destination application.

2. Choose the desired date in the time-phased grid, making sure to match the data in the grid with the correct rows from the table before copying this information and pasting it to the destination application.

3. Enter the column headings for both the table information and the time-phased data into the destination application.

Linking Data Between Applications

The previous section discussed how to make static copies from one application to another, unlinked copies that will not change if the source data changes. You are now going to learn how to paste a value from one application into another application that will change and update based on the changes of the source document. These are known as *linked references*. You can update a linked reference to show the changes in the value stored in the source document.

Linking Project Data Fields from External Sources

When pasting a link from an external data source into a Project table, you can use another application, such as Excel or Word, where you can maintain reference data efficiently, or you can link from another Project document. For instance, you could use an Excel workbook to keep track of resource names and cost rates, linking that document to your Project document.

Follow these steps to link Project field values to values stored in other sources:

1. Choose your source data, such as a cell or range of cells in an Excel worksheet. You can choose a single value or several values; if choosing several values, confirm that the order of the values you are copying matches the order of the values in the table into which you are pasting your data.

2. Copy the data to the Clipboard.

3. Activate Project and choose which view has the table with the columns arranged to match the order of the data you will be copying into Project.

4. Choose the row in the table that will receive the data.

5. Select the Task tab, Clipboard, Paste Special, opening the Paste Special dialog box, as shown in Figure 26.5.

6. Select the Paste Link option.

Figure 26.5
You can specify the format for the data that will be pasted into a receiving file using the Paste Special dialog box.

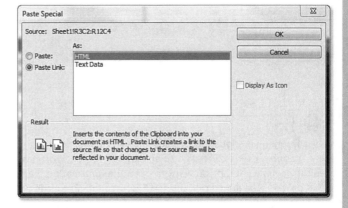

7. Select Text Data in the As box as the type of link, if you want the data to become text in the table. Project attempts to convert text data into numeric data in the number field, or into a date in the date field.

8. Click OK to set up the link. Project displays, by default, a small triangle in the lower-right corner of each cell linked to a source for its data. You can see the link indicator for the Name, the Standard Rate, and the Overtime Rate values in Figure 26.6. The resource names and cost rate information have been dynamically linked to an Excel worksheet, where the resource information is maintained.

tip

Select the Paste Link option button before you choose a format for the pasted data in the As box. If you change the link option, you can change the options in the As box.

note

If the Gantt Chart view is open, the Paste Special dialog box contains more options in the As box than if the Resource Sheet view were open, as shown in Figure 26.5. You can select the Worksheet or Picture option if you want to paste the data as a picture object in the graphical area (see "Placing Objects into Project," later in this chapter). With the Gantt Chart view, for instance, either of these options would create a graphical object in the bar chart area of the view.

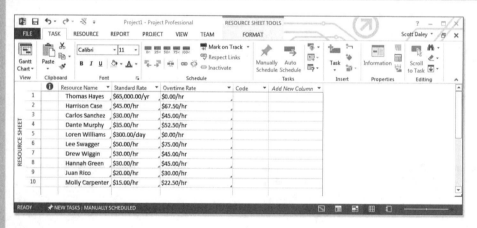

Figure 26.6
Project indicates which cells in a table are linked cells by a small triangle in the lower-right corner of the cell.

tip

Usually when you double-click a resource cell, Project opens the Resource Information dialog box. However, if you double-click a cell linked to an external source, Project opens the external source so you can view or edit the source data. If you want to open the Information dialog box for the task, resource, or assignment that contains the linked cell, use the Resource tab, Properties, Information command.

If you expect to see a link indicator, but do not, go to the File tab, Options Advanced, Display and make sure that the OLE Links Indictors check box is in use.

If you try to paste a link that contains mismatched data, you receive an object linking and embedding (OLE) error message to let you know the operation cannot be completed. Unlike with the regular Paste command, if data is mismatched while you are pasting a block of values, Project stops the operation and removes all the values that might have been pasted during the operation. These values are grouped together because the block of cells is considered one link. If even one cell has a mismatch, the entire block of data will be ignored.

➡ *For additional information about attaching hyperlinks, **see** the "Attaching Hyperlinks to Tasks" section on **p. 168** of Chapter 6.*

Refreshing Linked Data in Project

When you save a project file that contains linked values, Project saves the current value of your linked files, as well as a reference to the source for the value. This means that when you open a file with linked values, Project shows the most recent values.

If you open a Project file that contains links to other files, Project asks if you want to reestablish those links upon opening the file. Project refreshes the values in the linked cells with the current values in the source files, as shown in Figure 26.7. If you choose Yes, Project retrieves the current or saved values of each link's source. If you choose No, Project opens the Project document and shows the last saved values for the linked cells. If you decide later to go back and update these links, you can.

Figure 26.7
If you open a Project file with links to other files, Project refreshes the links or uses the last values saved in the Project file.

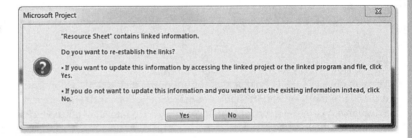

To update the linked values of a Project document at any time, add the Edit Links command (under All Commands) to the Quick Access toolbar and select it to open the Links dialog box. Your source application does not need to be open when your linked values are refreshed. When you open the Links dialog box, it lists all the external links in the current document, as shown in Figure 26.8.

The Links list displays the path of the source, the document type of the source file, and the update status of each link. All three items are displayed in greater detail at the bottom of the dialog box for the selected link. If you do not see these items on display, you might need to use the Update Now button. When the filename and link reference are too long, the path to the source will be condensed. Links in Project to external data sources utilize Dynamic Data Exchange (DDE) to manage the source and target locations of the data. The source is usually referred to as the DDE Server.

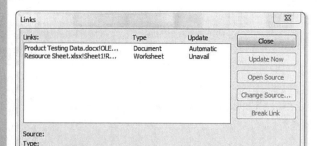

Figure 26.8
The Links dialog box shows you all the external sources of linked data in a project.

The chosen item in the Links list shows the path to the file condensed, because it is too long for the display, as shown in Figure 26.8. The details also show the filename and the location of linked data in the file, as well as the cell range. The type has been identified as a Microsoft Word Document, and the update status is Automatic, which means you do not have to click the Update Now button if you want to refresh the values in Project. If it was set to Manual, you would have to use the Update Now button to refresh the values.

If your update status is set to Automatic, and the file is open in memory and supports an automatic update, changes in the source appear immediately in the document while it too is open in memory. However, some source applications do not support the automatic update choice, and the Update column at the top of the dialog box shows Unavail (short for Unavailable). The update status is also set to Unavail when the Project document has not been updated during the current editing session.

 tip

When an object's Update field at the bottom of the dialog box has the Automatic button set, and you want to change to the Manual button, do not make the change if the update status for the link in the list is unavailable. You need to update the link with the Update Now button before any changes are made to the updating method.

 note

There is only one link reference in the Links dialog box for a whole range of Excel cells pasted in the link operation, as shown in Figure 26.8. If you want to maintain each of the cells as separate links, you need to copy and paste each cell independently.

Follow these steps if you want to update links to external sources:

1. Open the Links dialog box (refer to Figure 26.8) by adding the Edit Links command to the Quick Access toolbar and selecting it.

2. Choose all the links you want refreshed.
3. Click the Update Now button. This refreshes all the data links you have chosen. The source for each selected link is searched for among the current values.
4. To open the application document named in the chosen link reference, click the Open Source button. You must choose only one link when using the Open Source button; multiple links are invalid. You can, however, open multiple linked source documents simultaneously by opening each of them independently. Here are some other options in the Links dialog box:
   - To remove a selected link, click the Break Link button. The current value remains in the link location, but the external source reference disappears.
   - To change the source of a selected link, click the Change Source button. This opens the Change Source dialog box, as shown in Figure 26.9. Use the Browse button to select another file to link to.

> **tip**
> When the Links command is grayed out, the document has no linked values.

Figure 26.9
Use the Change Source dialog box to redefine a link's source.

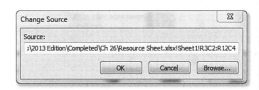

> **tip**
> Although you can browse the files directly to find the filename of a new source to link to, you might also need to establish the location within the new source file to finish the change. Because of this fact, it is usually better to paste new links over the old ones, instead of using the Change Source dialog box.

Deleting Links to External Sources

As mentioned in the previous section, when you break a link to an external source, Project saves the current value that was linked, but disassociates the value from the external source. Likewise, if you try to type over a field value already linked to an external source, you are warned that the link will be lost, and then given the choice to proceed or cancel the entry. Select No if you want to cancel your editing changes and keep the link. If you select Yes, the Dynamic Data Exchange (DDE) link reference will be lost. You can, however, undo the change using the Edit, Undo command.

If you want to delete the data and its link to an external source, select the file whose link you want removed and go to Edit, Clear, Contents, or use Ctrl+Del. You are asked to confirm your deletion.

tip

If you delete the link in a cell that is part of a block of linked values, the link for all the cells in that block will be removed, not just for one cell. Use the Edit, Undo command to restore these links if they are deleted accidentally.

Identifying Tasks or Resources with Links Attached

You can find out which of your tasks or resources use linked data from other sources by filtering them. Choose the Linked Fields filter from the Filters drop-down list in either a task view or resource view. You can also find the linked values by looking for the links indicator triangle in the lower-right corner of the cells.

Pasting Links to Project Data in Other Applications

Both Microsoft Excel and Microsoft Word accept pasted links to individual data cells in Project tables. To copy a single linked value into one of these applications, display a table with a cell for the value you want to use, select the cell, and use the Copy command. After you have completed the copy, activate either Word or Excel, go to the Paste Special command, and select the Paste Link option to paste the data as text. To copy a block of values, make sure you modify a table in Project so the values you choose to copy are adjacent to one another, just as you copied from another application into Project. Choose the entire block and, as before, go to Paste Special and use the Paste Link command to enter the block of values into Word or Excel. A pasted block of data is treated as a single entity in both applications, and when you update the links in Project, all the values of the block are updated.

 note

There can be formatting issues related to displaying the Project data in other applications. For instance, the duration fields can display the duration in minutes, multiplied by 10 (so an hour appears as 600), and the work fields display the work as minutes, multiplied by 1,000 (so an hour appears as 60,000). These durations can also be considered text by other applications because the unit can be copied with the value. You should process the data after copying it to provide a meaningful display for the users.

Working with Objects

Microsoft uses the term *object* to represent data, usually a group of data or a special format for data that has been formatted by another application. Objects are most frequently used to show graphical data, such as placing Excel charts, PowerPoint slides, sound files, video clips, or other graphics into Project. You can also use the Gantt Chart view or the Network Diagram view from Project and place them into other applications.

note
Many of the commands referenced in this chapter have to be added to the Quick Access Toolbar manually. Does this mean that Microsoft intends to remove these features one day? Probably. But Project 2013 still supports them because they are useful in many different project management organizations.

Pasting Objects

As with text data, you can copy data as an object from an external application and paste it as an object in Project by using the Special command. You could, for instance, paste an Excel chart into the Gantt Chart view. If you use the Paste Special command, the chart can be linked back to its originating Excel document. As with linked text data, you can update a linked object, either automatically or manually, depending on the settings you use in the Links dialog box.

When the object is not linked, but placed permanently into a client document and cannot be updated, it is called an *embedded* object. An embedded object is stored in the client document, and because the format is foreign to the client application, any editing of the embedded object requires activating the originating application. After editing is finished and the originating application is closed, the revised object remains in the client application.

After an object has been pasted, you can move and resize it using Project, as if it were a piece of clip art. It is also possible to edit some object formats directly from within Project by double-clicking on the object. For instance, if an Excel chart has been pasted in as a linked object, as shown in Figure 26.10, you can double-click the object to open Excel for editing. When you close Excel and save any changes, the revised object will be visible in Project.

If the chart in Figure 26.10 were embedded, instead of linked, double-clicking would open the object for editing, and Excel's Ribbon would be visible instead of Project's Ribbon, as shown in Figure 26.11. You would still, however, be working within Project. After you make your changes, click outside the object onto the Project workspace to exit from editing mode, and return to Project's Ribbon.

 note
While in editing mode, you can switch from Project to another application; when you return, your editing mode is still active, so you can continue with your changes.

When you paste a media object into Project, such as a video clip or sound file into the Gantt Chart, it shows up as an icon, and you must double-click it to activate and run the media.

When Project is a source or an origin, and you paste copies of data cells from the Gantt Chart view table into another application document as text, every row of task information becomes a row of ordinary text in the document. If, however, you copy the selection as an object, it is displayed as a graphic figure in the client document.

Figure 26.12 shows how the same Project task rows have been pasted as both text and as a picture object into a Microsoft Word document. The task field text appears as simple table in Word. The graphic of the tasks include the Gantt Chart view table cells, plus the taskbars and the timescale above the taskbars. You can read more about this in "Placing Objects into Other Applications," later in this chapter.

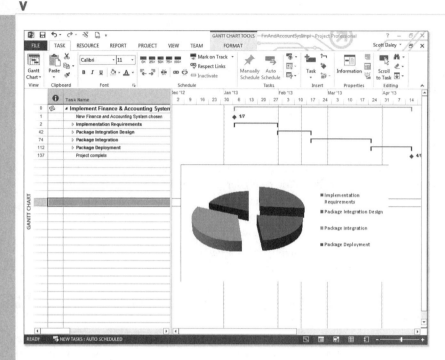

Figure 26.10
You can use Project data for each phase, paste-linked into an Excel worksheet, and that data can be used to create an Excel chart, which can be paste-linked back into Project as an object on the Gantt Chart view.

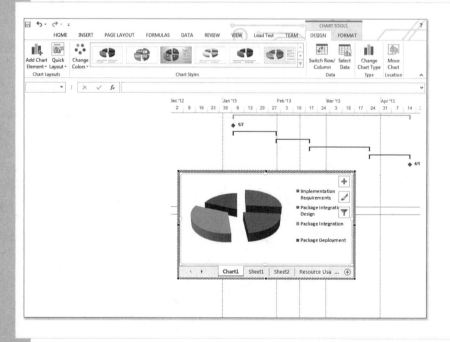

Figure 26.11
If you double-click on an embedded chart, it is opened for editing within Project, but using the source application, such as Excel in this example.

Figure 26.12
With
Microsoft
Word, you
can show
the same
informa-
tion as
both pasted
text and as
a Project
image on
the same
page of a
document.

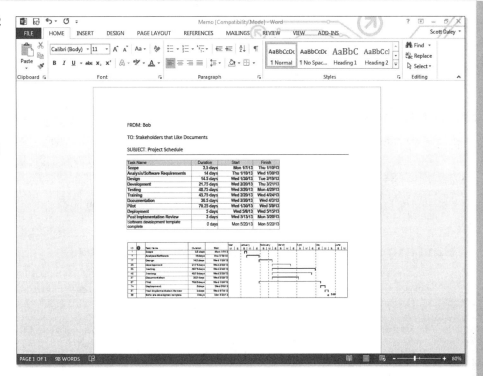

Inserting Objects

To place objects into a client document, use the Object command (Object is not available by default in the Ribbon; it must be added to the Quick Access Toolbar). This command inserts existing files that have been created by an originating application into the client document. You have the choice of the object being linked or embedded.

With the Object command, you can also open an originating application from within the client document. This lets you create new embedded objects that exist only within the client document. You could, for instance, insert a new, blank Excel spreadsheet into a Project document; whatever data you want to enter into the spreadsheet, you could do so using Excel.

When you are finished, you can click on the Project workspace in the background, and the object remains embedded in Project. The data only exists saved in the Project document. You could also insert a Project object into Word or Excel, such as a Gantt Chart you want to update and use for multiple meetings. When you are finished updating, click outside the object, and it remains embedded in the container document.

Placing Objects into Project

Objects of all sorts can be placed directly into views. Although this is very old functionality, there are still good reasons to, for example, paste a spreadsheet object into your Gantt chart if you regularly refer to the spreadsheet when looking at your Gantt chart.

You can paste or insert objects into Project in four locations:

- The graphics area of the Gantt Chart view

- The Notes box of the Task, Resource, or Assignment Information Form view

- The special task Objects box of the Task Form view, or the resource Objects box of the Resource Form view

- The Header, Footer, or Legend area of a view's Page Format dialog box

Pasting Objects in the Gantt Chart View

The Gantt Chart view is the primary view when looking at a graphically depicted Project file. You can enhance this view by pasting objects from other applications into the timescale area. Follow these steps to paste an object into the Gantt Chart view:

1. Activate the originating application and then select the source data, copying it to the Clipboard.

2. Activate Project (the client application) and open a Gantt Chart view.

3. Select the Task tab, Clipboard, Paste, Paste Special to open the Paste Special dialog box, as shown in Figure 26.13.

4. Select Paste if you want to embed the object, or Paste Link if you want to link it.

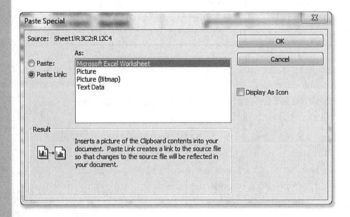

Figure 26.13
Use the Paste Special dialog box to embed or link objects into Project.

5. With the As list, you have the option to include the application's name. You might also have the option called Picture. These choices produce picture images that look similar. The originating application's name option enables you to open the object in the originating application and to edit or modify the object. With the Picture option, Project places a picture of the object into the document that cannot be edited with the client application. In short, select the originating application's name if you want to be able to go back and edit the object in Project, or select Picture if you do not want it to be editable.

6. Click OK to paste the image into the document.

After the object is in the Gantt Chart view, you can move and resize it as you like. To move it, simply click the object to select it, dragging it to a new position. To resize the object, select it and drag its resizing handles to change the size. If you want to remove the object, select it and press the Delete key.

> **tip**
>
> When you resize a picture object, regardless of whether it is linked, you might cause the picture to appear distorted. This is because resizing can cause the horizontal and vertical dimensions to change proportionally relative to one another. To keep the dimensions in proportion, hold down the Shift key as you drag the object's corner handles.

> **caution**
>
> Keep in mind that you cannot undo resizing or deleting of an object. Make sure to save your Project document before you begin experimenting with either of these actions.

> **tip**
>
> When you have more than one object placed on the Gantt Chart view, you can scroll through your objects quickly by using the Tab key. You can use the Tab key to select any other objects in that pane, one at a time.

Inserting Objects in the Gantt Chart View

You saw the examples used in the previous section, where the data of an object was created as part of an originating application document and then copied and pasted to the client application. Another option you can use is the Insert Object command, to place a linked or embedded copy of an entire source document into the client document as an object. Keep in mind that embedding an entire source document into Project increases the Project document's file size, and your embedded document will be cut off from updates to the original source document.

Another option when using the Object command is that you can create an object without using an existing file. You could create a new object by using the formatting capabilities for originating applications that support Microsoft OLE 2.0 or higher. You can open the originating application's interface from within Project to create the new data. After the origin is closed, the object remains embedded in Project.

To insert an object, add the Object command to the Quick Access bar and click on it. Project opens the Insert Object dialog box, as shown in Figure 26.14. Your default option button is Create New, which enables you to create a new, embedded object using one of the listed applications in the Object Type box. If the data has already been created and saved, select Create from File to insert a linked or embedded copy of the source data.

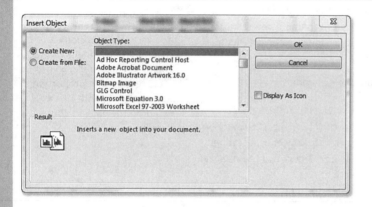

Figure 26.14
You have the option of creating an object from scratch within Project, using the Insert Object dialog box.

You could, for instance, embed in a new Excel object in the Gantt Chart view a worksheet that shows budgeted (baseline) and current gross margin data for a project. You would follow these steps to create a new worksheet object:

1. Activate the Gantt Chart view in the top pane of the combination view.

2. Go to the Object command (which must be added to the Quick Access toolbar) to open the Insert Object dialog box. It might take some time for this dialog box to appear because Project needs to prepare a list of all originating applications on your system that support OLE 2.0 or higher.

3. Select Create New, which is the default.

4. Select which originating application you want to use from the list in the Object Type list. In this case, you would select Microsoft Excel Worksheet.

5. Select the Display as Icon box if you want to see only an icon, instead of the worksheet object in the Gantt Chart view. After the object is inserted, you can double-click the icon to show the object's contents. This is a good choice if you have little room for objects in the graphical area of your Gantt Chart view. In this case, use the check box.

 tip
It is usually a good idea to use Display as Icon when you are first inserting an object. With the Display as Icon option, Project opens Excel into its own window, enabling you to enter and format your Excel data. You also have full access to Excel's features. After the data has been entered and formatted, it is easy to convert the object to be shown as a mini-worksheet. If you decide not to use the Display as Icon option, the object appears in a small window within the graphics area of the Gantt Chart view, making editing difficult. Not all of the Excel commands are available either.

6. Click OK to insert your new object. If you selected the Display as Icon box, Project opens an Excel window that you can use to create a worksheet.

7. You can now enter your data and edit and format the spreadsheet so that it appears as you want in the Gantt Chart view.

8. After your worksheet is finished, go to File, Close and Return to *filename* (where *filename* is the name of the Project document in which you inserted the object). The icon for your object is now displayed in the Gantt Chart view, as shown in Figure 26.15.

When you select the Display as Icon box, Project shows you what that icon will look like in the small space directly under the Display as Icon check box. It is not always an icon; it is often a word, such as *Chart* or *Document*.

 tip

You have the option of changing what the icon looks like if you do not like it or want it to stand out more. To do this, click the Change Icon button. When the Change Icon dialog box appears, either select a predesigned icon or browse for a graphic to use.

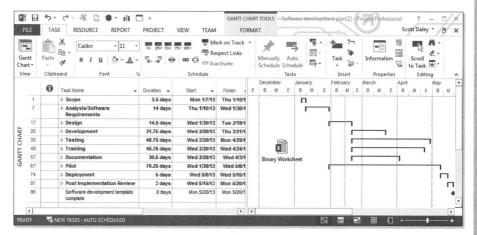

Figure 26.15
You can display any data you want, such as relevant cost and gross margin data, on the Gantt Chart view. Here, the worksheet object is shown as an icon.

After the object is embedded into Project, you can double-click it to open or edit the data; plus, you can convert the object from an icon to a displayed worksheet instead.

Follow these steps to convert the object from icon to worksheet:

1. Add the Convert command to the Quick Access toolbar.

2. Select the object by clicking on it.

3. Use the Convert button on the Quick Access toolbar to open the Convert dialog box, as shown in Figure 26.16.

4. Clear the Display as Icon check box, and click OK. Your icon now appears as a small worksheet, as you can see in Figure 26.17.

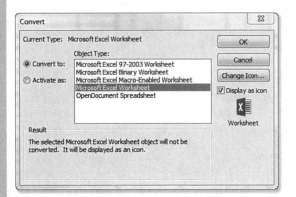

Figure 26.16
You can use the Convert dialog box to change the display of an object from an icon to a formatted data worksheet.

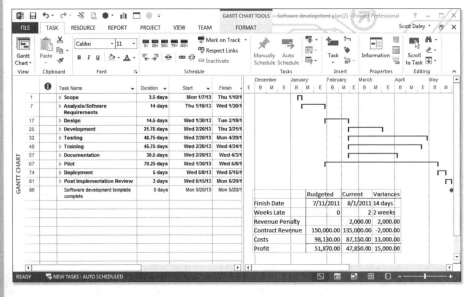

Figure 26.17
Your icon from Figure 26.15 is now converted into a worksheet object, which displays the relevant cost and gross margin data.

In the previous example, you created a new object and inserted it into the Gantt Chart, using the Object command. If you have a preexisting file that you want to place into the Gantt Chart, simply follow these steps:

1. Activate the Gantt Chart view in the top pane of a combination window.

2. Click the Object command, added to the Quick Access toolbar, to open the Insert Object dialog box.

3. Select the Create from File option. This opens a File text box and a Browse button, as shown in Figure 26.18.

Figure 26.18
You can insert external document files as objects into Project using the Insert Object dialog box.

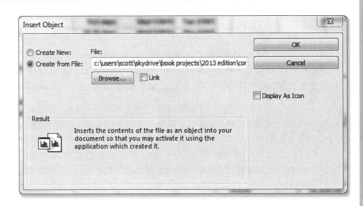

4. You can either enter the file's path name manually or use the Browse button to find and open the file.

5. Select the Link check box to insert a linked copy of the file's data. If you want to embed a copy that will not update, do not use the Link check box.

6. Choose the Display as Icon check box for the file to appear as an icon, instead of as a worksheet.

7. Click OK to create the object.

If you want to open or edit the object, double-click it.

> **note**
>
> Use the Edit Links command, which must be added to the Quick Access toolbar, to manage linked objects as described earlier in this chapter in the "Refreshing Linked Data in Project" section.

Placing Objects in the Notes Field

You can place objects into the Notes field for assignments, individual tasks, or resources. The Notes field is a great place to keep track of links to supporting documents stored elsewhere on your computer or in your organization's network. You could, for instance, insert into a note a group of objects, shown as icons, that link to documents defining authorization, budget, and scope for your project.

➡ *For more information on placing objects into the Notes field,* **see** *the "Inserting Object in Notes" section on* **p. 165** *of Chapter 6.*

Placing Objects in the Task or Resource Objects Box

There are three standard task form views (the Task Form, the Task Details Form, and the Task Name Form) you can use to display an Objects box. An Objects box is a spot where you can place a data object you want to associate with a task—a specific place for objects. Likewise, there are two standard resource form views (the Resource Form and the Resource Name Form) that can also be used to display an Object box that you can associate with a resource. To access the Object box, right-click a blank area of the Task Form and select it from the context menu.

➡️ *For additional information about custom reports,* **see** *Chapter 20, "Reports Part I: 2013 Reports," **p. 625.***

You can use either the Paste or Paste Special command to paste objects into an Object box. Unlike pasting notes, you can also paste links to objects by using the Paste Special command. In addition, you can use the Insert Object command to place linked or embedded objects into an Objects box.

As another option, Project offers a task Objects field and a resource Objects field. When you display an Objects field in a table, it shows the number of objects stored in the Objects box for that task or resource. The Objects field's main use is in filters; you use it to identify tasks or resources that have objects in their Objects boxes. You can use the standard filters of Tasks with Attachments and Resources with Attachments when choosing which tasks or resources have an Objects field with a value of greater than zero, or a Notes field that contains text. You can also build a custom filter to show records that have objects stored in their Objects boxes.

➡️ *For additional information about custom filters,* **see** *the "Creating and Customizing Filters" section on **p. 729** of Chapter 22.*

In Figure 26.19, a Task Form view has been set up under the Gantt Chart view, with the Objects box shown in the details area. The previous example of the gross margin worksheet has been used as the display in the Objects box.

The Gantt Chart view table has been modified to show the Objects field. You can see that two objects are attached to this resource. To see the next object, you need to use the scrollbar to scroll down.

Follow these steps to paste an object into the Objects field:

1. Go to the originating application and select the object, and copy it into the Clipboard.

2. Activate Project and then open one of the task or resource form views, depending on what kind of record you are pasting your object into.

3. Right-click anywhere outside a field box on the form, and select Objects from the shortcut menu.

4. Select the Objects field in the bottom of the form by clicking it. A thick black border appears around the field, letting you know it has been selected. You can see an example of that in Figure 26.20.

5. Go to the Task tab, Clipboard, Paste, Paste Special to open the Paste Special dialog box.

6. Select either Paste or Paste Link, depending on if you want to embed the item or link it.

7. Select the format option from the As list box.

8. Click OK to finish pasting the object.

If you want to insert an object into the Objects box, choose the Objects box and click Object (which you must have added to the Quick Access Toolbar) to open the Insert Object dialog box. You can now use the dialog box options as mentioned previously for inserting an object into notes and in the Gantt Chart view.

You can also place multiple objects into the Objects box. The first object you paste or insert appears first and is automatically selected. When you insert additional objects, Project places them below whichever one is selected, usually the first. After you have inserted a new object, the object is not automatically displayed or selected; you must scroll down to see the newly placed object. If you insert a second object, and do not scroll down and select it, when you insert a third, it will be placed between the first and second. This continues until you change which object is selected.

Figure 26.19
Project presents objects that are attached to an individual task or resource in the Objects field.

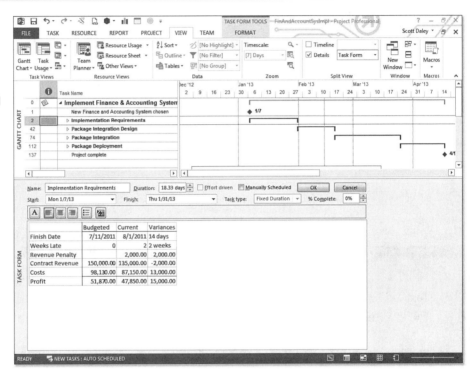

 tip

If you have an Objects box with multiple objects in it and want to change the order in which they appear, use the Cut and Paste tools to move the objects around. Select which object you want moved, and use the Edit, Cut (Ctrl+X) command. Next, choose which object you want your recently cut object to appear after, and use Edit, Paste or Paste Special. If the object you are moving is not formatted as a simple picture object, you must use the Paste Special command to retain its format.

The Objects box scrollbar does not scroll through a single object; instead, it jumps from object to object. So, if you have an item that is too large for the area it is displayed in, you have to try another option to see it. You can increase the size of the form, or open it in the originating application. You cannot, however, resize any objects that are pasted into the Objects box. If your object has been pasted as a picture, and you cannot see all of it, you need to resize the picture with the object's originating application, if possible.

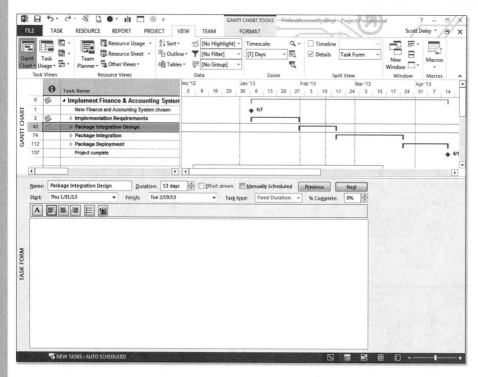

Figure 26.20
Select the
Objects
field of
the Task
Form view,
before
pasting or
inserting
objects
into it.

To delete an object from the Objects box, simply select said object and press the Delete key, removing the object from your document.

Placing Objects into Other Applications

Project uses several different and distinctive graphic views that can be effective when pasted into other applications. You can copy any of the following views:

- All the Gantt Chart views

- The Timeline view

- The Network Diagram and Detailed Network Diagram views

- The Calendar view

- The Task Usage and Resource Usage views

- The Resource Graph view

- The Calendar view

- Any of the sheet views, such as the Task Sheet or Resource Sheet view

You can copy most of these views by using the Task tab, Clipboard, Copy command or Copy Picture button. In the case of the Gantt Chart view, you need to format your view precisely and select Copy Picture. If you want to paste a linked object into another application, or embed a Project object that can be edited, you have to use the Copy command. The Copy Picture command lets you paste only an unlinked picture. You can see from the following descriptions which results you get when using the different commands:

- To paste a static, unlinked picture object or to create a GIF file to include on a web page, use the Copy Picture command. This enables you to precisely control the date range to include timescale views, and you can resize easily without seriously distorting the fonts.

- To paste an object that is linked to the source document in Project, use the Copy command. You can paste the object as a linked picture object, or a linked Project object. There is little difference between these two options. You can update both to show changes in the timescale data for any tasks included in the original picture, and you can double-click either type of object to open the Project document that is the source of the link. There are, however, limitations to this object type:

  - You cannot change the tasks or resources that have been included in the original picture without deleting the object and starting over.

  - You have limited control over the date range included, if the view contains a timescale.

  - To have total control over what is being displayed in the object, you should capture the view using the Copy command, and paste it as an unlinked Project object. Your data cannot be updated, and the entire project is embedded into the other application, which increases the file size dramatically. However, you have total control over what is displayed in the object image. You can even change the view, change the formats, and use the filters.

 note

You cannot use Project to copy the Relationship Diagram view or any of the form views. If you want a copy of these views, you must use either the Windows Print Screen command or a third-party screen capture program.

 note

The Timeline view cannot be pasted as an object into another application. The Timeline export is slightly different than other views; simply right-click on the timeline and choose For Email, For Presentation, or Full-Size. The Timeline view is available to other applications through the Clipboard.

Using the Copy Picture Command to Copy a View

The Copy Picture command is the best way to prepare a static picture object for inserting into other applications. It is also the only way to create a GIF format for use with web browsers. Select the Task tab, Clipboard, Copy, Copy Picture.

➡ *For additional information about modifying toolbars,* **see** *Chapter 22, "Customization Almost Beyond Reason: Views, Tables, Filters, Groups, Fields, Toolbars, Menus, and Forms," on* **p. 699.**

When preparing the view in Project before making a copy, you have several options in the Copy Picture dialog box that offer control over what is included in the image. Use these guidelines when you are arranging to copy a view:

■ It is best to set up whatever view you plan to copy so that it is contained in one screen. Project enables you to capture larger areas, but it becomes more difficult to get the results you want as the image gets larger.

■ If your view includes a table, you should prepare the columns that are displayed and the rows that need to be selected. You can use any of these techniques to prepare a table:

■ Only completely visible columns are included in the picture. You should, therefore, arrange the display of columns as you want them to appear in the picture. Also, be sure that the vertical split bar is not covering up any part of the rightmost column you want included in the picture.

■ You have the option with the Copy Picture dialog box to include the rows that are visible on the screen, or only the rows you have previously selected. To include selected rows, click at least one cell in each row you want included. If you choose nonadjacent rows, your image will only contain the rows you have selected.

■ If you choose a summary task row, its subtasks will not be included in the image. They have to be selected separately as well.

■ If your view has a timescale, you will get your best results by compressing the date range you want to include in the picture onto no more than two or three screens. You can create a picture that includes more screens of the timescale if you want. However, the printed image can be no wider than 22 inches. You will need to zoom out the timescale if you want to get a very large date range into the image successfully.

■ When copying the Task Usage or Resource Usage view, make sure your cells in the grid are at least 100% of their normal size. If not, you might see many cells filled with pound symbols (#), indicating the data cannot be displayed, even though you can see the values on the screen. If you need to fix the cell size, go to Format, Timescale, and you can set the value in the Size box to 100% or greater.

■ When you are copying the Calendar view, one of the Network Diagram views, or the Resource Graph view, Project includes only the current screen in the picture. You need to prepare the display to fit onto one screen before you capture your picture.

The Copy Picture dialog box, shown in Figure 26.21, offers options that vary depending on the view you are copying. With all views, you have choices about the format in which the picture is rendered, including the following:

■ Select the For Screen option if you want to paste the picture into another application to simply be viewed onscreen.

■ Select the For Printer option if you want to paste your picture into an application for printing. The format is determined by the printer you have selected in Project at the time you save the picture. If you change printers before you print, you should recopy the picture.

- Select the To GIF Image File option if you want to use the picture in a web page. Your image is saved in a GIF-format file that most web browsers can display. You need to enter the path and filename for the file being created. You can use the Browse button to search the directory structure or search for a filename you might be replacing.

Figure 26.21
You can use the Copy Picture dialog box to tailor the image you copy, enabling you to set up what it includes and how it is rendered.

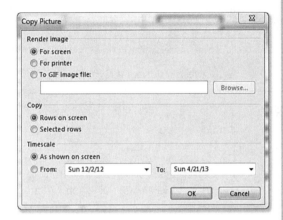

If the view you are copying includes a table, such as a Gantt Chart view or a Task or Resource Sheet view, you have the choice to include the following:

- **Rows on Screen**—Only the rows that are visible when you actually take the picture

- **Selected Rows**—Only the rows you have selected at least one or more cells in, before using the Copy Picture command

If your view contains a timescale, such as the Gantt Chart view or the Task or Resource Usage view, you have a choice of the following:

- You can use the dates shown onscreen, meaning that you must arrange the timescale onscreen as you want it to appear in the picture, and then capture only that range of dates in your picture.

- You can use a range of dates you specify in the From and To date boxes.

 tip

If you are selecting a date range with the Gantt Chart view, you should include at least one time unit before the From date and several after the To date. Many taskbars have graphic elements that extend beyond the start and finish dates of the task. This is especially true for bar text, such as resource names, that are displayed to the right of the taskbar. If you do not add these extra time units to the date range, the data in your picture might appear to be cut off.

Use these steps to copy a view to the Clipboard:

1. Use the guidelines listed earlier in this section to set up the view you want to copy.

2. Use the Copy Picture button on the Task tab, Clipboard, Copy menu to open the Copy Picture dialog box, as shown in Figure 26.21.

3. Select either For Screen, For Printer, or To GIF Image File. If you use To GIF Image File, you need to supply the path and filename for the GIF file in the text box.

4. If you are taking a picture of a table display, select either Rows on Screen or Selected Rows.

5. If there is a timescale in the display, either choose As Shown on Screen or fill in the From and To dates. You should add an appropriate number of time units before the From and after the To selections to prevent your image from being incorrectly cropped.

6. Click OK to save your picture.

The maximum size for a picture is 22 inches by 22 inches when using the For Screen or For Printer option. If the number of tasks you have selected or the date range specified for the timescale causes the picture to be greater than 22 inches in either direction, Project alerts you with the Copy Picture Options dialog box, as shown in Figure 26.22. If, however, you are using the To GIF image file option, you can create a GIF image up to 100 inches by 100 inches. A GIF image, however, is static, and best used for a website. When copying and pasting images to be placed in other applications, use the For Screen option.

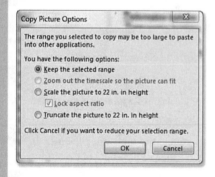

Figure 26.22
If your picture exceeds 22 inches in either dimension, you must decide what you want to do with it using the Copy Picture Options dialog box.

You have the following options with the Copy Picture Options dialog box:

- Select the Keep the Selected Range option if you want to use the picture anyway, although you might experience some distortion.

- Select the Zoom Out the Timescale So the Picture Can Fit option to have Project automatically change the timescale units, enabling the date range to fit within the maximum dimensions.

- Select the Scale the Picture to 22 Inches in Height option, and Project compresses the date range to fit within 22 inches without changing the timescale units. You can also choose the Lock Aspect Ratio check box if you want to keep the proportions intact during the scaling.

- Select the Truncate the Picture to 22 Inches in Height option if you want Project to use only the date range and rows in the table that fit.

- Select Cancel if you want to begin again with using the Copy Picture command.

You will get the best picture, in most cases, if you select Cancel and go back and manually adjust the timescale so the picture will fit. You might save a little time by selecting the Zoom Out the Timescale So the Picture Can Fit option and then pasting the picture to see what timescale unit is needed. You can manually zoom out the actual timescale when you capture the picture again.

When you open the application where you plan to paste your picture, select the location of the picture and use the Edit, Paste command (or Ctrl+V). You have the Paste Special command available, but it produces the same end result—pasting the picture as a picture object.

The object now appears with a border and resizing handles. You can change the height and width proportionally by using the corner handles.

Consultants' Tips

"Legacy" Features

Significant portions of this chapter have a distinctly pre-Project Server, pre-SharePoint orientation. Many of the more modern features of Project assume a highly collaborative and interconnected state; the features discussed here are oriented toward the individual project manager, working with a standalone project file. To the extent that this describes your situation, or to the extent that these features make your life easier, use them.

File Sizes

As previously mentioned, copying and pasting all of this information from one application to another can result in the creation of very large files. Imagine a Project file that has an embedded logo in each of its reports, an Excel chart embedded in the Gantt view, and several Word documents embedded into the Notes field of one or more tasks. Depending on the choices made when creating these embedded objects and the size of the original files, a .mpp's file size could easily grow very large, very quickly.

Creating the objects as links can be a viable alternative that results in a smaller-sized file, with the caveat that you need to be diligent about maintaining the links. For instance, what happens if you decide to reorganize your computer's Windows folder structure and inadvertently move a document that you created a link to in a .mpp file?

These techniques do work effectively and you should use them, but just make sure to exercise caution.

INDEX

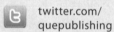
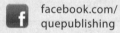
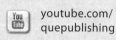
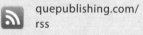

Project 2013

IN DEPTH

Que

Scott Daley

FREE
Online Edition

Safari
Books Online

Your purchase of *Project 2013 In Depth* includes access to a free online edition for 45 days through the **Safari Books Online** subscription service. Nearly every Que book is available online through **Safari Books Online**, along with thousands of books and videos from publishers such as Addison-Wesley Professional, Cisco Press, Exam Cram, IBM Press, O'Reilly Media, Prentice Hall, Sams, and VMware Press.

Safari Books Online is a digital library providing searchable, on-demand access to thousands of technology, digital media, and professional development books and videos from leading publishers. With one monthly or yearly subscription price, you get unlimited access to learning tools and information on topics including mobile app and software development, tips and tricks on using your favorite gadgets, networking, project management, graphic design, and much more.